Developing Cultural Sensitivity in Psychosexual Therapy

Developing Cultural Sensitivity in Psychosexual Therapy is a pioneering compilation that provides a comprehensive exploration of the intricate relationship between cultural diversity and human sexuality.

Featuring contributions from renowned psychosexual therapists and medical experts from Asia, the Middle East, Africa, and Europe, each chapter will delve into the unique challenges, practices, and insights related to psychosexual work within specific cultural contexts, particularly with a range of diverse communities. The book offers a rich tapestry of real-life scenarios and illustrations in work with a range of diverse clients including Black, LGBTQ, Orthodox Jew, Muslim, Observant Hindu, Sikh, and more. A great deal of attention is given to the seamless integration of scientific data with socio-cultural realities, treating readers to an immersive exploration that transcends conventional boundaries. Arguing that psychosexual relational therapy is historically impacted by colonialism, the book challenges a "one size fits all," mono-normative, Eurocentric approach, offering instead how to integrate social justice concerns both practically and philosophically.

This unique synthesis of scholarly insight, lived experience, and clinical expertise makes this book a compelling read for any psychosexual or relational therapist.

Bernd Leygraf is the Chief Executive Officer at Naos Institute, Consultant Psychotherapist, and Course Director for LDPRT. He is the only Consultant Psychotherapist in his field. He co-authored the first MSc in Humanistic Psychotherapy as well as the first Master's program in Psychosexual & Relationship Therapy in the UK. He also authored as well as led several Master's programs in the UK, primarily at South Bank University, Middlesex University, Westminster, and the University of Surrey.

Dr. Bishurul Hafi NA, MD (Dermatology & Venereology), DNB, LDPRT (UK), ADPRT (NAOS), FECSM (Belgium), is a COSRT Registered Psychosexual and Relationship Therapist in India. He is an author of the ESSM syllabus for Sexual Medicine, holds a Fellowship in Sexual Medicine, and has been an invited speaker at multiple national and international conferences.

Dr. NA Uvais, MBBS, DPM, PGDMLE, IFAPA, FRSPH, FRSB, is a psychiatrist and interdisciplinary leader, recognized as an International Fellow of the American Psychiatric Association (IFAPA). His unique profile combines elite scientific research membership (Sigma Xi) with fellowships in public health (FRSPH) and biology (FRSB).

'This book is an essential read as it helps clinicians develop their practice beyond the common and reductive white Western middle-class Anglophone viewpoint. Contributions from international top practitioners make it a rich book, and a vital resource for all sex therapists working with diverse populations.'

Silva Neves *is a psychosexual and relationship therapist, author of* Sexology: The Basics

'*Developing Cultural Sensitivity in Psychosexual Therapy* is a rare and generous offering to the field. It invites practitioners into a shared ethical and relational project, to practise psychosexual therapy with communities, rather than on them, as subjects. The book models how psychosexual work itself can heal, by listening across borders, learning across traditions, and valuing subjectivity and distributed knowledge over hierarchical expertise. Bringing together theory, clinical reflections, and implications for practice, this thoughtfully curated collection is highly recommended for psychosexual and relationship therapists, educators, and allied professionals. More than a source of knowledge, it challenges us to envision a practice rooted in mutual respect, humility, and collaboration.'

Mamood Ahmad *is a UKCP psychotherapist, and author of* A New Introduction to Counselling and Psychotherapy: Embedding Context, Diversity and Equity into Practice

'In a world where sexuality is too often filtered through Western narratives, this book offers a courageous and necessary widening of the lens. Bringing together voices from diverse cultures, faiths, and clinical traditions, it challenges the illusion of universality in psychosexual theory and practice. Each chapter reveals how history, identity, power, and place shape the ways people love, desire, and heal. This is not just a collection of insights—it is a call to rethink the very foundations of our work as therapists. With honesty and depth, the contributors illuminate pathways toward a more inclusive, decolonised, and culturally attuned understanding of sexual wellbeing. This book invites readers to listen more carefully, practice more humbly, and honour the rich human diversity at the heart of psychosexual care.'

Dr. Amr El Meliegy, *MESSM founder and 1st president, professor of Andrology, Sexology & STIs Cairo University*

Developing Cultural Sensitivity in Psychosexual Therapy

Global Perspectives

Edited by Bernd Leygraf,
Bishurul Hafi NA, and NA Uvais

Routledge
Taylor & Francis Group
LONDON AND NEW YORK

Designed cover image: Getty Images © ssnjaytuturkhi

First published 2027
by Routledge
4 Park Square, Milton Park, Abingdon, Oxon OX14 4RN

and by Routledge
605 Third Avenue, New York, NY 10158

Routledge is an imprint of the Taylor & Francis Group, an informa business

British Library Cataloguing-in-Publication Data
A catalogue record for this book is available from the British Library

ISBN: 978-1-041-00734-0 (hbk)
ISBN: 978-1-041-00733-3 (pbk)
ISBN: 978-1-003-61138-7 (ebk)

DOI: 10.4324/9781003611387

Typeset in Times New Roman
by Newgen Publishing UK

To the One that unites all—
Thou art Being and Breath,
and what Thou art shall never be destroyed.
This work is offered in recognition of the unity that underlies human diversity.
Across cultures and traditions, in the expressions of intimacy, longing, and love,
we encounter reflections of a common essence.

Contents

Acknowledgements

I wish to extend my gratitude to Routledge for their vision and support in bringing this work into being. My professional journey has been immeasurably enriched by the wisdom, encouragement, and collaboration of colleagues within my professional network, particularly Dr. John Dodd and Jo Coker at COSRT, LDPRT (Jean Miller, Judi Keshet-Orr, David Piner, Effie Soultani, Giuseppe Picuccio), and at the Naos Institute.

I am deeply indebted to my co-authors and collaborators—true giants in the field—with special thanks to Dr. Bishurul Hafi NA, whose insight and companionship have greatly shaped this work.

My teachers: Dr. David Schnarch, Dr. Joan Lachkar, Dr. Joseph Zinker

Beyond the professional sphere, I am blessed by the friendship and love of those who have stood beside me. Rev Achim Reinstaedtler, Rt. Rev David Charlesworth OSB, Ben Mckie, Rev Malcolm Bruce, Judi Keshet-Orr, Judith Hemming, Marina and Dan Cantacuzino, and above all my alpha and omega, Jaap Westerbos—your presence in my life has been a source of joy, strength, and inspiration.

To all of you: this book carries traces of your influence, and my gratitude is boundless.

Contributor Biography

Saquib Ahmad is a Consultant Psychotherapist fully accredited by the British Association of Behavioural and Cognitive Psychotherapies and EMDR UK and Ireland in CBT and EMDR. He is the founder and managing director of Fighting Fear, which offers psychological support, supervision, seminars, and workshops to professionals and the general public on various mental health topics.

Mohammad Shamsul Ahsan, MBBS, FCPS (Psych), MPhil (Psych), FECSM (Sexual Medicine), ECPS (Sexology), ICAP-I, Associate Professor, Department of Psychiatry, BSMMU, President of South Asian Society for Sexual Medicine.

Lukasz Birycki (he/him) is a COSRT-registered psychosexual and relationship therapist, trainer, and accredited coach with almost two decades of experience. He has worked across the NHS, charities, NGOs, and community settings, supporting people from diverse and often marginalized backgrounds.

Alice Einloft Brunnet, PhD, is an Associate Professor in Clinical Psychology at Paris Nanterre University and private psychologist and psychotherapist. Her main research interests are: 1) trauma, 2) refugee and migrant mental health, 3) grief, 4) processual approach in psychopathology, and 5) cognitive behavioral therapy.

Divine Charura, MBE, DCounsPsych, CPsychol, AFBPsS, UKCP reg. Psych, SFHEA, Counselling Psychologists and Psychotherapist, Professor of Counselling Psychology, Psychotherapy Supervisor and Independent Trainer.

Jo Coker, AccCOSRT(Sen), AccCOSRT (Sup), MBPsS FCOSRT, Counselling Psychologist, Director of Therapy and Training Standards, COSRT.

Joanne M Collins, is a Family and Systemic Psychotherapist. Her background includes teaching in the field of Social Care in educational and workplace settings and working clinically with traditionally marginalized and high-risk groups. These groups classically include young people who have experienced trauma, neglect and other abuses.

Amira Eldeeb is a dedicated Psychosexual and Relationship Therapist in Cairo, Egypt, with a strong focus on fostering healthier connections for individuals and couples. She is a Corporate Trainer and Master Coach at Mars Venus Coaching USA, and the CEO and Founder of Adam & Eve Garden LLC.

Wafaa Eltantawy is passionate gynecologist, counselor, and therapist, accredited by COSRT. She is an expert in psychosexual and relationship therapy, whilst also being a GMC licensed medical doctor with extensive clinical experience in sexual medicine. She developed her tireless work ethic at Mansoura University Medical School in Egypt (graduating in 1982) and developed her career in the UK NHS, acting as lead for one of London's busiest psychosexual clinics. She has also provided relationship therapy over the past 6 years both in the UK and in Egypt.

Caleb Jacobson is an internationally recognized clinical psychologist, sex therapist, and Bible scholar. He is the author of *Sex Therapy with Religious Patients: Working with Jewish, Christian, and Muslim Communities*. Jacobson is the founder of the School of Sex Therapy and currently serves as President of the International Association of Psychosexual Therapists.

Ramesha Jayaneththi is a postdoctoral researcher at the Institute of Social Movements, Ruhr University of Bochum, Germany. She also served as a lecturer at the University of Peradeniya, Sri Lanka. Her research interests are nationalism, historiography, Gender, identity politics, and Buddhist Temple lands.

Vinicius Jobim Fischer has a Master's in Sexological Sciences, specialized in individual and couple clinical sexology and a PhD in Psychology. He is a European certified psycho-sexologist (ECPS–EFS/ESSM) and works as a clinical psychologist and psychotherapist at the University of Luxembourg and at the center for Psychotherapy of the Neuropsychiatric Hospital center (CHNP). His main research interests are clinical sexology, sexual health, and emotion regulation.

Fatema Tuj Johora Joti, MBBS, MD (Child and Adolescent Psychiatry), Registrar: National Institute of Mental Health and Hospital.

Judi Keshet-Orr, Founder and Course Director for LDPRT. Director Relationship Resolve.

Justyna Kulczyk-Lewinska (she/her) is a Clinical Sexologist, COSRT-accredited Psychosexual and Relationship Psychotherapist and Registered Supervisor, Founder of JKL Therapy Centre, and Course Director of the Advanced Diploma in Psychosexual and Relationship Therapy at NAOS.

Bernd Leygraf, Chief Executive Officer at Naos Institute, Consultant Psychotherapist, Course Director LDPRT, Fellow NCIP, Fellow NCPS, Fellow COSRT (www.psychosexualtraining.org.uk and www.naos-institute.com).

Fatemeh Mafi is a general practitioner and a Fellow of the European Committee of Sexual Medicine (FECSM). She graduated with a London Diploma in Psychosexual and Relationship Therapy, accredited by the College of Sexual and Relationship Therapists (COSRT), in 2020, enabling her to integrate psychosexual talking therapy techniques with the medical management of sexual difficulties.

Urvashi Malhotra has practiced as a clinical psychologist and been a successful HR professional and coach, over a 22 year career. In her practice as a clinical psychologist, she works with individuals and couples as they negotiate the challenges of each stage of their lives. And this working through the rough patches together is what brings meaning and satisfaction to her clinical work.

Shobha Managoli is a NIMHANS Alumnus, Head of Parenting Practices at Parentof Solutions Pvt Ltd, a psychotherapist, subject-matter expert, consultant, trainer, mentor and author based out of Bengaluru, with over 30 years of experience. Her interest in the field of psychology and the opportunities lying unexplored in this field give her the motivation to work with different groups using psychological principles and theories, creating models, tools, and techniques to handle issues in daily life.

Keeley Mardon is a seasoned therapist with extensive expertise across various realms of psychotherapy. She holds the titles of Relationship & Psychosexual Therapist, Trauma Therapist, Energy Healer, EMDR Practitioner, and Clinical Supervisor. As a Senior Accredited Member of the National Counselling Society (NCP), an Accredited Member of the National Counselling Society (NCS), and a Registered Member of the College of Sexual and Relationship Therapists (COSRT), Keeley's credentials reflect her unwavering commitment and proficiency in her field.

Oberdan Marianetti is a psychologist, sexologist, founder of Dr. OM & Associates and scientist with over 30 years' experience in optimizing human potential. Based in Singapore, he is a recognized authority on integrating Western therapeutic models with Asian cultural values, offering distinctive insight into intimacy, identity, and leadership in a globalized world.

Leuza Mubassara, MBBS, MPH (Epidemiology), the Department of Psychiatry, Bangladesh Medical University, Dhaka.

Bishurul Hafi NA, Psychosexual and Relationship Therapist and sexual medicine expert, Mindtone Clinic, India.

Maha Nasrallah-Babenko is passionate about helping people live, love, and sexually connect more deeply and authentically. She is also the author of the book *The Integrated Guide to Treating Penetration Disorders in Women: Transforming Sexual Relationships from Fear to Confidence*. She is a licensed Psychologist in California (US) and has been practicing as a Psychosexual and Relationship Therapist since 2010.

Tiga-Rose Nercessian (she/her) is a multi-neurodivergent, multi-certified, accredited Sex & Relationship Psychotherapist, of Armenian-French extraction. She is also a researcher and specialist trainer for a variety of psychotherapy training institutions, focusing on supporting neurodivergent adults to have happy and healthy intimate relationships. Tiga-Rose is currently writing a neurodivergent sex book.

ML Ng is a senior psychiatrist and sexual health expert from China. He has dozens of high-quality peer reviewed publications in English and Chinese languages. He is a seasoned teacher worked in various medical colleges in psychiatry and sexology departments. Currently he is Clinical Co-director, Asian Academy of Family Therapy, Hong Kong.

Julie Sale is the Founding Director and Principal of the Contemporary Institute of Clinical Sexology, (CICS), a UK-based training institute providing qualification pathways in psychosexual and relationship psychotherapy. Julie is a United Kingdom Council for Psychotherapy (UKCP) Registered and Accredited Psychotherapist, Senior Accredited Member of the National Counselling and Psychotherapy Society, (NCPS), Senior Accredited Member of the College of Sexual and Relationship Therapists, (COSRT), Certified Member of the International Association of Psychosexual Therapists, (IAPST) and COSRT Accredited Supervisor.

Jodie Slee is a qualified psychotherapist specializing in Psychosexual, Relationship Therapy and EMDR therapy.

NA Uvais, MBBS, DPM, PGDMLE, IFAPA, FRSPH, FRSB, Full Member, Sigma Xi: He is a psychiatrist and interdisciplinary leader, recognized as an International Fellow of the American Psychiatric Association (IFAPA). His unique profile combines elite scientific research membership (Sigma Xi) with fellowships in public health (FRSPH) and biology (FRSB). This rare synthesis of clinical, research, and population health expertise defines his work as a scholar-physician dedicated to advancing mental health from the laboratory to the global community.

Foreword

Judi Keshet-Orr
Founder, London Diploma in Psychosexual & Relationship Therapy

It is a privilege to introduce this remarkable volume. As founder of the London Diploma in Psychosexual and Relationship Therapy, and as someone who has worked in this field for many decades, I have witnessed the gradual but steady evolution of our discipline. What began as a practice largely rooted in physiology and technique has expanded into a far more nuanced and multifaceted enterprise. This book captures that transformation and takes it further. It offers a truly global conversation that challenges assumptions, broadens horizons, and redefines what psychosexual therapy can and should be.

This work is ambitious in scope and generous in spirit. It moves confidently across continents and contexts, drawing together clinicians whose voices are rarely heard alongside one another. Contributors from Asia, Europe, Africa, and the Americas weave together histories, practices, and personal narratives that resist the tired notion that one size fits all. The volume is unique not only in its breadth of regions but also in its commitment to reflexivity. Each chapter reminds us that therapy is not conducted in a vacuum. It is embedded in culture, history, language, politics, and the lived experiences of communities. The courage of this book lies in its insistence that these contexts are not distractions from the "real" work of therapy—they are the work.

One of the most striking features of this collection is its deliberate disruption of what we might call the Eurocentric clinical canon. Too often, sexological literature has been dominated by Western models that universalize their own assumptions. This volume does something different. It listens outward. It asks what changes when we take the world seriously—when we allow the practices of Sri Lanka, the narratives of migrant workers in the Gulf, the traditions of Jewish communities, or the lived realities of Black British clients to reshape our frameworks. It honors local mores without romanticizing them, and it refuses to flatten cultural difference into checklists of "competence." Instead, it models cultural humility: the willingness to remain curious, to question ourselves, and to learn from those we serve.

For clinicians, the implications are profound. This book invites us to expand the kinds of questions we ask during assessment, to listen for meanings of shame, pride, and consent that may differ from our own, and to explore how migration histories, family structures, or religious narratives shape sexual identity and distress. It encourages us to seek supervision that is intercultural, where countertransference linked to race, class, gender, or faith can be openly explored. It asks us to regard humility training not as optional, but as integral to good practice.

Psychosexual therapy has too often been imagined as a matter of identifying dysfunction and applying techniques to cure it. This book insists on something broader and more humane. It reminds us that therapy is about dignity, about recognizing the cultural resonance of every intervention, and about fostering equity in access and outcomes. It challenges us to view our work not only as service to individuals but also as contribution to communities, especially in a world where mobility, displacement, and transnational belonging are increasingly the norm.

As readers make their way through these pages, they will be challenged, stretched, and inspired. They will encounter clinical vignettes that do not resolve neatly, theories that do not align perfectly, and voices that do not always agree. That, I believe, is the point. Growth happens in the tension between perspectives. Empathy deepens when we allow ourselves to be unsettled.

This book is a gift to the field. It will expand the knowledge base of practitioners, foster richer supervision conversations, and equip therapists to meet clients with greater compassion and competence. Most importantly, it signals a shift in our discipline toward a more inclusive, culturally sensitive, and globally aware psychosexual therapy.

I have no doubt that readers will finish this volume not only with new tools but with a renewed sense of responsibility: to meet clients where they are, to honor the worlds they come from, and to walk alongside them with respect and care.

Chapter 1

Introduction

Bernd Leygraf and Bishurul Hafi NA

Introduction by Bernd Leygraf

When I first entered clinical training, the case material we studied was filled with physiological detail and technical precision. The body was dissected, measured, and described in minute accuracy: blood flow, hormonal shifts, muscular contraction, orgasmic phases. Yet, for all its anatomical richness, the literature was strangely silent on something equally present in every consulting room—culture. Bodies were mapped, but lives were barely mentioned. What I learned was that desire, inhibition, or pain appeared as symptoms. What I came to understand much later is that they arrive carrying far more: languages with untranslatable words, religious prohibitions that echo across generations, migration stories marked by grief or separation, laws that render some loves illegal, and family scripts that regulate who may touch, speak, or choose.

If our frameworks cannot accommodate this complexity, our clients end up negotiating with a model instead of being met by a therapist. It was this realization that shifted my own practice and ultimately inspired the frame of this volume.

What Culture Brings into the Room

Consider what truly enters a therapeutic space when a couple sits down. A Turkish migrant couple in Germany may present with difficulties in sexual initiation, but what is unspoken are the layers of displacement, the stigma attached to seeking therapy, and the way German vocabulary feels both foreign and inadequate to capture intimacy. An Indian migrant worker in the Gulf may speak of "performance difficulties," yet beneath this lie fears of digital intimacy, the risk of private images being exposed, and the silent negotiation between religious devotion and sexual longing. In each of these cases, the presenting complaint cannot be separated from the cultural, legal, and social frameworks in which the clients live.

DOI: 10.4324/9781003611387-1

Four Themes Shaping This Volume

Across the chapters of this book, several themes appear again and again. They form the intellectual and clinical scaffolding of what follows.

Cultural Humility Rather than Cultural Certainty

This book does not offer a checklist of how to treat "clients from X culture." Instead, it offers questions that must be asked. What does "normal" mean in this particular family? How is consent understood in a context where hierarchy is strong? Which words for body parts are available, and which remain unsayable? These questions remind us that therapy is not about mastering every possible culture but becoming skilled at learning within any culture. Cultural humility literature teaches us that humility is not ignorance—it is a disciplined openness, a willingness to learn from our clients, and to allow their worlds to reshape our formulations.

Ethics as Method

It is tempting to think of culture as an add-on, something to be addressed before we move to the "real" work of technique. But as the chapters here demonstrate, the ethical stance is the method. Negotiating language carefully, building transparent alliances, pacing interventions to respect safety and modesty—these are not peripheral. They are the very levers that allow cognitive restructuring, sensate focus, pelvic floor retraining, or medication collaboration to take place. Ethics and technique cannot be separated.

The Clinician's Self as Instrument

Therapists are not neutral observers. Many of us are migrants ourselves, between languages, between nations, or between professions. We carry our own loyalties, superstitions, and wounds. These will surface in the room, sometimes subtly, sometimes not. Good supervision practices remind us to engage with these reactions not as failures but as resources. Reflexivity—naming our position, being transparent about our limits, noticing when transgenerational histories shape our responses—is central. Cultural humility again plays a role: we cannot erase our context, but we can use it thoughtfully, in service of the client.

The Realities of Present Practice

This book does not confine itself to history or abstract theory. It speaks to the digital age of intimacy, where clients negotiate relationships through WhatsApp, dating apps, and AI-driven platforms. It speaks to the intersections of faith and sexuality, to the ordinary lives of LGBTQIA+ clients, to inequities in healthcare between the Global North and South, and to the colonial legacies that still structure laws and attitudes today. Real clients live within these realities, and effective therapy must respond to them.

For Whom This Book Is Written

This volume will speak differently to different audiences. Clinicians will find case vignettes that do not resolve into neat solutions, reminding us that outcomes are sometimes modest but deeply meaningful—safer boundaries, deeper kindness, or courage to leave. Trainers and supervisors will find a blueprint for curricula that integrate anatomy with anthropology, pharmacology with reflective writing, skill practice with cultural critique. Commissioners and policymakers will see arguments for access models that do not punish cultural difference with longer waiting times or poorer care. Researchers will find here not only questions worth asking but also a reminder that rigorous methods need not be extractive or colonial.

An Invitation

To early-career therapists, I say this: you will not finish this book having "learned the cultures." You may, however, finish knowing how to learn with the person in front of you. Begin every assessment with humility, let your client's lived experience correct your assumptions, and remember that your steadiness and curiosity are themselves interventions. To seasoned colleagues, I say: many of us were trained to treat culture as noise in the data. The chapters that follow remind us that culture often is the data. Updating our frameworks is not an admission of past error; it is fidelity to our best tradition—we improve because we keep listening.

If you encounter tension between viewpoints in these chapters, do not rush to resolve it. Tension is what allows bodies to move, and it is also what allows ideas to grow. This book asks us to sit with that tension, to allow it to reshape our practice, and to see therapy not as a universal model, but as a global conversation.

Introduction by Bishurul Hafi

I was born and raised in a community where life was lived in stark binaries: right and wrong, permitted and forbidden, honor and shame. These categories shaped not only behavior but imagination itself. Sexuality was not spoken of openly, and when it was mentioned, it appeared as a shadow—something dangerous, something to guard against. These early experiences gave me clarity, but they also built walls around how I understood the human condition.

When I entered the world of medicine and, eventually, psychosexual health, those walls were shaken. My training took me far from Kerala, into lecture halls of the International Society for Sexual Medicine and the London Diploma in Psychosexual and Relationship Therapy in the UK. I encountered frameworks rooted in Western science—rich, rigorous, and liberating in many ways. They gave me diagnostic tools, therapeutic strategies, and a language to discuss sexual health. But they also presented me with dilemmas I was not prepared for. What I had learned as "norms" in those settings often clashed with the cultural and moral fabric of the communities I came from.

A Case That Changed Me

I remember a middle-aged woman in Kerala who came to me with hypoactive sexual desire disorder. Following my training, I recommended masturbatory exercises to help her reconnect with her body. What seemed an evidence-based suggestion to me landed as a shock to her. She looked at me with disbelief, her silence heavier than any words. In that instant, I realized how easily a therapist could alienate a client if cultural context was ignored. The intervention, however scientifically sound, had no chance of being effective because it did not honor her world. That moment became a turning point. It taught me that cultural humility is not optional—it is central. Evidence must be translated, adapted, and sometimes even reimagined for it to be meaningful.

Carrying the Past into the Room

As I continued in practice, I realized that my challenges were not limited to cultural difference between client and therapist. History itself was alive within me. During training, I formed a close friendship with a Portuguese colleague. But to my surprise, I suddenly felt unable to interact with him. I was confused until I explored it in therapy. What surfaced was not personal dislike but the residue of colonial trauma. My homeland had been colonized by the Portuguese centuries ago, and stories of battles and resistance were part of the cultural memory I had inherited. Though I had never lived those events, they lived in me. The same subtle resistance appeared when working with British colleagues, shaped by another layer of colonial history.

These unconscious residues shaped how I related to others professionally. They reminded me that therapy is not only shaped by the here-and-now but also by histories that echo silently in the present. For clinicians, this has profound implications. Our relationships with colleagues and clients may carry traces of these inherited wounds, and if we do not reflect on them, they risk distorting our work.

Science and Culture: Not Opposites, but Partners

At first, I framed my dilemma as a conflict between science and culture. Should I be loyal to the values of my community or to the principles of Western evidence-based practice? With time, I learned this was the wrong question. Science is not fixed dogma. It offers probabilities and guidelines, not universal truths. Its application must always take place in human contexts. Culture, too, is not a barrier to science but the terrain in which science must take root. The task is not to choose between them but to translate between them—to adapt, reframe, and find the bridge that allows both to work together.

Toward a Global Perspective

It was through these reflections, and conversations with my mentor Bernd Leygraf, that the idea for this book was born. We envisioned a global perspective in psychosexual therapy—one that recognizes the universality of human needs for intimacy, desire, safety, and connection, while honoring the particular languages, traditions, and histories that give those needs shape. This means treating sexual health not as a checklist of dysfunctions to cure but as an arena where dignity, identity, and meaning are negotiated.

An Invitation

I write this introduction not as someone who has resolved every tension but as someone still living them. My hope is that, as you read this volume, you will recognize your own inheritances—whether cultural, historical, or personal—and reflect on how they shape your practice. This is not a manual with rigid answers, nor a manifesto imposing one worldview. It is a dialogue, sometimes harmonious and sometimes uncomfortable, between diverse perspectives. If you approach these chapters with humility, curiosity, and courage, I believe they will expand not only your knowledge but also your capacity to meet clients where they truly live: in the specific intersections of their bodies, histories, and worlds.

Chapter Synopsis

This volume, *Global Perspectives on Psychosexual Therapy*, is designed as both a resource and a provocation. It resists the Eurocentric universalism that has long shaped psychosexual theory and practice, foregrounding instead the multiplicity of sexual lives, the force of history, and the weight of context. The book argues that to practice responsibly, clinicians must hold two positions at once: that sexual health is a universal human concern, and that sexuality is always lived in specific cultural, linguistic, political, and historical frameworks.

Our aims are threefold. First, to challenge the assumption that Western models of sexology can be simply exported to all settings. Second, to foreground debates on decolonization, intersectionality, and systemic inequities as central rather than peripheral to psychosexual care. And third, to equip practitioners, educators, and policymakers with practical tools for culturally inclusive and politically attuned work.

The volume is structured into four main sections.

1. Foundational Global Perspectives

We begin with two chapters by Bernd Leygraf, which lay the intellectual foundations for the book. The first explores how individualist and collectivist cultures frame intimacy and sexuality differently, drawing on examples from Sri Lanka, India, and Latin America. Here, cultural scripts are shown not as background detail but as active forces shaping desire, distress, and therapeutic encounters. The second turns to the language of sexology, engaging with Heike Bauer's scholarship to show how words, metaphors, and vocabularies carry histories of power. This section asks us to notice not only what is said in therapy but also what cannot be said in certain cultural contexts. Together, these chapters establish the principle that therapy cannot be separated from the cultures and languages in which it is practiced.

2. *UK Perspectives*

The next section situates psychosexual therapy within the UK, where the field has undergone rapid transformation over the last three decades. Jo Coker offers a reflective overview of theoretical and cultural shifts during this period, mapping how changes in social attitudes and clinical training have reshaped practice. Keeley Mardon examines the intersection of class and masculinity, showing how working-class men's lived realities complicate therapeutic engagement. Julie Sale turns to pedagogy, interrogating discrimination in training contexts and offering strategies for embedding equity into curricula. Dr. Joanne Collins explores Black sexuality, insisting on the necessity of addressing racism and systemic inequality in psychosexual work. Finally, Professor Divine Charura critiques the colonial legacies embedded in the field and advances decolonizing approaches that reframe therapy as contextually responsive and globally accountable. Collectively, these chapters reveal a UK landscape that is far from homogenous, marked by intersectional challenges and the ongoing struggle to build inclusive practice.

3. *Global Perspectives and Local Realities*

From the UK we expand outward to international contexts, where sexuality is inseparable from politics, family structures, and cultural scripts.

- In **China**, contributors examine the persistence of conservative sexual politics, highlighting how state regulation shapes private lives.
- In **Singapore**, law, culture, and sexuality intersect in a tightly controlled political climate, presenting distinctive challenges for therapy.
- In **Bangladesh**, the extended family system takes center stage, particularly the influence of in-laws on intimacy and relational dynamics.
- In **India**, Dr. Bishurul Hafi traces the history of psychosexual therapy from traditional frameworks through colonial disruptions to contemporary practice, while a companion chapter explores the impact of diaspora and transnational migration on Indian couples abroad.
- In **Armenia**, attention turns to neurodiversity, with a call to recognize neurodivergent sexual expression as valid and diverse.
- In **Poland**, the legacy of post-Soviet transition is explored, showing how political shifts shape therapeutic possibilities.

- In **Pakistan**, the focus is on gay Muslims, navigating repression, faith, and sexual identity.
- Two chapters from **Germany and Hungary**, by Caleb Jacobs, turn to Jewish contexts: one on the use of sex aids and embodiment, the other on therapeutic engagement with Jewish couples, framed by diaspora, memory, and modernity.

Across these contributions, recurrent themes emerge: migration as a force reshaping intimate lives, colonial legacies that continue to structure law and stigma, systemic inequities in healthcare, and the pressures of digital intimacy in a rapidly changing world.

4. Cultural Frameworks

The final section turns to Sri Lanka, where eight traditional forms of marriage offer a radically different lens on kinship and intimacy. By foregrounding this history, the chapter destabilizes Western assumptions about the nuclear family and monogamous marriage as the default relational template. It challenges therapists to consider how alternative frameworks of union and belonging might broaden our understanding of relationality.

More Than an Edited Collection

This book is not simply an anthology of regional case studies. It is conceived as a living dialogue across continents and disciplines. Each chapter is written in conversation with the others, not to produce consensus, but to hold tension productively. Migration, colonialism, inequities, and digital shifts are not side notes—they are the throughlines of contemporary psychosexual life.

Taken together, these chapters argue for a practice that is at once universal and particular: universal in recognizing human needs for intimacy, consent, pleasure, and safety; particular in honoring the histories, languages, and political realities in which those needs are pursued and denied.

Positioning the Volume

This volume sits at the crossroads of several urgent conversations in sexual health, psychotherapy, and global mental health. For too long, psychosexual therapy has been shaped by a Eurocentric canon that assumes its frameworks can travel unchanged across borders. This book responds by locating psychosexual work within wider debates on **cultural humility**, **decolonization**, and **intersectionality**.

Rather than offering a checklist of "what to do with clients from X culture," the collection insists on something deeper: a global dialogue grounded in reflexivity. Cultural humility reminds us that we do not master cultures; we learn with and from those who live them. Decolonization challenges us to recognize the colonial residues in law, training, and clinical language, and to imagine practices that are no longer tethered to those legacies. Intersectionality ensures that we attend to the way sexuality is always entangled with class, race, gender, migration, ability, and faith.

The contribution of this book is not only theoretical but profoundly practical. It widens assessment beyond the individual to include kinship systems, migration stories, religious meanings, and digital risks. It reframes interventions so they can be adapted for modesty, privacy, and cultural language. It proposes supervision and training structures that make room for therapists' own histories and vulnerabilities. And it calls attention to systemic inequities, reminding us that access to psychosexual care is itself shaped by policy and power.

The intended audience is broad.

- **Clinicians** will find clinical vignettes that illuminate how cultural scripts shape desire, shame, and intimacy.
- **Educators and supervisors** will discover frameworks for training that move beyond transmission of knowledge to the cultivation of humility and reflexivity.
- **Policymakers and commissioners** will encounter arguments for access models that do not punish cultural or linguistic difference with poorer care.
- **Researchers** will find both critical questions and methodological provocations for building a global evidence base.

Our call to action is clear: to reimagine psychosexual therapy as context-sensitive and globally interconnected. This means seeing culture not as an "add-on" but as central clinical data; recognizing that ethical stance is itself technique; and holding steady the paradox that sexuality is universal and yet always particular.

If there is a single thread running through these chapters, it is this: psychosexual therapy in the twenty-first century must be globally aware, historically informed, and ethically humble. Only then can it serve clients not as abstractions, but as whole people whose sexual lives are bound up with family, community, history, and hope.

Chapter 2

Not All Road Signs Are in English

Bernd Leygraf

Colonialism is usually defined in relation to territory and it is claimed that we are now in a post colonial era. The position of this paper is that colonialism continues to operate to this day, albeit in more insidious forms—transposing ideas, concepts, philosophies such as those represented by Eurocentric, North US counseling and therapy models and with it variations of gender, sex, and relationship models onto different, less individualistic and more collectivist cultures. The 1990s saw the challenges of feminism, heteronormativity, LGBTIQ, and more recently GSRD and has enabled us to re-define conventional notions of sex, relationships, and gender. However, in the international arena via human rights LGBTIQ discourses have made themselves the barometer to determine who the "good liberal" countries versus the "bad backward" are. These racist undertones imply that indigenous as well as "black and brown cultures" have not been civilized enough to tolerate gay and lesbian people (Abbas 2012), forgetting that, regional terminologies and definitions of sexuality predate Eurocentric discourses on GSRD and cannot be compared. We hope to offer a corrective to the pervasive idea that Western concepts of sex, sexuality, and gender were transmitted around the world, as if the West have ownership and monopoly on those. Our position is that sex, gender, and relationships concepts do not travel well in time or space and for Anglophone discourses in order to fully align itself to social justice pursuits it needs to demonstrate a higher degree of cultural awareness.

Introduction

Colonialism, as a historical force, is often assumed to be a phenomenon of the past—an era characterized by the conquest and control of territories. However, colonialism has transformed into more insidious forms, particularly through cultural and intellectual hegemony. One of the most pervasive examples of this is the global spread of Western psychosexual therapy models, which have reinforced a dominance over how sexuality and mental health are conceptualized worldwide

This chapter begins by unpacking how modern psychosexual therapy remains rooted in Eurocentric assumptions. It explores how foundational figures such as Freud, Kinsey, and Hirschfeld shaped a framework that, though presented as

DOI: 10.4324/9781003611387-2

universal, reflects Western cultural biases. These biases prioritize individual autonomy, rigid identity categories, and secular perspectives on sexuality—often clashing with collectivist traditions and religiously informed understandings of gender and relationships.

Colonial Legacies in Sexology

The historical foundations of sexology were deeply intertwined with colonial enterprises. As Liat Kozma's (2015) "Translating Sexology, Writing the Nation" illustrates, European sexological theories were often translated into non-Western languages in ways that aligned with nationalist projects, thus shaping new socio-political discourses on sexuality. Hebrew and Arabic translations of European texts, for example, not only introduced Western scientific discourses but also reinforced emerging nationalist ideals that framed certain sexual behaviors as "modern" while others were deemed regressive or backward.

Similarly, Howard Chiang's (2015) "Data of Desire" examines the introduction of Western homosexuality discourse in Republican China, where these ideas were not simply absorbed but were instead adapted through the lens of Confucian familial values. This underscores the central argument of this chapter: psychosexual therapy must move beyond the transplantation of Western frameworks and acknowledge the cultural negotiations that shape its global impact.

The Eurocentric Roots of Psychosexual Therapy

Western psychosexual therapy assumes that concepts like sexual identity, gender expression, and relationship structures are universally applicable. However, as James P. Wilper (2015) discusses in "Translation and the Construction of a 'Uranian' Identity," translation itself plays a crucial role in shaping sexual identity categories. Western sexology sought to define and categorize sexuality in rigid terms, but when these ideas were translated across linguistic and cultural borders, they were often reinterpreted in ways that Western theorists did not anticipate.

Critiquing the Secular Bias in Psychosexual Therapy

One of the core critiques of mainstream psychosexual therapy is its inherent secular bias. Hunt (2022) argues that counselling and psychotherapy can fail clients when they do not take religion and spirituality seriously. Rather than treating faith as a marginal or outdated concern, Hunt suggests that therapists need to recognise how deeply religious and spiritual commitments can shape a client's identity, moral world, relationships, and experience of distress. In this sense, a therapy model that assumes secular Western values as the default may unintentionally marginalise faith-based clients and reproduce a form of cultural imperialism.

Heike Bauer's (2015) "Suicidal Subjects: Translation and the Affective Foundations of Magnus Hirschfeld's Sexology" highlights a related issue—the emotional narratives that shaped early sexology were filtered through Western scientific frameworks, often disregarding alternative understandings of mental health and sexuality that were deeply embedded in religious and cultural traditions. This oversight continues today in psychosexual therapy, where religious understandings of sexuality are often viewed as barriers to psychological well-being rather than as legitimate frameworks in their own right.

Structure of the Chapter

This chapter is organized as follows:

- **Historical Context:** Exploring the roots of Western psychosexual therapy and its expansion through colonial and nationalist projects.
- **Mismatches Between Western Therapy Models and Non-Western Norms:** Examining the limits of individualism in therapy, the cultural inapplicability of Western identity labels, and the failure to engage with religious frameworks.
- **The Role of Human Rights in Perpetuating Western Norms:** Investigating how global human rights discourses have reinforced Western sexual frameworks and the resistance that emerges in response.
- **Towards a Decolonial Approach:** Proposing alternative models that respect non-Western epistemologies and advocate for culturally sensitive psychosexual therapy practices.

Through this structure, we will critically analyze the ways in which psychosexual therapy has been complicit in upholding Western cultural dominance and argue for a more pluralistic, context-sensitive approach that moves beyond rigid, Eurocentric assumptions.

The Eurocentric Foundations of Psychosexual Therapy

Historical Development and Global Expansion

The development of psychosexual therapy is deeply intertwined with Euro-American intellectual traditions, particularly those established by key figures such as Sigmund Freud, Magnus Hirschfeld, and Alfred Kinsey. These theorists laid the groundwork for a scientific approach to human sexuality that would later be exported worldwide, often without consideration for local cultural contexts.

Freud, Hirschfeld, and Kinsey: Foundational Figures

Sigmund Freud's psychoanalytic theory introduced the concept of sexuality as a central element in human psychological development. His works, including *Three Essays on the Theory of Sexuality* (2000), positioned sexual desire as a fundamental driver of human behavior. Freud's theories on repression and the unconscious became influential in Western psychotherapeutic approaches to sexuality. However, his emphasis on the nuclear family and individual psychological conflict did not easily translate into cultures where collectivism and extended kinship networks were dominant.

Magnus Hirschfeld, a German physician and sexologist, was one of the earliest advocates for sexual minorities, coining terms such as "third sex" to describe non-heteronormative sexual identities. His work, including *The Sexual History of the World War* (1930), sought to apply scientific analysis to human sexual diversity. However, Hirschfeld's framework remained steeped in European social and political norms, which limited its applicability outside of Western contexts.

Alfred Kinsey, through his groundbreaking studies *Sexual Behavior in the Human Male* (1948) and *Sexual Behavior in the Human Female* (1953), sought to quantify sexual behavior through empirical research. His introduction of the Kinsey Scale challenged the binary notion of sexual orientation. Yet, Kinsey's studies primarily reflected American sexual experiences and categories, often disregarding the culturally specific understandings of sexuality in non-Western societies.

The Assumption of Universal Applicability

The works of Freud, Hirschfeld, and Kinsey assumed a universality that did not account for the wide variety of sexual norms and identities across different cultures. Western sexology was often presented as an objective science, but, as Kozma (2015) illustrates, its adaptation into non-Western contexts was far from neutral. Rather than serving as a tool for pure knowledge dissemination, sexology was frequently shaped by colonial and nationalist ideologies, influencing how sexuality was understood in emerging nation-states.

Kozma's research highlights how Hebrew and Arabic translations of European sexology were instrumental in reshaping local attitudes toward sexuality. These translations did not merely import Western scientific knowledge but selectively integrated aspects that aligned with national identity projects, while omitting or modifying others to fit cultural and moral frameworks. This process underscores how psychosexual therapy, as rooted in Euro-American traditions, was often imposed on non-Western societies without full recognition of indigenous sexual epistemologies.

Sexology as a Tool of Colonial Influence

Sexology was not merely a scientific endeavor but was also tied to colonial and nationalist projects, shaping how sexuality was perceived and regulated in different cultural contexts. The imposition of Western categories of sexual identity onto non-Western societies often occurred in tandem with broader colonial efforts to "modernize" indigenous populations.

Case Study: Hebrew and Arabic Translations of European Sexology (Kozma 2015)

Kozma (2015) examines how European sexological texts were adapted into Hebrew and Arabic in the 1930s. These translations were not neutral scientific imports; instead, they served specific nationalist and cultural agendas.

For example, in the Hebrew adaptation, sexology was used to define modern Jewish identity, aligning sexual norms with Zionist ideals of nation-building and cultural revival. Discussions of sexual health, reproduction, and family structure were framed in ways that supported the Jewish nationalist movement, reinforcing particular gender roles and expectations. Certain aspects of European sexology that did not align with these nationalist objectives were modified or omitted altogether.

Similarly, in Arabic translations, European sexology was reshaped to fit Islamic moral frameworks and nationalist narratives. While some aspects of sexology were integrated into public health and medical discourses, topics that conflicted with religious and cultural values were softened or excluded. This selective adoption highlights the way sexology, far from being a neutral field of study, was actively translated to serve political and ideological interests.

Case Study: Republican China's Adaptation of Western Homosexuality Discourse (Chiang 2015)

Howard Chiang's (2015) "Data of Desire: Translating (Homo)Sexology in Republican China" explores how Western sexology was introduced into China during the early twentieth century. Rather than simply adopting Western categories of sexual identity, Chinese intellectuals and policymakers reshaped these ideas to align with existing Confucian and social structures.

Western sexology often framed homosexuality as an inherent, fixed identity. However, in Republican China, homosexuality was interpreted through the lens of familial and societal obligations. Rather than seeing same-sex desire as an individual identity, as in Western contexts, it was often understood as a social practice that could exist within the broader framework of Confucian familial duty.

Chiang's research underscores how non-Western societies did not passively accept Western sexological theories but instead engaged in a process of negotiation and reinterpretation. The adaptation of Western homosexuality discourse in China challenges the idea that psychosexual therapy, as informed by Western sexology, can be universally applied without regard for cultural and historical contexts.

The historical development and expansion of psychosexual therapy were deeply rooted in Euro-American intellectual traditions. Figures such as Freud, Hirschfeld, and Kinsey established frameworks that, while influential, often failed to account for the diversity of sexual cultures across the world. The assumption of universal applicability meant that these ideas were often imposed upon non-Western societies without full consideration of local contexts.

Furthermore, as seen in the case studies of Hebrew, Arabic, and Chinese adaptations of sexology, the translation of Western sexual knowledge was not neutral but deeply shaped by nationalist and colonial agendas. These processes demonstrate the necessity of critically examining how psychosexual therapy continues to reflect Eurocentric biases and why a more pluralistic approach is essential.

The Mismatch Between Western Therapy Models and Non-Western Cultural Norms

The Limits of Individualism in Therapy

Western psychosexual therapy is deeply rooted in the principles of individual autonomy, self-determination, and personal choice. These principles, while central to Western psychological thought, often clash with collectivist cultural values that emphasize interdependence, familial obligations, and social harmony. In many non-Western societies, the well-being of the individual is intrinsically linked to their relationships within the family and community.

Case Study: Therapy in Confucian Societies (Chiang 2015)

Chiang's (2015) analysis of the translation of Western sexology into Republican China provides a useful framework for understanding how Western therapeutic models can fail to align with Confucian social structures. In China, Confucian ethics prioritize familial duty and social cohesion over individual self-expression. When Western sexology was introduced to Republican China, its emphasis on personal sexual identity clashed with Confucian ideals, which viewed sexuality through the lens of family continuity and social responsibility.

Therapists trained in Western models often found themselves at odds with their clients' cultural realities. Western psychosexual therapy encouraged individuals to prioritize personal sexual identity, but in Confucian societies, maintaining harmony within the family often took precedence. As Chiang illustrates, therapy models that ignored these cultural frameworks were often ineffective and alienating for clients who did not view their sexual identity as an isolated personal trait but rather as a factor interwoven with familial and social obligations.

Case Study: Muslim and Hindu Perspectives on Sexuality and Relational Identity

In Muslim and Hindu traditions, sexuality is often deeply integrated with spiritual, familial, and societal structures. Islamic teachings, for example, frame sexuality within the bounds of religious morality, emphasizing modesty and the sanctity of marriage. Similarly, Hindu thought often conceptualizes sexuality within a dharmic framework, where sexual behavior is linked to spiritual duty, social roles, and familial obligations.

Western psychosexual therapy, with its focus on self-actualization and personal identity, frequently disregards these perspectives. Therapy models that encourage individuals to detach from cultural or religious constraints in pursuit of self-defined sexual identity often cause distress for clients from Muslim and Hindu backgrounds, as they fail to acknowledge the interwoven nature of sexuality, spirituality, and duty. A culturally sensitive approach to therapy would require an understanding of these traditions rather than imposing Western ideals of autonomy and self-expression.

The Cultural Inapplicability of Western Sexual Identity Labels

Western sexual identity categories, including LGBTQ+ labels, emerged from specific historical and social movements in the West. These categories are often presented as universal frameworks, but they do not always align with how gender and sexuality have been historically understood in other cultural contexts.

Western LGBTQ+ Categories as Cultural Constructs

James P. Wilper (2015), in "Translation and the Construction of a 'Uranian' Identity," explores how Western sexual identity categories were formed through translation and scientific discourse. The term "Uranian," which was an early Western label for homosexuality, had to be translated across different languages and cultural settings. However, as Wilper demonstrates, these translations often distorted or reshaped local understandings of sexuality rather than accurately reflecting indigenous sexual identities.

In many non-Western societies, sexual identity is not understood as a fixed personal trait but rather as a social or relational phenomenon. For instance:

- In many indigenous African cultures, same-sex practices have historically existed without rigid sexual identity labels.
- In South Asia, the hijra community exists outside Western gender binaries, reflecting a historical recognition of gender fluidity that predates LGBTQ+ categories. In South Asia, the hijra community exists outside Western gender binaries, reflecting a historical recognition of gender fluidity that predates LGBTQ+ categories. Boyce and Khanna (2011) similarly show that South Asian male-to-male sexual subjectivities cannot be neatly mapped onto Western identity categories, because terms such as hijra and kothi emerge from specific social, cultural, and political contexts. Bose and Bhattacharyya (2007) also demonstrate that sexuality in contemporary India has been shaped through local political, cultural, and social debates that cannot be reduced to imported Western categories.
- In Japan, male-male relationships were historically viewed through the nanshoku tradition, which was framed within Buddhist and samurai cultural contexts rather than through the lens of personal identity.

Despite this, Western therapy models frequently impose fixed identity categories that do not account for these cultural histories, leading to misrepresentation and alienation of non-Western individuals seeking therapy.

Therapy's Inability to Address Religious Frameworks

Western psychosexual therapy has often positioned itself as secular, rational, and scientific, frequently dismissing or marginalizing religious perspectives. This has led to an increasing disconnect between therapy models and clients from faith-based backgrounds.

J. Hunt (2022) and the Neglect of Religion in Therapy

J. Hunt (2022) discusses the growing hostility between psychology and religion, particularly in how mainstream psychological discourse often dismisses religious beliefs as irrational or outdated. This bias is particularly evident in psychosexual therapy, where religious perspectives on sexuality are often viewed as restrictive or pathological.

Faith-based cultures, particularly non-Western religious traditions, do not separate sexuality from morality and spirituality in the way that secular psychology does. Many religious clients experience a profound conflict when Western therapy encourages them to detach from religious teachings in order to embrace Western models of sexual identity. This approach not only alienates clients but also reflects a deeper epistemic bias within psychosexual therapy that privileges secular worldviews over religious ones.

Heike Bauer's "Suicidal Subjects" and Hirschfeld's Struggles to Translate Sexuality Within Religious Moralities

Heike Bauer's (2015) "Suicidal Subjects: Translation and the Affective Foundations of Magnus Hirschfeld's Sexology" explores how Magnus Hirschfeld, one of the early pioneers of sexology, encountered challenges when trying to reconcile his scientific findings with religious moral frameworks. Hirschfeld, a staunch advocate for sexual minorities, faced resistance from religious authorities who viewed his work as contradicting moral doctrine. However, rather than dismissing religious perspectives outright, Hirschfeld attempted to engage with them, albeit unsuccessfully.

Bauer's analysis highlights a critical issue in psychosexual therapy: its failure to meaningfully engage with religious epistemologies. Rather than acknowledging the legitimacy of religious understandings of sexuality, Western therapy often frames them as barriers to progress. This not only isolates religious clients but also reinforces the Eurocentric bias of psychosexual therapy as a discipline.

The Western emphasis on individualism in psychosexual therapy often clashes with collectivist cultural norms, leading to a fundamental mismatch in therapeutic effectiveness. The assumption that LGBTQ+ identity labels are universally applicable disregards the diverse ways in which sexuality and gender have been conceptualized across cultures. Additionally, therapy's secular bias has resulted in a growing alienation of religious clients who find that their perspectives are dismissed rather than understood.

To create a more inclusive and effective psychosexual therapy model, therapists must:

- Recognize the limitations of Western individualism in non-Western cultural contexts.
- Avoid imposing rigid LGBTQ+ categories on societies with different historical and cultural understandings of sexuality.
- Engage with religious perspectives rather than dismissing them as obstacles to psychological well-being.
- Understand that a pluralistic approach that respects non-Western epistemologies and religious frameworks is necessary to decolonize psychosexual therapy and make it more applicable to diverse global populations.

The Role of Human Rights Frameworks in Perpetuating Western Norms

Western Human Rights as a Benchmark for Sexual Progressivism

The globalization of human rights discourse has led to the widespread adoption of Western frameworks for defining sexual rights and freedoms. While human rights advocacy aims to promote equality and justice, it often operates on the assumption that Western norms are the universal benchmark for sexual progressivism. Corrêa, Petchesky, and Parker (2008) are important to this discussion because they examine the relationship between sexuality, health, and human rights while also showing that sexual-rights discourse is shaped by political, cultural, and social struggles rather than by neutral universal principles. Mutua (2002) offers a useful framework for this critique, arguing that human-rights discourse can reproduce Eurocentric assumptions when it presents Western liberal norms as universal standards for non-Western societies. This assumption creates tensions when these norms are imposed on societies with different cultural, religious, and historical understandings of sexuality and identity.

One of the central critiques of human rights frameworks in the context of sexual identity is their reliance on liberal individualism. The notion that sexual rights must be centered on self-identification and personal autonomy is deeply rooted in Western thought. However, in many non-Western societies, sexuality is intertwined with collective cultural values, familial obligations, and spiritual traditions. When Western organizations advocate for LGBTQ+ rights in these contexts, they often do so without considering how these identities are understood locally, leading to resistance and unintended cultural consequences.

Case Study: LGBTQ+ Activism in Africa and Its Unintended Cultural Consequences (Brian James Baer, "Translating Sexology in Late-Tsarist and Early-Soviet Russia")

Brian James Baer (2015), in "Translating Sexology in Late-Tsarist and Early-Soviet Russia," discusses how Western sexological discourses were translated and adapted in Russia, often with significant shifts in meaning. Similarly, the promotion of Western LGBTQ+ activism in African nations has led to unintended consequences. In many African countries, same-sex relationships have existed historically, but they were often conceptualized differently from Western identity-based frameworks.

Western LGBTQ+ advocacy, which frames same-sex relationships within rigid identity categories, has in some cases exacerbated tensions rather than fostering acceptance. Governments and religious institutions, perceiving LGBTQ+ rights as an external imposition, have responded with increased crackdowns and legal restrictions. This backlash underscores the risks of applying Western human rights benchmarks universally without engaging in meaningful dialogue with local communities and understanding their cultural histories.

In countries such as Uganda and Nigeria, the criminalization of same-sex relationships has been framed as a defense against Western moral imperialism. Activists working within these nations often face a dilemma: advocating for LGBTQ+ rights in a way that aligns with international human rights frameworks can alienate local populations, while ignoring these frameworks risks cutting off access to international support. This case study highlights the necessity of moving beyond one-size-fits-all approaches and developing human rights strategies that respect cultural specificity.

Resistance and Local Adaptations

While Western human rights discourses have been influential, they have not been passively accepted. Local activists often engage in a process of negotiation, adapting global discourses to fit their cultural contexts. This form of resistance challenges the assumption that Western sexual norms should serve as the universal standard for human rights.

How Local Activists Negotiate Western and Indigenous Understandings of Sexuality

Many local activists and scholars in non-Western contexts seek to bridge the gap between Western human rights frameworks and indigenous understandings of sexuality. This is evident in:

- **South Asia:** The legal recognition of the hijra community in India, Pakistan, and Bangladesh is an example of how gender diversity has been integrated into human rights discourse through culturally relevant frameworks rather than direct Western importation. Bose and Bhattacharyya (2007) further demonstrate that sexual politics in contemporary India have been shaped through local debates around normativity, activism, culture, and identity, rather than through a simple adoption of Western LGBTQ+ frameworks.

- **Latin America:** Indigenous activists in countries such as Mexico and Peru advocate for sexual rights using frameworks that emphasize collective well-being and social responsibility rather than solely focusing on individual identity.
- **Middle East and North Africa:** Activists working in Islamic contexts often frame discussions of sexual rights within Islamic ethics rather than using secular Western rights-based discourse, which would likely face greater resistance.

These approaches illustrate the complexity of integrating sexual rights advocacy into diverse cultural landscapes. Rather than imposing Western frameworks, effective activism must emerge from within communities, drawing on existing cultural, religious, and historical narratives.

The Risk of Epistemic Violence When Western Models Erase Local Frameworks

Epistemic violence occurs when dominant knowledge systems erase or marginalize alternative ways of knowing. In the context of sexual rights, the insistence on Western categories and norms can lead to the erasure of indigenous sexual identities and traditions. This erasure can take several forms:

- **Forcing Binary Gender Norms:** Many indigenous cultures historically recognized non-binary genders, but the Western LGBTQ+ framework, which often relies on binary categories, can obscure these histories.
- **Redefining Same-Sex Relationships:** Many societies had fluid and context-dependent understandings of same-sex relationships, but Western activism often insists on rigid identity-based categorizations.
- **Disregarding Religious Perspectives:** In societies where religious doctrine plays a fundamental role in shaping understandings of sexuality, purely secular rights-based advocacy can be perceived as an attack on cultural and spiritual traditions.

To avoid epistemic violence, human rights activism must engage with local knowledge systems and traditions rather than dismissing them as outdated or oppressive. This requires a nuanced approach that prioritizes dialogue and adaptation over imposition.

Western human rights frameworks have played a significant role in advancing sexual rights globally, but their universal application has often led to tensions, resistance, and unintended consequences. The assumption that Western norms represent the pinnacle of sexual progressivism overlooks the complexity of cultural differences and indigenous knowledge systems.

As seen in the case of LGBTQ+ activism in Africa, efforts to promote Western sexual identity categories have, at times, resulted in increased repression rather than acceptance. Meanwhile, local activists continue to adapt and negotiate these frameworks to align with their cultural realities, demonstrating that sexual rights advocacy must be flexible and contextually informed.

To create a more effective and inclusive approach to sexual rights, future efforts should:

- Recognize that Western human rights norms are not universally applicable.
- Engage with local cultural and religious traditions rather than dismissing them.
- Support locally-led initiatives that integrate human rights within indigenous epistemologies.

By acknowledging the limitations of a Western-centric approach and fostering intercultural dialogue, human rights advocacy can move toward a more respectful and inclusive model that honors the diversity of human experiences.

Towards a Decolonial Approach in Psychosexual Therapy

Recognizing Diverse Epistemologies

The dominance of Western psychosexual therapy is built upon specific epistemologies—ways of knowing and understanding sexuality—that prioritize individual autonomy, secularism, and identity-based frameworks. However, these approaches fail to recognize that sexuality is understood differently across cultures, with many non-Western societies integrating relational, spiritual, and community-centered perspectives. Drawing on decolonial approaches to knowledge production, Smith (2012) argues that Indigenous epistemologies must be treated as valid systems of knowledge rather than as cultural supplements to Western theory.

To move away from a one-size-fits-all approach, psychosexual therapy must embrace epistemic diversity, acknowledging that:

- Sexuality is often interwoven with spirituality in many cultures, where religious traditions shape understandings of desire, morality, and relationships.
- Non-Western cultures frequently prioritize communal and familial well-being over personal sexual identity.
- The Western focus on fixed sexual identity categories does not account for societies with fluid or relational understandings of sexuality.

Expanding Training for Therapists to Include Alternative Knowledge Systems

A critical step toward decolonizing psychosexual therapy is reforming therapist training to include a broader range of epistemologies. This means:

- Incorporating indigenous and religious perspectives into academic curricula.
- Educating therapists on how different societies construct and regulate sexuality.
- Developing culturally specific therapeutic models that align with local understandings of sexual well-being.

Translating Therapy, Not Transplanting It

One of the key mistakes of Western psychosexual therapy is its tendency to transplant Western models into non-Western societies rather than translating them in ways that respect local values. The history of sexology provides valuable lessons in this regard—Western sexual theories have been reinterpreted, adapted, or resisted in different cultural contexts rather than being adopted wholesale.

Lessons from Sexology's Historical Translations

The study of sexuality has always involved translation—both linguistic and conceptual. As seen in:

- Liat Kozma's research on Hebrew and Arabic translations of European sexology illustrates how sexological ideas were reshaped to fit nationalist and moral frameworks.
- Howard Chiang's work on Republican China highlights how homosexuality was interpreted through Confucian ethics rather than Western individualist models.
- James P. Wilper's study of Uranian identity demonstrates that sexual identity categories are not static but evolve through cultural and linguistic translation.

Respecting Non-Western Relational Models and Sexual Ethics

Psychosexual therapy must shift from imposing Western relational models—centered on personal identity and autonomy—to acknowledging:

- **Collectivist Relational Structures:** In many cultures, relationships are seen as obligations within extended kinship networks rather than expressions of personal identity.
- **Spiritual and Ethical Sexuality:** Religious and philosophical traditions influence sexual ethics, shaping ideas of desire, duty, and morality.

- **Alternative Gender and Sexual Categories:** Many non-Western societies have long recognized non-binary or third-gender identities outside the Western LGBTQ+ framework.

Recommendations for a More Inclusive Psychosexual Therapy

To build a decolonial psychosexual therapy model, practitioners and institutions must take deliberate steps to acknowledge and integrate cultural and epistemological diversity. Below are key recommendations:

Decentering Western Norms

- Rethink therapy models to accommodate collectivist and faith-based perspectives rather than centering on individualism and secularism.
- Move beyond the assumption that Western sexual identity categories are universally applicable.
- Recognize that mental and sexual well-being are deeply embedded in cultural and historical contexts rather than being biologically or psychologically predetermined.

Integrating Faith-Based Perspectives

- Acknowledge the legitimacy of religious frameworks in shaping sexual ethics and identity.
- Train therapists to work with clients whose sexual struggles are framed by spiritual and moral concerns rather than imposing secular perspectives.
- Engage with religious leaders and communities to foster culturally relevant therapeutic approaches.

Expanding Language and Identity Categories

- Challenge the assumption that Western LGBTQ+ categories are the only valid way of understanding gender and sexuality.
- Recognize and respect indigenous and historical sexual identities that do not fit within Western terminology.
- Encourage flexible identity models that reflect relational, fluid, and context-dependent understandings of sexuality.

Rethinking Human Rights in Therapy

- Avoid cultural imperialism in global advocacy efforts by working within local epistemologies rather than imposing external norms.

- Shift from a top-down imposition of sexual rights to community-led dialogues that respect diverse ways of knowing and regulating sexuality.
- Support legal and policy changes that are informed by cultural histories and lived experiences rather than solely relying on Western human rights discourses.

A decolonial approach to psychosexual therapy requires a fundamental rethinking of how sexual knowledge is produced, taught, and applied. Instead of treating Western sexology as a universal science, therapy must acknowledge that different cultures have distinct, valid ways of understanding sexuality and relationships.

By integrating diverse epistemologies, translating rather than transplanting therapeutic models, and fostering inclusivity in identity and relational frameworks, psychosexual therapy can move towards a model that truly respects the plurality of human sexual experience.

Conclusion

Summary of Key Arguments

This chapter has critically examined the ways in which Western psychosexual therapy models have been shaped by Eurocentric assumptions and how their global application has often resulted in cultural misalignment. The historical dominance of Freud, Kinsey, and Hirschfeld set the foundation for a sexological framework that prioritizes individual autonomy, fixed identity categories, and a secular worldview—concepts that do not always translate well into non-Western contexts.

The universalization of these models has been challenged by the processes of cultural translation, as evidenced by case studies such as the adaptation of sexology in Hebrew and Arabic nationalist discourses (Kozma) and the reinterpretation of homosexuality within Confucian social ethics in Republican China (Chiang). Additionally, the imposition of Western LGBTQ+ identity categories has often erased indigenous understandings of gender and sexuality (Wilper), while the global human rights framework has, at times, led to unintended cultural resistance rather than acceptance (Baer).

The chapter has also addressed the failure of Western therapy to integrate religious frameworks, as seen in Hunt's critique of therapy's neglect of religion and spirituality and Bauer's exploration of the struggles to reconcile religious moralities with early sexological theories..

The Necessity of Decolonizing Psychosexual Therapy

Given the limitations of Western psychosexual therapy in diverse cultural contexts, there is a pressing need to move towards a decolonial approach—one that recognizes the plurality of ways in which sexuality, gender, and mental health are understood across societies. This means:

- Moving beyond rigid identity categories to embrace fluid, relational, and culturally embedded understandings of sexuality.
- Shifting from a Eurocentric focus on individual self-actualization to a model that accounts for collectivist and faith-based perspectives.
- Challenging the universal applicability of Western human rights frameworks in favor of community-driven approaches to sexual well-being.
- Expanding therapist training to include indigenous and non-Western epistemologies, ensuring that therapy is contextually relevant and respectful of diverse cultural traditions.

Emphasizing a Culturally Pluralistic Approach Moving Forward

A truly inclusive psychosexual therapy model must be culturally pluralistic, acknowledging that different societies conceptualize sexuality, gender, and relationships in distinct ways. Rather than imposing a singular framework, therapy should be adaptive, responsive, and attuned to the historical, social, and spiritual dimensions of human sexuality.

Moving forward, efforts to reform psychosexual therapy should focus on:

- **Promoting Interdisciplinary Collaboration:** Engaging anthropologists, religious scholars, and indigenous knowledge keepers in the development of more inclusive therapeutic models.
- **Redefining Sexual Identity in Therapy:** Recognizing that sexual identity is not always fixed or individualistic but can be relational and fluid.
- **Encouraging Localized Therapeutic Practices:** Supporting mental health practitioners in developing culturally specific approaches to sexual well-being.
- **Respecting Religious and Ethical Frameworks:** Acknowledging that spirituality and sexual ethics play a vital role in shaping human experiences of intimacy and desire.

By embracing these principles, psychosexual therapy can evolve into a field that truly serves the diverse needs of global populations, fostering healing, understanding, and respect across cultural boundaries.

References

Abbas, A.A. (2012). Clash of Dominant Discourses and African Philosophies and Epistemologies of Education. In Abdi, A.A. (Ed.), *Decolonizing Philosophies of Education* (pp. 113–128). Rotterdam: Sense Publishers.

Baer, Brian James. Translating Sexology in Late-Tsarist and Early-Soviet Russia: Politics, Literature, and the Science of Sex. In Bauer, H. (Ed.), *Sexology and Translation: Cultural and Scientific Encounters across the Modern World* (2015). Temple University Press.

Bauer, Heike. Suicidal Subjects: Translation and the Affective Foundations of Magnus Hirschfeld's Sexology. In Bauer, H. (Ed.), *Sexology and Translation: Cultural and Scientific Encounters across the Modern World* (2015). Temple University Press.
Bose, Brinda, and Subhabrata Bhattacharyya, eds. (2007). *The Phobic and the Erotic: The Politics of Sexualities in Contemporary India*. Calcutta: Seagull Books.
Boyce, Paul, and Akshay Khanna. (2011). Rights and representations: Querying the male-to-male sexual subject in India. *Culture, Health & Sexuality*, *13*(1), 89–100.
Chiang, Howard. (2015). Data of Desire: Translating (Homo)sexology in Republican China. In H. Bauer (Ed.), *Sexology and Translation: Cultural and Scientific Encounters across the Modern World*. Philadelphia: Temple University Press.
Corrêa, Sonia, Rosalind Petchesky, and Richard Parker. (2008). *Sexuality, Health and Human Rights*. London and New York: Routledge.
Freud, Sigmund. *Three Essays on the Theory of Sexuality* (2000). New York: Basic Books.
Hirschfeld, Magnus. *The Sexual History of the World War* (1930). New York: Panurge Press.
Hunt, J. (2022). Ignoring religion is a form of cultural imperialism. *Therapy Today*, September, 34–36. Lutterworth, Leicestershire, UK: British Association for Counselling and Psychotherapy.
Kinsey, Alfred. *Sexual Behavior in the Human Male* (1948). W. B. Saunders.
Kozma, Liat. (2015). Translating Sexology, Writing the Nation: Sexual Discourse and Practice in Hebrew and Arabic in the 1930s. In H. Bauer (Ed.), *Sexology and Translation: Cultural and Scientific Encounters across the Modern World*. Philadelphia: Temple University Press.
Mutua, Makau. (2002). *Human Rights: A Political and Cultural Critique*. Philadelphia: University of Pennsylvania Press.
Smith, Linda Tuhiwai. (2012). *Decolonizing Methodologies: Research and Indigenous Peoples* (2nd ed.). London: Zed Books.
Wilper, James P. (2015). Translation and the Construction of a "Uranian" Identity: Edward Prime-Stevenson's [Xavier Mayne's] *The Intersexes* (1908). In H. Bauer (Ed.), *Sexology and Translation: Cultural and Scientific Encounters across the Modern World* (pp. 216–232). Philadelphia: Temple University Press.

Chapter 3

Types of Cultures and Their Impact on Therapy

Bernd Leygraf

Introduction

Psychosexual therapy has long been shaped by the cultural and linguistic translation of sexual norms, yet this process has historically reinforced dominant Western narratives while silencing non-Western frameworks. The translation of sexual and gender identities is not a neutral act; it carries with it the ideological weight of the languages, cultures, and political structures that frame it. As such, the expansion of Western psychosexual therapy has often resulted in a form of epistemic colonization, where non-Western understandings of sexuality and therapy are marginalized or erased in favor of Euro-American norms.

Western psychosexual models, developed primarily through Freudian, Kinseyan, and postmodern sexological frameworks, have been disseminated globally through a language of universality. However, as José Santaemilia (2017) and Brian James Baer (2017) argue, these models are not culturally neutral but are embedded within a specific ideological and historical trajectory. The very process of translating sexological concepts into different linguistic and cultural contexts reveals the limitations of a universalist framework.

The Eurocentric Bias in Western Psychosexual Models

Western psychosexual therapy has historically been developed within Euro-American cultural contexts, prioritizing individualism, self-expression, and secularism as its foundational principles. These models assume a binary understanding of gender and sexuality, reinforcing norms that may not align with the epistemologies of collectivist, spiritual, or indigenous cultures. For instance:

- Western models assume that sexuality is a fixed and personal identity, whereas many non-Western societies view sexuality as fluid, situational, or relational.
- Therapy frameworks emphasize self-discovery and autonomy, often conflicting with cultural traditions where family, religion, and social harmony take precedence.

DOI: 10.4324/9781003611387-3

- LGBTQ+ identity categories, which are historically rooted in Western socio-political movements, may not translate effectively into non-Western cultural discourses.

Baer and Kaindl (2017) highlight that the global transmission of sexual norms often operates under an implicit assumption of Western sexual progressivism, whereby non-Western approaches to sexuality are cast as either backward or underdeveloped. This epistemological imbalance reflects a colonial legacy in which Western theories dominate psychosexual discourses worldwide, effectively shaping how sexual and therapeutic identities are constructed across different cultural landscapes.

Translation as an Ideological Tool in Psychosexual Therapy

José Santaemilia (2017) argues that translation plays a central role in shaping how sexuality is understood across cultures. The linguistic transfer of psychosexual terminology is never a neutral process; rather, it is shaped by power dynamics, cultural assumptions, and the hegemonic influence of Western discourse. For example:

- Terms like "homosexuality" and "gender identity," originating in European sexological discourse, have been translated into multiple languages but often with significant shifts in meaning that reflect local cultural tensions.
- Western therapeutic concepts like "coming out" are framed as essential milestones in personal development, yet in many societies, sexual identity is not necessarily tied to public self-declaration.
- Translation often involves mistranslations or erasures of non-Western sexual traditions, reinforcing Western ideological dominance over global sexology.

The act of translating sexology is thus deeply political, as it determines what sexual knowledge is preserved, transformed, or erased when moving across cultural and linguistic boundaries. This has significant implications for psychosexual therapy, where non-Western cultural and spiritual frameworks may be excluded from therapeutic discourse due to linguistic and ideological bias.

Argument: The Need for a Decolonial Perspective in Psychosexual Therapy

The expansion of Western psychosexual therapy, though often framed as scientific and neutral, is an example of cultural hegemony. As Baer (2017) demonstrates, the transmission of sexological knowledge often functions as a one-way process, with Western models dictating the terms of psychosexual understanding. This dynamic silences indigenous, religious, and collectivist perspectives on sexuality, many of which offer alternative and equally valid understandings of gender and desire.

A decolonial perspective requires rethinking how therapy is practiced and conceptualized across cultures. Rather than imposing universalist models, psychosexual therapy must acknowledge local sexual epistemologies, allowing for a multiplicity of therapeutic approaches that respect cultural differences. This includes:

- Recognizing non-Western understandings of sexuality that do not conform to Euro-American identity politics.
- Reframing therapy not as a means of "fixing" deviations from Western norms but as a collaborative dialogue between cultures.
- Addressing linguistic biases in sexological translation and developing therapeutic language that is inclusive of non-Western perspectives.

The cultural and linguistic translation of sexuality plays a pivotal role in shaping psychosexual therapy, yet it has historically reinforced Western epistemic dominance. By recognizing the Eurocentric biases embedded in therapy models, we can begin to develop more inclusive and culturally responsive approaches to sexual well-being. As Santaemilia and Baer illustrate, translation is not simply a means of transferring information but a tool of ideological framing that determines whose sexual knowledge is validated or erased. Moving forward, psychosexual therapy must embrace a decolonial, multilingual, and cross-cultural lens that respects the diversity of global sexual epistemologies.

The Cultural and Linguistic Dimensions of Therapy

Translation as a Site of Power and Resistance

Language is a central force in shaping psychosexual therapy models, influencing how sexuality and identity are constructed across different cultural contexts. The linguistic dominance of English in psychosexual research and therapy has led to an imbalance in knowledge production, where Western definitions of sexuality become the universal standard, marginalizing alternative epistemologies.

Translation, rather than being a neutral act, serves as a site of power and resistance, determining which sexual identities are recognized, which are distorted, and which are erased entirely. As Eva Nossem (2017) discusses, lexicography—the practice of dictionary-making—plays a significant role in shaping dominant narratives around sexual identity. Dictionaries codify language and determine which terms become legitimized, reinforcing the conceptual frameworks of dominant cultures while marginalizing non-Western sexual identities.

Case Study: Lexicography and the Exclusion of Non-Western Sexual Identities (Nossem, 2017)

Nossem's analysis reveals how Western-centric dictionaries and lexicons frame LGBTQ+ identities in ways that often fail to reflect local understandings of gender and sexuality. For example:

- Many non-Western gender identities, such as hijra in South Asia or two-spirit in Indigenous North American cultures, are either mistranslated or absent from dominant linguistic frameworks.
- Western terms such as "homosexual" and "transgender" have been imposed on non-Western cultures, often displacing indigenous categories that carry different social and spiritual meanings.
- The process of defining terms in dictionaries reinforces a hierarchical structure where Western categories are seen as universal, while indigenous identities are viewed as deviations or cultural anomalies.

This linguistic dominance has a direct impact on psychosexual therapy. Suppose therapy relies on language to frame personal identity and psychological well-being. In that case, the exclusion of non-Western terms from lexicons means that non-Western clients may struggle to articulate their experiences within a Western-dominated therapeutic space. This highlights the need for a decolonial approach to translation in therapy, one that acknowledges multiple ways of understanding sexuality and identity rather than imposing Eurocentric norms.

Beyond Either/Or: Confronting Binary Therapy Models

Western psychosexual therapy has long been shaped by binary frameworks that position gender and sexuality within rigid, oppositional categories. These models are deeply embedded in a Euro-American tradition of individualism, which often clashes with the collectivist and relational frameworks found in many non-Western societies.

Brian James Baer (2017) critiques the ways in which translation has been used to enforce rigid Western sexual identities onto non-Western cultures. He highlights how sexuality and gender are often framed within a binary logic—masculine/feminine, heterosexual/homosexual—leaving little room for the fluid, context-dependent identities that exist in many cultures.

Case Study: Mistranslation of Gendered Terms in Russian Queer Discourse (Baer, 2017)

Baer's analysis of queer discourse in Russia provides a compelling example of how translation can impose rigid binaries where none originally existed. Some key issues include:

- The Russian language contains gendered linguistic structures that do not always align with Western categorizations of gender and sexuality. Attempts to translate Western queer terminology into Russian often force the adoption of rigid identity labels that do not reflect local experiences.
- Western identity categories such as "gay" or "lesbian" may not fully align with how same-sex desire is understood within Russian cultural contexts, yet translations frequently frame these identities in ways that conform to Western norms.

- The translation of sexual identity terms from English into Russian often results in loss of meaning, as certain concepts do not have direct equivalents, leading to either erasure or forced adaptation.

Baer's case study underscores the epistemic violence that can occur when Western models of therapy are uncritically transplanted into non-Western settings. By forcing clients to conform to rigid identity categories that may not align with their lived realities, psychosexual therapy can become a tool of cultural domination rather than an inclusive, healing practice.

How Binary Thinking Limits Cross-Cultural Therapy

The imposition of binary frameworks within therapy has several negative consequences:

- It excludes cultural understandings of gender and sexuality that do not fit neatly into Western paradigms.
- It fails to accommodate relational models of identity, where sexual and gender expression may be shaped by family, spiritual beliefs, and community roles rather than personal autonomy alone.
- It creates barriers for non-Western clients, who may struggle to express their sexual and gender identities in a therapeutic language that does not reflect their lived experience.

To challenge these limitations, psychosexual therapy must move beyond an either/or approach and embrace a spectrum-based, culturally responsive model. This means:

- Recognizing that gender and sexuality exist on a continuum, rather than within rigid categories.
- Valuing indigenous and non-Western understandings of identity, rather than erasing them through mistranslation.
- Training therapists to be linguistically and culturally competent, so they can engage with clients in ways that respect their cultural frameworks.

The cultural and linguistic dimensions of therapy are often overlooked, yet they play a fundamental role in shaping how sexual identities are framed, understood, and treated in psychosexual therapy. The dominance of English in psychosexual discourse and the rigid binaries imposed through translation reinforce Western epistemic control over global sexuality studies. As Nossem and Baer illustrate, translation is a site of power where identities are either legitimized or erased. Moving forward, psychosexual therapy must adopt a multilingual, culturally adaptive approach that resists the imposition of rigid Western norms and embraces the diversity of global sexual epistemologies.

The Mismatch Between Western Therapy Models and Non-Western Cultural Norms

The Role of Ethnography in Understanding Sexuality

Psychosexual therapy models often rely on Euro-American assumptions about identity, sexuality, and mental health, leading to an epistemic disconnect when applied in non-Western settings. Ethnography offers a crucial counterbalance by documenting how sexuality is lived, negotiated, and conceptualized in different cultural frameworks.

Evren Savci (2017) explores this issue through the lens of queer translation and ethnography, emphasizing how sexual identities are not universally understood but rather socially and historically contingent. The application of Western therapy frameworks in non-Western societies often fails to account for this local variability, leading to therapeutic approaches that are misaligned with the lived realities of clients.

Case Study: Turkish Queer Identities and the Failure of Western Therapy Models (Savci, 2017)

Savci's ethnographic study of Turkish queer identities highlights the ways in which Western psychosexual therapy fails to account for localized understandings of gender and sexuality. Key findings include:

- The Western fixation on "coming out" as a therapeutic goal does not translate well in Turkish cultural contexts, where queer individuals often navigate family, religious, and communal obligations differently than in the West.
- The imposition of rigid LGBTQ+ identity categories—such as "gay" or "lesbian"—erases more fluid and relational ways of experiencing sexuality in Turkish culture.
- Therapeutic language around "individual empowerment" often contradicts collectivist cultural norms, where personal identity is deeply interwoven with family expectations and community belonging.

Savci's work reveals that therapy needs to be adaptive, rather than assuming that Western psychological models are inherently superior. Instead of forcing clients into Western paradigms, psychosexual therapy must integrate ethnographic knowledge to create culturally relevant approaches that acknowledge localized frameworks of gender and sexuality.

Queering Therapy: Moving Beyond Universal Assumptions

Western therapy models frequently operate under the assumption that sexuality and identity must be expressed in fixed, individualist terms. This perspective, however, ignores the cultural relativity of sexual norms and often imposes hegemonic understandings of queerness onto non-Western societies. Therapy, then, becomes a performance of Western norms rather than a genuine engagement with the client's lived reality.

Michela Baldo (2017) examines how translating Butler's (2004) *Undoing Gender* into Italian serves as a case study in resisting these universalist assumptions. Baldo argues that translation is never a neutral process, and that dominant therapy discourses can be reinterpreted rather than imposed through careful engagement with local epistemologies.

Case Study: The Translation of Undoing Gender into Italian (Baldo, 2017)

Baldo's analysis of *Undoing Gender*'s translation into Italian provides a striking parallel to the failures of Western psychosexual therapy in non-Western cultural contexts:

- The original English text operates within a specific intellectual tradition—one that assumes readers share a particular understanding of gender performativity.
- In translating the text into Italian, certain concepts had to be adapted, as direct equivalents for Butler's arguments did not exist in Italian feminist and LGBTQ+ discourse.
- Rather than enforcing a one-to-one correspondence, the translation engaged with local frameworks of gender and sexuality, leading to new interpretations rather than a simple replication of Butler's ideas.

This example is crucial for psychosexual therapy: instead of assuming Western models should be transplanted unchanged, therapy must be contextualized and translated in ways that reflect local sexual epistemologies. The act of translation—whether linguistic or conceptual—must be a negotiation rather than a form of intellectual colonialism.

How Therapy Can Adapt Instead of Impose

The failures highlighted in these case studies suggest that Western psychosexual therapy must move towards a decolonial, adaptive model by:

- Engaging in ethnographic research to understand how sexuality is conceptualized in different cultures before applying therapeutic frameworks.
- Resisting the impulse to universalize Western understandings of queerness, gender, and sexuality in therapeutic discourse.
- Incorporating translation as an active, interpretative process, rather than assuming that Western sexual theories can be imposed unchanged in other cultural settings.

- Training therapists in cross-cultural competency, ensuring that they recognize the diversity of sexual experiences and frameworks across global societies.

The mismatch between Western therapy models and non-Western cultural norms is not just a theoretical issue—it has real consequences for how therapy is practiced and how clients experience treatment. Ethnographic studies, such as Savci's work on Turkish queer identities, demonstrate the harmful effects of applying Western therapeutic concepts without adaptation. Meanwhile, Baldo's work on the translation of *Undoing Gender* illustrates the potential for reinterpreting rather than imposing dominant discourse. If psychosexual therapy is to become truly inclusive, it must embrace cultural plurality, linguistic adaptability, and a commitment to ethnographic engagement rather than universalist assumptions.

The Linguistic Barriers to Inclusive Therapy

The Impact of Translation on LGBTQ+ Identity Formation

Language plays a crucial role in shaping LGBTQ+ identities, yet translation is often an imperfect and ideologically charged process that can alter, erase, or distort identity labels. Psychosexual therapy, which relies heavily on linguistic clarity, struggles when dealing with concepts that do not have direct equivalents across languages. Translation is not just about transferring meaning—it is about shaping reality.

Eva Nossem (2017) explores how queer terminologies shift and transform when moved between languages. The difficulty of translating "queer" across cultural and linguistic boundaries demonstrates how therapy can unintentionally enforce Western-centric LGBTQ+ identity categories that do not align with local experiences.

Case Study: The Challenges of Translating "Queer" (Nossem, 2017)

Nossem's analysis highlights significant barriers in translating "queer," which reflects broader issues in LGBTQ+ identity formation across languages:

- Many languages lack a direct equivalent for "queer," leading to translations that either strip away its political and fluid meanings or replace it with rigid identity markers.
- In languages where "queer" does exist, it is often understood differently, losing its original resistance to binary identities and heteronormativity.
- In some cultures, attempts to introduce "queer" into lexicons face social and political pushback, making it difficult for LGBTQ+ individuals to access affirming therapeutic spaces.

The failure of therapy to address fluid and relational sexual identities outside Western constructs is deeply tied to these linguistic issues. When therapeutic frameworks assume that sexuality and gender exist as fixed categories, they marginalize clients whose cultures do not subscribe to these rigid distinctions.

For instance:

- Non-Western conceptualizations of gender and sexuality (e.g., South Asian hijra, Indigenous two-spirit identities) often do not conform to Western LGBTQ+ terminology, creating misalignment in therapy.
- Translation can impose fixed labels where fluidity exists, pushing individuals into categories that do not reflect their lived experiences.
- Therapists trained in Western models may struggle to recognize identity expressions that lack direct linguistic representation in English, creating a disconnect between client and therapist.

Decolonizing the Language of Therapy

If therapy is to be truly inclusive, it must actively resist the linguistic hierarchies that reinforce Western epistemologies. Nossem (2017) argues that lexicography—the creation of dictionaries and standardized terminologies—plays a fundamental role in shaping how sexuality and gender are defined globally. By controlling which terms are included and how they are defined, lexicographical translation can either validate or erase non-Western identities.

Case Study: The Erasure of Non-Western Gender Identities in Lexicography (Nossem, 2017)

Nossem provides a critical examination of how non-Western gender identities are often excluded from dictionaries, leading to:

- The invisibilization of Indigenous and non-Western gender expressions by framing them as "cultural anomalies" rather than valid identities.
- The translation of gender categories in a way that forces them into Western, binary molds, removing the fluidity and social significance that they hold in local contexts.
- The dominance of English-language terms in LGBTQ+ discourse, reinforcing Western narratives as the global standard for sexual identity formation.

How Therapy Can Avoid Reinforcing Linguistic Hierarchies

A truly decolonial approach to therapy must challenge the assumption that Western psychosexual terminology represents a universal framework. This requires:

- Incorporating multilingual perspectives in therapeutic training, ensuring that therapists are familiar with non-Western sexual and gender epistemologies.

- Rejecting rigid identity labels in favor of more flexible, relational understandings of sexuality that reflect cultural and linguistic diversity.
- Engaging with lexicographical activism to promote the inclusion of diverse gender and sexual identities in language frameworks, ensuring that therapy does not erase non-Western experiences.

Linguistic barriers in therapy are not just technical issues of translation—they are sites of power that determine which identities are recognized and which are erased. Nossem's research highlights the deep impact of language on LGBTQ+ identity formation and the ways in which Western-dominated lexicography reinforces Eurocentric norms in psychosexual therapy. If therapy is to be truly inclusive, it must go beyond Western linguistic frameworks and embrace a decolonial, multilingual approach that validates diverse sexual and gender identities.

Towards a Decolonial Model of Psychosexual Therapy

The continued dominance of Western psychosexual therapy models has created a gap in accessibility and inclusivity for individuals whose experiences of gender, sexuality, and relationships exist outside of Euro-American frameworks. A decolonial approach to psychosexual therapy must center linguistic plurality, cultural specificity, and alternative epistemologies, ensuring that therapy is adaptable rather than imposed as a rigid system. This section explores two key components of a decolonial approach: expanding therapist training and developing a queer, multilingual, and culturally adaptive therapy model.

Expanding Therapist Training and Cross-Cultural Competency

For psychosexual therapy to be effective on a global scale, it must equip therapists with the knowledge and skills to navigate non-Western conceptualizations of gender, sexuality, and identity. This requires an expansion of therapist training to include:

- Local sexual epistemologies and histories, ensuring therapists understand the cultural significance of sexuality beyond Western categories.
- Linguistic training in queer translation, allowing for a nuanced approach to working with clients who conceptualize identity differently.
- Ethnographic sensitivity, enabling therapists to work within culturally specific relational and familial structures rather than assuming individualist models of therapy.

José Santaemilia (2017) highlights the challenges of translating LGBTQ+ terminology into Arabic, a case that underscores the need for culturally competent therapist training. Western sexual identity categories such as "lesbian," "gay," and "bisexual" do not always have direct equivalents in Arabic and are often translated in ways that erase local understandings of same-sex relationships and non-binary identities. Therapy training must address these linguistic and epistemological gaps so that therapists can:

- Engage with non-Western gender and sexual categories on their own terms rather than forcing Western definitions.
- Recognize how language mediates identity formation, ensuring that translations reflect lived realities rather than foreign impositions.
- Develop culturally appropriate therapeutic interventions, acknowledging the role of faith, kinship, and social belonging in shaping LGBTQ+ experiences outside of the West.

Moving beyond Western psychological frameworks means rethinking therapy's fundamental assumptions about sexuality and mental health. Many cultures conceptualize sexuality as relational and fluid, rather than as an innate, fixed identity, yet most Western therapy models continue to operate under the assumption that sexual orientation and gender identity must be static, individualistic, and self-determined. Expanding therapist training to include non-Western epistemologies ensures that therapy is not an act of cultural erasure but a process of negotiation and understanding.

The Need for a Queer, Multilingual, and Culturally Adaptive Therapy Model

A truly decolonial psychosexual therapy model must be queer, multilingual, and culturally adaptive, rejecting the idea that Western therapeutic paradigms hold universal applicability. This requires an approach that treats translation as an act of resistance and adaptation, rather than as a simple process of linguistic substitution.

Brian James Baer (2017) discusses the reinterpretation of queer narratives in non-Western translation, revealing how queer discourses are not simply borrowed but reshaped in response to local sociopolitical realities. His analysis highlights the limitations of Western psychosexual therapy models when applied globally:

- In Russia, translations of queer discourse have historically been adapted to fit existing cultural and political frameworks, leading to shifts in meaning that depart significantly from Western narratives.
- Queer identity categories often undergo strategic reinterpretation, where terms like "gay" or "transgender" take on different connotations depending on social context.
- Therapy models that rely on Western identity labels may fail to engage with clients whose sense of self does not align with these frameworks, making treatment less effective.

Baer's findings suggest that psychosexual therapy must incorporate non-Western sexual and relational frameworks, ensuring that therapy is linguistically and culturally flexible rather than rigidly imposed. This means:

- Adopting multilingual therapeutic practices, where clients can explore sexuality and identity in their own linguistic and cultural terms.
- Recognizing indigenous and non-Western relational models, such as kinship-based gender roles in South Asian hijra communities or the social rather than biological determination of gender in many Indigenous cultures.
- Rejecting the demand for assimilation into Western categories, instead allowing clients to define their identities according to their cultural and historical contexts.

A culturally adaptive therapy model acknowledges that sexuality is not a singular experience but a deeply contextual one. Western therapy models that insist on individualized narratives of self-discovery and identity affirmation risk alienating clients who experience sexuality as relational, social, or even spiritual. A multilingual and queer approach to therapy ensures that therapy is not merely a Western export, but a globally relevant practice that adapts to the needs of diverse communities.

Moving towards a decolonial psychosexual therapy model requires a fundamental shift in how therapy is conceptualized and practiced. Expanding therapist training to include linguistic and cultural fluency ensures that therapy is not an imposition of foreign frameworks but a collaborative process rooted in mutual understanding. Similarly, embracing queer, multilingual, and culturally adaptive therapy models allows therapy to serve a broader, more diverse range of clients without forcing them to conform to Western identity paradigms.

Baer and Santaemilia's research reveals that translation is never neutral—it is an act of power, adaptation, and resistance. If psychosexual therapy is to truly serve global populations, it must move beyond Western linguistic and epistemological hierarchies and towards a model that values linguistic and cultural diversity. Only by doing so can therapy become a meaningful tool for healing, rather than a site of epistemic colonialism.

Conclusion

Psychosexual therapy has long been shaped by the forces of translation and cultural hegemony, operating under the assumption that Western understandings of sexuality and gender can be universally applied. However, the process of translation is far from neutral; it is a site where power, ideology, and cultural specificity converge. As explored throughout this chapter, translation can both expand and restrict the ways in which identities are recognized, often reinforcing Eurocentric frameworks while marginalizing non-Western perspectives. The dominance of Western psychosexual models has led to an epistemological imbalance, where non-Western sexual and gender identities are either erased, forcibly categorized into rigid identity structures, or rendered unintelligible within dominant therapeutic discourses.

A queer, decolonial approach to psychosexual therapy must recognize and resist these hegemonic translations, prioritizing linguistic and cultural plurality as fundamental principles. By acknowledging that gender and sexuality are deeply contextual phenomena, rather than fixed, universal experiences, therapy can become more inclusive and responsive to diverse ways of knowing. Rather than assuming that identity is inherently linked to Western frameworks of selfhood, autonomy, and individual expression, psychosexual therapy must be open to relational, spiritual, and collective understandings of identity that exist outside of Western paradigms. The field must critically interrogate the colonial histories embedded in its theories and practices, ensuring that therapy does not become an extension of cultural imperialism but a tool for self-determination across different linguistic and social realities.

Throughout this chapter, the research of Santaemilia, Baer, Nossem, Baldo, and Savci has illuminated the ways in which therapy can be adapted, rather than imposed, through careful and conscious engagement with translation and cultural context. Santaemilia's analysis of Arabic LGBTQ+ terminology demonstrates how linguistic adaptation is not a simple transfer of meaning but a complex negotiation that shapes identity itself. Baer's exploration of Russian queer discourse highlights how Western sexual identity categories are reinterpreted in different socio-political settings, resisting direct translation. Nossem's work on lexicography and power reveals the systematic exclusion of non-Western identities in dictionary-making, a process that profoundly influences the language available in therapeutic settings. Baldo's case study on the translation of *Undoing Gender* into Italian provides a clear example of how translation does not merely transmit ideas but transforms them, offering new ways of conceptualizing gender. Savci's ethnographic research on Turkish queer identities exposes the failure of Western therapy to accommodate non-Western relational models, demonstrating the urgent need for culturally responsive therapeutic practices.

The necessity of a queer, multilingual, and culturally adaptive model of psychosexual therapy is not just an academic concern—it is a practical imperative for ensuring that therapy serves rather than marginalizes diverse populations. This requires a fundamental shift in the way therapists are trained, urging professionals to become critically aware of the linguistic hierarchies and cultural translations that shape their practice. Applying Western therapeutic norms indiscriminately is no longer sufficient; instead, therapy must be actively translated into diverse cultural and linguistic frameworks, with a deep respect for indigenous and non-Western epistemologies.

Ultimately, psychosexual therapy must evolve beyond a universalist model that assumes its frameworks are neutral or universally beneficial. The future of the field lies in collaborative knowledge production, where voices from marginalized and colonized communities play a central role in shaping therapeutic discourse. Decolonizing psychosexual therapy does not mean rejecting Western insights entirely, but rather placing them in dialogue with multiple traditions of knowledge, allowing for an ethical, inclusive, and dynamic practice. Translation must be approached not as an act of dominance, but as a means of opening up possibilities for meaningful cross-cultural exchange. By embracing this approach, psychosexual therapy can truly move towards a model that does not impose sexuality and gender frameworks, but rather translates them in ways that affirm diverse lived experiences.

References

Baer, Brian James. "Beyond Either/Or: Confronting the Fact of Translation in Global Sexuality Studies." In Brian James Baer and Klaus Kaindl (Eds.), *Queering Translation, Translating the Queer: Theory, Practice, Activism*. Routledge Advances in Translation and Interpreting Studies. New York: Routledge, 2017.

Baer. Brian James and Kaindl, Klaus (Eds.), *Queering Translation, Translating the Queer: Theory, Practice, Activism*. Routledge Advances in Translation and Interpreting Studies. New York: Routledge, 2017.

Baldo, Michela. "Queer Translation as Performative and Affective Undoing: Translating Butler's *Undoing Gender* into Italian." In Brian James Baer and Klaus Kaindl (Eds.), *Queering Translation, Translating the Queer: Theory, Practice, Activism*. Routledge Advances in Translation and Interpreting Studies. New York: Routledge, 2017.

Bassi, Serena. "Displacing LGBT: Global Englishes, Activism and Translated Sexualities." In Olga Castro and Emek Ergun (Eds.), *Feminist Translation Studies: Local and Transnational Perspectives*. New York: Routledge, 2017, pp. 235–248.

Butler, Judith. *Undoing Gender*. New York and London: Routledge, 2004.

Nossem, Eva. "Queering Lexicography: Balancing Power Relations in Dictionaries." In Brian James Baer and Klaus Kaindl (Eds.), *Queering Translation, Translating the Queer: Theory, Practice, Activism*. Routledge Advances in Translation and Interpreting Studies. New York: Routledge, 2017.

Santaemilia, José. "Sexuality and Translation as Intimate Partners? Toward a Queer Turn in Rewriting Identities and Desires." In Brian James Baer and Klaus Kaindl (Eds.), *Queering Translation, Translating the Queer: Theory, Practice, Activism*. Routledge Advances in Translation and Interpreting Studies. New York: Routledge, 2017.

Savci, Evren. "Ethnography and Queer Translation." Brian James Baer and Klaus Kaindl (Eds.), *Queering Translation, Translating the Queer: Theory, Practice, Activism*. Routledge Advances in Translation and Interpreting Studies. New York: Routledge, 2017.

Chapter 4

History of Psychosexual Therapy Work

Bishurul Hafi NA and NA Uvais

Introduction

Psychosexual therapy is a specialized form of intervention designed to help individuals and couples address sexual concerns and dysfunctions by integrating medical, psychological, and relational perspectives. This form of therapy is not limited to the physical aspects of sexual health but also takes into account the emotional, psychological, and relational dimensions that influence sexual well-being. The evolution of psychosexual therapy is deeply rooted in the development of medicine, philosophy, psychology, and shifting social norms surrounding human sexuality.

The history of this field reveals a gradual yet profound transformation, starting from ancient traditions and beliefs about sexuality, progressing through early medical and psychological understandings, and eventually giving rise to contemporary sexual medicine practices. Understanding the trajectory of psychosexual therapy involves examining how cultural, social, and scientific perspectives on sexuality have shaped therapeutic practices, leading to a more holistic and integrated approach to sexual health today.

Throughout this chapter, we will explore the historical milestones that have contributed to the development of psychosexual therapy. By tracing its evolution from ancient views on sexuality, such as those found in the Kama Sutra and Traditional Chinese Medicine, to the groundbreaking work of modern sex therapists, we can better understand the complex interplay of biology, psychology, and culture that has shaped the practice. We will also discuss the impact of key figures, such as Masters and Johnson, Havelock Ellis, and Helen Kaplan, whose work helped transform psychosexual therapy into a recognized discipline within sexual medicine.

Additionally, clinical vignettes will be provided to illustrate how these historical theories have been applied in practice and how psychosexual therapy continues to evolve in response to contemporary challenges in sexual health.

DOI: 10.4324/9781003611387-4

Ancient and Classical Foundations

Eastern Concepts

Sexuality has long been regarded as an essential aspect of health, vitality, and overall well-being across many ancient cultures. In ancient India, sexuality was integrated into a broader understanding of life, love, and relationships. The *Kama Sutra*, written by the scholar Vatsyayana around the 3rd century CE, is often misunderstood as merely a guide to sexual positions. In reality, it serves as a comprehensive treatise on love, relationships, and the emotional and psychological aspects of intimacy. This ancient text emphasized the importance of emotional compatibility, communication, and sensual pleasure in human interactions. It marked one of the earliest recognized efforts to consider the psychological dimensions of sexual health, recognizing that physical intimacy cannot be separated from emotional connection. The Kama Sutra provided insights into the role of pleasure and mutual respect in fostering healthy relationships, shaping attitudes toward sexuality that would persist for centuries (Vatsyayana, 1962).

Furthermore, Traditional Chinese Medicine (TCM) and Taoist philosophy also placed great importance on the connection between sexuality and vitality. In TCM, sexual health was seen as intrinsically linked to the balance of life energy, or qi, and the proper flow of jing (sexual essence). Taoist texts, such as those by the philosopher Laozi, emphasized the idea that sexual energy should be cultivated and preserved, as it was believed to contribute to long life and spiritual health. This holistic view of sexuality not only focused on physical pleasure but also on the spiritual and energetic aspects of sexual expression, highlighting the importance of balance between body, mind, and spirit for overall well-being (Needham, 2000).

Ancient Indian and Chinese texts suggest that sexuality was considered an essential part of human health and not merely a private or taboo subject. By recognizing the psychological, emotional, and spiritual facets of sexuality, these cultures laid the groundwork for more comprehensive and integrated views of sexual health, which would later influence modern psychosexual therapy.

Greco-Roman Views

In the classical Greco-Roman world, sexuality and love were often explored in both philosophical and medical contexts. Greek philosophers, such as Plato, engaged in deep discussions about love and desire in works like *The Symposium*. In this dialogue, Plato explored the nature of love (eros) and how it transcends mere physical attraction to encompass intellectual and spiritual connection. Plato's depiction of love suggested that it could lead to a greater understanding of the self and the divine, reflecting early philosophical thinking about the psychological and existential significance of human sexuality (Plato, 1999).

In contrast to the philosophical views of Plato, the medical understanding of sexuality in the Greco-Roman period was largely influenced by the works of

Hippocrates and Galen. Hippocrates, often regarded as the father of Western medicine, suggested that sexual health was closely tied to the balance of bodily humors—blood, phlegm, yellow bile, and black bile. According to Hippocratic theory, an imbalance in these humors could result in sexual dysfunction or a lack of libido. Similarly, Galen, a prominent Roman physician, extended Hippocrates' ideas, proposing that both physical and psychological factors were important in understanding sexual health. Galen believed that an imbalance of the humors, particularly blood, could lead to sexual issues such as impotence or infertility (Galen, 1951; Hippocrates, 2002).

Both Hippocrates and Galen's medical frameworks represented a somatic approach to sexual problems, where dysfunctions were seen as physiological issues that could be corrected through the restoration of bodily balance. These early theories laid the foundation for later medical interpretations of sexual dysfunction, influencing the medicalization of sexuality that would emerge in the modern era.

While the Greco-Roman world did not have the same holistic understanding of sexuality as seen in Eastern philosophies, their contributions were instrumental in shaping the trajectory of sexual health, particularly through their focus on the body and its relationship to sexual function. Over time, these views would evolve and merge with more psychologically and emotionally attuned approaches to therapy, as seen in the development of psychosexual therapy.

Medieval Islamic and European Thought

Islamic Contributions to Sexual Health

During the Islamic Golden Age (8th to 14th century), scholars in the Islamic world made significant contributions to the field of sexual health, blending medical knowledge with philosophical and ethical considerations. Two key figures in this area were Avicenna (Ibn Sina) and Al-Razi, both of whom incorporated sexual health into their extensive medical works.

Avicenna, in his renowned medical text The Canon of Medicine (1025), explored human sexuality from both a physiological and psychological perspective. He emphasized the importance of balanced sexual activity for overall health and longevity, stating that sexual function was closely tied to both physical well-being and mental equilibrium. Avicenna highlighted the role of proper sexual activity in maintaining bodily health, suggesting that it could serve as a form of exercise that rejuvenated the body and mind. His work also discussed the causes of sexual dysfunction, including both physical ailments and psychological factors, such as anxiety and emotional trauma. These early medical insights into the relationship between sexual health and psychological well-being laid important groundwork for the development of psychosexual therapy (Avicenna, 2007).

Al-Razi (Rhazes), another significant Islamic physician, wrote extensively about sexual health in his work Kitab al-Hawi (The Comprehensive Book). Al-Razi acknowledged that sexual health could be affected by various physical conditions, such as hormonal imbalances and infections, as well as emotional and mental factors. He also explored the treatment of sexual dysfunction and infertility, offering a blend of medical and psychological approaches. Al-Razi's contributions to sexual health were progressive for his time, and he is credited with introducing ideas that considered not only the physical aspects of sexual health but also the emotional and relational components (Ullmann, 1978).

These scholars' works were pivotal in integrating sexuality into the broader fields of medicine and psychology, advocating for a holistic approach to sexual well-being. Their insights laid the foundation for future explorations into psychosexual therapy, where the interconnectedness of the body and mind would become central to understanding sexual function.

Medieval European Views on Sexuality

In medieval Europe, sexuality was primarily understood through the lens of Christian doctrine, which often framed sexual activity within moralistic and reproductive confines. The Church's teachings emphasized chastity, procreation, and the sanctity of marriage, while condemning practices that deviated from these ideals, such as masturbation, extramarital affairs, and homosexuality. Despite this moral framework, there were ongoing medical discussions about sexual health and dysfunction, particularly within the context of marriage.

Medical texts from the medieval period, often written by scholars influenced by both ancient Greek and Roman thought, continued to explore issues like infertility, impotence, and libido disorders. These texts often attributed sexual dysfunction to imbalances in bodily humors, a theory dating back to Hippocrates and Galen, and they recommended a variety of treatments ranging from dietary changes to herbal remedies. The work of Hildegard of Bingen, a medieval abbess, healer, and mystic, is particularly notable in this context. She wrote about the importance of balance in sexual relationships and recommended natural remedies for conditions like impotence and infertility, acknowledging that both physical and spiritual factors contributed to sexual health (von Bingen, 1998).

While medieval Christian views generally emphasized the reproductive purpose of sex, there were also subtle acknowledgments of the emotional and relational aspects of sexuality. For example, St. Thomas Aquinas argued that sexual pleasure within marriage could be justified if it served the higher purpose of procreation, suggesting that a balance between moral purpose and physical pleasure was necessary for a healthy sexual relationship (Aquinas, 1993). This recognition of the complex nature of sexuality set the stage for future discussions on sexual well-being, which would later evolve into more comprehensive and integrated models of psychosexual therapy.

Despite the moral constraints imposed by religious teachings, the continued exploration of sexual health during the medieval period laid the groundwork for later advancements in understanding the psychological, emotional, and physical aspects of sexuality. These discussions, though limited by the cultural and religious context of the time, began to integrate the mind and body in ways that would later be expanded upon by modern psychosexual therapy.

Enlightenment and 19th-Century Shifts

The 18th and 19th centuries were pivotal in shaping modern views on sexuality, as increasing medical and psychological inquiry began to pathologize sexual behavior while also opening the door to a broader understanding of human sexual diversity. This era marked a significant shift from religious and moralistic views on sexuality to a more clinical and scientific perspective. However, this shift also reflected the moral and societal constraints of the time, particularly within the Victorian era.

Richard von Krafft-Ebing and the Medicalization of Sexual Behavior

One of the most influential figures during this period was Richard von Krafft-Ebing, a German psychiatrist whose work *Psychopathia Sexualis* (1886) is often regarded as one of the foundational texts in the history of sexual medicine. Krafft-Ebing's work sought to categorize and understand what he considered to be "sexual deviations" or behaviors outside the traditional norms of heterosexual reproduction.

Krafft-Ebing's contributions to the field were groundbreaking in that he was among the first to document and attempt to classify sexual behaviors that deviated from what was considered normal, such as sadism, masochism, homosexuality, and transvestism. He viewed these behaviors through a pathological lens, presenting them as disorders that were largely defined by the presence of social and moral transgressions. However, Krafft-Ebing's contributions also laid the groundwork for modern psychology and sexology, helping to establish a clinical vocabulary for discussing sexual differences and issues.

It is important to note that while Krafft-Ebing's work was instrumental in shaping the early field of sexual medicine, his categorization of non-heteronormative sexual behaviors as "perversions" reflected the social stigma of the time, framing these practices in a negative light. The moral judgment that underpinned his views would later be critiqued by more progressive thinkers like Havelock Ellis, who advocated for a more empathetic and less judgmental view of sexual diversity (Krafft-Ebing, 1899).

Havelock Ellis and the Emergence of Sexual Diversity

In contrast to Krafft-Ebing's medicalized and pathologized approach to sexual behavior, Havelock Ellis offered a more humanistic and empathetic perspective on sexuality in his work Studies in the Psychology of Sex (1897). Ellis was an English physician and one of the first to advocate for a non-judgmental, scientific approach to human sexuality, proposing that sexual diversity was a natural variation of human experience rather than a deviation or disorder.

Ellis's research covered a wide range of topics, including homosexuality, masturbation, sexual fetishes, and gender identity. He recognized that sexual behaviors, even those deemed unconventional, did not necessarily imply pathology. Instead, he believed that these variations could be understood as part of the spectrum of human sexual expression. His work helped lay the foundation for understanding sexuality in a more inclusive and nuanced way, contributing to the gradual acceptance of sexual diversity in medical and psychological circles.

Ellis's approach was also one of empathy. He actively rejected the moralistic and punitive stance that often accompanied discussions of non-normative sexual behaviors, advocating for greater understanding and acceptance. This humanistic shift was critical in the development of psychosexual therapy, which would later adopt a more open and therapeutic approach to addressing sexual concerns, including those related to sexual orientation and gender expression (Ellis, 1900–1928).

Ellis's work is significant in that it helped frame sexual issues within a psychological and social context, as opposed to solely a medical one. By considering sexual issues as part of the human experience, rather than as problems to be fixed, Ellis encouraged a more holistic understanding of human sexuality that would later be expanded upon by sex therapists.

The Victorian Context and the Medicalization of Sexuality

The medicalization of sexuality in the 19th century was also shaped by the moral and cultural attitudes of the Victorian era. During this period, social mores dictated that sexuality, especially female sexuality, was to be repressed, and any deviation from this norm was seen as morally corrupt or a sign of psychological dysfunction. The rise of scientific inquiry into sexuality, spearheaded by figures like Krafft-Ebing and Ellis, coincided with a time when Victorian society was both fascinated by and fearful of sexual expression.

In this context, the medical profession played a central role in framing sexual issues as medical problems that required intervention. Conditions such as hysteria, frigidity, and impotence were medicalized, and treatments ranged from psychotherapy to physical therapies, often aimed at repressing or controlling sexual desires rather than understanding them. This reflects the tension between the emerging medical understanding of sexuality and the prevailing societal norms that sought to regulate and suppress sexual expression (Foucault, 1978).

The medicalization of sexuality in the Victorian era also gave rise to the psychoanalytic theory of sexuality, which would be developed further in the early 20th century. This framework introduced the idea that unconscious desires, particularly repressed sexual urges, could have a profound impact on mental health and behavior. This theory, while evolving into a more nuanced understanding of sexual issues, also contributed to the pathologization of many forms of sexual expression that were not aligned with heterosexual norms (Freud, 2000).

Clinical Vignettes: The Victorian Experience

To understand the lived experience of individuals during this time, we can consider clinical vignettes based on the historical accounts of patients treated by physicians during the 19th century.

In one example, a woman, whom we will call Elizabeth, came to a Victorian-era physician with complaints of anxiety, nervousness, and a lack of sexual desire. The doctor, following the standard medical approach of the time, diagnosed her with "female hysteria," a condition commonly attributed to sexual repression. Elizabeth was treated with a variety of methods, including pelvic massages, which were believed to alleviate her symptoms by stimulating sexual arousal. While this treatment was designed to address her perceived sexual dysfunction, it also reflected the era's understanding of women's sexual health as secondary to societal expectations of modesty and propriety.

In a separate case, Henry, a man struggling with what was diagnosed as "sexual excess," was treated by Krafft-Ebing's contemporaries using a similar pathologized approach. Henry's sexual desires were seen as excessive and perverse, and he was prescribed treatments aimed at curbing his libido, such as cold baths and rest. His experiences highlight the way sexual expression, particularly outside of heteronormative boundaries, was often medicalized and treated as a disorder rather than a natural variation (Krafft-Ebing, 1899).

Legacy and Modern Implications

The legacy of 19th-century sexual medicalization and its impact on psychosexual therapy cannot be understated. The work of Krafft-Ebing and Ellis helped move the conversation about sexuality from a moral or religious framework to a more medical and psychological one. While Krafft-Ebing's pathologizing approach has been critiqued for its negative framing of sexual diversity, Ellis's more humanistic views laid the groundwork for modern psychosexual therapy, which seeks to understand sexual concerns as part of the broader human experience, rather than as disorders to be fixed.

By the end of the 19th century, the seeds were sown for the development of a more empathetic and scientific approach to treating sexual concerns, one that would continue to evolve into the integrated psychosexual therapy practices we recognize today.

Freud, Psychoanalysis, and Sexual Drives

Sigmund Freud, often considered the father of modern psychoanalysis, made groundbreaking contributions to the understanding of sexuality, shaping much of the field of psychosexual therapy. Freud's theories on libido, psychosexual development, and neurosis represented a major shift in how sexual behavior was understood, moving it from purely biological explanations to one that included unconscious processes and early childhood experiences.

Freud's work introduced the idea that sexual development was not just about physical maturation but was also deeply influenced by emotional and psychological factors. His exploration of the unconscious mind and its impact on behavior was revolutionary, suggesting that many of our sexual behaviors were not fully conscious but instead rooted in repressed desires and unresolved conflicts.

Freud's Theories on Libido and Psychosexual Development

Freud's three essays on sexuality (1905), a landmark work in the history of psychology, introduced the concept of libido as a driving force behind human behavior. Freud suggested that libido, or sexual energy, was not limited to just physical or genital sexual expression but was also an important factor in shaping emotional and psychological development throughout life. He theorized that early childhood experiences played a crucial role in forming sexual identity and adult sexual behavior. Freud's psychosexual stages of development, which include the oral, anal, phallic, latent, and genital stages, proposed that unresolved conflicts during these stages could lead to neurosis and sexual dysfunctions later in life.

One of Freud's most famous concepts is the Oedipus complex, which he described as the unconscious desire of a child to possess the opposite-sex parent and a corresponding rivalry with the same-sex parent. Freud believed that unresolved feelings during the phallic stage could lead to long-term effects on sexual behavior and relationships in adulthood. This concept, along with many others in Freud's work, introduced a psychological dimension to sexual dysfunction, suggesting that sexual difficulties were not just about physical health but also about unconscious conflicts and emotional blocks.

Despite the groundbreaking nature of his ideas, many of Freud's theories have been critiqued over time, particularly his emphasis on infantile sexuality and his gendered views. Freud's work was also seen as being overly focused on male sexuality, leading to a lack of attention to female sexual experiences. Nonetheless, his work laid the foundation for later psychoanalytic theories and highlighted the significance of the unconscious in shaping sexual behaviors and desires.

The Role of Sexual Repression in Neurosis

One of Freud's most influential contributions to psychosexual therapy was his assertion that sexual repression was at the heart of many psychological disorders. Freud believed that repressed sexual desires could manifest as neuroses, leading to symptoms such as anxiety, depression, and compulsive behaviors. This connection between sexual repression and mental illness was a radical idea at the time and marked a significant departure from previous views that only focused on physical causes of sexual dysfunction.

Freud's ideas about sexual repression were tied to his broader theories about civilization and culture. In his work *Civilization and Its Discontents* (1930), Freud argued that social and cultural norms often required the repression of natural sexual desires, leading to feelings of frustration and conflict. He suggested that the repression of sexuality was a necessary but harmful part of societal functioning, as it allowed for social order but also led to psychological distress.

Wilhelm Reich and Body-Oriented Therapy

Wilhelm Reich, one of Freud's early followers, expanded on Freud's ideas and made important contributions to the development of psychosexual therapy. Reich was a psychoanalyst who became increasingly interested in the body's role in emotional expression, particularly as it related to sexual health. He is best known for developing orgone therapy, which emphasized the connection between sexual energy and physical health.

Reich's theories extended Freud's concept of the libido but emphasized the importance of orgasm as a means of emotional release and personal healing. Reich believed that the body could hold emotional tension and that sexual release through orgasm could help alleviate psychological distress. He introduced the concept of muscular armor, which referred to the physical tension that developed in response to repressed emotions, particularly sexual ones. Reich's work was some of the first to incorporate bodywork into psychosexual therapy, seeing the body as not only the site of sexual function but also a key component of emotional healing.

Reich's ideas were controversial and often met with skepticism, but his work laid the groundwork for later developments in body-oriented psychotherapy and humanistic approaches to sexual health. His emphasis on sexual liberation as a means of emotional release was particularly influential during the sexual revolution of the 1960s.

Clinical Vignettes: The Psychoanalytic Influence

To understand the impact of Freud's and Reich's theories in practice, consider a clinical vignette based on historical treatments:

- In the early 20th century, a woman named Eleanor sought psychoanalytic therapy due to a longstanding issue with sexual frigidity. She had been married for several years, but she experienced a lack of desire for her husband. Freud's influence on her therapist's approach was evident, as the therapist began by exploring Eleanor's early childhood experiences, particularly focusing on any unresolved conflicts with her father. Eleanor's therapist hypothesized that her lack of sexual desire stemmed from unconscious sexual repression, particularly the result of early childhood trauma and a sense of guilt about her sexual feelings.

- In another case, Robert, a middle-aged man, was referred to therapy for impotence. His symptoms had appeared after a series of stressful life events, but he had also been experiencing intense guilt around his sexual desires. The therapist, influenced by Reich's ideas, helped Robert explore the connection between his emotional state and his sexual dysfunction. Robert's therapy involved working through his unconscious guilt around sexuality while also incorporating physical relaxation techniques to release muscular tension. As he worked through his emotional and physical blocks, Robert's symptoms improved, demonstrating the therapeutic importance of addressing both the mind and body in treating sexual issues (Reich, 1942).

Legacy of Freud and Reich in Psychosexual Therapy

The influence of Freud and Reich continues to shape psychosexual therapy today. Freud's focus on the unconscious mind, early childhood experiences, and the role of sexual repression has provided essential tools for therapists working with sexual dysfunctions, particularly those involving deeply rooted emotional conflicts. Meanwhile, Reich's body-oriented approach helped pave the way for modern body psychotherapy techniques, which are now widely used in the treatment of sexual and relational issues.

However, both Freud's and Reich's theories have been critiqued over the years. Freud's emphasis on sexual development and his deterministic views on sexuality have been questioned, particularly regarding his ideas about female sexuality. Reich's orgone therapy and focus on orgasm as a therapeutic tool also remain controversial. Despite these critiques, their contributions to psychosexual therapy are undeniable, and their work opened up new avenues for understanding and treating sexual concerns in ways that continue to influence contemporary therapy.

Freud and Reich's theories marked a turning point in the development of psychosexual therapy. Freud's work on libido and psychosexual development introduced a psychological framework for understanding sexual behavior, while Reich's integration of body-oriented therapy broadened the scope of psychosexual work to include the physical dimension of sexual health. Together, their contributions laid the foundation for the more integrated and multidisciplinary approaches used in psychosexual therapy today. In the next section, we will examine the work of Masters and Johnson, who shifted the focus of sex therapy to the physiological and behavioral dimensions of sexual health.

The Masters and Johnson Revolution

The 1960s marked a pivotal moment in the history of psychosexual therapy with the groundbreaking work of William Masters and Virginia Johnson. As one of the most influential couples in the field of sexual medicine, their research transformed the way sex therapy was practiced and understood. Prior to their contributions, the study of sexual dysfunctions was largely theoretical or anecdotal. Masters and

Johnson's empirical, evidence-based research introduced a new level of scientific rigor to the field of sex therapy, and their work remains foundational to contemporary practices.

The Birth of the Sexual Response Cycle

Before Masters and Johnson, sexual health was often seen as a more moral or philosophical issue rather than a physiological one. Masters, an obstetrician and gynecologist, and Johnson, a clinical psychologist, began studying the physiological aspects of human sexual response in the early 1960s. They established a laboratory where they closely observed individuals and couples during sexual activity to measure physiological changes, such as heart rate, blood pressure, and genital arousal, during different stages of sexual activity.

Their work resulted in the Sexual Response Cycle, a model that categorizes sexual activity into four distinct phases: excitement, plateau, orgasm, and resolution. This model provided a clear, physiological framework for understanding human sexual function. Their research demonstrated that sexual response was not only a psychological experience but also a complex, coordinated physiological process. This was revolutionary, as it moved beyond earlier theories that mostly focused on psychological or moral interpretations of sexual behaviors.

Human Sexual Response and Human Sexual Inadequacy

In their landmark books, *Human Sexual Response* (Masters and Johnson, 1966) and Human Sexual Inadequacy (Masters and Johnson, 1970), Masters and Johnson provided a detailed exploration of sexual dysfunctions, introducing a more structured way to classify and understand sexual difficulties. For the first time, sexual problems like erectile dysfunction, premature ejaculation, vaginismus, and anorgasmia were framed in terms of observable physiological responses rather than moral or psychiatric disorders.

Masters and Johnson's work also emphasized the importance of sexual communication and the need for mutual understanding between sexual partners. Their research demonstrated that many sexual dysfunctions were not necessarily rooted in individual pathology but were often related to relationship dynamics, misunderstandings, or learned behaviors. This approach was radical because it shifted the focus of treatment from individual therapy to couple-based interventions. This emphasis on communication and mutual understanding helped couples address their sexual concerns in a non-judgmental, collaborative way.

Sensate Focus: A Behavioral Intervention

One of Masters and Johnson's most significant contributions was the development of sensate focus, a behavioral technique that remains one of the most widely used therapeutic approaches for treating sexual dysfunctions. Sensate focus encourages couples to engage in non-sexual touch and gradually build sexual intimacy without the pressure of performance. This technique emphasizes mindfulness and body awareness, which helps couples reconnect with their sexual experiences in a less anxiety-driven way.

Sensate focus involves structured exercises where couples explore each other's bodies with the goal of increasing sensitivity and pleasure. The idea is to gradually reduce anxiety around sexual performance and create a more relaxed environment for sexual exploration. By focusing on pleasure and physical sensations rather than on orgasm or sexual performance, sensate focus aims to reduce the emotional and psychological barriers that often lead to dysfunction. The technique has been shown to be effective in treating a wide range of sexual dysfunctions, including erectile dysfunction, premature ejaculation, and female orgasmic disorder ((Weiner & Avery-Clark, 2017).

The Empirical Approach to Sexual Problems

Masters and Johnson's work was groundbreaking because it shifted the study of sex from speculative theories to empirical research (Masters & Johnson, 1970). They gathered data from over 10,000 sexual encounters in their laboratory, making their findings highly reliable and scientifically validated. Their studies were among the first to provide quantitative data on sexual behaviors and responses, which was previously difficult to assess. This objective approach to sexual health helped to demystify many of the anxieties surrounding sex and provided clinicians with a solid foundation for treatment.

Their research also made it clear that sexual dysfunctions were not unique to one gender or sexual orientation. Both men and women, regardless of sexual preference, could experience sexual difficulties. By observing a wide variety of individuals and couples, Masters and Johnson were able to demonstrate that sexual dysfunction was a normal part of human experience, not something to be ashamed of. This insight helped reduce the stigma surrounding sexual issues and encouraged many people to seek therapy.

Clinical Vignettes: The Impact of Masters and Johnson's Work

To illustrate the clinical impact of Masters and Johnson's work, consider the case of David, a 40-year-old man who sought therapy for erectile dysfunction. David had been married for 10 years and had difficulty maintaining an erection during intercourse. His physician had told him that the issue was psychological, but David felt ashamed and unsure about his ability to perform sexually. In therapy, Masters and Johnson's sensate focus technique was introduced. Through structured exercises with his partner, David was able to shift his focus away from performance anxiety and toward physical sensation and intimacy. Over time, David's erectile dysfunction improved, as he learned to communicate more openly with his partner and reduced the pressure he felt during sex.

Similarly, Sandra, a 35-year-old woman experiencing vaginismus, was referred for sex therapy after several unsuccessful attempts at intercourse. Sandra's condition was characterized by involuntary tightening of her pelvic muscles, making penetration painful and difficult. Sandra had avoided sexual intimacy for years due to fear and discomfort. Through Masters and Johnson's approach, Sandra worked with her therapist on relaxation techniques and body awareness, gradually desensitizing the fear and discomfort associated with penetration. By using sensate focus and communication exercises, Sandra was able to overcome her fears and eventually enjoyed a fulfilling sexual relationship with her partner.

The Legacy of Masters and Johnson's Work

The contributions of Masters and Johnson to psychosexual therapy were transformative. Their scientific and empirical approach to sexual health provided much-needed evidence and structure for the field. Their pioneering work in classifying sexual dysfunctions and introducing behavioral therapy techniques laid the groundwork for modern sexual medicine and sex therapy. Today, evidence-based interventions like sensate focus, cognitive-behavioral therapy, and mindfulness techniques continue to shape how sexual dysfunctions are treated in clinical settings.

Masters and Johnson's research also paved the way for a more holistic view of sexuality, considering it as a natural and important part of human well-being rather than something to be stigmatized or pathologized. Their work opened the door for therapists to view sexual issues as opportunities for growth and improvement, rather than as shameful problems to be hidden away.

The work of William Masters and Virginia Johnson in the 1960s and 1970s revolutionized the field of psychosexual therapy. By introducing empirical research, classifying sexual dysfunctions, and creating behavioral interventions like sensate focus, they made significant strides in reducing the stigma surrounding sexual problems and promoting healthier, more open conversations about sex. Their influence continues to resonate today, as modern sexual medicine and therapy continue to build on their pioneering contributions to understanding and treating sexual dysfunctions. In the next section, we will explore the work of Helen Singer Kaplan, who integrated behavioral and psychodynamic approaches to create an even more comprehensive model for treating sexual problems.

The Kaplan Model and Integrated Therapy

In the 1970s, Helen Singer Kaplan made a groundbreaking contribution to psychosexual therapy by introducing an integrated approach to treating sexual dysfunctions. Building upon the work of Masters and Johnson, Kaplan combined behavioral therapy with psychodynamic psychotherapy to create a more holistic treatment model that addressed both the physical and psychological aspects of sexual health. Her work marked a pivotal moment in the history of sex therapy, as it acknowledged the complex and multifaceted nature of sexual dysfunctions and introduced a more comprehensive framework for understanding and treating these issues.

Kaplan's Triphasic Model of Sexual Response

Kaplan's most significant contribution to sexual therapy was her triphasic model of sexual response, which expanded upon the linear model of sexual function proposed by Masters and Johnson. The triphasic model highlighted three essential components of sexual functioning: desire, arousal, and orgasm. What set Kaplan's model apart was her recognition of desire as a distinct phase, separate from arousal and orgasm. This focus on desire was a significant shift in the way sex therapy approached sexual dysfunctions.

Before Kaplan's work, sexual response was typically understood as a linear progression from arousal to orgasm, with little attention paid to the psychological dimension of desire. Kaplan recognized that sexual desire could be influenced by a variety of factors, including psychological, emotional, and relational dynamics, and that it was just as important as physical arousal and orgasm in sexual health. By adding desire as a separate phase, Kaplan's model provided a more nuanced understanding of sexual response and dysfunction. According to Kaplan (1974), sexual desire often involves complex emotional and psychological components, including personal values, relationship dynamics, and individual histories of sexual experiences.

Kaplan's model proposed that sexual problems could arise in any of the three phases, and thus interventions needed to target not just the physical symptoms but also the psychological and emotional aspects of sexuality. For example, a person experiencing erectile dysfunction might have a problem with the arousal phase, while a person with low libido might be struggling with the desire phase. By focusing on all three aspects of sexual response, Kaplan's model allowed for a more comprehensive treatment approach.

Integrating Psychodynamic Therapy with Behavioral Techniques

Kaplan's approach was notable for blending psychodynamic therapy with behavioral sex therapy. While Masters and Johnson focused primarily on the behavioral aspect of sexual dysfunction, Kaplan acknowledged that psychological factors, such as anxiety, fear, guilt, and past trauma, could play a significant role in sexual difficulties. In particular, Kaplan's approach incorporated the psychodynamic understanding that unconscious conflicts, often rooted in early childhood experiences, could affect adult sexual functioning (Kaplan, 1974).

Kaplan's therapy was active and directive, meaning that therapists would provide clear, structured interventions to address sexual problems. This was a contrast to traditional psychodynamic approaches, which tend to focus more on exploration and insight. By actively engaging clients in therapy, Kaplan was able to help individuals not only understand their sexual difficulties but also take concrete steps to overcome them. For instance, sensate focus exercises, pioneered by Masters and Johnson, were integrated into Kaplan's therapeutic model, along with psychodynamic techniques aimed at uncovering unconscious fears or repressed emotions that might be contributing to the sexual dysfunction.

Treating Desire Disorders and the Role of Communication

Kaplan's integrated model proved especially effective in treating desire disorders, which were often challenging to address with purely behavioral techniques. Desire disorders, such as hypoactive sexual desire disorder (HSDD), involve a lack of interest in or desire for sex, and are often linked to complex psychological and relational factors. Kaplan's focus on desire allowed therapists to explore issues like relationship dissatisfaction, emotional intimacy, stress, and sexual trauma, which could all contribute to a lack of desire (Leiblum, 2007).

Therapy, according to Kaplan, needed to focus not only on the physical components of sexual desire (such as arousal and orgasm) but also on the emotional and relational dimensions. Many clients with desire issues may have unspoken or unacknowledged emotional needs or may have communication barriers with their partners. Kaplan's therapeutic approach emphasized the importance of communication, especially between partners, in building a healthy sexual relationship. By encouraging clients to openly discuss their sexual desires, concerns, and anxieties, Kaplan's model aimed to improve both sexual satisfaction and relationship quality.

Addressing Sexual Dysfunction through an Interdisciplinary Approach

Kaplan's model laid the groundwork for the interdisciplinary approach to sexual medicine that is commonly used today (Lipshultz et al., 2016). By combining psychodynamic principles with behavioral therapy, she created a model that addressed the physical, emotional, and relational aspects of sexual dysfunction. Modern sex therapy continues to build upon this biopsychosocial model, which considers the biological, psychological, and social factors that influence sexual health (Bancroft, 2008).

Kaplan's work also demonstrated the importance of collaboration between professionals from different fields of expertise. Sex therapists, medical doctors, psychologists, and even physical therapists can all contribute to a comprehensive treatment plan for sexual dysfunction. This interdisciplinary approach ensures that all aspects of a client's sexual health are addressed and that the therapist tailors interventions to the specific needs of the individual or couple (Bancroft, 2008).

Clinical Accounts: The Impact of Kaplan's Approach

To illustrate the impact of Kaplan's approach, consider the case of Emily, a 35-year-old woman experiencing low sexual desire. Emily had been in a relationship for several years, and although her partner was emotionally supportive, she found it difficult to feel sexually interested. Emily felt frustrated and anxious about her lack of desire, and her self-esteem began to suffer. In therapy, Kaplan's approach allowed Emily to explore both the psychological and emotional aspects of her sexual difficulties. Through discussions, it became clear that Emily had unresolved issues related to body image and past sexual trauma, both of which were inhibiting her sexual desire.

Using Kaplan's model, Emily's therapist worked with her to address these emotional barriers while also introducing techniques like sensate focus to reduce performance anxiety and foster greater intimacy with her partner. Over time, Emily reported feeling more comfortable in her body and more connected to her partner, which significantly improved her sexual desire and overall relationship satisfaction.

Similarly, John, a 42-year-old man struggling with erectile dysfunction and performance anxiety, benefited from Kaplan's integrated model. John's physical symptoms were compounded by deep-seated fears about his sexual performance, which had been fueled by past experiences of sexual rejection. Kaplan's approach helped John address both his physical symptoms and his psychological barriers, allowing him to engage in more fulfilling and confident sexual experiences.

Kaplan's Legacy in Modern Therapy

Helen Singer Kaplan's integrated approach to sexual therapy remains an influential model in the field of sexual medicine and sex therapy. By combining behavioral techniques with psychodynamic therapy, Kaplan's work provided a more comprehensive framework for understanding and treating sexual dysfunctions. Her emphasis on desire, communication, and emotional intimacy continues to shape the way therapists approach sexual problems today.

Her approach laid the foundation for the multimodal treatment strategies that are now common in sex therapy. Modern practitioners often incorporate elements of cognitive-behavioral therapy, mindfulness, psychodynamic therapy, and even mindfulness-based techniques into their work, reflecting Kaplan's interdisciplinary approach. Furthermore, Kaplan's focus on patient-centered care and tailored interventions ensures that treatment remains personalized and responsive to each individual's needs.

In summary, Helen Singer Kaplan's work marked a transformative moment in the evolution of sex therapy. Her triphasic model and integrated approach continue to provide valuable insights and practical tools for therapists working with individuals and couples facing sexual dysfunctions.

The Rise of Sex Therapy as a Profession

Sex therapy, which has roots in the early works of pioneers like Masters and Johnson and Helen Kaplan, began to emerge as a recognized clinical specialty in the 1980s and 1990s. This marked a turning point in the treatment of sexual dysfunctions, as the focus expanded from individual treatment models to more structured, evidence-based therapeutic approaches. As research into sexual health and therapy grew, professional organizations like the Society for Sex Therapy and Research (SSTAR) and the American Association of Sexuality Educators, Counselors and Therapists (AASECT) formalized standards for training and ethics. These organizations played a crucial role in establishing sex therapy as a professional discipline, ensuring that therapists were adequately trained and held to high ethical standards.

Standardization and Professional Recognition

The development of standardized training and certification processes marked a critical step in professionalizing sex therapy. Before this period, there were no consistent guidelines or recognized credentials for therapists working with sexual dysfunctions, leading to a wide variation in practice and expertise. With the establishment of SSTAR and AASECT, a formal framework for certification and ethical practice in sex therapy was created, and therapists who wished to work in this field were required to undergo rigorous training. These organizations also began to advocate for greater recognition of sex therapy as an essential mental health specialty.

The 1980s and 1990s also saw the growth of specialized graduate-level programs and training workshops dedicated to sex therapy. These programs often included coursework in human sexuality, sexual dysfunctions, and therapeutic techniques, along with supervised clinical practice. This formal education allowed therapists to acquire the necessary expertise to treat a wide range of sexual issues, from psychological barriers to physical dysfunctions.

The Development of Manualized Treatments

As the field of sex therapy expanded, manualized treatment protocols began to emerge. These treatment protocols were designed to address common sexual dysfunctions such as premature ejaculation, vaginismus, hypoactive sexual desire disorder, and erectile dysfunction. By standardizing the treatment process, manualized approaches provided a systematic and evidence-based way of addressing sexual issues. The manualized approach also helped to move sex therapy into the realm of scientific validity by applying methods that could be tested and replicated across diverse populations.

For example, cognitive-behavioral therapy (CBT) became widely adopted in sex therapy for its structured, goal-oriented approach to treating sexual problems. CBT was particularly useful for treating sexual anxiety, performance fears, and negative sexual beliefs. Mindfulness-based therapies, which focus on increasing awareness of bodily sensations and emotions in the present moment, were also integrated into treatment. These approaches aimed to reduce stress and performance anxiety, which are common barriers to healthy sexual functioning.

Manualized treatments provided a step-by-step framework for addressing sexual issues, including detailed instructions for therapists and clients. This helped both parties feel more confident in the therapeutic process and enabled therapists to work more efficiently with patients. For example, sensate focus, a technique originally developed by Masters and Johnson, was adapted and incorporated into manualized programs. Sensate focus involves gradual, non-demanding physical contact between partners, which helps reduce anxiety and build emotional and sexual connection.

Evidence-Based Interventions

With the professionalization of sex therapy came an increasing emphasis on evidence-based interventions. Therapists began to rely more heavily on research and scientific studies to guide their treatment plans. This shift was crucial in ensuring that sex therapy remained grounded in scientifically valid approaches and continued to evolve with advances in sexual medicine and psychology.

During this time, the therapeutic community began to embrace the concept of relational therapies, which focus on improving communication and intimacy between sexual partners. These therapies acknowledged that sexual problems often have a relational component, where dissatisfaction or dysfunction may arise due to issues of emotional connection, communication barriers, or unresolved conflicts between partners. Relational therapies encouraged collaborative approaches to sexual healing, empowering both partners to work together on their sexual well-being.

Additionally, interventions like sex education and behavioral modification techniques were also incorporated into sex therapy. These techniques help individuals and couples develop a better understanding of their bodies, desires, and sexual preferences, promoting a healthier, more open approach to sexuality. As a result, therapists were able to offer a more holistic treatment approach that addressed both individual concerns and relationship dynamics.

Clinical Vignettes: The Impact of Professional Sex Therapy

To understand the impact of sex therapy during this period, consider the case of Sarah, a 30-year-old woman who had been experiencing vaginismus, a condition where involuntary muscle spasms make vaginal penetration painful or impossible. Sarah had struggled with this condition for several years, experiencing emotional distress and isolation. Despite numerous attempts at seeking help, she had not found a therapist who understood the complexity of her situation. However, after being referred to a certified sex therapist, Sarah was introduced to sensate focus exercises and cognitive-behavioral therapy.

Through regular sessions, Sarah and her partner learned to gradually explore intimacy without the pressure of intercourse. The therapist emphasized communication skills and helped Sarah address the underlying anxiety that had contributed to her vaginismus. Over the course of several months, Sarah's symptoms began to improve, and she regained confidence in her ability to experience pleasure without fear or pain. Her case is a testament to the power of manualized treatment protocols and evidence-based interventions in helping individuals overcome sexual dysfunctions.

Similarly, consider the case of Mark, a 40-year-old man struggling with premature ejaculation. Mark had been embarrassed by his condition for years, feeling inadequate and frustrated. He had attempted to avoid intimacy altogether, fearing that he would not be able to perform. After seeking therapy, Mark worked with a certified sex therapist who introduced him to CBT techniques aimed at changing his performance anxiety. Through relaxation exercises, behavioral modification, and discussions about his relationship dynamics, Mark was able to regain control over his sexual function and experience greater satisfaction with his partner.

The Continued Evolution of Sex Therapy

The professionalization of sex therapy in the 1980s and 1990s represented a significant step forward in the field of sexual medicine. As the field continued to evolve, sex therapy became an established discipline within mental health and medicine, and its reach expanded beyond the clinical setting to include community-based education and outreach.

The continued integration of various therapeutic approaches, including CBT, mindfulness, and relational therapy, ensured that sex therapy remained adaptable and responsive to the needs of clients. Today, sex therapists work with individuals and couples facing a wide range of sexual issues, from sexual dysfunctions to relationship difficulties to concerns about sexual identity and orientation. The field's emphasis on both research and compassionate care ensures that therapy remains grounded in scientific understanding while also taking into account the unique experiences of each client.

The rise of sex therapy as a profession was a crucial turning point in the history of psychosexual therapy. By formalizing the training and ethical standards for practitioners, developing evidence-based treatment protocols, and fostering interdisciplinary collaboration, sex therapy became a trusted and effective tool for addressing sexual concerns. From the introduction of manualized treatments to the integration of cognitive-behavioral therapy and mindfulness techniques, the field has grown to encompass a wide array of therapeutic approaches, all of which continue to help individuals and couples navigate the complex landscape of human sexuality. As the field of sex therapy continues to grow and evolve, it will no doubt remain a vital component of modern sexual medicine.

Contemporary Psychosexual Therapy and Sexual Medicine

In contemporary psychosexual therapy, the focus has expanded beyond individualistic models of treatment to a more integrated approach. This modern framework, known as the biopsychosocial model, incorporates biological, psychological, social, and cultural factors, recognizing that human sexuality is complex and multifaceted. As sexual health and dysfunction continue to be understood from a holistic perspective, sexual medicine and therapy have evolved to treat not just the body or mind, but the intricate relationship between the two, as well as the environmental and societal influences that shape sexual experiences.

Biopsychosocial Framework

The biopsychosocial model of sexual health integrates the biological, psychological, and social dimensions of sexual functioning. This approach recognizes that disorders like erectile dysfunction, genito-pelvic pain, and anorgasmia are not solely medical issues but rather arise from a complex interplay of physiological, emotional, and social factors. For example, erectile dysfunction is no longer seen merely as a consequence of physical illness like cardiovascular disease but also as something potentially influenced by stress, anxiety, and relationship dynamics.

Medical treatments for sexual dysfunctions, such as medications for erectile dysfunction, are now considered only one part of the solution. These interventions are often paired with psychotherapy, behavioral therapy, and relationship counseling to address the emotional and relational components of the issue. Therapists and doctors work together to assess the various contributors to sexual dysfunction, providing a more comprehensive approach to treatment.

A common approach in sexual medicine today is the integration of biological treatments (e.g., pharmacological treatments) and psychological therapies (e.g., cognitive-behavioral therapy) to address the multifactorial nature of sexual dysfunctions. The DSM-5, the diagnostic manual used by clinicians, reflects this shift by classifying sexual disorders in a way that distinguishes distressing dysfunctions from normal variations (American Psychiatric Association, 2013). By doing so, it recognizes that some variations in sexual desire or functioning are part of the natural spectrum of human sexuality, while others may require therapeutic intervention.

Clinical Vignette: Consider the case of James, a 50-year-old man who has been diagnosed with erectile dysfunction. After initial assessments, it became clear that James' condition was not just due to age-related factors or diabetes, but also influenced by work-related stress and a strained relationship with his wife. Through a biopsychosocial approach, his treatment plan included medication to address the physical side of erectile dysfunction, combined with couples therapy to address communication issues with his partner and stress management techniques to address his work-related anxiety. Over time, this integrated approach resulted in significant improvements in both James' sexual function and his relationship satisfaction.

Cognitive and Mindfulness-Based Approaches

Therapies in contemporary psychosexual practice have evolved to include a broader range of psychological interventions. Cognitive restructuring, emotional regulation, and mindfulness-based approaches have been shown to be highly effective in addressing sexual dysfunctions, particularly in women. Brotto and Basson (2014) provide empirical support for this approach, showing that group mindfulness-based therapy can improve sexual desire and related aspects of sexual functioning in women. MBCT combines mindfulness techniques with cognitive-behavioral therapy, helping individuals become more aware of their sexual experiences and reduce negative emotional responses, such as anxiety and self-criticism, that often interfere with sexual desire. Brotto et al. (2021) further support this approach through a randomized trial showing that group mindfulness-based cognitive therapy and supportive sex education can both improve symptoms of female sexual interest/arousal disorder.

Mindfulness approaches help clients focus on the present moment and foster a non-judgmental awareness of their bodies and sexual sensations. This technique is particularly useful in treating conditions like female sexual arousal disorder, where women may experience a disconnect between their emotional state and physical responses. Through mindfulness exercises, women can develop a greater sense of body awareness and acceptance, which in turn can improve sexual function and satisfaction.

Furthermore, these approaches not only focus on reducing performance anxiety but also work to promote a deeper connection between partners, encouraging couples to cultivate intimacy in a supportive, non-pressured environment.

Clinical Vignette: Take Lina, a 37-year-old woman experiencing low sexual desire and arousal difficulties. After exploring her case, it became clear that anxiety, self-criticism, and an emotional disconnect from her partner were significant contributing factors to her condition. Lina began MBCT, learning to focus on the sensations in her body and the emotional intimacy with her partner, rather than obsessing over performance. After several months of practice, Lina reported improved desire, increased pleasure, and a deeper connection with her partner. This case highlights how mindfulness-based therapy can empower individuals to reclaim their sexual health by focusing on emotional regulation and present-moment awareness.

Critiques and Expansions

While contemporary psychosexual therapy has made tremendous strides in integrating multiple therapeutic modalities, criticism has also emerged, particularly regarding the medicalization of sex. Scholars like Leonore Tiefer have critiqued the field's emphasis on diagnosing and treating sexual issues as medical problems, arguing that this perspective may overlook the broader socio-cultural and psychological aspects of sexuality. Tiefer (2006) further develops this critique by showing how female sexual dysfunction was shaped through disease-mongering and medicalization. Tiefer has argued for a more nuanced, pleasure-centered approach to sexual therapy that considers gender dynamics, power relations, and sexual scripts (Tiefer, 2004). These aspects, she suggests, play a fundamental role in how people experience their sexuality.

The New View Movement, as it is known, emerged from these critiques, advocating for a shift away from strictly medical models and encouraging a focus on pleasure, agency, and sexual autonomy. This approach places greater emphasis on empowerment, encouraging individuals to explore and define their sexuality without being confined to traditional medical diagnoses. For example, the New View movement has brought attention to the impact of sexual trauma, gender inequality, and cultural norms on sexual functioning, highlighting the importance of understanding these influences in psychosexual therapy.

While medical approaches have been helpful in treating certain sexual dysfunctions, The New View challenges the idea that all sexual issues can be solved with a one-size-fits-all medical solution. Instead, it calls for a more holistic, contextual, and empowerment-focused approach to therapy. This has led to increased interest in culturally informed practices and a broader exploration of sexual rights, pleasure, and agency in therapy.

Clinical Vignette: Consider David, a 45-year-old man who has struggled with erectile dysfunction for several years. After being prescribed medication by his doctor, David was still not satisfied with his sexual life, feeling that the medication didn't address the emotional distance he had developed with his wife. He began working with a therapist who was trained in New View principles. Together, they explored how societal expectations and gender norms around masculinity and sexual performance were affecting David's relationship with his body and his partner. With guidance, David and his wife were able to break free from rigid sexual scripts and focus on emotional intimacy and pleasure, leading to greater satisfaction in their sexual life. This case highlights how the New View framework can help individuals and couples find fulfillment by moving beyond medical interventions and addressing emotional and cultural factors.

The contemporary landscape of psychosexual therapy is marked by a deep understanding of sexual health that integrates biological, psychological, social, and cultural perspectives. The biopsychosocial model has allowed sexual medicine to address the multifactorial nature of sexual dysfunction, moving away from purely physical explanations to include psychological and relational factors. Mindfulness-based therapies, cognitive restructuring, and integrated approaches have proven effective in helping individuals and couples overcome sexual challenges.

Simultaneously, the critique of medicalization and the rise of New View approaches have expanded the scope of sexual therapy, urging practitioners to address the cultural, social, and emotional dimensions of sexuality. As the field continues to evolve, it remains committed to providing more holistic, empowerment-focused, and scientifically grounded interventions that reflect the complexity and diversity of human sexual experiences.

Cultural and Global Perspectives

Sexual health is not just a medical or psychological issue; it is deeply shaped by the norms and cultural contexts in which people live. The way sexuality is understood, expressed, and treated varies greatly from one culture to another. Local attitudes, customs, and traditions influence how individuals experience sexual issues, how they seek treatment, and how they communicate about their sexual health. This is especially evident in regions like India, where cultural attitudes toward sex are often intertwined with religious, societal, and familial expectations.

In India, sexual health issues are often clouded by taboos, myths, and shame. Despite the growing awareness of sexual health in urban centers, where evidence-based care is more accessible, there is still a significant gap in knowledge in rural areas. Many people in these areas rely on unqualified practitioners or myths passed down through generations, leading to the perpetuation of misinformation. For instance, conditions like Dhat syndrome, which is a cultural diagnosis in India for men who experience anxiety about their semen loss, are often misunderstood and inadequately addressed by conventional medical professionals.

Despite the challenges, Indian sexual medicine practitioners are increasingly blending medical expertise with culturally sensitive counseling. This integration is essential for addressing the complex issues faced by individuals who are navigating sexual health challenges within a cultural context that may not always be open to open discussions about sexuality. The approach of combining pharmacotherapy (e.g., medications for erectile dysfunction or hormonal imbalances) with psychosocial counseling is becoming more common, especially when treating disorders like Dhat syndrome or non-organic erectile dysfunction. This blend of medical and therapeutic approaches helps address not just the physiological aspect of sexual health but also the emotional and cultural factors that may be influencing the individual's experience.

One of the strengths of this integrated approach is the growing recognition that sexual dysfunction is not only a biological issue but one that involves emotional, psychological, and sociocultural dimensions. For example, a man suffering from erectile dysfunction may have a physiological condition such as vascular disease but may also be experiencing performance anxiety, guilt, or cultural shame that exacerbates his symptoms. By addressing both the physical and emotional dimensions of the issue, the therapy becomes more effective in providing lasting solutions.

Clinical Vignette: Take the case of Ravi, a 42-year-old man from a rural town in India who sought treatment for erectile dysfunction. Ravi's condition was not only caused by diabetes, but also by intense performance anxiety and cultural shame surrounding his sexuality. Ravi felt that his inability to perform sexually diminished his masculinity, leading to deep feelings of inadequacy and guilt. His condition had gone untreated for years, as he had sought help from a local practitioner who attributed his symptoms to spiritual causes and prescribed herbal treatments. Ravi's treatment plan involved a combination of medications to address his physical symptoms and psychological counseling to explore the deeper emotional and cultural factors influencing his condition. Through this integrated approach, Ravi was able to understand the relationship between his physical health and the cultural pressures he faced, leading to significant improvement in both his sexual function and his self-esteem.

In addition, organizations such as the South Asian Society for Sexual Medicine (SASSM) are helping to formalize and elevate the field of sexual medicine in India and other South Asian countries. These organizations provide specialized training programs for practitioners, equipping them with the knowledge and tools necessary to provide culturally sensitive and evidence-based care. As a result, sexual medicine is increasingly becoming a recognized specialty, and more people are seeking treatment for sexual health concerns in a way that is both medically sound and culturally respectful.

Cultural Sensitivity and Challenges

Sexual health interventions in cultures with strong traditions of silence around sexuality require careful, culturally sensitive approaches. In many societies, discussions about sex are seen as taboo, especially within the context of marriage and family life. In India, for example, conversations about sexuality are often intertwined with moral and religious judgments. Traditional beliefs regarding chastity, modesty, and the role of women in sexual relationships have shaped societal norms, creating a challenging environment for individuals seeking help for sexual health issues. These norms can perpetuate harmful beliefs such as the idea that sex should only be for procreation or that women should not enjoy sex.

Despite these challenges, there are signs of progress. Some therapists and clinicians are helping to normalize the conversation around sexuality by integrating sexual education into public health campaigns and clinical practice. By using a culturally respectful approach, they help individuals and couples discuss and address sexual issues in a way that aligns with both their cultural values and modern medical understandings.

The Future of Sexual Medicine in India

The field of sexual medicine in India is evolving, and the continued efforts of organizations like SASSM are essential to advancing the profession. Training programs, conferences, and research initiatives are helping to bridge the gap between Western practices and traditional cultural understandings of sexuality. Indian clinicians are beginning to embrace evidence-based practices while also recognizing the importance of cultural context when diagnosing and treating sexual dysfunctions. This evolving integration allows for a more comprehensive, nuanced approach to sexual health that is responsive to the cultural and individual needs of patients.

A Global Lens on Sexual Health

Beyond India, cultural norms around sex and sexuality vary greatly across different regions of the world. In Africa, for instance, issues like polygamy, female genital mutilation, and sexual violence can deeply affect sexual health and well-being. In Western societies, shifting views on gender, sexual orientation, and sexual rights have created new challenges and opportunities for psychosexual therapy. Cultural competence is a critical skill for sex therapists worldwide, allowing them to provide interventions that are not only scientifically sound but also respectful of the values and beliefs of the individuals they serve.

Sexual health is shaped by the confluence of biology, psychology, and culture. While India and other countries in South Asia face particular challenges in addressing sexual health due to cultural taboos, these challenges are also opportunities for growth and development in sexual medicine. As more people in these regions seek culturally informed, evidence-based care, the field of sexual medicine will continue to evolve, offering more effective and respectful treatments for sexual dysfunctions. With the help of organizations like SASSM, and the dedication of clinicians to holistic care, the future of sexual health looks promising, not just in India, but globally.

Conclusion

The history of psychosexual therapy is a story of transformation, beginning in the realms of mysticism and taboo and gradually evolving into a scientifically grounded and compassionate approach to sexual well-being. Over the centuries, ideas about sexuality have shifted, from being seen as a moral or spiritual issue to being understood as a complex interplay of biological, psychological, and sociocultural factors. This evolution has not been without its challenges, but the journey from taboo to understanding reflects a growing acceptance and acknowledgment of the importance of sexual health as an integral part of overall well-being.

Pioneers such as Masters and Johnson, Helen Kaplan, and Havelock Ellis were instrumental in shaping psychosexual therapy into the clinical discipline it is today. Their groundbreaking work in understanding sexual dysfunction, sexual response, and the emotional and relational aspects of sexuality laid the foundation for the contemporary field of sexual medicine. Masters and Johnson's focus on the physiological aspects of sexual response and their development of behavioral techniques like sensate focus helped to demystify sexual issues and made sex therapy more accessible to individuals and couples. Kaplan's integration of psychodynamic psychotherapy with behavioral approaches added a new dimension to therapy by addressing both the psychological and physical aspects of sexual health.

Today, psychosexual therapy is a recognized and respected field within sexual medicine. Modern practitioners draw on a range of disciplines, including neuroscience, psychology, behavioral science, and cultural studies, to offer holistic, patient-centered interventions. These professionals are better equipped than ever to treat individuals with sexual concerns, ranging from low libido and erectile dysfunction to psychosexual trauma and sexual orientation issues. The continued evolution of the field has been aided by advancements in technology, such as online therapy and the use of digital tools like teledildonics, which allow people to access treatment in ways that were previously unimaginable. Online therapy in particular has opened new avenues for individuals who might otherwise have faced geographical or social barriers to treatment, enabling more people to receive the care they need.

In parallel with these technological advances, there is a growing global awareness of sexual rights, sexual diversity, and the importance of gender equality in sexual health. As society's understanding of sexuality broadens, so too does the ability of psychosexual therapy to meet the diverse needs of patients. Today's therapists are increasingly aware of the social and cultural contexts that shape their patients' sexual experiences. As sexual norms continue to evolve, psychosexual therapy must adapt to keep pace with new understandings and emerging needs. Issues such as sexual autonomy, consent, identity, and pleasure are gaining more attention, challenging traditional models and pushing the boundaries of what is understood as normal sexual behavior.

At the same time, it is important to acknowledge the rich history of psychosexual therapy, which provides a foundation upon which current and future practitioners can build. The foundational work of Freud, Reich, and Ellis continues to influence contemporary theory, while the more humanistic approaches pioneered by Kaplan and Brotto offer invaluable insights into sexual functioning, desire, and intimacy. By acknowledging the historical milestones and integrating them into modern practice, clinicians can ensure that their work is both rooted in tradition and open to innovation.

Ultimately, the future of psychosexual therapy lies in a continued dialogue between past and present, tradition and innovation. As sexual medicine advances, it is crucial that therapists remain flexible and adaptable, integrating new research findings and technologies while staying attuned to the evolving cultural attitudes surrounding sexuality.

With this dual approach, psychosexual therapy will continue to grow and evolve, helping individuals and couples navigate the complexities of their sexual and emotional lives. Through compassionate, scientifically informed care, sexual well-being can be fully recognized as an essential aspect of overall health, ensuring that individuals not only understand their bodies and desires but also find acceptance, healing, and fulfillment in their sexual relationships.

As we look toward the future, psychosexual therapy will undoubtedly face new challenges. However, by embracing the diversity of sexual experiences, maintaining cultural sensitivity, and pushing the boundaries of what is known, the field is poised to offer even more innovative solutions for those seeking sexual well-being.

In conclusion, the history of psychosexual therapy underscores its growth from a mysterious, taboo subject to an integrated and vital part of modern medicine and mental health. Recognizing the rich legacy of the field, alongside its continuous evolution, ensures that psychosexual therapy will continue to meet the diverse needs of patients, empowering them to live fuller, more satisfying lives.

References

American Psychiatric Association. *Diagnostic and Statistical Manual of Mental Disorders*. 5th ed. (DSM-5). Arlington, VA: American Psychiatric Publishing; 2013.

Aquinas T. *The Summa Theologiae: Complete English Edition*. Translated by Fathers of the English Dominican Province. New York, NY: Benziger Bros; 1993.

Avicenna. *The Canon of Medicine*. Translated by Laleh Bakhtiar. Chicago, IL: Kazi Publications; 2007.

Bancroft J. *Human Sexuality and Its Problems*. 3rd ed. Edinburgh, UK; Elsevier Health Sciences; 2008.

Brotto, L. A., & Basson, R. (2014). Group Mindfulness-based Therapy Significantly Improves Sexual Desire in Women. *Behaviour Research and Therapy*, *57*, 43–54.

Brotto, L. A., Zdaniuk, B., Chivers, M. L., Jabs, F., Grabovac, A., Lalumière, M. L., Weinberg, J., Schonert-Reichl, K. A., & Basson, R. (2021). A Randomized Trial Comparing Group Mindfulness-based Cognitive Therapy with Group Supportive Sex Education and Therapy for the Treatment of Female Sexual Interest/Arousal Disorder. *Journal of Consulting and Clinical Psychology*, *89*(7), 626–639. https://doi.org/10.1037/ccp0000661.

Ellis H. *Studies in the Psychology of Sex*. Philadelphia: F.A. Davis Company; 1900–1928.

Foucault M. *The History of Sexuality: Volume 1. An Introduction*. Translated by R. Hurley. Pantheon Books; 1978.

Freud S. *Three Essays on the Theory of Sexuality*. Translated by James Strachey. New York: Basic Books; 2000.

Galen. *A Translation of Galen's Hygiene: De sanitate tuenda*. Translated by R. M. Green. Springfield, IL: Charles C. Thomas; 1951.

Hippocrates. *Aphorisms and Prognostics*. Translated by Francis Adams. Project Gutenberg; 2002.

Kaplan HS. *The New Sex Therapy: Active Treatment of Sexual Dysfunctions*. New York: Brunner/Mazel; 1974.

Leiblum SR, Rosen RC. *Principles and Practice of Sex Therapy*. 4th ed. New York: Guilford Press; 2007.

Lipshultz LI, Pastuszak AW, Goldstein AT, Giraldi A, Perelman MA (Eds.). *Management of Sexual Dysfunction in Men and Women: An Interdisciplinary Approach*. New York: Springer; 2016.

Masters WH, Johnson VE. *Human Sexual Response*. Boston: Little, Brown and Company; 1966.

Masters WH, Johnson VE. *Human Sexual Inadequacy*. Boston: Little, Brown and Company; 1970.

Needham J. *Science and Civilisation in China*, Volume 6: Biology and Biological Technology. Cambridge: Cambridge University Press; 2000.

Plato. *The Symposium*. Translated by Christopher Gill. London: Penguin Classics; 1999.

Razi A. Kitab al-Hawi (Liber Continens). Translated excerpts available in: M. Ullmann *I slamic Medicine*. Edinburgh: Edinburgh University Press; 1978.

Reich W. *The Function of the Orgasm*. New York: Orgone Institute Press; 1942.

Tiefer, L. (2004). *Sex Is Not a Natural Act and Other Essays* (2nd ed.). Boulder, CO: Westview Press.

Tiefer, L. (2006). Female Sexual Dysfunction: A Case Study of Disease Mongering and Activist Resistance. *PLoS Medicine*, *3*(4), e178. https://doi.org/10.1371/journal.pmed.0030178

Vatsyayana. *Kama Sutra*. Translated by Sir Richard Burton and F.F. Arbuthnot. New York: Modern Library; 1962.

von Bingen, H. *Physica: The Complete English Translation of Hildegard von Bingen's Classic Work on Health and Healing*. Translated by P. Throop. Rochester, VT: Healing Arts Press; 1998.

von Krafft-Ebing R. *Psychopathia Sexualis: With Especial Reference to the Antipathic Sexual Instinct*. Translated by F.J. Rebman. New York: Rebman Company; 1899.

Chapter 5

Cultural Sensitivity and the Clinical Use of Sexual Health Aids

Caleb Jacobson

Introduction

Within the mind's eye of many, sex toys—or sexual health aids, as they will be referred to in this chapter—are often imagined as novelty items found in dirty, dingy sex shops. These are the types of shops where one might park behind the building to avoid being seen entering. The prevailing notion is that these items are cheaply made, fashioned to appear as genitalia, and feature crude images and text on their packaging. Yet, this taboo, which is often overemphasized, and the faulty cognitions concerning the modern state of sexual health aids have caused many to neglect the benefits these items can offer for medical, psychosexual, and relational issues.

Sexual health aids have long played a multifaceted role in human history, serving as instruments of both pleasure and necessity. From the use of olive oil as a lubricant starting in 350 BC (Miranda et al., 2019) to the teledildonics of the modern era (Jannini et al., 2012), these tools have evolved alongside shifting societal norms, technological advancements, and medical understandings. Despite this, stigma surrounding their use persists, perpetuated by outdated cultural attitudes that overshadow their significant therapeutic potential. Yet, clinicians should be aware that this is a rapidly shifting narrative that can be observed throughout a global context. For example, during the COVID-19 pandemic, increased sales of sex toys highlighted their growing normalization as essential tools for self-care and intimacy (Arafat & Kar, 2021).

This chapter will help strip away the taboo that often enshrouds sexual health aids by giving a historical and cultural perspective that predates modern stereotypes. Additionally, the potential benefits of incorporating sexual health aids within clinical practice, in both psychosexual and relationship therapy, will be discussed, as well as cultural and ethical aspects that clinicians must be aware of when discussing these tools with patients. The aim is to assist clinicians in incorporating sexual health aids within their clinical practice in a way that is not only empirically based but also culturally informed and sensitive to the needs of the patient.

DOI: 10.4324/9781003611387-5

A Brief History of Sex Toys

Sex toys, broadly defined as objects or devices designed to enhance sexual pleasure, have a rich and multifaceted history that spans centuries and traverses cultures. Their development not only reflects evolving societal attitudes toward sexuality but also highlights shifts in gender roles, medical understanding, and technological innovation. Evidence of early sex toys dates back to prehistoric times, with phallic objects crafted from stone, bone, and ivory (Levi-Strauss, 1969). These artifacts, often associated with both ritualistic and sexual purposes, illustrate the intertwined nature of spirituality and sexuality in early human societies.

In ancient Greece and Rome, sexual health aids were more openly integrated into daily life and cultural norms. The Greeks, for instance, used dildos known as "olisbos," crafted from materials such as wood, leather, and even bread (Halperin, 1990). These societies regarded such devices as a natural extension of sexual expression. This cultural openness was further reflected in the elaborate erotic art and literature of the time, which celebrated diverse sexual practices. However, with the rise of Christianity in medieval Europe, sexual expression became tightly regulated. The Christian Church's view of non-procreative sexuality as sinful led to the suppression of discussions about and use of sexual aids (Jacobson, 2025). Despite this, clandestine use persisted, as evidenced by surviving manuscripts and artifacts, suggesting that private sexual behaviors were less affected by public dogma than official narratives might imply.

The Renaissance, characterized by its revival of classical knowledge and humanistic values, marked a gradual loosening of stringent sexual mores. Anatomical drawings by figures like Leonardo da Vinci demonstrate a renewed interest in understanding human sexuality and reproduction (Carroll, 2025). This period laid the groundwork for the eventual commercialization of sex toys. The Industrial Revolution of the 19th century was pivotal in this regard, introducing mechanization and mass production. The late 1800s saw the invention of electric vibrators, initially developed by British physician J. Mortimer Granville as medical devices for treating "hysteria" in women, a diagnosis that encompassed a wide array of psychological and physical complaints (Lieberman, 2016; Maines, 2001). These vibrators, once confined to physicians' offices, eventually became accessible to the public, catalyzing the emergence of the commercial sex toy industry.

The 20th century ushered in dramatic advancements in the design and accessibility of sex toys, paralleling broader societal changes. The sexual revolution of the 1960s and 1970s, spurred by the feminist movement and greater sexual liberation, fueled a surge in the availability of products aimed at enhancing female sexual pleasure (Rubin, 1993). Companies began offering a diverse array of products tailored to different needs and preferences. Later, the advent of the internet in the late 20th and early 21st centuries revolutionized the market by enabling discreet purchasing and access to a wide variety of products and information (Attwood, 2007). This era also introduced teledildonics and interactive devices, such as vibrators that could sync with MP3 players or virtual reality systems, underscoring the integration of technology into intimacy (Jannini et al., 2012). Moreover, specialized devices emerged to address the needs of individuals with disabilities or those recovering from medical procedures, further bridging the gap between sexual pleasure and health care (Rodríguez & Méndez, 2022).

The COVID-19 pandemic amplified these trends, as lockdowns and physical distancing measures disrupted traditional forms of intimacy. Global sales of sex toys soared, reflecting a growing recognition of these products as tools for maintaining sexual wellness and emotional connection during periods of isolation. For instance, sales in New Zealand tripled during the pandemic, highlighting a societal shift toward the normalization of sexual health aids as essential self-care items (Arafat & Kar, 2021). This surge in demand underscores the resilience of human sexuality and the adaptability of sexual health products in meeting diverse needs during times of crisis.

A Brief History of Lubricant

Sexual lubricants, substances crafted to reduce friction and enhance comfort during sexual activity, have a long and intriguing history that mirrors broader shifts in societal attitudes toward sexuality, health, and pleasure. Their development and use provide valuable insights into the evolving understanding of sexual wellness across cultures and epochs. The earliest known uses of sexual lubricants date back to ancient civilizations, where natural substances were prized for their functionality and availability. In ancient Greece, olive oil was widely used as a lubricant, appreciated for its smooth texture and ease of access (Miranda et al., 2019). Meanwhile, in ancient China, physicians documented the application of silk oil and ginseng-based preparations, which were believed to enhance sexual pleasure and address dryness, reflecting an early recognition of the connection between sexual comfort and health (Korda et al., 2010; Potenza et al., 2023; Yang et al., 2020).

The Middle Ages in Europe saw a decline in open documentation of sexual lubricants, shaped by dominant religious and cultural attitudes that often repressed discussions of sexuality. However, records from this period suggest that animal fats and plant-derived oils continued to be used discreetly, particularly among those with access to such resources (Brundage, 1987; Bullough & Bullough, 1995). The Renaissance, with its revival of classical knowledge and more permissive attitudes toward human sexuality, brought a renewed interest in personal lubricants. Texts from the period indicate that natural oils and animal-based fats remained popular for facilitating sexual activities, highlighting an enduring practical approach to sexual health (Miranda et al., 2019).

The Industrial Revolution marked a turning point in the history of sexual lubricants, with advancements in medical and chemical industries leading to the creation of more refined and accessible products. Petroleum jelly, or Vaseline, introduced in the late 19th century, was initially marketed for its medicinal properties but quickly gained popularity as a sexual lubricant due to its smooth, long-lasting texture (Lieberman, 2016; Lieberman & Schatzberg, 2018). The mid-20th century heralded further innovation with the advent of water-based lubricants like KY Jelly, which provided a safe, non-staining alternative to petroleum-based products. These water-based options were particularly significant in medical and safer sex contexts, as they were compatible with latex condoms, addressing concerns about material degradation and promoting safer sexual practices (Laumann et al., 1994).

The sexual revolution of the 1960s and 1970s catalyzed a more open discourse around sexual health and pleasure, fostering increased acceptance and use of lubricants. This era also saw the rise of products designed specifically for sexual activities, emphasizing their role in enhancing intimacy and reducing discomfort (Rubin, 1993). The late 20th and early 21st centuries brought diversification in lubricant formulations, introducing silicone-based and hybrid options that offered varied textures and extended durations. These advancements catered to an expanding range of preferences and needs, including hypoallergenic formulations, organic products, flavored lubricants, and those designed to mimic natural bodily fluids (Lieberman, 2016)). These innovations underscored a growing focus on inclusivity and individualization in sexual wellness.

Today, sexual lubricants occupy a prominent place in the broader landscape of sexual health products, supported by a market that continues to innovate and respond to consumer demands. The destigmatization of sexual health and wellness has contributed to the normalization of lubricant use, framing these products as essential tools for enhancing sexual experiences and promoting comfort. Studies have highlighted their role in facilitating both pleasure and function, making them integral to modern sexual practices (Herbenick et al., 2013).

As with sex toys, the history of lubricants reflects broader societal shifts in attitudes toward sexuality, health, and innovation. From the natural substances of antiquity to the sophisticated chemical formulations of today, their evolution underscores the importance of sexual health and the human pursuit of enhanced intimacy and pleasure. This narrative offers a compelling window into the intersections of culture, medicine, and technology in the ongoing exploration of sexual wellness.

Inclusion of Sexual Health Aids in Clinical Practice

Psychosexual therapists will often, and sometimes instinctively, give enthusiastic encouragement to patients concerning the incorporation of a sex toy in their intimate life. Though often the clinician is unaware of the scientific and clinically proven benefits of such suggestion. Nevertheless, the integration of sexual health aids into clinical practice represents an important and growing trend in modern healthcare, reflecting their demonstrated effectiveness in addressing a variety of sexual health concerns and improving overall quality of life. These tools, ranging from vibrators to dilators and teledildonic devices, have been increasingly recognized by clinicians as valuable therapeutic interventions, educational resources, and solutions for reducing barriers to care. By incorporating these aids into healthcare settings, providers can create more inclusive and supportive environments for addressing sensitive sexual health issues with precision and compassion.

One of the key advantages of offering sexual health aids in clinical settings is the ability to mitigate the embarrassment or confusion patients often experience when attempting to purchase these products from retail outlets. Many individuals face stigma or discomfort in exploring or discussing their sexual needs, which can impede treatment adherence and hinder outcomes. By providing sexual health aids directly within a clinical framework, patients are not only afforded privacy but also receive tailored guidance on their use. For instance, a clinician might recommend and demonstrate the use of a vibrator, which has been shown to improve blood flow and alleviate pain for a patient with vulvodynia, or suggest a dilator set to a patient recovering from pelvic surgery as a means of preventing scarring and maintaining vaginal elasticity (Miles & Miles, 2021; Rodríguez & Méndez, 2022). These approaches allow patients to make informed decisions, empowering them to engage with their sexual health in a proactive and therapeutic manner. Of course, these demonstrations do not and should not include the actual use of the toy by the clinician or the patient and instead should focus on how the product functions and explanation of how to properly use the tool for maximum therapeutic benefit.

Sexual health aids also serve as powerful educational tools, enriching therapy and counseling sessions. Devices such as vibrators and dildos can facilitate discussions about anatomy, arousal, and sexual pleasure, fostering a deeper understanding of the body. This educational approach is particularly valuable for individuals with limited knowledge of sexual health or those who experience guilt or shame around solo sex. By reframing self-exploration as a healthy and normal practice, clinicians can help patients overcome anxiety and cultivate a more positive relationship with their sexuality. For example, a therapist might use a sexual health aid as a visual aid to demonstrate clitoral anatomy and its central role in orgasm, demystifying sexual function and encouraging self-acceptance (Tomnay et al., 2021). These interactions provide patients with the knowledge and confidence needed to navigate their sexual experiences with greater ease and satisfaction.

Incorporating sexual health aids into therapeutic care can also strengthen the therapeutic alliance between clinicians and patients. Addressing patient needs through tangible, practical solutions reinforces a clinician's commitment to holistic care, building trust and fostering open communication. For instance, clinicians may recommend remote-controlled devices or teledildonics to couples in long-distance relationships, offering practical tools to maintain intimacy and connection despite physical separation (Jannini et al., 2012). These devices not only enhance sexual engagement but also serve as a reminder of the clinician's role in addressing both emotional and physical dimensions of patient well-being.

Further, the inclusion of sexual health aids in clinical practice represents a pivotal shift toward normalizing discussions around sexual health and validating these tools as legitimate therapeutic interventions. By integrating sexual health aids into care plans, clinicians can deliver innovative solutions that improve sexual health, foster self-awareness, and enhance patients' overall well-being. This approach not only advances therapeutic goals but also contributes to destigmatizing conversations about sexuality, enabling patients to lead healthier, more fulfilling lives.

Sexual Health Aids and Sexual Functioning

Sexual health aids, including vibrators, dildos, and other devices, play an essential role in helping individuals explore and understand their sexuality. These tools provide a safe and accessible means for self-exploration, empowering individuals to discover their sexual responses, preferences, and areas of heightened sensitivity. For instance, vibrators can help individuals identify erogenous zones such as the clitoris, nipples, or perineum, enabling them to better understand the types of stimulation they find most pleasurable. This self-awareness is particularly transformative for individuals who have experienced sexual shame or who lack comprehensive education about their bodies. Research has demonstrated that women who use vibrators are more likely to engage in health-positive behaviors, such as regular gynecological exams and genital self-examinations, underscoring the broader health benefits of these tools beyond sexual pleasure (Herbenick et al., 2009). Furthermore, sexual health aids are embraced by individuals across diverse sexual orientations and identities. For example, lesbian and bisexual women frequently incorporate vibrators into partnered sexual activities to facilitate orgasms, reflecting a playful and subversive approach to sexuality that normalizes and celebrates sexual exploration (Herbenick et al., 2010).

Beyond enhancing sexual pleasure and self-discovery, sexual health aids are instrumental in addressing sexual dysfunctions and promoting overall sexual well-being. Vibrators, in particular, are often recommended for individuals with pelvic floor disorders due to their ability to improve blood flow, enhance pelvic circulation, and strengthen pelvic floor muscles. This makes them particularly effective for managing conditions such as incontinence, vaginal atrophy, and vulvodynia. For women experiencing vulvodynia, vibrators can provide pain relief through vibration-induced desensitization. This therapeutic process involves gradually introducing non-painful sensations to the vulvar area, helping the nervous system recalibrate and reduce pain responses over time. Women who use vibrators for these purposes often report significant improvements in their ability to engage in activities that were previously uncomfortable, such as tampon use, gynecological exams, or penetrative sex (Dubinskaya et al., 2023).

In the context of post-cancer recovery, sexual health aids are equally vital. Women undergoing pelvic radiation frequently face challenges such as vaginal scarring and reduced elasticity, which can impede comfort and sexual function. In these cases, vibrators and vaginal dilators are used to gently stretch the vaginal tissue, maintain elasticity, and prevent adhesions, ultimately improving comfort during sexual activity. These tools are typically introduced gradually, starting with smaller sizes and increasing in diameter as comfort improves, allowing patients to regain confidence and a sense of normalcy in their sexual lives (Miles & Miles,

2021). Similarly, for men recovering from surgeries, such as prostate or colorectal cancer procedures, devices like the Tenuto by MysteryVibe are designed to promote localized blood circulation and support erectile function. These devices deliver targeted stimulation to penile tissue, improving blood flow and sensitivity over time, which can be particularly beneficial in the recovery process (Rodríguez & Méndez, 2022).

Sexual health aids also address broader issues of equity in sexual satisfaction, such as the orgasm gap—the disparity in orgasm frequency between men and women during partnered sexual activity. Research highlights that vibrators and similar devices significantly increase the likelihood of orgasm for women by providing consistent and direct clitoral stimulation, a critical factor for most women to achieve orgasm (Herbenick et al., 2015). Unlike manual stimulation or penetrative sex, vibrators offer customizable settings for intensity, patterns, and rhythm, allowing users to find the stimulation that suits them best. When incorporated into partnered sexual activities, these tools not only enhance pleasure but also encourage open communication about needs and desires, fostering deeper intimacy and satisfaction. By bridging gaps in pleasure, sexual health aids promote equity in relationships, challenging longstanding disparities in sexual satisfaction and deepening the emotional connection between partners.

These tools are not only effective in enhancing sexual pleasure but also in fostering healing, confidence, and a sense of agency over one's sexual health. Their accessibility, versatility, and adaptability make sexual health aids indispensable in both personal and clinical contexts. As such, they are vital in promoting a holistic approach to sexual wellness, enriching the lives of individuals and couples alike.

Sexual Health Aids within a Relationship

Within the context of relationships, sexual health aids serve as transformative tools for enhancing intimacy, fostering open communication, and deepening mutual pleasure. When thoughtfully integrated, these devices can help couples explore new dimensions of their sexual connection, enriching both physical and emotional closeness. Vibrators, for instance, are commonly incorporated into partnered sexual activities to provide targeted stimulation that enhances arousal and significantly increases the likelihood of orgasm, particularly for women. This application can bridge the orgasm gap, addressing disparities in orgasm frequency between men and women during partnered sex. Couples who introduce these tools into their relationships often report greater satisfaction, as open discussions about preferences and boundaries create opportunities for deeper intimacy and trust (Herbenick et al., 2015). For example, a heterosexual couple might experiment with a clitoral vibrator during intercourse, discovering that its use not only enhances pleasure but also sparks candid conversations about mutual needs and desires.

For some couples, however, the introduction of sex toys may evoke complex dynamics. In heterosexual relationships, women may worry that the use of vibrators or other sexual aids could threaten their male partners' sense of sexual competence or masculinity. Despite these initial concerns, many couples ultimately find that using sex toys together fosters playfulness and mutual enjoyment. This dynamic is especially evident among lesbian, bisexual, and queer women, who are more likely to view shared use of sexual health aids positively. For these couples, sex toys often represent a way to challenge traditional sexual norms and explore new forms of pleasure and connection, highlighting their subversive and liberating potential (Herbenick et al., 2010).

Technological advancements have further broadened the possibilities for incorporating sex toys into relationships, particularly for couples navigating the challenges of long-distance dynamics. Teledildonic devices, which can be remotely controlled via apps or internet connections, enable one partner to interact with the other's device in real time, creating opportunities for shared intimacy and interactive sexual experiences despite physical separation. These tools have become particularly valuable for couples in geographically distant relationships, providing a practical means of maintaining both emotional and sexual connection. For example, during the COVID-19 pandemic, when lockdowns and travel restrictions kept many couples apart, teledildonics allowed partners to preserve intimacy, demonstrating the evolving role of technology in supporting relationships (Jannini et al., 2012).

The shared use of sexual health aids in relationships also requires careful attention to hygiene and safety. Research emphasizes the importance of thoroughly cleaning shared toys and using protective barriers, such as condoms, to minimize the risk of infections like bacterial vaginosis and candida. Proper maintenance ensures that couples can enjoy the benefits of these tools without compromising their sexual health. For instance, a couple using a shared dildo might implement a routine of cleaning it with antibacterial solutions after each use or employing condoms when alternating between partners to prevent cross-contamination (Döring & Pöschl, 2018). These practices underscore the importance of combining pleasure with responsibility in the use of sexual health aids.

As societal attitudes toward sex toys continue to evolve, more couples are embracing these tools as an integral part of their relationships. The stigma once associated with sexual health aids has diminished significantly, empowering couples to view them as valuable resources for enhancing intimacy and mutual exploration. By facilitating open communication, addressing sexual challenges, and introducing playful and creative elements into the bedroom, sex toys contribute to healthier, more fulfilling partnerships. For many couples, these tools represent not only a source of physical pleasure but also an opportunity to deepen emotional bonds and approach their sexual relationship with renewed confidence and joy (Herbenick et al., 2009).

Cultural and Ethical Considerations within Clinical Practice

Incorporating sexual health aids into clinical practice demands a nuanced understanding of cultural and ethical complexities. Clinicians must balance patient values, cultural norms, and potential stigma with the need to provide evidence-based care that upholds professional integrity. Research underscores the importance of approaching these discussions with cultural humility, creating an inclusive space where diverse sexual experiences are validated. By ensuring that recommendations for sexual health aids align with patients' personal and cultural beliefs, clinicians foster trust and encourage open communication (Döring & Pöschl, 2018).

A key ethical consideration in this context involves informed consent and transparency. When discussing or prescribing sexual health aids, clinicians must clearly outline their therapeutic benefits and proper use, empowering patients to make informed decisions about their care. The practice of offering these products within a clinical setting is particularly debated, as it addresses barriers like embarrassment or confusion while raising concerns about potential conflicts of interest. Jannini et al. (2012) highlight that while selling sexual aids in healthcare settings provides patients with privacy and access to reliable tools, it can create power imbalances and perceptions of coercion. To address these risks, clinicians are advised to maintain clear professional boundaries by offering patients alternative purchasing options and focusing on education to enhance autonomy and informed decision-making.

Cultural attitudes toward sexual health aids vary significantly, often shaping how patients perceive these tools. For example, in religious or conservative cultural contexts, sex toys may carry stigmas or be viewed as inappropriate. Clinicians can navigate these sensitivities by reframing sexual health aids as tools for medical or relational enhancement rather than as recreational items. For instance, emphasizing the use of vibrators for improving pelvic floor health or alleviating pain during intercourse can make these devices more acceptable to patients who might otherwise reject them on moral or cultural grounds (Jannini et al., 2012).

Gender norms and relationship dynamics also influence receptiveness to sexual health aids. Male partners may perceive vibrators or similar devices as threats to their sexual competence, which can introduce tension into relationships. Clinicians can address such concerns by highlighting the collaborative benefits of sexual aids, positioning them as tools to enhance mutual satisfaction and intimacy. Facilitating open discussions about how these devices can strengthen relationships helps to reduce resistance and promote shared understanding. For example, educating couples on how vibrators can enhance sexual experiences for both partners provides a pathway to integrating these aids in a way that strengthens their connection (Herbenick et al., 2010; Rodríguez & Méndez, 2022).

Practical cultural dilemmas also arise in addressing stigma or taboos associated with sexual health aids. Patients from conservative or religious backgrounds may resist discussing or using these tools due to associations with immorality or impropriety. In such cases, clinicians should adopt a patient-centered approach that respects personal and cultural boundaries while ensuring informed consent. Jannini et al. (2012) recommend strategies such as active listening, framing recommendations in culturally congruent terms, and exploring alternative therapies. Providing culturally aligned resources, such as referrals to faith-based counselors or community advocates, can further support patients in navigating these challenges (Döring & Pöschl, 2018).

By fostering cultural competence and sensitivity in their practice, clinicians establish an environment where patients feel supported and empowered to address their sexual health needs. Furthermore, adhering to the highest professional and ethical standards in psychosexual care allows clinicians to actively challenge biases and reduce discomfort surrounding intimate wellness tools like sexual health aids. These efforts not only enhance therapeutic outcomes but also build trust and collaboration between clinicians and patients, cultivating a respectful and effective therapeutic relationship.

Case Example: William

William, a 24-year-old white male, presents with difficulty ejaculating during intercourse, a problem he has experienced for several years. He initially believed this issue was related to his involvement in casual hookups, to which he confesses feeling anxiety and shame about. Currently single, William has a "friend with benefits," Alison, with whom he is beginning to develop feelings. He is concerned that his inability to ejaculate with her may hinder the development of a deeper relationship. William sought sex therapy following a referral from his primary care physician.

Initial Interaction

In my assessment process, I employ Ecological Systems Theory to evaluate the various environmental, familial, cultural, ethnic, and religious factors that may influence the patient's sexual development and conceptualization of sexuality. This assessment also involves a thorough exploration of the patient's sexual history, as well as their current understanding of sex, sexuality, and gender.

Through this process, it emerged that William was raised in the Southern United States in a Christian household. He described his family as being actively involved in the local Baptist church during his early years, although discussions regarding sexuality were notably absent from the family dynamic. He recalled that the prevailing messages from his religious community emphasized sexual abstinence and avoidance of sexual engagement until marriage. William's first sexual experience occurred during his time in college, though he admitted to viewing pornography beginning at the age of 14, an activity that he associated with significant feelings of shame in his formative years.

Following his initial sexual experience, William reported a pronounced compulsion to engage in sexual activity frequently, which he described as an addictive urge. In an effort to enhance his physical attractiveness and thereby increase his sexual opportunities, he began a rigorous regimen of physical exercise at the university gym. While he did not enter into any serious romantic relationships during his college years, William engaged in numerous casual sexual encounters with women whom he found intriguing, noting that the pursuit or "chase" of potential partners was a considerable source of sexual excitement for him.

Initially, William did not experience difficulty with ejaculation during sexual encounters; however, this issue developed later in his college years and has progressively exacerbated. In earlier instances, he viewed his inability to orgasm as a "gift," believing it allowed him to prolong sexual encounters and provide greater satisfaction to his partners. However, in his current emotionally intimate relationship with Alison, this difficulty with orgasm has become a significant point of distress. William conveyed that Alison perceives his inability to ejaculate as an indication of either a lack of attraction to her or an inability to be sexually satisfied by her, which has led to heightened tension in their relationship. He expressed concern that this issue could undermine the potential for a deeper connection with her.

Regarding his sexual expression, William disclosed that he engages in frequent masturbation, often multiple times per day, which he reports finding highly pleasurable. He noted that he no longer experiences the guilt or shame associated with pornography use that characterized his adolescent years. Notably, William affirmed that he is generally able to ejaculate during masturbation, suggesting that his difficulty with orgasm may be more specifically linked to sexual intercourse, rather than a pervasive issue with ejaculation itself.

Clinical Assessment and Treatment

Initially, one might consider the guilt and shame associated with sexual behavior stemming from William's early Christian upbringing as a significant contributing factor to his current difficulties. However, in this case, it appeared that these feelings were secondary to the primary issue at hand, given that William had engaged in sexual activity for several years without presenting any ejaculatory difficulties initially. Furthermore, he no longer identifies religious influences as a significant factor in his current sexual functioning. Nevertheless, it remains prudent to revisit these religious and cultural influences prior to discharge to ensure that they do not emerge as an underlying concern in the future.

As William was referred to therapy by his primary care physician, I inquired about any medical interventions he had undergone, particularly regarding any potential physiological causes of his ejaculatory difficulties. William confirmed that he had recently consulted with a urologist, who ruled out any significant medical issues contributing to his sexual concerns. I also took the opportunity to assess relational factors, though William had not experienced any serious, long-term relationships, which helped rule out relational dynamics as a primary contributor. My inquiry shifted to his masturbatory habits and pornography consumption, as William reported no significant difficulty ejaculating while viewing pornography, though he did mention that it sometimes took longer than usual. He shared that he typically masturbates 2–3 times per day, though this may occasionally be reduced due to his schedule or travel.

Further exploration revealed that William sometimes requires specific mental imagery—namely, recalling past pornography he had watched—to achieve a fully erect penis. He also disclosed that he does not use lubricants, such as lotions or saliva, during masturbation. The absence of lubrication and his repetitive grip patterns during masturbation were critical factors in understanding his sexual difficulties. Typically, when males engage in frequent masturbation, their grip tends to become progressively tighter with each session. This was true for William, who had developed a tight grip, which, coupled with the lack of lubrication, resulted in a sensory experience that was not replicable during sexual intercourse. A lubricated vagina could not mimic the tightness and friction he had grown accustomed to during masturbation, leading to significant difficulty reaching orgasm with a partner.

The primary cause of William's ejaculatory issues, therefore, appeared to be his habitual, overly tight grip and the absence of lubrication during masturbation. To address this, the recommended course of treatment focused on modifying his masturbatory practices. I suggested that he refrain from masturbation for a period of two weeks to reset his habitual patterns. Upon reengaging in masturbation, I advised him to use a sexual health aid designed to simulate the sensations of intercourse more effectively. It was essential that he select a product with a rigid outer shell, which would prevent him from adjusting the tightness by altering the external pressure, a behavior that contributed to the issue. Products such as the Tenga Cup, Tenga Flip, Arcwave Pow, and Fleshlight were recommended as suitable options. Additionally, I emphasized the importance of using ample lubrication to reduce friction and facilitate a more natural, varied sensory experience.

In the therapeutic setting, the focus was directed toward exercises aimed at increasing William's present-moment awareness during sexual interactions. This involved reducing his reliance on pornography as his primary means of sexual expression, encouraging him instead to engage more fully with imagination and fantasy. We also explored the potential psychological impacts of his religious and environmental upbringing, particularly in relation to guilt and shame surrounding sexuality. These discussions aimed to ensure that any residual negative associations with sexual behavior could be addressed, thus fostering a more healthy and integrated approach to his sexual life.

Treatment Outcome

After two and a half months of therapy, William's difficulty with ejaculation gradually dissipated, largely as a result of incorporating sexual health aids into his routine. By using products designed to replicate the sensations of intercourse, combined with ample lubrication, William was able to break the cycle of tight gripping and friction that had previously hindered his ability to achieve orgasm during sexual encounters with a partner. This intervention allowed him to overcome the physical barriers he had been experiencing.

Furthermore, William has been able to engage in meaningful and fulfilling sexual activity with Alison, free from the distress and tension that had previously characterized their interactions. The therapeutic focus on improving his masturbatory hygiene and introducing more varied sensory experiences through the use of sex toys and lubrication has not only addressed his ejaculatory difficulties but also enhanced his overall sexual satisfaction. Additionally, shifting his focus toward imagination and fantasy during masturbation has strengthened his erections, allowing him to experience more robust and consistent arousal.

As a result of these changes, William has reported being more present and engaged during sexual interactions with Alison. This increased presence has improved his ability to connect with her emotionally and physically, fostering a deeper and more satisfying relationship. Overall, the combination of behavioral modifications, psychological interventions, and the use of sexual health aids has contributed to a significant improvement in William's sexual functioning and his overall sense of well-being.

Conclusion

The evolution of sexual health aids reflects humanity's enduring pursuit of pleasure, intimacy, and wellness. From the phallic objects of prehistoric societies to the teledildonics and organic lubricants of today, these tools have adapted to meet the shifting demands of culture, medicine, and technology. For example, the normalization of sex toys and lubricants during the COVID-19 pandemic underscores how societal barriers to discussing sexual health have diminished, allowing these products to be seen as legitimate instruments for self-care and connection (Arafat & Kar, 2021). Their integration into clinical practice also highlights the growing acceptance of these aids as therapeutic interventions, bridging the gap between medical care and holistic sexual wellness (Jannini et al., 2012; Rodríguez & Méndez, 2022).

The inclusion of sexual health aids in clinical settings requires navigating ethical complexities, including concerns about professional boundaries and the risks of perceived coercion when offering these products directly (Jannini et al., 2012). By maintaining cultural humility and adopting patient-centered approaches, clinicians can create supportive environments that empower individuals to embrace their sexual wellness journeys (Döring & Pöschl, 2018).

As society continues to destigmatize discussions about sexuality, the role of sexual health aids will only grow in importance. Their history, rich with examples of human ingenuity and resilience, underscores their capacity to foster healing, promote equity in pleasure, and enrich relationships. By recognizing their value in both personal and professional contexts, we contribute to a more inclusive and compassionate understanding of sexual health.

References

Arafat, S. M. Y., & Kar, S. K. (2021). Panic buying of sex toys during COVID-19 pandemic lockdown: An exploratory analysis. *Journal of Psychosexual Health*, *3*(1), 1–4.

Attwood, F. (2007). Sluts and riot girls: Female identity and sexual agency. *Journal of Gender Studies*, *16*(3), 233–247.

Brown, P. R. (2008). *The body and society: Men, women, and sexual renunciation in early Christianity*. Columbia University Press.

Brundage, J. A. (1987). *Law, sex, and Christian society in Medieval Europe*. University of Chicago Press.

Bullough, V. L., & Bullough, B. (1995). *Sexual attitudes: Myths and realities*. Prometheus Books.

Carroll, M. (2025). The renaissance of reproductive science: Leonardo da Vinci's anatomical contributions. *Reproductive Sciences*, 32, 575–599. https://doi.org/10.1007/s43032-024-01772-9

Döring, N., & Poeschl, S. (2018). Sex toys, sex dolls, sex robots: Our under-researched bedfellows. *Sexologies: European Journal of Sexology*, *27*(3), e51–e55.

Dubinskaya, A., Horowitz, R., Scott, V., Anger, J., & Eilber, K. (2023). Is it time for doctors to Rx vibrators? A systematic review of pelvic floor outcomes. *Sexual Medicine Reviews*, *11*(1), 15–22. https://doi.org/10.1093/sxmrev/qeac008

Halperin, D. M. (1990). *One hundred years of homosexuality: And other essays on Greek love*. Routledge.

Herbenick, D., Barnhart, K. J., Beavers, K., & Benge, S. (2015). Vibrators and other sex toys are commonly recommended to patients, but does size matter? Dimensions of commonly sold products. *The Journal of Sexual Medicine*, *12*(3), 641–645.

Herbenick, D., Reece, M., Sanders, S., Dodge, B., Ghassemi, A., & Fortenberry, J. D. (2009). Prevalence and characteristics of vibrator use by women in the United States: Results from a nationally representative study. *The Journal of Sexual Medicine*, 6(7), 1857–1866. https://doi.org/10.1111/j.1743-6109.2009.01318.x

Herbenick, D., Reece, M., Schick, V., Sanders, S. A., Dodge, B., & Fortenberry, J. D. (2010). Sexual behavior in the United States: Results from a national probability sample of men and women ages 14–94. *The Journal of Sexual Medicine*, *7*(Suppl 5), 255–265. https://doi.org/10.1111/j.1743-6109.2010.02012.x

Herbenick, D., Schick, V., Reece, M., Sanders, S. A., Sanders, S. A., Smith, N., Dodge, B., & Fortenberry, J. D. (2013). Characteristics of condom and lubricant use among a nationally representative probability sample of adults ages 18–59 in the United States. *The Journal of Sexual Medicine*, 10(2), 474–483. https://doi.org/10.1111/jsm.12021

Jacobson, C. (Ed.). (2025). *The Routledge International Handbook of Sex Therapy and Religion*. Routledge. https://doi.org/10.4324/9781003268017.

Jannini, E. A., Limoncin, E., Ciocca, G., Buehler, S., & Krychman, M. (2012). Ethical aspects of sexual medicine: Internet, vibrators, and other sex aids: Toys or therapeutic instruments? *The Journal of Sexual Medicine*, *9*(12), 2994–3001.

Korda, J. B., Goldstein, S. W., & Sommer, F. (2010). Sexual medicine history: The history of female ejaculation. *The Journal of Sexual Medicine*, 7(5), 1965–1975. https://doi.org/10.1111/j.1743-6109.2010.01720.x

Laumann, E. O., Gagnon, J. H., Michael, R. T., & Michaels, S. (1994). *The social organization of sexuality: Sexual practices in the United States*. University of Chicago Press.

Levi-Strauss, C. (1969). *The raw and the cooked: Introduction to a science of mythology*. Harper & Row.

Lieberman, H. (2016). Selling sex toys: Marketing and the meaning of vibrators in early twentieth-century America. *Enterprise & Society*, 17(2), 393–433. https://doi.org/10.1017/eso.2015.97

Lieberman, H., & Schatzberg, E. (2018). A failure of academic quality control: The technology of orgasm. *Journal of Positive Sexuality*, 4(2), 24–47. https://doi.org/10.51681/1.421

Maines, R. P. (2001). *The technology of orgasm: "Hysteria," the vibrator, and women's sexual satisfaction.* The Johns Hopkins University Press.

Miles, K., & Miles, S. (2021). Low dose, high frequency movement-based dilator therapy for dyspareunia: Retrospective analysis of 26 cases. *Sexual Medicine*, *9*(3), 100344.

Miranda, E. P., Taniguchi, H., Cao, D. L., Hald, G. M., Miranda, E. P., Cao, D. L., Hald, G. M., Jannini, E. A., & Mulhall, J. P. (2019). Application of sex aids in men with sexual dysfunction: A review. *The Journal of Sexual Medicine*, *16*(6), 767–780. https://doi.org/10.1016/j.jsxm.2019.03.265

Potenza, M. A., Montagnani, M., Santacroce, L., Charitos, I. A., & Bottalico, L. (2023). Ancient herbal therapy: A brief history of Panax ginseng. *Journal of Ginseng Research*, 47(3), 359–365. https://doi.org/10.1016/j.jgr.2022.03.004

Rodríguez Martínez, J. E., Alcaina, J., & Agullo, R. (2022). Preliminary results from a multicenter study on the use of a new device for the treatment of genito-pelvic pain disorders. *Journal of Sexual Medicine*, *19*, S102–S122.

Rubin, G. (1993). Thinking sex: Notes for a radical theory of the politics of sexuality. In H. Abelove, M. A. Barale, & D. M. Halperin (Eds.), *The lesbian and gay studies reader* (pp. 3–44). Routledge.

Tomnay, J., Vaisey, A., Malta, S., Goller, J. L., Temple-Smith, M., Bourchier, L., Lau, A., Chow, E. P. F., & Hocking, J. S. (2021). Love during lockdown: Findings from an online survey examining the impact of COVID-19 on the sexual health of people living in Australia. *Sexually Transmitted Infections*, *97*(5), 357–362. https://doi.org/10.1136/sextrans-2020-054688

Yang, L., Hou, A., Zhang, J., Wang, S., Man, W., Yu, H., Zheng, S., Wang, X., Liu, S., & Jiang, H. (2020). Panacis Quinquefolii Radix: A review of the botany, phytochemistry, quality control, pharmacology, toxicology and industrial applications research progress. *Frontiers in Pharmacology*, 11. https://doi.org/10.3389/fphar.2020.602092

Chapter 6

Cultural Considerations for Effective Psychosexual Therapy with Jewish Individuals and Couples

Caleb Jacobson

Introduction

Judaism significantly shapes individuals' core values, social interactions, and perspectives on sexuality, intimacy, and gender roles. Not a monolithic entity, Judaism encompasses a diverse range of beliefs, customs, and practices varying across denominations and individual communities (Jacobson, 2024; Satlow, 2020). Such diversity ranges from Orthodox communities' emphasis on strict adherence to laws of modesty and family purity (Frydman, 2022; Hartman & Marmon, 2004; Ribner & Rosenbaum, 2005) to the more liberal interpretations found within Reform Judaism (Carpenter & Kaplan, 2015), presenting unique challenges for psychosexual therapists. As noted, clinicians must thoughtfully navigate these differences while providing culturally competent care (Jacobson, 2024).

Therapists frequently encounter biases when engaging with religious populations, often interpreting religious and sexual regulations, such as those concerning menstrual purity, premarital abstinence, or sexual modesty, as inherently restrictive or sex-negative (Chandler, Sennott, & Constantinides, 2019; Friedman, 2019). Such biases risk alienating Jewish patients, who may see these regulations not as oppressive but as spiritually meaningful practices that enhance marital intimacy (Hartman & Marmon, 2004; Ribner & Kleinplatz, 2007; Westheimer & Mark, 2020). Misunderstanding these nuances can weaken therapeutic alliances, prompting patients to feel alienated rather than supported.

Moreover, Judaism often emphasizes sexuality as inherently positive within specific contexts, actively promoting marital intimacy as a vital aspect of emotional, physical, and spiritual health (Satlow, 2020; Westheimer & Mark, 2020). Rabbinic texts, for instance, emphasize sexuality not merely as a means for procreation but as essential for emotional connection and marital harmony (David & Weitzman, 2015; Satlow, 2020). Thus, recognizing the affirmative role religion can play in sexual and relational fulfillment is crucial for clinicians working with Jewish populations.

This chapter examines these critical cultural considerations, beginning by exploring Judaism's substantial influence on identity formation and personal development through the lens of Bronfenbrenner's Ecological Systems Theory (Jacobson,

DOI: 10.4324/9781003611387-6

2024). By adopting this framework, the multilayered, systemic impact of Judaism on individuals' sexual identities and behaviors becomes clear. Subsequent sections will delve into specific topics, including marital and non-marital sexual norms, homoeroticism, sexuality in advanced age, and practices around menstrual separation and ritual immersion, to provide therapists with deeper insights and practical strategies explicitly tailored for effective psychosexual therapy with Jewish individuals and couples.

Judaism as a Cultural Influence

Judaism is not merely a religion but a cultural system deeply embedded in the development of individuals, shaping their worldview, values, and social interactions. Unlike secular cultural identities, Judaism integrates religious law (*halakha*), historical continuity, communal belonging, and shared traditions that span generations (Jacobson, 2024). This cultural influence is particularly strong because Judaism is both an ethno-religious identity and a lived experience, shaping how individuals engage with family, community, and broader society (Satlow, 2020).

Understanding Judaism as a cultural system is essential for psychosexual therapists, as religious and communal norms influence individual and relational experiences of sexuality, intimacy, and gender roles. Jewish cultural identity manifests in diverse ways, from Orthodox communities that adhere to strict *halakhic* regulations on marital intimacy and gender separation to more liberal Jewish movements that embrace evolving gender roles and sexual ethics (Ribner & Rosenbaum, 2005; Westheimer & Mark, 2020). Misunderstanding this diversity can create barriers in therapy, as Jewish patients may perceive therapeutic models as incongruent with their lived realities (Jacobson, 2024).

A case described by Ribner & Kleinplatz (2007) involves a young Orthodox Jewish woman referred to sex therapy following ongoing sexual dysfunction within her marriage. The therapist initially assumed the patient's discomfort was due to repressive religious norms. However, further exploration revealed that the woman derived a strong sense of spiritual fulfillment from adhering to taharat hamishpacha and found the mikveh process deeply affirming. The true source of her distress stemmed from inadequate premarital education and anxiety about communication with her spouse, issues rooted in communal silence around sex, not in religious doctrine itself. Once this was clarified and culturally competent strategies were applied, including involving a culturally informed female educator, therapeutic outcomes improved significantly (Ribner & Kleinplatz, 2007, p. 448).

Bronfenbrenner's Ecological Systems Theory provides a helpful framework for understanding the multilayered cultural impact of Judaism on individuals and communities. By analyzing the interaction between personal, familial, communal, and societal influences, clinicians can better appreciate how Jewish cultural identity informs psychosexual experiences and challenges (Bronfenbrenner, 2005; Kitchen, Bethell, & Rehkopf, 2019).

Ecological Systems Theory and Jewish Identity

Bronfenbrenner's model outlines five interconnected layers that shape individual development: the microsystem, mesosystem, exosystem, macrosystem, and chronosystem. Judaism, as both a faith and a cultural tradition, operates within each of these layers, influencing personal identity, relationships, and communal interactions.

Microsystem: Family and Early Identity Formation

The microsystem consists of the immediate environment, such as family, which plays a foundational role in transmitting Jewish values, rituals, and traditions. From an early age, Jewish children are immersed in religious and cultural practices, including reciting blessings, keeping kosher, lighting Shabbat candles, and celebrating holidays like Passover and Hanukkah. These familial customs create a consistent rhythm of life, embedding religious meaning into daily routines and contributing to early identity formation (Westheimer & Mark, 2020). In more observant communities, early gender role expectations are reinforced through family interactions, influencing beliefs about modesty, marital intimacy, and appropriate sexual conduct (Hartman & Marmon, 2004).

Mesosystem: Integrating Jewish Identity Across Social Structures

The mesosystem reflects the interplay between various microsystems, such as how interactions between family, school, and synagogue reinforce Jewish cultural norms. A child attending a Jewish day school while participating in synagogue youth programs experiences a cohesive environment where religious teachings, social development, and identity formation align. In Orthodox communities, education often emphasizes *halakhic* teachings on marriage, gender roles, and family purity, which significantly shape attitudes toward sexuality and intimate relationships in adulthood (Frydman, 2022; Ribner & Rosenbaum, 2005).

In a case reported by Friedman (2019), a Modern Orthodox adolescent male sought therapy for compulsive masturbation and anxiety about violating *halakhic* norms. He was raised in a tightly integrated mesosystem, attending a yeshiva, living in an observant household, and participating in synagogue life. The school's abstinence-based sex education and religious messaging had strongly shaped his internalized sexual ethics. During therapy, it became clear that his anxiety was less about sexual behavior itself and more about perceived moral failure and anticipated shame from his religious community. Treatment focused on helping him reframe his understanding of religious accountability while introducing psychoeducational material that aligned with Modern Orthodox perspectives. Involving a posek (religious legal authority) in consultation helped reinforce that therapy was not undermining his faith but supporting his health (Friedman, 2019, pp. 934–936).

Exosystem: Institutional and Communal Influences

Jewish institutions, including synagogues, community centers, and advocacy organizations, indirectly shape individual experiences by providing resources, communal expectations, and social structures that reinforce Jewish identity. For instance, Jewish community centers offer marriage preparation courses, family purity classes, and support groups for couples experiencing sexual dysfunction, integrating cultural values into psychosexual education (Hartman & Marmon, 2004; Westheimer & Mark, 2020). These institutions also influence norms regarding sexual health, intimacy, and marital expectations, which can affect how individuals approach therapy and seek guidance for relational concerns (Jacobson, 2024).

Macrosystem: Cultural Values and Religious Worldview

At the macrosystem level, Judaism functions as part of a broader cultural framework that shapes collective attitudes toward ethics, sexuality, and social responsibility. A key Jewish concept at this level is *tikkun olam* (repairing the world), which underscores the ethical dimension of Jewish life, influencing perspectives on relationships, family, and social justice (Colwell, Pollard, & Pollard, 2015; Jacobson, 2024). Additionally, Jewish law historically shaped attitudes toward sexual ethics, including the regulation of marital relations, prohibitions on extramarital sex, and expectations surrounding modesty and procreation (Satlow, 2020). These deeply embedded cultural norms continue to influence contemporary Jewish communities, even as liberal movements reinterpret traditional teachings in response to changing societal values (Schreiber, 2016).

Chronosystem: Adaptation Over Time

The chronosystem highlights how Jewish culture and identity evolve in response to historical and societal changes. The Jewish diaspora has led to diverse expressions of Judaism, with Ashkenazi and Sephardic communities developing distinct traditions, liturgical practices, and approaches to gender and sexuality (Olszewska, El-Shaarawi, & Yilmaz, 2019). Additionally, major societal shifts, such as feminist movements, LGBTQ+ advocacy, and advances in reproductive health, have influenced contemporary Jewish debates on gender roles, sexual ethics, and marital expectations (Schreiber, 2016; Robinson, 2016). In Orthodox and Ultra-Orthodox communities, these shifts often result in increased efforts to preserve traditional values. In contrast, more progressive Jewish movements embrace new interpretations of *halakha* to accommodate evolving cultural norms (Jacobson, 2024).

By applying Bronfenbrenner's Ecological Systems Theory to Jewish identity, clinicians can gain a deeper understanding of the interconnected cultural, religious, and social influences shaping Jewish individuals' experiences of intimacy, sexuality, and relationships. Recognizing these complexities allows therapists to offer culturally competent interventions that respect Jewish values while addressing psychosexual concerns effectively.

Impact on Family and Community

Within Jewish communities, family and communal structures are pivotal in shaping individual identity, reinforcing cultural continuity, and fostering psychosocial resilience. The family serves as the primary conduit for transmitting Jewish values, including respect for elders, prioritization of education, and commitment to communal welfare. The extended family structure, a characteristic feature of many Jewish communities, strengthens intergenerational ties, further embedding religious and cultural traditions across generations (Friedman, 2019; Ribner & Rosenbaum, 2005). These familial bonds shape personal and relational development, particularly in regard to intimate relationships, marriage, and gender roles (Hartman & Marmon, 2004; Westheimer & Mark, 2020).

Jewish communal life extends beyond the family unit, significantly contributing to individual psychosocial resilience. Institutions such as synagogues, Jewish community centers, and educational programs provide critical social structures that reinforce cultural identity and offer a framework for social support (Jacobson, 2024). These communal settings function as integral microsystems within Bronfenbrenner's Ecological Systems Theory, playing an active role in an individual's personal development and psychological well-being (Bronfenbrenner, 2005; Kitchen, Bethell & Rehkopf, 2019).

Particularly in times of emotional or relational crisis, Jewish communal support systems can provide essential emotional and social resources, helping individuals and couples navigate personal struggles while maintaining a sense of belonging and religious identity. Studies show that social support networks reduce stress and enhance coping mechanisms, making them particularly relevant in psychosexual therapy (Harandi, Taghinasab, & Nayeri, 2017). For Jewish individuals and couples, these support networks help mitigate distress related to sexual dysfunction, marital discord, or conflicts between religious values and personal experiences (Friedman, 2019; Ribner & Kleinplatz, 2007).

Ribner & Rosenbaum (2005) documented a case involving an ultra-Orthodox couple referred for therapy after six months of an unconsummated marriage. Both partners adhered strictly to halakha and were embedded in a tight-knit family and synagogue communities. Due to communal expectations and shame, they delayed seeking therapy, hoping a religious mentor would resolve the issue. The couple reported high relational warmth but experienced extreme anxiety regarding sexual intimacy, driven in part by community-based modesty norms and a complete lack of sexual education. Therapy involved structured, *halakha*-compliant sexual education and modified sensate focus exercises that accommodated *taharat hamishpacha*. With appropriate cultural adaptations and permission from a rabbinic advisor, the couple achieved full sexual function over time (Ribner & Rosenbaum, 2005, pp. 343–344).

Psychosexual therapists must thoughtfully integrate familial and communal influences into their therapeutic approach, recognizing that Jewish identity is often deeply intertwined with cultural and religious frameworks. Understanding these connections enables therapists to work more effectively with Jewish individuals and couples, ensuring that interventions respect and incorporate the patient's religious and communal values (Jacobson, 2024).

Cross-Influence of Religion and Society

The relationship between religion and society is reciprocal, with each continuously influencing the other. This dynamic is particularly evident in Judaism, where religious practices have adapted over time in response to societal shifts while also contributing significantly to broader cultural and ethical norms (Jacobson, 2024; Robinson, 2016).

Jewish law and traditions have historically evolved in response to external influences, including migration, persecution, and social change. For example, contemporary Jewish denominations, such as Reform and Conservative movements, have increasingly embraced inclusivity and gender equality, reflecting broader cultural movements toward social justice and progressive values (Schreiber, 2016). In contrast, Orthodox and Ultra-Orthodox communities have maintained traditional gender roles and family structures, emphasizing adherence to *halakha* as a means of preserving religious continuity amidst societal transformation (Westheimer & Mark, 2020). These differences illustrate the broad spectrum of Jewish responses to modernity and cultural change.

Conversely, Jewish values have significantly influenced societal norms, particularly in regions with substantial Jewish populations. Core Jewish principles, such as the emphasis on education, family cohesion, and ethical responsibility, have played a foundational role in shaping legal, social, and educational policies in various countries (Donin, 2019; Robinson, 2016). The Jewish concept of *tikkun olam* (repairing the world) has particularly resonated beyond religious contexts, influencing global movements focused on human rights, environmental sustainability, and social justice (Jacobson, 2024).

A case described by Jacobson (2024) involved a gay man raised in a Modern Orthodox community who entered therapy due to intense internal conflict surrounding his sexual orientation. Though no longer observant, he remained culturally and emotionally tied to his Jewish identity. He expressed grief over the alienation he felt from his family and synagogue and described internalized homophobia shaped by years of exposure to *halakhic* prohibitions. Therapy focused on integrating his sexual identity with his cultural heritage, using supportive Jewish texts from progressive denominations and community-based LGBTQ+ Jewish advocacy organizations. This dual approach, while addressing both psychosocial and spiritual needs, helped him reclaim aspects of his Jewish identity while fostering self-acceptance (Jacobson, 2024, Ch. 3).

Jewish resilience in adapting to societal pressures is evident throughout history. The development of the Talmud, for example, exemplifies Judaism's capacity to preserve religious teachings while adapting to changing socio-political conditions. During periods of exile and persecution, Jewish scholars compiled and codified oral traditions into written form to ensure continuity in religious practice despite external challenges (Steinsaltz, 2006). This adaptability underscores the balance Judaism maintains between preserving tradition and responding to new realities, a dynamic that remains relevant in contemporary discussions about sexuality, gender roles, and family structures (Robinson, 2016).

Understanding this intricate interplay between Jewish religious traditions and societal influences is crucial for psychosexual therapists. Jewish patients may struggle with conflicts between their religious identity and societal expectations, particularly regarding issues such as LGBTQ+ inclusion, premarital relationships, and evolving gender roles (Jacobson, 2024). By recognizing these reciprocal influences, clinicians can enhance their cultural competence, fostering therapeutic environments that acknowledge religious values while addressing the personal and relational concerns of Jewish individuals and couples.

Judaism as a Diverse Culture

Judaism is frequently misrepresented as a uniform religious or cultural identity, a perspective that wrongly assumes shared beliefs, customs, and norms across all Jewish individuals. This misconception disregards Judaism's significant internal diversity, encompassing variations in beliefs, customs, practices, and ideological expressions among different communities and denominations (Jacobson, 2024). Judaism comprises a broad spectrum of practices and interpretations, including liberal denominations such as Reform and Conservative, as well as more conservative streams such as Modern Orthodox, Hasidic, and Ultra-Orthodox (Haredi) communities (Carpenter & Kaplan, 2015; Hartman & Marmon, 2004; Ribner & Rosenbaum, 2005).

Within these diverse groups, attitudes toward sexuality, gender roles, marriage, and intimacy can vary considerably, often shaped by distinct historical, cultural, and theological influences. For example, Orthodox and Ultra-Orthodox communities emphasize religious law (*halakha*) and traditional gender roles, whereas Reform and Conservative Judaism tend to adopt progressive views on gender, sexuality, and relationship dynamics (Satlow, 2020; Westheimer & Mark, 2020). These internal variations highlight the complexity and richness inherent within Judaism as both a religion and a cultural identity. However, Judaism is frequently misrepresented or oversimplified in psychotherapeutic settings, where clinicians may apply broad assumptions without considering this diversity. Such misconceptions can lead to ineffective therapeutic interventions or compromised therapeutic relationships, causing Jewish patients to feel misunderstood or alienated (Friedman, 2019; Jacobson, 2024).

In a case referenced by Friedman (2019), a sex therapist working with a Conservative Jewish couple assumed that the wife's discomfort with sexual activity stemmed from internalized religious guilt. However, upon further inquiry, it was revealed that the couple rarely engaged with Jewish law and did not observe family purity practices. The patient clarified that her anxiety was instead due to past sexual trauma unrelated to her Jewish identity. The therapist's initial framing caused the patient to feel misunderstood, delaying progress. Once this assumption was corrected, therapy shifted toward trauma-informed care and significantly improved outcomes (Friedman, 2019, pp. 937–938).

Therefore, therapists must recognize and appreciate this internal diversity within Judaism, cultivating a nuanced understanding that respects and integrates patients' distinct religious and cultural experiences. Clinicians must remain flexible, ensuring that therapeutic interventions align sensitively with the patient's lived experience while acknowledging that Jewish identity is multifaceted and deeply personal (Jacobson, 2024). A deeper appreciation of these variations fosters a more potent therapeutic alliance and enhances the effectiveness of psychosexual therapy.

Judaism: A Dual Identity

Judaism represents a dual identity framework, encompassing both cultural and religious dimensions, each rich in nuance and variability. Cultural Judaism is often associated with traditions, historical experiences, languages such as Yiddish or Ladino, and a sense of communal belonging that exists independently of religious observance (Olszewska, Twardowska, & Katny, 2019). Religious Judaism, on the other hand, primarily emphasizes adherence to Jewish law (*halakha*), spiritual practices, and theological beliefs (Steinsaltz, 2006). While these cultural and religious identities frequently intersect, they remain distinct and may be expressed differently across individuals and communities.

For instance, individuals identifying primarily with cultural Judaism may vigorously participate in holiday celebrations, Jewish literature, and communal rituals without regular synagogue attendance or strict observance of religious laws. Secular Jews may uphold Jewish cultural traditions as a reflection of heritage rather than religious doctrine. In contrast, religiously observant Jews may rigorously maintain laws regarding diet (*kashrut*), Sabbath observance (*Shabbat*), and family purity (*taharat hamishpacha*) while engaging less with secular aspects of Jewish culture such as art, literature, or historical identity (Jacobson, 2024; Steinsaltz, 2006).

This dual identity framework has significant implications for psychosexual therapy. A clinician working with a Jewish patient cannot assume uniform adherence to religious norms or secular Jewish cultural practices. A patient may experience sexual concerns within marriage that are influenced by strict religious teachings, while another may struggle with cultural expectations surrounding dating or family roles that exist outside of religious frameworks (Ribner & Rosenbaum, 2005; Westheimer & Mark, 2020). These varied expressions of Jewish identity necessitate a clinical approach that recognizes each patient's distinct integration of religious and cultural elements, avoiding assumptions about uniformity within Judaism.

A case presented by Ribner & Kleinplatz (2007) involved a secular Jewish woman in her mid-30s who sought therapy due to sexual dissatisfaction in a long-term relationship. Although she did not identify as religious, she described a strong cultural connection to Judaism, regularly attending holiday gatherings and engaging with Jewish art and literature. During therapy, it emerged that her discomfort around sexual expression stemmed not from personal values but from implicit messages about female modesty and sexuality absorbed during her childhood in a culturally conservative Sephardic Jewish household. Therapy involved disentangling inherited cultural scripts from her personal values. By validating her secular Jewish identity and exploring how her cultural legacy shaped her relational dynamics, the therapist helped her gain clarity and sexual confidence (Ribner & Kleinplatz, 2007, pp. 448–450).

By acknowledging the complexity of Jewish identity, therapists can cultivate culturally sensitive interventions that validate the patient's lived experience. This approach ensures that therapy remains respectful of the patient's background while addressing psychosexual concerns within a context that feels authentic and relevant to their personal and communal identity (Jacobson, 2024).

The Diversity of Beliefs and Practices

The diversity within Judaism becomes particularly evident when examining attitudes toward Jewish law and practice. Denominations such as Orthodox, Conservative, Reform, Reconstructionist, and secular forms of Judaism differ notably in their interpretation and application of *halakha*, reflecting a broader spectrum of theological and cultural viewpoints (Hartman & Marmon, 2004; Jacobson, 2024). These differences manifest in various ways, particularly in regard to sexuality, gender roles, and marital intimacy. Understanding these variations is crucial for psychosexual therapists, as rigid assumptions about religious adherence can lead to ineffective interventions or alienation of Jewish patients.

One of the most significant areas of divergence is in the observance of family purity laws (*taharat hamishpacha*), which regulate marital intimacy based on menstrual cycles. Orthodox Judaism views these laws as divinely ordained commandments fundamental to marital sanctity and personal holiness. These laws include the mandatory observance of *niddah*, during which a woman refrains from physical intimacy with her husband until she immerses in a ritual bath (*mikveh*) following menstruation (Hartman & Marmon, 2004; Ribner & Rosenbaum, 2005). Hasidic and ultra-Orthodox communities often impose additional stringencies, such as heightened physical separation between spouses during *niddah* (Frydman, 2022).

In contrast, Conservative and Reform Judaism approach *taharat hamishpacha* with greater flexibility. Conservative Judaism often acknowledges the spiritual and historical value of these laws while allowing for modified observance. Reform Judaism, however, generally regards these practices as non-obligatory, emphasizing personal autonomy in determining their relevance (Jacobson, 2024; Westheimer & Mark, 2020). Many Jewish individuals outside of Orthodox circles may have limited awareness or engagement with these practices, which therapists must consider when addressing issues of intimacy and sexual function.

In a study by Ribner & Rosenbaum (2005), a therapist worked with a newlywed Modern Orthodox couple experiencing difficulties initiating sexual intimacy. The husband strictly adhered to taharat hamishpacha and was distressed that his wife, though raised in a Conservative home, felt alienated by the niddah restrictions. She viewed the mandated abstinence as punitive and outdated. The therapist collaborated with a Modern Orthodox rabbi who clarified permissible leniencies within halakha and worked with the couple to establish mutually acceptable practices around immersion and intimacy. By bridging denominational perspectives, the therapist preserved both partners' religious integrity and improved their relational satisfaction (Ribner & Rosenbaum, 2005, pp. 345–346).

Additional religious laws impacting sexuality, such as prohibitions against masturbation, extramarital sex, and non-procreative sexual acts, are similarly interpreted with significant variation. While Orthodox Judaism often strictly adheres to these prohibitions, more progressive denominations may adopt more lenient or symbolic interpretations (Ribner & Kleinplatz, 2007; Satlow, 2020). These diverse perspectives highlight the importance of tailoring clinical approaches to individual beliefs and practices rather than making broad assumptions based on religious affiliation (Jacobson, 2024).

Thus, clinicians must assess each patient's specific religious and cultural background, engaging in open dialogue rather than assuming uniform adherence to Jewish sexual ethics and practices. Doing so ensures that therapy remains patient-centered and culturally competent.

The Pitfall of Generalization

A primary clinical risk when treating Jewish patients is presuming a fixed correlation between Jewish identity and specific religious or cultural behaviors. Therapists may erroneously assume patient familiarity with or adherence to traditional laws, leading to misunderstandings, therapeutic misalignment, or patient alienation (Hartman & Marmon, 2004). Jewish identity is complex, and levels of observance vary widely, even within the same denominational affiliation.

For instance, a therapist may assume that all Orthodox Jewish patients strictly observe *taharat hamishpacha*. However, even within Orthodox communities, levels of observance can differ. Some couples may follow all laws meticulously, while others may engage in private modifications that deviate from strict *halakhic* requirements (Ribner & Rosenbaum, 2005).

In *Sex Therapy with Religious Patients* (Jacobson, 2024), a case is described involving a therapist who, upon learning that a client was Modern Orthodox, preemptively structured the treatment plan around assumptions of strict adherence to *halakha*, including presumed rejection of masturbation, oral sex, and non-procreative touch. The client, however, identified as spiritually Orthodox but personally lenient and non-observant in sexual matters. She felt shamed and misunderstood by the therapist's assumptions, nearly terminating treatment. After this rupture, the therapist engaged in cultural humility, asking open-ended questions about how the client personally navigated her Jewish identity. This shift in approach restored trust and allowed therapy to continue productively (Jacobson, 2024, Ch. 4).

Similarly, therapists may assume that Jewish patients avoid premarital sex. However, research shows that many modern Orthodox Jews engage in premarital intimacy, albeit with varying degrees of conflict or negotiation between personal values and religious teachings (Carpenter & Kaplan, 2015; Frydman, 2022).

Moreover, Jewish patients from non-Orthodox backgrounds may not have received formal religious education regarding Jewish sexual ethics or *halakha*. A therapist working with a Jewish patient experiencing sexual dysfunction might assume a lack of sexual knowledge due to religious conservatism when, in fact, the patient may have never been exposed to traditional Jewish teachings on intimacy at all (Jacobson, 2024; Westheimer & Mark, 2020). This misalignment between therapist assumptions and patient experiences can weaken the therapeutic alliance and hinder treatment effectiveness.

To avoid these pitfalls, clinicians should adopt an open, curious stance when engaging Jewish patients in discussions about their religious and cultural backgrounds. Asking exploratory questions, such as, "How does your religious or cultural background shape your views on intimacy?" allows therapists to gather individualized information without making assumptions (Jacobson, 2024). Additionally, utilizing patient-centered, nonjudgmental inquiry fosters therapeutic rapport, reduces the risk of alienation, and promotes patient engagement by acknowledging each individual's unique experiences and practices (Ribner & Kleinplatz, 2007).

By prioritizing personalized assessments over generalizations, therapists can ensure that their clinical approach remains culturally sensitive, allowing Jewish patients to feel understood and supported in navigating their psychosexual concerns.

Implications for Clinical Practice

Acknowledging Judaism's internal diversity has direct implications for clinical practice. Therapists working with Jewish individuals and couples benefit significantly from an awareness of how religious and cultural identities shape patients' worldviews and presenting issues (Hartman & Marmon, 2004). For instance, attitudes toward religious rituals, such as *taharat hamishpacha* (family purity laws), can provide clinicians with critical insight into patients' relational dynamics, personal values, and areas of potential conflict or distress (Ribner & Rosenbaum, 2005). Furthermore, the intersection of religious belief and sexual health can be complex, as Jewish patients may experience internalized guilt, communal pressure, or struggles reconciling personal desires with religious teachings (Ribner & Kleinplatz, 2007).

Clinicians who adopt a stance of cultural humility, recognizing and respecting the internal diversity of Judaism, are better positioned to build trust and therapeutic rapport. Jewish patients often expect therapists to acknowledge their cultural and religious background without judgment or assumption, and failure to do so can lead to disengagement from therapy (Jacobson, 2024). Clinicians enhance therapeutic engagement and treatment efficacy by facilitating a respectful environment in which patients feel their identities are understood (Westheimer & Mark, 2020).

A patient-centered approach requires therapists to actively explore, rather than assume, the role that Judaism plays in their patients' lives. While some Jewish individuals may strictly observe *halakha*, others may identify culturally rather than religiously, leading to highly individualized attitudes toward intimacy and sexuality (Satlow, 2020). Open-ended inquiry allows therapists to assess religious significance without making assumptions. Questions such as "*How does your Jewish identity influence your views on relationships and sexuality?*" or "*What role do religious teachings or cultural expectations play in your intimate relationships?*" help clinicians tailor interventions that align with the patient's beliefs and values (Jacobson, 2024).

Friedman (2019) describes a case involving a married Ultra-Orthodox couple who sought therapy due to severe sexual dysfunction. The couple had not consummated their marriage after nearly a year. The therapist, rather than assuming a fixed level of *halakhic* adherence, asked open-ended questions about the couple's personal practices, comfort, and religious understanding. It was revealed that the husband experienced significant anxiety around "halakhically correct" intercourse and feared the spiritual consequences of "doing it wrong." The therapist worked closely with both partners and, when appropriate, consulted with a rabbinic advisor the couple trusted. Tailored psychoeducation was provided in a sensitive, gender-specific format. With this respectful, collaborative approach, the couple gradually developed physical and emotional intimacy, leading to successful consummation and reduced distress (Friedman, 2019, pp. 934–937).

Clinicians must also be aware of common misconceptions regarding Jewish sexuality. One prevalent myth is that Orthodox Judaism is inherently restrictive toward sexuality; in reality, *halakha* often frames sexual intimacy as a sacred and vital component of marital life (Westheimer & Mark, 2020). In some cases, however, religious teachings may contribute to sexual dysfunction, such as anxiety around sexual performance or fear of violating religious laws (Ribner & Rosenbaum, 2005). For instance, Orthodox couples struggling with unconsummated marriages often experience distress due to a lack of sexual education combined with *halakhic* concerns about proper sexual conduct (Frydman, 2022). Understanding these religious influences allows therapists to provide sensitive, tailored interventions that validate patients' religious values while addressing their psychosexual concerns.

A culturally attuned clinical approach ensures that therapeutic interventions respect, rather than challenge, religious values. By integrating Jewish identity into therapy in meaningful ways, therapists can help patients navigate personal and relational challenges while maintaining a sense of religious and cultural integrity. This approach fosters a therapeutic environment where Jewish patients feel understood, validated, and empowered to engage in psychosexual therapy that aligns with their beliefs and lived experiences.

Judaism and Sexuality

Judaism, deeply embedded in individual development, significantly influences views on sex, sexuality, and gender. As Jacobson (2024) emphasizes, Jewish perspectives on these topics are rooted in religious texts and traditions while also reflecting the cultural diversity within Jewish communities. Judaism often regards sexuality as a divine gift integral to human connection and spiritual purpose. However, its interpretation and application vary widely across different Jewish movements, illustrating the complex interplay between tradition and modernity.

Sexuality in Jewish Thought

Central to Judaism's view on sexuality is the concept that sexual expression is both a physical and spiritual act. Traditional Jewish texts, such as the Talmud, frame sexuality within the bounds of marriage, emphasizing its role in fostering intimacy and fulfilling the commandment to "be fruitful and multiply" (Genesis 1:28). Sexual activity is not merely tolerated but celebrated as a mitzvah (commandment) when practiced in a marital context, highlighting the religion's sex-positive stance within specific parameters (Berkovits, 1976; Jacobson, 2024).

Unlike certain religious traditions that view celibacy as a form of holiness, Judaism encourages sexual fulfillment within marriage as an obligation that serves both procreation and marital unity (Westheimer & Mark, 2020). The Talmud even mandates sexual frequency based on a husband's occupation, ensuring that wives receive consistent physical intimacy, underscoring the expectation of mutual pleasure in Jewish marital relationships (Satlow, 2020).

In a clinical case reported by Ribner & Kleinplatz (2007), a therapist worked with an Orthodox couple experiencing low sexual desire. The husband reported a belief that sex was primarily for procreation and that his wife's pleasure was not essential. The therapist introduced classical *halakhic* sources (e.g., Ketubot 61b) that obligate a husband to provide sexual satisfaction to his wife, grounded in the mitzvah of onah (conjugal duty). This reframe, coming from within Jewish tradition, shifted the husband's perception dramatically. He began engaging more attentively, and his wife, feeling more valued, reciprocated with greater interest and vulnerability. The couple reported substantial improvements in intimacy and marital satisfaction (Ribner & Kleinplatz, 2007, pp. 447–448).

However, Jewish perspectives on sexuality are not static. Rabbinic authorities throughout history have debated issues such as contraception, sexual pleasure, and non-procreative sex, with rulings evolving based on cultural and societal contexts (Ribner & Kleinplatz, 2007; Westheimer & Mark, 2020). This flexibility allows

Judaism to maintain its traditional values while simultaneously engaging in modern discussions on sexual health and relationships.

Family Purity Laws

The laws of family purity (*taharat hamishpacha*) provide a key example of Judaism's nuanced approach to sexuality. These laws, rooted in Leviticus 15, mandate periods of sexual abstinence during and immediately following menstruation, followed by ritual immersion in a *mikveh* (ritual bath). For many Orthodox Jews, these practices foster spiritual renewal and enhance marital intimacy by introducing cycles of separation and reunion (Friedman, 2019).

In Orthodox communities, adherence to *taharat hamishpacha* is seen as essential to maintaining both religious observance and marital harmony. Many couples report that the structured periods of separation strengthen desire and emotional connection, reinforcing the idea that Jewish law enhances rather than restricts marital intimacy (Hartman & Marmon, 2004; Ribner & Rosenbaum, 2005). However, for some, particularly those in ultra-Orthodox communities, these laws can introduce anxiety and strain in marital relationships, especially if education about sexuality is limited or if one partner experiences distress related to the observance of these laws (Ribner & Kleinplatz, 2007).

In a longitudinal study by Hartman & Marmon (2004), one Orthodox couple reported that adherence to *taharat hamishpacha* initially created tension. The wife experienced anxiety and a sense of impurity during menstruation, while the husband misinterpreted the laws as requiring emotional distance. During sex therapy, the clinician explored these beliefs and introduced alternative interpretations found in rabbinic and feminist Jewish literature, which view niddah not as punishment but as a rhythm of renewal. The couple began using the abstinence period to build emotional intimacy, plan spiritual experiences together, and engage in non-sexual closeness. Their sexual satisfaction improved significantly once they felt spiritually aligned and mutually respected within *halakhic* boundaries (Hartman & Marmon, 2004, pp. 395–396).

In liberal Jewish movements such as Reform and Conservative Judaism, these laws are often reinterpreted or set aside entirely, reflecting a focus on personal autonomy and evolving gender roles (Jacobson, 2024; Westheimer & Mark, 2020). Some Jewish women in these communities reclaim *mikveh* as a spiritual practice unrelated to menstruation, using it to mark significant life transitions rather than as a mandated element of sexual practice (Hartman & Marmon, 2004). These varying interpretations illustrate the broader diversity in how Judaism approaches sexuality across denominations.

Sexuality and Diversity Within Judaism

Judaism's perspectives on sexuality are not uniform and vary significantly among its denominations. Orthodox Judaism generally maintains traditional views, often opposing premarital sex, same-sex relationships, and nonbinary gender expressions. By contrast, Reform and Conservative Judaism frequently adopt more inclusive stances, supporting LGBTQ+ rights and emphasizing individual conscience over strict adherence to Jewish law (Jacobson, 2024).

It has been highlighted that these differences illustrate a broader tension within Judaism between tradition and adaptation (Jacobson, 2024). For example, while Orthodox interpretations of texts such as Leviticus 18:22 view homosexuality as prohibited, progressive Jewish communities increasingly embrace inclusive readings that affirm diverse sexual orientations and gender identities (Satlow, 2020). This shift is reflected in Reform and Reconstructionist synagogues, which officiate same-sex marriages and advocate for LGBTQ+ inclusion in all areas of Jewish life (Schreiber, 2016).

In Jacobson (2024), a therapist recounts working with a gay Orthodox man who remained deeply committed to his religious practice. He presented with depressive symptoms linked to his internalized belief that living openly as a gay man would invalidate his connection to Judaism. Rather than pressuring the client to "resolve" his sexual orientation or religious belief, therapy focused on identity integration. This included reviewing alternative Orthodox rabbinic voices (e.g., Rabbi Steven Greenberg) and connecting him to support groups like Eshel, which serve LGBTQ+ Orthodox Jews. The client reported that recognizing he was not alone and could retain his religious observance while exploring his sexuality reduced his self-hatred and allowed him to begin building meaningful relationships (Jacobson, 2024, Ch. 5).

Additionally, debates regarding premarital sex reveal evolving attitudes within Judaism. While Orthodox Judaism generally forbids non-marital sexual activity, surveys suggest that many modern Orthodox Jews engage in premarital relationships but navigate them within a framework of religious ethics and discretion (Carpenter & Kaplan, 2015; Ribner & Rosenbaum, 2005). By contrast, Reform Judaism largely accepts premarital sex as a matter of personal autonomy, provided it is conducted within a framework of mutual respect and emotional well-being (Jacobson, 2024).

These variations in sexual ethics reflect Judaism's broader adaptability to modern social and cultural trends. However, they also underscore the necessity for clinicians to approach Jewish patients with sensitivity, avoiding assumptions about their beliefs or practices. A therapist working with a Jewish patient should assess their specific religious and cultural background rather than relying on denominational labels alone (Jacobson, 2024).

Gender and Sexuality in Jewish Communities

Gender roles, historically distinct in traditional Judaism, have also undergone significant transformation. Orthodox Judaism often preserves defined roles for men and women in religious and family life, emphasizing male leadership in ritual and legal decision-making. In contrast, women traditionally oversee family and home responsibilities (Westheimer & Mark, 2020). This division extends to sexual expectations, where men are often seen as obligated to provide sexual satisfaction to their wives. At the same time, female sexuality is sometimes framed within the context of modesty and purity (Ribner & Kleinplatz, 2007).

However, the Reform and Conservative movements have actively challenged these traditional structures, advocating for egalitarianism and expanding leadership roles for women and LGBTQ+ individuals (Schreiber, 2016). Many progressive Jewish communities now ordain female rabbis, welcome LGBTQ+ clergy, and incorporate gender-inclusive liturgical language, reflecting broader societal changes in gender and sexuality (Jacobson, 2024).

In a clinical report by Frydman (2022), a Modern Orthodox couple presented with sexual dissatisfaction linked to differing expectations around gender roles. The wife, who held a graduate degree and worked full-time, struggled with pressure from her extended family to prioritize domestic responsibilities. The husband adhered more closely to traditional expectations, viewing himself as the primary religious and sexual decision-maker. Therapy revealed that the wife's resentment and emotional withdrawal were directly impacting sexual desire. Through culturally sensitive couples therapy, they renegotiated household roles, shared religious obligations more equitably, and validated each other's identities. This relational shift allowed them to rebuild sexual intimacy and improve mutual respect (Frydman, 2022, pp. 365–367).

Jewish feminist scholarship has further contributed to these shifts by critically examining traditional texts and advocating for a reinterpretation of Jewish law regarding women's sexual agency and bodily autonomy (Hartman & Marmon, 2004). These changes demonstrate that Jewish communities are not monolithic in their views on gender and sexuality. Instead, they exist on a continuum between the preservation of tradition and adaptation to contemporary values.

For clinicians, these ongoing transformations mean that Jewish patients may have varying degrees of comfort with traditional gender roles and sexual expectations. A culturally competent approach requires therapists to explore how gender and sexuality intersect with each patient's Jewish identity, ensuring that therapeutic interventions align with their personal and communal beliefs (Jacobson, 2024).

Therapist's Responsibility when Working with Jewish Patients

Working with religiously Jewish patients can present unique challenges for sex therapists, particularly when navigating the boundaries and values that patients bring into therapy. These boundaries, often informed by Jewish law and cultural norms, may seem restrictive or antiquated from a secular perspective. However, as Jacobson (2024) emphasizes, therapists must resist the temptation to interpret these boundaries as inherently sex-negative. Instead, they must adopt a culturally sensitive approach that respects the patient's values and avoids imposing their own biases.

Jewish patients often integrate their religious beliefs into their understanding of intimacy, viewing sexuality as both a divine gift and a regulated act within the framework of Jewish law (Westheimer & Mark, 2020). While some patients may struggle with religious teachings that feel limiting or at odds with personal desires, others find deep meaning in these traditions, using them to guide their sexual and relational lives (Friedman, 2019; Satlow, 2020). A therapist's role is to facilitate conversations that allow Jewish patients to explore their sexuality in a way that honors their beliefs rather than positioning religious frameworks as obstacles to sexual health.

Understanding Boundaries Within Jewish Contexts

Jewish patients often approach sexuality through a framework informed by both religious texts and communal norms. For example, practices such as *taharat hamishpacha* (family purity laws) involve periods of sexual abstinence and ritual immersion, which may be misunderstood by therapists unfamiliar with their spiritual significance. These laws are not intended to suppress sexuality but to sanctify it, reinforcing intimacy within a sacred context (Friedman, 2019). In Orthodox communities, adherence to these laws is seen as essential to maintaining both religious observance and marital harmony, often enhancing the cyclical nature of desire and reconnection (Hartman & Marmon, 2004; Ribner & Rosenbaum, 2005).

However, in more liberal Jewish movements, *taharat hamishpacha* is often approached as an optional practice, with individual autonomy dictating whether and how these traditions are observed (Jacobson, 2024). Some Jewish women have reclaimed *mikveh* (ritual immersion) as a spiritual practice unrelated to menstruation, instead using it to mark life transitions or personal milestones (Hartman & Marmon, 2004). These diverse expressions of religious tradition highlight the importance of assessing each patient's unique relationship with Jewish law and cultural expectations rather than making assumptions based on their religious affiliation.

It has been noted that many sex therapists, particularly those with secular or progressive worldviews, may find it difficult to reconcile their professional training with patients' religiously informed perspectives on sex (Jacobson, 2024). This difficulty is compounded by the broader cultural tendency to view religion as an obstacle to sexual health (Chandler et al., 2019). However, dismissing or pathologizing these values risks alienating religious patients and undermining the therapeutic alliance. Instead, therapists should strive to understand the ways in which Jewish patients integrate their religious beliefs into their sexual and relational lives, ensuring that interventions align with the patient's values and lived experience.

Recognizing and Addressing Therapist Bias

Therapists must take responsibility for recognizing their own biases and the ways these may impact their work with Jewish patients. As explained in *Sex Therapy with Religious Patients* (2024), therapists often encounter three common forms of bias:

1. **A sense of superiority over religious patients**: Some therapists unconsciously assume that religious patients are repressed or uninformed about sexual health due to their adherence to religious norms. This attitude can lead to condescension, which alienates patients and weakens the therapeutic relationship.
2. **Projecting their own experiences onto the patient**: Therapists who have had negative personal experiences with religion may unintentionally impose their own perspectives onto their Jewish patients. For example, a therapist who left a strict religious upbringing might assume that all religious Jewish patients experience their faith as oppressive, thereby misinterpreting their patients' relationship with religious observance.
3. **Viewing the patient as embodying negative aspects of the therapist's past religious trauma**: Some therapists, particularly those with prior religious affiliations, may struggle to separate their personal history from their work, leading to unconscious biases that affect clinical decision-making (Salem & Hijazi, 2019).

A case discussed in *Sex Therapy with Religious Patients* (Jacobson, 2024) describes a therapist who initially dismissed a Hasidic client's concerns about nighttime ejaculation (Keri) as excessive religious anxiety. The client believed these emissions rendered him spiritually impure and unworthy of prayer or intimacy the following day. The therapist, a secular clinician, interpreted this as pathological scrupulosity and attempted CBT interventions without cultural grounding. The client withdrew emotionally and nearly terminated treatment. Upon supervision, the therapist re-engaged the client using a culturally respectful approach, integrating *halakhic* texts and facilitating consultation with a trusted rabbi. The client reported feeling "seen," and therapy progressed as he gained tools to manage religious concerns without shame or alienation (Jacobson, 2024, Ch. 6).

For instance, a therapist who assumes that a Jewish patient's boundaries around premarital sex or same-sex relationships are inherently damaging may unconsciously impose their own values, leading to tension or mistrust. Conversely, therapists who approach these boundaries with curiosity and respect are more likely to create a safe, supportive space for exploration and growth. Rather than dismissing religious values, therapists can explore how patients navigate tensions between faith and sexuality, helping them reconcile conflicts in a way that aligns with their beliefs (Jacobson, 2024).

Emphasizing Cultural Competence and Ethical Practice

Cultural competence is a cornerstone of ethical practice when working with Jewish patients. This requires not only a willingness to understand Jewish beliefs and practices but also a commitment to integrating these into the therapeutic process. Jacobson (2024) advocates for using the patient's religious worldview as a resource rather than a barrier, leveraging their cultural and spiritual framework to promote sexual health and well-being.

For example, therapists might explore how sacred texts or community teachings can support a patient's efforts to navigate sexual challenges within their faith tradition. A patient struggling with sexual guilt may find relief in learning that Jewish law does not universally condemn sexual pleasure but often frames it as a positive, sacred experience (Westheimer & Mark, 2020). Similarly, couples facing intimacy issues within Orthodox settings may benefit from discussing Jewish teachings that emphasize marital satisfaction as a religious obligation (Satlow, 2020).

Moreover, therapists must be mindful of the unique pressures faced by Jewish patients, particularly those from Orthodox communities. These patients often live within tightly knit social networks where deviations from religious norms can result in stigma or ostracism. Understanding this context helps therapists balance empathy with advocacy, supporting patients in ways that respect both their individual needs and their communal obligations (Ribner & Kleinplatz, 2007).

Ultimately, an effective therapist does not seek to change a patient's religious beliefs but rather to help them explore and integrate their sexual and relational experiences within the framework of their faith. By prioritizing cultural humility, open-ended inquiry, and nonjudgmental engagement, therapists can ensure that Jewish patients feel respected and supported in addressing their sexual health concerns in a way that aligns with their values and identity.

Effective Therapeutic Intervention When Working with Jewish Patients

When working with Jewish patients, clinicians must carefully navigate the intersection of therapeutic techniques and religious observance. As Jacobson (2024) explains, interventions that conflict with Jewish law can create significant barriers, particularly for Orthodox patients who adhere strictly to religious guidelines. It is essential for therapists to approach treatment with sensitivity and adaptability, ensuring interventions align with the patient's cultural and spiritual framework.

Jewish patients often seek therapy with concerns rooted in both personal and religious contexts, making a culturally competent approach vital for treatment success (Friedman, 2019). A therapist's role is not to challenge or alter a patient's religious beliefs but to integrate evidence-based interventions in ways that respect Jewish law while promoting positive sexual health. By understanding *halakhic* considerations and adapting interventions accordingly, clinicians can foster trust, increase treatment adherence, and help Jewish patients navigate their sexual concerns in alignment with their values (Jacobson, 2024).

Consideration of Interventions: The Start-Stop Method

The start-stop method, a widely used intervention for premature ejaculation, involves repeated stimulation and withdrawal to develop ejaculatory control.

While clinically effective, this technique presents *halakhic* challenges for observant Jewish men, as it typically requires self-stimulation, which is prohibited under Jewish law due to the prohibition against wasting semen (*Zera Levatala*) (Berkovits, 1976; Jacobson, 2024). The foundation for this restriction stems from interpretations of Genesis 38:9-10, in which Onan's act of spilling semen outside of procreative intercourse was condemned (Friedman, 2019). Later rabbinic literature, including the *Shulchan Aruch*, reinforces this prohibition, viewing male masturbation as a serious transgression (Jacobson, 2024).

However, as with many areas of Jewish law, flexibility within *halakha* can sometimes be found when addressing medical or psychological concerns, provided interventions align with religious principles. In cases where premature ejaculation impairs marital intimacy, some rabbinic authorities allow for modifications to the standard start-stop method (Westheimer & Mark, 2020). These modifications aim to maintain adherence to Jewish law while addressing clinical concerns in a manner that remains respectful of religious boundaries.

One adaptation that respects *halakha* boundaries is the partner-assisted start-stop method, in which the patient's spouse takes an active role in guiding stimulation and withdrawal. This approach ensures that all sexual activity occurs within the context of marriage and without unnecessary waste of semen (Jacobson, 2024). In cases where even this adaptation remains problematic, therapists can introduce alternative interventions, such as the squeeze technique or paced penetration training, which do not involve ejaculation outside of vaginal intercourse (Ribner & Rosenbaum, 2005).

In a study by Ribner & Rosenbaum (2005), a Haredi couple sought help for premature ejaculation but were concerned that conventional behavioral techniques (like solo start-stop training) violated *halakhic* prohibitions on masturbation. The therapist consulted with a rabbinic authority and implemented a modified, partner-assisted version of the technique during permitted periods of intimacy. The couple was educated about semen retention and ejaculatory control in a medically accurate yet halakhically sensitive way. Over time, they gained better control, and intimacy improved, with both partners expressing deep appreciation for the therapist's religious respect and discretion (Ribner & Rosenbaum, 2005, pp. 344–345).

Additionally, therapists working with Orthodox Jewish men should be mindful of psychological distress surrounding masturbation prohibitions. Many religious patients experience guilt, anxiety, and shame surrounding ejaculation control, often leading to avoidance behaviors that can exacerbate sexual dysfunction (Ribner & Kleinplatz, 2007). Therapists should employ psychoeducation to help patients understand that Jewish law does not prohibit seeking medical or psychological assistance for sexual health concerns. In some cases, collaboration with religious authorities can help patients navigate permissible solutions while adhering to their beliefs (Satlow, 2020).

By integrating religious sensitivity with clinical expertise, therapists can ensure that interventions remain both effective and culturally appropriate. This approach not only respects the patient's spiritual commitments but also fosters greater marital collaboration, reinforcing intimacy through shared responsibility and communication (Jacobson, 2024).

Family Purity Laws and Sensate Focus Therapy

Sensate focus therapy, a foundational technique in sex therapy, encourages couples to engage in non-demand sensual touching to reduce performance anxiety and build intimacy. However, *taharat hamishpacha*, which mandates periods of abstinence during and following menstruation, can complicate the implementation of this intervention (Friedman, 2019). These laws, rooted in Leviticus 15, emphasize ritual purity and require physical separation during menstruation until the woman immerses in a *mikveh* before resuming intimacy (Hartman & Marmon, 2004).

For Orthodox and Ultra-Orthodox couples, adherence to these laws means that traditional sensate focus exercises, which often involve gradual physical exploration, may not be feasible at all times. Instead, therapists must adapt the intervention by incorporating non-physical intimacy exercises that can be practiced during periods of abstinence. These can include:

- Verbal affirmations and emotional intimacy-building exercises
- Mindfulness and guided meditation together
- Joint planning of future intimate experiences
- Exploring shared fantasies and expectations through open dialogue

In a clinical review by Friedman (2019), a therapist worked with an observant couple whose sexual relationship was marked by performance anxiety and a lack of emotional closeness. The wife felt especially distant during the niddah period, interpreting it as a time of "disconnection" rather than spiritual preparation. The therapist introduced non-touch-based sensate focus tasks for niddah phases, guided fantasy sharing, intimate conversation rituals, and emotional check-ins, followed by progressive physical touch exercises post-mikveh. These practices helped the couple view the menstrual cycle as a time of emotional building rather than restriction. They reported greater overall intimacy and reduced anxiety around sexual "resumption" (Friedman, 2019, pp. 935–936).

By structuring therapy in a way that acknowledges and accommodates religious guidelines, therapists can maintain treatment effectiveness while ensuring that interventions remain halakhically permissible. Moreover, therapists working with Jewish couples must consider the psychological impact of ritual immersion, as some women may experience *mikveh* as either a meaningful spiritual renewal or as an anxiety-inducing obligation (Hartman & Marmon, 2004; Ribner & Rosenbaum, 2005). Exploring these emotions in therapy can help couples strengthen communication and reduce potential tension surrounding these practices.

Creativity and Professional Growth

Adapting therapeutic interventions to align with Jewish laws and values requires a high degree of creativity, ultimately benefiting the clinician's professional development. Jacobson (2024) emphasizes that working within culturally specific frameworks fosters innovation, encouraging therapists to think critically and develop a broader range of interventions. This adaptability enhances not only the therapeutic alliance but also the clinician's ability to address diverse needs across patient populations.

Cultural humility plays a critical role in therapist self-growth. Engaging with multiple worldviews enriches the therapeutic process, allowing clinicians to approach challenges from new perspectives. Working with Jewish patients provides an opportunity for therapists to refine their ability to integrate religion, sexuality, and clinical best practices in a respectful and effective manner (Chandler et al., 2019).

Jacobson (2024) describes the experience of a secular therapist who began working with ultra-Orthodox Jewish clients through a community mental health center. Initially hesitant, the therapist struggled to reconcile psychosexual interventions with strict *halakhic* boundaries. Over time, through rabbinic consultation and patient collaboration, she modified approaches like sensate focus and assertiveness training to align with cultural norms (e.g., delaying physical touch stages until after mikveh). This process challenged the therapist's assumptions and expanded her therapeutic toolkit. She reflected that this experience made her more adaptable, more respectful in inquiry, and ultimately more effective across all patient populations, not just religious ones (Jacobson, 2024, Ch. 7).

Moreover, clinicians must recognize that Jewish patients, particularly those from tightly knit Orthodox communities, often experience unique communal pressures surrounding sexuality. In these settings, deviations from religious norms can result in stigma or ostracism, requiring therapists to balance empathy with advocacy (Ribner & Kleinplatz, 2007). Understanding this dynamic helps therapists provide support in a way that respects both individual needs and communal obligations.

As Salsman et al. (2005) highlight, integrating patients' spiritual and cultural frameworks into therapy can significantly enhance psychological adjustment and treatment outcomes. By adopting a patient-centered approach, prioritizing cultural humility, and remaining flexible in adapting interventions, therapists can effectively support Jewish patients in navigating sexual and relational concerns while remaining true to their religious beliefs.

Conclusion

Working with Jewish patients presents a unique opportunity for therapists to expand their cultural competence and develop creative therapeutic strategies. Judaism's influence on individual development, extending across familial, community, and societal levels, profoundly shapes perceptions of sex, sexuality, and gender. As

Jacobson (2024) underscores, therapists must recognize that Jewish identity is neither monolithic nor static; it encompasses diverse practices and beliefs influenced by religious, cultural, and social factors. By approaching Jewish patients with cultural humility and sensitivity, therapists can build trust and foster meaningful therapeutic relationships.

Effective interventions require both respect for Jewish laws and the ability to adapt traditional therapeutic techniques to align with religious values. For example, reframing the start-stop method to include a patient's spouse or modifying sensate focus therapy to accommodate *taharat hamishpacha* demonstrates the power of thoughtful, culturally aware adaptations (Friedman, 2019; Jacobson, 2024). Such interventions not only address patients' clinical needs but also validate their spiritual and cultural identities, enhancing the overall therapeutic outcome.

Beyond the immediate therapeutic benefits, working with Jewish patients enriches the clinician's professional development. The need for creativity in addressing culturally specific challenges fosters innovation and adaptability, which can be applied across diverse patient populations. Engaging with multiple worldviews broadens therapists' perspectives, ultimately contributing to a more inclusive and effective practice.

As this paper has shown, respecting the cultural and spiritual identities of Jewish patients is not merely an ethical obligation but a valuable opportunity for growth. By integrating Jewish frameworks into therapy, clinicians can enhance the therapeutic alliance, improve outcomes, and expand their own professional capacities, illustrating the profound benefits of culturally competent care.

References

Berkovits, E. (1976). *Jewish women in time and Torah*. KTAV Publishing House.

Bronfenbrenner, U. (2005). *Making human beings human: Bioecological perspectives on human development*. Sage Publications.

Carpenter, K., & Kaplan, D. E. (2015). Non-marital sex in reform Judaism: Reconciling theory with reality. *Sexuality & Culture*, *19*(4), 916–927. https://doi.org/10.1007/s12119-015-9294-1

Chandler, D., Sennott, S. L., & Constantinides, D. M. (2019). *Sex therapy with erotically marginalized clients: Nine principles of clinical support*. Taylor & Francis Group.

Colwell, J., Pollard, A., & Pollard, A. (2015). *Readings for reflective teaching in early education*. Bloomsbury Academic.

David, B. E., & Weitzman, G. A. (2015). Sexuality in advanced age in Jewish thought and law. *Journal of Sex & Marital Therapy*, *41*(1), 39–48. https://doi.org/10.1080/0092623X.2013.811451

Donin, H. H. (2019). *To be a Jew: A guide to Jewish observance in contemporary life*. Basic Books.

Friedman, S. (2019). Assessing and treating sexual dysfunctions in Orthodox Jewish couples: A summary of 41 consecutive cases. *Mental Health, Religion, & Culture*, *22*(9), 930–942. https://doi.org/10.1080/13674676.2019.1688269

Frydman, S. D. (2022). The quick shift: Orthodox Jewish women's early marital sexual experience. *Sexual and Relationship Therapy*, *37*(3), 360–376.

Harandi, T. F., Taghinasab, M. M., & Nayeri, T. D. (2017). The correlation of social support with mental health: A meta-analysis. *Electronic Physician*, *9*(9), 5212–5222.

Hartman, T., & Marmon, N. (2004). Lived regulations, systemic attributions: Menstrual separation and ritual immersion in the experience of Orthodox Jewish women. *Gender and Society*, *18*(3), 389–408.

Jacobson, C. (2024). *Sex therapy with religious patients: Working with Jewish, Christian, and Muslim communities*. Routledge.

Kitchen, K. A., Bethell, C. D., & Rehkopf, D. H. (2019). Social determinants of health: Toward a unified framework for understanding complex interactions. *Health Affairs*, *38*(3), 392–400.

Olszewska, Z., El-Shaarawi, N., & Yilmaz, S. (2019). The politics of religious identity: Islam, Judaism, and diaspora communities. *Journal of Ethnic and Migration Studies*, *45*(2), 193–212.

Olszewska, Z., Twardowska, K., & Katny, M. (2019). The politics of religious identity: Islam, Judaism, and diaspora communities. *Journal of Ethnic and Migration Studies*, *45*(2), 193–212.

Ribner, D. S., & Kleinplatz, P. J. (2007). The hole in the sheet and other myths about sexuality and Judaism. *Sexual and Relationship Therapy*, *22*(4), 445–456. https://doi.org/10.1080/14681990701297797

Ribner, D. S., & Rosenbaum, T. Y. (2005). Evaluation and treatment of unconsummated marriages among Orthodox Jewish couples. *Journal of Sex & Marital Therapy*, *31*(4), 341–353. https://doi.org/10.1080/00926230590950244

Robinson, G. (2016). *Essential Judaism: A complete guide to beliefs, customs, and rituals*. Simon & Schuster.

Salem, D. E., & Hijazi, A. M. (2019). Therapist bias and religious trauma: Addressing past experiences in clinical settings. *Journal of Counseling and Development*, *97*(4), 478–492.

Salsman, J. M., Brown, T. L., Brechting, E. H., & Carlson, C. R. (2005). The link between religiousness and health: A review of recent literature and directions for future research. *Journal of Counseling Psychology*, *52*(4), 504–512.

Satlow, M. L. (2020). *Tasting the dish: Rabbinic rhetorics of sexuality*. Brown Judaic Studies.

Schreiber, E. (2016). Jewish perspectives on gender and sexuality. *Journal of Jewish Ethics*, *2*(1), 89–112.

Steinsaltz, A. (2006). *The essential Talmud*. Basic Books.

Westheimer, R. K., & Mark, J. (2020). *Heavenly sex: Sexuality and the Jewish tradition*. New York University Press.

Chapter 7

Navigating Sexuality: Ethical Perspectives and Therapeutic Practices in the Islamic World

Amira Eldeeb

Introduction

Sexuality is a fundamental part of human life, but how we understand and practice it is deeply shaped by culture, ethics, and faith. Just as Western perspectives on sexuality are grounded in certain philosophical and psychological paradigms, Islamic traditions have their own guiding principles. Some of these values align with modern Western frameworks—such as the importance of consent, mutual satisfaction, and marital harmony—while others differ significantly, reflecting a worldview that integrates spirituality, ethics, and social responsibility (Rahman, 2009).

From an Islamic perspective, sexuality is not merely a biological function or a personal choice—it is a trust from Allah (Amanah) that carries social and spiritual implications. This trust is governed by key ethical principles, including *Ikhtilat* (gender mixing), *Hayaa'* (modesty), and *Khalwah* (seclusion between unrelated men and women). These concepts, often misunderstood outside of Islamic discourse, shape both the lived experiences of Muslim individuals and the therapeutic frameworks that serve them (Hathout, 1995). For therapists working in Muslim communities, these principles are not just theoretical, they impact how clients engage with therapy, what they feel comfortable discussing, and how therapy sessions should be structured to respect cultural and religious sensitivities.

One of the most striking differences between Islamic and Western approaches to sexuality is the role of modesty (Hayaa'). In many contemporary settings, openness about sexuality is often encouraged as a way to reduce shame and promote self-awareness. However, in Islamic traditions, Hayaa' is seen as a moral compass, not a barrier to education or therapy. Imam Al-Ghazali describes Hayaa' as a safeguard for the soul, ensuring that sexual discussions take place within ethical boundaries that preserve dignity and respect (Al-Ghazali, Ihya Ulum al-Din, Vol. 4). This does not mean that sex education is absent in Islamic cultures; rather, it has historically been integrated into religious teachings, family life, and community structures in a way that maintains modesty (Nasir, 2016).

This chapter explores the evolution of sex education in Islamic contexts, the unique ethical considerations in psychosexual therapy, and how Muslim clients and practitioners navigate contemporary challenges in sex therapy. It also provides

DOI: 10.4324/9781003611387-7

practical recommendations for therapists working with Muslim clients, ensuring that therapy is both effective and culturally sensitive.

Sex Education: The Islamic Perspective

Historically, sex education in Muslim societies was not a taboo subject—it was structured, intentional, and values-drive. Islamic scholars such as Ibn Qayyim and Al-Ghazali wrote extensively on marital intimacy, reproductive health, and the ethics of sexual relations. Traditional Islamic teachings encouraged comprehensive sex education within appropriate contexts—marriage preparation, family discussions, and religious study (Ibn Qayyim, Zaad al-Ma'ad). Unlike modern secular models that often separate sex education from spirituality, Islamic teachings integrated sexual knowledge with moral and ethical guidance, ensuring that individuals understood not just the physical aspects of sexuality but also its emotional, social, and spiritual dimensions (Haque, 2004).

However, over time, cultural shifts, colonial influences, and modernization have altered how sex education is approached in many Muslim societies. In some regions, discussions about sexuality became stigmatized, leading to gaps in knowledge, increased sexual anxiety, and reluctance to seek therapy for sexual concerns. In contrast, other Muslim-majority countries have begun to reintroduce structured, values-based sex education that aligns with both Islamic ethics and modern psychological research (Rashid, 2018).

Bridging the Gap: Culturally Responsive Sex Therapy

One of the core challenges in providing psychosexual therapy to Muslim clients is bridging the gap between religious values and therapeutic approaches. Many conventional models of sex therapy do not account for the spiritual dimensions of sexuality, often focusing solely on psychological and physiological factors (Abu-Raiya, 2020). While these approaches can be beneficial, they may feel incomplete or even inappropriate for Muslim clients who view sexuality through a moral and religious lens.

As a therapist working in Muslim communities, I have witnessed firsthand how these gaps impact clients' willingness to seek therapy, their comfort in discussing sexual issues, and the overall effectiveness of interventions. Some of my female clients refuse to see male therapists, fearing that such interactions could be *haram* (forbidden). Conversely, I have had male clients specifically choose a female therapist because they feel more comfortable discussing emotional intimacy with a woman, yet these same clients object to their wives seeing male therapists. These gendered dynamics can complicate therapy, but they also present an opportunity for culturally adaptive approaches.

One approach I have found particularly effective is joint male-female therapist collaboration. In one case, I worked alongside a male colleague to counsel a couple struggling with marital intimacy. The husband worked with the male therapist, while the wife worked with me, and we coordinated their therapy plan. This approach respected their religious sensitivities while ensuring they received comprehensive care. This case, along with others, highlights how culturally sensitive therapy models can enhance trust and improve therapeutic outcomes in Muslim communities.

The Ethical Framework of Sexuality in Islam

Sexuality in Islam is not merely a private matter; it is deeply embedded in ethical, social, and spiritual dimensions. Unlike secular approaches that often prioritize personal autonomy, Islamic teachings present sexuality as a responsibility toward Allah, oneself, and one's spouse. This ethical framework balances human desires with spiritual accountability, ensuring that sexual health is approached with both moderation and moral integrity (Ibn Qayyim, Zaad al-Ma'ad).

Sexuality as a Natural Aspect of Life

Islam does not view sexuality as something shameful or sinful when practiced within its ethical and legal boundaries. Instead, it is recognized as a natural human need that, when fulfilled appropriately, becomes a means of spiritual reward and emotional well-being (Al-Ghazali, Ihya Ulum al-Din). The Quran describes marital intimacy as a divine gift and source of tranquility:

> They are a garment for you, and you are a garment for them…
>
> (Quran 2:187)

This verse illustrates how sexual relationships are meant to provide emotional and physical closeness, symbolizing protection, comfort, and mutual fulfillment. Imam Ibn Qayyim expands on this, stating that sexual intimacy is not just a physical act but a means of strengthening love and mercy within marriage (Zaad al-Ma'ad).

From a therapeutic perspective, this understanding helps Muslim clients overcome guilt, shame, or misinformation about sexuality. Many individuals enter marriage with limited knowledge about intimacy, often due to cultural taboos rather than Islamic teachings. As therapists, acknowledging Islam's positive stance on marital intimacy can be an essential step in helping clients navigate sexual concerns without fear or shame.

The Balance Between Desire and Modesty (Hayaa')

Modesty (Hayaa') is a defining feature of Islamic ethics—it governs how individuals interact, dress, and speak about intimate matters. The Prophet Muhammad (peace be upon him) said:

> Every religion has a defining characteristic, and the defining characteristic of Islam is Hayaa'.
>
> (Ibn Majah, 2014, Hadith 4181)

However, Hayaa' does not mean ignorance. Islamic scholars, including Al-Ghazali and Ibn Qayyim, emphasized that modesty should not prevent the pursuit of necessary knowledge (Al-Ghazali, Ihya Ulum al-Din). For example, the Prophet (peace be upon him) himself addressed sexual matters openly when necessary, ensuring that both men and women had access to proper guidance.

One of the challenges therapists encounter is clients feeling uncomfortable discussing sexual issues due to cultural shame. While modesty is valuable, excessive avoidance of these topics can lead to sexual dissatisfaction, anxiety, and even marital problems (Rashid, 2018). A therapist working with Muslim clients must strike a balance; ensuring discussions remain respectful and within Islamic boundaries, while also providing accurate, essential information.

Therapeutic Approaches to Modesty in Sex Therapy

- Using culturally sensitive language: Instead of using explicit terms, therapists can use Islamic terminology and metaphors to convey sexual health concepts in a way that aligns with Hayaa'.
- Normalizing the discussion: Clients often feel relieved when they realize that Islamic teachings do not suppress sexual knowledge but rather guide it ethically.
- Providing private and secure spaces: Ensuring that therapy sessions feel safe and non-judgmental, so clients feel comfortable discussing their concerns.

The Role of Marriage in Managing Desires

Marriage in Islam is seen as the ethical framework for fulfilling sexual needs. The Prophet (peace be upon him) emphasized marriage as a protection from both emotional distress and sinful temptations:

> O young people! Whoever among you can afford to get married, let him do so, for it helps lower the gaze and guard chastity.
>
> (Bukhari, 2007, Hadith 5066)

Islamic teachings encourage sexual fulfillment within marriage, ensuring that spouses view intimacy as a right and responsibility. This perspective is essential in therapy, especially when dealing with low sexual desire, mismatched libidos, or marital dissatisfaction. Therapists can help clients by: encouraging open communication between spouses to discuss their emotional and physical needs; providing Islamic perspectives on intimacy to reassure clients that their desires are normal and encouraged within marriage; addressing sexual anxieties rooted in misinformation and replacing them with Islamic teachings that emphasize love, mercy, and mutual fulfillment.

Understanding Ikhtilat, Khalwah, and Their Impact on Therapy

Many Muslim clients experience internal conflicts about therapy settings, particularly when seeing a therapist of the opposite gender. This is due to Islamic guidelines on gender interactions, which are designed to prevent inappropriate relationships and emotional attachments (Haque, 2004).

Ikhtilat (Gender Mixing) in Therapy

- Islamic ethics permit necessary interactions between men and women when there is a clear purpose, such as education, business, or medical treatment.
- However, cultural interpretations vary; some clients may feel uneasy discussing personal matters with a therapist of the opposite gender.

Khalwah (Seclusion) and Therapy Sessions

- Khalwah is prohibited, meaning a man and woman who are not mahram (lawful kin) should not be alone in a private setting.
- In therapy, this means ensuring transparency, such as leaving doors slightly open or having a chaperone present when necessary.
- For conservative clients, alternatives like same-gender therapy or online sessions can be effective solutions.

Islamic ethics provide a structured, values-based approach to sexuality, emphasizing the balance between fulfilling desires and maintaining modesty.

Historical Perspectives on Sex Education in Islam

Sex education in Islam has historically been comprehensive, structured, and deeply integrated into religious and ethical teachings. Unlike the modern assumption that discussions on sexuality were absent in Muslim societies, classical Islamic scholarship demonstrates that sex education was both encouraged and considered necessary for marital harmony, family well-being, and spiritual growth (Nasir, 2016). Early Muslim scholars, including Imam Al-Ghazali, Ibn Qayyim, and Ibn Hazm, addressed sexual health, intimacy, and marital relationships with scientific depth and ethical clarity.

Sex Education During the Time of the Prophet (Peace Be Upon Him)

Islamic sex education is rooted in the teachings of the Prophet Muhammad (peace be upon him), who openly addressed marital intimacy, hygiene, and sexual rights between spouses. The Prophet's guidance balanced modesty with the need for accurate knowledge, ensuring that both men and women had a proper understanding of their rights and responsibilities in marriage.

The Role of the Prophet in Sex Education

One of the most notable aspects of Prophetic teachings on sexuality is that women felt comfortable seeking guidance on intimate matters. The wives of the Prophet (peace be upon him), particularly Aisha (may Allah be pleased with her), played a crucial role in transmitting knowledge about female sexuality and marital intimacy (Bukhari, Hadith 2494).

For example, Aisha (may Allah be pleased with her) reported:

> The best women are those of the Ansar. They do not let their shyness prevent them from seeking knowledge about religion.
>
> (Muslim, Hadith 332)

This hadith highlights how early Muslim women actively sought knowledge on sexual matters, and their modesty did not prevent them from understanding their rights and obligations. Unlike many modern cultural taboos that discourage such discussions, Islamic tradition encouraged open learning about intimacy within the right context.

The Contributions of Classical Islamic Scholars

Medieval Islamic scholarship provided detailed discussions on sexual health, marital intimacy, and reproductive rights, combining scientific insights with ethical guidance.

Imam Al-Ghazali (1058–1111 CE): The Ethics of Sexual Intimacy

Imam Al-Ghazali, one of the most influential scholars in Islamic history, discussed sexual ethics extensively in Ihya Ulum al-Din (The Revival of Religious Sciences). He emphasized the importance of mutual satisfaction in marital intimacy; the role of sexual pleasure in strengthening the marital bond; and the need for sexual education to prevent marital discord. He writes:

> A man must be considerate toward his wife's desires, for neglecting this will create dissatisfaction and disrupt marital harmony.
>
> (Al-Ghazali, Ihya Ulum al-Din, Vol. 2)

This perspective contradicts modern misconceptions that Islamic teachings are restrictive regarding sexual fulfillment. On the contrary, classical scholars encouraged discussions on sexual health and pleasure within the framework of marriage.

Ibn Qayyim Al-Jawziyya (1292–1350 CE): The Science of Sexual Health

Ibn Qayyim expanded on these discussions in Zaad al-Ma'ad, providing a psychological and physiological approach to sexual health. He wrote about the emotional and physical benefits of healthy sexual relations; the impact of unresolved sexual tension on mental health; and how Islamic medicine supports reproductive well-being. He emphasized that neglecting sexual satisfaction in marriage could lead to emotional detachment and dissatisfaction, reinforcing the importance of communication and intimacy.

Ibn Hazm (994–1064 CE): The Emotional and Psychological Aspects of Love and Desire

Ibn Hazm, an Andalusian scholar, authored Tawq al-Hamama (The Ring of the Dove), a book dedicated to love, relationships, and the psychology of desire. He described: The natural human inclination toward love and intimacy. How emotions and sexual attraction shape relationships. The ethical boundaries that Islam sets for expressing love and desire. His work provides a profound psychological insight into relationships, making it one of the earliest Islamic texts exploring emotional intelligence in love and marriage.

The Role of Families and Communities in Sex Education

Historically, families, scholars, and religious institutions played a significant role in delivering sex education. The methods used included:

- **Parental Guidance:** Parents were expected to gradually educate their children about puberty, hygiene, and marital intimacy in an age-appropriate manner.
- **Islamic Study Circles:** Scholars provided structured discussions on marital rights, sexual health, and ethical relationships.
- **Medical and Religious Texts:** Islamic physicians wrote books detailing reproductive health, contraception, and sexual well-being (Haque, 2004).

Unlike today's Western-style sex education, which often emphasizes individual autonomy, Islamic sex education historically framed sexuality within the context of responsibility, ethics, and social well-being.

Contemporary Challenges in Muslim Sex Education

Despite this rich historical tradition, modern Muslim communities face significant challenges in addressing sexuality. These include:

- **Cultural Stigmas**: Many Muslim-majority societies have adopted cultural taboos that make discussions on sexuality uncomfortable.

- **Misinformation**: Some individuals enter marriage with little to no knowledge about sexual health due to a lack of proper education.
- **Western Influence vs. Islamic Ethics**: Many sex education programs fail to consider Islamic values, creating resistance among Muslim parents and educators.

A young Muslim couple sought therapy due to sexual dissatisfaction in their marriage, but both felt uncomfortable discussing the issue. The husband believed that talking about intimacy was inappropriate, while the wife had received no prior sex education and felt ashamed about her concerns.

Solution: Using historical Islamic texts, I reassured them that Islam encourages sexual fulfillment in marriage. I shared Hadiths and scholarly opinions to normalize their concerns, which allowed them to openly communicate and seek appropriate guidance. This case highlights how culturally sensitive sex education rooted in Islamic teachings can transform relationships.

The Need for a Modern, Islamically Integrated Sex Education Model

Given these challenges, there is a growing need for a structured, Islamically integrated approach to sex education that: (1) respects Islamic ethics while providing medically accurate information; (2) encourages open discussions within a values-based framework; and (3) equips therapists, educators, and families with culturally appropriate tools.

This would ensure that Muslims receive comprehensive sexual education without compromising their faith.

Current Attitudes and Practices in Muslim Communities Toward Sex Therapy

Despite Islam's historically open and structured approach to sex education, contemporary attitudes toward sexuality and sex therapy in Muslim communities often reflect cultural barriers, misinformation, and hesitation toward professional intervention. Many Muslim clients approach sex therapy with uncertainty, influenced by social expectations, religious misunderstandings, and a lack of accessible, faith-sensitive professionals (Rashid, 2018).

The Stigma Around Seeking Sex Therapy

Sex therapy is still a taboo topic in many Muslim societies, largely due to cultural stigmas rather than religious prohibitions. Although Islam encourages mutual satisfaction in marriage, many clients struggle to seek help due to societal pressures, shame, or the fear of being judged (Haque, 2004).

Common Barriers to Seeking Therapy

- Shame and Embarrassment: Many Muslim clients fear that discussing sexual concerns will bring shame to themselves or their families.
- Perceived Religious Guilt: Some believe that experiencing sexual issues is a spiritual failing rather than a medical or psychological concern.
- Lack of Trust in Therapy: Many therapy models do not incorporate Islamic values, leading to hesitation in seeking Western-based sex therapy.

A married woman experiencing low sexual desire due to past trauma sought therapy but felt guilty about needing help. She believed that having such difficulties reflected a weakness in her faith. Through therapy, I introduced Islamic perspectives on healing, self-compassion, and emotional well-being, helping her reframe her struggle as a human experience rather than a religious failure. Over time, she embraced therapy without guilt and found healing in both faith and psychological intervention. Many Muslim clients need religiously informed therapy approaches that reduce guilt and shame, making them feel that seeking help is a step toward self-improvement, not a sign of weakness.

The Influence of Culture vs. Islamic Teachings

A critical issue in Muslim communities is the conflation of culture with Islamic teachings. Many beliefs surrounding sex education and therapy are rooted in cultural taboos rather than religious guidance (Nasir, 2016).
Examples of cultural misconceptions include:

- Sex is only for procreation. While Islam recognizes both pleasure and procreation as valid purposes of intimacy (Quran 30:21).
- Women should not express sexual needs. While Islamic teachings emphasize mutual pleasure and fulfillment in marriage (Bukhari, Hadith 4793).
- Discussing sexual problems is shameful. While Islam encourages knowledge-seeking in all aspects of life, including sexuality (Muslim, Hadith 332).

The therapeutic strategy needed is correcting misinformation.

When working with Muslim clients, educating them on the difference between cultural expectations and religious principles helps ease their anxiety and encourage open discussions. An example is a Muslim couple experiencing a lack of intimacy believed that discussing their needs was inappropriate. By introducing Islamic teachings that emphasize communication and mutual fulfillment, they felt reassured that seeking help aligned with their faith, not against it. Many Muslim clients need clarity on what Islam actually teaches about sexuality, rather than relying on cultural interpretations that create unnecessary barriers to therapy. Muslim clients approach sex therapy with a complex mix of cultural hesitation, religious concerns, and personal insecurities. Understanding their fears, debunking myths, and providing faith-sensitive guidance can empower them to seek help without shame.

Strategies for Working with Muslim Couples

- Encourage open communication within Islamic values: Many couples hesitate to express sexual concerns due to modesty.
- Normalize discussions while respecting boundaries of modesty and respect.
- Integrate religious guidance into therapy: Highlight Islamic teachings on mutual pleasure, rights, and responsibilities (Bukhari, Hadith 4793).
- Respect the couple's gender preferences in therapy: Some couples may prefer joint male-female therapist teams.

A Muslim couple experiencing marital dissatisfaction due to a lack of emotional and physical intimacy sought therapy with me. The wife struggled to express her needs, and the husband believed he was fulfilling his role by providing financially. I Introduced Islamic teachings on emotional and physical connection. Encouraged the couple to discuss their needs openly in a structured way. Provided culturally appropriate intimacy-building exercises. Islamic-based marriage counseling helps Muslim couples navigate emotional and sexual well-being in a way that aligns with their faith. Working with Muslim clients in sex therapy requires a deep understanding of religious values, cultural sensitivities, and ethical boundaries. By integrating Islamic perspectives into therapy, professionals can create safe, respectful, and effective therapeutic spaces.

Key Takeaways for Therapists:

- Understand and respect Islamic ethics on sexuality.
- Address shame and stigma using faith-sensitive approaches.
- Adapt therapy models to align with gender and privacy preferences.
- Provide structured, culturally appropriate sex education.
- Offer couples therapy that integrates religious and psychological insights.

By bridging the gap between Western therapeutic models and Islamic ethics, therapists can support Muslim clients in achieving healthier, more fulfilling intimate relationships.

Future Developments:

- Expansion of Islamic-informed sex therapy training for Muslim mental health professionals.
- More accessible online resources for faith-based sex education.

- Collaborations between religious scholars and psychosexual therapists to provide holistic guidance.

For therapists, educators, and counselors working within Muslim communities, it is crucial to:

- Educate yourself on Islamic teachings on intimacy to build credibility and trust.
- Respect cultural sensitivities while encouraging open and necessary conversations.
- Use religiously appropriate language and references to align therapy with clients' faith-based values.
- Advocate for structured sex education in Muslim communities, addressing misconceptions and gaps in knowledge.
- Develop therapy models that integrate both science and spirituality, ensuring clients feel respected, understood, and empowered.

By embracing these principles, professionals can create a transformative impact, helping Muslim clients navigate their sexual health and relationships with confidence, faith, and psychological well-being.

This chapter aimed to bridge the gap between Islamic teachings and modern psychosexual therapy, providing a framework for ethical, faith-sensitive therapeutic practices. With the right knowledge, cultural awareness, and respect for religious principles, therapists can create a safe, informed, and empowering space for Muslim clients to explore sexual health and well-being without fear or shame.

> Verily, with hardship comes ease.
>
> (Quran 94:6)

Sexual health challenges can feel overwhelming, but through knowledge, faith, and compassionate therapy, healing and fulfillment are always possible.

References

Abu-Raiya, H. (2020). *Islamic Psychology and Mental Health: Theory and Practice*. New York: Routledge.

Al-Ghazali, I. (n.d.). *Ihya Ulum al-Din [The Revival of the Religious Sciences*]. Beirut: Dar al-Kutub al-Ilmiyyah.

Bukhari, M. I. (2007). *Sahih al-Bukhari*. Dar El-Salam. Cairo.

Haque, A. (2004). *Psychology from an Islamic Perspective*. Virginia: International Institute of Islamic Thought.

Hathout, H. (1995). *Reading the Muslim Mind*. Plainfield, IN: American Trust Publications.

Ibn Majah, M. (2014). *Sunan Ibn Majah*. Cairo: Dar al-Ta'sil.

Ibn Qayyim Al-Jawziyya, M. (n.d.). *Zaad al-Ma'ad fi Hady Khayr al-Ibad*. Beirut: Dar al-Kutub al-Ilmiyyah.

Nasir, M. (2016). *Sexual Ethics in Islam: Feminist Reflections on Qur'an, Hadith, and Jurisprudence*. Massachusetts: Harvard University Press.

Rahman, F. (2009). *Major Themes of the Qur'an*. Chicago, IL: University of Chicago Press.

Rashid, S. (2018). *Muslim Sexual Ethics and Therapy Approaches*. Oxford: Oxford University Press.

Chapter 8

Through the Looking Glass

Reflections from an Anglophone Therapist on Their Personal, Psychosexual, Cultural, and Spiritual Journey from 1960s to 2026

Jo Coker

Upbringing in 1950s–1960s Britain

I am a White, middle-class woman born in the 1950s and raised in the 1960s United Kingdom, an era defined by the aftermath of World War II. The cultural context of my upbringing was heavily shaped by societal norms that were, at that time, largely unquestioned. These norms were rooted in a post-war ethos that emphasized stability, conformity, and adherence to rigid gender roles. As a young woman, my path was clearly defined, I was to receive an education to a certain level, secure a modest job (but not a career), marry a suitable man, and then devote myself to supporting his career and raising children.

The moral code I was raised with was profoundly shaped by conservative values, largely reinforced by the Church of England, which emphasized duty, submission, and the sanctity of marriage. These values told me that women were expected to serve as pillars of domesticity and modesty and that the concept of divorce was out of the question, even in the face of marital discord. The notion of a woman's worth being tied to her domestic role and her ability to be a "good wife and mother" was omnipresent. Women who did not fulfil this role were often judged harshly by society.

Pre-marital sex was viewed as morally wrong and often seen as a sign of moral failure. As I grew up, I internalized the belief that any deviation from this strict framework, particularly in terms of sexuality, was a woman's fault. This was in alignment with what has been termed the "Eve Syndrome," where women were blamed for moral lapses, particularly in relation to sexual matters (Koessler, 1987). The pressures to conform to these gendered expectations were immense, but I did not fully understand their grip on my life until much later.

Early Life: A Time of Limited Understanding and Shifting Values

Growing up in a remote area and attending a single-sex boarding school in 1960s Britain, my early life was shaped by a profound lack of sexual education and understanding. The environment in which I was raised provided little to no opportunity to

DOI: 10.4324/9781003611387-8

discuss sex, relationships, or even emotions in a meaningful way. Biology lessons focused on the anatomy of dogfish and frogs, leaving little room for discussions around human sexuality. These early years epitomized what is often referred to as "the silence around sex education," where any mention of sexuality, especially outside the heterosexual norm, was either ignored or suppressed (Tolman, 2002).

At this point, the assumption was that everyone was heterosexual, and the concept of alternative sexual orientations was largely unexplored. The occasional murmurs about two teachers being "lesbians" were met with confusion and dismissive curiosity. Lesbian relationships, when they did come up, were not framed as legitimate emotional or sexual partnerships but as curiosities or anomalies, further reinforcing the lack of validation for same-sex love in mainstream culture (Fletcher, 2008). This was a period in which there was little room for exploration beyond the prescribed norms, and any feelings or connections that strayed from the expected heterosexual path were marginalized and misunderstood.

Sexuality itself was poorly explained in schools, and the process of menstruation was awkwardly handled without guidance or proper education. I recall the chaotic and almost comical attempts by girls in my dormitory to navigate menstruation without any support, using a large tub of Vaseline to "help" with tampons, an incident that highlights the confusion and secrecy that pervaded the topic of female sexuality. This reflects what McKellar and Smith (2019) discuss in the context of adolescence: the pervasive discomfort and lack of proper guidance during formative sexual years that can leave individuals confused and ill-prepared for future sexual health.

The moment I discovered "The Hitchhiker," a book passed between peers, was one of those rare instances when a glimpse into a broader sexual world outside the constraints of school rules presented itself. This book, which depicted sexual encounters and explored same-sex relationships, felt like a thrilling escape from the silence and suppression surrounding sexuality in my life. At 16, it was an eye-opening experience that juxtaposed my sheltered upbringing with the reality of sexual exploration. The feelings it stirred were not easily expressed in the confines of our tightly controlled school environment, leading to further repression. As Fine and McClelland (2006) argue, the expression of sexual desire in adolescence is often subjected to shame, silencing, and punishment in environments where sexual behavior is considered transgressive, especially for young women.

This particular instance became a point of punishment, both for the book's contents and for the sexual feelings it aroused. This aligns with Sanchez and Kiefer's (2007) findings, which illustrate that young women often face moral judgment and disciplinary action when exploring or expressing sexual curiosity, particularly in contexts that challenge traditional sexual norms. Our "transgression" was met with harsh discipline and a lengthy lecture on the moral dangers of deviating from the conservative sexual values of the time.

Parallel to these experiences, I also grew up witnessing the complexities of my mother's life, which further shaped my understanding of relationships and gender roles. My mother's tumultuous marriage to a violent man and her eventual escape and divorce in 1966 was a pivotal experience. At that time, divorce was still viewed as a social stigma, and my mother faced profound isolation and shunning from friends and family. The stigma of divorce (Kay-Flowers, 2019) and the moral judgment that accompanied it deeply impacted my childhood. The effects of this social isolation, which both my mother and I endured, left lasting marks on my identity and my understanding of what it meant to navigate societal expectations.

Despite these challenges, my mother displayed remarkable resilience. As she rebuilt her life and held her head high in the face of public shame, I began to see how societal norms could impose unjust expectations on individuals, particularly women. Her ability to challenge societal expectations, even in small but profound ways, such as showing up at my school with a new partner and unapologetically rejecting the stigma around her divorce, was a model of defiance that would shape my own beliefs. It is through this early exposure to my mother's strength that I began to understand the intersection between social stigma and individual empowerment, an understanding that would later influence my therapeutic work with individuals dealing with stigma and identity challenges (Link & Phelan, 2001).

Ultimately, this section illustrates the profound impact of growing up in an environment that provided little room for sexual exploration or discussion, as well as the difficulties of navigating societal expectations about gender roles and relationships. These early life experiences, marked by shame, silence, and moralizing, created the foundation of my later work, where I would be driven to understand the emotional and psychological effects of sexual repression, particularly for those who, like me, grew up in environments where sexual identity and exploration were neither encouraged nor openly discussed.

The Start of Professional Life: A Journey of Sexual Awakening and Cultural Exposure

Having grown up in a relatively isolated and rule-bound environment, I moved to London at 18 to begin nursing training. This was a monumental shift in my life, an immersion into a vibrant, chaotic, and often overwhelming city. Coming from a background where freedom was limited, and the social fabric was homogenous, the urban environment of London presented both a culture shock and a profound sense of freedom. This transition from a strictly controlled upbringing to the relative autonomy of the city is reflective of what Marcia (1966) describes as the "identity crisis" faced by individuals in early adulthood when they are exposed to new, unfamiliar social and cultural environments.

In London, the social atmosphere was very different, and for the first time, I felt liberated from the constant scrutiny that had defined much of my life until then. I could move about freely, make my own choices, and explore the city's diverse array of activities. This exposure to different lifestyles and attitudes was transformative, although it was tempered by certain limitations, especially around sexual health. For example, obtaining birth control required falsely claiming that marriage was imminent, despite the shared understanding that the real reason was to engage in sexual activity. This reflects the contradictory messages about sexuality that permeated the cultural atmosphere at the time, particularly the tension between the burgeoning sexual liberation of the 1960s and the continued societal expectations regarding sexual morality (Bruley, 2017).

Despite the newfound freedom, I also encountered the limitations of this freedom. There was still judgment and shame surrounding sexual expression, especially for women. My peers and I often felt the weight of societal expectations when it came to sex and relationships. The concept of heteronormative sexual scripts, which assume heterosexuality as the norm and place women in the role of submissive participants in sexual activity, was still deeply embedded in our interactions and in the educational system (Gagnon & Simon, 2005). As Laumann (1994) discusses, these scripts often set up unrealistic expectations for both genders, creating internal conflicts about what was acceptable in sexual exploration.

During my nursing training, I encountered patients from diverse backgrounds, which provided a cultural education that I had never received in the small community I was brought up in. The exposure to patients from various ethnicities, sexual orientations, and cultural traditions broadened my understanding of human sexuality, race, and gender. The diversity within the hospital environment allowed me to begin to understand the complexities of human relationships that extended far beyond the limited scope I had previously encountered. However, despite my personal efforts to be non-judgmental, I was often aware of the cultural biases I carried with me, inherited from my upbringing. These were the unconscious biases that many individuals of my generation struggled to identify and unpack. The popular Rogerian approach (Rogers, 1957) to non-directive therapy, which emphasized empathy, congruence, and unconditional positive regard, resonated with me as I navigated this multicultural environment, even though I was still in the process of recognizing and confronting my own biases.

Sexual awakening also played a role in this period of my life, albeit in an awkward and shame-laden manner. The experience of sexual exploration at this stage was both clandestine and fraught with guilt. The sexual double standard, which demands that women experience sexual activity with an air of modesty while men's sexual exploration is often seen as a rite of passage, was pervasive (Tolman, 2002). One of my early encounters with sexual devices, such as the vibrator, was one of confusion and amusement, highlighting my naiveté and the lack of comprehensive sex education I had received.

A pivotal moment during my training involved an encounter with Katarina Petrova, a sex worker who was admitted to the hospital for end-stage cancer care. Katarina's life and personality were a sharp contrast to the conservative environment in which I had been raised. She was confident, glamorous, and unapologetically sexual. Her frank discussions about her experiences with sex and sexuality were revelatory. As Foucault (1978) argues, sexuality is not simply a personal experience but a social construct that is shaped and regulated by society. Katarina, through her stories, exposed the contradictions and limitations in how sex was perceived and talked about in medical and social contexts. Her willingness to openly discuss sexual desires and preferences in the face of a terminal illness challenged the medical profession's tendency to treat patients solely for their physical health while neglecting their emotional and sexual well-being (Wang et al., 2022).

Katarina's openness was cathartic for her, and her ability to speak freely about her sexuality in a hospital setting, where patients are often treated in asexual terms, was transformative. She encouraged us to think about sexuality as more than just a physical act, to think about it in emotional and personal terms. She was one of the first people who introduced me to the idea that sex could be empowered, pleasurable, and a source of personal growth rather than something inherently shameful or confined to a marital context. Her stories of her life as a sex worker helped me understand the intersectionality of sex, identity, and profession, and her refusal to conform to societal judgment inspired me to be more open-minded in my professional life.

This experience shaped my future work and led me to become increasingly interested in psychosexual and relationship therapy. Katarina taught me, without meaning to, that the medical profession's narrow focus on curing disease often overlooks the broader, more nuanced aspects of human experience, particularly sexuality and identity. Her legacy, in a sense, was to highlight the psychosocial dimensions of sex that had been absent in my earlier training and education.

Moving on Professionally: Paths That Shape the Journey

As I navigated my professional career, several formative experiences shaped my development as a clinician and eventually guided me toward specializing in psychosexual and relationship therapy. In each of these moments, I was confronted with the intersectionality of societal issues, such as race, class, and gender, that impacted both my work and my understanding of human relationships. These experiences revealed my "learning edges," where my personal biases and professional experiences began to join and thanks to excellent teaching I began to develop my skills and grow in my new specialisms, limitations were exposed, sparking my desire to pursue deeper training and self-reflection in the field of psychosexual and relationship therapy.

Confronting Racial Inequality in Toxteth

One pivotal moment occurred in the early 1980s when I was working in Toxteth, Liverpool, during the civil disturbances in 1981. This area, historically marked by tensions between the local police and the Black community, was facing racial and economic challenges. The riots in Toxteth were a direct result of long-standing systemic inequalities, particularly issues related to stop-and-search laws, which disproportionately targeted Black individuals. For me, it was the first time I truly became aware of how structural inequality operates within the healthcare system and society at large and how it shapes the lives of marginalized individuals (Nazroo, 2024).

At the time, I found myself grappling with guilt and an overwhelming sense of incongruence as a White clinician working in a predominantly Black community. My upbringing in a predominantly White, middle-class environment had shielded me from understanding the complexities of racial dynamics, and my initial attempts to bridge this gap often felt awkward and unacknowledged. According to Sue et al. (2007), clinicians often struggle with transference and countertransference when working with clients from different cultural backgrounds as well as unintentionally committing microaggressions. These emotions, stemming from both personal biases and professional expectations, influenced my clinical approach and initially hindered my ability to form authentic connections with patients.

It was through these difficult experiences that I began to appreciate the importance of cultural humility, the understanding that as a clinician, I must continuously question my assumptions and actively engage in learning about the lived experiences of those from diverse backgrounds.

Supporting Teenage Mothers in Inner-City Leeds

Another defining chapter of my professional journey occurred when I worked in Leeds with teenage mothers, a group that was often stigmatized and misunderstood. As a health visitor, I provided support to these young women, as part of a governmental objective (Public Health England, 2018). Many of whom were raising children in poverty without significant family support. Most were living in substandard housing, facing social isolation, and grappling with the challenges of teenage pregnancy. Society's judgmental stance toward these young mothers was palpable. They were labeled as irresponsible or immoral, with narratives that stigmatized their sexuality and their decisions to become mothers. Negative stereotypes about teenage pregnancy, as discussed by SmithBattle (2013), often overshadow the resilience and strength these young women exhibited. The assumptions that these women were unfit to be parents simply because of their age and poverty were not only incorrect but also damaging. Through my work with them, I realized how the social construction of teenage motherhood as a negative phenomenon influenced the care they received. This taught me a great deal about the psychological impact of stigmatization and the importance of providing services that empower rather than further marginalize.

One particular incident that stands out involved a 16-year-old girl who, after a traumatic home birth, expressed her disillusionment with the healthcare system. She refused hospital care, and nearly lost her baby, believing that the medical system was untrustworthy. This was a common sentiment among the mothers I worked with, who often felt ignored or misunderstood by medical professionals. This experience deepened my understanding of mistrust in healthcare systems among disenfranchised populations and highlighted the necessity of culturally responsive care that acknowledges the lived experiences of vulnerable individuals (Shukla et al., 2025).

Encountering the Complexities of Sexual Identity and Conversion Therapy

A third experience that shaped my career trajectory occurred in a wealthy Essex household where I was supporting a family struggling with the challenges of a disabled child. During one visit, the distraught mother confided in me that her husband had contracted an STI from an affair with a male colleague which had been passed to her. The emotional fallout from this revelation was immense. Her husband, who had previously expressed anti-gay sentiments, was devastated by his actions and sought conversion therapy in an attempt to reconcile his sexuality with his desired identity and save his marriage.

As someone who had little experience with the complexities of sexual identity and the psychological aspects of conversion therapy, I felt both helpless and inadequate in offering the support this family needed. My lack of knowledge about the psychosocial consequences of conversion therapy, an approach now widely condemned as harmful, left me feeling overwhelmed. The psychological harm caused by attempts to alter sexual orientation, especially when compounded by the family dynamics at play, was something I did not fully comprehend at the time, but it devastated this family who never recovered.

In retrospect, I understand that my inability to adequately address the emotional turmoil surrounding sexual orientation and conversion therapy was a key turning point as it became clear that in order to provide competent care to individuals experiencing confusion or distress related to their sexual identity, I needed a deeper understanding of gender identity, sexuality, and the ethical considerations surrounding conversion therapy.

These formative experiences led me to question and ultimately reshape my approach to therapy. The transition from health visiting to psychosexual and relationship therapy was not just a change in career focus, it was a profound personal shift in my understanding of the intersectionality of human experiences, particularly as they relate to sexuality, identity, and societal expectations. Over the years, these encounters shaped me as a clinician, reinforcing the importance of cultural competence, empathy, and a non-judgmental stance when working with diverse populations.

My professional development was not just about acquiring new skills or knowledge; it was as much about confronting my own personal biases and prejudices, ongoing self-reflection and personal therapy.

A Time of Change: Navigating Growth

As my career progressed, I increasingly found myself reflecting on the evolving landscape of psychosexual and relationship therapy. The earlier experiences I had in working with diverse communities, across race, gender, and sexual orientation, served as the foundation for a deeper inquiry into human behavior, relationships, and sexuality. I became increasingly aware of the impact of societal norms and the changing discourse on topics such as gender and sexuality. These reflections ignited my desire to pivot in my career, moving from general healthcare roles to psychosexual and relationship therapy.

Through years of dedicated study and training, I gradually transformed my professional focus, acquiring the academic and therapeutic tools needed to engage with complex psychosexual issues. This section will delve into the personal transformation that took place alongside the larger societal shifts I experienced as a therapist, highlighting the professional milestones that defined my journey into psychosexual and relationship therapy.

Revisiting Education: A Return to the Classroom

After several years in community healthcare and early child-rearing, I decided to return to education, motivated by a growing desire to understand human psychology and its profound influence on relationships and sexuality. Starting as an undergraduate student in psychology, I laid the groundwork for my future postgraduate specialization in counseling psychology. This foundational education offered a structured introduction to psychological theories, which significantly impacted my understanding of human development, identity, and relational dynamics.

Continuing with postgraduate studies in counseling psychology, I expanded my knowledge of clinical supervision, mediation, and psychosexual and relationship therapy. The combination of these fields created a comprehensive approach to therapeutic practice, one that integrated psychological understanding with sexual health and relationship dynamics.

By immersing myself in advanced psychosexual and relationship therapy training, I was able to access the knowledge and therapeutic frameworks that had previously eluded me and I progressed professionally. The once fragmented pieces of my professional experiences began to align as I made connections between psychological theory, cultural norms, and clinical training in practice. My educational journey served as a turning point, enabling me to see the interconnectedness of human sexuality and mental health in new ways.

As a clinician, this period marked the start of an evolving understanding of identity, not only my own as a White middle-class woman but also the identities of my clients, which were often influenced by race, culture, gender, and sexual orientation. This period of study also gave me tools to better navigate cultural differences in therapeutic relationships as I began to reflect critically on my own cultural biases and how they shaped my approach to therapy (Sue et al., 2007).

Shifting from Practice to Teaching

As my clinical work advanced, I moved into supervision, teaching, clinical training, placement management and consultancy, before finally working for the specialist professional body, the College of Sexual and Relationship Therapy (COSRT), where I became their Director of Therapy and Training. While my early career had been deeply influenced by rigid, Eurocentric perspectives, by the time I reached this role, the discourse on sexuality, relationships, and identity had become far more inclusive and diverse. I dedicated myself to educating new therapists about the complexities of multiculturalism, sexuality, gender fluidity, and the expanding definitions of healthy sexual expression. In the process, I worked diligently to ensure that those entering the field would have the knowledge and cultural competence required to meet the needs of diverse clients, competencies that I had not had as a young woman.

This transition also highlighted the necessity of reflective practice in psychosexual and relationship therapy, something that I believe is crucial for all therapists no matter how experienced.

The Impact of the Equality Act 2010: New Legal Frameworks for Diversity

During this phase of professional development, I witnessed the evolution of legal frameworks that increasingly influenced the profession. One of the most significant shifts came with the enactment of the Equality Act (2010), which sought to integrate diversity and inclusion into every aspect of UK society, including healthcare and therapy. The Act unified several pieces of anti-discrimination legislation, extending protections to various marginalized groups, including those based on race, gender, disability, and sexual orientation (Equality Act, 2010).

As I worked in the therapy field, the changing legislation not only reshaped the professional environment but perhaps also reinforced the importance of cultural competence and diversity training for therapists. The Act underscored the ethical responsibility of therapists to challenge discriminatory practices and ensure equitable access to care for all clients. While the law set a strong foundation for equal rights, the practical application of this legislation within psychosexual and relationship therapy required continuous reflection on the part of clinicians, especially those from more traditional or privileged backgrounds.

Understanding Race, Identity, and White Privilege

Throughout my career, one of the most pertinent and pivotal concepts I encountered was White privilege. Growing up in a predominantly White, middle-class environment, I was never truly made aware of how privilege, based on race, class, and other factors, affected the lived experiences of others. It was not until I worked in diverse settings, particularly in inner-city areas like Toxteth and Leeds, that I began to critically examine how racism and systemic oppression shaped not only the lives of my clients but also my approach to therapy.

In more recent times the increased rise in anti-colonialism fanned by the Windrush scandal (Home Office, 2024) and the 2020 Black Lives Matter riots (UK

Parliament, 2021) further raised this issue. We as a nation and in particular therapists, began to understand and learn about White privilege.

This exploration of White privilege and racial identity in therapy led me to confront the limitations of traditional therapeutic models, which often ignored the cultural contexts and unique experiences of non-White clients (Mackintosh, 2003). For example, I began to recognize that Western models of therapy, which assumed a certain cultural homogeneity, were insufficient for understanding the nuanced emotional and psychological needs of Black, Asian, and ethnically diverse clients. To address these shortcomings, organizations like the Black, African, and Asian Therapy Network (BAATN), have developed and have been instrumental in pushing for a more inclusive and anti-oppressive approach to therapy as well as providing education to therapists.

More recently the Coalition for Inclusion and Anti-Oppressive Practice, which brings together organizations with a shared mission to improve diversity within the counseling, psychotherapy and psychological therapy professions are having an impact. Their "Race is Complicated Toolkit" (Williams & Menyié, 2024) aims to help the UK counseling and psychotherapy sectors better understand and address race and diversity as well as support in the objective of inclusion and improved training.

Gender, Sexuality, and Relationship Diversity: The Evolving Landscape

One of the most profound changes in recent years has been the increased recognition and development of Gender, Sexuality, and Relationship Diversity (GSRD). In the early years of my career, many therapeutic models were based on heteronormative assumptions and binary gender norms. GSRD was not something that was openly discussed, and therapists were often unprepared to address the different needs of LGBTQ+ individuals or those with non-traditional relationship structures. Today, however, sexual orientation, gender identity, and relationship configurations are acknowledged as fluid, diverse, and worthy of respect and affirmation in the therapeutic setting. The recognition and de-stigmatization of Gender, Sexuality, and Relationship Diversity (GSRD) has transformed the landscape. The legal recognition of same-sex marriage, the rise of transgender rights, and the growing acceptance of polyamory and kink have radically altered the way therapy is approached. Another key turning point occurred in 2000 when homosexuality was no longer a criminal offense in the UK military, representing another shift in societal norms (Osborne & McGill, 2024).

Organizations which have developed such as Pink Therapy and Stonewall have played a pivotal role in advocating for the rights of LGBTQ+ individuals, ensuring that their needs are met within the healthcare and therapy systems. These movements have helped de-stigmatize non-heteronormative sexualities and relationships, empowering individuals to embrace their authentic selves without fear of discrimination.

In recent times perhaps one of the most important developments has been Memorandum of Understanding on Conversion Therapy (2024 v2) which is a joint document signed by over 25 health, counseling and psychotherapy organizations which aims to end the practice of conversion therapy in the UK, and which has provided a clear stance against the unethical practice of conversion therapy, whether in relation to sexual orientation or gender identity. Safe and ethical clinical practice requires the therapist to ensure they have sufficient specialist knowledge of GSRD and not to favor any one sexual orientation or gender identity over another or attempt to "convert" individuals' sexual orientation or gender identity (). These shifts are part of the larger cultural movement to respect differences and ensure equal rights for all individuals, regardless of their gender or sexual identity.

This shift has also seen the rise of more inclusive clinical practices in psychosexual and relationship therapy and an increase in education. Many of my colleagues have welcomed these changes and sought to learn and understand the diverse lifestyles and therapeutic needs of clients with non-binary or fluid gender sexual identities which may differ from their own. While these changes may present a learning curve for the clinician, they are essential for ensuring that therapists offer culturally competent and affirmative care to all individuals, regardless of sexual, gender, and relationship identity.

As a psychosexual therapist, I have witnessed firsthand how language and terminology around sexuality and gender have evolved during this time and how important it is to stay abreast of these changes to remain culturally in tune and competent. However, for many therapists of my generation, navigating this shift in language and concepts, especially with terms like "queer," "non-binary," and "pansexual," has been a difficult but necessary process. As these terms have become part of mainstream discourse, we are learning how to incorporate them into our practice without perpetuating harm or misunderstanding (Osborne & McGill, 2024). The struggle with terminology is one that reflects a broader shift in society's growing understanding of human diversity and the need for constant learning and growth as professionals.

The Changing Landscape of Relationships and Divorce

The growing acceptance of divorce and the evolving approach to personal relationships has been a huge change in my lifetime and one I welcome having seen the stigma my Mother faced in the 1960s. While divorce is still somewhat stigmatized, particularly for female single parents, as society continues to equate good parenting with two parent norms (Carroll, 2018), it is increasingly seen as a legitimate choice for those in unhealthy or unsatisfactory marriages. Divorce in the 1950s and 1960s was seen as a moral failure, especially for women, but over the decades, it has become more normalized and less shameful. However, it is important to acknowledge that single parents, particularly women, often face financial hardship and mental health challenges as a result of society's persistent expectations around family structures and gender roles (Kim et al., 2023).

Despite the increased recognition of divorce, single-parent and blended families still struggle with deeply ingrained cultural assumptions about family norms. One of the ongoing challenges is society's tendency to equate good parenting with the two-parent family structure. For example, UK statistics reveal that one in four children is raised in a single-parent household (ONS, 2019), yet society continues to idealize the nuclear family as the standard for raising children. As a psychosexual and relationship therapist, this disconnect remains a topic that requires further exploration and research to understand the unique challenges faced by single-parent families, especially regarding mental health and the social stigma they often endure.

Professional Bodies and Collaborative Growth

In recent years I have noticed significant changes within the psychosexual and relationship therapy field. Today, professional bodies are working more collaboratively, fostering interdisciplinary learning and networking through coalitions, committees, and political interest groups. The increasing focus on equality and diversity within the field is a testament to the changing societal values. These collaborations and networking efforts are essential for expanding the scope of psychosexual and relationship therapy to meet the needs of a more multicultural and diverse society.

The growth of psychosexual and relationship therapy training has also been remarkable, with many institutions developing courses to meet the increasing demand for well-trained therapists. COSRT and other professional organizations have been at the forefront of this progress, ensuring that therapists have access to rigorous training and practical tools to address the evolving needs of clients. The rise of diverse student populations, with increasing participation from individuals of different races, sexual orientations, and gender identities, is an encouraging development. This diversity will help enrich the profession and promote the cultural competence that is critical for modern therapists.

Going Forward: Welcoming Change in Psychosexual and Relationship Therapy

Reflecting on my journey, the person I was in the 1960s seems like a distant figure, almost unrecognizable compared to the person I am today. My identity has evolved significantly since then, shaped not only by personal growth but also by the socio-cultural shifts that have transformed the UK and the wider world. As a White woman living in 2025, I have seen how society and the psychosexual and relationship therapy professions have grown to embrace a more diverse, inclusive, and open approach to identity, gender, sexuality, and relationships. As a clinician, I have learned to recognize the intersectionality of our multi-faceted identities and how it profoundly this influences the way we approach sexuality, gender, relationships, culture, race, and well-being. This has led to more inclusive and compassionate care, but it also requires a willingness to reflect critically on the ways in which therapists may inadvertently uphold privilege or perpetuate harm.

As we continue to evolve, I am committed to adapting my practice to meet the needs of all individuals, regardless of identity, background, or experience. This journey of personal and professional growth has not only made me a more competent clinician but also a more culturally humble and empathetic practitioner, better equipped to engage with clients in a world that continues to change in ways that are both exciting and challenging.

As I continue to reflect on this transformation, I remain grateful for the lessons I have learned from patients, service users, and colleagues who challenged my preconceived notions and pushed me to re-evaluate my beliefs. Their perspectives and experiences have broadened my view and have been essential in my journey toward a more inclusive, compassionate, and culturally competent practice. I am thankful that I did not conform to the societal expectations of my youth, which prescribed a very specific role for women. The societal shifts I have witnessed in the field of psychosexual and relationship therapy have led me to understand how individual agency, self-determination, and authenticity can be powerful forces in creating healthier, more fulfilling relationships.

The Need for Reflection and Adaptation in the Future of Psychosexual and Relationship Therapy

As we look to the future of psychosexual and relationship therapy, it is critical that we, as practitioners, continue to engage in self-reflection, education, and professional development to stay in tune with the rapidly changing landscape of identity, gender, sexuality, and relationships. It is essential that we avoid complacency and instead remain open to new ideas and challenges presented by clients, peers, and societal shifts.

The challenges of terminology and the nuances of language will continue to be a source of tension, particularly as the linguistic landscape continues to evolve and very quickly. While it can be difficult to keep up with the rapid pace of change in language and labels, it is crucial that therapists engage in ongoing learning to better serve their clients. The goal is not perfection but a commitment to growth, empathy, and respect.

A new development is of course artificial Intelligence (AI). Chatbots and apps like ChatGPT were not developed initially for therapy but are now being widely used. AI offers instantly available help, which is cheap, often free, and there is of course no fear of human judgment. It is also available 24 hours a day, thus, it provides those who cannot afford face-to-face therapy with the possibility of support. Prescott and Hanley (2023) reflect that many practitioners are already beginning to use the technology to support their practice both clinical and supervisory. As such we can say it will be here to stay, and our task will be how our professions relate to this development and embrace this positively while also being aware of the negative aspect that may evolve.

As I reflect on my own journey as a psychosexual and relationship therapist, I recognize the profound changes I have experienced personally and professionally. The adaptation to new social and cultural norms has been a transformative process, and I am proud to see how far the profession has come. However, there is still much work to be done. Therapists today face the challenge of navigating rapidly shifting cultural landscapes while ensuring that inclusive, respectful, and affirmative care is provided to all clients.

I look forward to continuing to contribute to this profession which has becomes more of a lifestyle than a career and providing compassionate care for people who are seeking healthier relationships and emotional well-being.

As John F. Kennedy said, "Change is the law of life, and those who look only to the past or present are certain to miss the future" and we must embrace future change with openness and hope in our heart.

Questions for Practice and Discussion

- Public protection has become a very important aspect of professional practice; how do we facilitate this? Should we push for regulation of our profession?
- What role should professional bodies play in enforcing ethical guidelines and ensuring public protection?
- In training abroad, how do we ensure we respect the culture of overseas students and any limits as to what is acceptable within their regional laws while ensuring a rigorous training?
- How can training programs adapt to better prepare therapists for cross-cultural psychosexual work in diverse contexts?
- How do we continuously reflect on and challenge our own biases as therapists, especially when working with diverse populations?

References

Bruley, S. (2017). "It didn't just come out of nowhere, did it?" The origins of the women's liberation movement in 1960s Britain. *Oral History*, 45(1), 67–78. www.ohs.org.uk/journal

Carroll, N. (2018). Lone mothers' negotiation of competing employment and parenting demands in the contemporary British context of "worker citizenship". *Contemporary Perspectives in Family Research* 13, 24–39.

Equality Act (2010). London: HMSO "in bibliography and" Equality Act (2010).

Fine, M., McClelland, S.I. (2006). Sexuality education and desire: Still missing after all these years. *Harvard Educational Review*, 76(3), 297–338.

Fletcher, L. (2008). *Historical romance fiction: Heterosexuality and performativity.* Burlington, VT: Ashgate.

Foucault, M. (1978). *The history of sexuality, volume 1: An introduction.* New York: Pantheon Books.

Gagnon, J.H., Simon, W. (2005). *Sexual conduct: The social sources of human sexuality* (2nd ed.). New York: Routledge

Home Office (2024). *The Historical Roots of the Windrush Scandal (2024): Independent Research Report Gov. Uk.*

Kay-Flowers, S. (2019). *Childhood experiences of separation and divorce.* Bristol, UK: Policy Press. Retrieved Nov 19, 2025.

Kim, A., Jeon, S., Song, J. (2023). Self-stigma and mental health in divorced single-parent women: Mediating effect of self-esteem. *Behavioral Sciences (Basel).* Sep 6; 13(9):744. doi: 10.3390/bs13090744. PMID: 37754022; PMCID: PMC10525459.

Koessler, K. C. (1987). The "eve" syndrome. *Manuscripts*, 56(2), Article 30.

Laumann, E.O. (1994). *The social organization of sexuality: Sexual practices in the United States.* Chicago: University of Chicago Press.

Link, B.G., Phelan, J.C. (2001). Conceptualizing stigma. *Annual Review of Sociology*, 27, 363–385.

Marcia, J.E. (1966). Development and validation of ego-identity status. *Journal of Personality and Social Psychology*, 3(5), 551–558.

McIntosh, P. (2003). White privilege: Unpacking the invisible knapsack. In S. Plous (Ed.), *Understanding prejudice and discrimination* (pp. xiii, 191–196, 609). New York, NY: McGraw-Hill.

McKellar, K., Sillence, E., Smith, M. (2019). Sexual health experiences, knowledge and understanding in low SES female teenagers: A diary approach. *Journal of Adolescence*, 73, 122–130.

Memorandum of Understanding on Conversion Therapy in the UK, Version 2 Revision A, Update 2024.

Nazroo, J. (2024). Race/ethnic inequalities in health: Moving beyond confusion to focus on fundamental causes. *Oxford Open Economics*, 3(Supplement_1), i563–i576,

ONS (2019). Families and households in the UK: 2019. *Statistical Bulletin.* www.ons.gov.uk

Osborne, A.K., McGill, G. (2024). The impact of the historic policy to ban homosexuality in the UK armed forces: The lived experience of LGBT + veterans. *Sexuality Research and Social Policy*, 21, 1123–1136. doi: 10.1007/s13178-024-00952-1.

Prescott, J. Hanley, T. (2023). Therapists' attitudes towards the use of AI in therapeutic practice: Considering the therapeutic alliance. *Mental Health and Social Inclusion*, 27(2), 177–185. doi: 10.1108/MHSI-02-2023-0020.

Public Health England (2018). *Teenage pregnancy prevention framework—Supporting young people to prevent unplanned pregnancy and develop healthy relationships.* London: PHE.

Rogers, C.R. (1957). The necessary and sufficient conditions of therapeutic personality change. *Journal of Consulting Psychology*, 21(2), 95–103.

Sanchez, D.T., Kiefer, A.K. (2007). Body concerns in and out of the bedroom: Implications for sexual pleasure and problems. *Archives of Sexual Behavior*, 36(6), 808–820.

Shukla, M., Schilt-Solberg, M, Gibson-Scipio, W. (2025). Medical mistrust: A concept analysis. *Nursing Reports*, Mar 17; 15(3):103.

SmithBattle, L.I. (2013). Reducing the stigmatization of teen mothers. *MCN: The American Journal of Maternal/Child Nursing*, Jul–Aug; 38(4): 235–241; quiz 242–243.

Sue, D.W., Capodilupo, C.M., Torino, G.C., Bucceri, J.M., Holder, A.M., Nadal, K.L., Esquilin, M. (2007). Racial microaggressions in everyday life: Implications for clinical practice. *American Psychologist*, May–Jun; 62(4):271–286.

Tolman, D.L. (2002). *Dilemmas of desire: Teenage girls talk about sexuality.* Cambridge: Harvard University Press.

UK Parliament (2021). *Black Lives Matter: New race inequalities commission and a London statue review*. London: House of Lords Library.

Wang, Y., Feng, W. (2022). Cancer-related psychosocial challenges. *General Psychiatry*, 35(5), e100871. doi: 10.1136/gpsych-2022-10087.

Williams, V., Menyié, Y. (2024). *Race is complicated—A toolkit for psychological therapies training*. Commissioned by The Coalition for Inclusion and Anti-Oppressive Practice. www.place2be.org.uk/about-us/our-policies/equity-diversity-and-inclusion/coalition-for-inclusion-and-anti-oppressive-practice/race-is-complicated-a-toolkit-for-psychological-therapies-training

Organizations and coalition resources

Pink Therapy, https://pinktherapy.com/

Stonewall, www.stonewall.org.uk/

COSRT, www.cosrt.org.uk/

Coalition for inclusion and anti-oppressive practice, www.place2be.org.uk/about-us/our-policies/equity-diversity-and-inclusion/coalition-for-inclusion-and-anti-oppressive-practice

The Black, African and Asian Therapy Network, www.baatn.org.uk/

Chapter 9

An Introduction to Global Perspectives on Therapy for Neurodivergent People

Tiga-Rose Nercessian

Introduction

Let me introduce Hiba, an autistic, Hausa 30-year-old who disliked bodily fluids but was too ashamed to tell their partner that this was why they kept avoiding sex. Meet Mary, a Chinese autistic woman, and JT, her Filipino partner with ADHD. They worried they had mismatched libidos but had been overlooking the cultural relevance of their neurodivergence and how it intersected with socially prescribed gender roles. And then there's Mayukh, a Bangladeshi trans man who was trying to work out his gender and sexuality through his newly diagnosed autistic lens.

This chapter was inspired by clients like these. In it, I aim to explore why people from diverse cultural backgrounds and with overlapping identities struggle to access psychosexual therapy. I also seek to address what we, as practitioners, can do to dismantle these barriers. This chapter calls for a paradigm shift in psychosexual therapy—one that is inclusive, culturally competent, neuro-affirmative, and client-centered. Specifically, it advocates for a deeper engagement with the lived experiences of neurodivergent individuals from the Global South, many of whom are navigating not just neurodivergence, but also intersecting marginalization related to race, gender, language, class, and colonially shaped mental health frameworks.

Before delving into the main discourse, let me briefly position myself socio-culturally. I write as a multi-neurodivergent, queer, white-passing, anglophone sex and relationship therapist in private practice. My personal background is multicultural, shaped by the diverse ethnic and socio-cultural heritages of my parents, as well as the countries and cultures in which I have lived. I acknowledge that certain aspects of my identity have conferred privileges I have not earned—privileges that are often invisible to those who hold them yet deeply impactful for those who do not. These intersections fundamentally shape both how I view the world and how I practice therapy.

As a teenager in the 1990s, I was inspired by the writings of Homi Bhabha and bell hooks, naively believing that greater cultural representation and academic decolonization were just around the corner. I anticipated a more just global discourse where mental health narratives reflected the pluralistic realities of our

DOI: 10.4324/9781003611387-9

world. Now, several decades on, we find ourselves in a unique position to assess the successes—and failures—of diversity and equality policies. The enduring dominance of white, Western, anglophone epistemologies in mental health fields, including psychosexual therapy, demands a more critical lens.

Although there is limited statistical data on global neurodivergent populations, some estimates do exist—particularly for ADHD, which I will use here as a focal point for clarity and brevity. In 2020, the global prevalence of persistent adult ADHD—defined as ADHD diagnosed in childhood and persisting into adulthood—was estimated at 2.6%. Meanwhile, symptomatic adult ADHD, or what is colloquially referred to as "late" or "adult-onset" diagnosis, stood at 6.8%, translating to roughly 140 million and 366 million adults, respectively (Song et al., 2021).

However, even within academic literature, these prevalence estimates vary considerably. In Arab countries, ADHD prevalence ranges between 0.5% and 19.6% (Alhraiwil et al., 2015). Data from Mainland China, Hong Kong, and Taiwan report rates of 6.5%, 6.4%, and 4.2%, respectively, with a pooled estimate of 6.3% (Liu et al., 2018). A Nigerian study on childhood ADHD observed that prevalence in other African countries such as South Africa, the Democratic Republic of Congo, and Ethiopia ranged from 5.4% to 8.7% (Chinawa et al., 2014). A broader meta-analysis placed the pooled prevalence of childhood and adolescent ADHD in Africa at 7.5% (Ayano et al., 2020). Evidence also suggests socioeconomic development may influence diagnosis rates, with higher prevalence reported in high-income countries (3%) compared to lower-middle-income countries (1.4%) (Popit et al., 2024).

These disparities may reflect not actual variation in incidence, but rather differential access to diagnostic frameworks, cultural recognition, and healthcare systems. The limitations of global ADHD prevalence data expose a deeper problem: a largely Eurocentric construction of diagnostic categories, often insufficiently validated across cultural contexts (Henrich et al., 2010).

Even for those who enjoy parsing data—myself included—the lack of cultural and linguistic representation in most research can be discouraging. The overwhelming majority of neurodivergent studies define participants in terms of age, sex, gender, and sometimes sexual orientation, but rarely include crucial identifiers such as first language, ethnicity, or cultural heritage. This gap not only skews the data but severely limits our understanding of neurodivergence in its global complexity.

This deficit is particularly troubling when one considers that 90% of the world's children and adolescents live in low- and middle-income countries, yet only about 10% of neurodevelopmental research is conducted there (Franz et al., 2017). This massive imbalance contributes to what Miranda Fricker (2007) termed epistemic injustice—in this context, the systematic exclusion of non-Western, non-anglophone perspectives from the knowledge production about neurodivergent experiences.

Language is also a major barrier in neurodivergent research. My own review was restricted to sources in English, French, and Spanish, despite identifying valuable publications in Russian, Arabic, and other languages. For example, Kelly et al.

(2024) found that in a systematic review on ADHD in women, 8% of the original 21,123 papers—nearly 2,000—were excluded solely because they were not written in English. This reflects a wider trend in which anglophone meta-analyses routinely exclude non-English studies, thereby reinforcing the dominance of English-speaking populations in neurodivergent discourse and research.

To put it bluntly: most of what we currently "know" about neurodivergence is based on white, affluent, English-speaking populations—research produced by and for individuals within that same demographic. Until very recently, this research was overwhelmingly conducted by white men in high-income countries. This entrenched imbalance amounts to an epistemic hegemony, privileging a narrow worldview while marginalizing the rest.

The remainder of this chapter seeks to interrogate this imbalance and offer pathways forward. It aims to shine a light on the systemic barriers that prevent neurodivergent individuals—particularly those from the Global South and multiply marginalized communities—from accessing equitable psychosexual care. It advocates for a recalibration of therapeutic models toward neuro-affirmative, anti-racist, and anti-oppressive approaches. These must not only respect neurodivergent lived experiences but be adaptable to the cultural, linguistic, and socio-political contexts in which those lives unfold.

What Are the Barriers Preventing the Global Majority of Neurodivergent People from Accessing Therapy?

Despite growing global recognition of neurodivergence, neurodivergent adults—particularly from low- and middle-income countries and minoritized ethnic groups—continue to face significant barriers in accessing effective psychotherapeutic services. These challenges are multifactorial and often compounded by systemic inequality, cultural stigma, and intersectional identity struggles. Drawing on the limited yet emerging research base, this section outlines five dominant barriers that restrict access to therapy for the global majority of neurodivergent individuals:

1. Access to culturally appropriate diagnostic services and assessment tools
2. Accessibility barriers to general therapeutic services
3. Communication problems with mental health professionals
4. Lack of social awareness and community support
5. Social isolation, shame, and stigma

Access to Culturally Appropriate Diagnostic Services and Assessment Tools

Take the case of Ester, an East African woman who sought an adult ADHD diagnosis after learning that her twins were both autistic with ADHD. Without a cultural frame of reference for her symptoms, Ester had previously internalized blame for her failed marriage, unaware that her undiagnosed hyperactivity clashed with strict gender norms about how wives should behave. Her story reflects the wider global reality: access to diagnostic services is not only uneven—it is often culturally misaligned.

Globally, neurodevelopmental diagnostic frameworks remain biased toward white, cisgender, Western male presentations (Loomes et al., 2017; Santos et al., 2022). The widely cited gender ratios for autism and ADHD—3:1 and 2.3:1 respectively—reflect structural diagnostic oversights rather than biological truths. Klefsjö et al. (2020) found that girls tend to be diagnosed later than boys, and require more clinical consultations to reach a diagnosis, due in part to subtler symptom profiles and gendered social masking strategies.

Cultural disparity further complicates timely diagnosis. In the United States, Latino children are diagnosed with autism on average 2.5 years later than white non-Latino peers (Zuckerman et al., 2014). Black children are also routinely diagnosed later, even when controlling for socioeconomic status, access to Medicaid, and symptom severity. These patterns are echoed across the Global South, where infrastructural underdevelopment and stigma severely restrict access to culturally congruent assessments.

Furthermore, diagnostic tools such as the ADOS-2 and ADI-R—deemed the "gold standard" in autism assessment—are rarely adapted for linguistic or cultural specificity. Most translations are confined to European languages, leaving African, Middle Eastern, and Southeast Asian populations vastly underserved (Olatunji et al., 2023). Without meaningful localization of these tools, many neurodivergent individuals are either misdiagnosed, underdiagnosed, or completely missed.

Accessibility Barriers to General Therapeutic Services

Globally, mental healthcare—including psychosexual therapy—is often financially inaccessible. Whether accessed through underfunded public systems or costly private providers, the financial barrier disproportionately affects individuals in low-income and marginalized communities (Patel et al., 2018). This is particularly pressing for neurodivergent individuals who may struggle with stable employment due to co-occurring learning difficulties or executive dysfunction (Barkley, 2015).

Even when therapy is theoretically available, structural design flaws impede neurodivergent access. For instance, online booking systems that require telephone calls may be inaccessible to individuals with auditory processing challenges, social anxiety, or phone phobia—a frequent occurrence in autism and ADHD (Levy & Perry, 2011). Attendance-based penalties, such as discharge from services after missed or late appointments, also fail to account for common neurodivergent traits like time blindness, poor working memory, or impaired planning skills (Brown, 2005).

Moreover, psychosexual therapy, considered a "specialist" or "secondary" service, is often omitted from national health priorities, particularly in Global

South contexts where sexual well-being is marginalized in public discourse. As a result, even when neurodivergent individuals access general mental health services, their psychosexual concerns remain overlooked or deprioritized (Fine & McClelland, 2006).

Communication Problems with Mental Health Professionals

Language remains one of the most overlooked yet significant barriers to therapy. In many postcolonial nations, dominant mental health frameworks and training continue to rely on colonial languages (e.g., English, French, Portuguese), creating significant access issues for those who are not fluent in these tongues. This linguistic gatekeeping restricts awareness, delays help-seeking, and often forces clients to articulate distress in a second or third language, limiting their expressive capacity and emotional nuance (Sue et al., 2009).

In the MENA region, ADHD is still widely viewed as a childhood condition, despite emerging evidence showing that most children diagnosed with ADHD continue to meet the criteria into adulthood (Safiri et al., 2023). This belief leads to a dearth of services tailored to adults, especially those without caregiving advocates. Adults who were previously supported by parents often flounder when expected to independently navigate a complex mental health system.

Culturally and linguistically, the terminology surrounding autism reveals profound differences in conceptualization. For example, the Chinese term "gūdúzhèng" (孤独症) translates to "loneliness disease," while "zìbìzhèng" (自闭症) means "closed-self disease"—both imply pathology and isolation. These conceptual framings influence family attitudes and public perceptions. In contrast, terms in Western languages like "autismo" (Spanish) or "autisme" (French) are more clinically neutral, yet still carry historical stigma rooted in pathologization.

Lack of Social Awareness and Community Support

*Priya, a North Indian woman in her twenties, self-diagnosed through social media platforms like TikTok—long before her family acknowledged her neurodivergence. Her parents initially sought help from faith healers, reflecting a cultural norm where psychological distress is interpreted through spiritual or metaphysical lenses (*Kudi et al., 2023*). Such practices are not inherently harmful but may delay formal diagnosis or necessary therapeutic intervention.*

In many regions of the world, neurodivergence is poorly understood or entirely unknown. Kapoor (2019) found that only 13% of survey respondents in India had heard of autism, compared with 100% in the United States. Furthermore, in cultures where family honor is paramount, visible neurodivergence can be seen as shameful, leading to minimization or denial of symptoms (Chinese Autism, 2020). The intersection of neurodivergence and non-conformity to gender norms—such as a lack of eye contact or rigid routines—often fuels greater ostracism, especially in conservative or patriarchal societies.

Community support structures, such as neurodivergent peer groups, are rare in the Global South. This exacerbates feelings of isolation and marginalization. Research shows that lack of social belonging and perceived burdensomeness are key predictors of self-harm and suicidality among autistic individuals (Pelton et al., 2023; Costa et al., 2020). Without neuro-affirming spaces and informed peer support, many neurodivergent adults retreat into isolation or become entirely disengaged from healthcare systems.

Social Isolation, Shame, and Stigma

Xavi, an indigenous Chilean engineer, was grappling with a sudden and overwhelming increase in his libido, leading to frequent concerns about being caught masturbating at work. He believed this was the only way to manage his heightened sexual urges, which were interfering with his ability to focus on his job. When he sought help from his general practitioner, he was met with dismissive, racialized humor—his GP joked about the stereotype of "horny Latino men." Xavi was shocked and left speechless, yet the GP suggested he try sex therapy. Upon discussing the situation with me, Xavi revealed that his heightened libido began shortly after his ADHD medication had been changed due to a national shortage of his usual prescription. This medication change turned out to be the cause of his increased sexual drive. After switching back to his previous medication, his libido returned to a more manageable level within weeks.

This case highlights not only the challenges neurodivergent individuals face in managing unexpected side effects, but also the compounded cultural and racial biases they encounter in healthcare settings. Xavi's experience is a vivid example of how intersectionality—where race, neurodivergence, and sexuality intersect—can contribute to the misdiagnosis and dismissal of valid concerns. His story reflects the critical need for therapists and healthcare providers to be culturally competent, to challenge harmful stereotypes, and to approach neurodivergent individuals' experiences with empathy and understanding, rather than perpetuating harmful narratives based on race and gender.

Stigma remains one of the most entrenched barriers to care. Neurodivergence is often pathologized as a failure to adhere to social, gender, or professional norms (Link & Phelan, 2001). For example, the same traits praised as "intellectual giftedness" in wealthy white boys may be labeled "disruptive" or "defiant" in Black, Indigenous, or low-income children. This cultural bias in labeling perpetuates disparities in both diagnosis and intervention (Skidmore, 2015).

In Chinese studies, 70% of parents of autistic children reported feeling discriminated against, primarily due to the culture's strong emphasis on conformity and family honor (Chinese Autism, 2020). Children without significant impairments—i.e., those considered "high-functioning"—are particularly at risk of being left without educational or social support, as their needs are often deemed invisible or invalid (Baimbridge Cotton, 2020).

Furthermore, social stigma often silences discussions about sexuality and bodily autonomy. This can be especially limiting for individuals who are neurodivergent and also identify as LGBTQIA+, non-binary, or gender diverse, as they must navigate additional layers of marginalization when addressing their psychosexual health (Strang et al., 2018).

In summary, neurodivergent individuals from the Global Majority face interlocking systemic, cultural, and practical barriers to accessing effective therapy—particularly psychosexual services. Diagnostic disparities, financial inaccessibility, linguistic obstacles, community disengagement, and deep-rooted stigma all contribute to their marginalization within therapeutic systems. A culturally nuanced, neuro-affirmative, and socially just therapeutic model is urgently needed to dismantle these barriers and deliver equitable care.

Neurodivergent Adults and Psychosexual Issues

Having outlined the key barriers that prevent neurodivergent individuals from accessing therapeutic services—particularly within psychosexual contexts—we can now turn our focus to what is known about the psychosexual lives and challenges faced by neurodivergent adults. While this area of research remains nascent, it is slowly expanding and revealing the unique complexities these individuals encounter in their intimate lives.

Early empirical work in this domain was scarce and anecdotal. The earliest published study investigating the sexual attitudes and knowledge of autistic adults dates only to 1991 and included a mere 21 participants (Ousley & Mesibov, 1991). Since then, the literature has grown incrementally but remains limited in both scale and inclusivity. Much of it focuses on Western, cisgender, white populations, thus failing to capture the global diversity of neurodivergent experiences. In this way, the field reproduces the epistemic injustice discussed earlier.

Studies on psychosexual functioning among neurodivergent populations often concentrate on deficits or pathologies. For example, Hancock et al. (2020) and Yew et al. (2021) focus primarily on communication challenges and difficulties with romantic relationship maintenance among autistic individuals. Other research shifts the lens to neurotypical partners, examining the stress or emotional burden they may face in relationships with neurodivergent individuals (Robin & Payson, 2005; Knies et al., 2020). Still, others focus on problematic outcomes such as risky sexual behavior, victimization, and even sexual perpetration—particularly in those with ADHD (Fang et al., 2010; Blanchard et al., 2022). While such findings are important for safeguarding and mental health, they perpetuate a deficit model that often fails to consider strengths, desires, and capacities for mutual pleasure and intimacy among neurodivergent individuals themselves.

Quantitative studies present some compelling—if not always encouraging—data. In one study, only 11.1% of autistic males reported satisfaction with their romantic relationships, compared to 63.8% of neurotypical counterparts; similarly, just 10.7% were satisfied with their sex lives, compared to 59.6% of neurotypical peers (Young & Cocallis, 2023). The disparity is notable and echoes a broader trend of under-recognized emotional and relational struggles. Bijlenga et al. (2018) similarly report that only 27% of male ADHD participants expressed satisfaction with their sexual lives, compared with 68% of neurotypical males. Beyond satisfaction, ADHD is also linked to impulsive sexual behavior, fluctuating libidos, and higher relational conflict (Barkley, 2015; Wymbs et al., 2021). These issues often go unrecognized or are misattributed to personality flaws rather than neurological divergence.

Furthermore, psychosexual research has reported higher rates of sexual dysfunction among neurodivergent individuals. These include low arousal, difficulty achieving orgasm, erectile dysfunction, and painful intercourse—symptoms often intensified by sensory sensitivities, performance anxiety, or challenges with emotional communication (Byers et al., 2013; Turner et al., 2019). Complicating matters further is the role of co-occurring conditions. For instance, anxiety disorders, depression, PTSD, and alexithymia—each disproportionately prevalent among autistic and ADHD populations—can exacerbate or mask psychosexual distress (Bird & Cook, 2013; George & Stokes, 2018).

That said, research is not uniformly bleak. A recent study by Yew et al. (2023) found that some autistic participants reported higher levels of perceived sexual and relationship satisfaction than neurotypical peers. These findings challenge prevailing assumptions and suggest that with supportive environments and affirming partners, neurodivergent individuals can experience deeply fulfilling relationships. Such outcomes underscore the need for therapeutic practices that are not only inclusive but also strength-based.

Intersectionality and Psychosexual Experience

As Kimberlé Crenshaw (1989) famously articulated, intersectionality is essential in understanding how various forms of oppression—such as racism, ableism, sexism, and homophobia—interact in the lives of marginalized individuals. This is especially pertinent in the context of neurodivergent adults.

Emerging research reveals that neurodivergent people are disproportionately likely to hold other minoritized identities. For example, autistic individuals are significantly more likely to identify as LGBTQIA+, particularly as transgender, non-binary, or queer (George & Stokes, 2018; Strang et al., 2018). Strang et al. (2021) found that gender-diverse identities were 7.59 times more common in autistic individuals than in the general population. These overlapping identities often create unique challenges in accessing sexual healthcare, education, and affirming therapeutic relationships.

Neurodivergent individuals are also more likely to live with co-occurring mental and physical health conditions. These include—but are not limited to—Ehlers-Danlos Syndrome (EDS), gastrointestinal disorders, immune dysregulation, and chronic fatigue syndromes (Strati et al., 2017; Wijsen et al., 2021; Riquelme et al.,

2022). Such conditions not only impact general well-being but can complicate sexual activity, body image, and communication within intimate partnerships.

These intersecting identities and challenges do not occur in isolation. Rather, they accumulate into what has been termed a "minority stress load" (Meyer, 2003)—a psychological burden that stems from repeated exposure to stigma, discrimination, and social exclusion. Minority stress theory, originally developed to explain the mental health disparities among LGBTQIA+ populations, has since been adapted to include disabled and neurodivergent groups (Botha & Frost, 2020). Understanding these intersecting pressures is critical to providing trauma-informed, client-centered psychosexual therapy.

Clinical Observations from Practice

While formal research remains limited, anecdotal data from private practice can provide meaningful insights. Although not generalizable, such observations highlight recurring psychosexual concerns among neurodivergent clients—particularly those with autism or ADHD.

For autistic adults, common issues include:

- Sensory sensitivities, such as aversion to bodily fluids, touch, or temperature changes.
- Rigid or narrow definitions of sex, which can inhibit exploration or adaptation in intimate settings.
- Temporal transition challenges, especially during initiation and conclusion of sexual activity.
- Executive functioning burdens, such as scheduling intimacy, remembering birth control, or managing mood fluctuations.
- Stress from routine disruptions, including travel or changes in sleeping arrangements, which can significantly impair sexual desire or comfort.

For clients with ADHD, common psychosexual issues include:

- Impulsivity or compulsivity, which may lead to risk-taking behaviors or difficulties with consent boundaries.
- Fluctuating libido, which may not match a partner's sexual rhythm.
- Erectile dysfunction or anorgasmia, potentially exacerbated by stimulant medications or stress.
- Distraction during sex, which can impair intimacy or emotional connection.
- Sensory hyposensitivity or hypersensitivity, impacting pleasure and discomfort thresholds.

Additionally, many neurodivergent individuals report chronic digestive issues—often undiagnosed or self-managed—which affect comfort, confidence, and physical readiness for sexual activity (Strati et al., 2017). As such, attending to physical comorbidities becomes an essential aspect of holistic psychosexual therapy.

Case Example: Raha

Raha, an Emirati cisgender woman, had long struggled with selective eating. Diagnosed with Avoidant/Restrictive Food Intake Disorder (ARFID) in adolescence, her sensory issues persisted into adulthood. In her early twenties, following an assisted marriage, she found herself unable to engage in oral sex despite an intellectual desire to do so. The issue became a point of conflict in her relationship and eventually led her to seek sex therapy.

Rather than interpreting her difficulty as psychological avoidance or repression, therapeutic work focused on mapping her sensory preferences. Raha disclosed an aversion to wet textures, noting that she only drank through straws and used oil-based cosmetics to avoid water on her skin. This sensory sensitivity, previously framed as "picky" or "difficult," was explored compassionately. Raha chose to undergo autism assessment and was formally diagnosed shortly after.

The diagnosis enabled her to reframe her experience and communicate more openly with her husband. Together, they developed a repertoire of alternative intimate activities that were pleasurable for both partners. Their story illustrates how sensory-informed therapy, self-awareness, and mutual consent can transform psychosexual outcomes.

Moving Forward

Taken together, the evidence shows that neurodivergent adults face a constellation of psychosexual issues that are insufficiently understood by the wider therapeutic community. Limited, inconsistent research findings, cultural erasure, and diagnostic overshadowing have kept these issues at the margins of both sexology and neurodevelopmental discourse.

To truly support neurodivergent individuals, psychosexual therapists must:

- Abandon deficit-based models.
- Embrace neurodivergence as a variation of human sexuality and intimacy.
- Adapt practice frameworks to reflect the sensory, emotional, and cognitive diversity of clients.
- Conduct further research—especially intersectional and Global South-focused studies—to enhance the depth and breadth of understanding in this critical area.

Why Is This Topic so Important Right Now?

This chapter was written during the inaugural weeks following the re-election of Donald Trump—an event emblematic of the broader global shift toward authoritarianism, ethnonationalism, and social conservatism. In such a sociopolitical climate, minoritized communities—including neurodivergent individuals—are experiencing increasing levels of precarity, fear, and exclusion from civic participation, healthcare, and education (Wong & Moorhouse, 2021). The intensification of systemic persecution makes the task of creating inclusive, equitable frameworks for psychosexual therapy not only a clinical imperative but a moral one.

Across many global contexts, identity-based marginalization prevents entire populations from contributing to or benefiting from dominant social understandings of health, identity, and human experience. Neurodivergent individuals—particularly those who are also racialized, queer, gender-diverse, or economically marginalized—are structurally denied opportunities to articulate and affirm their realities. This phenomenon is an example of hermeneutical injustice, a form of epistemic injustice coined by philosopher Miranda Fricker (2007), which refers to the systemic gaps in shared interpretive resources that prevent marginalized individuals from making sense of their experiences.

As Coady (2017) explains, epistemic injustice occurs when "the voices, experiences, and problems of marginalized individuals, communities, and societies are not being taken seriously," often due to the dominant group's control over institutional and epistemological structures. For neurodivergent people, especially those from the Global Majority, this often manifests as a lack of culturally or linguistically accessible diagnostic frameworks, underrepresentation in research, and mischaracterization in public discourse.

Moreover, these injustices are not merely theoretical. They result in tangible harms: delayed diagnoses, exclusion from research samples, inaccessible therapeutic services, and even interpersonal invalidation during clinical encounters. In the realm of psychosexual therapy, this becomes especially urgent, as intimacy, identity, and embodiment are deeply personal and vulnerable aspects of human life that require safety, affirmation, and contextual understanding (Botha, 2021).

The neurodiversity movement, emerging primarily from autistic self-advocacy communities, offers a counter-narrative to medicalized and deficit-based discourses. Rather than framing neurodivergence as a pathology to be cured, the movement recognizes it as a natural and valuable variation of human cognition and behavior (Kapp et al., 2013). This perspective aligns with broader global movements toward epistemic justice and decolonial thought, which challenge the Eurocentric, ableist structures of knowledge production and professional practice (Santos, 2014).

Indeed, the call for intellectual decolonization is inseparable from the call for neuro-affirmative practice. Just as colonial ideologies historically framed Indigenous, Black, and Global South ways of knowing as primitive or irrational, contemporary psychiatric systems often pathologize neurodivergent modes of communication, perception, and self-expression. Therapists who fail to question these norms risk perpetuating the very systems of exclusion their clients are navigating (Titchkosky, 2007).

This is why culturally grounded, anti-oppressive, and neuro-affirming frameworks in psychosexual therapy are essential at this juncture. They not only validate neurodivergent lived experience but also reconfigure what counts as knowledge, competence, and health. In doing so, they contribute to the larger struggle against epistemic violence and toward inclusive liberation.

As Fricker (2007) and later scholars (Medina, 2013; Kidd et al., 2017) have argued, responding to epistemic injustice requires cultivating epistemic humility, testimonial sensitivity, and the active redistribution of credibility. For psychosexual therapists, this might mean privileging client narratives over diagnostic scripts, validating culturally specific understandings of intimacy, or challenging their own epistemological assumptions in supervision and training contexts.

This topic matters urgently today because the intersection of neurodivergence, sexuality, and marginalization is both under-theorized and under-resourced. A truly inclusive psychosexual practice must go beyond therapeutic technique; it must be rooted in the political, epistemological, and ethical project of justice.

What Can We Do as Practitioners to Improve Psychosexual Therapy for Neurodivergent People?

As a practitioner passionate about neurodivergent clients, it can feel overwhelming to tackle the multifaceted challenges they face in accessing therapy. However, a more pragmatic approach suggests that these challenges can be addressed by focusing on interventions at three levels: macro, community, and practice. This multi-layered framework offers a way forward, from systemic advocacy to personal therapeutic practice.

Macro Level: Government, Training Institutions, and Regulatory Bodies

At the macro level, much of the work begins with dismantling the entrenched medical and charity models of disability. In most mental healthcare settings, neurodivergence is often conceptualized as something to be fixed, treated, or managed. This is in stark contrast to the social model of disability, which frames neurodiversity as a natural variation of human experience rather than a pathology (Shakespeare, 2013). Shifting to a social model that embraces neurodivergence as part of the natural spectrum of human experience would fundamentally reshape how neurodivergent clients are perceived and treated.

To enact this paradigm shift, we must engage in advocacy, research, and the development of support networks that challenge and educate these outdated models of disability. This includes pressuring governmental bodies, educational institutions, and professional organizations to adopt updated frameworks for neurodiversity that emphasize neuro-affirmation and social inclusion. Institutions like the World Health Organization (WHO) and the American Psychological Association (APA) have recognized the importance of rethinking neurodivergence; however, more research is needed to explore the lived experiences of neurodivergent individuals, particularly within the context of psychosexual issues (Kapp et al., 2013).

For example, the misdiagnosis or late diagnosis of autism and ADHD, particularly in women and racial minorities, has been well-documented (Zukerman et al., 2015; Loomes, 2017). Expanding diagnostic criteria and improving diagnostic tools to ensure inclusivity is a crucial step toward improving access to psychosexual therapy. This requires a more intersectional approach to research, exploring not just neurodivergence but also how race, class, and gender influence diagnostic experiences (Crenshaw, 1989). Moreover, exploring how neurodivergence intersects with gender identity can illuminate the unique challenges faced by gender-diverse neurodivergent individuals (Strang et al., 2018).

Community Level: Professional Peers and Personal Communities

On a community level, practitioners have the opportunity to contribute to culturally appropriate community-based interventions that integrate both professional care and indigenous knowledge. For instance, in India, mental health interventions for women have found success by incorporating family- and community-oriented activities such as sanghas or faith-based groups (Weaver et al., 2023). These culturally sensitive interventions can be expanded to include activities that are already familiar and meaningful to the community, like yoga classes, group fitness walks, and even watch parties for popular films. Integrating psychosexual education into these spaces can help bridge gaps between clinical care and community support.

At the professional peer level, therapists can work together to develop culturally competent, neuro-affirmative therapeutic practices. This includes advocating for anti-racist, anti-ableist, and anti-oppressive approaches in training programs and professional networks. Working with colleagues to build these frameworks ensures that a collective shift happens across therapeutic spaces.

The need for cross-cultural competence in working with neurodivergent clients cannot be overstated. Practitioners should recognize how cultural nuances and norms may influence how clients approach therapy, especially when discussing intimate topics like sex and relationships (Tervalon & Murray-Garcia, 1998). For instance, understanding that certain neurodivergent experiences are interpreted differently across cultures can help therapists avoid making assumptions based on dominant Western frameworks of care.

Practice Level: Your Psychosexual Therapy Practice

At the practice level, therapists can implement a range of strategies to better support neurodivergent clients. Below are several practical suggestions for therapists looking to improve their psychosexual practice.

Take a Truly Client-Centered Approach

The cornerstone of effective therapy is to genuinely understand the world from the client's perspective. For neurodivergent individuals, this means suspending personal biases and preconceptions about what constitutes "normal" sexuality. Each neurodivergent client brings unique experiences of sex and intimacy that may be misunderstood or mislabeled by mainstream society. By embracing individual differences—including co-presentations like alexithymia, aphantasia, hyperfantasia, and synesthesia—therapists can help clients better understand how their brains process sensual and sexual stimuli (Mundy & Sigman, 2006). A key element of client-centered therapy is recognizing that neurodivergent clients may experience sensory sensitivities, different emotional processing, and differing relationships with intimacy (Fletcher-Watson, 2019).

Help Clients to Explore Their Unique Sensory Sensitivity Profile

Neurodivergent individuals often experience sensory input differently. For instance, an individual with autism may be hypersensitive to touch, making physical intimacy overwhelming (Leekam et al., 2007). Practitioners can help clients understand how they process sensory information and explore how sensory sensitivities—whether hypo- or hypersensitive—affect intimate interactions. This could involve using multiple sensory modalities in therapy (e.g., visual, auditory, tactile) to help clients articulate how different sensory inputs affect their sexual experiences. Sensory awareness can be integrated into psychosexual therapy to provide practical solutions that align with the client's needs.

Support and Explore Their Self-Diagnosis

Self-diagnosis is a powerful tool for neurodivergent clients, but it often carries years of frustration and shame. Many neurodivergent individuals, particularly in under-resourced communities, may not have formal diagnoses, or may have been misdiagnosed for years (Cummings et al., 2023). Practitioners should approach self-diagnosis with curiosity and validation, acknowledging the process of self-discovery as an important part of the therapeutic journey. By respecting and affirming clients' self-diagnoses, therapists can foster a strong therapeutic alliance and create a space where clients feel safe to explore intimate issues without fear of judgment.

Consider a Developmental/Strengths-Based Approach

Societal stigma often causes neurodivergent individuals to internalize negative self-beliefs. Many are taught to focus on their limitations rather than their strengths. In therapy, a strengths-based approach can encourage clients to focus on their abilities and coping strategies (Russell & McNulty, 2011). This approach is particularly helpful for clients with Rejection Sensitivity Dysphoria (RSD) or Pathological Demand Avoidance (PDA), as it builds resilience and confidence in their unique capabilities. For neurodivergent individuals, focusing on abilities rather than deficits promotes a more empowered and affirming therapeutic experience.

Model Access and Communication Options

One significant barrier for neurodivergent individuals is accessing therapy in ways that suit their communication preferences. Many neurodivergent individuals struggle with phone calls, for instance, and prefer to book appointments online or communicate via email or voice notes (Jokinen et al., 2022). Offering these options—along with body doubling, collaborative form completion, and clear communication of boundaries—can create a more accessible and supportive therapeutic environment. Therapists should explicitly state the available communication options and clarify expectations to avoid misunderstandings.

Offer Advocacy Support

Therapists must advocate for neurodivergent clients' rights in all areas of life, including intimate relationships and sexual autonomy. Many neurodivergent individuals experience internalized ableism and shame, making it difficult to assert their desires or boundaries in intimate settings. Practitioners can support clients by providing resources and tools to help them navigate these challenges, including training in sexual self-advocacy and access to supportive communities. Additionally, therapists should be ready to challenge any institutional ableism or discrimination that clients may face in their daily lives.

Decolonize Neurodivergence

To truly support neurodivergent clients, it is essential to recognize the intersectionality of neurodivergence with other social identities, such as race, gender, sexuality, and class (Mackenzie et al., 2021). Historical and systemic oppression, particularly colonialism, has shaped how neurodivergent people are perceived and treated in different cultures. For example, in many Global South contexts, neurodivergent individuals may face not only cultural stigma but also gendered oppression and racial discrimination (Santos, 2014). Practitioners should engage with decolonial and intersectional frameworks to understand how these dynamics influence a client's experience of intimacy and sexuality. Providing culturally relevant and neuro-affirmative resources, including educational materials on neurodivergent conditions, is one practical way to foster greater acceptance and understanding.

Conclusion

In conclusion, this chapter has underscored the urgent need for a profound paradigm shift within psychosexual therapy, advocating for a more inclusive, culturally sensitive, and neuro-affirmative approach. Through the vignettes of individuals like Hiba, Mary, JT, and Mayukh, we have illustrated the diverse and often complex psychosexual issues faced by neurodivergent people in accessing therapeutic support. These narratives highlight critical barriers, including diagnostic disparities, access to care, communication challenges, societal stigma, and the unique psychosexual presentations of neurodivergent individuals. This exploration reveals a stark reality: existing therapeutic models frequently fail to accommodate the needs of neurodivergent people, often perpetuating epistemic injustice and further marginalizing these populations (Fricker, 2007).

The concept of epistemic injustice, as discussed earlier in this chapter, underscores how the voices and experiences of neurodivergent individuals—especially those from marginalized communities—are often invalidated or overlooked in the broader discourse on sexuality and mental health. In practice, this manifests as a significant gap in mental healthcare, leaving neurodivergent individuals with limited access to the psychosexual support they need to navigate their intimate relationships and sexual identities (Coady, 2017).

Moreover, this chapter emphasizes the necessity of moving beyond the medicalized and deficit-based views of neurodivergence toward a social model that affirms neurodiversity as a natural variation of human experience (Shakespeare, 2013). Such a shift requires systemic change at governmental, institutional, and societal levels. Educational institutions, healthcare providers, and regulatory bodies must revise their frameworks and practices to integrate a neuro-affirmative, anti-racist, and anti-ableist approach to neurodivergent individuals, recognizing the intersectionality of race, gender, class, and neurodivergence (Crenshaw, 1989). Research should continue to explore and validate the lived experiences of neurodivergent people, particularly within the context of psychosexual therapy, so that services can be designed to meet their unique needs (George & Stokes, 2018).

For practitioners, it is essential to adopt a client-centered approach that validates and recognizes the unique sensory and emotional experiences of neurodivergent individuals. By approaching therapy with a focus on strengths, individual preferences, and cultural relevance, therapists can better support neurodivergent clients in navigating psychosexual issues. This also includes challenging societal stigma, promoting neurodivergent rights, and integrating neurodiversity-affirming principles into therapy. Sensory sensitivities, impulse control issues, and different temporal experiences of sexuality, for example, must be acknowledged as integral aspects of the therapeutic process (Mundy & Sigman, 2006; Byers et al., 2013).

The urgency of this shift is further emphasized by the current global socio-political climate, where marginalized communities—especially neurodivergent individuals—continue to face systemic oppression and vulnerability (IARSCLCE,

2018). These individuals are often denied the opportunity to engage fully in societal life, including the experience of fulfilling and satisfying intimate relationships. As such, neurodivergent people remain at the intersection of multiple forms of oppression, both cultural and structural. By integrating neurodiversity-affirming approaches into psychosexual therapy, practitioners can contribute to a more equitable, inclusive, and just therapeutic landscape. This requires us, as therapists and practitioners, to challenge long-standing societal norms, build more neuro-inclusive frameworks, and ensure that neurodivergent individuals have the space and tools they need to understand and express their sexual identities with dignity, autonomy, and support.

As we move toward this transformative future, it is vital to embrace a more inclusive and culturally responsive approach to therapy. In doing so, we can begin to dismantle the barriers that have long denied neurodivergent individuals their right to experience fulfilling, meaningful, and authentic intimate lives. This approach will not only improve therapeutic outcomes but will also contribute to a broader societal shift that values and respects the diversity of human minds, bodies, and experiences.

References

Alhraiwil, N. J., Ali, A., Househ, M. S., Al-Shehri, A. M., & El-Metwally, A. A. (2015). Systematic review of the epidemiology of attention deficit hyperactivity disorder in Arab countries. *Neurosciences (Riyadh, Saudi Arabia)*, 20(2), 137–144. https://doi.org/10.17712/nsj.2015.2.20140678

Ayano, G., Yohannes, K., & Abraha, M. (2020). Epidemiology of attention-deficit/hyperactivity disorder (ADHD) in children and adolescents in Africa: A systematic review and meta-analysis. *Annals of General Psychiatry*, 19, 21. https://doi.org/10.1186/s12991-020-00271-w

Bambridge-Sutton, G. (2020, November 7). The problems facing autistic people in modern China. *Psychology Today*. www.psychologytoday.com/us/blog/politics-and-disability/202011/the-problems-facing-autistic-people-in-modern-china

Barkley, R. A. (Ed.). (2015). *Attention-deficit hyperactivity disorder: A handbook for diagnosis and treatment* (4th ed.). Guilford Press.

Bijlenga, D., Vroege, J. A., & Stammen, A. J. M. (2018). Prevalence of sexual dysfunctions and other sexual disorders in adults with attention-deficit/hyperactivity disorder compared to the general population. *ADHD Attention Deficit Hyperactivity Disorder*, 10, 87–96. https://doi.org/10.1007/s12402-017-0237-6

Bird, G., & Cook, R. (2013). Mixed emotions: The contribution of alexithymia to the emotional symptoms of autism. *Translational Psychiatry*, 3(7), e285. https://doi.org/10.1038/tp.2013.61

Blanchard, A., Wymbs, B. T., Marshall, A. D., & Ranson, L. M. (2022). Adult ADHD and intimate partner violence: A systematic review. *Journal of Attention Disorders*, 26(11), 1391–1410. https://doi.org/10.1177/10870547211073471

Botha, M. (2021). Academic, activist, or advocate? Angry, subjective and biased, or a voice for reform? Righting the ship of academic autism research. *Autism*, 25(8), 2127–2131. https://doi.org/10.1177/13623613211043744

Botha, M., & Frost, D. M. (2020). Extending the minority stress model to understand mental health problems experienced by the autistic population. *Society and Mental Health*, 10(1), 20–34. https://doi.org/10.1177/2153330X19826191

Brown, T. E. (2005). *Attention deficit disorder: The unfocused mind in children and adults*. Yale University Press.

Byers, E. S., Nichols, S., & Voyer, S. D. (2013). Challenging stereotypes: Sexual functioning of single adults with high functioning autism spectrum disorder. *Journal of Autism and Developmental Disorders*, 43(11), 2617–2627. https://doi.org/10.1177/1362361311431950

Chinese Autism. (2020). *Autism and Chinese culture*. Chinese Autism Community Interest Company. https://chineseautism.org.uk/autism-chinese-culture/

Chinawa, J. M., Ezeudu, C., Manyike, P. C., Obi, I. E., & Ujunwa, F. A. (2014). Prevalence of attention deficit hyperactivity disorder (ADHD) in Nigerian children: A systematic review. *Journal of Epidemiology*, 2014, 1–7. https://doi.org/10.1155/2014/694764

Coady, D. (2017). Epistemic injustice and distributive injustice. In M. Fricker & S. Kidd (Eds.), *The Routledge handbook of epistemic injustice* (pp. 77–89). Routledge. https://doi.org/10.4324/9781315212043-6

Costa, A. P., Loor, C., & Steffgen, G. (2020). Suicidality in adults with autism spectrum disorder: The role of depressive symptomatology, alexithymia, and antidepressants. *Journal of Autism and Developmental Disorders*, 50(10), 3585–3597. https://doi.org/10.1007/s10803-020-04433-3

Crenshaw, K. (1989). Demarginalizing the intersection of race and sex: A Black feminist critique of antidiscrimination doctrine, feminist theory and antiracist politics. *University of Chicago Legal Foum*, 1989, 139.

Cummings, S., Dhewa, C., Kemboi, G., & Young, S. (2023). Doing epistemic justice in sustainable development: Applying the philosophical concept of epistemic injustice to the real world. *Sustainable Development*, 31(3), 1965–1977. https://doi.org/10.1002/sd.2497

Fang, X., Massetti, G. M., Ouyang, L., Grosse, S. D., & Mercy, J. A. (2010). Attention-deficit/hyperactivity disorder, conduct disorder, and young adult intimate partner violence. *Archives of General Psychiatry*, 67(11), 1179–1186. https://doi.org/10.1001/archgenpsychiatry.2010.137

Fine, M., & McClelland, S. I. (2006). Sexuality education and desire: Still missing after all these years. *Harvard Educational Review*, 76(3), 297–338.

Fletcher-Watson, S., Adams, J., Brook, K., Charman, T., Crane, L., Cusack, J., ... & Pellicano, E. (2019). Making the future together: Shaping autism research through meaningful participation. *Autism*, 23(4), 943–953. https://doi.org/10.1177/1362361318786721

Franz, L., Chambers, N., von Isenburg, M., & de Vries, P. J. (2017). Autism spectrum disorder in sub-saharan Africa: A comprehensive scoping review. *Autism Research: Official Journal of the International Society for Autism Research*, 10(5), 723–749. https://doi.org/10.1002/aur.1766

Fricker, M. (2007). *Epistemic injustice: Power and the ethics of knowing*. Oxford University Press.

George, R., & Stokes, M. A. (2018). Sexual orientation in autism spectrum disorder. *Journal of Autism and Developmental Disorders*, 48(10), 3469–3477

Hancock, G., Stokes, M., & Mesibov, G. (2020). Differences in romantic relationship experiences for individuals with an autism spectrum disorder. *Sexuality and Disability*, 38(2), 231–145. https://doi.org/10.1007/s11195-019-09573-8

Henrich, J., Heine, S. J., & Norenzayan, A. (2010). The weirdest people in the world? *Behavioral and Brain Sciences*, 33(2–3), 61–83.

IARSCLCE. (2018). A brief guide to epistemic (in)justice. *Epistemic Justice*. https://epistemicjusticeiarslce2018.wordpress.com/a-brief-guide-to-epistemic-injustice-justice/

Jokinen, J., Wallin, L., & Dennhag, I. (2022). A systematic review of the relationship between neurodiversity and psychosexual functioning in individuals with autism spectrum disorder (ASD) or attention-deficit/hyperactivity disorder (ADHD). *Psychology & Sexuality*, 13(3), 567–584. https://doi.org/10.1080/19419899.2022.2043603

Kapoor, A. K. (2019, March 14–15). Comparison of autism awareness levels in the US and India [Poster presentation abstract]. In *European Autism Congress*, Zagreb, Croatia. Autism Open Access.

Kapp, S. K., Gillespie-Lynch, K., Sherman, L. E., & Hutman, T. (2013). Deficit, difference, or both? Autism and neurodiversity. *Developmental Psychology*, 49(1), 59–71.

Kellaher, D. C. (2015). Sexual behavior and autism spectrum disorders: An update and discussion. *Current Psychiatry Reports*, 17, 25. https://doi.org/10.1007/s11920-015-0562-4

Kelly, C. A., Kelly, C., & Taylor, R. (2024). Review of the psychosocial consequences of attention deficit hyperactivity disorder (ADHD) in females. *European Journal of Medical and Health Sciences*, 6(1), 10–20. https://doi.org/10.24018/ejmed.2024.6.1.2033

Kidd, J. D., Jackman, K. B., Barucco, R., Dworkin, J. D., Dolezal, C., Arbuckle, M. T., ... & Bockting, W. O. (2017). Understanding the intersection of gender identity, neurodiversity, and mental health outcomes. *Journal of Clinical Child & Adolescent Psychology*, 46(6), 841–854.

Klefsjö, U., Kantzer, A. K., Gillberg, C., & Billstedt, E. (2020). The road to diagnosis and treatment in girls and boys with ADHD – gender differences in the diagnostic process. *Nordic Journal of Psychiatry*, 75(4), 301–305. https://doi.org/10.1080/08039488.2020.1850859

Knies, K., Bodalski, E., & Flory, K. (2020). Romantic relationships in adults with ADHD: The effect of partner attachment style on relationship quality. *Journal of Social and Personal Relationships*, 38(1), 42–64. https://doi.org/10.1177/0265407520953898

Kudi, S. R., Khakha, D. C., Deb, K. S., Lata, K., & Kumar, H. (2023). Role of faith healers in the treatment of severe mental illness in India. *International Journal of Community Medicine and Public Health*, 10(12), 4774–4780. https://doi.org/10.18203/2394-6040.ijcmph20233778

Leekam, S. R., Nieto, C., Libby, S. J., Wing, L., & Gould, J. (2007). Describing the sensory abnormalities of children and adults with autism. *Journal of Autism and Developmental Disorders*, 37(5), 894–910. https://doi.org/10.1007/s10803-006-0218-7

Levy, A., & Perry, A. (2011). Outcomes in adolescents and adults with autism: A review of the literature. *Research in Autism Spectrum Disorders*, 5(4), 1271–1282. https://doi.org/10.1016/j.rasd.2011.01.023

Link, B. G., & Phelan, J. C. (2001). Conceptualizing stigma. *Annual Review of Sociology*, 27(1), 363–385. https://doi.org/10.1146/annurev.soc.27.1.363

Liu, K., Xu, Y., Yan, C., Deng, X., Li, T., & Jin, C. (2018). The prevalence of attention deficit/hyperactivity disorder among Chinese children and adolescents. *PloS One*, 13(8), e0201099.

Loomes, R., Hull, L., & Mandy, W. P. L. (2017). What is the male-to-female ratio in autism spectrum disorder? A systematic review and meta-analysis. *Journal of the American Academy of Child & Adolescent Psychiatry*, 56(6), 466–474. https://doi.org/10.1016/j.jaac.2017.03.013

Mackenzie, A., Russell, A. J., Shah, P., & Gaigg, S. B. (2021). Empathic accuracy and cognitive and affective empathy in young adults with and without autism spectrum disorder. *Journal of Autism and Developmental Disorders*, 52, 1–15. https://doi.org/10.1007/s10803-021-04936-w

Medina, J. (2013). *The epistemology of resistance: Gender and racial oppression, epistemic injustice, and resistant imaginations*. Oxford University Press. https://doi.org/10.1093/acprof:oso/9780199929023.001.0001

Meyer, I. H. (2003). Prejudice, social stress, and mental health in lesbian, gay, and bisexual populations: Conceptual issues and research evidence. *Psychological Bulletin*, 129(5), 674–697. https://doi.org/10.1037/0033-2909.129.5.674

Milton, D. (2022, June). Socially situating the lives of autistic people: The double-empathy problem [Seminar presentation]. ACRE – BPS Seminar Series, United Kingdom.

Mundy, P., & Sigman, M. (2006). Joint attention, social competence and developmental psychopathology. In D. Cicchetti & D. J. Cohen (Eds.), *Developmental psychopathology: Vol. 1. Theory and method* (2nd ed., pp. 293–332). John Wiley & Sons, Inc.

Olatunji, G., Faturoti, O., Jaiyeoba, B., Toluwabori, A. V., Adefusi, T., Olaniyi, P., Aderinto, N., & Abdulbasit, M. O. (2023). Navigating unique challenges and advancing equitable care for children with ADHD in Africa: A review. *Annals of Medicine and Surgery*, 85(10), 4939–4946. https://doi.org/10.1097/MS9.0000000000001179

Ousley, O. Y., & Mesibov, G. B. (1991). Sexual attitudes and knowledge of high-functioning adolescents and adults with autism. *Journal of Autism and Developmental Disorders*, 21(4), 471–481. https://doi.org/10.1007/BF02206871

Patel, V., Saxena, S., Lund, C., Thornicroft, G., Baingana, F., Bolton, P., Chisholm, D., Collins, P. Y., Cooper, J. L., Eaton, J., Herrman, H., Herzallah, M. M., Huang, Y., Jordans, M. J. D., Kleinman, A., Medina-Mora, M. E., Morgan, E., Omigbodun, O., Prince, M., . . . Wolpert, M. (2018). The Lancet Commission on global mental health and sustainable development. *The Lancet*, 392(10157), 1553–1598. https://doi.org/10.1016/S0140-6736(18)31612-X

Pelton, M. K., Crawford, H., Bul, K., Robertson, A. E., Adams, J., de Beurs, D., Rodgers, J., Baron-Cohen, S., & Cassidy, S. (2023). The role of anxiety and depression in suicidal thoughts for autistic and non-autistic people: A theory-driven network analysis. *Suicide & Life-Threatening Behavior*, 53(3), 426–442. https://doi.org/10.1111/sltb.12954

Popit, S., Serod, K., Locatelli, I., & Stuhec, M. (2024). Prevalence of attention-deficit hyperactivity disorder (ADHD): Systematic review and meta-analysis. *European Psychiatry*, 67(1), e68. https://doi.org/10.1192/j.eurpsy.2024.1786

Riquelme, I., Riquelme, P., & Mories, L. (2022). Association between Ehlers-Danlos syndrome, hypermobility spectrum disorders, and autism spectrum disorder: A systematic review. *Journal of Clinical Medicine*, 11(16), 4668.

Robin, A. L., & Payson, E. (2005). The impact of ADHD on marriage. *The ADHD Report*, 10(3), 9–14. https://doi.org/10.1521/adhd.10.3.9.20553

Russell, V. M., & McNulty, J. K. (2011). Frequent sex protects intimates from the negative implications of their neuroticism. *Social Psychological and Personality Science*, 2(2), 220–227. https://doi.org/10.1177/1948550610387165

Safiri, S., Mousavi, S. E., Nejadghaderi, S. A., Noori, M., Sullman, M. J. M., Amiri, S., & Kolahi, A.-A. (2023). The burden of attention-deficit hyperactivity disorder (ADHD) in the middle East and North Africa Region, 1990 to 2019. *Journal of Attention Disorders*, 27(13), 1433–1447. https://doi.org/10.1177/10870547231187161

Santos, B. de S. (2014). *Epistemologies of the South: Justice against epistemicide*. Paradigm Publishers.

Santos, S., Ferreira, H., Martins, J., Gonçalves, J., & Castelo-Branco, M. (2022). Male sex bias in early and late onset neurodevelopmental disorders: Shared aspects and differences in Autism Spectrum Disorder, Attention Deficit/hyperactivity Disorder, and Schizophrenia. *Neuroscience and Biobehavioral Reviews*, 135, 104577. https://doi.org/10.1016/j.neubiorev.2022.104577

Shakespeare, T. (2013). *Disability rights and wrongs revisited*. Routledge.

Skidmore, S. T. (2015). Cultural bias in the diagnosis of ADHD. *Journal of Attention Disorders*, 19(3), 203–215.

Song, P., Zha, M., Yang, Q., Zhang, Y., Li, X., & Rudan, I. (2021). The prevalence of adult attention-deficit hyperactivity disorder: A global systematic review and meta-analysis. *Journal of Global Health*, 11, 04009. https://doi.org/10.7189/jogh.11.04009

Strang, J. F., Kenworthy, L., Dominska, A., Sokoloff, J., Kuschner, E. S., Crissman, S., ... & Wallace, G. L. (2018). Increased gender variance/transgender identification in autism spectrum disorder. *Archives of Sexual Behavior*, 47(7), 2597–2606.

Strang, J. F., van der Miesen, A. I., Caplan, R., Hughes, C., Guy, L., Edwards-Leeper, L., Pleak, R. R., Spack, N., White, B. A., & Anthony, L. G. (2021). Both sides of the screen: A qualitative study of clinical care experiences of transgender and gender diverse autistic and/or ADHD youth and their parents. *Journal of Clinical Child & Adolescent Psychology*, 50(6), 841–854. https://doi.org/10.1080/15374416.2021.1965116

Strati, F., Cavalieri, D., Albanese, D., Fornasari, G., Pizza, F., De Giorgi, R., & Biagi, E. (2017). New evidences on the altered gut microbiota in autism spectrum disorders. *Microbiome*, 5(1), 24.

Sue, S., Zane, N., Nagayama Hall, G. C., & Berger, L. K. (2009). The role of culture and cultural techniques in psychotherapy: A critique and reformulation. *Asian American Journal of Psychology*, S(1), 3–14. https://doi.org/10.1037/1948-1985.S.1.3

Tervalon, M., & Murray-García, J. (1998). Cultural humility versus cultural competence: A critical distinction in defining physician training outcomes in multicultural education. *Journal of Health Care for the Poor and Underserved*, 9(2), 117–125. https://doi.org/10.1353/hpu.2010.0233

Titchkosky, T. (2007). *Reading resistance: Discourses of exclusion in desegregation and inclusion*. University of Toronto Press.

Turner, D., Briken, P., Schöttle, D. (2019). Sexual dysfunctions and their association with the dual control model of sexual response in men and women with high-functioning autism. *Journal of Clinical Medicine*, 8(4), 425. https://doi.org/10.3390/jcm8040425

Weaver, L. J., Karasz, A., Muralidhar, K., Jaykrishna, P., Krupp, K., Madhivanan, P. (2023). Will increasing access to mental health treatment close India's mental health gap? *SSM – Mental Health*, 3, 100184. https://doi.org/10.1016/j.ssmmh.2022.100184

Wijsen, L., Vlieger, A. M., Rommelse, N. N., Franke, B., & Hoekstra, P. J. (2021). Gastrointestinal problems in children and adolescents with attention-deficit/hyperactivity disorder: A systematic review. *European Child & Adolescent Psychiatry*, 30(7), 1017–1031.

Wong, J. P. H., & Moorhouse, A. (2021). Mental health and well-being of East Asian autistic adults: A scoping review. *Autism*, 25(8), 2147–2160. https://doi.org/10.1177/13623613211022241

Wymbs, B., Canu, W., Sacchetti, G., & Ranson, L. (2021). Adult ADHD and romantic relationships: What we know and what we can do to help. *Journal of Marital and Family Therapy*, 47(3), 664–681. https://doi.org/10.1111/jmft.12475

Yew, R. Y., Hooley, M., & Stokes, M. A. (2023). Factors of relationship satisfaction for autistic and non-autistic partners in long-term relationships. *Autism: The International Journal of Research and Practice*, 27(8), 13623613231160244. https://doi.org/10.1177/13623613231160244

Yew, R., Samuel, P., Hooley, M., Mesibov, G., & Stokes, M. (2021). A systematic review of romantic relationship initiation and maintenance factors in autism. *Personal Relationships*, 28(4), 777–802. https://doi.org/10.1111/pere.12397

Young, S., & Cocallis, K. (2023). A systematic review of the relationship between neurodiversity and psychosexual functioning in individuals with Autism spectrum disorder (ASD) or attention-deficit/hyperactivity disorder (ADHD). *Neuropsychiatric Disease and Treatment*, 19, 1379–1395. https://doi.org/10.2147/NDT.S319980

Zuckerman, K. E., Sinche, B., Mejia, A., Cobian, M., Becker, T., & Nicolaidis, C. (2014). Latino parents' perspectives on barriers to autism diagnosis. *Academic Pediatrics*, 14(3), 301–308. https://doi.org/10.1016/j.acap.2013.12.004

Zuckerman, K. E., Sinche, B., Mejia, A., Cobian, M., Becker, T., & Nicolaidis, C. (2015). Diagnosing autism spectrum disorder in Latino children: Guiding voices from parents. *Journal of Health Care for the Poor and Underserved*, 26(2), 527–547. https://doi.org/10.1353/hpu.2015.0061

Chapter 10

The Journey of Psychosexual Therapy from the Middle East to the West

Maha Nasrallah-Babenko

Introduction and Author Positionality

When I first began my formal training in London, completing a PhD in psychology while studying to become a psychosexual and relationship therapist, I did not anticipate how profoundly the process would reshape both my worldview and my practice. By that point I had already been living in London for three years, yet entering a structured program where sexuality, intimacy, and relationships were openly examined alongside peers from vastly different cultural and religious backgrounds pushed me into new terrain. I began to realize that many of the beliefs I had absorbed growing up in Beirut, even the ones I thought I had long rejected, still lingered quietly beneath the surface. Some of these views had been shaped by Lebanon's unique blend of progressiveness and tradition, where cosmopolitan openness coexists with deeply conservative attitudes about sexuality, gender, and family. Training in a multicultural environment forced me to see that certain judgments and assumptions I carried about myself and about others were not as neutral as I had once believed.

The exposure was both unsettling and deeply transformative. Being asked to confront personal biases in a professional setting sharpened my awareness of how unconscious beliefs can shape the therapy room. It became clear to me that cultural competence is not simply about memorizing facts about a given group but about cultivating a posture of humility and curiosity. I learned that listening deeply to clients' stories teaches far more than any textbook could, precisely because each client's experience is never identical to the stereotype of their culture, faith, or nationality. The therapeutic encounter required me to move past assumptions and into the more difficult but more rewarding practice of asking, waiting, and learning directly from the client in front of me.

This realization has continued to guide my journey as I have practiced across multiple cities and cultural contexts, from Beirut to Dubai and Abu Dhabi, and later in New York City, Southern California, and Colorado. Each of these settings brought its own cultural scripts, societal expectations, and legal restrictions around sex, intimacy, and identity. The shifts demanded constant adaptation, not only in therapeutic strategies but also in language, framing, and pacing. While

DOI: 10.4324/9781003611387-10

my professional role remained consistent, the way I could practice it responsibly changed according to the cultural and legal realities of each place. These experiences reinforced for me that psychosexual therapy cannot be lifted out of its social context. What works in one community might feel irrelevant, disrespectful, or even unsafe in another.

I approach the work today with a clear stance. My practice is client-centered, meaning that the client's voice and lived experience take priority over preconceived models. It is culturally responsive, recognizing that sexuality is inseparable from culture, faith, law, and family systems. It is rights-respecting, holding firmly to the principle that all people deserve safety, dignity, and the possibility of fulfilling sexual lives. This position is consistent with the World Health Organization's (2006) framing of sexual health as involving physical, emotional, mental, and social well-being in relation to sexuality. And it is trauma-informed, acknowledging that many clients carry histories of shame, fear, or direct harm that must be approached gently and without judgment.

In this chapter, I share lessons from my journey of practicing psychosexual therapy in the Middle East and the West. I begin with reflections on the limits of cultural assumptions and the importance of humility in therapeutic encounters. I then explore the nuances of arranged marriages and the common challenges couples face with unconsummated unions. I devote special attention to the treatment of vaginismus, an issue I encountered repeatedly across clients from conservative religious backgrounds, and reflect on how to adapt evidence-based care in culturally sensitive ways. From there, I expand to the broader themes of shame, sexual identity, and LGBTQ clients, showing both the differences and common threads that appear across cultural settings. Later sections discuss the practical and ethical challenges of doing this work in restrictive environments, including resource gaps, media dilemmas, and the scarcity of trained medical professionals. Finally, I reflect on what these experiences reveal about both the differences that divide cultures and the deep commonalities that bind us together as human beings seeking connection, safety, and love. It is important to note that the names of the clients and other details in the clinical vignettes presented in the chapter have been changed to protect the clients' identity.

Contexts and Contrasts: Practicing Across Cities and Systems

Working as a psychosexual therapist and coach/consultant across five very different regions—Beirut, Dubai and Abu Dhabi, New York City, Southern California, and Colorado—has meant entering into distinct legal frameworks, healthcare systems, and cultural climates. Each place shaped not only the concerns clients brought into therapy but also the therapeutic strategies that were possible, safe, and effective. At the same time, certain threads remained constant: shame, secrecy, and the longing for intimacy were present everywhere, even if expressed differently.

Beirut was where my roots lay and where I returned after my training in London. Lebanon's capital is at once cosmopolitan and traditional. There are pockets of great openness, particularly among younger urban populations, yet sexuality remains highly taboo in many families and religious communities. Homosexuality is criminalized under Article 534 of the Penal Code, although enforcement has become inconsistent in recent years. Premarital sex is often hidden, and sexual education in schools is minimal. In this environment, many clients sought therapy because they could not consummate their marriage, or because they were struggling with sexual pain, arousal, and other dysfunctions that had gone untreated for years. Many clients also sought therapy for premature ejaculation or erectile difficulties. Therapy-seeking was often kept secret, even from family members. Access to medical professionals who were supportive and informed about sexual health was inconsistent, which made referrals a challenge.

Dubai and Abu Dhabi presented another layer of complexity. The United Arab Emirates is highly international, with a large expatriate population and a modern healthcare system. Yet it is also governed by conservative laws and cultural norms. Extramarital sex is illegal, and LGBTQ identities remain heavily stigmatized and punishable under the law. Many of my clients were from South Asian or Middle Eastern backgrounds, often in arranged marriages where sexual inexperience was the norm. A significant number of women sought therapy for vaginismus, reflecting the deep cultural messages of shame, fear, and secrecy surrounding sex. Here, therapy often had to be carefully framed as medical or marital support rather than sexual exploration. Conversations about pleasure or desire were usually deferred until after couples were able to establish basic sexual function. At the same time, the thriving expatriate community meant that some clients were more comfortable speaking about intimacy and actively sought therapy for relationship enhancement.

New York City could not have been more different. In a city celebrated for diversity and openness, clients experienced a wide range of concerns: exploring kink and BDSM practices, navigating polyamory, improving communication, or simply seeking greater sexual satisfaction. The legal framework was permissive, and the healthcare system, while expensive, offered more specialist referrals and resources. LGBTQ clients were often more open, though they still carried the weight of family rejection or cultural stigma. Compared to the Middle East, where therapy was often about survival—overcoming pain, consummating marriage, or protecting safety—clients in New York were also interested in seeking to thrive, to deepen intimacy, or to expand the boundaries of their sexual expression.

Southern California brought another shift. The cultural climate was progressive, and many clients were open to integrating mindfulness, holistic health, and alternative healing into therapy. This openness to mindfulness-based work aligns with Brotto and Basson's (2014) findings that group mindfulness-based therapy can improve sexual desire and related aspects of sexual functioning in women. The proximity to academic institutions and sexual health networks provided rich referral possibilities, from medical doctors to pelvic floor specialists to sex-positive community groups. At the same time, the high cost of living and healthcare disparities meant that not all clients could access comprehensive care. Even in such an open environment, cultural and religious stigma persisted in some parts of the state where some families carried conservative messages about sex.

Colorado offered yet another contrast. While progressive in many areas, it also has strong pockets of conservatism. Clients here experience a mix of sexual challenges from sexual trauma to common sexual dysfunctions such as orgasmic difficulties or a mismatch in desire, and gender identity issues. For the most part, support and resources regarding sexuality are readily available in and around major cities.

Reflecting across these regions, what stands out most clearly is that the same conditions—vaginismus, erectile dysfunction, desire discrepancy, struggles with sexual identity—appeared everywhere. Atallah et al. (2016) similarly emphasize that ethical and sociocultural factors must be considered when assessing sexual function and dysfunction across diverse cultural contexts. What differed was how clients understood their struggles, how openly they could seek help, and which therapeutic strategies would feel safe and respectful. For example, in Dubai, I needed to frame body-based exercises in terms of overcoming fear and preparing for marriage, while in California, the same exercises could be introduced as tools for enhancing pleasure and intimacy. What remained constant was the necessity of cultural humility: never assuming that my professional expertise outweighed the client's lived reality, and always seeking to align therapy with their values, beliefs, and readiness.

Learning to See: Color-Racial Blindness, Bias, and Cultural Humility

Early in my career I learned how easily well-intentioned therapists can fall into the trap of assuming they "know" what a client's cultural or religious background means for their sexual life. This is a kind of color-racial blindness that can appear not only in relation to race but also in relation to culture, faith, and tradition. It happens when therapists overlook the impact of systemic prejudice or assume that cultural differences are irrelevant in the therapy room. Research has shown that multicultural and diversity training helps reduce these attitudes, which are measured by tools like the Color-Blind Racial Attitudes Scale (CoBRAS) (Neville et al., 2000). High scores on this scale reflect a denial of racial prejudice or an underestimation of structural racism, and by extension, they reflect a failure to notice how deeply inequality shapes people's intimate and relational lives.

What training taught me—and what clinical practice reinforced—is that cultural competence is not a static skill set that can be checked off once and for all.

Rather, it is a continuous process of cultural humility. This approach is consistent with Tervalon and Murray-García's (1998) distinction between cultural humility and cultural competence, where humility is understood as an ongoing process rather than a fixed achievement. Humility means staying curious, asking questions respectfully, and being open to having our assumptions corrected by the lived realities of the people we serve. It means recognizing that two clients from the same community can carry very different values, beliefs, and practices when it comes to sex and intimacy.

For example, before working with couples in Dubai, I assumed that arranged marriages always involved little to no choice for the partners. With time, I learned that many couples in such marriages do in fact have the opportunity to get to know each other and make a choice, even if within the framework of family guidance. This realization reminded me to suspend my own narratives and ask, instead, about the specific meanings a couple assigns to their relationship. What feels empowering to one client may feel restrictive to another, even within the same cultural tradition.

In psychosexual therapy, humility also requires the use of practical micro-skills. Rather than assuming that a Muslim couple avoids premarital sex, it is better to ask about how their faith informs their sexual choices and whether they feel aligned with or conflicted about those teachings. Instead of presuming that a client from a conservative background will find certain body-based exercises inappropriate, it is safer to check in about what feels acceptable, modest, or shame-inducing. Even the words we use—such as choosing "intimacy" or "marital closeness" instead of "sex" in some contexts—can make the difference between a client feeling understood or feeling alienated.

Therapists can also name their own positionality when relevant. Sharing with a client that I was raised in Beirut, or that I have worked across both Middle Eastern and Western contexts, sometimes helps open the door for them to clarify how their own experience may be similar or different. It signals that the therapy room is a place where complexity is welcome and assumptions are open to challenge.

Humility, then, is not about erasing cultural difference but about learning to see more clearly. It is about trading certainty for curiosity, stereotypes for respectful inquiry, and professional authority for collaboration (Table 10.1).

Arranged Marriages, Consent, and First-Night Expectations

Arranged marriages are often reduced in Western discourse to a single stereotype: two people who are forced into marriage without choice or voice. While forced marriage is a real and harmful phenomenon that must be named clearly, many arranged marriages include consent, gradual courtship, and genuine affection. In reality, there is wide variation in how families introduce potential spouses, how much autonomy young people have, and how much time is spent building a

Table 10.1 Curiosity-Forward Questions That Replace Assumptions

Area of exploration	*Curiosity-forward questions*	*Purpose in psychosexual therapy*
Religious Observance	"How does your faith or spirituality shape the way you think about intimacy?"	Allows client to define the role of religion in their sexual life instead of therapist assuming.
Family and Upbringing	"What messages about sex and relationships were most present in your home growing up?"	Brings forward early sexual scripts that may still shape present struggles.
Cultural Scripts	"In your community, what do people say a 'good partner' should be like? How does that fit or not fit with your own values?"	Identifies external pressures versus personal beliefs.
Comfort with Language	"Are there words for body parts or sexual activities that feel more comfortable for you to use here?"	Reduces shame and ensures respectful dialogue.
Gender and Roles	"How do you and your partner divide roles in your relationship? Do these roles feel chosen or expected?"	Explores gender dynamics without stereotyping.
Therapist Transparency	"I may not share your cultural background, but I want to understand what is most important for you. What should I know so that I can be respectful?"	Names therapist positionality and centers client expertise.

bond before marriage. What unites many of these unions, however, is the cultural expectation that penetrative intercourse will occur immediately after the wedding ceremony. This expectation, often unspoken but deeply ingrained, creates enormous pressure on couples who have had little or no prior sexual experience.

For therapists, it is essential to hold the nuance. Arranged marriage itself is not inherently pathological, and many couples in arranged marriages enjoy strong partnerships. What often causes distress is the script that demands immediate consummation, regardless of readiness, knowledge, or emotional comfort. Simon and Gagnon's (1986) concept of sexual scripts is useful for understanding how cultural expectations shape what clients believe sex should mean, when it should occur, and how partners should perform. This script is intensified for women who have been taught that their virginity is the family's honor, and that they must endure pain or fear on their wedding night. The psychological burden of these expectations is often compounded by silence, shame, and lack of sexual education.

Vignette 1: Inaya and Abdul

Inaya and Abdul were a young couple I met in Dubai. Their families had introduced them, and after several months of getting to know each other, they chose to marry. By the time they arrived in therapy, they had been married for eight months and were still unable to consummate their relationship. Inaya experienced severe vaginismus, while Abdul struggled with erectile difficulties fueled by performance anxiety. Neither had received any meaningful sexual education, and both felt they were failing at something that "should" be natural and effortless.

As we worked together, it became clear that Inaya was deeply fearful of penetration, while Abdul internalized the belief that his masculinity depended on sexual performance. Both carried the heavy weight of the first-night expectation: that intercourse was mandatory, immediate, and the ultimate proof of a successful marriage. Therapy involved reframing this script. Instead of focusing on intercourse as the measure of success, we emphasized communication, gradual exploration, and mutual consent. Inaya was introduced to body-awareness and relaxation exercises that did not begin with genital touch but instead with simple practices of breath and grounding. Abdul learned strategies to manage anxiety and began to see himself not as a failure but as a supportive partner in a shared journey. Over time, they were able to shift their goal from "proving" marriage through intercourse to cultivating intimacy at their own pace (Table 10.2).

Table 10.2 Cultural Scripts Often Encountered Around Marriage and Sex

Cultural script	*Common client experience*	*Therapist response*
"Sex must happen on the wedding night."	Pressure, fear, and traumatic first experiences.	Normalize pacing, reframe intimacy as a process, validate consent at every step.
"Pain is normal for women at the beginning."	Endurance of distress, silence about vaginismus or dyspareunia.	Provide psychoeducation that pain is not inevitable, introduce body-based interventions.
"A man's value lies in sexual performance."	Erectile difficulties, anxiety, feelings of failure.	Reframe masculinity around care, patience, and emotional presence.
"Virginity is proof of family honor."	Guilt, fear, and secrecy around premarital sexual experiences.	Explore impact of these beliefs, separate personal identity from imposed values.
"Sex is only for reproduction."	Limited exploration of desire or pleasure.	Expand definitions of sexuality, introduce concepts of intimacy and mutual satisfaction.

Holding these scripts in awareness allows therapists to respect cultural contexts while also protecting safety, autonomy, and wellbeing. This is not about erasing tradition, but about creating space for couples to experience intimacy as consensual and life-enhancing rather than pressured and traumatic.

Sexual Pain and Unconsummated Marriage: Evidence-Based Care

Across much of the Middle East and South Asia, unconsummated marriage is one of the most frequent reasons couples seek psychosexual therapy. In clinical practice, it is striking how often these cases are linked to vaginismus or what the DSM-5 now refers to as Genito-Pelvic Pain/Penetration Disorder (GPPPD) (American Psychiatric Association, 2022). The American College of Obstetricians and Gynecologists (2019) similarly emphasizes that female sexual dysfunction requires careful clinical assessment and management rather than reduction to a single physical or psychological cause. Women from conservative or religious backgrounds are particularly vulnerable because they grow up with little or no sexual education, are taught that sex is shameful or dangerous, and are expected to have penetrative intercourse immediately after marriage.

Prevalence estimates vary, but several studies suggest that vaginismus is significantly more common in Arab and South Asian populations compared to Western clinical samples. In Turkey, for example, rates of vaginismus among women presenting with sexual dysfunction have been reported as high as 42% (Doğan et al., 2009). Similar findings appear across clinical discussions of unconsummated marriage, where vaginismus and erectile difficulties are frequently reported as major contributing factors (Krishnappa et al., 2024). Although epidemiological data is still limited, the high demand for treatment highlights an urgent need for culturally sensitive, evidence-based care. Kurban et al. (2021) further highlight the psychological dimensions of vaginismus treatment and the need to address associated emotional factors rather than relying only on physical explanations.

Differentials in Sexual Pain

It is essential to differentiate between vaginismus, dyspareunia, and other causes of sexual pain. Bergeron et al. (2015) also frame female sexual pain disorders as multifactorial conditions shaped by biomedical, psychological, relational, and interpersonal factors. Dyspareunia can stem from medical factors such as infections, dermatological conditions, endometriosis, or hormonal changes, while vaginismus is primarily characterized by involuntary tightening of the pelvic floor muscles in anticipation of penetration, often rooted in fear and avoidance (Reissing et al., 2003). Pukall et al. (2016) define vulvodynia as a prevalent and impactful genital pain condition, further supporting the need to distinguish it from vaginismus and other penetration-related disorders. Misdiagnosis is common, and women are frequently subjected to unnecessary procedures, including hymenectomy, which does little to address the underlying psychosexual and fear-avoidance mechanisms.

Vignette 2: Haifa

Haifa was a 26-year-old woman from Saudi Arabia who came to therapy after two years of marriage without consummation. She described a deep fear of penetration, and even the thought of touching her genitals caused shame and panic. Her husband was supportive, but the couple both carried the burden of family expectations and social pressure. Initially, Haifa could not even bring herself to look at her vulva.

The therapeutic work began not with sexual pleasure exercises but with safety training. I framed each step not as an attempt to "perform" sexually, but as a way for her nervous system to learn that her body could be approached without harm. We started with grounding exercises, guided relaxation, and simple hand placement over clothing. Over time, Haifa was able to progress to mirror work, external touch, and eventually the gradual use of dilators. Goldfinger et al. (2019) further support the use of structured, gradual dilator therapy as part of treatment for sexual pain conditions. Her husband participated by practicing communication and supportive touch outside of penetrative goals. This reframing helped shift the meaning of therapy away from shame and toward healing.

Vignette 3: Shayna

Shayna, an Orthodox Jewish woman from New York, came to therapy with nearly identical fears, despite her very different background. Like Haifa, she had received little sexual education and was expected to have intercourse on her wedding night. The attempt left her traumatized, with severe pain and bleeding, and she avoided further intimacy. What stood out was how similar her fears, guilt cycles, and body responses were to the Muslim women I had worked with in the Gulf.

Her journey followed a similar progression: body mapping, gentle desensitization, and gradual exposure framed as safety rather than pleasure. While the cultural context differed—Shayna's community pressures were couched in Jewish law rather than Islamic norms—the underlying dynamics were remarkably alike. These parallels highlight how sexual shame, silence, and lack of education can transcend religious and national boundaries.

Critique of Non-Evidence-Based Interventions

One of the most troubling patterns I observed in the Gulf was the routine recommendation of hymenectomy for women with vaginismus. The assumption was that a "tight hymen" caused penetration difficulties, and that surgical removal would resolve the problem. In reality, most women continued to experience pain and fear after the procedure, because the underlying phobic response and muscle tension

Table 10.3 Myths and Evidence in Vaginismus Care

Myth	*Evidence-based understanding*	*Therapist response*
"The hymen is too tight, it must be cut."	Hymenal rigidity rarely causes vaginismus. The problem lies in fear and pelvic floor tension.	Provide psychoeducation, discourage unnecessary surgery, focus on exposure and relaxation.
"Pain is normal for women in the beginning."	Pain is not inevitable and can signal dysfunction. Early painful experiences often worsen vaginismus.	Normalize pleasure as possible and desirable, validate that pain is not a necessary part of intimacy.
"She just needs to relax and try harder."	Vaginismus is a conditioned fear response, not a matter of willpower.	Teach evidence-based desensitization strategies, avoid blame.
"It is purely psychological."	Psychological, relational, and physiological factors interact. Pelvic floor dysfunction may play a role.	Adopt a biopsychosocial model and refer to physiotherapy if indicated.
"Vaginismus only happens in conservative cultures."	It occurs globally, though prevalence may be higher in contexts of silence and shame.	Acknowledge universal vulnerability, while adapting care to cultural context.

were never addressed. These women not only carried the trauma of an invasive and unnecessary surgery, but also the disappointment of continued sexual dysfunction.

Evidence-based care makes it clear that vaginismus is best treated through a biopsychosocial approach that includes education, gradual exposure, pelvic floor relaxation, and involvement of the partner when appropriate (Pacik, 2011; ter Kuile et al., 2007). The International Consultation on Sexual Medicine (2015) also recommends careful diagnosis and multidisciplinary management of sexual pain disorders. Morin et al. (2017) further support the role of pelvic floor physical therapy within multidisciplinary care for provoked vestibulodynia and related sexual pain presentations. The International Consultation on Sexual Medicine (2015) also recommends careful diagnosis and multidisciplinary management of sexual pain disorders. Medical co-management may be needed to rule out organic causes of pain, but therapy should avoid pathologizing or retraumatizing clients (Table 10.3).

Shared Roots of Shame Across Religions and Cultures

One of the most striking realizations from working across different regions is how shame, secrecy, and moral judgment around sexuality transcend religious, cultural, and geographic boundaries. At first glance, it might seem that Muslim, Jewish, and

Christian clients present very different stories about sexual struggles. The rituals, vocabulary, and teachings may differ, but underneath, there is a remarkable similarity: people raised in conservative traditions often internalize messages that sex is dangerous, sinful, or purely for procreation, and that desire is something to be suppressed.

These messages shape not only behavior but also emotional and physical responses. When sexual contact is attempted, especially within the context of marriage, individuals may experience anxiety, guilt, or fear that blocks arousal or makes intimacy painful. For some, these early experiences create a lifelong association between sex and danger.

Vignette 4: Mark

Mark was a man in his forties who grew up in a small Christian community in the American Midwest. He presented to therapy with delayed ejaculation that had persisted throughout his marriage. At first, he described the problem in purely functional terms: he was frustrated that he could not climax with his wife, even though he could during masturbation.

As we explored further, Mark shared that his upbringing was filled with subtle but powerful shaming messages about sex. Whenever the topic arose, his parents would respond with disgust or avoidance, reinforcing the idea that sexual thoughts were dirty. In his church community, sex was framed strictly as something a woman does for her husband, not as an act of shared pleasure. He carried an unspoken conflict between his natural curiosity about sex and the heavy moral codes of his upbringing.

Over time, it became clear that his delayed ejaculation was not simply a medical or functional issue but a manifestation of deep internal conflict. His desires often involved scenarios that went against what he had been taught was acceptable, and his body responded with inhibition when those feelings arose in the marital bed. Therapy focused on helping him untangle these layers of shame and repression, slowly introducing the idea that desire itself was not inherently sinful. This process required a careful balance: respecting Mark's religious values and sense of morality while also making space for him to explore authentic expressions of sexuality.

Cross-Cultural Similarities

What was striking about Mark's story is how similar it felt to the narratives I had heard in Beirut, Dubai, or from Orthodox Jewish women in New York. While the cultural language differs, the underlying emotional experience often echoes the same themes: fear of divine punishment, fear of bringing shame to the family, or fear of being "dirty" if one expresses sexual desire. Whether it is a Muslim woman terrified on her wedding night, an Orthodox Jewish bride overwhelmed by the expectation of intercourse, or a Christian man paralyzed by guilt about his fantasies, the common thread is the moral framing of sexuality as something that must be tightly controlled.

These similarities do not erase the differences. Each faith tradition contains its own complexities, interpretations, and lived realities. In Islam, concepts like modesty and honor shape sexual narratives; in Judaism, laws around family purity add structure to marital intimacy; in Christianity, teachings on chastity and gender roles can heavily influence expectations. Therapists must be careful not to flatten these differences into a single universal story. Yet acknowledging the shared emotional burden of shame helps clients feel less alone and creates a bridge of empathy across cultural divides.

Pacing Conversations About Pleasure

A lesson I learned repeatedly is that introducing pleasure into the therapeutic conversation must be paced according to the client's readiness, values, and safety. For some, beginning therapy with an emphasis on sexual enjoyment would feel overwhelming, inappropriate, or even threatening. With women like Haifa or Shayna, who were terrified of even touching their bodies, the first task was not to talk about pleasure but to help them feel safe.

The same applied with Mark. Directly encouraging him to pursue fantasies that conflicted with his beliefs would have backfired, reinforcing his shame. Instead, therapy began with validating his faith and moral framework, while gently inviting curiosity about whether desire could coexist with his values. Only after trust and safety were established could we shift toward discussions of pleasure as a legitimate and meaningful part of intimacy.

This gradual, client-led pacing is crucial. It prevents retraumatization, respects cultural and religious frameworks, and ultimately leads to more sustainable therapeutic change.

LGBTQ Clients Across Legal and Cultural Ecologies

When working with LGBTQ clients, the legal and cultural environment they live in profoundly shapes both their presenting concerns and the therapeutic process. A man in Beirut questioning his sexuality faces very different risks than a man in London or Los Angeles. Yet their inner struggles often share common threads: fear of rejection, fear of losing family ties, and fear of living a life that does not align with who they truly are.

In restrictive contexts, homosexuality may be criminalized, or at the very least heavily stigmatized. ILGA World (2023) documents the continuing global variation in laws affecting LGBTQ people, making legal context a central consideration in therapeutic safety planning. Clients from these environments frequently enter therapy with high levels of fear and secrecy. Their concerns are not simply about identity but about survival: whether they will be arrested, ostracized, or disowned if their sexual orientation or gender identity is revealed. Meyer's (2003) minority stress model is useful here because it explains how prejudice, stigma, concealment, and social stress can harm the mental health of lesbian, gay, and bisexual clients. In permissive contexts, where legal protections exist, fear does not disappear. It shifts toward internalized shame, family rejection, or difficulty reconciling long-held beliefs with emerging desires. In both settings, the therapist becomes a vital safe space, often the only place where the client can speak openly about their sexuality.

Vignette 5: Matthew

Matthew was a middle-aged man from the United Kingdom who had been married for over twenty years when he first entered therapy. On the surface, he and his wife sought support to address growing distance in their marriage. As we worked together, Matthew began to share more about himself. With time, he disclosed that he had always been attracted to men but had suppressed these desires throughout his life. He explained that growing up in a conservative environment during the 1970s, being open about his sexuality felt impossible. Marriage to a woman seemed like the only acceptable path.

Now, decades later, the strain of repression had become too heavy. Therapy provided him a confidential, non-judgmental space to explore what it might mean to honor his attraction to men while still caring for his wife and children. For Matthew, the challenge was not only about whether to come out, but about how to live authentically without causing undue harm to the people he loved. His situation reflected the complexity many LGBTQ clients face: the negotiation of personal truth against relational and societal obligations.

Ethical Care in Restrictive Environments

Cases like Matthew's take on added weight in countries where homosexuality is criminalized or culturally condemned. Clients there may not even feel safe to name their desires. The therapist's role is not to encourage disclosure in unsafe contexts but to help the client weigh risks carefully and develop safety plans if needed.

A cornerstone of ethical care is refusing to participate in any form of conversion therapy. The United Nations Human Rights Council (2020) similarly identifies so-called conversion therapy as a harmful practice that raises serious human-rights concerns. The American Psychological Association (2009) likewise rejects efforts to change sexual orientation and emphasizes ethical, affirmative responses to clients experiencing distress around sexuality. Requests for such interventions sometimes emerge in restrictive contexts where clients feel torn between their religious or cultural values and their sexuality. While empathy for this inner conflict is crucial, therapists must remain clear that sexual orientation is not a disorder to be treated. The task instead is to support the client in finding realistic pathways to safety, authenticity, and self-acceptance within the constraints of their environment.

Confidentiality becomes paramount. Therapists must consider how notes are kept, how telehealth sessions are secured, and how records might be accessed by authorities. At times, referral to specialized support networks or discreet community groups may provide clients with the sense of belonging they cannot find in their immediate surroundings. In particularly high-risk contexts, therapists may need regular supervision to process the ethical dilemmas and emotional weight of the work.

Practical Strategies for Supporting LGBTQ Clients

- **Confidentiality and Documentation:** Keep records minimal, focusing on therapeutic goals without unnecessary detail that could endanger the client if disclosed.
- **Safety Planning:** Explore what might happen if family or community members discover the client's sexuality, and identify safe responses in advance.
- **Telehealth Privacy:** Use secure platforms and confirm that the client is in a safe physical space before discussing sensitive topics.
- **Informed Consent:** Be transparent about the limits of confidentiality, particularly in regions where therapists may be compelled to report certain disclosures.
- **Supervision and Peer Support:** Seek guidance when navigating ethical gray zones, especially when client safety and cultural respect seem in tension.
- **Community Resources:** Where possible, connect clients to LGBTQ-affirming organizations, even if only virtually, to reduce isolation and build resilience (Table 10.4). For transgender and gender-diverse clients, WPATH (2022) provides standards of care that reinforce the importance of affirming, individualized, and ethically grounded support.

Speaking in Public: Media and Education in Conservative Environments

In conservative cultural contexts, media engagement can be both an opportunity and a minefield for psychosexual therapists. On the one hand, public platforms allow therapists to normalize conversations about intimacy, dispel harmful myths, and reach individuals who may never seek therapy in private. On the other hand, each word is scrutinized not only for its content but for its potential to challenge entrenched religious or cultural values.

When I appeared on Arab television programs, for example, it was not possible to use the Arabic equivalent of the word "sex." Instead, I would refer to "intimacy" or "marital life," terms that were palatable to the audience and still conveyed essential meaning. The choice of language is not a superficial adjustment. It represents a delicate balance between providing accurate sexual health education and respecting cultural sensibilities. It also acknowledges the therapist's personal safety, since speaking too directly about prohibited or taboo topics can invite not only criticism but also threats.

Table 10.4 Ethical Decision Points With LGBTQ Clients in Restrictive Contexts

Ethical domain	*Therapist considerations*
Confidentiality	Minimize record detail; clarify limits of privacy with client; protect session notes.
Documentation	Use neutral language in files; avoid labels that could expose client if records are read.
Telehealth Privacy	Ensure secure platforms; confirm physical privacy before sensitive discussions.
Risk and Safety Planning	Discuss potential exposure scenarios; co-create safe responses and contingency plans.
Referral Options	Identify discreet, affirming networks or online communities where possible.
Conversion Therapy Requests	Validate client distress but decline to provide; reframe focus to safety and self-worth.
Supervision and Support	Regularly process ethical dilemmas with peers or supervisors to avoid isolation.

This dilemma extends to social media. In societies where homosexuality is illegal or where women's sexual autonomy is tightly controlled, posts about sexual rights or pleasure can be misinterpreted as advocacy for behaviors that are culturally condemned. A therapist might fear being accused of "promoting" homosexuality or encouraging immorality, despite providing only evidence-based information. Preparing for this possibility requires careful planning: clarifying one's intent, using disclaimers when needed, and being selective about which topics to introduce first.

A common strategy is sequencing sensitive content. Early efforts may focus on safer subjects such as relationship communication, the importance of consent, or managing anxiety in intimacy. As trust grows and audiences demonstrate readiness, more sensitive issues such as sexual orientation or gender identity may be addressed, often framed in terms of compassion and health rather than politics.

Even with preparation, backlash is possible. Misinterpretation is almost inevitable when messages travel across diverse communities with different levels of comfort and understanding. Anticipating negative responses, developing a crisis plan, and having supportive networks in place are crucial for therapists who engage in public education. Speaking in public about sexuality in conservative environments is not simply about wording. It is about embodying cultural humility, protecting oneself, and finding ways to keep important conversations alive without causing harm.

Resource Gaps and Interprofessional Collaboration

Beyond the media landscape, another pressing challenge in conservative regions is the lack of accessible resources for sexual health. Therapists may have the skills and knowledge to support clients, but without proper tools and referral options, progress is limited. Pascoal and Raposo (2023) are relevant here because they discuss how sexual problems are managed by other professionals, reinforcing the need for coordinated referral pathways and interprofessional collaboration.

Books on sexual health are often difficult to access, either because they are not translated into local languages or because importing them is restricted. Online purchasing may not be feasible, and even when possible, clients may fear family members discovering their orders. Something as simple as recommending a self-help text becomes complicated by these realities.

The scarcity of medical devices and therapeutic tools is equally challenging. Vaginal dilators, which are central to evidence-based treatment for vaginismus, may be nearly impossible to obtain in some regions. In certain countries, sex toys are criminalized, and even lubricants can be unavailable or of poor quality. Some clients resort to underground markets, which expose them to unsafe or overpriced products, while others wait until they travel abroad to purchase what they need. Therapists often find themselves coaching clients through creative yet safe alternatives, always balancing practicality with safety.

Perhaps the most serious barrier lies in interprofessional collaboration. In many Middle Eastern or South Asian settings, gynecologists, urologists, and general practitioners receive little to no training in sexual health. Female clients, in particular, face dismissive or harmful medical care. For example, some women with vaginismus are advised to undergo hymenectomy under the mistaken belief that a "tight hymen" causes their pain. Not only is this procedure ineffective for most cases, but it can also retraumatize clients and reinforce the belief that their bodies are defective. Male clients with erectile difficulties may be told to simply "relax" or are given medications without psychological assessment, ignoring the relational or anxiety-based contributors.

The responsibility for psychosexual therapists is twofold: first, to build a vetted referral network of providers who understand or are at least open to learning about sexual health, and second, to advocate for clients within the medical system when necessary. This may mean writing referral letters that explain the psychological dimensions of a condition, documenting harmful medical advice, or gently educating a physician about evidence-based approaches. Over time, these collaborations can begin to create pockets of competence within otherwise underprepared health systems.

For clients who relocate to or from different regions, building cross-border referral ecosystems can be lifesaving. A woman starting vaginismus therapy in Dubai may later move to Canada or the UK, and continuity of care depends on her therapist's ability to connect her with qualified professionals abroad. Similarly, diaspora communities may return to home countries during visits, seeking therapists who understand both their cultural context and modern treatment pathways.

Interprofessional collaboration is not a luxury in psychosexual therapy. It is a necessity. Without it, clients are left to navigate fragmented systems that often perpetuate harm. By actively networking, advocating, and educating, therapists can extend the reach of their work beyond the therapy room, ensuring clients receive comprehensive and compassionate care across disciplines and borders.

A Practice Framework for Culturally Sensitive Psychosexual Therapy

One of the key lessons from working across such varied settings is that there can be no single template for psychosexual therapy. Each case requires flexibility, cultural awareness, and a willingness to hold space for values that may differ significantly from the therapist's own. Still, certain principles can guide the work and provide structure, even in environments that feel uncertain or constrained.

Assessment with Cultural Depth

The starting point is always assessment, but in cross-cultural psychosexual work, assessment must go beyond medical history or sexual function checklists. It requires careful inquiry into cultural context, religious meaning, acculturation experiences, and personal safety. Questions about how sexuality was taught in childhood, what role religion plays now, and what expectations are tied to marriage or partnership can uncover powerful influences on presenting difficulties. Elements from the Cultural Formulation Interview (American Psychiatric Association, 2022) are especially helpful, such as asking clients to describe their own understanding of the problem and how their community views it.

Collaborative Goal Setting

Goal setting must always be collaborative, but in multicultural contexts, it is essential that goals align with the client's values. A woman who sees dilator work as "masturbation" may not accept pleasure as a goal, but she may be motivated by the desire to reduce pain or to experience closeness with her spouse. Respecting this distinction is not about avoiding conversations on pleasure forever but about meeting the client where she is.

Interventions with Flexibility

Once goals are set, interventions can be flexed to fit modesty, privacy, and pacing needs. Communication training can be tailored for couples who have never spoken openly about intimacy. Intimacy scaffolding may begin with non-sexual touch exercises before progressing toward sexual contact. Trauma-informed graded exposure is especially relevant in cases of vaginismus or delayed ejaculation, where fear and shame underlie the symptoms. Partner involvement can be transformative, but in some contexts, individual work is safer until trust is established.

Documentation and Ethics in High-Risk Settings

In restrictive environments, documentation requires special care. Therapists must weigh the need for accurate records with the potential risks if notes were subpoenaed or accidentally disclosed. Using neutral clinical language while ensuring continuity of care is one practical strategy. Confidentiality, informed consent, and careful discussion of risks are not optional—they are the foundation of ethical practice when the stakes for clients can include family rejection, reputational damage, or even legal consequences.

This framework does not promise easy answers. Instead, it offers a way of thinking that prioritizes cultural respect, clinical rigor, and human dignity, regardless of setting.

Consolidated Clinical Vignettes

The five case examples described earlier illustrate how cultural sensitivity plays out in practice.

- **Inaya and Abdul** showed that arranged marriages are not always forced or loveless, and that therapy for unconsummated marriage required addressing both vaginismus and performance anxiety while respecting the couple's bond.
- **Haifa** highlighted the importance of pacing exercises in a way that did not trigger shame, framing them as medical treatment for safety rather than pleasure.
- **Shayna** demonstrated how similar fears and scripts can appear across very different cultures, with Orthodox Jewish and Muslim women echoing one another's struggles with guilt and sexual pain.
- **Mark** illustrated how repression and shame that we sometimes see in a strict Christian upbringing could contribute to developing delayed ejaculation, reminding us that conservative sexual scripts are not bound by geography.
- **Matthew** offered a glimpse into the hidden lives of LGBTQ clients, whose safety and self-acceptance depend heavily on legal and cultural contexts. His case reminded us of the need for safety planning, confidentiality, and compassion in guiding clients through identity disclosure and relational transitions.

What carried across all these stories was the power of shame, secrecy, and silence to generate distress, and the ability of culturally sensitive, client-centered therapy to open doors toward safety and healing. What differed was the language used, the pacing of interventions, and the ethical considerations shaped by local laws and norms.

Training, Supervision, and Therapist Sustainability

Culturally responsive psychosexual therapy does not happen by accident. It requires intentional training, ongoing supervision, and active self-reflection.

Cultural Humility as a Lifelong Discipline

Therapists cannot expect to "master" cultural competence, because culture itself is dynamic and each client's experience is unique. What can be cultivated is cultural humility: a stance of curiosity, openness, and willingness to learn from clients rather than assuming expertise. This requires constant self-examination and an acceptance that mistakes will happen, paired with the courage to repair them.

Supervision for Countertransference and Moral Distress

Working across value systems often stirs up strong countertransference. A therapist may feel anger at oppressive norms, grief at the suffering of LGBTQ clients, or helplessness when medical colleagues perpetuate harm. Without supervision, these feelings can erode empathy and lead to burnout. Supervision provides a space to process moral distress, examine biases, and strengthen the capacity to stay grounded with clients.

Protecting Therapist Safety

In regions where open discussion of sexuality can provoke backlash, therapists themselves can be at risk. Engaging in media or public education requires careful preparation, risk assessment, and support networks. Therapists should never feel pressured to take risks they are not comfortable with. Protecting one's own safety is not only valid but necessary for sustaining the work long-term.

Training Modules for the Next Generation

Formal training programs should include structured modules on cross-cultural psychosexual therapy. These should cover global perspectives on sexuality, legal and ethical dilemmas, strategies for working in resource-limited settings, and tools for navigating stigma. Case-based learning, including exposure to stories like Inaya, Haifa, Shayna, Mark, and Matthew, can help trainees grapple with the complexities they will face in practice.

Sustainability in this work means more than preventing burnout. It means cultivating resilience, grounding practice in ethical clarity, and maintaining faith in the transformative power of therapy. When therapists continue learning, seek supervision, and protect their own well-being, they are better equipped to accompany clients through some of the most vulnerable and courageous journeys of their lives.

Conclusion

Looking back across my journey as a psychosexual therapist and coach, from Beirut to Dubai, Abu Dhabi, London, New York, Southern California, and Colorado, I am struck most by how much sameness lies beneath what appear at first to be stark differences. Every setting had its own cultural scripts about marriage, sexuality, and gender. Every community had its own boundaries about what could and could not be spoken aloud. And yet, in the therapy room, clients revealed needs that were profoundly similar: the need to feel safe in their own bodies, the need to connect deeply with their partners, and the longing to be accepted without shame.

Working across cultures has taught me that difference matters. The words we use, the pace at which we introduce therapeutic exercises, and the kinds of goals we set must all be aligned with the client's cultural, religious, and social reality. It is never enough to apply evidence-based methods without adaptation. At the same time, sameness matters too. Shame, secrecy, fear, and longing are not confined to one faith or one region. Recognizing these shared threads helps us to normalize struggles while still honoring cultural distinctions.

For psychosexual therapy to truly serve diverse populations, three commitments must travel together. This commitment also aligns with the World Association for Sexual Health's (2014) declaration that sexual rights are grounded in dignity, equality, privacy, and freedom from violence and discrimination.

The first is **cultural humility**: an openness to being taught by clients, a willingness to suspend assumptions, and an understanding that culture is dynamic, not fixed. The second is **ethical clarity**: a steadfast refusal to collude with harmful practices such as conversion therapy, a commitment to confidentiality and safety, and a respect for universal human rights even in restrictive environments. The third is **evidence-based practice**: ensuring that interventions are grounded in research and clinical knowledge, whether that means rejecting unnecessary hymenectomies, using trauma-informed graded exposure for vaginismus, or scaffolding intimacy communication in couples.

The path forward requires more than individual therapists adapting to their clients. It calls for building **regional capacity** so that culturally sensitive, rights-affirming sexual health services are available within communities rather than only in large metropolitan centers or Western countries. It requires partnerships with medical colleagues, educators, policymakers, and community leaders to create ecosystems where sexual health can be addressed safely, respectfully, and effectively.

If there is one lesson I hope readers will carry from this chapter, it is that psychosexual therapy is never simply about sex. It is about human dignity, cultural respect, and the courage to accompany clients as they navigate the most intimate intersections of body, belief, and identity. Whether in Beirut or Colorado, the task remains the same: to offer safety, to honor values, to bring evidence to bear, and to help people reclaim their right to intimacy, pleasure, and connection.

References

American College of Obstetricians and Gynecologists. (2019). Female sexual dysfunction. *ACOG Practice Bulletin No. 213.*

American Psychiatric Association. (2022). *Diagnostic and statistical manual of mental disorders* (5th ed., text rev.; DSM-5-TR). American Psychiatric Publishing.

American Psychological Association. (2009). *Report of the APA task force on appropriate therapeutic responses to sexual orientation.* APA.

Atallah, S., Johnson-Agbakwu, C., & Rosenbaum, T., et al. (2016). Ethical and sociocultural aspects of sexual function and dysfunction in both sexes. *Journal of Sexual Medicine, 13*(4), 591–606. https://doi.org/10.1016/j.jsxm.2016.01.021

Bergeron, S., Corsini-Munt, S., Aerts, L., Rancourt, K., & Rosen, N. O. (2015). Female sexual pain disorders: A review of the literature on etiology and treatment. *Current Sexual Health Reports, 7*(3), 159–169. https://doi.org/10.1007/s11930-015-0053-y

Brotto, L. A., & Basson, R. (2014). Group mindfulness-based therapy significantly improves sexual desire in women with sexual interest/arousal disorder. *Journal of Sexual Medicine, 11*(7), 1767–1781. https://doi.org/10.1111/jsm.12599

Doğan, S. (2009). Vaginismus and accompanying sexual dysfunctions in a Turkish clinical sample. *The Journal of Sexual Medicine, 6*(1), 184–192. https://doi.org/10.1111/j.1743-6109.2008.01048.x

Goldfinger, C., Pukall, C. F., Gentilcore-Sanders, A., McLean, L., & Chamberlain, S. (2019). A prospective study of dilator therapy for provoked vestibulodynia. *Journal of Sexual Medicine, 16*(9), 1441–1453. https://doi.org/10.1016/j.jsxm.2019.05.011

ILGA World. (2023). *State-sponsored homophobia report.* International Lesbian, Gay, Bisexual, Trans and Intersex Association. https://ilga.org

International Consultation on Sexual Medicine. (2015). *Recommendations for the diagnosis and treatment of sexual pain disorders.* ICSM.

Krishnappa, P., Manfredi, C., Jayaramaiah, S., Ditonno, F., Matippa, P., Shah, R., & Moncada, I. (2024). Unconsummated marriage: A systematic review of etiological factors and clinical management. *The Journal of Sexual Medicine, 21*(1), 20–28. https://doi.org/10.1093/jsxmed/qdad146

Kurban, D., Eserdag, S., Yakut, E., & Mishra, P. C. (2021). The treatment analysis of the patients suffering from vaginismus and the correlation with the psychological issues. *International Journal of Reproduction, Contraception, Obstetrics and Gynecology, 10*(4), 1328–1336. https://doi.org/10.18203/2320-1770.ijrcog20211107

Meyer, I. H. (2003). Prejudice, social stress, and mental health in lesbian, gay, and bisexual populations: Conceptual issues and research evidence. *Psychological Bulletin, 129*(5), 674–697. https://doi.org/10.1037/0033-2909.129.5.674

Morin, M., Carroll, M. S., & Bergeron, S. (2017). Systematic review of randomized controlled trials of pelvic floor physical therapy for women with provoked vestibulodynia. *Sexual Medicine Reviews, 5*(3), 295–322. https://doi.org/10.1016/j.sxmr.2017.03.002

Neville, H. A., Lilly, R. L., Duran, G., Lee, R. M., & Browne, L. (2000). Construction and initial validation of the color-blind racial attitudes scale (CoBRAS). *Journal of Counseling Psychology, 47*(1), 59–70. https://doi.org/10.1037/0022-0167.47.1.59

Pacik, P. T. (2011). Vaginismus: Review of current concepts and treatment using Botox injections, bupivacaine injections, and progressive dilation with the patient under anesthesia. *Aesthetic Plastic Surgery, 35*, 1160–1164. https://doi.org/10.1007/s00266-011-9737-5

Pascoal, P. M., & Raposo, C. F. (2023). How sexual problems are managed by other professionals. In *Midwifery and sexuality* (pp. 345–354). Springer. https://doi.org/10.1007/978-3-031-18432-1_29

Pukall, C. F., Goldstein, A. T., Bergeron, S., Foster, D., Stein, A., Kellogg-Spadt, S., & Bachmann, G. (2016). Vulvodynia: Definition, prevalence, impact, and pathophysiological factors. *The Journal of Sexual Medicine, 13*(3), 291–304. https://doi.org/10.1016/j.jsxm.2015.12.021

Reissing, E. D., Binik, Y. M., Khalifé, S., Cohen, D., & Amsel, R. (2003). Etiological correlates of vaginismus: Sexual and physical abuse, sexual knowledge, sexual self-schema, and relationship adjustment. *Journal of Sex & Marital Therapy, 29*(1), 47–59. https://doi.org/10.1080/713847095

Simon, W., & Gagnon, J. H. (1986). Sexual scripts: Permanence and change. *Archives of Sexual Behavior, 15*(2), 97–120. https://doi.org/10.1007/BF01542219

ter Kuile, M. M., van Lankveld, J. J. D. M., de Groot, E., Melles, R., Neffs, J., & Zandbergen, M. (2007). Cognitive-behavioral therapy for women with lifelong vaginismus: Process and prognostic factors. *Behaviour Research and Therapy, 45*(2), 359–373. https://doi.org/10.1016/j.brat.2006.03.013

Tervalon, M., & Murray-García, J. (1998). Cultural humility versus cultural competence: A critical distinction in defining physician training outcomes in multicultural education. *Journal of Health Care for the Poor and Underserved, 9*(2), 117–125. https://doi.org/10.1353/hpu.2010.0233

United Nations Human Rights Council. (2020). *Report of the Independent Expert on protection against violence and discrimination based on sexual orientation and gender identity: Practices of so-called "conversion therapy" (A/HRC/44/53)*. United Nations.

World Association for Sexual Health. (2014). *Declaration of sexual rights*. www.worldsexualhealth.net/was-declaration-on-sexual-rights

WPATH. (2022). *Standards of care for the health of transgender and gender diverse people, version 8*. World Professional Association for Transgender Health. www.wpath.org

World Health Organization. (2006). *Defining sexual health: Report of a technical consultation on sexual health, 28–31 January 2002*. WHO.

Chapter 11

Psychosexual Work in Singapore

Oberdan Marianetti

Introduction

Singapore is a modern city-state, vibrant, rich, full of opportunities and still growing. It is a relatively independent country, having obtained its independence from Malaysia only in 1965.

As of September 2024, Singapore counts about 6 million inhabitants, with about 3.6 million Singapore citizens, and the rest a mixture between Permanent Resident and Non-resident population. The country boasts four official languages (English, Mandarin, Malay, and Tamil), in line with its vibrant multi-cultural mix. According to the latest census, which the country releases every 10 years, of the citizen population, 75% are ethnically Chinese, 15% Malay, 7.5% Indian, and the remainder other ethnicities. Singapore's cultural landscape is heavily influenced by its Chinese majority, rooted in Confucian values like filial piety and meritocracy. This foundation shapes much of the country's mainstream identity, even as it harmoniously coexists with other cultural traditions.

These values, particularly filial piety (孝), inform family structures and intergenerational expectations, often shaping how individuals view selfhood, duty, and relationships (Ho, 1996; Lim, 2021). At the same time, Singapore's developmental narrative, focused on technocratic governance and moral conservatism, has been shown to reinforce a cautious public discourse around sexuality and identity (Tan, 2014).

Against this backdrop, psychosexual and relationship therapy in Singapore unfolds within a context shaped by cultural conservatism, colonial legacies, and strong state influence. The city-state's unique socio-political framework, marked by rapid modernization, strict regulation, and a national narrative of multicultural harmony, often obscures the more complex, private struggles individuals face in navigating identity, intimacy, and desire.

Singapore's history of British colonialism, followed by post-independence nation-building, has produced what scholars have described as a "managed diversity" model—one that celebrates multiculturalism publicly while maintaining strict social controls, particularly around race, religion, and sexuality (Chua, 2003; Heng

DOI: 10.4324/9781003611387-11

& Devan, 1992). This balancing act often renders issues like sexual expression and queer identity invisible within official discourses.

This chapter offers a Singaporean perspective on the evolving practice of psychosexual and relationship therapy, particularly as it interfaces with diverse cultural expectations and norms. Drawing from both clinical experience and lived case studies, it explores the interplay between Western therapeutic models, which prioritize individual autonomy, expression, and emotional honesty, and Eastern values that often center around family obligation, social harmony, and restraint. These tensions are especially evident in how clients manage personal needs, relational expectations, and social taboos.

Therapists practicing in Singapore must navigate a landscape in which personal expression is often constrained by deeper cultural imperatives: to uphold family honor, avoid shame, and maintain a respectable social image. Even well-educated individuals may sometimes lack basic sexual literacy. Queer clients, in particular, encounter added layers of marginalization, as various pressures continue to silence their identities and experiences.

Research shows that Singaporean youth often experience a gap between formal sex education and real-world needs, with many turning to digital spaces for answers, only to encounter further stigma or misinformation (Wee & Parker, 2020). Meanwhile, queer individuals, especially those from religious families, frequently encounter microaggressions and institutional erasure, even in therapeutic settings (Leong et al., 2019).

The chapter also addresses the therapist's own role, especially in a society where race, class, and colonial histories subtly inform perceptions of authority, professionalism, and legitimacy. Issues such as language use, cultural fluency, and perceived alignment with Western or local worldviews all influence the therapeutic encounter. For example, a foreign-trained clinician may be both respected for their expertise and questioned for their cultural fit.

This dynamic reflects a postcolonial ambivalence toward Western knowledge systems: admired for their prestige, yet often viewed as incompatible with local lived realities (Seth, 2009). Therapists, therefore, operate not only as clinicians but as cultural translators, negotiating credibility, trust, and positionality in every session.

Through anonymized case narratives, such as a woman who chooses to remain in a sexless marriage to maintain family harmony, or a high-functioning couple who need stick-figure diagrams to initiate conversations about sex, this chapter highlights the emotional and relational costs of silence, shame, and systemic pressures. It reveals how even within a highly developed and cosmopolitan city, intimate lives remain shaped by powerful, often unspoken cultural scripts.

In response, this chapter advocates for a culturally attuned, decolonized approach to therapy that acknowledges both shared human struggles and the distinct contours of life in Singapore. The aim is not to reject Western frameworks, but to adapt and place them meaningfully within local contexts, allowing for a therapeutic space that honors clients' cultural identities while gently challenging the norms that constrain their growth.

This requires an intersectional and critically reflective practice—one that understands clients not as isolated individuals, but as members of complex cultural, familial, and political ecosystems (Moodley & Palmer, 2006). The work of therapy in Singapore, then, is not only clinical but cultural, ethical, and generative.

Western Training in an Eastern Context

The foundations of psychosexual and relationship therapy in Singapore are predominantly drawn from Western theoretical frameworks, many of which prioritize individual autonomy, verbal expression of emotions, and a linear understanding of psychological development. These assumptions often clash with the lived realities of clients in an Asian context, where indirect communication, collective identity, and the preservation of social harmony take precedence. As a result, therapists trained in the West frequently find themselves in a double bind: equipped with powerful tools that may not quite "fit" the cultural expectations or internal worlds of the clients they aim to serve.

This "cultural mismatch" between Western models and non-Western lived experiences is well documented in cross-cultural psychotherapy literature (Moodley, 2007; Sue & Sue, 2012). While models such as humanistic and psychodynamic therapy focus on individuation and the primacy of internal conflict, many Asian cultural systems conceptualize selfhood relationally, with the individual nested within family, kinship, and social obligation structures (Ho, 1995; Kirmayer, 2007). This difference significantly shapes how emotional distress is understood, communicated, and resolved.

Much of the early training I received was based on models such as cognitive behavioral therapy (CBT), attachment theory, psychodynamic work, and sensate focus exercises, often taught through a lens that assumed sexual openness, access to language for desire, and a willingness to challenge familial or religious norms. In practice, however, many local clients, even highly educated ones, arrive in therapy without the conceptual or emotional vocabulary to talk about sex, intimacy, or emotional needs. It is not uncommon, for example, to ask a client who can clearly articulate the pain in their relationship what they need, only to be met with a genuine blank stare and a hesitant, "I don't know." Asking a client to "express what they want" or "set boundaries" with a parent or spouse may not only feel alien, but also threaten their sense of duty, loyalty, or belonging.

Therapists working cross-culturally must recognize that concepts such as "needs articulation" and "boundary-setting" are not culturally neutral but stem from Western ideals of assertiveness and self-actualization. In Confucian-informed cultures, relational hierarchy and harmony are often prioritized over individual preferences, and overt boundary-setting may be interpreted as disrespectful or selfish.

In one early case, a client who presented with low sexual desire described herself as "lazy in bed." Only after some investigation and careful reframing did she begin to realize a sense of emotional detachment and obligation, rather than desire, in her sexual relationship.

Over time, I found myself adapting core concepts using everyday metaphors and culturally resonant language. Rather than speaking of "emotional awareness," for example, a term that often landed awkwardly, I began referring to "the car dashboard" to illustrate the importance of regularly monitoring the state of our system, to ensure it performs its required functions well, even when those functions primarily involve serving others.

This kind of metaphorical translation is a key strategy in culturally responsive therapy. Research supports that using familiar cultural symbols or analogies can increase engagement and help clients integrate abstract psychological concepts (Pedersen, 2008). Metaphors serve as cognitive bridges, translating therapeutic goals into culturally accessible meaning.

Similarly, Confucian values such as filial piety, social hierarchy, and duty to the collective are not simply "obstacles" to be challenged, but deeply held beliefs that shape one's identity and decision-making. Therapists must be cautious not to pathologize these values. Instead, there is a need to work alongside them: to help clients find agency without severing ties, to assert needs without dishonoring their elders, and to craft intimacy in ways that feel authentic within their worldviews.

This echoes the principles of culturally adapted psychotherapy, where the goal is not to displace cultural identity but to work within its framework (Chun, 2003). For example, rather than framing family loyalty as a hindrance to personal growth, therapists can guide clients to explore how loyalty can be expressed in new, less self-sacrificing ways—thereby preserving values while reducing psychological burden.

This cultural translation is not only a task within the therapist–client relationship, but also an internal negotiation for therapists trained in Western institutions. As someone who studied in the West, from Western professors and Western literature, I often found myself questioning my instincts, wondering whether what I was offering was truly suitable for my Asian clients. Over time, I came to understand that cultural translation requires exploration on two distinct levels: process and content.

As a Western-trained professional who grew up in Europe, I am generally comfortable with speaking up and with more direct forms of communication. From a process perspective, I had to adjust quickly, toning down my approach and resorting to more direct interventions only when the circumstances called for or allowed them. Eventually, it felt natural to adapt my therapeutic style to better match local expectations.

However, it was not so easy to align with local norms when it came to content. The case of Jane (a pseudonym) clearly illustrates the struggle I encountered as a therapist when I first faced this reality.

When I met Jane, she was in her mid-thirties, a generally healthy woman who exercised regularly and took care of her physical well-being. She worked as a marketing executive in a large corporation and, as part of her job, frequently traveled within the region. On one such trip, Jane found herself sitting on the window ledge of her hotel room, dangling her legs ten floors from the ground. Thankfully, she had the presence of mind to call the hotel reception for help.

Upon her return to Singapore, Jane began therapy with me.

She displayed signs of burnout, depression, and general exhaustion. Her life dream was to become an artist, an aspiration she still held dear, despite having worked in the corporate world for over a decade. In line with practices common in many Asian cultures, Jane allocated a portion of her salary to her parents, even though she came from a wealthy family and her parents frequently encouraged her to stop sending money.

Through our sessions and her deep introspection, it became clear that the main reason Jane remained in her corporate role was to continue this financial support. She was modest in her lifestyle, and would have willingly adjusted to a simpler life in pursuit of her artistic goals.

Toward the end of our work together, I offered Jane a thought experiment. I suggested she imagine visiting her parents and offering them a choice: on one hand, to continue receiving financial support, labeled with the risk that this might one day lead her to suicide; on the other, to stop the support, accompanied by her own guilt and shame, but more likely leading to health and happiness.

Without hesitation, Jane replied that her parents would clearly choose the second option, her well-being over money. Yet despite this conscious clarity about her preference, Jane decided to discontinue therapy. By her own admission, she could not bring herself to abandon the cultural expectation of financial contribution, even though her parents neither needed nor wanted it.

This was the first time I had to confront cultural beliefs so deeply ingrained and so diametrically opposed to my own, and to ask myself how far I should go in challenging them.

Unlike the process-level adjustments I made earlier in my practice, it took longer to clarify my stance in this case. I eventually came to the conclusion that, regardless of cultural context, if a client is at risk of self-destruction or suicide, I will actively challenge the beliefs contributing to that risk.

This decision aligns with an ethical stance in multicultural counseling: that cultural relativism cannot override the duty of care when a client's safety is at stake (APA, 2017). Ethical practice must strike a balance between cultural sensitivity and client welfare—recognizing that culture may inform suffering, but should not shield it from intervention.

Since then, I have continued to use this approach, tempering it with the softer, less direct process I've adopted locally. When paired with compassion and empathy, I have found clients to be more open to challenging their own core limiting beliefs, even when doing so means confronting deeply held cultural norms.

When unfamiliar with the local context, it is all too easy for foreign therapists to label client dynamics as "avoidant," "enmeshed," or "co-dependent," without appreciating that multigenerational households, shared finances, and deference to parental authority are normative in many Asian cultures. Without cultural sensitivity, even well-intentioned therapists can inadvertently reinforce a sense of inadequacy or cultural dissonance.

This highlights the risk of pathologizing cultural norms through the lens of individualistic frameworks. Terms like "enmeshment" or "codependency" carry moral undertones that may unfairly stigmatize collectivist ways of relating (Tummala-Narra, 2015). Therapists must be vigilant about the cultural biases embedded in diagnostic and conceptual language.

In this light, ongoing professional development must involve more than just updating therapeutic models. It requires a critical re-examination of the values embedded within those models, and a reflection on how (and whether) they resonate in an Eastern setting.

Ultimately, effective therapy demands more than textbook expertise. It calls for humility, cultural fluency, and a willingness to unlearn, an openness to questioning which parts of one's training genuinely serve the client, and which need to be reimagined through a local lens. This is not about diluting the work; it is about making it meaningful, accessible, and respectful, so that healing, growth, and connection can emerge within a cultural frame that feels safe, not foreign.

As the field of global mental health expands, there is growing recognition that effective practice must include "decentering" Western paradigms and co-creating models grounded in the lived experiences of diverse populations (Fernando, 2012; Watters, 2010). Cultural fluency is not a static competence but a lifelong process of reflexivity, humility, and relational attunement.

Cultural Norms and the Sacrificing of Needs

In Singapore, as in many parts of Asia, the undercurrents of culture run deep through the fabric of individual identity and relational life. While the city-state is often portrayed as a modern, globalized hub, its accepted behaviors remain shaped by a rich confluence of Confucian, Malay-Muslim, Indian, and colonial British influences. Within this hybrid cultural landscape, psychosexual and relationship therapy becomes entangled in an intricate web of unspoken obligations, intergenerational expectations, and what might be termed the politics of silence.

In collectivist societies, identity is constructed not as a separate, autonomous self but as deeply relational—a self-in-context (Markus & Kitayama, 1991). As a result, expressions of distress often take socially acceptable forms like somatic complaints or role fatigue rather than overt emotional disclosure (Kleinman & Good, 1985).

Themes of silence, duty, and the suppression of needs are not simply individual coping strategies, they are culturally sanctioned responses to maintaining social harmony and family reputation. In particular, the concept of "saving face" (known in various forms across Chinese, Malay, and Indian communities) plays a central role in shaping clients' willingness to articulate distress, especially when that distress concerns sexuality or relational dissatisfaction.

"Face" (面子 or muka) is both a psychological and sociopolitical concept. It encapsulates a person's moral standing and the family's honor in public space.

Losing face, therefore, carries both individual and communal consequences (Ho, 1976; Ting-Toomey, 2005), leading to a cultural imperative to suppress personal conflict, particularly if it threatens social equilibrium.

Edith, a woman in her early forties, exemplifies the quiet toll such norms can take. She first came to therapy not with a presenting issue of sexual dissatisfaction, but with vague complaints of fatigue and a lack of "motivation in life." Only gradually, after a period of building trust, did her narrative begin to surface. A Chinese Singaporean and the eldest daughter in her family, Edith had lived her life according to what she called "the rules": be filial, don't bring shame, stay married, and put others before yourself. Her marriage of over twenty years was marked by emotional distance and a complete absence of sexual intimacy for over a decade.

Despite the profound loneliness she described, Edith found it difficult to name what she wanted. "I don't think about what I need," she once said, "because it's not practical. You just carry on." This kind of internalized minimization of self is often viewed, within her community, as a virtue, evidence of being a "good wife" and "dutiful daughter." Even in therapy, the language Edith used was cautious, tentative. There were no declarations, only hints: "Maybe I just feel a bit... invisible / unimportant / unwanted."

Such hesitancy reflects what has been termed *cultural alexithymia*—a collective discomfort with articulating affective states, often reinforced by gender norms and intergenerational expectations (Cheung & Lau, 1982). For women in particular, the idealization of self-sacrifice often becomes a psychological double-bind: to express need is to appear selfish; to remain silent is to become invisible.

Such narratives are not unusual. In Singaporean society, particularly among the older generation and more traditional families, there remains a strong emphasis on collectivism. The individual's needs are often subordinated to the family's reputation, the relationship's continuity, or the avoidance of conflict. For women, especially, sexuality is commonly framed through the lens of duty, either as a wife responsibility or as something not to be discussed at all. The silence around these issues is not merely a lack of vocabulary; it is a protective strategy. Speaking openly about one's desires or discontent can be seen as selfish or even shameful.

This tension is compounded by a lingering postcolonial moral conservatism, where sexuality is monitored both socially and institutionally (Oswin, 2010). As such, psychosexual expression is entangled in a politics of respectability, particularly for women, who are expected to perform compliance to preserve familial and societal honor.

In practice, therapists working within this context must develop a heightened sensitivity to what is not being said. The therapeutic space may be the first place where clients like Edith are invited to speak their truth, not only to their therapist, but to themselves. It is not uncommon for clients to struggle with guilt simply for expressing a desire for more, more intimacy, more recognition, or even the right to feel unhappy.

The concept of "sacrifice" emerges frequently in such sessions. Clients speak of having sacrificed dreams, careers, freedoms, and emotional needs for the sake of family or harmony. Yet the cultural scripts that elevate these sacrifices rarely offer a corresponding space to mourn what was lost. Edith, for instance, initially rejected the idea of grieving her unmet needs. "It would be ungrateful," she said. "My husband is a good man. He doesn't hit me. He provides."

In this context, gratitude functions as a moral contract that often prevents critical self-reflection. The "good enough" narrative operates as a defense against acknowledging emotional deprivation, particularly when care and obligation are culturally framed as moral duties rather than negotiable relational needs (Held, 2002). The moral hierarchy of needs is shaped by cultural scripts that elevate duty and diminish desire.

Such internal conflicts can present a challenge for therapists who have been trained in Western models of individual fulfilment and assertiveness. Encouraging clients to "prioritize their needs" or "claim their pleasure" can feel tone-deaf or even destabilizing when set against a cultural backdrop where such moves are seen as disruptive, disloyal, or narcissistic. Instead, the therapeutic task becomes one of gentle enquiry, creating a space where clients can begin to acknowledge their own needs without feeling they are betraying their values or communities.

Therapy, in this context, becomes less about confrontation and more about reclamation: reclaiming language for desire, permission for boundaries, and compassion for the self. For Edith, the breakthrough did not come with a dramatic decision to leave her marriage, but in the quiet realization that her feelings mattered. She began to see that silence was not neutral; it had been her way of surviving, yes, but it had also kept her unseen. "Maybe," she said in one session, "I don't have to disappear just to keep the peace."

This therapeutic shift—from endurance to emergence—parallels broader feminist critiques of silent suffering as a mode of cultural virtue (Gilligan, 1982). Rather than dismantle tradition, therapists can help clients re-negotiate its terms, finding space for voice within the structure of loyalty.

This reframing, of silence not as strength but as sacrifice, offers a path forward. In bringing stories like Edith's to the fore, we challenge the dominant therapeutic narratives and create space for culturally attuned models that honor both individual truth and collective context. In places where the road signs are not in English, and where speaking up feels like a betrayal, therapy must learn to listen in a different key.

Listening "in a different key" involves attuning to subtext, metaphor, gesture, and even omission. It is about recognizing that silence, when culturally conditioned, is not a void but a message (Tseng & Streltzer, 2008). The therapist's role is to decipher that language, not to overwrite it.

Sexual Literacy and the Myth of Educated Competence

In Singapore's deeply stratified society, where educational attainment, professional status, and material success are heavily valued, there persists a curious and often invisible gap: the assumption that high intellectual or professional accomplishments would automatically grant emotional or sexual competence. While there is an important part that intellect plays in learning the knowledge and skills of emotional and sexual attunement, the mixing of intellectual capital with intimacy literacy is not just misleading; it is a clinical blind spot that therapists must actively resist.

This conflation of academic success with emotional maturity reflects what Bourdieu (1986) might term *symbolic capital*—the assumption that one form of privilege (education, profession) seamlessly translates into others, including psychosexual sophistication. In practice, however, psychosexual development often remains disconnected from formal education systems in Singapore and globally (Alldred & David, 2007).

Time and again, clients present from middle- or upper-middle-class backgrounds with degrees, careers, and apparent "togetherness," yet their lived experiences reveal profound gaps in psychosexual understanding, gaps often accompanied by shame, silence, and deeply internalized myths.

It is more common than one might expect to encounter young, accomplished local couples, healthy, affectionate, and committed to building a fulfilling life together, who, after a decade or more in relationship, present with quiet distress: "We want to have children," or "We want to enjoy each other sexually," followed by the revealing admission that they have not been able to achieve full penetrative intercourse.

The case of a young married couple, both lawyers, graduates of a prestigious university, married for two years, illustrates this starkly. They initially came to therapy because they wanted children and were concerned that conception hadn't happened despite "trying." On further enquiry, it became clear they had not had penetrative sex at all. In fact, neither of them quite knew how to. The language was cautious, the assumptions vague. When gently asked what "trying" entailed, the couple hesitated before the husband admitted, "We lie together, but I am not sure how to enter."

Both were visibly distressed, not only by their difficulties, but by the realization that they were, by all accounts, unaware of basic sexual anatomy. There was no known trauma, no religious repression, and no pathology, just a deep and sincere lack of sexual knowledge and exploration. They had been left to "figure it out," with neither having the conceptual or embodied vocabulary to begin. In session, I resorted to drawing stick figures, with arrows and labels, to explain the basic mechanics of penetrative sex. Even then, their reaction was not one of amusement, but relief tinged with disbelief, this is what no one had told them.

Such experiences reveal what UNESCO refers to as a global failure in *comprehensive sexuality education*—one that disproportionately affects conservative and academically competitive societies, where sex education is either biologically reductionist or absent altogether (UNESCO, 2018). In Singapore, formal sex education continues to focus largely on abstinence, STI prevention, and reproductive health, with little to no engagement with desire, pleasure, communication, or consent.

When I asked gently whether they had tried looking anything up online, they looked alarmed. "Oh no, no," said the wife, "we don't want to leave any trace of visiting those sites." Her husband nodded. "We didn't want to get into trouble." In that moment, what emerged was a quiet but striking dissonance between their intellectual and professional competence and their uncertainty in navigating sexual knowledge. These were not individuals lacking in resources, they were well-traveled, well-educated, and legally trained. Yet the enduring sensitivities around sex, shaped by cultural norms, privacy concerns, and familial silences, had made this aspect of their lives feel opaque and fraught with hesitation.

Their reluctance also reflects the residual fear stemming from Singapore's strict regulatory environment surrounding sexuality and media. While private consumption of pornography is not actively policed, the *Undesirable Publications Act* technically prohibits possession of obscene material, and the broader cultural climate remains morally conservative. This legal ambiguity reinforces internalized censorship, particularly among clients from status-conscious backgrounds.

While viewing sexually explicit content online is not, in itself, a criminal offence in Singapore, the broader legal framework around pornography remains restrictive. The possession, distribution, production, and sale of such material are explicitly illegal. This legal ambiguity, coupled with a general climate of caution, means that many clients hesitate to access even educational resources online, fearing unintended legal or social repercussions.

This case, like many others I have witnessed, exposes a widespread myth that because one possesses an intellect and good education, one should automatically, perhaps naturally, be knowledgeable and skilled in the emotional, relational, and sexual domains.

For high-functioning couples like this one, shame becomes doubly layered. There is the obvious discomfort around sexual inadequacy, but also a meta-shame: shame about having shame. They are embarrassed not only by their lack of experience, but by what this lack might imply about their competence, their adulthood, or their "worldliness." In a culture where reputation and image account for much, to admit confusion about sex is to risk puncturing the carefully crafted façade.

Psychologists have described this phenomenon as *imposter syndrome in intimacy*—where individuals fear being "found out" for not knowing what they are expected to already embody (Brunning, 2018). This fear is intensified by societal expectations that competence in one domain (e.g., career) should naturally extend to relational ones, especially in high-achieving environments.

Another couple, Lydia and Marcus, also lawyers, also highly educated, presented with "communication issues," only for it to emerge later that they, too, had not had penetrative sex since marriage. Both carried unspoken fears that they were "doing it wrong," but neither felt they could broach the topic. "It sounds ridiculous now," Lydia later said, "but we genuinely thought maybe something was wrong with us… or maybe we were just supposed to wait." Marcus added, "I was too ashamed to ask. It's like, we're supposed to know."

Their story echoed similar themes: the central myth that sex equals penetration, the absence of reliable or shame-free resources, and the tendency for high-achieving clients to intellectualize their distress rather than sit with emotional or bodily discomfort. Therapy involved not only deconstructing myths, but gently expanding their understanding of sex as a spectrum of relational, emotional, and physical experiences, none of which had been modeled for them in any meaningful way.

The reliance on penetration as a default metric of sexual normalcy reflects heteronormative scripts often reinforced by abstinence-focused education and media censorship (Tolman, 2002). Without exposure to diverse models of sexual expression, many clients equate "healthy sex" with reproduction or performance rather than connection or pleasure.

Class privilege, in these cases, paradoxically functioned both as a protective barrier and a limiting one. It shielded these clients from certain forms of societal scrutiny, but also reinforced their reluctance to ask "basic" questions or admit perceived ignorance. Their education had taught them how to excel in exams and present legal arguments, but not how to name desire, navigate sexual initiation, or embrace the inevitable vulnerability of erotic life.

For therapists, this underscores the urgent need to de-link professional or academic status from assumed sexual competence. It also calls for a more nuanced understanding of how state narratives, censorship fears, and class-based performance anxieties shape psychosexual development in Singapore. When shame is compounded by the fear of state visibility, even curiosity becomes risky.

This reinforces the need for therapists to hold space where *epistemic humility* is normalized—where clients are free to say "I don't know" without it destabilizing their sense of identity. Shame in these contexts is not just intrapsychic, but sociocultural and class-coded (Ahmed, 2004).

Therapy, in this context, must do more than teach mechanics. It must offer a place where clients can admit they don't know, without judgement, without fear, and without the burden of always having to seem "put together." In that sacred space of not-knowing, healing and discovery can begin, not just of anatomy, but of the self in relation to others.

To truly meet clients where they are, therapists must deconstruct not just sexual myths but the elitist epistemologies that shame people for not already knowing. Sex education—whether formal or therapeutic—must offer permission to begin again, to explore from the body, not just the book.

Queer Invisibility and the Lingering Shadow of 377A

The repeal of Section 377A in Singapore in 2022 was a historic legal moment, but for many queer individuals, especially youth, its symbolic victory did not translate into immediate safety, visibility, or affirmation. The long shadow cast by 377A, a colonial-era law criminalizing sex between men, continues to shape public discourse, familial dynamics, and clinical practice. Its cultural residue lingers in classrooms, religious communities, and dining rooms, where silence and moral disapproval often replace open dialogue.

As scholars such as Lim (2021) has noted, while 377A was rarely enforced in the latter decades of its existence, its performative power lay in its symbolic criminalization of queer identity. This produced a culture of quiet erasure—a societal stance where "tolerance" replaced acceptance, and queerness remained something to manage or mute, rather than affirm.

For queer clients, therapy in Singapore remains a complex and sometimes risky space. Despite increased awareness, psychosexual and relationship therapy still operates within a society where queerness is frequently pathologized, erased, or moralized, often within families themselves. Religious values, in particular, are deeply embedded in the social psyche, and frequently invoked as the reason why queer identities cannot be accepted. In this context, therapists are often navigating not only the inner world of the client, but also the deeply entrenched belief systems of those around them.

One case stands out as a harrowing illustration of these pressures. A teenage boy, just 17 at the time, was brought into therapy by his mother after she found him in the midst of a suicide attempt at home. The event was shocking for her, and it marked the first time she recognized the depth of his pain. As the sessions unfolded, the history behind his mental health struggle became heartbreakingly clear.

When the boy was just eight years old, he had indirectly come out to his mother, not in explicit terms, but through questions and comments that signaled his budding awareness of being different. Rather than respond with curiosity or support, his mother reacted with a firm moral stance, informed by her strong religious beliefs. She told him that "God does not allow that kind of behavior," that "it's just a phase," and that with enough prayer and discipline, he would grow out of it.

For the next nine years, this was the climate he lived in: one of conditional love and silent policing. He was never abused, never cast out, but also never seen. His queerness became the thing that could not be acknowledged. At church, he was taught that to be gay was to be broken. At home, the message was more subtle, but equally damaging: that he could be loved, so long as he was not that.

This experience echoes what Meyer (2003) defined as *minority stress*: the chronic psychological toll that results from stigma, concealment, and internalized oppression. For many queer individuals in Singapore, this stress is compounded by a collectivist culture that equates conformity with virtue and deviance with familial dishonor.

By the time he arrived in therapy, his sense of self-worth had been eroded. He described feeling "like a ghost in my own family," someone who existed only in parts, always careful, always afraid. Therapy began with stabilizing his suicidal ideation, but the deeper work involved helping his mother confront a truth she had long resisted: that her theology, however well-intended, had become a life-threatening force in her son's life.

At one pivotal session, the question was posed to her directly: *Would you rather have a queer son, or no son at all?* The silence that followed was unbearable. But it was also a turning point. It cracked something open in her, not just guilt, but grief. Grief for the years she had lost trying to correct what was never broken. Grief for the trust she had unknowingly shattered. And eventually, a softening.

"I never stopped loving him," she said. "I just didn't know how to love this part." That distinction, between loving the child and loving the *whole* child, became central to their therapeutic work. Slowly, painfully, she began to shift. Not toward full understanding, perhaps, but toward acceptance. Not toward affirmation yet, but away from rejection.

This case speaks to the enduring cultural, religious, and legal legacies that queer individuals in Singapore must navigate. The repeal of 377A did not dismantle the structures that upheld it, namely, a deep discomfort with non-normative identities, often reinforced by conservative religious institutions and filial duty. Queerness remains largely invisible in schools, rarely discussed in family settings, and still presented as controversial in the public sphere.

While Singapore's official discourse promotes a narrative of "multicultural harmony," it continues to exclude queer perspectives from public institutions like education and healthcare. This selective inclusion results in what queer theorist Jasbir Puar calls *homonationalism*: where a state may decriminalize queerness without actually affirming or protecting it.

In the therapeutic room, this invisibility becomes a kind of trauma in itself. Queer clients frequently struggle not just with external rejection, but with internalized shame so profound that even imagining a future becomes difficult. Many come to therapy not because they are queer, but because they are exhausted from hiding it. For youth, especially those still financially and emotionally dependent on unsupportive families, the risks of coming out can be existential.

Therapists must tread carefully in such terrain. Affirmation cannot be assumed; it must be built. Safety must be co-created, moment by moment. Working with families, particularly religious ones, requires cultural humility, patience, and sometimes, a painful kind of honesty. The question is not whether the family is "ready" to accept a queer child, but whether the cost of their resistance is one they are truly prepared to bear.

These family dynamics mirror what scholars have identified as *conditional belonging*—a status queer people are granted only when they suppress or mask their identities in order to maintain harmony (Yue & Zubillaga-Pow, 2012). In clinical terms, it becomes a balancing act between empathic attunement and gentle truth-telling, where the therapist acts not as an advocate for one identity, but as a mediator of life-affirming connection.

For this mother, it took nearly losing her son to begin seeing him. For the son, it took immense courage to stay alive long enough to be seen. Their story reminds us that queer visibility in therapy is not simply about identity labels or political correctness, it is about survival. Until the family, faith, and therapy can all become places of refuge rather than harm, the legacy of 377A will remain alive, even without its legal teeth.

The work of decolonizing therapy in Singapore must therefore include a queer lens—one that recognizes not only the systemic erasure of non-heteronormative lives, but also the intimate violences of silence, denial, and conditional love.

Youth, Digital Spaces, and the New Sexual Consciousness

Singapore's youth are coming of age in a landscape marked by contradiction. On one hand, they are more digitally connected, globally exposed, and rhetorically "woke" than any generation before them. On the other, they are still embedded within traditional social systems—schools, families, and religious institutions—that often reproduce conservative or restrictive values around gender, sexuality, and relationships. Within this tension, young people develop a duality of moving fluently between liberal digital subcultures on one hand, and the more conformist expectations of home and society, all while internalizing the dissonance in silence.

This duality aligns with what Turkle (2011) refers to as the "*split screen self*"—a generation performing differently across multiple platforms, not out of inauthenticity, but survival. In Singapore, where collectivist expectations remain strong, this split is both cultural and psychological.

In a society where households are often multi-generational, and youth frequently live at home with parents and grandparents until marriage, they are left to navigate two deeply contrasting worlds, often alone.

Nowhere is this more evident than in their relationship with sexuality. While formal sex education in Singapore remains largely heteronormative, risk-focused, and biologically reductive, digital platforms have become informal classrooms for exploring desire, identity, and community. Social media, forums, anonymous chat sites, fanfiction platforms, and streaming services offer young people narratives and images that diverge sharply from what they are told in school or at the dinner table. For many, the internet is the first place they encounter sex as something pleasurable, diverse, and emotionally complex, rather than dangerous, deviant, or shameful.

These online spaces function as "counter-publics" (Fraser, 1990), where marginalized identities find voice and solidarity. For many Singaporean youth, especially queer or neurodiverse individuals, the internet is not escapism but lifeline.

This digital literacy does not always translate smoothly into embodied or relational confidence. A young client in his mid-20s once described the experience as being "educated and clueless at the same time." Online, they could quote feminist texts, debate kink ethics, or explain the nuances of gender fluidity. Offline, they had never spoken to their parents about sex, didn't know how to ask for consent in real life, and felt paralyzed by the fear of being found out. "It's like living in two different worlds," they said. "I'm queer online, and quiet offline."

Another client in her early thirties, active in the kink community, echoed this quiet split. “My church friends think I’m a virgin,” she said, half-laughing, half-resigned. “They could never imagine I’ve already had sex, let alone that I’m involved in BDSM.” The dissonance between her embodied sexual expression and the persona she maintained in other parts of her life wasn’t just about secrecy; it was about managing safety, belonging, and the invisible calculations required to exist across radically different moral landscapes.

These stories reflect what sociologist Erving Goffman (1959) described as *front-stage and back-stage identity management*. In contemporary terms, they underscore the emotional labor of code-switching not just across cultures or languages, but across moral worlds.

This bifurcation creates both empowerment and anxiety. On the one hand, digital spaces can be profoundly validating, especially for those whose identities are marginalized in mainstream Singaporean discourse—queer youth, neurodiverse individuals, or those exploring alternative relationship structures. On the other hand, these same youths must continually manage the risks of being seen, outed, or misunderstood in their offline environments. The performance of normalcy becomes second nature; code-switching, a survival skill.

Therapy with these clients requires a recognition that their knowledge is not necessarily linear or integrated. They may be more articulate than their parents about gender politics but still deeply confused about their own desires. They may be emotionally intelligent but completely unpracticed in relational vulnerability. They may know the right vocabulary, but lack the internal permission to use it. Holding space for this complexity, without slipping into either idealization or condescension, is key.

The therapist’s role here is not to decode or instruct, but to co-create a space where these seemingly fragmented selves can coexist and converse. This work is deeply integrative, and often developmental in nature (Siegel, 2020).

Generational shifts are also becoming increasingly apparent within the family systems therapists work with. Some parents, particularly those under 50, are more open than their own parents were, but still carry anxieties about “losing control” or “corrupting innocence.” Often, when young people come out or speak about sex at home, the concern is less about the content and more about the perceived threat to authority, tradition, or family cohesion. The child becomes a symbol of change the parent is not ready for.

Even parents who take a more open, developmentally attuned approach, introducing conversations about relationships and sexuality in thoughtful, comprehensive ways, may find themselves caught in an intergenerational bind. Their efforts can be met with judgment from their own parents, who may view such openness as inappropriate, dangerous, or even morally suspect. In these moments, the liberal parent becomes the new target of shame, implicitly framed as having failed in their parental role. The message is not just that their approach is wrong, but that they are inadequate, irresponsible, or corrupting—a projection that can be deeply destabilizing.

In some cases, youth themselves internalize these contradictions, resulting in deep ambivalence. A client in his early twenties, who identified as bisexual, once said: "I'm proud of who I am, but I also wish I wasn't. It would just be easier." Such sentiments speak not to confusion about identity, but about the burden of navigating it within a context that offers little affirmation. For these clients, therapy is not simply a space of education, it is a space of coherence—a place where they can hold their many selves together without splitting.

This speaks to the therapeutic aim of *psychological integration*—the ability to honor multiple identities without disowning any. As Winnicott (1960) suggested, mental health is not the elimination of complexity, but the capacity to tolerate it.

Clinically, working with digitally fluent youth challenges therapists to stay current without becoming performative. It is not enough to be "accepting"; we must be fluent in the cultural texts that shape their realities, from TikTok discourse to Reddit communities to the politics of Instagram. At the same time, we must model something rare in their world: slowness, presence, reflection and the acceptance of not-knowing. In an age of instant commentary and curated selfhood, the therapeutic space may be one of the few places where youth are invited not just to be heard, but to truly listen to themselves.

Singaporean youth are not waiting for permission to change; they are already changing. What they lack is not access to information, but access to integration—to safe, guided, and reflective processes that help them make sense of their experiences across the digital and physical worlds. The role of therapy, then, is not to pull them back to tradition, nor to push them toward progress, but to walk alongside them as they navigate the messy, creative, and often contradictory space in between.

The Invisible Therapist: Perspective and Power

In Singapore's therapy landscape, where titles, credentials, and social status carry significant weight, the identity of the therapist often plays an unspoken yet influential role in the client's sense of safety, trust, and engagement. This is especially salient in psychosexual and relationship therapy, where issues of vulnerability, shame, and cultural values are already present in the room.

With a doctorate in clinical sexology and prior experience in the corporate world, I often find myself being chosen by clients who feel reassured by my formal credentials and perceive an alignment with their own professional struggles. In a society where educational pedigree and business cards stacked with post-nominal letters confer legitimacy, the therapeutic alliance is frequently shaped before the first session even begins.

In Singapore's meritocratic society, where institutional legitimacy is closely tied to perceived expertise, this phenomenon reflects what Foucault (1977) called the "*technologies of power*"—where knowledge and authority are fused into structures that determine who is allowed to speak, and who is believed when they do.

At the same time, race and perceived cultural affinity influence the way clients relate to the therapist. In multiple instances, clients have stated, sometimes with disarming frankness, that they trusted me more simply because I am Caucasian and Western-trained. This bias operates alongside the assumption that foreign-trained therapists may be more "open-minded," more affirming, or less bound by local taboos.

But the reverse also holds true. Other clients have initially hesitated to book a session with me, concerned that I might not "get it," that my background would render me unfamiliar with the intricate dance they navigate in their daily lives and culture. Only after being referred by a trusted friend, or reassured by shared values during the first few sessions, did they begin to engage meaningfully.

This duality, being both idealized and mistrusted, illustrates the complexity of therapist positionality. It challenges the ideal of therapeutic neutrality and underscores the importance of acknowledging who we are in the room, and how that shapes the therapeutic process.

It is not enough to be competent; one must also be culturally fluent. And even then, fluency is not sameness. I have found that being transparent about my training, experience, and approach, while remaining curious about the client's context, creates the kind of therapeutic humility that builds genuine rapport.

Hooks (1994) describes this stance as *engaged pedagogy*—the practice of teaching and learning through mutual vulnerability and dialogue, rather than rigid hierarchy. In therapy, this means showing up as fully human, not omniscient expert.

In this work, the therapist is not a blank slate. We are mirrors, often reflecting the very hierarchies, assumptions, and aspirations that clients bring with them. To be aware of this is not to apologize for our presence, but to use it thoughtfully, to create a space where trust can be earned not through similarity, but through integrity.

The therapeutic relationship in Singapore, especially in psychosexual and relationship therapy, is rarely free of socio-cultural projection. Rather than resist this, I have learned to name it when appropriate, to explore it when it serves the work, and to step back when my presence becomes a distraction. The goal is not to erase myself from the work, but to allow space for the client's world to expand within it.

Emotional Restraint and the Performance of Strength

Emotional expression in Singapore is often shaped by a cultural ethos that equates emotional restraint with strength, maturity, and self-control. In therapy, this manifests as a consistent hesitancy, or even incapacity, to articulate feeling states, even when clients are otherwise articulate, introspective, and highly functioning.

Clients frequently present with a range of complaints—fatigue, insomnia, panic attacks, communication breakdowns, obsessive thoughts—all of which point to significant emotional turmoil. Yet when invited to explore the emotional dimensions of their experience, they often respond with cognitive explanations, factual recounting, or strategic redirection. A question such as, "How did that make you feel?" is met with "I think…" followed by justifications, timelines, or blame. Others simply shrug and say, "I don't know."

Over time, I learned to adapt my language to better meet clients where they were. Reframing the question as "What impact does that have on you?" often elicited a less defensive and more accessible response. It allowed space for the client to reflect without immediately needing to access unfamiliar emotional vocabulary. This linguistic pivot often became a small but critical shift in the therapeutic dynamic, offering an entry point to emotional terrain previously marked as off-limits or irrelevant.

This approach reflects what cultural psychologist Kirmayer (2007) calls *narrative sensitivity*—an ability to enter a client's worldview through language that honors their meaning systems without prematurely imposing Western emotional constructs.

However, in many cases, I've had to entirely abandon the emotional line of enquiry in early sessions, recognizing that the client lacked not only the vocabulary but also the psychological permission to "go there." Many had never been encouraged to develop an emotional lexicon. Emotional detachment had become not only a survival skill but a badge of honor, proof of resilience, stoicism, and maturity.

For men in particular, this performance of strength is deeply entwined with traditional ideals of masculinity. Vulnerability is conflated with weakness, and emotional openness is seen as indulgent, dramatic, or unnecessary. Women, too, often conflate emotional containment with moral superiority—self-control is interpreted as grace, particularly within the familial or caregiving roles that many women occupy.

Clients may describe major life events with startling detachment. One woman spoke about discovering her husband's affair in flat, dispassionate terms, as if reading from a news report. When asked whether she had spoken to anyone about it, she shook her head and said, "What's the point? It won't change anything." Her pain was evident, but tightly sealed behind a wall of narrative control. She didn't need a therapist to tell her what she already knew; what she feared was being asked to feel what she had so carefully avoided.

For these clients, therapy must become a space where feeling is not forced, but offered. Where emotion is not extracted, but gently mirrored. The aim is not catharsis for its own sake, but reconnection to self. Many clients have learned to succeed by amputating parts of their emotional life, and therapy is often the first environment where these parts can begin to re-emerge without shame.

The emotional habits my clients bring into therapy often echo, if not directly shape, the emotional dynamics in their intimate relationships. Partners frequently describe feeling emotionally isolated, even when the relationship appears functional or harmonious on the surface. They speak of conversations that are efficient but rarely vulnerable, conflicts that are managed but never truly resolved, and moments of closeness that feel fleeting or conditional. In this context, love is expressed through acts of service, duty, or material provision, rarely through verbal affirmation, emotional availability, or shared reflection. For many, emotional restraint becomes a kind of relational blueprint: protective, familiar, and quietly erosive.

This echoes what Gottman and Gottman (1999) describe as emotional disengagement, a state in which partners become polite strangers, living parallel lives under the guise of peace.

Over time, these patterns can lead to a subtle but persistent form of disconnection. Partners may stop asking for emotional engagement, not out of acceptance, but resignation. Sexual intimacy, too, can become strained—not because of lack of attraction or affection, but because emotional distance seeps into physical space. I've worked with couples who care deeply for one another but no longer know how to reach across the silence. In such cases, therapy becomes not only a site of individual healing but a quiet intervention into relational paralysis—a place where clients begin to practice emotional presence, first with themselves, and eventually, with each other.

I have found that emotional breakthroughs, when they come, are rarely dramatic. They often appear as small shifts, a pause, a tear, a change in breath. A client once responded to the question "Where does that land in you?" with a long silence, then said simply, "That hurts more than I thought it would." For someone unused to naming their feelings, this was a profound act of courage.

Another client, a high-ranking executive in his fifties, initially dismissed therapy as "a bit indulgent." He came for "stress management" but slowly revealed the emotional cost of decades of self-suppression. "I don't even know what I want anymore," he admitted, "only what's expected." Therapy for him became an act of slow re-humanization—not in opposition to his competence, but alongside it.

Emotional strength, in many Singaporean narratives, is defined by endurance. To feel less is to suffer less. But what many of my clients eventually realize is that emotional numbing does not reduce pain, it simply delays its reckoning. Therapy invites them into a different kind of strength: one that does not suppress emotion, but can sit with it, name it, and learn from it.

In a culture where emotional restraint is rewarded and vulnerability remains stigmatized, the therapist's role is both radical and restorative. We offer not just tools, but presence. Not just coping strategies, but new ways of being. And in doing so, we affirm that feeling is not a failure of control—it is a gateway to connection, both with oneself and with others.

Conclusion: Reframing, Not Replacing

Psychosexual and relationship therapy in Singapore does not unfold on a blank slate. It is shaped by centuries of cultural memory, religious scripts, state narratives, and the quiet but powerful codes of family and social life. Therapists working in this space must learn not only the models of therapy, but the meanings behind the silence, the stories behind the sacrifice, and the shame behind the smile.

Culture, as Kirmayer (2007) reminds us, is not simply background context—it is the very medium through which distress is understood and healing is made possible. In this sense, therapy in Singapore is not conducted *in spite of* culture but *through* it.

This chapter has explored the lived realities of clients navigating love, sex, and identity in a context that often privileges duty over desire and harmony over honesty. From the woman who chose a sexless marriage to preserve family honor, to the lawyers who had never been taught how to have sex, to the teenager who almost ended his life for being gay, these stories reveal a deep and often invisible suffering, one that cannot be resolved through imported frameworks alone.

But neither is the solution to abandon Western models. Instead, what is needed is a culturally attuned, critically reflective, and decolonized approach, one that honors both the universality of emotional struggle and the particularities of cultural context. Therapy must be a space of translation, not transplantation. A space where clients can name their truths in a language that feels their own.

This calls for what Das (2007) terms "*vernacular healing*"—a way of engaging suffering that respects the local grammar of meaning and pain. Therapy, then, becomes less about applying techniques and more about co-creating language for what was previously unspeakable.

As therapists, our role is not to liberate clients from culture, but to help them live within it with more awareness, choice, and connection. We are cultural companions, not cultural critics. We help clients ask: What do I want to keep? What no longer serves me? What might I reclaim or reimagine?

In a society where the road signs are not always in English, therapy must listen in more than one language—literal and metaphorical. It must listen for silence, for metaphor, for gesture, and for grief. And it must offer, in return, not just insight, but safety, permission, and the slow unfolding of self.

The true work of therapy, especially in Singapore's psychosexual context, is not about loud declarations of freedom, but quiet revolutions of selfhood—carefully negotiated in the presence of cultural gravity.

In Singapore, as elsewhere, the work of therapy is not only clinical. It is cultural, ethical, and, ultimately, human.

References

Ahmed, S. (2004). *The cultural politics of emotion*. Edinburgh University Press.

Alldred, P., & David, M. E. (2007). *Get real about sex: The politics and practice of sex education*. Open University Press.

American Psychological Association. (2017). *Ethical principles of psychologists and code of conduct* (2002, amended effective June 1, 2010, and January 1, 2017). www.apa.org/ethics/code

Bourdieu, P. (1986). The forms of capital. In J. G. Richardson (Ed.), *Handbook of theory and research for the sociology of education* (pp. 241–258). Greenwood Press.

Brunning, L. (2018). The distinctiveness of polyamory. *Journal of Applied Philosophy*, *35*(3), 513–531. https://doi.org/10.1111/japp.12240

Cheung, F. M., & Lau, B. W. K. (1982). Situational variations of help-seeking behavior among Chinese patients. *Comprehensive Psychiatry*, *23*(3), 252–262.

Chua, B. H. (2003). *Communitarian ideology and democracy in Singapore*. Routledge.

Das, V. (2007). *Life and words: Violence and the descent into the ordinary*. University of California Press.

Fernando, S. (2012). Race and culture issues in mental health and some thoughts on ethnic identity. *Counselling Psychology Quarterly*, *25*(2), 113–123. https://doi.org/10.1080/09515070.2012.674098

Foucault, M. (1977). *Discipline and punish: The birth of the prison* (A. Sheridan, Trans.). Pantheon Books.

Fraser, N. (1990). Rethinking the public sphere: A contribution to the critique of actually existing democracy. *Social Text*, (25/26), 56–80. https://doi.org/10.2307/466240

Gilligan, C. (1982). *In a different voice: Psychological theory and women's development*. Harvard University Press.

Goffman, E. (1959). *The presentation of self in everyday life*. Doubleday.

Gottman, J. M., & Gottman, J. S. (1999). *The seven principles for making marriage work*. Crown Publishing.

Held, V. (2002). Care and the extension of markets. *Hypatia*, *17*(2), 19–33.

Heng, G., & Devan, J. (1992). State fatherhood: The politics of nationalism, sexuality and race in Singapore. *Gender & Society*, *6*(4), 481–502. https://doi.org/10.1177/089124392006004005

Ho, D. Y. F. (1976). On the concept of face. *American Journal of Sociology*, *81*(4), 867–884. https://doi.org/10.1086/226145

Ho, D. Y. F. (1995). Selfhood and identity in Confucianism, Taoism, Buddhism, and Hinduism: Contrasts with the West. *Journal for the Theory of Social Behaviour*, *25*(2), 115–139. https://doi.org/10.1111/j.1468-5914.1995.tb00269.x

Ho, D. Y. F. (1996). Filial piety and its psychological consequences. In M. H. Bond (Ed.), *The handbook of Chinese psychology* (pp. 155–165). Oxford University Press.

Hooks, B. (1994). *Teaching to transgress: Education as the practice of freedom*. Routledge.

Kirmayer, L. J. (2007). Psychotherapy and the cultural concept of the person. *Transcultural Psychiatry*, *44*(2), 232–257. https://doi.org/10.1177/1363461506070796

Kleinman, A., & Good, B. (Eds.). (1985). *Culture and depression: Studies in the anthropology and cross-cultural psychiatry of affect and disorder*. University of California Press.

Leong, D. Y., Wong, H. B., & Chia, W. Y. (2019). Queer lives in Singapore: An analysis of cultural erasure. *Asian Journal of Social Psychology*, *22*(2), 164–175. https://doi.org/10.1111/ajsp.12345

Lim, S. S. (2021). Digital intimacy, parenting, and sexual silences in Singapore. *Journal of Children and Media*, *15*(1), 36–49. https://doi.org/10.1080/17482798.2020.1815222

Markus, H. R., & Kitayama, S. (1991). Culture and the self: Implications for cognition, emotion, and motivation. *Psychological Review*, *98*(2), 224–253. https://doi.org/10.1037/0033-295X.98.2.224

Meyer, I. H. (2003). Prejudice, social stress, and mental health in lesbian, gay, and bisexual populations: Conceptual issues and research evidence. *Psychological Bulletin*, *129*(5), 674–697. https://doi.org/10.1037/0033-2909.129.5.674

Moodley, R. (2007). (Re)placing multiculturalism in counselling and psychotherapy. *British Journal of Guidance & Counselling*, *35*(1), 1–22.

Moodley, R., & Palmer, S. (Eds.). (2006). *Race, culture and psychotherapy: Critical perspectives in multicultural practice*. Routledge.

Oswin, N. (2010). Sexual tensions in modernizing Singapore: The postcolonial and the intimate. *Environment and Planning D: Society and Space*, *28*(1), 128–141. https://doi.org/10.1068/d15308

Pedersen, P. B. (2008). Ethics, competence, and professional issues in cross-cultural counseling. In P. B. Pedersen, J. G. Draguns, W. J. Lonner, & J. E. Trimble (Eds.), *Counseling across cultures* (6th ed., pp. 5–20). SAGE Publications.

Seth, S. (2009). *Subject lessons: The Western education of colonial India*. Duke University Press.

Siegel, D. J. (2020). *The developing mind: How relationships and the brain interact to shape who we are* (3rd ed.). Guilford Press.

Sue, D. W., & Sue, D. (2012). *Counseling the culturally diverse: Theory and practice* (6th ed.). John Wiley & Sons.

Tan, K. P. (2014). *Governing global-city Singapore: Legacies and futures after Lee Kuan Yew*. Routledge.

Ting-Toomey, S. (2005). The matrix of face: An updated face-negotiation theory. In W. B. Gudykunst (Ed.), *Theorizing about intercultural communication* (pp. 71–92). Sage.

Tolman, D. L. (2002). *Dilemmas of desire: Teenage girls talk about sexuality*. Harvard University Press.

Tseng, W.-S., & Streltzer, J. (Eds.). (2008). *Cultural competence in health care*. Springer.

Tummala-Narra, P. (2015). Cultural competence as a core emphasis of psychoanalytic psychotherapy. *Psychoanalytic Psychology*, *32*(2), 275–292. https://doi.org/10.1037/a0034041

Turkle, S. (2011). *Alone together: Why we expect more from technology and less from each other*. Basic Books.

UNESCO. (2018). *International technical guidance on sexuality education: An evidence-informed approach* (Rev. ed.). UNESCO. https://unesdoc.unesco.org/ark:/48223/pf0000260770

Watters, E. (2010). *Crazy like us: The globalization of the American psyche*. Free Press.

Wee, L. E., & Parker, M. (2020). Sex education and sexual health knowledge in Singapore: A review. *Asian Journal of Social Science*, *48*(3), 355–374. https://doi.org/10.1163/15685314-04803002

Winnicott, D. W. (1960). Ego distortion in terms of true and false self. In D. W. Winnicott (Ed.), *The maturational processes and the facilitating environment: Studies in the theory of emotional development* (pp. 140–152). Karnac Books.

Yue, A., & Zubillaga-Pow, J. (Eds.). (2012). *Queer Singapore: Illiberal citizenship and mediated cultures*. Hong Kong University Press.

Chapter 12

Redefining Intimacy: Colonial Influence on Love, Sexuality, and Family in Sri Lanka Under British Rule

Ramesha Jayaneththi

Introduction

Expressions of sexuality and the very notion of family vary significantly across cultures and regions. Understanding these differences requires an exploration of diverse representations of sexuality in various societies. Such studies expand the discourse on emotions like love and sexuality, offering deeper insights into their evolving meanings. Historians, in particular, can examine these concepts across different contexts and historical periods, revealing how interpretations of love and sexuality have been fluid rather than universal.

Murray Bowen conceptualized the family as an emotional unit characterized by intricate and collective interactions. He observed that families exert such a profound influence on their members' thoughts, feelings, and behaviors that individuals often seem to exist under the same "emotional skin" (The Bowen Center, 2021). Traditionally, family has been regarded as an extension of the conjugal bond, but this raises the question: Is marriage, in the conventional sense, essential to forming a family?

The conceptualization of love and sexuality is inherently dynamic, shaped by changing social norms and historical contexts. These are not merely personal emotions but socially constructed realities influenced by external forces. Feelings such as love, jealousy, and sexual acceptance—or rejection—have varied across time and space. Distinct differences can be observed between Western and Eastern conceptions of family and sexuality. As Santhushya Fernando et al. (2018: 10) explain:

> Sexuality is an intrinsic part of life and connotes the totality of a human being. Unlike the word "sex," which represents a physiological act or the rigid categorizations into which human beings are often placed, sexuality encompasses the most intimate feelings and deepest longings of individuals to find sexual expression and meaningful relationships—not only with others but also with their own identities.

The historiography of emotions has emerged as a pivotal field in historical research, significantly reshaping the study of love, jealousy, and sexuality. While

DOI: 10.4324/9781003611387-12

early studies touched upon these themes, the late 20th century witnessed the formal development of the history of emotions as a distinct academic discipline. By the 2000s, this field—sometimes referred to as the history of feelings—had gained traction in Western universities.

Pioneers such as Lucien Febvre and Peter Gay played a crucial role in introducing new perspectives to the study of emotions, human interactions, and intimate relationships. Febvre's seminal 1941 article, *Sensibility and History: How to Recreate the Affective Life of the Past*, remains foundational to this field. He argued that emotions should be taken seriously as complex mental states that go beyond mere physical responses. He encouraged scholars to investigate the portrayal of emotions in conduct books, court records, paintings, sculpture, music, and literature. In a call for collective scholarly engagement, Febvre wrote:

> I am asking for a vast collective investigation to be opened on the fundamental sentiments of man and the forms they take. What surprises we may look forward to!
>
> (Febvre & Folca, 1973: 12)

His insights into emotional contagion and ritual remain particularly relevant to contemporary discussions on wandering feelings—the transmission and transformation of emotions across cultures and historical periods.

> The emotions became a sort of institution. They were controlled in the same way as a ritual. Many of the ceremonies practised by primitive peoples are simulated situations with the obvious aim of arousing in all, by means of the same attitudes and gestures, one and the same emotion, welding them all together in a sort of superior individuality and preparing them all for the same action.
>
> (Febvre & Folca, 1973: 15)

In succeeding decades, the discipline broadened and established itself as a distinct area. Thereafter, the history of emotions became methodologically related to newer historiographical approaches, including the history of concepts, historical constructivism, cultural history, and the history of the body (Burke, 2008). This new historiographical discussion is founded on the concept that not only the manifestation of emotions but also the feelings themselves are taught, comparable to the sociology of ethnology of emotions. Feelings, as well as their expression, are shaped and changed by culture and history. Emotions can be traced as social significance and intensity have varied historically and culturally. As a result, many historians in this field believe that "feeling is as basic a category of history as class, race, or gender" (Bailey, 2016: 164).

In recent years, a variety of distinct methodological aspects have been considered to develop this field. Some historians of emotions have used the term "*emotionology*" to refer to the historical study of emotional norms and values. After 2000, the history of emotions' methodological spectrum has been widened to encompass performative, constructivist, and theoretical perspectives. As Bailey describes, emotional habitus, emotional practice, and emotive are three of the most important methodological notions nowadays. There are other phrases like emotional community, emotional regime, or emotional style that indicate the distinct range and dedication of emotional cultures, as well as terms like emotional broker or emotional go-between that represent the cultural translation and mediation of feelings (Bailey, 2016: 164–165).

In 1985, the social historians Peter and Carol Stearns developed the word *emotionology* to explain the emotional norms sustained in historical societies and gave one of the most successful methodological techniques (Stearns & Stearns, 1985). Barbara Rosenwein, another significant historian of emotions, has demonstrated that historical actors' emotional experiences are shaped not just by regimes, but also by a range of groups with "a shared stake, interest, values, and aspirations" (Rosenwein, 2006: 24). On the other hand, *Sex Before the Sexual Revolution: Intimate Life in England 1918–1963*, published by Steven Szreter and Kate Fisher, is a more traditional single-country study that challenges the popular assumption that couples' sex lives prior to the sexual revolution were unsatisfied and a cause of shame. They demonstrate that prior to the 1960s, the prevalent societal silence regarding sex allowed couples to establish their own hidden meanings and private habits, boosting closeness between them (Szreter & Fisher, 2010).

By comparing classic medieval European courtly love writings with contemporary analogues outside of Europe, William Reddy aims to find the foundations of a particularly Western notion of passionate love. In 2012, he published *The Making of Romantic Love: Longing and Sexuality in Europe, South Asia, and Japan, 900–1200 CE*. This research addresses a variety of modern issues and argues that Europe or the West evolved a distinct culture of romantic love that, once exported, went on to revolutionize the practices of "traditional" nations across the world has become a cliché. Reddy's work provides a comparative examination, concluding that the West has acquired a unique understanding of the connection between love and sexual desire. Comparing different regions and cultures, Reddy demonstrates that, just like in other aspects of life, people make culturally validated decisions about what they want and how they want to get it. Sexual desire appears to be an emotion triggered by a variety of culturally specific judgments about cleanliness, prosperity, health, and partners who correspond to gender stereotypes (Reddy, 2012).

Another advantage of the history of love and sexuality is that historians must look for women's writings and private materials that are often overlooked in event-driven political histories. Recent outstanding works like Claire Langhamer's *The English in Love* give a nuanced picture of shifting love relationships in twentieth-century Britain and have highlighted these kinds of neglected love histories in less popular materials. With this literature survey, it is evident that the study of love and sexuality, as well as the history of emotions, is gaining increasing interest in academic circles. Hundreds of articles and books have been released to investigate this subject. However, in South Asia, the topics of love and sexuality as well as their emotional paradigms have received little attention. Therefore, this chapter will examine the changes in emotional history in Sri Lanka and its peculiar traditions of love and sexuality.

Throughout the pre-modern era, Asian societal hierarchies and family structures classified love and sexuality differently from contemporary European civilization. As a result, Europeans who traveled and represented European culture were puzzled by strange local customs in new colonies. With newly established colonial legacies, general behavioral patterns of pre-modern Asian people were questioned and subjected to change. These inquiries were sparked by travel diaries and biographies of European travelers and civil servants. The political future of South and Southeast Asian colonies was influenced by these new perspectives. On the other hand, it was viewed as the white author's burden to justify the Empire and its ethno-political frame through colonial knowledge-building projects. Therefore, studying, interpreting, and controlling emotional structures in society became an essential element in colonial social policy. Obviously, in India, social reforms were considered the white man's burden. As Kipling traces in *On the City Wall* (1901):

> It [India] will never stand alone, but the idea is a pretty one, and men are willing to die for it, and yearly the work of pushing and coaxing and scolding and petting the country into good living goes forward.
>
> (Kipling, 2013)

Later, Max Weber introduced Indian people as "uncultured masses" and described the matter as one of the a-literate (Thapar, 2018: 124–125). Therefore, the eagerness to advance these uncultured people in South Asia became a part of colonial political projects.

Colonial economic, social, and political processes collectively introduced colonial modernity to South Asian communities. Through various educational institutions and the expansion of print media, modern sensibilities and habits were gradually disseminated and popularized among the masses. As a result, colonial modernity had both direct and indirect consequences on the everyday lives of South Asians, reshaping their personal worldviews and emotional frameworks.

Within the broader colonial political landscape, the colonial government actively sought to regulate human bodies and emotions through various policies. These cultural interventions were often justified by colonial writers, whose works became integral to the discourse of Orientalism. Their attempts to portray the Orient as an exotic and unfamiliar cultural space, characterized by peculiar human behaviors, played a crucial role in shaping the relationship between the Orient and the Occident.

As Edward Said (1979: 2) observed, while these representations of the Orient were largely products of Western imagination, they nonetheless served a critical function. By constructing the East as an exotic and inferior counterpart, the West was able to define itself in opposition, reinforcing its own identity and perceived superiority.

> Orientalism can be discussed and analyzed as the corporate institution for dealing with the Orient dealing with it by making statements about it, authorizing views of it, describing it, by teaching it, settling it, ruling over it: in short, Orientalism as a Western-style for dominating, restructuring, and having authority over the Orient. It helped the European culture to gain strength and identity in contrast to the image of the Orient.
>
> (Said, 1979: 3)

As he further emphasized,

> the creation of "Orient" through various documents and media helped to maintain the relationship between Occident and Orient as a relationship of power, of domination, of varying degrees of a complex hegemony.
>
> (Said, 1979: 4)

The socio-cultural analyses of colonies came forward through many private and official publications. That can be understood as colonial knowledge-building projects.

These intellectual endeavors laid the foundation for the collective notion of distinguishing Europeans as "us" and non-Europeans as "them." The colonial administration reinforced European supremacy and framed Asian societies as inherently backward, drawing upon European cultural interpretations of the Orient. Colonial officials overseeing the documentation of the East contributed anthropological perspectives to Western academic discourse, embedding racial, caste, and class-based categorizations into their narratives.

These observations were not confined to private memoranda but extended to official colonial censuses, which were used to classify individuals and analyze social behaviors. By identifying patterns across different racial or caste groups, colonial authorities sought to legitimize their rule and assert control. Over time, these studies came to be regarded as objective representations of colonial societies. Consequently, official and informal colonial discourses became deeply interconnected, shaping governance strategies. The colonial administration used these orientalist frameworks to draft new laws and regulations aimed at controlling the colonial "other." Thus, orientalist scholarship not only enriched Western academic knowledge but also directly served the administrative machinery of empire.

In Sri Lanka, all three colonial powers—the Portuguese, Dutch, and British—perceived the island's society as a distinct social system, yet indigenous customs and behaviors were often ridiculed. The European perspective on love and sexuality led to significant misinterpretations of pre-modern Sri Lankan practices, frequently labeling them as immoral or unethical. The indigenous family structure and sexual norms, particularly the prevalence of polyandry and polygamy alongside conventional family arrangements, were regarded with both curiosity and condemnation by colonial observers.

Colonial writers frequently noted the flexible sexual principles among the Sinhalese, viewing them as fundamentally opposed to European norms. These practices were deemed savage and uncivilized, reinforcing the colonial mission of "civilizing" the colonized. The transformation of social behaviors among Sri Lankans can be understood through a dual-layered process: the tension between traditional Sinhalese sexual norms and colonial attitudes highlights the diverse ways human emotions manifest across civilizations. When an entrenched cultural system in a colony encountered external pressures—whether through direct enforcement or subtle incentives—the colonized often adapted to the imposed behavioral patterns over time.

As Santhushya Fernando et al. explain in relation to Sri Lankan society:

> Human beliefs, practices and taboos on sexuality have varied in different periods of time in different parts of the world, with what was considered "normal" or "abnormal" at the time, often being controlled by a complex and constantly changing plethora of factors. These factors include the dominant culture, religion, politics and the media. For instance, how and how much one chose to reveal or conceal them, have often been politicized and commoditized based on when and where one lived. This is especially true for women.
>
> (Fernando et al., 2018: 15)

Likewise, colonialism brought direct and indirect influences on the community behaviors of Sri Lankans that tallied with the modernization process.

In numerous colonial publications, many conceptual narrations could be found to illustrate these cultural clashes between Sri Lankans and the colonizers. To understand the critical views of colonial writers on Sri Lankan marriage and sexuality, there were many examples that could be evaluated. Robert Knox (1641–1720) was a notable writer in colonial Sri Lanka who spent nine years as an outdoor prisoner in the Kandyan kingdom. Knox and other sailors were taken by islanders when their ship was wrecked, despite the fact that the Dutch colonizers had established dominance in many parts of the coastal area of the country. Knox was imprisoned by the royal officers of the kingdom in the central highlands and kept in a tiny hamlet. When his fellow European colleagues married local women and settled down, Knox spent his time in this village in Kandy as a devout Christian. His sole desire was to flee and return to England. Therefore, from the beginning, Knox viewed this society as an inferior social order compared to his own society and he enthusiastically described the notion of love and sexuality of the local Sinhalese as a wicked tradition. His devotion to Christianity and the influences he gained from contemporary English society made him critical of the strange sexual behaviors of the people. Thus, the descriptions of Knox should be understood parallel with some elucidations of family and sexuality in seventeenth-century England.

Alice Brabcová highlights that in seventeenth-century England, marriage and sexual morals played a crucial role in shaping society, as the family—centered around a married couple—was the fundamental social, economic, and political unit (Brabcová, 2006). The Christian social order reinforced the notion of the husband's authority over his wife, children, and servants, legitimizing it as part of a divinely ordained hierarchy. Women, perceived as physically, intellectually, morally, and even spiritually inferior to men, were subjected to an unquestioned patriarchal structure. In English society, marriage was not only a means of legalizing sexual relations but also a pathway to securing social status. A woman's respectability and prestige were entirely dependent on marriage, leaving little room for independent existence.

During his time in England, Robert Knox was deeply influenced by these Christian ideals, viewing marriage as the only legitimate institution through which love and sexuality could be expressed. Consequently, women who did not conform to this model were seen as lacking in virtue and moral standing.

In his book *An Historical Relation of the Island Ceylon, in the East-Indies* (1681), Knox provided a strikingly different portrayal of marriage and sexuality in Sri Lanka. He observed that

> both women and men (in Kandy) do commonly wed four or five times before they can settle themselves to their contentation [sic].

His description of Sinhalese family structures and what he perceived as their relaxed sexual norms was accompanied by harsh criticisms, particularly towards women and their approach to love and relationships. Knox interpreted these practices through his own cultural lens, concluding that there was

> nothing so common as whoredom

in Sinhalese society. His account exemplifies how colonial observers often imposed their own moral frameworks onto non-European societies, reinforcing stereotypes of cultural superiority while misinterpreting the complexities of indigenous social customs.

> Indeed, here no public whores are allowed by the authority. In the city, some that have followed that trade, have oftentimes by the king's order been severely punished by whipping and having their ears and hair cutoff. But in private few or none can exempt themselves… Indeed, the public trade would be bad and hardly maintained them that exercised it, the private one being so great. And I also think they be all whores, yet they abhor the name of Vesou, which is whore.
>
> Neither do they in their anger reproach one another with it, unless they should lay with a man of inferior quality to themselves. And the woman reckons herself as much obliged to the man for his company, as he does to her for hers. In these affairs, the woman is very expert (it being their continual practice) to keep their design from the husband's knowledge: though by his own experience he cannot

> be ignorant of women's devices. And unless he catches them in the act he doth not much trouble himself a Cuckold; Cuckolds [sic] being so common, that is not here regarded
>
> (Knox, 1681: 92)

Knox's depiction reflects the patriarchal biases common to both colonial European and indigenous Sri Lankan societies, where women's sexuality was viewed with suspicion and moral judgment. His observations reinforced the stereotype of Sinhalese women as morally lax, perpetuating a narrative that justified colonial intervention. Such attitudes echo findings in cross-cultural research on gender and sexuality, where patriarchal social structures often regulate female sexuality through social sanctions and stigma (Connell, 2005; Kandiyoti, 1988).

Knox further recounts:

> It is law here, that if a man catches another in bed with his wife, he may, be it whosoever, kill him and her if he pleases. It has so happened that the man has come to the door when another has been within with his wife, there being no way to escape, the woman has taken a pan of hot ashes, and as he opened the door, her husband being entering, cast them in his eyes, and so she and her bed-fellow made an escape.
>
> (Knox, 1681: 92)

This harsh legal stance reflects the complex interplay between sexuality, honor, and violence in historical Sri Lankan society, paralleling similar norms in other patriarchal cultures (Nussbaum, 1999). The emphasis on honor and control of female sexuality often precipitates gender-based violence, a phenomenon still relevant in contemporary psychosexual therapy when addressing trauma related to cultural norms (Kitzinger, 2005).

European colonial writers frequently framed love, sexuality, emotions, and marriage in Sri Lanka through a lens that pathologized any deviation from European norms as uncivilized. Modern historians view Knox's accounts as partial, anecdotal, and influenced by hearsay rather than empirical observation (Obeyesekere, 1967; Pieris, 1956). Yet, some scholars appreciate these writings as alternative perspectives offering insight into the fluidity and diversity of social and emotional relationships in pre-colonial Sri Lanka (Kemper, 1980).

Despite relatively open romantic and sexual practices before colonization, Sri Lankan culture maintained formal marriage practices with ceremonies and customs. Knox noted:

> But enough of this Ribaldry, let us turn away to more honest practices. To speak of their marriages, which make the bed lawful. There are not many ceremonies used in or about the same. Here is no wooing for a wife. The parents commonly make the match, and in their choice regard more the quality and descent than the beauty. If they are agreed all is done. The match being thus made, the man

> carries or sends to the woman her wedding clothes; which is a cloth containing six or seven-yard length, and a linen waste-coat wrought with Blue and Red. If the man be so poor that he cannot buy a cloth, it is the custom to borrow one… The day being come[sic], he attended with his friends goes to her house, which is always in the evening, and bring provisions and sweet-meats with him according to his ability, towards the charge of the wedding… Then the bride and bridegroom both eat together in one dish, which is to intimate that they are both of one rank and quality, and sometimes they tie their thumbs together, but not always and night go to sleep together.
>
> (Knox, 1681: 91–92)

This passage highlights how Sinhalese marriage rituals emphasized social equality and communal bonding, contrasting with the more elaborate European ceremonies (Hayley, 1923). The practice of eating from one dish symbolized unity, a motif resonant with symbolic interactionist theories about ritual and social cohesion (Durkheim, 1912).

Clinical Vignette

In psychosexual therapy, understanding such cultural symbolism is vital. For instance, a client from a Sri Lankan working-class background described anxiety surrounding sexual intimacy. Through exploring cultural traditions and family expectations, the client realized his internal conflict stemmed from inherited values around marital roles and communal identity, rather than personal desire alone. Recognizing these cultural scripts allowed therapeutic work to foster healthier intimacy patterns by validating cultural identity while addressing individual emotional needs (Sue & Sue, 2016).

F.A. Hayley (1923) noted that elaborate wedding ceremonies were more common among upper-caste and affluent families, and that matriarchal marriage traditions existed among some highland Sinhalese, illustrating the regional and social diversity of matrimonial practices (Hayley, 1923: 155, 167).

Marriage in early Sri Lanka was a regulated social institution governed by legal and customary norms, playing a key role in maintaining social order. Steven Kemper (1980) emphasized that caste boundaries heavily influenced marriage choices and sexual selection, reinforcing structured social stratifications.

Kemper also observed:

> To be sure, some Indie characteristics have held fast in Sinhalese society. Marriage has been legitimated only within the caste group, and while society has tolerated a high caste man's having extramarital relations with a low caste woman, a high caste woman taking a low caste lover has been in peril of her life. But, on the whole, traditional Kandyan society seems to have been almost indifferent to Indie strictures on sexuality.
>
> (Kemper, 1980: 302)

This reflects the complex gendered and caste-based double standards that regulated sexual behavior, similar to findings in South Asian gender studies (Chakravarti, 1993).

Significantly, Sri Lankan concepts of love, sexuality, and marriage were distinct from Indian norms, particularly Hindu practices where women's virginity and virtue were highly emphasized and socially policed (Ludden, 1999). Sri Lankan Sinhalese society exhibited more fluid sexual customs, which attracted orientalists' attention and critique.

Western writers, unfamiliar with Sinhalese marital customs, sought to depict these practices, which were different from those in their own societies. Due to various socioeconomic factors, Sri Lanka developed several distinctive marriage practices, with polygamy and polyandry becoming socially accepted norms. One well-known example was Ekageikema, a polyandrous system practiced among the Kandyan Sinhalese. One of the earliest records of this practice can be found in a Portuguese source. Joao Ribeiro, a Portuguese captain who served during the final years of Portuguese rule in Ceylon, described this unique marital tradition in 1685.

> The marriages of the Sinhalese are celebrated in a very ridiculous way. When a young girl is about to be married to a man of the same rank as herself (for it is not allowed for men or women to marry either above or below their caste,) she first agrees as to the conditions and acquaints her relations with what she has done, and they have to consider whether they are contended with those terms: if they are satisfied, a great repast is prepared and the ceremony is concluded. The first night of consummation is allotted to the husband, the second to his brother, the third to the next brother, and so on as far as the seventh night, when if there be more brothers, the remainder are not entitled to the privilege of the eldest six. These first days being past, the husband has no greater claim on his wife than his brothers have; if he finds her alone, he takes her to himself, but if one of his brothers be with her, he cannot disturb them. Thus, one wife is sufficient for a whole family and all their property is in common among them; they bring their earnings into one general stock, and the children call all the brothers indifferently their fathers.
>
> (Ribeiro, 1847: 64)

According to Sri Lankan vernacular sources, such as the *Rajavaliya*, the practice of polyandry was not only common among rural Sinhala families but was also observed in some royal households. During the Kotte Kingdom in the fifteenth century, for instance, a king and his brother were both married to the same princess, and the marriage continued without issue. The queen was publicly honored (Wimalasurendra Thero, 1995: 74). As such, the polyandry system in pre-colonial Sri Lanka was widely accepted, and a woman's virtue was not judged by the number of husbands she had.

In addition to polyandry, there were other unconventional sexual practices in the Kandyan Kingdom. These practices were often linked to social and political power and were particularly prevalent among the upper-caste classes. Knox noted,

> In some cases, the man will permit their wives and daughters to lye {sic} with other men. And that is, when intimate friends or great men chance to lodge at their houses, they commonly will send their wives or daughters to bear them company in their chamber. Neither do they reckon their wives to be whores for lying with them that are as good or better than themselves.
>
> (Knox, 1681: 92)

This illustrates that polyandry was practiced both within and outside of marriage in certain situations. British census officer Denham noted in the 1911 Census Review that living with multiple husbands in one household was becoming increasingly rare but still occurred in certain areas of the Kandyan provinces. In these cases, several brothers would marry a single woman and continue living together as a family. However, this did not mean that all the brothers shared the same wife in the same way; instead, the husbands would say, "we earn our living in the same house," while the wife would reply, "I cook rice for all of them" (Ceylon at the Census of 1911: 329–330). Their children received the benefits of parenthood from all fathers, and the wife and her children enjoyed equal marital rights.

The most intriguing aspect of the polyandry practice was that the wife had the authority to refuse the admission of a second husband, even if he were the brother of the first. The consent of the wife's family was required for such a union to take place (Armour, 1861: 9). In addition, local families had established fair rules concerning the ownership and inheritance of property among these polyandrous households. British civil servants and judges often recorded how property laws were linked to these customs, highlighting the impartiality of property transfers to children, irrespective of the number of husbands. As D'oyly observed, when one of the husbands passed away, the woman retained all the rights that would normally be granted to a widow, including her late husband's share of the estate (D'oyly, 1975: 163). After the death of a parent, the children of these joint unions were entitled to claim their deceased father's portion of the property (Pieris, 1956: 170). Thus, the practice of polyandry in pre-colonial Sri Lanka reflected a unique understanding of love, sexuality, and property rights, with a focus on communal and practical arrangements rather than emotional connections.

Several scholars have explored the socio-economic context of polyandry in Sri Lanka, noting that imbalanced sex ratios due to factors like infanticide, war, and disease may have contributed to the practice. Additionally, in rural areas, farmers were often called upon to serve as soldiers or in other government roles, leaving the remaining brothers to care for the family and manage agricultural tasks. This system helped maintain social stability. The geographical context of the Kandyan region, with its hilly terrain and limited arable land, also played a role. Families were faced with the challenge of passing down land through generations, and polyandry allowed for a more efficient system of inheritance by preventing the division of land into smaller, unmanageable parcels. In this way, socio-economic needs rather than emotional connections drove sexual behaviors and family structures. However, as Steven Kemper and Tambiah argue, polyandry in Sri Lanka cannot be reduced to a purely economic arrangement. Instead, it reflects a Sinhalese approach to reconciling subsistence needs with sexuality, an approach that contrasts with the more conventional norms of monogamy (Kemper, 1980: 300).

Clinical Vignette

During a psychosexual therapy session, a middle-aged male client from a Kandyan lineage reflected on the silence around his grandmother's polyandrous marriage. As a child, he remembered asking why his grandmother had "two husbands," and being told to keep quiet. This silence led to confusion and shame around intimacy in his adult life. Therapy helped him explore how deeply embedded societal norms and transgenerational messages around propriety and silence had influenced his own experiences of sexual identity and belonging. This exemplifies how inherited, unspoken legacies around familial structures can shape psychosexual well-being across generations (Fonagy et al., 2003; Levant et al., 2009).

In contrast, polygamy was also a well-established tradition among certain segments of the Sinhalese population. Both men and women had the freedom to have multiple partners, with men often maintaining several wives. As noted in *Armour's Grammar of the Kandyan Law*, polygamy, like polyandry, was not restricted by a set number of spouses. However, a woman could not take a second husband without her first husband's consent, while a man could take a second wife without his first wife's approval (Armour, 1861: 9). These marital practices presented challenges for the British when they attempted to introduce the Marriage Registration Act in 1859. Even after the law was enacted, many native officers, especially those of high rank, found it difficult to adapt to the new monogamous norms, as they had multiple wives (Ceylon Administration Reports, 1868: 235–236). Kemper referred to these peculiar marriage traditions as *family socialism*, in which shared property, labor, and sexuality were integral to the family structure. He noted that polyandrous households, much like polygynous ones, were marked by the sharing of resources and responsibilities, contributing to a form of communal living (Kemper, 1980: 310).

The social acceptance of polygamy shifted over time as Sri Lankans came into contact with British marriage customs. In later years, some villagers in the Kandyan region associated polyandry with sacrifice, sharing, and solidarity, seeing it as a reflection of brotherly, if not sisterly, behavior. In contrast, polygamy was increasingly viewed as morally questionable, bordering on prostitution, and thus earned a lower social standing (Kemper, 1980: 315). The changing perspectives on love, sexuality, and marriage in the face of British influence highlighted the difference between the socio-economic motivations underlying these practices and the more emotional, commitment-based views common in European societies. In a colonial context, sexual relationships were often viewed as socially constructed, with various forms of sexuality emerging in different cultural settings. The acceptance of these diverse sexual practices in Sri Lanka was based on respect for the relationship rather than conformity to Western notions of marital fidelity.

Ralph Pieris observed that, in Kandyan society, sexual and marital relationships were not fetishized or romanticized. They were seen as casual, inevitable aspects of life, and even extramarital affairs were generally tolerated. Marriage, however, was regarded as a sacred and indissoluble bond (Pieris, 1956: 197). In wedding ceremonies, caste and wealth were significant factors, often influencing the manner in which weddings were celebrated. Interestingly, the bridegroom's concern over whether his bride was a virgin was often negligible, a sentiment shared by Knox, who observed that Sinhalese men did not prioritize whether their wives were virgins at the time of their marriage (Knox, 1681: 92).

Despite the prevalence of polyandry and polygamy, family bonds remained strong in pre-colonial Sri Lanka. As John Davy noted in 1821, "Among few people, I believe, are family attachments more strong and sincere. There is little to divert or weaken them" (Davy, 1821: 289). Knox also observed that Sinhalese men were not typically jealous of their wives and that even the highest-ranking women in the land freely conversed with any men they pleased, even in the presence of their husbands (Knox, 1681: 92). This freedom of sexual expression in pre-colonial Sri Lanka set the Sinhalese apart from other cultures, offering a level of liberty in sexual relationships that was uncommon in other parts of the world.

At the village level, while people may have gossiped about or criticized such practices, there was little interference with the free choices made by individuals in matters of marriage or separation. British court reports reveal that fathers sometimes kept a separate portion of land for daughters who had experienced difficulties in their marriages and returned home (Armour, 1861: 33; Hayley, 1923: 370; *Niti Niganduwa*, 1880; Sawers, 1826: 7). A daughter who divorced or was destitute was entitled to family support, unless she had dishonored the family in some way (Obeyesekere, 1967: 43). Marriage was seen as a sincere contract, but one that could be dissolved without animosity if necessary. Kemper further emphasized that these marriage customs were flexible, uncertain, and subject to revision, reflecting a broader trend in the Kandyan community (Kemper, 1980: 303).

Nevertheless, there was one strict social rule in Kandyan society: relationships between individuals of different castes were not permitted. Inter-caste sexual relationships were severely punished, and anyone found engaging in such behavior would face legal consequences. If an upper-caste man kept a woman of a lower caste, the king would issue a warning to end the relationship and punish the woman. These penalties were even more severe when women had relations with lower-caste men, often resulting in death (Armour, 1861: 8). Illegitimate children, particularly those born of low-caste mothers, were excluded from inheriting their father's property unless there was a written deed or verbal agreement witnessed by respected individuals (Pieris, 1956: 202).

The British officers' observations painted a complex picture of love and sexuality in Sri Lanka, one that differed significantly from European norms. In contrast to the rigid, morality-driven systems of Victorian Britain, relationships in Sri Lanka were shaped more by caste hierarchies and kinship systems than by adherence to strict sexual codes. The socio-cultural fabric of pre-colonial Sinhalese society thus allowed for a broader and more diverse range of sexual and marital practices. As Steven Kemper (1980) argued, these customs reflected a distinctively Sinhalese approach to managing intimacy, sexuality, and kinship—grounded in social functionality rather than conformity to Western ideals of romantic monogamy.

The latitude of relationships permitted in Sri Lankan society—particularly in the "coming and going of women," as Yalman phrased it—was intricately linked to kinship structures. Cross-cousin marriage, for instance, played a central role in organizing both relational expectations and the emotional architecture of family life. In this context, kinship terminology and the separable property rights of men and women operated as mechanisms of social coherence. While elite groups emphasized descent-based social difference, in practical terms these distinctions were often redundant. Families were structured around a wide range of flexible marriage arrangements, shaped by geography, class, and lineage (Kemper, 1980: 307).

This structural flexibility extended to marital dissolution. In both customary and legal terms, the Kandyan marriage system allowed for separation at the discretion of either spouse. Armour's Grammar of Kandyan Law (1861) provides insight into this dynamic: a husband could dismiss his wife at will, with or without cause, and a wife held the reciprocal right to divorce her husband. In such cases, the wife was typically returned to her natal village along with any property or dowry she had brought into the marriage. The absence of permanent shared marital property underlined a legal recognition of individual economic autonomy.

Two principal marriage forms governed these arrangements: Deega and Beena. In a Deega marriage, the wife moved into her husband's home and relinquished her claim to natal family property, while in Beena, the husband resided with the wife's family and often accessed her inheritance. Importantly, in Beena marriages, the wife and her kin retained the authority to expel the husband if the union proved unsatisfactory (Armour, 1861: 13).

When children were involved, additional provisions applied. If the wife was separated without fault, she was entitled to maintenance until the child was of age to be transferred to the father's household. However, if the wife initiated separation without justifiable cause, the husband had no such obligation to support her (Armour, 1861: 14). These detailed protocols suggest that while Sri Lankan marriage law reflected patriarchal traditions, it also included robust safeguards for women's property and personal rights—nuances often overlooked in colonial interpretations.

British administrative reports and judicial records from the colonial era reveal the intricacy of these family systems. Far from being static or primitive, the Kandyan marital customs were highly adaptive, offering a socially sanctioned framework for both union and dissolution. Despite entrenched boundaries related to caste, class, and gender, the Kandyan system demonstrated a notable degree of equity in matters of marital autonomy and resource allocation.

Clinical Vignette

In contemporary psychotherapeutic practice, echoes of this marital flexibility can still surface. One female client, originally from a Kandyan lineage, shared her confusion about marital loyalty and separation. Her parents had divorced amicably, with her mother retaining land and continuing family ties independently. In therapy, she gradually realized how this matrilineal resilience, embedded in her heritage, offered a foundation for asserting boundaries in her own romantic life. Understanding these cultural legacies can be crucial in psychosexual work with Sri Lankan clients, where identity, history, and emotional inheritance intersect.

Transformation of Sinhalese Family and Sexuality During the Colonial Era

Over the course of 450 years of colonial rule, Sri Lanka underwent profound socio-cultural transformations. Western ideals, religious values, and juridical concepts infiltrated local traditions, fundamentally altering how love, marriage, and sexuality were conceptualized and practiced. Colonial administrations introduced Western-style education, Christianity, and legal reforms that reshaped everyday life, particularly in relation to intimate and familial structures. The modernization process, coupled with colonial administrative enforcement, compelled many Sri Lankans to gradually conform to European norms and moral expectations.

The earliest phase of colonial intervention began with the Portuguese, whose marriage systems were grounded in Catholic doctrine. While their influence remained largely confined to coastal regions, it marked the beginning of institutional regulation over local matrimonial traditions. The Dutch, who followed, imposed even more rigid frameworks. According to Bulten et al. (2018: 58), Dutch colonial authorities reduced the number of prohibited kinship degrees and permitted cousin marriages within Christian communities, while simultaneously forbidding unions with non-Christians.

Moreover, Dutch administrators aggressively policed sexual morality. Adultery, particularly when committed by married women, was criminalized and punishable by exile. Divorced individuals judged guilty of infidelity were prohibited from remarrying, effectively ostracizing them from society. These punitive moral codes were internalized through colonial education systems, which served to indoctrinate native populations into Protestant ethical values. Schools and churches functioned not only as centers of learning but as institutions of sexual and marital regulation.

The Dutch also institutionalized marriage registration through a formalized two-step process. Initially, the couple's intent to marry was announced by a village schoolmaster and read aloud for three consecutive Sundays during church services. If no objections were raised, the marriage was validated in church. However, in certain areas such as Galle, this final step was often informally bypassed (Bulten et al., 2018: 64), reflecting regional variation in compliance and enforcement.

These early colonial interventions laid the groundwork for even more structured regulation under British rule. After securing full control of the island in 1815, the British introduced sweeping legal reforms, aimed at integrating both coastal and Kandyan marriage customs into a unified framework. British administrators, influenced by the ideology of the "White Man's Burden," deemed Sinhalese customs—especially polyandry and informal unions—as insufficiently "civilized." In their view, regulating personal relationships was essential not only for social order but for moral uplift. Consequently, personal life, particularly sexuality and kinship, became central to the imperial civilizing mission.

Christian priests were given legal authority to officiate marriages under new marriage registration laws passed in 1822. Initially, the British allowed for regional legal variations, particularly in Kandyan provinces, which retained a semi-autonomous legal status under the 1815 Kandyan Convention. However, with increasing efforts to standardize legal practices, this autonomy was gradually dismantled. Ordinances No. 6 of 1847 and No. 3 of 1870 served to harmonize disparate marriage laws, reinforcing Victorian ideals across the island.

A turning point came with the 1859 Kandyan Marriage Registration Ordinance, which officially invalidated traditional ceremonial marriages. From this point on, only registered marriages were legally recognized. Ordinance No. 3 of 1870 expanded this mandate island-wide, stripping Kandyan marriage systems of their legal autonomy and replacing them with British legal constructs (Dissanayake, 1963: 8–20). The erosion of indigenous marital customs was thus not incidental but strategically codified through colonial legal reforms.

To enforce these sweeping changes, colonial authorities employed a dual strategy. On one side were formal institutions—courts, registrars, and local magistrates—tasked with imposing compliance. On the other were informal but powerful cultural agents: missionaries, educators, vernacular writers, and capitalist elites. These figures functioned as emissaries of modernization, using pulpits, pamphlets, and publications to propagate the vision of a monogamous, nuclear family as the cornerstone of a civilized society.

Christian missionaries, in particular, were instrumental. They openly denounced polyandry and polygamy, urging converts to embrace registered, monogamous unions. Their moral authority grew in tandem with their institutional presence, and they increasingly regarded themselves as custodians of Sri Lankan ethical reform. Churches became centers not only of worship but also of ideological transformation, with marriage sermons doubling as cultural indoctrination.

In therapy, a middle-aged Sri Lankan woman recounted feeling shame surrounding her parents' unregistered union. Despite their long-standing cohabitation and social recognition as a married couple, the lack of legal validation—imposed by colonial-era standards—had left her questioning the legitimacy of her own birth. Through psychodynamic exploration, she came to understand that her family's practices were historically grounded in Kandyan custom rather than moral failure. This shift helped her reconcile personal identity with ancestral legacy, a common therapeutic task in postcolonial societies.

Recent scholarship has highlighted how American and British missionaries dedicated their lives to shaping native women into "ideal Christian brides." Their mission went beyond merely legalizing marriages; they sought to instill discipline in women. This was seen as a part of the so-called "white man's burden," and figures like Mrs. Harriet Winslow, a missionary in Eastern Sri Lanka, took an active role in these reformative efforts. In her memoir, she reflects on the challenges she faced:

> Great hostility to the education of girls by the Tamil people and the fear of breaking caste made it difficult at first to induce girls to become boarding pupils. But eventually, the school began to attract pupils and supply native teachers and wives for the pastors. The mission permitted the girls to remain in school until they received "an eligible offer" of marriage.
>
> (Robert, 1997: 119)

Before Mrs. Winslow's death in 1833, twelve girls from her school had converted to Christianity and married Christian husbands, thus becoming models for Tamil Christian marriage life. She described these unions as "the loveliness of domestic virtue in the midst of abounding vice," illustrating the moral transformation missionaries sought to bring about in Sri Lanka (Winslow, 1835: 273). Some later scholars have also lauded these social changes, viewing the missionaries as pioneers who introduced "new vistas of progress and possibility."

As Alagiyawanna (1991/92: 1) notes,

> The missionaries brought with them not only their religion but also a whole culture—the entire gamut of attitudes and feelings; the discipline of developing modern societies, and a set of social, economic, and political ideas which were new to the East.

These missionaries were not merely religious reformers; they were cultural agents, working to destabilize traditional systems while simultaneously presenting new possibilities for progress in Sri Lanka, India, and beyond.

This shift in moral and social values was further reinforced by legal regulations governing marriage and property rights. Through these regulations, the British administration instilled a Victorian ethical hegemony within Sri Lankan society, which quickly transformed the cultural norms surrounding relationships. Virtue, chastity, and virginity became expected in nineteenth-century Sri Lankan culture, particularly concerning women. Some vernacular poetesses even extolled the virtue of young brides, urging them to maintain their chastity as a necessary condition for a successful marriage (Jayaneththi, 2013). This shift in societal expectations was directly tied to the legalization of marriage and the subsequent modernization of the island. As Emily Burrill (2015: 2) explains, "Marriage binds individuals to each other, just as it binds married persons to larger social, religious, and political communities."

The influence of Westernization on Sri Lankan society during the nineteenth century led to a radical transformation in local attitudes towards love, sexuality, and family structures. Among the newly educated upper class, including some Kandyan chiefs, there was strong support for these Western ethical frameworks. Figures like Jeronis Pieris and James Alwis criticized traditional Kandyan marriage practices, particularly polyandry and polygamy. Pieris, for example, condemned polygamy as a "brutal practice," while Alwis observed that among the Kandyan Sinhalese, marriage was treated as a matter of little importance. He claimed that many native Sinhalese, even those who had converted to Christianity, did not grasp the "sacredness" of marriage, particularly in rural areas where "white man's foot never trod" (Roberts, 1975: 28).

These reformers believed that the solution to these "barbarous" customs lay in converting the population to Christianity and enforcing new marital norms based on Christian teachings. Over time, the pressure to register marriages in accordance with these Western norms increased, particularly in the Kandyan region, where many locals initially resisted. However, as British officers sought to enforce compliance, even local agents were made to understand the importance of registering marriages. Some local officers were even threatened with the loss of their positions unless they adhered to the new marriage regulations (Meththananda, 2006: 150).

Despite the resistance, these institutional efforts ultimately succeeded in establishing marriage as a legally recognized institution, aligning with the Western ethical framework. Missionaries and other agents of colonialism used newspapers, pamphlets, and other forms of media to promote these new ideas about marriage and sexuality. These changes were perceived as a sign of progress, and many Sri Lankans, influenced by both colonial authorities and local reformers, began to reconfigure their cultural practices to align with these new ideals.

Some Buddhist reform leaders, such as Anagarika Dharmapala, also praised the new ethical standards imposed by colonialism, even as they critiqued the morality of native customs. As Guruge (1965) explains, these leaders promoted a new way of life based on Western ideals, which led to a re-evaluation of traditional values, particularly concerning love and sexuality. Vernacular publications, in particular, became sites of intense debate between old and new practices, with the Buddhist code of virtues being reinterpreted in light of colonial influences. This shift in thinking led to a new emphasis on the importance of virginity and chastity, particularly for women, as part of a larger effort to modernize Sri Lankan society.

Clinical Vignette

A young Sinhalese woman, recently engaged, entered therapy grappling with intense guilt over a premarital sexual relationship. Raised in a Buddhist household yet educated in a Christian school, she expressed confusion over conflicting values surrounding chastity, honor, and love. Therapy helped her identify how Victorian moral standards—imported during the colonial period and reinforced by school curricula—had taken root in her psyche. By disentangling these inherited beliefs from her personal values, she began to reclaim a healthier and more authentic understanding of her sexuality.

In the post-independence era, Sri Lanka has undergone significant changes, including a broader discourse around love and sexuality. Contemporary debates now include the recognition of transgender people, whose experiences of gender and sexuality have also shaped the ongoing discussion. However, even as these modern ideas take root, Sri Lankan society remains anchored in traditional moral codes, particularly regarding marriage and sexuality. As C. Lynch (2007: 9) notes, "many Sinhala Buddhists consider women to be the agents who will hold the nation together." These moral codes continue to influence the institution of marriage, even as it faces new challenges in the context of modern societal transformations. Despite increasing opportunities for women in education and the workforce, Sri Lanka's family law remains outdated, with same-sex marriages and civil unions still unrecognized. Furthermore, the country continues to stigmatize divorce, where individuals who undergo it are often seen as morally suspect.

Bruce Caldwell observes that, in comparison to the rest of South Asia, Sri Lanka's transition to a Western model of marriage has led to lower birth rates and fertility levels. He argues that the decline of the family-based society, and the shift to an economic system emphasizing individual attributes, has eroded the centrality of family involvement in marriage decisions. Nevertheless, these changes have had significant implications for how Sri Lankans now view love, sexuality, and marriage.

Today, Sri Lankan society is facing new challenges as the notion of love and sexuality continues to evolve. While the country has made strides in addressing issues such as gender roles and the recognition of diverse sexualities, it still grapples with its colonial legacy in shaping attitudes towards relationships. The traditional parameters surrounding marriage, family, and sexuality remain influential, and Sri Lanka's legal and social structures continue to reflect the complex interplay of colonial, religious, and cultural forces that have shaped the nation's moral identity.

Conclusion

The exploration of love, sexuality, and family in pre-colonial and colonial Sri Lanka reveals a complex, layered history that challenges Eurocentric narratives about morality, intimacy, and social order. Far from being monolithic or primitive, indigenous Sri Lankan practices around marriage—such as polyandry, polygamy, and fluid kinship structures—reflected pragmatic responses to geography, economy, and social cohesion. These practices not only provided stability but also embodied a distinct emotional and relational ethos that privileged communal responsibility over rigid gender binaries or romantic exclusivity.

Colonial encounters disrupted this equilibrium. Western missionaries, legal reforms, and Victorian moral codes reconfigured what it meant to be a spouse, a parent, a woman, or a man in Sri Lankan society. Through the mechanisms of religious conversion, legal standardization, and cultural propaganda, colonial powers reframed native intimacy as backward and immoral, advocating instead a sanitized ideal rooted in chastity, monogamy, and Christian domesticity. As this chapter has shown, these imposed norms were not adopted passively; they were resisted, contested, and selectively incorporated by local communities, producing hybridized cultural forms that continue to shape contemporary Sri Lankan understandings of love and family.

From a psychosexual perspective, the colonial reshaping of relational norms left emotional residues that persist in modern Sri Lankan society—shame around sexuality, the policing of female virtue, caste-based taboos, and an enduring discomfort with non-traditional family structures. As clinical observations suggest, individuals navigating their identities today often struggle with the internalized contradictions of these inherited values. Therapy, historical literacy, and cultural scholarship all offer routes through which these psychic legacies can be understood and, gradually, unlearned.

Ultimately, this chapter underscores the importance of rehistoricizing love and intimacy—not as timeless, universal feelings, but as cultural artifacts shaped by power, politics, and resistance. In doing so, it becomes possible to imagine a decolonial future where emotional authenticity is not constrained by imported ideologies, but informed by local histories, lived experiences, and a broader human capacity for relational diversity.

References

Alagiyawanna, K. L. V. (1991/1992). The Social Impact of Missionary Activities in Sri Lanka in the Early 19th Century. *Journal of the Royal Asiatic Society of Sri Lanka New Series*, 36, 1–12.

Armour, J. (1861). *Armour's Grammar of the Kandyan Law: Methodically Arranged and Digested, with a Copious Index, Glossary, and Appendix*. Colombo: Printed at the "Examiner" Press.

Bailey, C. (2016). Review: The History of Emotions. *Contemporary European History*, 25(1), 163–175.

Brabcová, A. (2006). *Marriage in Seventeenth-Century England: The Woman's Story*. Plzeň: University of West Bohemia.

Bulten, L., et al. (2018). Contested Conjugality: Sinhalese Marriage Practices in Eighteenth-Century Dutch Colonial Sri Lanka. *Annales de démographie historique*, 135(1), 51–80.

Burke, P. (2008). *What Is Cultural History?* Cambridge: Polity Press.

Burrill, E. (2015). *States of Marriage: Gender, Justice, and Rights in Colonial Mali*. Athens: Ohio University Press.

Caldwell, B. (1999). *Marriage in Sri Lanka: A Century of Change*. New Delhi: Hindustan Publishing Corporation.

Ceylon Administration Reports. (1868). Colombo: Ceylon Government Press.

Chakravarti, U. (1993). Conceptualising Brahmanical Patriarchy in Early India: Gender, Caste, Class and State. *Economic and Political Weekly*, 28(14), 579–585.

Connell, R. W., & Messerschmidt, J. W. (2005). Hegemonic Masculinity: Rethinking the Concept. *Gender & Society*, 19(6), 829–859.

Connell, R. W., & Messerschmidt, J. W. (2005). Hegemonic masculinity: Rethinking the concept. *Gender & Society, 19*(6), 829–859. https://doi.org/10.1177/0891243205278639

Davy, J. (1821). *An Account of the Interior of Ceylon, and of Its Inhabitants: With Travels in the Island*. London: Longman.

D'oyly, J. (1975). *A Sketch of the Constitution of the Kandyan Kingdom* (L. J. B. Turner, Ed.). Dehiwala: Tisara Prakasakayo Ltd.

Denham, E. B., & Cottle, H. C. (1911). *Ceylon at the Census of 1911: Being the Review of the Results of the Census of 1911*. Colombo: Government Printer.

Dissanayake, T. B., & de Soysa, A. B. C. (1963). *Kandyan Law and Buddhist Ecclesiastical Law*. Colombo: Dharmasamya Press.

Durkheim, É. (1995). *The Elementary Forms of Religious Life*. New York: Free Press.

Febvre, L., & Folca, K. (1973). *A New Kind of History and Other Essays*. New York: Harper & Row.

Fernando, S. et al. (2018). *Montage of Sexuality in Sri Lanka*. Colombo: College of Community Physicians of Sri Lanka.

Fonagy, P. (2003). The Developmental Roots of Borderline Personality Disorder in Early Attachment Relationships: A Psychoanalytic Perspective. In J. J. Skodol & E. B. Steuart (Eds.), *Borderline Personality Disorder: Etiology and Treatment* (pp. 291–314). Washington, DC: American Psychiatric Publishing.

Guruge, A. (1965). *Return to Righteousness: A Collection of Speeches, Essays, and Letters of the Anagarika Dharmapala*. Colombo: Ministry of Education and Cultural Affairs.

Hayley, F. A. (1923). *A Treatise on the Laws and Customs of the Sinhalese*. Colombo: Government Printers.

Jayaneththi, R. (2013). Women's Attitudes and Their Social Status as Discovered from the Poems in Colonial Sri Lanka. In M. Somathilake (ed.), *Sarathi* (pp. 123–165). Colombo: Ministry of Cultural Affairs.

Kandiyoti, D. (1988). Bargaining with patriarchy. *Gender & Society, 2*(3), 274–290. https://doi.org/10.1177/089124388002003004

Kemper, S. (1980). Polygamy and Monogamy in Kandyan Sri Lanka. *Journal of Comparative Family Studies*, 11(3), 299–323.

Kipling, R. (2013). *On the City Wall*. California: Createspace Independent Publishing Platform.

Kitzinger, C. (2005). "Speaking as a Heterosexual": (How) Does Sexuality Matter for Talk-in-Interaction? *Research on Language and Social Interaction, 38*(3), 221–265.

Knox, R. (1681). *An Historical Relation of the Island Ceylon in the East-Indies*. London: The Royal Society.

Levant, R. F., et al. (2009). Gender Differences in Alexithymia. *Psychology of Men & Masculinity*, 10(3), 190–203.

Ludden, D. (1999). *An Agrarian History of South Asia*. Cambridge: Cambridge University Press (The New Cambridge History of India, Vol. IV.4).

Lynch, C. (2007). *Juki Girls, Good Girls: Gender and Cultural Politics in Sri Lanka's Global Garment Industry*. Ithaca, NY: ILR Press.

Meththananda, T. (2006). *The Implementation of the Marriage Registration Ordinance in 1859. Sambavana*. Peradeniya: University of Peradeniya.

Miller, J. (2012). Identity, Sexuality and Commercial Sex among Sri Lankan Nnachchi. In A. Nichols (Ed.), *Sexualities*, 15(5–6), 554–569.

Nussbaum, M. C. (1999). Women and Equality: The Capabilities Approach. *International Labour Review*, *138*(3), 227–245.

Obeyesekere, G. (1967). *Land Tenure in Village Ceylon: A Sociological and Historical Study*. Cambridge: Cambridge University Press.

Pieris, R. (1956). *Sinhalese Social Organization: The Kandyan Period*. Peradeniya: Ceylon University Press Board.

Reddy, W. M. (2012). *The Making of Romantic Love: Longing and Sexuality in Europe, South Asia, and Japan, 900–1200 CE*. Chicago: University of Chicago Press.

Ribeiro, J. (1847). *History of Ceylon – 1685* (G. Lee, Trans.). Colombo: The Government Press.

Robert, D. L. (1997). *American Women in Mission: A Social History of Their Thought and Practice*. Macon: Mercer University Press.

Roberts, M. (1975). *Facets of Modern Ceylon History: Through the Letters of Jeronis Pieris*. Colombo: Hansa Publishers Ltd.

Rosenwein, B. H. (2006). *Emotional Communities in the Early Middle Ages*. Ithaca: Cornell University Press.

Said, E. W. (1979). *Orientalism*. New York: Vintage Books.

Sawers, S. (1826). Memoranda and Notes on the Kandyan Law of Inheritance, Marriage, Slavery, etc. In F. A. Hayley (Ed.), *A Treatise on the Laws and Customs of the Sinhalese* (pp. 566–677). Colombo: Government Printers.

Stearns, P. N., & Stearns, C. Z. (1985). Emotionology: Clarifying the History of Emotions and Emotional Standards. *The American Historical Review*, 90(4), 813–836.

Sue, D. W., & Sue, D. (2016). *Counseling the Culturally Diverse: Theory and Practice* (7th ed.). Hoboken, NJ: Wiley.

Szreter, S., & Fisher, K. (2010). *Sex Before the Sexual Revolution: Intimate Life in England, 1918–1963*. Cambridge: Cambridge University Press.

Thapar, R. (2018). Revisiting Max Weber's Religion of India. *Max Weber Studies*, 18(1), 122–139.

Wimalasurendra Thero, Rev. (1995). *The Rajavaliya* (B. Gunasekara, Trans.). New Delhi: Asian Educational Services.

Winslow, H. L., & Winslow, M. (1835). *A Memoir of Mrs. Harriet Wadsworth Winslow: Combining a Sketch of the Ceylon Mission*. New York: Leavitt, Lord & Co.Web Resource.

The Bowen Center. (2021). Introduction: Eight Concepts. Retrieved from: https://thebowencenter.org/theory

Chapter 13

Unveiling Intimacy: Exploring Hindu Perspectives in Therapy

Urvashi Malhotra

Introduction

India's association with sexuality and love evokes images of classical paintings and intricate temple carvings at Khajuraho, where couples and groups are depicted in various forms of intimacy. These visual narratives reflect an ancient cultural comfort with sexual expression, rooted in sacred texts like the *Kamasutra*, which offers detailed guidance on relationships, sexual compatibility, and courtship rituals (Pande, 2022; Vatsyayana, 2002).

Hindu mythology celebrates love, sensuality, and passion as sacred forces. Krishna is revered as the eternal lover, whose divine charm and flute captivated countless devotees. Shiva, in his form as *Ardhanarishwara*, embodies the fusion of masculine and feminine energies. In temples across India, worshippers offer prayers to the Shivalinga, a symbolic union of the phallus (linga) and the yoni (vulva), signifying the cosmic balance and unity of creation (Ancient Origins, 2019).

Ancient Indian literature and sculpture also celebrated women as autonomous sexual beings. The Nayika, or heroine, is depicted in classical poetry and art as a woman who is confident in her desires and an equal partner in pleasure. Many temple sculptures were didactic, intended to educate youth about physical relationships and marital roles through sacred aesthetics (Mason, 2004; Pande, 2022).

However, attitudes toward sexuality have changed dramatically over the centuries. Religious epics and scriptures such as the Ramayana and the Vedas began to reflect more restrictive ideas about female agency and purity. A well-known example is Sita's *agni pariksha*, a trial by fire she was compelled to undergo to prove her chastity after her abduction by Ravana. The symbolism of this test not only underscored public scrutiny of women's virtue but also institutionalized the idea that women's purity must be defended and validated, often at the cost of their dignity (Ray, 2017).

The Vedas, composed and transmitted by Brahmin men over centuries, established a patriarchal social order through the concept of *varna*. Society was divided into four hereditary castes: Brahmins (priests and scholars), Kshatriyas (warriors and rulers), Vaishyas (merchants and agriculturists), and Shudras (laborers and service providers) (Chakravarti, 1993; Joshi, 2017). This stratification permeated

DOI: 10.4324/9781003611387-13

domestic life, with joint family systems emphasizing obedience to familial hierarchy and the containment of women's autonomy (Rathore and Meena, 2022).

Over time, these hierarchical structures became deeply entrenched. Texts such as the Manu Smriti, composed in the first century CE, formalized gender inequality by asserting that women should be under the control of their fathers, husbands, or sons at all stages of life. Although women occasionally held ritual roles, they were denied property rights and social independence (Doniger and Smith, 1991).

Yet, amidst this rigidity, alternative philosophies such as Tantra emerged. Tantra promoted spiritual democratization and integrated sexuality, meditation, and bodily awareness as paths to enlightenment. Unlike mainstream Brahmanical doctrine, which tended to suppress sexual discourse, Tantric practices validated sexuality as a sacred force and challenged caste exclusivity (Doniger, 2009).

During colonial rule, British administrators and Christian missionaries reinforced conservative Vedic ideals and marginalized Tantric traditions. While colonial legislation contributed to the abolition of practices like child marriage and *sati*, it also introduced Victorian norms that stigmatized sexual expression. Public conversations about sex became taboo, and sex education was systematically neglected (Doniger, 2009).

One persistent issue in contemporary Hindu society is the disparity in the value placed on male and female children. Sons are often preferred for their role in continuing the family name and performing ancestral rites, while daughters are viewed as financial liabilities due to dowry expectations and marriage costs. India's national gender ratio, with only 943 women for every 1000 men, reflects this imbalance and the lingering effects of gender-biased social norms (Census of India, 2011).

Even as society evolves, many Hindu customs surrounding marriage, gender roles, and intergenerational responsibilities remain strong. Until recent decades, arranged marriages within the same caste and community were considered standard. However, Hindu society today includes at least four active generations, each practicing vastly different interpretations of culture. Older generations tend to preserve inherited traditions. Middle-aged couples often inhabit nuclear family arrangements, adapting rituals to modern sensibilities. Young adults, particularly those aged 15 to 24, show greater distance from tradition and are more likely to engage in premarital relationships, influenced by globalization and exposure to Western sexual norms through social media (Bhargava, 2020; Chakravorty et al., 2021).

While many still choose partners based on caste, language, and religious alignment, younger generations increasingly select their own spouses, sometimes in defiance of parental expectations. This generational divide creates tension, particularly for those navigating sexual identity, autonomy, and intimacy in relationships.

Hindus currently comprise approximately 79% of India's population, or 1.1 billion of its 1.43 billion citizens (World Population Review, 2025). Practices among Hindu communities are highly diverse, shaped by regional, linguistic, caste-based, and generational factors. As a result, challenges in intimacy and sexuality vary widely.

This chapter presents two case studies that illustrate how Hindu couples from nuclear family systems grapple with inherited values and cultural expectations in intimate relationships. These cases highlight the psychological tug-of-war between collectivist values, caste norms, and modern ideals of intimacy and partnership. As D'Cruz and Bharat (2001) note, the concept of the "adaptive extended family" helps explain why even geographically separated families exert a powerful influence over couples' lives.

For psychosexual therapists working with Hindu clients, cultural fluency is essential. By understanding the mythological, historical, and social narratives embedded in Hindu thought, clinicians can better support individuals and couples in negotiating a path that honors both personal desires and cultural obligations.

Case Studies

Case Study 1: Ajanta and Saurabh

Ajanta and Saurabh are an educated Brahmin couple in their thirties who recently returned to India after several years in the United States. Married for eight years and raising two children, they present as financially stable but report that their relationship has grown emotionally distant and sexually disconnected. Their main concern during therapy is the lack of romance and intimacy in their marriage.

Ajanta had a sexually fulfilling relationship before marriage but chose not to marry her former partner due to religious differences. That past experience has left her longing for deeper sexual satisfaction. Saurabh, on the other hand, had no sexual experience before marriage. His understanding of intimacy was shaped by limited exposure to pornography and conversations with male friends. He grew up believing the common cultural myth that masturbation without intercourse could weaken one's body, a belief often linked to the Indian construct of Dhat syndrome (Jadhav and Weiss, 1994; Om Prakash et al., 2014).

Ajanta desires a more passionate sexual relationship. Over time, their disagreements have become circular, often ending with Ajanta expressing frustration over Saurabh's lack of initiative and comparing him unfavorably to their more sexually open peers.

Understanding the Cultural Context

The Brahmin community is historically regarded as the highest in the Indian caste hierarchy, belonging to the *varna* of priests and scholars (Iriye, 1979). Marriages within this group are expected to maintain purity of bloodline, language compatibility, and adherence to astrological matching. Even today, many Brahmin families expect ritual compliance, vegetarian diets, and a commitment to spiritual discipline (Chakravarti, 1993).

Historically, much of India's normative literature—especially religious and moral texts—was authored by Brahmin men. As such, early Sanskrit literature often portrayed women as beings who were emotionally volatile, sexually impulsive, and in need of male control (Chakravarti, 1993; Ray, 2017). Although modern couples may no longer accept these views, many still witnessed similar dynamics in their own families. Fathers were often distant and authoritarian. Mothers, especially in traditional households, were financially dependent and focused on caregiving.

Public affection was rarely displayed, and conversations about sex or intimacy were considered taboo. For many, including Saurabh, emotional vulnerability and sexual expression within marriage remain underdeveloped skills.

Ajanta's Perspective

Ajanta grew up in a progressive household where women were highly educated and economically independent. As a third-generation professional, she was not influenced by the traditional requirement that women remain virgins before marriage. Her family encouraged rational thinking and respected personal choice, which gave her the space to develop her own beliefs about love, intimacy, and tradition.

Ajanta's views on sexual intimacy were shaped both by her personal experiences and by media portrayals. The idea of being a virgin on the first night of marital intimacy, holds deep cultural significance in Indian society (Ray, 2017). In some communities, a blood-stained sheet is still presented to demonstrate the bride's virginity. While Ajanta rejected such rituals, she remained open to preserving symbolic traditions that felt meaningful.

In therapy, she expressed frustration over her unmet needs and her husband's limited emotional expression. She wanted to feel desired and missed the sexual confidence she experienced in her prior relationship.

Saurabh's Perspective

Saurabh respected Ajanta's autonomy and had no issues with her premarital sexual history. However, his sexual development was shaped by deeply traditional values. Raised in a modest household, he followed strict Brahmin customs—vegetarianism, fasting, and mantra chanting—as part of daily life.

A key internal conflict for Saurabh stemmed from religious messages that discourage sexual indulgence. In some Hindu texts, *brahmacharya* (celibacy) is extolled as a virtue, and ejaculation is considered a loss of vital energy (Kar et al. 2021).[1] These messages, common in orthodox circles, promote sex primarily as a duty for procreation, not pleasure.

At the same time, Saurabh appreciated Ajanta's emotional and intellectual depth. He wanted to be a better partner but lacked a framework to understand intimacy beyond physical acts. His guilt over sexual inadequacy compounded his reluctance to initiate, reinforcing a cycle of avoidance and resentment.

Clinical Assessment and Intake Process

Therapists working with modern Hindu couples must carefully explore the intersection of tradition and modernity. Ajanta and Saurabh's case is illustrative of how personal histories, family structures, and gender expectations collide within marital intimacy.

In therapy, an effective intake process involves conducting individual sessions before joint interventions. This allows therapists to uncover deeply embedded cultural beliefs that may not surface in the presence of a partner.

Some critical areas to explore include:

- The cultural meaning of their wedding rituals, and whether any caused discomfort or disagreement
- Each partner's previous sexual experience and the sources of their knowledge (e.g., sex education, peer discussion, religious instruction)
- Internalized myths, such as semen loss and sexual "purity" standards
- Gender expectations within their families of origin
- Their communication patterns around intimacy
- Sexual preferences, arousal styles, and perceived barriers
- Their beliefs about parenting, household roles, and financial decision-making.

Psychoeducation should be provided using frameworks like the PLISSIT model (Reisman, 2015) to discuss levels of permission, limited information, specific suggestions, and intensive therapy when needed.

Ajanta and Saurabh were open to understanding one another's emotional and physical needs. Over several sessions, the therapist facilitated structured dialogues, addressed myths about masturbation and sexual performance, and introduced couple exercises focusing on sensuality rather than intercourse.

In one pivotal session, Ajanta was asked to describe moments when she felt most desired. She recalled a time early in their relationship when Saurabh had made her breakfast in bed and read poetry aloud to her. For her, these non-sexual gestures were deeply arousing and emotionally fulfilling.

Saurabh, in turn, was encouraged to discuss his fears of sexual inadequacy. He shared a memory of being mocked by older cousins for asking questions about sex. This moment became a gateway into exploring his relationship with shame and performance anxiety.

The couple began practicing sensate focus exercises, which removed the goal of penetration and emphasized pleasure, touch, and connection. This helped reframe their intimacy not as a performance, but as a process of mutual exploration.

Over time, they reported improved communication, less tension around sex, and greater comfort with discussing fantasies and desires. Saurabh noted that his understanding of sexual pleasure had expanded beyond physical release. Ajanta shared that she felt heard, respected, and emotionally connected—more than she had in years.

Case Study 2: Jyothi and Dheeraj

Jyothi and Dheeraj are a young, healthy, professionally secure couple living in Delhi. They had not engaged in penetrative sex after nearly one year of their arranged marriage. Neither partner had been in a romantic relationship nor had any prior sexual experience. Despite achieving orgasm individually and during non-penetrative sexual play, they experienced difficulties with intercourse. The persistent issue of erectile dysfunction, with no clear medical explanation, and rising interpersonal conflict brought them to therapy.

Understanding the Context

Dheeraj's family visited frequently, often accompanied by extended relatives. As a newly married woman, Jyothi was expected to host these gatherings, cook elaborate meals, and dress in traditional attire. Dheeraj's mother played an active role in shaping these expectations, often selecting Jyothi's clothing and influencing household decisions. His father, too, remained closely involved, advising the couple on financial matters and asserting his opinion on key life decisions, including Dheeraj's choice of bride.

Jyothi's parents rarely visited. This pattern reflected the Indian cultural construct of *paraya dhan*, a belief that daughters, once married, belong to their husband's family and home (Khatri, 1975). This created an uneven dynamic, where Jyothi had little familial support while being closely monitored by her in-laws.

Couple Dynamics

Two significant themes emerged during assessment. The first involved Dheeraj's struggle with performance anxiety. Although capable of arousal and orgasm during foreplay and masturbation, he experienced shame and embarrassment during attempts at penetration. The recurring difficulty eroded his confidence and intensified his anxiety around sexual activity.

Jyothi's frustration compounded the problem. She believed Dheeraj was not making enough of an effort to improve his "inadequate" sexual skills. When attempts at penetration failed, she would sometimes end the experience abruptly, saying, "There is no point in this." For days afterward, she would withdraw emotionally, unable to articulate her disappointment.

The second theme centered around the influence of Dheeraj's family. Initially, Jyothi was optimistic about connecting with her in-laws. However, Dheeraj's behavior would change markedly during their visits. Normally an equal participant in domestic life, he became passive and deferential in front of his parents. Jyothi perceived this shift as a betrayal of the egalitarian relationship she hoped to build. Their arguments intensified over time, especially when Dheeraj failed to stand up for her.

Although Dheeraj sympathized with Jyothi, he found it difficult to confront his parents. As the only son, he felt a strong sense of *dharma*,[2] or duty, to care for their needs. He was caught between honoring his wife's need for boundaries and fulfilling his filial obligations. The emotional tug-of-war created immense stress, and Dheeraj feared an open conflict between his wife and his parents could fracture the family.

Case Formulation: The Ganesha Complex

This couple's struggles may be viewed through the lens of the Ganesha complex, a concept proposed by psychoanalyst Sudhir Kakar (2005). In Hindu mythology, Ganesha—the son of Shiva and Parvati—guards his mother while she bathes, refusing his father's entry. In a moment of fury, Shiva beheads him, unaware of the boy's identity. Ganesha is later resurrected with the head of an elephant, and Parvati never forgives Shiva for harming her son.

Ganesha is portrayed as deeply loyal to his mother and emotionally unbound from a partner, symbolizing arrested development in individuation. In Indian families, this dynamic may emerge as a strong maternal attachment that complicates marital relationships.

In Dheeraj and Jyothi's case, several features of this complex were evident:

- **Conflicting priorities**: Dheeraj prioritized his parents' needs over his wife's emotional well-being, leading to resentment.
- **Boundary challenges**: There was regular interference by Dheeraj's family in major decisions, including financial planning and household roles.
- **Incomplete individuation**: Both partners had moved directly from living with their families to living with each other. Dheeraj maintained stronger ongoing ties to his family than Jyothi.
- **Cultural guilt**: Dheeraj struggled to assert himself against his parents' expectations, fearing that doing so would be disrespectful and unfilial.
- **Intimacy disruption**: Jyothi's frustration with family interference and sexual disappointment led her to withdraw, which only deepened the emotional disconnect.
- **Sexual inexperience**: Though both partners had sexual desire and some physical responsiveness, the absence of sexual education, coupled with performance anxiety, hindered successful intercourse.

Therapeutic Interventions

The clinical approach focused on four key areas (Malhotra, 2022):

Improving Communication and Conflict Management

Therapy began with teaching the couple to identify micro-conflict patterns and respond with emotional resilience. They practiced naming their emotions, listening with empathy, and validating each other's vulnerability. These steps were essential in establishing psychological safety.

Setting Boundaries

Sessions focused on exploring how cultural guilt shaped their choices. Dheeraj examined the emotional weight of breaking from his upbringing, while Jyothi explored her struggle to adapt to expectations she had never agreed to. They were guided to clarify what values they would want their children to learn, which helped realign their priorities and support healthier boundaries with extended family.

Strengthening Couple Identity

The therapist encouraged shared rituals and time away from family influences. Whether through travel, decision-making about household roles, or joint financial planning, these activities helped the couple build a sense of partnership. They learned to push back gently but firmly when family expectations became intrusive.

Psychoeducation and Sensate Focus

The couple received structured psychoeducation around sexual functioning, arousal cycles, and the distinction between desire and performance. Sensate focus techniques were introduced to shift attention away from penetration and toward pleasure, comfort, and intimacy. Over time, they practiced non-goal-oriented physical intimacy, exploring erogenous zones and preferences for touch.

As trust and relaxation increased, the couple began to enjoy their physical connection without the pressure of intercourse. Eventually, their relationship became more sexually fulfilling and they were able to consummate the marriage.

Clinical Reflection

Jyothi and Dheeraj's case illustrates how traditional family roles, caste values, and lack of sexual experience can shape and sometimes strain modern Hindu marriages. The intersection of cultural constructs such as *paraya dhan*, *dharma*, and the Ganesha complex presents therapists with nuanced dynamics that go far beyond individual pathology (Kakar, 2005; Ray, 2017).

The couple's ability to eventually renegotiate boundaries and improve intimacy highlights the therapeutic potential of culturally sensitive interventions. For Indian therapists and global clinicians working with Hindu couples, it is crucial to understand the sociocultural scripts that continue to influence even the most educated and progressive families.

Discussion

When we broadly examine the generations of adult Hindus living in society today, we find distinct and often conflicting approaches to intimacy, gender roles, and marital expectations. The older generations have typically adhered to age-old customs, rooted in religious texts and family traditions. The middle generations, particularly those raised during India's economic liberalization, began to shift toward conjugal and nuclear family structures. Many individuals in this group attempt to strike a balance between honoring their heritage and adapting to modern life. Meanwhile, the youngest generation has taken a more explicit turn toward personal freedom, including openness about sexual exploration and autonomy in partner choice (Bhargava, 2020; Chakravorty et al., 2021).

The two case studies explored in this chapter reflect the challenges faced by modern Hindu couples in their twenties and thirties. These couples often experience a tug-of-war between the values modeled by their parents and their own evolving beliefs. Their struggles are not only interpersonal but also deeply shaped by societal expectations about caste, gender, marriage, and duty.

For example, couples like Ajanta and Saurabh may experience inner conflicts about intimacy and sexual pleasure, especially when their religious upbringing discourages open discourse about sex. Saurabh's inherited beliefs about sexual restraint, for instance, stem from a blend of cultural messages and sacred texts that associate semen retention with moral purity. Ajanta, by contrast, brings to the relationship a different experience, one informed by individual freedom and the desire for mutual pleasure. Such mismatches are not uncommon and are shaped by intergenerational shifts in how sexuality is perceived and discussed.

In the second case, Dheeraj and Jyothi illustrate how familial attachments can interfere with marital intimacy. Dheeraj's emotional bond with his parents, particularly his mother, reflects what has been termed the Ganesha complex (Kakar, 2005). This dynamic often involves unresolved individuation, especially among sons who remain psychologically fused with their maternal family system. As seen in this couple, the failure to set boundaries with extended family led to repeated emotional distancing and sexual dysfunction.

The dilemmas these couples face are emblematic of the broader societal transition. Many contemporary Hindu couples are caught between *dharma* (duty to family and tradition) and emerging values such as equality in gender roles, sexual agency, and autonomous relationship boundaries. Parental attachments, caste-based injunctions, and inherited customs continue to shape the emotional and sexual dynamics of these relationships. The case of Dheeraj's prioritization of family harmony over spousal intimacy demonstrates how such conflicts can create long-term strain if not consciously addressed.

The outlook of Gen Z in India differs considerably. In urban centers, many young people are sexually active during their teenage years, often exploring multiple relationships before settling down. However, this openness is usually concealed from parents and elders. It is also associated with emotional challenges, such as loneliness, anxiety, and relationship burnout after repeated breakups (Chakravorty et al., 2021; Bhargava, 2020). For therapists, this means that younger clients may appear emotionally resilient on the surface but carry hidden distress related to secrecy, rejection, or loss of trust.

Understanding Hindu psychosexual perspectives requires a historical and cultural lens. The *Kamasutra*, ancient temple carvings, and erotic sculptures all point to an earlier cultural openness around sexuality (Vatsyayana, 2002). However, over time, particularly with the rise of Vedic orthodoxy and the codification of social norms in texts like the *Manu Smriti*, women's roles were gradually restricted, and sexual discourse became more conservative. The arrival of Victorian values during colonial rule further entrenched the repression of sexual expression, casting practices like Tantra as backward and immoral (Doniger, 2009).

In clinical practice, intake and assessment with Hindu couples and individuals should include open-ended, culturally sensitive questions. Therapists should explore caste norms, wedding customs, family structures, and personal interpretations of key concepts such as *dharma*, purity, and honor. Particular attention should be paid to beliefs around virginity, sexual knowledge, consent, and gender dynamics. Even when couples live apart from their families, the adaptive extended family continues to play a powerful emotional and psychological role in their decision-making (D'Cruz and Bharat, 2001; Khatri, 1975).

Effective therapeutic intervention must consider these intergenerational dynamics. With couples, interventions should blend psychoeducation, sexual skill-building, and boundary-setting strategies. Techniques like sensate focus, communication training, and values clarification can help couples navigate guilt, develop autonomy, and rebuild intimacy. For younger adults, particularly those navigating early sexual experiences, interventions may need to focus on self-awareness, consent, emotional regulation, and managing the psychological toll of secrecy or relationship disappointment.

Finally, therapists working in this context must recognize that sexual and relational concerns are rarely only personal. They are deeply embedded in collective values, historical narratives, and enduring family systems. When addressed with cultural empathy and clinical insight, therapy can empower Hindu individuals and couples to integrate tradition with personal growth, helping them build relationships that are both rooted and resilient.

Notes

1 A more severe form of this culture-bound syndrome called Dhat syndrome is seen across the Indian subcontinent (Kar et al. 2021). The four *Vedas* mention masturbation as a wasteful exercise and, when experienced with intensity, young men complain of feeling tired, guilty, and anxious due to masturbation or experiencing nightfall. Erectile dysfunction and premature ejaculation share a high correlation with Dhat syndrome as well (Om Prakash, Kar and Rao, 2014). Wig (1960) coined the term "Dhat" syndrome (Om Prakash and Rao, 2010).

2 In Hinduism, *dharma* is the religious and moral prescription of individual social duties matched with the individual's life-stage. Salvation or *moksha* is promised for the faithful execution of these role-based duties. The stage for younger men is *brahmacharya* or chaste students. The next stage, *grihastha*, is where getting married, having children, and looking after all family members are the duties of the householder. Older men are expected to move to detachment by becoming forest dwellers (*vanaprastha),* moving to *sanyas* (complete renouncement) (Doniger, 2009).

References

Ancient Origins (2019). What is a lingam and how does it represent Shiva? In: Ancient origins: unravelling the mysteries of the past [website]. www.ancient-origins.net/history-ancient-traditions/lingam-shiva-0012871 (accessed 8 April 2025).

Bhargava JM (2020). *Stoned, Shamed, Depressed.* Gurugram: HarperCollins (https://harpercollins.co.in/product/stoned-shamed-depressed/, accessed 10 April 2025).

Census of India (2011). Office of the Registrar General and Census Commissioner, India Ministry of Home Affairs, Government of India. (https://censusindia.gov.in/census.website/, accessed 8 April 2025).

Chakravarti U (1993). Conceptualising Brahmanical patriarchy in early India: gender, caste class and state. *Economic and Political Weekly*, 28(14):579–85. (www.jstor.org/stable/4399556).

Chakravorty S, Goli S, & James KS (2021). Family Demography in India: Emerging Patterns and Its Challenges. *SAGE Open*. 11. 215824402110081. https://doi.org/10.1177/21582440211008178

D'Cruz P & Bharat S (2001). Beyond Joint and Nuclear: The Indian Family Revisited. *Journal of Comparative Family Studies*, 32:167–94. https://doi.org/10.3138/jcfs.32.2.167

Doniger W (2009). *The Hindus: An Alternative History*. Oxford: Oxford University Press. (www.google.co.in/books/edition/The_Hindus/nNsXZkdHvXUC, accessed 8 April 2025).

Doniger W, Smith BK (1991). *The Laws of Manu*. New Delhi, India: Penguin Classics. (https://books.google.co.in/books?id=9hS_n4bb_iAC&source=gbs_book_other_versions_r&cad=1, accessed 8 April 2025).

Iriye A (1979). *The World of Asia*. Forum Press: 106.

Jadhav S, Weiss M (1994). Historical perspectives on Dhat syndrome. *NIMHANS Journal*, 12(2):117–24.

Joshi N. (2017). Caste system in ancient India. In: World history encyclopedia [website] (www.worldhistory.org/article/1152/caste-system-in-ancient-india/, accessed 8 April 2025).

Kakar S (2005). Hindu myth and psychoanalytic concepts: the Ganesh complex. In: Chang SC, Nishizono M, Tseng W-S, editors. *Asian Culture and Psychotherapy: Implications for East and West*. University of Hawaii Press. www.degruyterbrill.com/document/doi/10.1515/9780824873868/html

Kar SK, Menon V, Yasir Arafat SM, Singh A, Das A, Shankar A, et al. (2021). Dhat syndrome: Systematic review of epidemiology, nosology, clinical features, and management strategies. *Asian J Psychiatry*, 65:102863. https://doi.org/10.1016/j.ajp.2021.102863

Khatri AA (1975). The Adaptive Extended Family in India Today. *Journal of Marriage and Family*, 37(3):633–42. https://doi.org/10.2307/350528

Malhotra U (2022). Case study. Couples therapy: impact of sociocultural factors on an unconsummated marriage. In: 23rd ISSM/SMSNA Joint Scientific Meeting, Miami, FL, 27–30 October 2022 [poster presentation]. (www1.statusplus.net/misc/posters/issm/issm-smsna2022/search/poster/270, accessed 8 April 2025).

Mason D (2004). Images of integration: the temples of India and their "erotic" sculptures. *Journal of Religious & Theological Information*. https://onlinelibrary.wiley.com/doi/10.1002/j.2632-3494.2004.tb00174.x

Om Prakash, Kar SK, Rao TSS (2014). Indian story on semen loss and related Dhat syndrome. *Indian Journal of Psychiatry*, 56(4):377–82. https://doi.org/10.4103/0019-5545.146532

Om Prakash, Rao TSS (2010). Sexuality research in India: an update. *Indian Journal Psychiatry*, 52(Suppl 1):S260–S263. https://doi.org/10.4103/0019-5545.69243

Pande A (2022). *The Nayika and Kama: She Takes Her Pleasure*. New Delhi: Speaking Tiger Books www.ibpbooks.in/the-nayika-and-kama-she-takes-her-pleasure/p/57942, accessed 8 April 2025)

Rathore J, Meena S (2022). A sociological study of changes in joint family. *International Journal of Trend in Scientific Research and Development*, 6(4):470–4. www.ijtsrd.com/papers/IJTSRD50067.pdf

Ray U (2017). "Idealizing motherhood": the Brahmanical discourse on women in ancient India (circa 500 BCE–300 CE). ProQuest LLC. Doctoral Thesis, SOAS, University of London, 1999.

Reisman Y (2015). Let's talk about taking a sexual history: The PLISSIT model. In: Reisman Y, Porst H, Lowenstein L, Tripodi F, Kiana PS, editors. *The ESSM Manual of Sexual Medicine*, 2nd ed. Amsterdam: Medix Publishers: 218 https://drive.google.com/file/d/1av Ft3lSbp-4txeMsOobBbMHA0DcTau1e/view

Vatsyayana M (2002). *The Original Kamasutra: Completely Illustrated.* Translated by Burton RF, Arbuthnot FF. Eastern Press, Mittal Publishing.

World Population Review. 2025. Hindu countries. World Population Review [website]. (https://worldpopulationreview.com/country-rankings/hindu-countries, accessed 8 April 2025).

Chapter 14

Navigating the Intersection of History, Trauma, and Cultural Stigma: Psychosexual Challenges in Contemporary Poland

Justyna Kulczyk-Lewinska and Lukasz Birycki

Introduction: The Invisibility and Otherness of Polish Identity

Polish identity has been profoundly shaped by historical experiences characterized by struggle, resilience, and survival. These factors exert a considerable influence upon the contemporary emotional and psychosexual experiences of Polish individuals. Although Polish people are recognized within the broader European cultural landscape, their distinctive cultural, historical, and political narratives frequently remain marginalized in global discourses concerning migration, trauma, and identity. Consequently, many Polish individuals, whether residing in Poland or as part of the diaspora, occupy an ambiguous social position, neither fully embraced by their home country nor completely integrated into host societies. This duality of invisibility and otherness significantly influences psychosexual well-being, identity formation, and interpersonal relationships.

Poland's turbulent history—marked by partitions, warfare, and prolonged foreign occupation—has cultivated a collective psyche rooted in endurance, emotional suppression, and silent suffering. Many Polish individuals grow up in environments where survival mechanisms predominate, resulting in coping strategies centered on emotional restraint, familial loyalty, and a profound sense of national duty. The scarcity of open emotional dialogue, compounded by insufficient psychosexual education, exacerbates generational trauma and complicates the development of secure emotional and sexual identities.

In therapeutic contexts, Polish clients frequently navigate tensions between dual identities—characterized by openness towards cultural diversity—and exclusive identities, which involve a rejection of multicultural influences. Individuals adhering to exclusive identities often exhibit parochial or nationalist attitudes, resist dialogues on diversity, and experience difficulty empathizing with those perceived as outsiders.

Transgenerational trauma is central to understanding these psychological complexities. Events such as the Second World War and subsequent communist oppression left profound psychological scars across Polish society, which continue to influence contemporary attitudes towards difference and otherness. Family

DOI: 10.4324/9781003611387-14

narratives often emphasize themes of self-preservation and suspicion, overriding tendencies towards inclusivity. Additionally, prejudices cultivated by communist-era propaganda persist, influencing contemporary perceptions of ethnic as well as sexual minorities and alternative ideologies.

The collapse of communism further intensified identity-related tensions, prompting a marked resurgence of nationalism within Polish society. This revival often manifests through resistance to multiculturalism, driven by fears regarding the dilution of traditional cultural values. Exclusive conceptions of Polishness, deeply embedded in notions of cultural purity, fuel ongoing anxieties concerning national identity and external influences.

These historical and cultural influences are particularly salient among adults who experienced childhood characterized by emotional neglect and emotional or instrumental parentification. Psychotherapist Joanna Flis (2023) conceptualizes this experience through the metaphor of the "basket of needs," highlighting how unmet emotional needs in childhood create enduring psychological deficits. For many Polish individuals, these emotional deficits originate from overly protective or emotionally immature parenting styles, rigid societal expectations, and oppressive educational practices, collectively contributing to persistent feelings of frustration, dissatisfaction, and emotional unfulfillment in adulthood.

Furthermore, upbringing in dysfunctional households or oppressive educational settings significantly affects adult behaviors and emotional well-being, manifesting as pervasive low self-esteem, relational difficulties, and chronic self-doubt, even amid apparent external achievements. Unaddressed, these emotional wounds perpetuate cycles of self-neglect and relational dysfunction. The phenomenon of "latchkey children"—children regularly left unsupervised due to parental economic pressures following the fall of communism—is particularly noteworthy. Widespread emotional and instrumental parentification during this period highlights the critical need for open dialogue addressing shared traumas to foster collective healing and resilience. Thus, the journey towards self-acceptance and emotional healing becomes essential. Acknowledging and understanding one's historical and emotional experiences facilitates the cultivation of healthier relationships and improved psychosexual well-being. Therapeutic interventions addressing unresolved emotional wounds offer practical means for individuals to repair their emotional deficits, leading to more fulfilling interpersonal relationships and greater emotional satisfaction.

Moreover, promoting generational dialogue is particularly relevant for those who grew up as latchkey children. The widespread phenomenon of children prematurely assuming adult responsibilities has left lasting psychological impacts, underscoring the necessity of open conversations about shared childhood experiences. Facilitating this dialogue can enhance emotional resilience, foster collective healing, and deepen communal understanding within Polish contexts.

Ultimately, this chapter examines the profound influence of historical and cultural contexts on Polish clients' emotional and sexual identities, interpersonal relationships, and psychological health. By acknowledging these distinctive cultural and psychological factors, psychosexual therapists can provide tailored support, empowering Polish individuals—particularly within diaspora communities—to overcome historical traumas and achieve meaningful personal growth.

Historical and Collective Trauma: The Psychological Legacy of Partitions, War, Communism, and Post-Communist Transitions

Poland's complex historical trajectory—including its partitions, experiences of war, communist rule, and subsequent post-communist transitions—has left a profound imprint on its collective psyche. These sociopolitical upheavals have not only shaped national identity but continue to influence individual psychological development, particularly in relation to psychosexual identity, relational functioning, and therapeutic engagement. For clinicians working with clients of Polish heritage, a nuanced understanding of these cultural-historical legacies is essential to establishing trust, fostering emotional safety, and enhancing therapeutic efficacy.

The Legacy of Partition: Suppressed Identity and Emotional Ruptures

Between 1772 and 1918, Poland experienced successive partitions by Russia, Prussia, and Austria, resulting in the loss of national sovereignty for over a century. This period was marked by forced assimilation into foreign political and cultural systems, alongside active resistance to cultural erasure. Families endured the suppression of Polish language, customs, and identity—circumstances under which emotional expression, particularly in intimate or vulnerable forms, became closely linked with subversion and defiance.

One lasting emotional legacy of this historical rupture is a culturally specific form of shame—*wstyd*—defined by an acute sensitivity to judgment, fear of public disgrace, and a drive towards self-monitoring. This dynamic continues to influence the inner lives of many Polish clients today, often manifesting as reluctance to express vulnerability, discuss sexuality, or seek emotional support. As Ehlers and Clark, (2000) note, cultural frameworks significantly shape trauma narratives and coping mechanisms. In therapeutic settings, this shame may surface as perfectionism, emotional inhibition, or avoidance—responses that, unless recognized and contextualized, can hinder relational and emotional progress.

World Wars and Soviet Occupation: Internalized Vulnerability and Institutional Distrust

Poland regained independence briefly in 1918, only to be ravaged by the devastations of the Second World War (1939–1945), including Nazi atrocities and Soviet incursions. The Holocaust, mass executions, forced relocations, and systemic violence inflicted enduring psychological trauma. Subsequent Soviet occupation

(1945–1989) further entrenched authoritarian values, demanding loyalty to the state and actively discouraging emotional expression, particularly those reflecting dissent, grief, or vulnerability.

These experiences embedded intergenerational patterns of hypervigilance, emotional suppression, and deep-seated mistrust in institutions. Vulnerability, under such conditions, was pathologized—equated with weakness or betrayal. For contemporary clients, these internalized beliefs may emerge as difficulties in expressing need, reluctance to trust the therapeutic process, or resistance to emotional openness. Volkan (2001) underscores the importance of historical consciousness in therapeutic work with culturally diverse populations. Psychoeducational approaches that contextualize client experiences within a framework of collective trauma can be instrumental in reducing shame and fostering resilience.

Post-Communist Transitions: Psychosexual Shame and Socioeconomic Pressure

The fall of communism in 1989 ushered in dramatic social and economic transformations. While new opportunities emerged, so too did heightened social expectations concerning success, duty, and sacrifice. The concurrent resurgence of Catholic conservatism significantly influenced public discourse on sexuality, reinforcing restrictive gender roles and psychosexual shame (Flis, 2023). The absence of comprehensive sex education during this period further contributed to confusion, misinformation, and emotional disconnect in relation to intimacy and desire. Cultural ideals such as *poświęcenie*—the valorization of self-sacrifice—reinforce traditional gender norms, promoting modesty and emotional suppression among women and stoicism and control among men. These narratives often manifest in therapeutic settings as relational difficulties or maladaptive coping strategies.

Clinical Vignette

Tomasz, a 42-year-old heterosexual Polish man, sought therapy after the breakdown of his second marriage. Despite professional success in construction management, he experienced symptoms of depression, erectile dysfunction, and a profound sense of emotional numbness. "I follow the rules, provide, don't cheat—and still, I lose everything," he lamented. Raised in a patriarchal, emotionally austere household in southern Poland, Tomasz's father, a former soldier, equated masculinity with stoicism, toughness, and control. Emotional expression was viewed as weak or feminine. Tomasz's two failed marriages reflected his struggle to form vulnerable, emotionally attuned connections. Both partners described him as cold and controlling. In therapy, Tomasz initially intellectualized his problems; emotional literacy was low, and affect was heavily defended. His case exemplifies how cultural norms and historical trauma shape psychosexual difficulties and relational patterns among Polish men.

Migration: Cultural Dislocation and Intergenerational Guilt

Migration introduces an additional layer of complexity to the therapeutic experiences of Polish clients. Many migrants face subtle forms of marginalization, linguistic barriers, and cultural alienation in host countries, while simultaneously managing the emotional burden of supporting families and preserving cultural identity across borders. This dual pressure can exacerbate feelings of displacement, invisibility, and guilt, complicating psychosexual well-being and identity development (Bhugra & Becker, 2005; Kirmayer et al., 2011).

Consider the case of Aneta, a Polish mother residing in Ireland, who experienced a profound sense of emotional erasure within her partnership, compounded by the expectation to serve as a cultural mediator for her extended family. Such roles often lead to emotional exhaustion and identity fragmentation (Bhugra & Becker, 2005). Therapists working with migrant clients can employ narrative therapy (White & Epston, 1990) to support the integration of past and present identities and somatic approaches to assist in reestablishing a sense of embodied agency amidst disconnection and stress (Ogden, Minton & Pain, 2006).

Iwona, a 38-year-old nurse, resides in Oxford but was born and raised in a conservative, rural region of southeastern Poland. She sought therapy to address chronic anxiety, emotional numbness, and a recurring fear of abandonment in relationships. Though she has built a relatively open queer life abroad, each return to Poland for family obligations induces profound psychological distress. "The moment I cross the border, I feel my body contract," she says. "I lower my voice, change how I walk. I disappear into the version of me they want to see."

Raised in a multigenerational household steeped in Catholic doctrine, Iwona absorbed deep messages linking bodily autonomy with sin, desire with corruption, and identity with duty. Her grandmother—widowed by war, hardened by survival—frequently recited aphorisms such as "*Trzeba cierpieć w milczeniu*" ("One must suffer in silence"), a phrase that still echoes in Iwona's inner dialogue. Her mother, emotionally distant and preoccupied with appearances, emphasized *poświęcenie*, especially for daughters: giving up personal wants to preserve family unity and respectability.

Iwona has never come out to her family, fearing *wstyd*—the kind of shame that not only implicates the individual but stains the family lineage. "If they knew," she says, "it would not just be about me—they would feel they had failed." This belief reveals the transgenerational transmission of shame and survival-based morality rooted in Poland's long history of foreign occupation and cultural erasure (Danieli, 1998; Flis, 2023). To be "other" is to betray what has been protected.

In her romantic life, Iwona is self-sacrificing and conflict-avoidant, choosing partners who are emotionally unavailable or themselves closeted. While Oxford offers legal and social freedom, her emotional template—formed through years of hiding, muting, and code-switching—remains rigid. Her desire for visibility is haunted by internalized fears of social ruin. Therapy focuses on helping her grieve the loss of a unified self, reconnect with bodily sensations, and separate inherited shame from authentic identity (Johnson & Greenberg, 1985).

Family Dynamics: Hierarchical Structures and Emotional Inhibition

Traditional Polish family structures tend to prioritize hierarchy, conformity, and interdependence, often at the expense of emotional openness. Historical oppression has shaped generational transmission of trauma, producing characteristic clinical presentations such as anxiety, hypervigilance, and internalized guilt (Danieli, 1998). Within these families, cognitive distortions—such as catastrophizing and dichotomous thinking—are frequently observed, reinforcing cycles of emotional suppression and self-criticism (Beck, 1976).

Therapeutic work with Polish clients may benefit from explicitly naming these culturally embedded patterns, reframing them not as individual failings but as adaptive responses to historical and familial contexts. For example:

- Catastrophizing may reflect a survival-oriented worldview inherited from generations exposed to instability and loss.
- Black-and-white thinking, such as the belief "If I am not perfect, I am a failure," often mirrors moralistic values tied to familial expectations of sacrifice and honor.

Normalizing these patterns within a culturally sensitive therapeutic framework can reduce shame, foster self-compassion, and open pathways for emotional growth (Neff, 2011).

Clinical Vignette

Ewa and Pawel, both in their early thirties, migrated from Cracow to London ten years ago. They sought couples therapy due to mounting conflict over parenting roles, emotional disconnection, and a diminishing sexual relationship. Ewa expressed feeling "invisible" and emotionally burdened, while Pawel described feeling "criticized no matter what I do." Their communication had become tense and transactional, with both partners feeling increasingly misunderstood.

Though their difficulties may seem familiar in a globalized, dual-income context, they are deeply shaped by Polish cultural legacies. Ewa was raised with the implicit ideal of the *Matka Polka*—a national archetype of the self-sacrificing, morally pure, and tireless mother who carries the emotional and physical weight of family and nation. Originating in the 19th century during the Partitions, when Poland was under foreign occupation, *Matka Polka* came to symbolize the ultimate patriot: a woman who preserves Polish identity, Catholic faith, and cultural continuity through suffering, endurance, and maternal devotion (Heinen, 2009; Imbierowicz, 2012; Fiałkowska, 2019).

In post-communist Poland, this figure remains deeply embedded in social expectations and family narratives. Ewa internalized this script early: to be a "good woman" meant to be strong, silent, modest, and giving—especially as a mother. Though she is educated and professionally ambitious, she feels chronic guilt about voicing needs, setting boundaries, or desiring emotional reciprocity. In therapy, she described sex as "just another task," shaped less by desire than obligation. "There's no space for me as a woman," she said, "only as a caretaker."

Pawel, raised in a more traditional family, internalized different but complementary values. His father—a quiet, emotionally distant man who worked long hours—modeled the ideal of the provider who expresses love through financial security rather than affection or presence. Pawel sees himself as doing "everything right" by working hard and avoiding vice, yet feels ill-equipped to meet Ewa's emotional needs. He fears being judged—by peers, family, and the local Polish community—if he is perceived as too vulnerable or too "controlled" by his wife. Therapy itself, in his view, initially represented weakness and failure.

Their social context exacerbates these tensions. Living in a Polish diaspora community in London, where cultural norms are often preserved more rigidly than in Poland itself, both Ewa and Pawel feel scrutinized. Ewa fears gossip and judgment from other Polish mothers if she appears dissatisfied or "ungrateful," while Pawel experiences pressure to maintain stoicism among male peers. The collective gaze of the community acts as a form of emotional surveillance, reinforcing gender roles and punishing deviation.

Therapeutically, their dynamic reflects a collision of inherited scripts: Ewa, torn between the *Matka Polka* ideal and her desire for mutuality and freedom; Pawel, shaped by post-war masculine stoicism and discomfort with affect. Their sexual disconnection mirrors a deeper difficulty with vulnerability, autonomy, and self-expression—dynamics rooted not only in their personal histories, but in centuries of Polish collective experience.

Psychosexual Therapy with Polish Clients: Cultural Legacies, Emotional Inheritance, and Therapeutic Possibility

The psychological experiences of Polish clients are deeply shaped by a complex sociohistorical matrix: the legacy of partitions, war, communism, post-communist transition, Catholic conservatism, and patterns of migration. These collective events have left emotional residues that continue to inform clients' identities, relational patterns, and psychosexual lives. Within this context, shame, silence, and sacrifice are often internalized not as individual pathology, but as inherited strategies of survival and belonging (Danieli, 1998; Flis, 2023). For therapists, working with Polish clients means not only understanding these legacies but engaging in culturally attuned, reflective practice that honors both individual agency and cultural embeddedness.

Clinical Themes and Cultural Scripts

Polish clients frequently present with symptoms that, at first glance, resemble universal human concerns—perfectionism, emotional avoidance, sexual inhibition, or relational conflict. However, these experiences often have culturally specific roots. The concept of *wstyd*—a uniquely Polish form of shame grounded in fear of social disgrace—frequently manifests as an unwillingness to express vulnerability or explore intimacy ((Wierzbicka, 1999; Scheff, 2000; Tokarska-Bakir, 2004). Similarly, gender roles shaped by *poświęcenie* (sacrifice), Catholic modesty, and post-communist societal expectations contribute to rigid self-concepts and relational scripts.

As illustrated in case studies throughout this chapter, these cultural narratives influence emotional development across a spectrum of clients—from heterosexual couples navigating diasporic pressures to LGBTQ+ individuals living double lives between countries and cultures (Heinen, 2009; Imbierowicz, 2012; Fiałkowska, 2019; Kulczyk-Lewinska & Birycki, 2025).

Reframing Shame and Emotional Expression

Shame-based thinking in Polish clients requires careful, culturally responsive interventions. Emotional expression is often perceived as self-indulgent or dangerous, particularly for men socialized within post-war masculine ideals or women raised under the enduring archetype of the *Matka Polka*—the idealized self-sacrificing mother who silently upholds family and national identity (Imbierowicz, 2012; Schultes, 2014).

Therapists must work to reframe vulnerability as strength, helping clients recognize emotional expression as a relational need rather than a moral failure (Brown, 2012). This work involves pacing, permission-giving, and cultural translation—ensuring that therapeutic language resonates with the client's values rather than inadvertently undermining them (Sue et al., 2009).

Therapist Reflexivity and Cultural Humility

As Hook et al. (2013) argue, cultural humility is not a static competency but an ongoing practice of self-awareness, curiosity, and relational attunement. Therapists must question their assumptions around empowerment, autonomy, and healing. For instance, the Western emphasis on assertiveness or sexual liberation may feel alien—or even shaming—to Polish clients who find safety in restraint, modesty, or family obligation (Kirmayer, 2007).

Rather than imposing ideals, clinicians must co-create therapeutic goals that feel meaningful within the client's cultural worldview. Success might mean expressing doubt without shame, naming desire without guilt, or initiating a difficult conversation after years of silence. In these moments, healing is not dramatic transformation but subtle reclamation (Sue, 2010).

Countertransference also requires attention. For therapists who share Polish heritage with clients, over-identification or silent collusion with cultural scripts may arise. Others may feel compelled to "rescue" clients from perceived cultural oppression. In either case, reflective practice is essential for maintaining a stance of empathy without projection, and care without coercion (Gelso & Hayes, 2007).

Narrative, Emotional, and Somatic Integration

Narrative therapy (White & Epston, 1990) is particularly effective for clients whose identities are entangled with inherited scripts around morality, femininity, masculinity, and duty. Encouraging clients to externalize problems and re-author their stories creates distance from internalized shame and opens space for agency. This approach is especially useful when working with constructs like *Matka Polka* or internalized ideals of stoic masculinity (Imbierowicz, 2012; Connell, 2020).

Emotionally focused therapy (Johnson & Greenberg, 1985) supports clients in reconnecting with disavowed emotional material, particularly in relational settings. As seen in the case of Tomasz earlier, insight alone was not sufficient—change occurred through emotionally safe experiences of being seen and understood.

Somatic interventions are vital for clients who have learned to dissociate from their bodies, either due to trauma or religious dualism that positioned the body as morally suspect (van der Kolk, 2014). Techniques such as grounding, breathwork, and mindful movement support the gradual re-inhabiting of the body—not for performance, but for presence (Levine, 2010).

Intergenerational Trauma and Cultural Psychoeducation

Providing psychoeducation about intergenerational trauma allows clients to recontextualize their experiences within broader historical narratives. In Polish families shaped by war, Soviet occupation, or migration, trauma was often transmitted not through stories, but through silence, vigilance, or sacrifice (Danieli, 1998). Clients may carry a diffuse sense of burden, anxiety, or guilt—what Danieli describes as "conspiracies of silence." These unspoken legacies contribute to emotional atmospheres in which certain feelings or desires are implicitly prohibited. Psychoeducation, when delivered with sensitivity, helps clients understand these patterns not as personal failings but as emotional inheritances that can be worked with and transformed.

Culturally Shaped Cognitions

Common cognitive distortions—such as all-or-nothing thinking, over-responsibility, or chronic self-criticism—must also be understood in cultural terms. Beliefs like "If I'm not perfect, I'm a failure" or "My needs are selfish" often reflect inherited schemas rooted in survival logic and moral duty (Beck, 1976; Young et al., 2003). These beliefs are not merely irrational—they once served a function.

Therapists should avoid prematurely challenging these cognitions. Instead, they should explore their origin, purpose, and emotional logic. This approach opens a more compassionate and collaborative process of transformation, where the client can discern what still serves them and what may be let go (Neff & Germer, 2017).

Conclusion

To work effectively with Polish clients in psychosexual therapy is to step into a space shaped not only by individual psychology but by the weight of history, the silences of families, and the unspoken codes of culture. Poland's collective experience—marked by partitions, occupation, war, communism, religious conservatism, and waves of migration—has cultivated emotional strategies centered on resilience, survival, and self-containment. These strategies, while often adaptive, also create profound challenges around intimacy, sexuality, and emotional expression.

Across generations, shame (*wstyd*), duty (*poświęcenie*), and control have become deeply ingrained cultural narratives. They shape not just what clients feel, but how they feel allowed to feel. In many Polish clients, one finds a particular kind of guardedness: the instinct to protect what is vulnerable, to endure rather than disclose, to comply rather than assert. In some, this manifests as perfectionism or stoicism; in others, as dissociation from the body or avoidance of desire. For therapists, recognizing these patterns as culturally inherited—not merely individually constructed—is essential to providing empathic and effective care (Hook et al., 2013).

Healing in this context often requires a redefinition of what change looks like. Western ideals of therapeutic progress—emotional fluency, assertiveness, sexual liberation—can sometimes feel jarring or alienating to clients whose cultural background prizes modesty, discretion, and emotional endurance. What might look like resistance or inhibition from one perspective may, from another, be understood as the expression of deeply held values shaped by generations of struggle and survival (Kirmayer, 2007; Brown, 2012).

Rather than framing these cultural scripts as obstacles to overcome, therapists are invited to approach them with curiosity, respect, and critical empathy. Clients may carry both loyalty and resentment towards these scripts—grateful for what helped their families survive, yet burdened by what those same narratives have cost them in emotional freedom or sexual authenticity. Therapy becomes the space where these ambivalences can be explored safely, without agenda or judgment (Sue et al., 2009).

This requires more than cultural "competence"; it calls for cultural humility and reflexivity. Therapists must regularly interrogate their own assumptions—about health, empowerment, agency, and growth. They must resist the temptation to project their own ideals of healing onto clients, especially when those ideals stem from psychological models rooted in individualism or secular liberalism. For example, a therapist who views assertiveness as inherently healthy may inadvertently pathologize a client's preference for indirect communication, failing to recognize it as a form of relational safety within a context that has long prioritized harmony over confrontation (Gelso & Hayes, 2007).

Crucially, therapists must be willing to sit with complexity and contradiction. A client may long for emotional closeness while fearing it. They may desire sexual agency while carrying generations of shame. They may want to break familial patterns while feeling paralyzed by guilt. Progress may look subtle: the ability to name an emotion without minimizing it; to tolerate pleasure without recoiling; to speak aloud a thought once unthinkable. These small acts of reclamation—of voice, of body, of desire—are profound acts of resistance against inherited silence (Neff & Germer, 2017).

In many Polish families, trauma is passed down not through explicit stories but through emotional atmosphere: tension that is never named, grief never mourned, and expectations never questioned. Clients often describe feeling "too much" or "not enough" without knowing why—carrying emotional burdens predating their own experiences. Therapy offers a language for this: a way to understand inherited guilt, fear, or vigilance not as personal flaws, but as emotional residues of a collective history alive in body and mind (Danieli, 1998).

A culturally attuned practice also requires attention to migration and displacement. Polish clients living abroad often navigate dual realities: the culture they left, and the one they now inhabit. For some, this brings freedom; for others, disorientation. Many live bifurcated lives—speaking differently, dressing differently, even moving differently depending on context. The pressure to maintain appearances for the family back home or to meet unspoken community standards can reinforce secrecy and emotional compartmentalization. Therapists must be attentive to the subtle toll of this "in-between-ness" (Kulczyk-Lewinska & Birycki, 2025).

Therapy, then, becomes not just a site of insight or resolution, but a sanctuary of witnessing. A place where silence can be interrupted with care. Where the therapist listens not only to what is said but to what has never been said. Where cultural values are not discarded but explored. Where the client is not asked to choose between self and family, tradition and freedom, but supported in finding a new relationship to these tensions—one that allows for more breath, more softness, more possibility.

Ultimately, the aim is not to liberate the client from culture, but to invite them into a more spacious relationship with it. Therapy becomes a place where inherited narratives are honored but not obeyed, where identity expands beyond what was modeled, and where intimacy—emotional, physical, relational—can be experienced not as risk, but as a fundamental human right.

This work is slow, relational, and deeply ethical. It demands that therapists hold space not just for trauma, but for history; not just for change, but for ambivalence. In doing so, therapy with Polish clients becomes an act of quiet transformation—a process of re-inhabiting what was once silenced, and of discovering, perhaps for the first time, what it means to be fully alive in one's own story.

References

Beck, A. T. (1976). *Cognitive therapy and the emotional disorders*. International Universities Press, New York, NY.

Bhugra, D., & Becker, M. A. (2005). Migration, cultural bereavement and cultural identity. *World Psychiatry*, *4*(1), 18–24.

Brown, L. S. (2012). *Cultural competence in trauma therapy: Beyond the flashback*. American Psychological Association, Washington, DC.

Connell, R. W. (2020). *Masculinities*. Routledge, Cambridge, UK.

Danieli, Y. (1998). *International handbook of multigenerational legacies of trauma*. Springer, New York, NY.

Ehlers, A., & Clark, D. M. (2000). A cognitive model of posttraumatic stress disorder. *Behaviour Research and Therapy*, *38*(4), 319–345.

Fiałkowska, K. (2019). "By education I'm Catholic": The gender, religion and nationality nexus in migration. *Central and Eastern European Migration Review*, *8*(2), 121–136. https://doi.org/10.17467/ceemr.2019.13

Flis, J. (2023). *Co ze mną nie tak? O życiu w dysfunkcyjnym domu, środowisku, w Polsce i o tym, jak sobie z tym (nie) radzimy*. Wydawnictwo Znak, Kraków, Poland.

Gelso, C. J., & Hayes, J. A. (2007). *Countertransference and the therapist's inner experience: Perils and possibilities*. Lawrence Erlbaum Associates, Mahwah, NJ.

Heinen, J. (2009). *Religion, politics and gender equality in Poland*. United Nations Research Institute for Social Development (UNRISD), Geneva, Switzerland.

Hook, J. N., Davis, D. E., Owen, J., Worthington, E. L., & Utsey, S. O. (2013). Cultural humility: Measuring openness to culturally diverse clients. *Journal of Counseling Psychology*, 60(3), 353–366.

Imbierowicz, A. (2012). The Polish mother on the defensive? The transformation of the myth and its impact on the motherhood of Polish women. *Journal of Education Culture and Society*, *1*, 140–152.

Johnson, S. M., & Greenberg, L. S. (1985). Emotionally focused couples therapy: An outcome study. *Journal of Marital and Family Therapy*, *11*(3), 313–317. https://doi.org/10.1111/j.1752-0606.1985.tb00624.x

Kirmayer, L. J. (2007). Psychotherapy and the cultural concept of the person. *Transcultural Psychiatry*, 44(2), 232–257.

Kirmayer, L. J., Dandeneau, S., Marshall, E., Phillips, M. K., & Jessen Williamson, K. (2011). Rethinking resilience from indigenous perspectives. *The Canadian Journal of Psychiatry*, *56*(2), 84–91.

Kulczyk-Lewinska, J., & Birycki, L. (2025). Navigating the intersection of history, trauma, and cultural stigma: Psychosexual challenges in contemporary Poland. *[Journal/Publisher]. Unpublished manuscript.*

Levine, P. A. (2010). *In an unspoken voice: How the body releases trauma and restores goodness*. North Atlantic Books, California.

Morgan, D. H. J. (2000). The gender of the household: Domestic labour and power. *Sociological Review*, *48*(2), 195–219. https://doi.org/10.1111/1467-954X.00220

Neff, K. D. (2011). *Self-compassion: The proven power of being kind to yourself.* William Morrow, New York, NY.

Neff, K. D., & Germer, C. K. (2017). Self-compassion and psychological well-being. In E. M. Seppälä, E. Simon-Thomas, S. L. Brown, M. C. Worline, C. D. Cameron, & J. R. Doty

(Eds.), *The Oxford handbook of compassion science* (pp. 371–385). Oxford University Press. https://doi.org/10.1093/oxfordhb/9780190464684.013.27

Ogden, P., Minton, K., & Pain, C. (2006). *Trauma and the body: A sensorimotor approach to psychotherapy*. W. W. Norton & Company, New York, NY.

Scheff, T. J. (2000). Shame and the social bond: A sociological theory. *Sociological Theory, 18*(1), 84–99. https://doi.org/10.1111/0735-2751.00089

Schultes, A. K. (2014). On the margins of religion/on the forefront of culture: The image of the Matka Polka (Polish mother) in contemporary Poland. *Journal of the Motherhood Initiative for Research and Community Involvement*, *5*(1), 96–112.

Sue, D. W., Capodilupo, C. M., Torino, G. C., Bucceri, J. M., Holder, A. M. B., Nadal, K. L., & Esquilin, M. (2009). Racial microaggressions and the power of cumulative stress. *Journal of Counseling & Development*, *87*(3), 329–339.

Sue, D. W. (2010). *Microaggressions in everyday life: Race, gender, and sexual orientation.* John Wiley & Sons, Hoboken, NJ.

Tokarska-Bakir, J. (2004). *Rzeczy mgliste: Eseje i studia*. Wydawnictwo Sejny.

van der Kolk, B. A. (2014). *The body keeps the score: Brain, mind, and body in the healing of trauma*. Viking, New York, NY.

Volkan, V. D. (2001). *Bloodlines: From ethnic pride to ethnic terrorism*. Farrar, Straus and Giroux, New York, NY.

White, M., & Epston, D. (1990). *Narrative means to therapeutic ends*. W.W. Norton & Company, New York, NY.

Wierzbicka, A. (1999). *Emotions across languages and cultures: Diversity and universals.* Cambridge University Press, Cambridge.

Young, J. E., Klosko, J. S., & Weishaar, M. E. (2003). *Schema therapy: A practitioner's guide*. Guilford Press, New York, NY.

Chapter 15

Put the Viagra Down

Keeley Mardon

Introduction: Defining the Working Class in the UK

In the United Kingdom, the term "working class" has historically referred to individuals engaged in manual, industrial, or low-wage service occupations. These roles are typically characterized by physical labor, repetitive or routine tasks, and minimal opportunities for upward mobility or career advancement (Crompton, 2008). Common professions within this demographic include builders, factory operatives, delivery drivers, cleaners, and care assistants. Such occupations often lack the economic and structural security found in professional or managerial roles and tend to be associated with limited access to higher education and lower income brackets.

However, the working class is more than an economic designation; it functions as a salient cultural identity. Many individuals continue to self-identify as working class even after experiencing upward mobility through education or employment. This persistent identification is often rooted in familial lineage, early life experiences, and community affiliations, reflecting the enduring social capital embedded in class-based norms and values (Savage et al., 2013). The lived reality of class is therefore shaped as much by cultural transmission as by occupational status.

Contemporary sociologists have increasingly moved away from viewing class purely through the lens of income or job type. In particular, the "Great British Class Survey" conducted by Savage and colleagues (2013) reconceptualized class as a multi-dimensional construct defined by three interrelated forms of capital: economic (material wealth, assets, income), social (networks, relationships, and connections), and cultural (patterns of taste, leisure activities, and cultural awareness). Within this framework, the traditional working class is typically identified by low levels of all three capitals and by distinct forms of cultural participation that differ markedly from middle-class norms.

Importantly, this classification system sheds light on the often-overlooked heterogeneity within the working class. It also emphasizes how structural inequalities and inherited disadvantage intersect with behavioral norms, coping mechanisms, and emotional expression. These are particularly relevant in therapeutic contexts

DOI: 10.4324/9781003611387-15

where assumptions based on social class can significantly influence treatment outcomes.

The political and media discourse surrounding the "working class" further complicates the picture. Frequently invoked during election cycles or in media portrayals of specific regions, the term is often used as a shorthand for particular voting behaviors or social values. Yet such depictions risk flattening the complex and diverse lived experiences of this demographic (Lawler, 2005).

Class and Access to Psychosexual Therapy

In the realm of psychosexual therapy, an awareness of class dynamics is not just beneficial but essential. Class influences a wide spectrum of psychosocial factors, including emotional expressiveness, attitudes towards intimacy, and help-seeking behavior. Working-class men, in particular, may have internalized norms that discourage vulnerability or emotional self-exploration, aligning instead with cultural values that emphasize stoicism, endurance, and autonomy (Seidler, 2006; Addis & Mahalik, 2003).

Furthermore, structural barriers, such as limited financial resources, less flexible work schedules, and fewer locally available mental health services, can restrict access to psychotherapy for working-class clients. Compounding these logistical challenges are psychological obstacles. Many individuals from this background view therapy as a resource designed primarily for the middle and upper classes. As a result, they may perceive the therapeutic space as alien or unwelcoming, especially when the therapist does not appear to reflect their cultural or social realities.

Therapists who remain attuned to these class-specific dynamics can play a pivotal role in facilitating access and engagement. By creating culturally sensitive and non-pathologizing spaces, therapists can enable clients from working-class backgrounds to articulate concerns that may otherwise remain unspoken. These include struggles with sexual identity, relationship dissatisfaction, erectile dysfunction, and internalized shame.

The therapeutic alliance is significantly strengthened when clinicians validate class-based experiences and recognize that psychosexual distress is often not rooted in individual pathology but in the cumulative pressures of cultural scripts, economic constraints, and gendered expectations. Sensitivity to these layers enhances the effectiveness of psychosexual therapy and supports a more inclusive, holistic model of psychological care.

A Little About Myself

As a 53-year-old Caucasian British woman, my understanding of psychosexual dynamics has been deeply shaped by my personal and professional journey. I grew up in a household with four brothers, three older and one younger, where gender roles were apparent and routinely reinforced. My early childhood unfolded in Leeds, a vibrant and diverse city in the north of England that, like many urban centers, contained stark contrasts in wealth and opportunity. When I was twelve, my family relocated to Gipton, a council estate marked by economic deprivation, close-knit communities, and a resilient working-class ethos.

This move was more than geographical; it was cultural. I was immersed in a community that was both materially constrained and emotionally rich. I witnessed firsthand how social class shaped expectations around behavior, gender identity, and interpersonal relationships. Within these working-class spaces, traditional gender scripts were pervasive. Boys were encouraged to be tough, emotionally self-contained, and physically capable. Men were expected to serve as breadwinners and protectors, rarely showing vulnerability, and certainly not discussing emotional or sexual concerns openly.

Masculinity in this setting was synonymous with stoicism, strength, and sexual dominance, norms that often left little room for emotional authenticity or relational complexity. These rigid expectations became embedded early and persisted throughout adolescence and adulthood, especially for those whose identities were interwoven with manual labor or physical skill. It is within this environment that many men developed their first, and often only, templates for understanding relationships, power, and self-worth.

These personal observations have since informed my therapeutic work, particularly in psychosexual settings. However, the question remains: do these cultural expectations still hold true today?

While much has evolved socially, economically, and legislatively, many of the core tenets of working-class masculinity remain intact. The economic decline of post-industrial Britain, particularly in the North, has had a devastating effect on working-class male identity. The collapse of manufacturing and mining industries not only led to widespread unemployment but also destabilized the foundational structures upon which male status had been historically built (Scourfield et al., 2012; Casey, 2016). Men who once found purpose, identity, and respect through their labor were left grappling with a profound sense of loss, both of livelihood and of self.

In the therapeutic room, these shifts frequently manifest in complex emotional presentations: depressive symptoms that are minimized or denied, sexual dysfunction that carries intense shame, or intimacy issues rooted in unacknowledged fear and emotional repression. Many clients come into therapy expressing frustration about their relationships, difficulties with erection or desire, or a pervasive sense of "not being good enough," yet remain disconnected from the deeper emotional or psychological wounds that underlie these experiences.

This is not surprising. Despite economic and social change, the cultural narrative of the "strong, silent man" continues to exert influence. Expressions of vulnerability are often interpreted as weakness, and the internalization of these ideals can create a dangerous dissonance between how men feel and how they believe they ought to feel. As a result, many suffer in silence, lacking both the language and permission to explore their emotional worlds.

From a clinical perspective, understanding the intersections between class, gender, and socio-economic change is crucial. Psychosexual therapists must acknowledge that male sexual issues such as erectile dysfunction or low libido are often not purely physiological in origin. Rather, they are frequently expressions of deeper existential dilemmas: identity disruption, relational ambivalence, or internalized masculine norms that restrict emotional literacy.

By bringing class-consciousness into therapeutic work, we can dismantle the myth of the isolated, malfunctioning male and begin to see him within the broader tapestry of structural pressures, cultural scripts, and psychological defenses. Empathic inquiry, narrative reframing, and collaborative exploration become tools not only for symptom relief but for identity reconstruction.

In essence, male psychosexual dysfunction must be contextualized within the lived realities of working-class men, many of whom have inherited a definition of masculinity that is no longer tenable in contemporary society, yet remains emotionally and psychologically binding.

Working with Masculine Energy in Psychotherapy

Within my psychotherapy practice, approximately 95% of my clients identify as male and come from working-class backgrounds. This demographic presents a distinct set of challenges, shaped not only by individual psychological histories but also by sociocultural narratives around masculinity, emotional expression, and class identity. Many of these men arrive at therapy carrying not just personal wounds, but also generational messages that silence vulnerability and define manhood in narrow, performance-based terms.

My therapeutic approach is to honor and welcome the masculine energy they bring into the room, while simultaneously drawing upon a conscious balance of both masculine and feminine energies within myself. This balance is not about gender roles or sexual identity, but about energetic dynamics that shape how we relate, express, and connect. When clients feel that both structure and softness are present, direction and containment alongside warmth and acceptance, it creates an environment of psychological safety. Within such a space, emotional honesty can emerge.

Masculine and Feminine Energy in Psychosexual Therapy

In the context of psychosexual therapy, the language of "masculine" and "feminine energy" provides a valuable framework for exploring emotional, relational, and sexual dynamics. These energies are not confined to biological sex or gender identity; rather, they represent archetypal qualities present in all individuals, regardless of how they identify. This concept is rooted in Jungian psychology and has been further developed by theorists like Moore and Gillette (1990), who described the masculine archetype as encompassing direction, action, purpose, assertiveness, and containment. In contrast, feminine energy embodies qualities such as receptivity, intuition, emotional fluidity, nurturing, and connection (Carl Jung Institute, 2020).

Therapeutically, this model allows clients to examine how internalized cultural roles and external expectations shape their emotional and sexual lives. A man who over-identifies with traditional masculine energy may exhibit traits like emotional stoicism, a fixation on sexual performance, or an aversion to vulnerability. Conversely, a diminished connection to the feminine within may hinder emotional intimacy, limit empathy, or fuel relational distance.

Drawing on Jung's (1959) concept of the anima, the inner feminine figure in a man's psyche, psychosexual therapy invites male clients to reclaim the emotional and intuitive parts of themselves that may have been disowned or devalued. Rebalancing this internal dynamic is not about becoming "less masculine" but about becoming more whole. When a man connects with both his inner structure and his inner sensitivity, he gains access to deeper levels of intimacy, mutuality, and self-acceptance (Estés, 1992).

This integrative perspective challenges dominant Western narratives that associate masculinity with detachment, invulnerability, and physical prowess. It also aligns with research in men's psychology that shows how adherence to rigid masculine norms is linked to poorer psychological functioning, including heightened anxiety, depression, and sexual dysfunction (Addis & Mahalik, 2003; Seidler, 2006).

In my clinical work, I often see that for many men, therapy represents the first time they have been given permission to reflect openly on their emotional and sexual experiences. By validating their masculine identity while also gently expanding it, I help them dismantle the internalized shame that often accompanies struggles with sexual health. This might include anxieties about erectile performance, difficulties with orgasm, or a lack of emotional connection with a partner. Many arrive expecting to "fix" a mechanical problem, only to discover that their difficulties are entwined with deeper emotional needs that were never allowed to be voiced.

In these moments, therapeutic healing begins not through performance strategies or behavioral modification, but through compassionate witnessing. When clients are met with attunement rather than judgement, their internalized sense of failure is replaced with the possibility of self-compassion. As they begin to explore both their masculine and feminine energies, they step into a fuller version of themselves, one capable of intimacy, vulnerability, and self-trust.

The therapeutic journey, then, becomes not just about resolving sexual dysfunction, but about transforming the very notion of what it means to be a man in today's world. For working-class men, whose cultural environments may discourage emotional exploration, this work is radical. And for many, it is life-changing.

Cultural and Societal Barriers

A significant contributor to the underutilization of psychosexual therapy among working-class men is the influence of entrenched cultural narratives. These narratives dictate how men are expected to understand, express, and manage both psychological distress and sexual dysfunction. In many British working-class communities, values such as stoicism, toughness, and emotional self-reliance remain central to masculine identity. Seeking help for emotional or sexual concerns is often perceived not as a strength, but as a failure to embody these ideals. The culturally ingrained adage that one should "just get on with it and don't moan" typifies this worldview (Robertson, Gough & Hanna, 2015).

Contrary to the assumption that men casually discuss their sexual lives with friends, evidence suggests otherwise. A 2022 YouGov survey reported that only 17% of British men felt comfortable discussing erectile dysfunction (ED) or low libido with close friends, compared to 37% of women who openly shared such concerns. Similarly, the Men's Health Forum (2023) highlighted that one in three men in the UK had never spoken to anyone about their mental health. This reluctance is even more pronounced among working-class men, who may perceive vulnerability as incompatible with their social and gendered identity.

These silences are not benign. When men internalize difficulties such as ED, emotional disconnection, or performance anxiety as personal inadequacies, it fosters shame, isolation, and self-criticism. Seidler et al. (2016) identify these patterns as psychological avoidance strategies that reinforce emotional suppression and block access to therapeutic support. In the psychosexual context, these defenses often manifest as difficulties with intimacy, avoidance of vulnerability, or a persistent sense of failure around sexual identity and performance.

As Kilmartin (2005) aptly notes, "Men often avoid therapy due to societal norms that equate vulnerability with weakness, fostering a culture where seeking help is perceived as a failure rather than a strength." For working-class men, these norms are deeply embedded, both interpersonally and structurally, and they pose a substantial barrier to emotional disclosure and help-seeking.

Erectile Dysfunction, Medical Support, and the Working Class

Prescription data over the past decade reveals a noteworthy pattern in how British men, particularly from working-class backgrounds, approach sexual dysfunction. Between 2009 and 2019, the number of general practitioner (GP) prescriptions for erectile dysfunction medications in England more than doubled, rising from approximately 2.1 million to 4.5 million prescriptions annually. Notably, this increase was disproportionately higher in the North of England, where prescription rates were approximately 50% higher than in London. In regions marked by socio-economic deprivation, prescription rates were 21% higher than in more affluent areas (Warwick Business School, 2022).

For example, in the 12 months leading up to June 2022, Blackpool recorded the highest prescription rate for ED medication in England, with 36 prescriptions per 100 men aged 18 and over. Doncaster followed closely with 30 prescriptions per 100 men (Blackpool Gazette, 2022; Doncaster Free Press, 2022). These statistics reflect a nuanced shift: on one hand, they suggest an encouraging reduction in stigma, with more men seeking medical help. On the other, they reveal how treatment continues to be shaped by masculine ideals that favor action and problem-solving over introspection or emotional engagement.

In this sense, the popularity of medications such as Viagra (sildenafil) among working-class men is not solely about sexual restoration. It also represents a compromise, a way of seeking help that does not require breaking masculine codes of silence or vulnerability. Consulting a GP and requesting a prescription fits the narrative of "taking action" and "fixing the problem," without delving into the emotional complexities that may underlie the dysfunction.

However, as psychosexual therapy repeatedly demonstrates, the use of ED medication alone is often insufficient. While sildenafil and similar drugs may facilitate physiological arousal, they rarely address the psychological roots of sexual dysfunction, such as performance anxiety, low self-worth, unresolved trauma, or relational dissatisfaction. In therapy, these unexamined aspects often surface as clients begin to explore their full emotional and relational context.

Indeed, the "little blue pill" can become a symbol of stoic resilience, quietly tolerated shame masked by pharmaceutical intervention. While it may offer temporary relief, it does so without challenging the emotional scripts that perpetuate distress. By contrast, therapeutic engagement provides space to reflect, feel, and reconstruct narratives about masculinity, sexuality, and identity in ways that are both healing and liberating.

The Stigma of Sexual Dysfunction

Sexual health, particularly erectile dysfunction (ED), remains enveloped in silence and stigma among working-class men in the UK. Deeply rooted cultural and gender norms often position male sexuality within the framework of virility, dominance, and emotional detachment. Consequently, any disruption to sexual performance is not merely experienced as a physiological issue but as a profound threat to masculine identity (White & Johnson, 2000; Galdas, Cheater & Marshall, 2005).

In these communities, traditional ideals of masculinity, centered on sexual performance, emotional stoicism, and physical strength, create an internalized script that discourages vulnerability. Admitting to a sexual difficulty such as ED is often experienced as emasculating. Even within close friendships, discussions about sexual health are rare. A culture of silence prevails, making it difficult for men to normalize or process their struggles. The prevailing message is clear: a "real man" does not fail sexually, and if he does, he certainly does not speak of it.

This internalization of stigma becomes especially problematic when sexual dysfunction arises. For many men, it precipitates a cascade of self-doubt, shame, and social withdrawal. The sense of having failed at something so intrinsically linked to manhood creates an emotional landscape of inadequacy, which often goes unspoken and unaddressed in personal relationships, let alone clinical settings. In therapy, this is frequently observed as resistance, avoidance, or defensive humor, all protective mechanisms to shield against deeper feelings of shame and exposure.

Pornography, Performance, and Unrealistic Expectations

A growing body of research highlights the impact of pornography in shaping male sexual expectations. Within the genre, men are portrayed as perpetually sexually potent, dominant, and physically unrelenting. These depictions contribute to the construction of unrealistic and often unachievable performance standards, particularly for men already grappling with body image concerns, stress, or sexual dysfunction (Rothman, Kaczmarek & Berent, 2021).

For many working-class men, who may lack access to comprehensive sex education or culturally attuned psychosexual resources, pornography becomes a primary reference point. Within this frame, ED is not just a medical condition but a personal and moral failure. When the body does not perform on demand, it is not seen as a signal to explore underlying emotional or relational dynamics, but rather as evidence of weakness or brokenness.

Within clinical work, this dissonance becomes particularly salient. Clients will often express confusion and frustration about their perceived inability to "measure up," despite being physically healthy or in otherwise stable relationships. These distorted expectations fuel performance anxiety, further exacerbating sexual difficulties and reinforcing avoidance patterns in both intimacy and therapeutic engagement.

Barriers to Seeking Help

Despite the wider availability of ED treatments, both prescription and over-the-counter, there remains a significant gap in help-seeking behaviors among men, particularly those from working-class contexts. A national survey reported that only 4% of men experiencing erection issues had consulted a pharmacist, and 76% indicated embarrassment as the primary barrier (Pharmacy Magazine, 2022). These figures align with clinical observations: even when services are available, internalized shame frequently deters men from accessing them.

In lieu of professional support, many men turn to self-medication or unregulated online markets. These alternatives offer a degree of anonymity and control, but often come with significant risks, ranging from harmful drug interactions to counterfeit medications containing unknown ingredients (PubMed, 2021). The preference for silent management over therapeutic exploration illustrates how deeply the stigma is embedded. For many, it is safer to risk bodily harm than emotional exposure.

Therapists working with this population must understand these barriers as not simply personal decisions but culturally and structurally reinforced patterns. Creating a space that validates clients' fears while gently challenging limiting beliefs is central to the work. Only then can men begin to uncouple their sense of worth from sexual performance and reframe intimacy as a shared, emotional experience rather than a solitary performance-based act.

Case Study: Paul's Journey to Therapy

Paul (pseudonym), a 40-year-old heterosexual white British man from a working-class background in the Northwest of England, presented for psychosexual therapy following the breakdown of his second marriage. After relocating to the South in his twenties and experiencing significant personal losses, including the recent death of his mother and earlier death of his father, Paul began to confront a lifelong struggle with erectile dysfunction (ED), a condition that had remained unaddressed for over two decades.

Paul had internalized a model of masculinity shaped by his working-class roots, where emotional vulnerability was viewed as weakness and sexual performance as the cornerstone of manhood. His self-perception was deeply enmeshed with his ability to satisfy a partner sexually, and when he found himself unable to do so, feelings of shame and inadequacy intensified. This is not unusual; research suggests that many working-class men view ED as a direct threat to masculine identity and, rather than exploring psychological dimensions, tend to medicalize the issue (White & Johnson, 2000; Johnson, 2019).

Paul's initial encounter with healthcare exemplifies this pattern. Like many in his demographic, he visited a general practitioner, who prescribed Viagra (sildenafil) without further inquiry into emotional or relational factors. While this temporarily offered hope, the effects were inconsistent and unsatisfying. Repeated visits to different GPs left him feeling disillusioned. One dismissive doctor reportedly advised, "You shouldn't have that problem at your age. Just carry on watching porn and don't worry." Such interactions compounded his shame and reinforced the idea that help-seeking was futile or even embarrassing.

Paul became increasingly resentful of his body. He described himself in early sessions as "useless" and "less of a man," phrases that reflected internalized gender norms associating erectile ability with self-worth (Seidler, 2006; Tiefer, 2004). He never discussed his ED with friends and initially saw therapy as irrelevant, believing that "real men" didn't need emotional support.

Reliance on Viagra: The "Fix-It" Masculinity Model

Paul's story mirrors the broader societal trend regarding the reliance on pharmaceutical solutions for psychosexual difficulties. The reclassification of sildenafil (Viagra) as an over-the-counter (OTC) medicine in the UK in 2018 contributed to a surge in sales, with over 7 million tablets sold between May 2020 and May 2021 (The Independent, 2022). Most users were aged 25–54, highlighting the increasing reliance among younger and middle-aged men.

While accessible medication can be an important tool, it is often mistaken for a comprehensive solution. The ease of acquiring Viagra from high-street pharmacies or online sellers appeals to men socialized to "fix" problems independently. However, this pattern rarely leads to meaningful resolution. It often bypasses the emotional and relational roots of dysfunction, reinforcing the belief that psychosexual issues are purely physical (Gifford, 2021; Tiefer, 2004).

The dark side of this convenience is the booming black market for unlicensed ED drugs. In 2019, the UK's Medicines and Healthcare products Regulatory Agency (MHRA) seized over 3.5 million counterfeit pills worth over £10 million (GOV.UK, 2019). These unregulated substances pose serious health risks and reflect how desperation, stigma, and misinformation drive risky behaviors.

Paul, like many, sought a "magic bullet" in Viagra. His early sessions focused narrowly on restoring physical function. Only gradually did therapy reveal how ED had become a conduit for deeper psychological pain, grief, unresolved trauma, relational insecurity, and the internalized belief that "a man must always be in control."

Prevalence, Stigma, and the Psychological Toll

ED is highly prevalent, affecting nearly 50% of men at some point in their lives (Johns Hopkins Medicine, 2024). In the UK specifically, recent findings indicate that approximately 41.5% of men report some level of erectile difficulty, with incidence increasing significantly with age (Li et al., 2022). Yet stigma continues to prevent open dialogue. According to a 2018 study by Atomik Research (2018), 31% of men in their thirties had experienced relationship breakdowns related to ED. Additionally, 36% reported a loss of self-confidence and deteriorated self-esteem (Gifford, 2021).

In the therapy room, men like Paul often reveal internalized scripts such as "You're not a real man if you can't get it up," or "You're broken." These narratives perpetuate shame, impede intimacy, and fuel emotional withdrawal. Without intervention, such men often live in a chronic state of relational disconnection, sexual anxiety, and emotional dysregulation (McCabe et al., 2016).

Paul's resistance to addressing childhood experiences or discussing emotions was typical. Like many working-class men, he had been taught to suppress vulnerability. His reluctance initially took the form of deflection and humor. Gradually, however, through the safety and attunement of the therapeutic alliance, he began exploring deeper wounds, grief over familial loss, abandonment fears, and early messages around masculinity and self-worth.

Psychotherapeutic Significance

Therapy helped Paul shift from a purely genital focus to a more integrated view of sexual well-being. Psychosexual therapy offered him a space where he could reframe ED not as a failure, but as a symptom pointing to unmet emotional needs. Through this reframing, Paul learned to separate his sexual function from his masculine identity and began to access previously buried emotions, fear, sadness, and tenderness.

Paul's case underscores a critical therapeutic principle: medication can be part of the solution, but healing from sexual dysfunction often requires addressing emotional history, internalized gender roles, and relational trauma. His journey exemplifies how therapeutic work can begin not with performance, but with permission to feel, to explore, and to be seen without judgment.

The Importance of Understanding Childhood

Broken Mirror Syndrome in Men: An Attachment-Based Perspective

In psychosexual therapy with working-class men, many clients present with an elusive but deeply felt experience, a sense that something essential within them is fractured. These men often report emotional numbness, difficulty with intimacy, or a disconnection between their achievements and their inner sense of worth. While not a formal clinical diagnosis, this internal fragmentation can be conceptualized through the metaphor of Broken Mirror Syndrome.

This metaphor describes the developmental and emotional consequences of growing up in an environment where a child's emotional experiences are not adequately mirrored, validated, named, or understood by caregivers. In such environments, the child's evolving self-concept is formed without the stabilizing reflection of attuned parental engagement. As a result, the emerging sense of self remains disjointed, vulnerable to collapse under emotional stress or interpersonal demands.

This concept resonates strongly with attachment theory (Bowlby, 1988), which posits that early interactions with primary caregivers create internal working models that shape future relationships, emotional regulation, and self-perception. Secure attachment, characterized by consistent responsiveness and emotional attunement, fosters resilience and emotional intelligence. Insecure attachment, however, especially in the form of emotional neglect, can distort the self's internal architecture (Ainsworth & Bowlby, 1991).

In clinical settings, men affected by this fractured development may show a reluctance to share emotions, a chronic need for control, or a compulsive pursuit of external validation, patterns often rooted in early experiences of unmet emotional needs. This emotional dysregulation may manifest in adulthood as sexual dysfunction, relational withdrawal, or chronic shame. Thus, Broken Mirror Syndrome is not a pathology in itself, but a developmental injury that shapes the lens through which these men relate to themselves and others.

Early Reflections and the Formation of the Self

British psychoanalyst Donald Winnicott (1967) emphasized the concept of the caregiver's face as the "first mirror" for the infant. Through the caregiver's response, smiling at joy, soothing distress, the infant begins to perceive itself as a coherent and emotionally valid being. This early mirroring forms the scaffolding upon which self-awareness and emotional literacy are constructed.

However, when this reflection is absent, inconsistent, or distorted, often due to parental emotional unavailability, mental illness, substance abuse, or intergenerational trauma, the child internalizes confusion, rejection, or shame. Over time, these early distortions become embedded as deep-seated beliefs: "My feelings don't matter," "I must not be weak," or "Connection is unsafe."

These dynamics are further complicated by societal gender norms. Levant, Hall and Rankin (2009) introduced the term Normative Male Alexithymia to describe a culturally reinforced difficulty among men in identifying and expressing emotions. Boys, especially those in working-class contexts, may be taught to suppress vulnerability in favor of stoicism and action. When this suppression intersects with early attachment injuries, it creates a powerful double bind: men not only lack emotional skills but are also socialized to view those skills as irrelevant or threatening to their masculinity.

Signs of the Broken Mirror

In therapeutic practice, the signs of Broken Mirror Syndrome often include:

- **Alexithymia**: Difficulty identifying or naming emotional states
- **Emotional detachment**: Numbness, disassociation, or an aversion to vulnerability
- **Relational difficulties**: Avoidance of closeness, fear of abandonment, or compulsive independence
- **Shame and inadequacy**: A persistent internal narrative of being "not enough"
- **Overcompensation**: A reliance on external validation through work, status, or control

These traits often underlie male presentations of sexual dysfunction, especially erectile dysfunction, where psychological factors such as performance anxiety and low self-worth play a central role. Fonagy et al. (2003) argue that the ability to mentalize, to understand and reflect on one's own and others' emotional states, is rooted in early caregiver mirroring. When this capacity is underdeveloped, adults may misinterpret emotional cues, struggle with self-awareness, and rely on rigid coping strategies in relationships and sexual expression.

In men from working-class environments, these internal struggles may be further exacerbated by cultural messages that prize toughness and emotional invulnerability (Seidler, 2006; Addis & Mahalik, 2003). Consequently, the result is not only a broken internal mirror, but a social environment that punishes attempts to repair it.

Understanding these developmental and sociocultural intersections is vital in psychosexual therapy. Therapeutic progress often begins not with interventions focused on sexual performance, but with a compassionate reconstruction of the client's self-concept, using empathy, validation, and relational safety to slowly replace distorted reflections with authentic, affirming ones.

Masculinity, Vulnerability, and the Social Mirror

One of the central aims in psychosexual therapy with men from working-class backgrounds is to redefine the narratives they have internalized about masculinity and vulnerability. These narratives often stem from both childhood experience and cultural reinforcement, fostering an ideal of the emotionally invulnerable, sexually dominant male. This construct, while socially valued in many communities, becomes a psychological trap, one that discourages emotional honesty and deters men from seeking help, especially for issues related to sexual functioning.

Levant and Richmond (2007) argue that traditional masculinity ideology, defined by toughness, emotional control, and anti-femininity, is strongly associated with maladaptive emotional regulation and poor mental health outcomes. In therapy, men are invited to critically examine and re-author these internalized masculine scripts. This process often involves surfacing long-buried emotions, grief, fear, tenderness, that were once perceived as weaknesses but are now recontextualized as valid expressions of strength.

A key therapeutic intervention in this space is narrative reconstruction, where the client begins to explore and rewrite the personal stories that have shaped their sense of identity and worth. As clients gain the emotional vocabulary and psychological permission to connect with their inner lives, many experience a sense of liberation. Vulnerability, once feared, becomes a bridge to deeper intimacy, resilience, and self-compassion (Brown, 2012; Addis & Mahalik, 2003).

One client, for instance, shared that after addressing early unmet emotional needs and confronting inherited masculine ideals, he was finally able to extend kindness and emotional generosity towards himself and others. This transformation reflects what Carl Rogers (1961) called the move towards congruence: a state in which a person's inner experiences are aligned with their outer expression.

Moving Towards Wholeness

The metaphor of the broken mirror, introduced earlier as a symbol of a fragmented sense of self, remains a guiding image in this therapeutic work. However, the goal is not to return the mirror to its original, unblemished state. Rather, therapy aims to support the client in integrating these fragmented aspects of self, recognizing that wholeness comes not from perfection but from acknowledgment and acceptance of every emotional shard.

This integrative approach draws from both psychodynamic and humanistic traditions, emphasizing emotional processing, reparation of early attachment injuries, and the development of authentic relational connection (Schore, 2012; Siegel, 2010). In practice, men are supported to grieve their unmet childhood needs, name their unspoken emotional experiences, and dismantle rigid gender expectations that have impeded their capacity for intimacy.

The therapeutic space is particularly critical for these men. As a practitioner, my role involves bearing witness without judgment, listening for what is not said as much as what is. The silence before an emotional disclosure, the guarded body language, the subtle deflection through humor, these are the cracks where deeper work begins. Men who have been taught to distrust emotion or associate sensitivity with shame are gently guided towards emotional literacy and self-compassion.

Many of my clients are highly articulate in logic and reason, yet emotionally underdeveloped, a dynamic referred to by Apter (1990) as "cognitive-emotional disconnection." By validating their emotional reality and challenging the performance-based model of masculinity, I create a space where clients can begin to reframe emotional vulnerability as strength, rather than liability.

Transgenerational Messages: Breaking the Cycle

The emotional rigidity seen in many working-class men is not simply personal; it is often transgenerational. That is, the beliefs and behaviors shaping their emotional lives have been passed down through generations of familial and cultural conditioning. Connell (2005) and Seidler (2007) emphasize that hegemonic masculinity is perpetuated not only through media and social institutions but also within families, often unconsciously.

These inherited scripts, "real men don't cry," "get on with it," "deal with it like a man," become internalized mandates that shape how men navigate relationships, emotions, and identity. Such messages begin early in life and are reinforced through both direct instruction and implicit modeling. Parents who were themselves emotionally suppressed often pass this dynamic onto their children, continuing a legacy of emotional avoidance and silence.

Breaking this cycle involves intergenerational work in therapy, where men are supported to recognize these inherited beliefs, understand their origins, and consciously choose new ways of relating to themselves and others. For many clients, this is the first time they have considered that their discomfort with emotion is not a flaw but a learned response to emotionally impoverished environments.

Working-Class Men, Alcohol, and Erectile Dysfunction

One of the most prevalent, yet underexplored, coping strategies used by men to manage emotional distress and performance anxiety is alcohol consumption. Particularly within working-class communities, alcohol serves multiple social and psychological functions: it offers escape, facilitates social bonding, and reinforces cultural identities of toughness and camaraderie (Wilkins, 2010).

However, alcohol use is also one of the most significant contributors to sexual dysfunction. A large-scale meta-analysis by Li et al. (2021), encompassing over 216,000 participants, confirmed a statistically significant relationship between regular alcohol use and erectile dysfunction, with chronic alcohol misuse being particularly detrimental. Physiologically, alcohol impairs vascular and hormonal processes essential for sexual functioning, notably reducing nitric oxide production and testosterone levels. Psychologically, it dampens arousal, impairs sexual responsiveness, and fosters dependence on external substances for emotional regulation.

Despite these well-established effects, alcohol-related sexual issues are rarely discussed openly. Cultural norms that valorize stoicism and sexual dominance deter men from acknowledging these difficulties, let alone seeking professional help. As a result, men often continue using alcohol to mask anxiety and self-doubt, unknowingly exacerbating the very issues they are attempting to escape.

In therapy, this pattern is addressed not only through psychoeducation but also through shame deconstruction. Clients are encouraged to recognize the emotional functions that alcohol is serving and explore healthier alternatives. For example, mindfulness-based interventions, emotional regulation training, and relational work around intimacy and self-worth can replace reliance on substances with internal resilience and emotional presence (Miller & Rollnick, 2013).

Case Study: John's Journey to Therapy

John (a pseudonym, shared with consent) was a 42-year-old, white British heterosexual man from a working-class background. His presenting concern in therapy was a long-standing struggle with emotional intimacy and sexual connection within his marriage. John's upbringing had been strongly influenced by conventional masculine norms. His father, a factory worker, frequently communicated the belief that "men should handle their own problems," while his mother, though affectionate, echoed the same ideology with statements like "Be strong, don't dwell on things." These early parental messages formed the foundation of John's internalized masculinity: one rooted in stoicism, emotional suppression, and independence.

In adulthood, these inherited norms manifested as a habitual withdrawal from emotional conflict. When tension arose in his relationship, John would shut down rather than risk vulnerability. Like many working-class men, he perceived therapy as a last resort, something for the weak or the privileged. He often repeated, "Therapy isn't for people like me. I should be able to sort this out on my own," a belief echoing Seidler's (2006) observations on how masculine identity is shaped by cultural pressures to appear self-reliant.

John's resistance softened only after years of encouragement from his wife, who expressed exhaustion at his emotional unavailability. Upon entering therapy, John presented with guarded body language, minimal eye contact, and a hesitancy to speak freely. These early sessions were crucial in establishing trust. Drawing from a strengths-based and person-centered approach (Rogers, 1961), I began by validating John's courage in seeking help. Reframing his decision as an act of strength, not weakness, helped shift his perception of therapy and of himself.

As the therapeutic alliance deepened, we worked with transgenerational patterns using narrative therapy techniques, metaphor-based exercises, and family genogram exploration (McGoldrick, Gerson & Petry, 2008). These methods illuminated the intergenerational transmission of emotional stoicism, helping John to contextualize his emotional avoidance not as personal failure but as inherited survival strategy.

Gradually, John began to recognize that his emotional needs were not liabilities. He learned that vulnerability was not a betrayal of masculinity but an integral part of being human. This shift enabled him to communicate more openly with his wife, express his fears without shame, and disentangle his sense of sexual adequacy from rigid performance expectations. As his internalized shame diminished, he even found humor and pride in his sexual growth, an indicator of affect regulation and self-acceptance (Levant & Richmond, 2007).

Returning to Paul: A Complex Healing Journey

Paul's journey, in contrast, was marked by profound trauma and longstanding emotional injury. As noted earlier, Paul, a 40-year-old white British heterosexual man, entered therapy with a history of emotional neglect, physical and sexual abuse, and multiple relational betrayals. These early adverse experiences left deep psychological imprints, which he carried silently into adulthood, manifesting as erectile dysfunction, low self-esteem, and pervasive shame.

Initially, Paul's help-seeking was directed towards medical solutions. Like many men socialized within a working-class framework, he approached his general practitioner for what he believed was a physical problem. This aligns with Johnson's (2019) assertion that sexual dysfunction is often medicalized among men who lack access to or awareness of psychotherapeutic alternatives. When medication (e.g., Viagra) failed to produce lasting improvement, Paul's internal distress escalated. Rather than perceiving erectile dysfunction as a multidimensional issue, he interpreted it as yet another personal failing.

Therapy offered Paul a new narrative space, one where his body was no longer the enemy but a site of unmet emotional need. Drawing on psychodynamic theory, particularly the concept of somatic transference (Lemma, 2016), we explored how Paul had come to displace unprocessed trauma onto his sexual functioning. His penis, as he described, had become the repository of his lifelong pain.

Therapeutic work focused on building safety, processing trauma, and reclaiming bodily agency. This took time and persistence. Through emotion-focused therapy, inner child work, and trauma-informed psychoeducation, Paul gradually came to see that his body had not failed him; it had merely adapted to survive unbearable experiences (Schore, 2012; Levine, 2010).

As Paul's sense of self-compassion grew, so did his ability to trust again. He redefined his masculine identity, not as someone who performs under pressure, but as someone who feels, connects, and relates. This therapeutic milestone was illustrated when, for the first time in years, Paul reported achieving and sustaining an erection during sex, not via medication, but through emotional safety, trust, and mutual presence.

Reflections on the Casework

Both John and Paul exemplify the powerful intersections between masculinity, psychosexual health, and early relational trauma. Where John's difficulties stemmed primarily from intergenerational conditioning around emotional stoicism, Paul's struggles were rooted in complex trauma and somatization. Yet, both narratives reflect a shared cultural backdrop, one in which emotional expression is constrained, vulnerability is pathologized, and sexual performance is hyper-valued.

These case studies demonstrate the critical role of relational safety in psychosexual therapy. A compassionate therapeutic alliance, attuned to class, culture, gender, and trauma, offers men an opportunity to rewrite internal scripts that have long dictated silence and suffering. In doing so, therapy becomes not just a clinical intervention, but a space of profound emotional reintegration.

Conclusion

This chapter has illuminated how the enduring reliance on Viagra among working-class British men, like Paul and John, speaks not only to the medicalization of erectile dysfunction (ED) but also to a deeper cultural impulse for quick fixes in the face of emotional complexity. While pharmacological interventions such as sildenafil can offer symptom relief, they seldom address the underlying psychological distress, trauma histories, and relational ruptures that often contribute to sexual dysfunction (Tiefer, 2004; McCabe et al., 2016).

To engage meaningfully with psychosexual challenges, we must adopt a holistic, multi-dimensional approach, one that foregrounds emotional literacy, dismantles the stigma surrounding male vulnerability, and honors the socio-cultural context from which these issues arise. Open conversations about sexual and emotional health, facilitated through culturally sensitive therapeutic practices, create opportunities for lasting transformation. This is particularly critical in working-class communities, where entrenched gender norms and structural inequalities continue to obstruct access to mental health support (Galdas, Cheater & Marshall, 2005; Wilkins, 2010).

At the heart of this work lies the "Broken Mirror Syndrome," a therapeutic metaphor capturing the psychic fragmentation that occurs when emotional needs go unrecognized in childhood. As theorized in Kohut's self psychology, the absence of empathic attunement in early life can lead to deficits in self-cohesion and identity (Kohut, 1977). This disrupted mirroring process, compounded by masculine ideals that pathologize vulnerability, leaves many men with internalized narratives of inadequacy, particularly around sexual competence and emotional expression.

Psychosexual therapy, grounded in attachment theory (Bowlby, 1988), mentalization (Fonagy et al., 2003), and relational psychodynamics, seeks to repair these internal ruptures. Through empathic witnessing, affect regulation, and re-authoring of internalized beliefs, men can begin to reintegrate dissociated parts of the self, reclaim agency over their bodies, and redefine their masculine identities. In doing so, the therapist does not simply address a dysfunction but supports the client in reconstructing a coherent and compassionate sense of self.

Importantly, this therapeutic process takes on heightened significance within the working-class demographic. As explored, these men often face intersecting barriers, economic precarity, societal marginalization, and inherited norms that conflate emotional suppression with strength (Connell, 2005; Seidler, 2006). Therapy thus becomes a site of quiet revolution: where inherited silence is met with voice, where shame is held with empathy, and where relational intimacy is reclaimed not through performance but through presence.

The stories of Paul and John offer powerful testimony to this process. Each journey illustrates how vulnerability, when met with therapeutic safety and cultural attunement, can be transformed into a wellspring of healing and authenticity. Through the dismantling of internalized shame and the expansion of emotional vocabulary, these men were not merely treated, they were seen, heard, and restored.

In a broader sense, psychosexual therapy for working-class men is not just about sexual health, it is about relational justice. It invites us to reimagine masculinity beyond stoicism and self-sacrifice, and towards a model that embraces emotional depth, mutuality, and embodied connection. By challenging dominant cultural myths, this work has the potential to ripple outward, nurturing not only individual healing but also stronger families, more emotionally literate partnerships, and more compassionate communities.

References

Addis, M.E. and Mahalik, J.R., 2003. Men, masculinity, and the contexts of help seeking. *American Psychologist*, 58(1), pp. 5–14.

Ainsworth, M.D.S. and Bowlby, J., 1991. An ethological approach to personality development. *American Psychologist*, 46(4), pp. 333–341.

Atomik Research, 2018. 50% of male Brits in their 30s suffer erectile problems. [online] Available at: www.atomikresearch.co.uk/50-of-male-brits-in-their-30s-suffer-erectile-problems [Accessed 10 May 2025].

Blackpool Gazette, 2022. Blackpool is the Viagra capital of England, according to new figures. [online] Available at: www.blackpoolgazette.co.uk [Accessed 8 May 2025].

Bowlby, J., 1988. *A Secure Base: Parent-Child Attachment and Healthy Human Development*. London: Routledge.

Brown, B., 2012. *Daring Greatly: How the Courage to Be Vulnerable Transforms the Way We Live, Love, Parent, and Lead*. New York: Gotham Books.

Carl Jung Institute, 2020. *Masculine and Feminine Energy in the Therapeutic Encounter*. Zurich: Jungian Thought Archive.

Casey, L. (2016) *The Casey Review: A Review into Opportunity and Integration*. London: Department for Communities and Local Government. Available at: www.gov.uk/government/publications/the-casey-review-a-review-into-opportunity-and-integration (Accessed: 7 April 2026.

Connell, R.W., 2005. *Masculinities*. 2nd ed. Cambridge: Polity Press.

Crompton, R., 2008. *Class and Stratification*. Cambridge: Polity Press.

Doncaster Free Press, 2022. More men prescribed erectile dysfunction drug Viagra in Doncaster than almost anywhere else in England. [online] Available at: www.doncasterfreepress.co.uk [Accessed 8 May 2025].

Estés, C.P., 1992. *Women Who Run with the Wolves: Myths and Stories of the Wild Woman Archetype*. New York: Ballantine Books.

Fonagy, P., Gergely, G., Jurist, E.L. and Target, M., 2003. *Affect Regulation, Mentalization and the Development of the Self.* New York: Other Press.

Galdas, P.M., Cheater, F. and Marshall, P., 2005. Men and health help-seeking behaviour: Literature review. *Journal of Advanced Nursing*, 49(6), pp. 616–623.

Gifford, B.E., 2021. Six in 10 hide erectile dysfunction from their partner. *Hypnotherapy Directory*, 21 October. [online] Available at: www.hypnotherapy-directory.org.uk/articles/six-in-10-hide-erectile-dysfunction-from-their-partner [Accessed 10 May 2025].

GOV.UK, 2019. Fake erection pills worth £10 million seized. [online] Available at: www.gov.uk/government/news/fake-erection-pills-worth-10-million-seized [Accessed 8 May 2025].

Johns Hopkins Medicine, 2024. Erectile dysfunction statistics. [online] Available at: www.hopkinsmedicine.org [Accessed 10 May 2025].

Johnson, A., 2019. Erectile dysfunction: Addressing the psychological component. *British Journal of General Practice*, 69(688), pp. 488–490.

Jung, C.G., 1959. *Aion: Researches into the Phenomenology of the Self.* Princeton: Princeton University Press.

Kilmartin, C., 2005. Depression in men: Communication, diagnosis and therapy. *Journal of Men's Health & Gender*, 2(1), pp. 95–99.

Kohut, H., 1977. *The Restoration of the Self.* New York: International Universities Press.

Lawler, S., 2005. Disgusted subjects: The making of middle-class identities. *The Sociological Review*, 53(3), pp. 429–446.

Lemma, A. 2014. *Minding the Body: The Body in Psychoanalysis and Beyond*. London: Routledge.

Levant, R.F., Hall, R.J. and Rankin, T.J., 2009. Male Role Norms Inventory–Short Form (MRNI–SF): Development, confirmatory factor analytic investigation of structure, and measurement invariance across gender. *Journal of Counseling Psychology*, 56(3), pp. 392–407.

Levant, R.F. and Richmond, K., 2007. A review of research on masculinity ideologies using the Male Role Norms Inventory. *The Journal of Men's Studies*, 15(2), pp. 130–146.

Levine, P.A., 2010. *In an Unspoken Voice: How the Body Releases Trauma and Restores Goodness*. Berkeley, CA: North Atlantic Books.

Li, J.Z., Maguire, T.A., Zou, K.H., Lee, L.J., Donde, S.S., and Taylor, D.G., 2022. Prevalence, comorbidities, and risk factors of erectile dysfunction: Results from a prospective real-world study in the United Kingdom. *International Journal of Clinical Practice*, Article 5229702 [online] Available at: https://pubmed.ncbi.nlm.nih.gov/35693549/ [Accessed 10 May 2025].

Li, S., Song, J.M., Zhang, K. and Zhang, C.L., 2021. A meta-analysis of erectile dysfunction and alcohol consumption. *Urologia Internationalis*, 105(11–12), pp. 969–985. https://doi.org/10.1159/000508171

McCabe, M.P., Sharlip, I.D., Atalla, E., Balon, R., Fisher, A.D., Laumann, E.O. and Segraves, R.T., 2016. Definitions of sexual dysfunctions in women and men: A consensus statement

from the Fourth International Consultation on Sexual Medicine. *The Journal of Sexual Medicine*, 13(2), pp. 135–143.
McGoldrick, M., Gerson, R., and Petry, S., 2008. *Genograms: Assessment and Intervention*. 3rd ed. New York: W. W. Norton & Company.
Men's Health Forum, 2023. *Key Data: Mental Health*. Available at: www.menshealthforum.org.uk/key-data-mental-health (Accessed: 7 April 2026).
Miller, W.R. and Rollnick, S., 2013. *Motivational Interviewing: Helping People Change*. 3rd ed. New York: Guilford Press. (motivationalinterviewing.org).
Moore, R.L. and Gillette, D., 1990. *King, Warrior, Magician, Lover: Rediscovering the Archetypes of the Mature Masculine*. New York: HarperCollins.
Pharmacy Magazine, 2022. Men suffering in silence: Erectile dysfunction and pharmacy. [online] Available at: www.pharmacymagazine.co.uk [Accessed 8 May 2025].
PubMed, 2021. Men's health and barriers to treatment in primary care: A review of behavioural factors. [online] Available at: https://pubmed.ncbi.nlm.nih.gov [Accessed 8 May 2025].
Robertson, S., Gough, B. and Hanna, E., 2015. *Men's Health Literacy: Advancing Evidence, Policy and Practice in Gendered Health Communication*. London: Palgrave Macmillan.
Rogers, C.R., 1961. *On Becoming a Person: A Therapist's View of Psychotherapy*. London: Constable.
Rothman, E.F., Kaczmarek, L. and Berent, E., 2021. Pornography and sexual dysfunction among young men. *Journal of Adolescent Health*, 68(2), pp. 227–234.
Savage, M., Devine, F., Cunningham, N., Taylor, M., Li, Y., Hjellbrekke, J., Le Roux, B., Friedman, S. and Miles, A., 2013. A new model of social class? Findings from the BBC's Great British Class Survey experiment. *Sociology*, 47(2), pp. 219–250.
Schore, A.N., 2012. *The Science of the Art of Psychotherapy*. New York: W.W. Norton & Company.
Scourfield, J., Fincham, B., Langer, S. and Shiner, M., 2012. Sociological autopsy: An integrated approach to the study of suicide in men. *Social Science & Medicine*, 74(4), pp. 466-473.
Seidler, V.J., 2006. *Transforming Masculinities: Men, Cultures, Bodies, Power, Sex and Love*. London: Routledge.
Seidler, V.J., 2007. *Rediscovering Masculinity: Reason, Language and Sexuality*. London: Routledge.
Seidler, Z.E., Dawes, A.J., Rice, S.M., Oliffe, J.L. and Dhillon, H.M., 2016. The role of masculinity in men's help-seeking for depression: A systematic review. *Clinical Psychology Review*, 49, pp. 106–118.
Siegel, D.J., 2010. *The Developing Mind: How Relationships and the Brain Interact to Shape Who We Are*. 2nd ed. New York: Guilford Press.
The Independent, 2022. Young men turn to Viagra as sexual performance anxiety rises. [online] Available at: www.independent.co.uk [Accessed 8 May 2025].
Tiefer, L., 2004. *Sex is Not a Natural Act and Other Essays*. 2nd ed. Boulder, CO: Westview Press.
Warwick Business School, 2022. Why have GP prescriptions for erectile dysfunction doubled in a decade?. [online] Available at: www.wbs.ac.uk [Accessed 8 May 2025].
White, A. and Johnson, M., 2000. Men making sense of their chest pain: A qualitative study. *Journal of Clinical Nursing*, 9(4), pp. 534–541.

Wilkins, D., 2010. *Untold Problems: A Review of the Essential Issues in the Mental Health of Men and Boys*. London: Men's Health Forum.

Winnicott, D.W., 1967. Mirror-role of mother and family in child development. In: Lomas, P., ed. *The Predicament of the Family: A Psycho-Analytical Symposium*. London: Hogarth Press, pp. 26–33.

Chapter 16

Healing Racialized Identities as Part of Couples Therapy

Joanne M Collins

Introduction

Trevor is a 60-year-old man. Early in the work Trevor explained that it was important to him that I was a black therapist. He had grown up with frequent visits to his home by the police, he was neglected in the education system as he didn't have any adult to fight for him and within his family he had cousins who had been raised by the care system. He was very aware of the real oppressive power of the system and the discourses society held for black men like him.

Part of his lived experience is that he had only ever dated white women, he would say that this was his "preference." Srinivasan (2018) describes preference as often shaped by societal hierarchies, discrimination, and oppressive norms, arguing that rigid preferences should be interrogated as part of a moral responsibility. As part of his sexual experience he had never ejaculated with a partner as part of their sexual practice. As a black man he felt that for some partners this inability was something they were happy with as they already had expectations of sexual prowess and sexual pleasure with black men. This was a complicated belief for him as he himself worked hard to "whiten" himself socially by reducing the markers of blackness that he could be associated with. He aimed to be part of the professional class and described himself as someone who dressed like Nigel Farage (he explained this as a tweed and countryside look). Importantly, he was not going to be the "deadbeat" or "unreliable" black man. All these worries consolidated as an unconscious wish to not have children. This presented as feelings of ambivalence on fatherhood and an inability to ejaculate during sex.

In further exploration of his ambivalence on fatherhood, he described a past troubled with physical abuse and neglect. As part of his own survival, he reflected on his experience and made a deliberate identification with whiteness (to attempt to pass) hoping this would allow him a better quality of life, one where he is safe. He wanted to distance himself from the brutality he witnessed Black people (including himself) suffered. Trevor developed a sexual script (Simon and Gagnon, 2003) based on racialized, patriarchal culture as well as his personal experiences of oppression and pain. An important part of the couple fit for him is the ability to have access to power, social mobility, and a different quality of life. His current

DOI: 10.4324/9781003611387-16

partner was unaware of all these concerns. How do you develop intimacy with another person when there is this vulnerable false self who is invested in staying hidden?

How do we as therapists help Trevor build a stronger sense of self that he can use in his relationships? A fundamental task would be enabling him to work through real oppression and constitutive experience of power that he has experienced in his life. We must consider transgenerational trauma and the legacy this has left for him. We also must address his identity concerns. What does it mean to be a black man in 21st century England. The insecurities presented in this case have mostly emerged from a relationship to white oppressive power. This oppressive power not only affected Trevor's life but that of his parents, siblings, and the estate where he spent his early years. Trevor is not thinking about who he is in relationship to these oppressive experiences but thinking in terms of the inevitability of his experience. He views all of his experiences outside of himself, and this will not support the building of a positive self-identity. How does he build a sense of self that includes him holding a less fragmented story of himself? How does he build a self that he is proud of that can sustain him as he continues his journey through life?

Trevor's case study is a complex one speaking to a number of different factors to include racial trauma, transgenerational trauma, and deep insecurity borne out of childhood neglect. Our narratives are constructed in a web of relationships to include significant others, cultural/religious context, socio-political contexts, and mediated within a historically defined time context. Interpretations and meaning making therefore must operate under the same complex interplay. In Trevor's case meaning making was part of creating an identity. One of being "other" to black people but sadly eventually othering himself into alienation.

As a black woman I am frequently invited to speak on the subject of "race" or issues pertaining to black people. This has its benefits and challenges. One such challenge is the risk of being reductionistic. We group people together based on superficial features and deny them complexity or nuance which keeps the narrative around their lives limited. The other and pertinent issue is the lack of attention to power. Power has a multiplicity of influences and expressions. The same power base which constructed society by gender, race, class, religion, and other demographics is often at the heart of oppressive experiences of traditionally subjugated groups. Therapy is not excluded from this expression of power; it is often a politicized response to pain and has its own structure also influenced by the society it occurs in. Trevor is an example of the type of client that therapy has historically failed because of its inattention to power issues. To acknowledge the destructive aspect of power for the client, means, as therapists, we need to acknowledge that this power is real. Power exists and is maintained by structures that therapists also benefit from. The professional's power to think about what is normal or to allow unexplored personal biases to implicitly guide the therapeutic process need to be examined by self and in a supervisory relationship.

My hope for this chapter is that it contributes to a conversation about colonial power and its impact on romantic and/or sexual relationships. Individuals are a microcosm of the society they inhabit so some of the wider societal attitudes, beliefs, and discourses are likely to be reflected in their interactions. Apart from the traditional reasons for choosing a romantic partner such as romantic love, sexual attraction, class based/social climbing, family and traditions, curiosity, to name a few. Some will choose partners based on navigating and healing from very real oppressive experiences. To "exoticize" and "other" someone is part of not seeing them in preference for another story, therapists must hold this in mind or we are not allowing clients the full experience that therapy offers, to truly meet yourself and another. What is intended here is an exploration of what is insufficiently explored within the therapeutic space.

Simon (2024) describes the difference between theories of self and stories of self. Theories of self are political with a person's problems being located within an individual and/or wider social system. She also highlights that some concepts of self are defined within colonial frameworks with inequality of power affecting all your human rights and human experience.

The black experience is one that is characterized by power and politics and the legacy of this experience speaks directly to the structures and frameworks we, as black people, have fought to resist. Colonial power, and the continued racism, shapes the self and its presentation in the world. It's my belief that many black people navigate their experience in relationship to this power so therapeutic work must consider and reflect on this navigation as part of the whole person experience. Du Bois (1903) created the idea of double consciousness to consider one of the ways that the black person navigates the experience of living in a white world. It emphasizes the idea that the black person is aware of always being observed by "whiteness." These navigations are part of the "stories of self."

Social Construction

In presenting Trevor I offered the idea of sexual script (Simon, 1973). Sexual script is one way to describe Trevor's attempt to construct a less painful narrative for himself leading to choosing a particular type of partner. At the heart of sexual script is an idea that sexuality is socially constructed. Sexual scripts specifically aim to shed light on the interplay of how people perceive sexual activity in addition with patriarchal and cultural forces that organizes social worlds.

Social constructionists are skeptical of "universal truth" and "universal knowledge." Both are sources of power. Ideas of objectivity and truth are replaced with subjectivity and curiosity to allow understandings to be expanded upon to normalize other truths and give them credence. As claims to truth and knowledge are central to a discussion of identity and power it becomes fundamental to the ethics of knowledge. "Truth" is often white and is the established baseline from which many explore the world. Identities are shaped and deemed healthy or not against this "truth" (Andrews, 2023; 2025). To question the basis and thus validity of the power we need to revisit the power paradigm (Meretoja, 2013). This means critically deconstructing texts and conversations to offer multiple realities/truths.

Within the context of sex, sexuality, and relationships there are a number of social constructions and stereotypes. In the interplay of race, sex, desire, and gender are constructions about beauty and desirability where often the blonde white women sit at the top of the hierarchy. Black men ignite some curiosity about penis size, sexual capability, and sometimes stories of danger. I am reminded here of Linford Christie, a Jamaican-born British athlete who is one of the most decorated British athletes ever but struggled to be taken seriously as an athlete as the focus was on his "lunch box" (describing his penis in his running shorts). In his documentary "Linford" he talked about how white women would walk up to him and grope him (sexual assault) then giggle. He was eroticized and reduced to his "lunchbox." At times he was in tears but the media did not yield.

Black women are often not considered beautiful, consider the reporting on former first lady Michelle Obama being compared to "ape in heels" via social media or Diane Abbott, a Black British MP—a 2017 review found that she had received almost half of all abusive tweets sent to female MPs. Black and Asian female MPs received 35% more abusive tweets than their white colleagues. The abuse was fundamentally racist, comparing her to an ape and or threating to rape her (Elgot, 2017). The Urban dictionary displays the term "black belt" used to describe having sex with a black person for the first time. These narratives do not try to humanize black people, they support an idea of us as "fair game," animals perhaps even savages.

As therapists, we listen as clients tell their stories and pay attention to the "how" and "what" of personal stories. Meretoja (2013) offers the idea that recognizing our entanglement in narratives allows us to acknowledge the fundamental role played by power within the experience of subjectivity and identity. Malcolm X's (1962) infamous response to allegations that the Nation of Islam were spreading hate was "Who taught you to hate the texture of your hair? Who taught you to hate the color of your skin to such an extent that you bleach to get like the White man? Who taught you to hate the shape of your nose?..." Narrative ideas communicate how an identity is negotiated and how power has shaped identity. The role of narratives in our lives has ethical, political, and cultural importance and they allow subjugated racialized and other voices to have a seat within the creation of meaning.

Burr (2003) highlights one critique of social construction in that it does not account for the emotional investment that people make in particular discursive positions. How does social construction account for "self," including desires, hopes, fantasies, and the role of choice or agency? A sense of agency is what gives us the ability to define ourselves in any given moment. Positioning theory offers a way to think about how we use our agency to position ourselves in conversations. Cultural narratives can be a source of resistance and resilience for individuals engaged in a process of creating identities that are complex (and use culturally adapted power paradigms), because cultural narratives then offer permission to be different or to think about difference (Lorde, 2012). With the help of the Black Power movement, we had counter narratives that included "black is beautiful" in response to the racist narrative that said all black people were ugly.

Luckmann (1966) drew on the perspective of symbolic interactionism to argue that people, through social practices, construct and maintain all social phenomena which they experience as natural. In this next case study I want to think about social construction and narratives with a couple. First, I'd like to introduce two ideas from therapists who have considered why couples choose each other for romantic relationships.

Couple's Framework

Couple fit is one framework for thinking about who and why we choose the other. Fundamental to this idea is a basic idea, I choose you because you give me what I need. You fulfill a need in me. If I am low in confidence or wish that I could live a bolder life I may find myself attracted to another who exudes this confidence and with this partner I feel a sense of wholeness. In my view this phenomenon is not limited to qualities we possess but can be expanded to think about the social fit. This experience will also have an unconscious element to it. With this in mind it becomes easier to explore the unmet need we choose when choosing a partner and ask how might ethnicity or other identity markers influence the choice of healing this unmet need.

Another more well-known author is Esther Perel. Perel (2007) speaks about when we choose a partner we choose a story. In this story we have roles that we've assigned to ourselves and our partners. These stories are laden with expectations often unexpressed until the couple experiences some conflict. In this conflict expectations rise to the surface leaving hurt, grief, and sometimes a loss of hope. Sadly, these expectations are connected to narratives, for example, what is a good man? What is a good woman? What are the expectations on black men, black women etc.? The baseline expectation can often be heavily culturally, socially, religiously, politically loaded as well as the influence of family beliefs. When we widen the influences what does it do to the person being subjected to them?

The discourse on whiteness is a discourse on power, entitlements, and acceptability. This is an enticing discourse to someone for whom being the "other" has led to deep insecurity. I will use a case study to make this point. Names have been changed to support anonymity.

Case Study Two

Teresa is a 35-year-old black woman of Caribbean descent raised in the UK who is married to Adam, a white Jewish man. They are both qualified professionals with demanding jobs. They agreed that she would stop working to offer full-time care to their two children. They have very different family of origin stories. Teresa's mother was the matriarch to a family of six children. Her father was not reliable, and her mother led without complaining. When Teresa and her sisters were old enough to be involved in the home they followed in their mother's footsteps. The men in the nuclear family (father and brothers) came to rely on the females for their functioning needs. The sisters have grown up to be equally matriarchal in their families, presenting as the stereotype "strong black woman." They do not complain, they make it happen, they don't express any vulnerability. Adam has a different family of origin story. His mother was passive and submissive despite being married to an unreliable man who, on more than one occasion, had put the family home at risk with his gambling. In their attraction, they chose what they needed, he chose a strong black woman, she chose a reliable man. Her basis for him being reliable is because he was white. As the relationship progressed and children entered their lives, he presented as more vulnerable/needy and she withdrew from him, reinvesting all her energy into her children. Both their cultural and religious stories inform different actions and different priorities.

What might be the hidden stories about gender for each culture? What does equity look like in each cultural frame? In her individual session Teresa explained that she chose white men because she wanted a family norm that included security, reliability, and safety. In this moment she is also admitting that she believes the constructs about black men. She is experiencing a sense of despair as her construction of relationship has not worked. Her ex-boyfriends, also white, were deeply unreliable. Part of the crisis that Teresa is having is that she, like Trevor, believed the constructions of black men. She thought that she was correcting a pattern of pain in her life by choosing another ethnicity and specifically by choosing white. Now she has to face the pain of older unmet needs, of being failed by the first black man in her life (her father) and the shame it brought to her to be part of a dysfunctional discourse assigned to black families. Facing the pain is partly a vulnerable position and she doesn't feel that she can do this right now. Meeting the pain can be a big part of the work when working with the effects of power. How do we help Teresa to feel safe enough to meet her grief and pain that she has lived as a black woman? This leads me to think more explicitly about power and in post-colonial times. What might this mean for black people?

In speaking about the life of the post-colonial subject Fanon (1967) writes on "the woman of color and the white man." He offers something pertinent here that applies to the struggle of both Trevor and Teresa. He says "... it is our problem to ascertain to what extent authentic love will remain unattainable before one has purged oneself of that feeling of inferiority..." Let us think more here on the experience of post-colonial life.

Power and Post-Colonial Thinking

At its simplest, power is the ability to direct and/or influence behavior. The Foucauldian idea of discourse (1980) has some relevance here as the colonial experience is one where a number of "truths" were created to define relations and experiences for black people. Systems were structured around these ideas to reinforce bias to create knowledge that reinforced their oppression. Power was delivered with brutality and maintained through social constructs and discourses which treated as fact that African was less than human. One such brutality is the commonplace rape of women in slavery (Andrews, 2025; Davis, 1981; Fanon, 1967).

Post colonial thinkers (Stuart Hall, Franz Fanon, etc.) have extensively explored and written about life in post-colonial times. This theory arose out of anti-colonial resistance and the increase in nonwestern perspectives on colonialism. It's a body of work and study of political and social change that highlights the social, psychological, and cultural inferiority in the wake of the experience of the colonized state as well as the struggle for cultural and political self-directedness. The statistics and outcomes on black lives continue to be impacted negatively. We have an increase in awareness about diversity but as Angela Davis (2015) has said "we have given black and brown people a slice of the capitalist pie… We have the difference that makes no difference" (Eckert, 2015).

One idea that post-colonial thinkers have highlighted to the colonial subject is how those with a colonial history can and must resist identities placed upon us (Hall, 2026; 1993). As a therapist I have an interest in how colonization has shaped our identities. Fanon (1967) is particularly relevant here as a psychiatrist because he emphasized ideas on what has been internalized for the African post-colonial experience. Key to his idea is the concept of an inferiority complex which sets up the white master and his way of being as the ideal baseline we should strive for. The African attempts to lighten himself with a hope of gaining access to better social experience. I would argue that this "attempt to lighten self" is part of a social construction of romantic relationships. It may also be important to note here that religion was fundamental to the colonial experience. Religion was the dominant education so to lighten oneself could also be seen as being closer to God. God was presented as white and he had a clear view on sex, relationships, and family structures. Romantic relationships are already socially constructed around expectations, behaviors, religion, and culture, but importantly there is an idea of an ideal partner. The ideal was white; however, the paradox is that the discourse forbade the mixing of black and white, creating some ambivalence and excitability for the forbidden.

Andrews (2023) writes on the psychosis of whiteness, as it is from this perspective that we have the baseline from which the world is understood. He argues that we can't educate ourselves out of it because it's so heavily structural we need something much more radical. The psychosis element of his concept highlights the illogical nature of this phenomenon. Psychosis as a diagnosis is made up from a number of subjective markers which the "other" has had to navigate; this whiteness is often grounded in western values and ethics and makes little to no effort in trying to understand "other." Fanon (1963) describes colonization as "… a systematic negation of the other person and a furious determination to deny the other person all attributes of humanity, colonialism forces the people it dominates to ask themselves the question constantly: 'In reality, who am I?'" For Fanon, if the impact of colonization on identity is not contested, this can create a mental pathology. Every effort is made to force the colonized person to admit the inferiority of his culture and in the extreme to see the imperfect nature of who they are as a person.

Couple Relationships and Power

Foreman and Dallos (1992) state that "couples do not just create any reality but create permutations of pieces of wider social realities." Wider constructions and patriarchal structures are entangled into the couple's belief systems. In the same way feminist scholars have taught about the impact of power on heteronormative (and queer) relationships. The social construction of men and women creates an imbalance in power and, depending on the lens that we use to analyze this, an important question must be whose construction has more power. As therapist we also need to understand that any power can be used to influence relationships. Srinivasan (2018), in her exploration "Right to sex", reminds us that the intersectional variations on oppression mean we cannot address patriarchal roots without considering race and class-based inflections. We must identify them and explore them or it could lead to resentments, among other challenges, in romantic relationships. These constructions and intersecting oppressions are especially important to acknowledge as they enter the bedroom as "personal preference." Who we have sex with is a political question (Srinivasan, 2018).

Rampage (1994) states that it's a widely held belief that the purpose of contemporary romance is to satisfy each partner's need for intimacy. From a feminist perspective she discussed three pre-conditions required to achieve this: (1) equity between partners, (2) empathy for each other's experience, and (3) willingness to collaborate around both meaning and action. This was not demonstrated in Trevor's or Teresa's relationship.

For a black couple, different power dynamics are at play. The black woman and the black man have both gendered and racialized constructs and expectations on them. Srinivasan (2018) explores Willis in *Lust Horizons* and raises important questions for consideration here, if we are challenging patriarchal structures we must ask "Why do we choose what we choose? What would we choose if we had real choice?"

Perel (2007) explores romantic relationships and focuses on the tension between love and desire, and the need to balance the known and unknown. She argues that modern relationships are complex and contradictory, and that we want many things from our partners. This idea will show itself more clearly in my final case study of Wendy and Aron.

Case Study 3

Wendy and Aron are a couple in their early forties. They have been together since they met in College (they are Black American). Wendy's family are black, working class and religious. She grew up in a single parent household and as the firstborn she was raised within a structure that told her she was responsible for the younger siblings and eventually her mother. Her mother was vulnerable due to a mental health condition for which there is no clear diagnosis. Wendy remembers her mother as vulnerable, not really able to offer much to the household and not making good decisions. Aron grew up with his grandparents because both his parents died when he was under the age of 10, due to alcohol-related concerns. Though he lived in his grandparents' home, he had the loving support of aunts, uncles, and cousins. He remembers being held and supported, he remembers "always being cared for and feeling safe." Wendy was always a carer, this was their couple fit. As time went on, Wendy had an affair, with someone who made her feel "visible and sexy." It was hard for her to end this affair and the feelings evoked were new and powerful to her. She wanted to be touched in a particular way by her husband but his story didn't facilitate that type of thinking in him. Both of them continued to be very successful black professionals, not the type of imagery sufficiently seen to be "the norm." They worked many years on cultivating a particular image of black family life and they also had children. The extended families wanted this relationship to work out with the family staying together. The pressure was with the wife to be strong; there was no expectation for the husband to change and the affair made many in his family more protective of him.

In this example I have chosen a black middle-class couple. Together since they were 20, they shared a belief in the importance of creating a black middle-class family, which they successfully achieved. They were not able to navigate successful sexual life or relationship intimacy. The tradition of her being the first-born female meant much was expected of Wendy. There wasn't a narrative that they agreed on that allowed her to be vulnerable. She is devoted to the narrative and up and until the affair, has spent 20 years being loyal to someone who, in her own admission, was never able to give her what she wanted. The affair was an attempt to be seen differently and therapy about the affair was a way to confront some of these truths but the narrative didn't expand to acknowledge her pain so she was still invisible. The social somehow overrode the personal. This example raises many points but I'll raise two here, one about gender and the black woman, the other about black middle-class families.

Collins (2000) describes the way black women have been thought about in American society. One idea is the superstrong "Black mother." In a context of institutionalized racism where African Americans have long aimed to present a united front to whites, many US blacks learn to police one another. This includes who black women date and whether they (black men) can be spoken about publicly in a negative way. Silence becomes both protective and defensive of black men. Black women must learn how to survive the sexual politics of intersecting oppressions while rejecting and transcending the same power relations. How do we raise and protect daughters in a society that doesn't value them? Not seen as beautiful, not the right color/shade, hair, etc. Black females must learn and navigate the domains of power in the community in which they exists. The dynamics set up the stage for the "strong black woman" archetype which I feel contributed to how Wendy ended up in crisis. As she revisited her relationship history, she realized that they shared the financial responsibility but she always did the emotional labor without reciprocity from her husband. She always put him first, she never complained, wanting to feel supportive to "a brother."

Life on the plantation shaped gender expectations for black people. Women were needed for their bodies to produce babies as well as the work they forcibly did in support of capitalism and slavery. It was easy to separate the family as members could be sold off so family norms expanded to include a sense of community (source). Black men were not allowed the traditional role of protector or provider and some have argued they were emasculated by this. The abolition of slavery did not bring rights to black people and white patriarchy, through racism, created structures that negatively impacted black families as often the black man was attacked, killed, imprisoned, or institutionalized. Many black families in the western world lived in slum conditions with poor access to housing, health, and financial resources. On a human level I could understand why many black people hoped for the institution of family to be a safe place for them where they could protect its members. With this history in mind The Cosby Show and a Different World were two powerful series that showed black people outside of the narrative of deprivation and struggle. On the show, black people were successful and living with a class-based privilege that many would not have experienced. One challenge to this is that they continued to perpetuate white patriarchy by allowing black actors in a white script on class and family life. It didn't allow us to see different family norms that were also valid ways of being.

Conclusion

When this offer came along, to contribute to a book that was going to start a conversation about the unsaid, untold, and unexplored in the interplay of race and sex and the many nuances that exist within these facets of life. It felt like an opportunity to begin a conversation. In closing, I want to return to this quote by Fanon (1967) "… it is our problem to ascertain to what extent authentic love will remain unattainable before one has purged oneself of that feeling of inferiority…" This is an important idea, as it speaks to healing we need to receive to be able to trust the love we receive. Outside ideas of toxic love, our inability to trust the love we find can cause us to keep picking and checking. When the structures have challenged your beauty and worth it can be hard to feel a right to love.

Discourse is a term that allows consideration to forms of knowledge and what is accepted as reality within a given society. Couple relationships are also shaped by the discourses that inform societal structure. Discourses hold stories about people that can be appealing to particular wounds. One way that people seek to heal themselves is in relationships, and romantic and/or long-term relationships can be a powerful source for growth and healing.

For some, to be accepted by a white partner is the ultimate in healing a fragile self which was the consequence of racist wounds as it offers a sense of self-worth. How do we think about racialized discourses when exploring the couple fit with black couples or couples where a partner is not white? If we don't make space to explore some of these ideas what is the impact to the intimacy between the couple? How does intimacy express itself with an old internalized power dynamic around race and other intersections? Social constructions can be deconstructed as part of the process of healing that also considers early years, wider belief systems, wider experiences of love and attachments. Therapists are also subject to these discourses and constructions, they need to make space to explore these and how they impact the work with couples.

Due to word restrictions this exploration has been limited. I have focused on what is happening for the black person, but the white (or other) person dating who chooses black can also be choosing something in the discourse. In my clinical work, for example, I have met white partners who assumed their black partner would have a higher sex drive or expected that the black partner would be a source of protection for them. This writing has also had a heteronormative focus and it would be helpful to also think about racialized discourses within the queer community.

Critical race theory is pivotal as it provides a framework to think about race and power within society. This fits in with my clinical work where I think about the socio-political, the psychological, and their impact between people on the type of relationships people have and the types of distress people may experience. The goal in therapy must be working towards a space where we facilitate deeper meetings and fuller experiences of the selves. An exploration of racialized discourses must be part of this work.

References

Andrews, K. (2023) *The Psychosis of Whiteness: Surviving the Insanity of a Racist World.* London: Penguin.

Andrews, K. (2025) *Nobody Can Give You Freedom: The Real Mission of Malcolm X.* London: Penguin.

Burr, V. (2003) *Social Constructionism.* (2nd Ed.). London and New York: Routledge.

Collins, P.H. (2000) *Black Feminist Thought: Knowledge, Consciousness, and the Politics of Empowerment.* Oxfordshire: Routledge.

Davis, A. (2015) Keynote from John Hope Franklin Symposium 2015. https://youtu.be/NpbxC8v4dxw?si=C3GlWaRRyaYlT_8N

Davis, Y. D. (1981) *Women, Race & Class.* USA: Penguin.

Dicks, H. (1983) *Marital Tensions: Clinical Studies Towards a Psychological Theory of Interaction.* London: Routledge.

Du Bois, W.E. (1903) *The Souls of Black Folk.* Chicago: Amazon Classics Edition.

Eckert, M. (2015) "Civil Rights Leader Angela Davis Speaks at Bovard", *Daily Trojan*, 23 February. Los Angeles, CA: University of Southern California. Available at: https://dailytrojan.com/news/2015/02/23/civil-rights-leader-angela-davis-speaks-at-bovard/

Elgot, J. (2017) Diane Abbott more abused than any other female MP during election. *The Guardian.* www.theguardian.com/politics/2017/sep/05/diane-abbott-more-abused-than-any-other-mps-during-election?CMP=share_btn_url

Fanon, F. (1963) *The Wretched of the Earth.* London: Penguin Books.

Fanon, F. (1967) *Black Skin, White Masks.* London: Pluto Press.

Foreman, S. and Dallos, R. (1992) Inequalities of Power and Sexual Problems. *Journal of Family Therapy*, 14, 349–369.

Foucault, M. (1980) *Power/Knowledge: Selected Interviews and Other Writings, 1972–1977*. Harlow: Longman.
Hall, S. (1994) 'Cultural Identity and Diaspora', in P. Williams and L. Chrisman (eds) *Colonial Discourse and Post-Colonial Theory: A Reader*. New York: Columbia University Press, pp. 392–403.
Hall, S. (2019) *Essential Essays, Volume 2: Identity and Diaspora*. Edited by David Morley. Durham, NC: Duke University Press. .https://doi.org/10.2307/j.ctv11smnnj. Accessed 11 April 2026.
Lorde, A. (2012) *Essay and Speeches by Audre Lorde: Sister Outsider*. New York: Crossing Press.
Luckmann, T. and Berger, P.L. (1966) *The Social Construction of Reality*. New York: Anchor Books.
Malcolm X. (1962) "Who Taught You To Hate?". Speech.
Meretoja, H. (2013) *The Travelling Concepts of Narrative*. Amsterdam: John Benjamins Publishing.
Perel, E. (2007) Reprint. *Mating in Captivity: Unlocking Erotic Intelligence*. New York: Harper Perennial.
Rampage, C. (1994) Power, Gender, and Marital intimacy. *Journal of Family Therapy*, 16:125–137. https://doi.org/10.1111/j.1467-6427.1994.00783.x
Simon, G. (2024, Spring) Stories of "Self". Ideology in Action. *Murmurations*: *Journal of Transformative Systemic Practice*, 7(1). doi: 10.28963/7.1.4.
Simon, W. (1973). *Sexual Conduct: The Social Sources of Human Sexuality* (2nd ed.). Routledge. https://doi.org/10.4324/9781315129242
Simon, W. and Gagnon, J. H. (2003). Sexual Scripts: Origins, Influences and Changes. *Qualitative Sociology*, 26(4), 491–497.
Sirinivasan, A. (2018) Does Anyone Have the Right to Sex? *London Review of Books*, 40(6), March 2018.

Chapter 17

Cultural Sensitivity and the Navigation of Sexualities and Relationships in Iran

Fatemeh Mafi

17.1 Of Symbols and Sentire: A Prelude to Cultural Sensitivity

The phrase "cultural sensitivity" comprises two key terms: culture and sensitivity. It is helpful to briefly reflect on the meanings I attribute to each of these terms, as well as my interpretation of what the conjunction of these two terms signifies, which will establish the tone for the subsequent discussions. These definitions are not intended to be rigid or exhaustive, but rather as working concepts to guide engagement with the themes explored throughout the chapter. However, before delving into the broader arguments of this chapter, I wish to begin by acknowledging that I approach this chapter from multiple professional standpoints: as a medical doctor, a psychosexual and relationship therapist, and an educator. The theme of cultural sensitivity is one that resonates profoundly across each of these roles, informing the way I engage with patients, clients, colleagues, and learners. Therefore, I will not restrict my reflections to any one of these domains in isolation; instead, I will allow insights from across medical, therapeutic, and educational contexts to inform the discussion where relevant.

As with many complex concepts, there exists a myriad of definitions for the term "culture." The definition of culture to which I adhere is that offered by Clifford Geertz (1973), who describes culture as a "historically transmitted pattern of meanings embodied in symbols, a system of inherited conceptions expressed in symbolic forms by means of which men communicate, perpetuate, and develop their knowledge about and attitudes toward life" (Geertz, 1973, p. 89). Geertz's interpretive approach has been widely adopted by scholars, including myself, who view culture as a system of shared symbolic meanings through which individuals navigate and make sense of the world. This definition of culture intricately connects the concept to some related constructs, including values, virtues, attitudes, traits, and norms. These elements, to some extent, constitute some of the cornerstones of the internal architecture of culture; those shared, often implicit, frameworks through which individuals interpret meaning and navigate their social and moral worlds. They also play a pivotal role in shaping how sexualities, gender roles, and interpersonal relationships are understood and experienced. While this interpretive framework

DOI: 10.4324/9781003611387-17

is useful for understanding shared systems of meaning, culture here is approached as dynamic, internally diverse, and continually negotiated rather than as a fixed or homogeneous system.

Building upon Geertz's definition of culture, it is noteworthy to highlight the concept of sexuality socialization, which is "the process of acquiring knowledge, norms, attitudes, cultural symbols and meanings, codes of conduct, and values about a wide range of topics concerning sex and sexuality" (Warner et al., 2020, p. 160). Research in this area predominantly focuses on the sources of sexual socialization, with particular attention given to the roles of parents, peers and media in shaping individuals' comprehension of their own sexualities and, consequently, their sexual conduct (Bleakley et al., 2009; Fletcher et al., 2015; Ward, 2016; Warner et al., 2020). Thus, if culture is, as Geertz suggests, a system of inherited meaning-making through which individuals come to understand themselves and their place in the world, then sexual socialization can be seen as a key mechanism by which cultural meanings surrounding sexuality are transmitted and sustained.

Having outlined my working definition of culture, I now turn to the concept of sensitivity. To grasp the meaning of sensitivity, not only within the context of psychosexual and relationship therapy but also in a broader and more nuanced sense, it is helpful to consider the term's etymological roots. Reiss (2019, p. 356) traces the word sensitive to the medieval Latin *sensitivus*, which in turn derives from the classical Latin *sentire*, meaning "to feel." The term "sensitive" encompasses a spectrum of meanings, ranging from physiological receptivity to emotional responsiveness. Reiss notes that sensitivity may refer to perceptual capacities, such as the eyes being sensitive to light, without implying any evaluative judgment. In this sense, sensitivity simply denotes a capacity for responsiveness to stimuli. However, Reiss (2019) aptly extends this understanding beyond the domain of sensory receptors, such as eyes, ears, or proprioceptors, to include the emotional realm, highlighting the ways in which individuals may be emotionally attuned or affected. Importantly, Reiss argues that the sensitivity of a topic can illuminate not only the complexity of the subject matter itself but also offer significant insights into characteristics of those who are responsive and engage with it. Sensitivity, then, pertains to both the content and the relational dynamics it evokes, which is especially relevant in therapeutic contexts, where the personal and the social, the emotional and the embodied, are often deeply entangled. While Reiss does not apply this framework directly to psychosexual and relationship therapy, his conceptualization of sensitivity offers a useful lens through which the relational, emotional, and embodied dimensions of therapeutic work may be understood.

Therefore, I perceive cultural sensitivity as the intersection of culture, understood as a historically transmitted framework of shared symbolic meanings, values, virtues and attitudes that individuals adhere to in order to make sense of their lives, and sensitivity, defined as the capacity to perceive, respond to, and engage with various stimuli, either physically or emotionally. Thus, within the context of psychosexual and relationship therapy, cultural sensitivity requires therapists to be aware of and responsive to the diverse cultural signifiers, symbols, narratives, values, and meanings that clients bring to therapeutic encounters. It is not merely an awareness or acknowledgment of cultural differences, but an active and intentional responsiveness to how these differences impact communication, relationship-building, therapeutic processes, and outcomes.

Being culturally sensitive involves recognizing that each therapeutic relationship is situated within specific cultural contexts, each characterized by unique values, beliefs, taboos, and interpretations concerning relationships, sexuality, intimacy, and personal identity. However, while familiarity with common cultural practices and how individuals generally make sense of the world may prove advantageous, it is essential to recognize that sensitivity toward specific cultural beliefs, practices, or values varies considerably among individuals from the same region and it could prove to be challenging to find two individuals, even with shared sociocultural backgrounds, who experience or interpret their cultural identities in precisely the same way. Therefore, when working with individuals from the same cultural background, therapists must exercise ongoing mindfulness and remain vigilant in adopting flexible and adaptive therapeutic techniques, consciously avoiding stereotyping, and engaging in continuous reflection on their practice.

While this chapter presents and explores various perspectives on values related to sexualities and relationships within the Iranian population, it is imperative to emphasize that these reflections are not intended to represent fixed, monolithic, or collectively applicable paradigms. Rather, they are provided to promote curiosity and encourage thoughtful engagement with the diverse and often complex cultural frameworks that may inform individuals' experiences. Recognizing the heterogeneity that exists within any cultural group is essential to avoiding reductive assumptions and stereotypes, ensuring that educational and therapeutic practices remain both respectful and responsive to individual variation. Furthermore, assessment tools, interventions, and therapeutic goals must be reexamined with each client to ensure their alignment with the individual's unique cultural context and lived experience, thereby facilitating therapeutic relationships that are not only effective but also profoundly meaningful and authentically client-centered. This approach also resonates with the concept of cultural humility, which emphasizes the importance of ongoing self-reflection, openness, and an awareness of the limitations inherent in any fixed notion of cultural competence (Tervalon & Murray-Garcia, 1998). In this sense, culturally sensitive therapeutic practice requires not the assumption of complete knowledge regarding another individual's cultural experience, but rather a continual willingness to engage thoughtfully and reflexively with the diverse meanings, values, and lived realities that clients bring into the therapeutic space.

17.2 Values Surrounding Sexualities and Relationships

In the remainder of this chapter, I draw upon some of the findings from my doctoral research thesis (Mafi, 2023), which explored the values underpinning cultural understandings of sexualities and relationships in contemporary Iran. These insights are complemented by reflections from my clinical experience as a psychosexual and relationship therapist, allowing for a more nuanced exploration of how such values manifest in therapeutic settings. The study examined the feasibility of implementing sexualities and relationships education programs in Iranian schools, focusing on the sociocultural context and the values that shape stakeholders' perceptions and practices. Primary data were collected through in-depth, semi-structured interviews with 55 stakeholders, comprising 25 parents and 30 members of school staff, including headteachers and classroom teachers. Supplementary insights were also drawn from online group discussions with young individuals, documentary analysis, and ethnographic observations and field notes. Employing a qualitative, multi-method approach guided by a critical realism framework, both thematic analysis for identifying patterns and grounded theory techniques for enhancing the coding process and revealing connections between codes were used, which enabled a rich exploration of the values shaping stakeholders' perspectives and broader cultural narratives surrounding sexualities and relationships within the Iranian context.

Educational institutions, such as schools, serve as one of the primary environments through which cultural patterns of meaning are transmitted. Through everyday activities and interactions with educators and peers, they can, to some extent, play a central role in shaping children's values, attitudes, and their conceptualizations of the world. What unfolds within schools, alongside the goals and aspirations embedded in child-rearing practices, offers a revealing window into a community's cultural fabric. Importantly, schools contribute significantly to the process of sexual socialization, even in contexts where formal sexualities and relationships education programs are absent or have a scarce presence, by conveying implicit messages through social interactions and the broader cultural environment they cultivate.

Since the interviews and the overarching focus of my doctoral research centered on school-based sexualities and relationships education, students were the primary population of interest. However, child-rearing goals and desires should be recognized as integral to this context, acting as a mirror to cultural values, shedding light on the beliefs and aspirations that shape not only educational priorities but also broader societal expectations. While the empirical focus remained within school settings, stakeholders' narratives often touched on themes of parenting, authority, discipline, and emotional development within the realm of sexualities and relationships, offering implicit yet powerful insights into the cultural beliefs that inform children's sexual socialization and society's conceptualization of sexuality and what constitutes a good relationship.

To facilitate the analysis of the findings, it was helpful to group the extracted values into clusters based on their shared characteristics. In clinical practice, particularly when addressing sexual difficulties, many practitioners are familiar with the biopsychosocial model of medicine, first proposed by George Engel (1977). Widely adopted by both therapists and physicians, this model offers a holistic perspective by considering any given issue through three interconnected lenses: biological, psychological, and social. However, I adhered to the critical realism's framework of Four-Planar Social Being, as developed by Bhaskar (2008), which introduces an additional dimension by proposing four distinct yet interrelated planes of human existence:

1. Material relations with nature in the physical reality of bodies and of the natural world.
2. Interpersonal subjective relationships between individuals and groups.
3. Broader social relations and inherited structures.
4. Inner being, the stratified personality, subjective agency, and ideas about the good life, the good society (Alderson, 2013, p. 62).

These planes are not discrete and isolated categories but rather interwoven dimensions of lived experience. Together, they provide a comprehensive view of one's experiences and a framework for understanding how individuals navigate meaning, identity, and relationality within their cultural contexts. In what follows, I examine each of Bhaskar's conceptual frameworks of Four-Planar Social Being in turn, outlining the values embedded within different layers of social being that emerged as particularly significant to the interviewees in my study in relation to sexualities and relationships.

17.3 Bodies, Boundaries, and the Weight of Visibility: Material Relations with Nature in the Physical Reality of Bodies and of the Natural World

Social phenomena, such as sexualities, unfold across multiple levels simultaneously and must be examined through various dimensions. The discussion opens with the most physically grounded and immediately observable layer, which Bhaskar conceptualizes as "material transactions with nature" (2016, p. 83), that is, real bodies, which involves examining the underlying values that influence how bodies are perceived and treated, how they are clothed or uncovered, desired or rejected, protected or deprived, and ultimately, how they are regulated, controlled, and surveilled.

Before delving into the discussion, I would like to begin this section, focused on bodies, by highlighting a crucial linguistic barrier. Across various contexts in Iran, the confusion around appropriate terms in Farsi for describing genitalia and sexual health issues emerges as a significant obstacle. Whether in school environments, family conversations, peer discussions, medical or therapeutic settings, there is a consistent lack of clarity around what vocabulary can be used to address sexual matters or refer to genitalia appropriately. This linguistic ambiguity not only hinders communication and leads to silence but also contributes to feelings of shame, discomfort, and misrecognition in both clinical and educational encounters. For psychosexual therapists, recognizing that cultural silences are value-laden is crucial: silence, in itself, is rarely empty; rather, it is full of meaning, shaped by what can and cannot be spoken in a given cultural context. With this in mind, this section explores the key themes that emerged from participants' reflections on how bodies are understood and managed in relation to cultural values and social expectations surrounding sexualities and relationships.

17.3.1 Health, Normalcy, and Obedience: Deconstructing Biomedical Authority

In conversations around sexuality, the concept of health often appears neutral or universally positive. In discussions with Iranian stakeholders, particularly parents, "Health" emerged frequently as a theme. Health appears to hold a particularly significant place within Iranian culture, to the extent that even when a practice is considered religiously or culturally impermissible, it is often widely accepted by clients and patients if reframed as a medical or health-related necessity, particularly when recommended or prescribed by a doctor. That being said, although the term "health" might open doors in some contexts, it could conceal deeply embedded taboos and anxieties in others.

During the interviews, it initially appeared that references to health commonly centered on physical well-being, with even the mental dimension frequently overlooked or excluded. However, what came to light was that health often emerged in conversation as culturally loaded, functioning as a proxy for moral and social norms. For example, stakeholders' desire for a child to be healthy or to display healthy conduct often implicitly signified being normal (as defined within their own understanding), proper, or obedient to social expectations. This framing revealed how biomedical discourse could mask or reinforce moral values. For example, teachers pointed out that while earlier generations may have relied solely on religious authority, moral messages were now often couched in scientific or health-based language to carry greater credibility, especially among young people. This shift reflected broader patterns of medicalization, where terms like health were used to police sexuality under the guise of objectivity.

The problem with such medicalization is that it can give way to pathologizing behaviors, identities, or desires that fall outside culturally sanctioned norms, thereby reinforcing stigma under the guise of clinical neutrality. In some cases, it may even lead to extreme measures being taken in an attempt to "treat" or "cure" sexual behaviors that are, in fact, entirely age-appropriate and consistent with typical developmental trajectories. A clear example that emerged in the interviews was the widespread pathologization of masturbation, often referred to in medicalized terms and linked to various unsubstantiated health risks. This "masturbation phobia," *defined as* "a social and historical phenomenon characterized by the scientific certainty that masturbation led inevitably to physical degeneration and mental derangement" (Egan & Hawkes, 2010, p. 24), was expressed by both parents and educators during interviews, as well as by some parents seeking help for their children in therapeutic sessions, who associated the act with physical or psychological harm, thereby reinforcing shame and anxiety around sexual autonomy and bodily exploration.

In therapeutic contexts, however, it is sometimes feasible to introduce some forms of self-exploration without explicitly labeling these practices as masturbation and by using terms such as genital familiarity or non-judgmental touch. Framing these exercises as part of a health or therapeutic routine often made them more acceptable to clients. At the same time, such reframing requires ongoing reflexivity and careful ethical consideration, particularly regarding transparency, informed consent, and the client's understanding of the therapeutic process, as well as careful attention to how these practices are understood and interpreted within the client's own moral, religious, and cultural frameworks. It is therefore important for therapists to explore clients' beliefs and restrictions surrounding such practices, including how these are personally defined, interpreted, and enacted within the context of their lived experience. Nonetheless, for many individuals, the presence of a partner could mentally alter the meaning and acceptability of a sexual act, regardless of the degree of the partner's involvement, with solo practices often perceived as inappropriate, unhealthy, or morally troubling. In culturally sensitive psychosexual therapy, it is essential to question what health signifies to clients, not merely as a clinical objective but as a value-laden ideal shaped by intersecting influences, including family expectations, religious beliefs, and sociopolitical dynamics.

17.3.2 Hayâ as Cultural Force: Understanding and Addressing Embodied Modesty and Shame

Another theme extracted from the data of my doctoral research centers on the concept of "Hayâ," a culturally embedded concept in Iran and numerous Islamic nations, which can be roughly translated as modesty or embarrassment. Particularly relevant to culturally sensitive psychosexual therapy, Hayâ functions for many individuals not only as a personal or internalized virtue but also as a performative cultural script that governs bodily comportment, visibility, and gendered interactions from an early age. It establishes norms around how bodies should be presented, how physical boundaries are maintained, and what forms of embodiment are considered appropriate or inappropriate.

The interviews demonstrated how the values of modesty and bodily restraint are materially and symbolically embedded in the child-rearing practices, social upbringing, and, consequently, the sexual socialization of Iranian students. Hayâ is expected to shape how children come to inhabit their bodies, how they comport themselves within gendered environments, and how they learn to navigate visibility and, particularly for girls, foster forms of invisibility. Participants in the study described how the value of Hayâ was conveyed through a combination of spatial, sartorial, and behavioral controls, all aimed at promoting bodily modesty in accordance with cultural expectations. These mechanisms included not only the structuring of classroom environments and routine references to standards of modesty but also highly specific bodily and aesthetic regulations. For instance, boys were required to keep their hair short, whereas girls were prohibited from grooming their eyebrows or removing facial hair. Both genders were mandated to wear school uniforms, often ill-fitting and disproportionately large for girls, to obscure bodily contours and minimize any indication of shape. Strict codes surrounding modest dress and restrained physical behavior were both informally expected and institutionally reinforced.

Some participants reflected on interventions and practices aimed at reducing the perceived desirability of children, such as prohibiting eyebrow grooming for girls and enforcing extremely short haircuts for boys, as justified and protective measures to deter unwanted attention or minimize the risk of sexual abuse. However, these measures were frequently founded on flawed assumptions that regulating one's appearance would reduce vulnerability. Such rationale diverts attention from the actions and accountability of perpetrators, reinforcing the harmful idea that the burden of prevention rests with the victim's appearance. Rather than empowering children with appropriate boundaries, these interventions inadvertently reinforce problematic ideas about blame and visibility. In the therapeutic context, such experiences may manifest as internalized guilt in victims of sexual abuse, difficulties in setting boundaries in relationships, or reluctance to assert bodily autonomy.

Furthermore, although these practices ostensibly promote modesty, they concurrently have unintended psychological consequences. Strict regulation of bodily appearance and expression, including measures that prevent younger individuals from perceiving themselves as subjects of desire, may contribute to the development of negative body image among youth. Girls, in particular, could internalize a sense of bodily shame and perceived undesirability, and learn to view their natural features as something to conceal or to alter. This early conditioning not only limits their bodily autonomy but also impacts their confidence and self-perception well into adolescence and adulthood. Within my clinical reflections, such internalized dissatisfaction with one's appearance may also elucidate the high and increasing rates of cosmetic surgery in Iran, although this phenomenon is likely shaped by multiple intersecting sociocultural factors (Kalantar Motamedi et al., 2016; Raisi et al., 2022). For psychosexual therapists, recognizing the long-term emotional imprint of these formative experiences is vital when supporting clients in reconstructing a healthier and more accepting relationship with their bodies.

In addition to outward appearance, interviewees remarked that speaking and laughing loudly, or slouching and displaying physical ease in the presence of others, could be regarded as indicators of insufficient Hayâ and modesty. Students were expected to move discreetly, speak softly, and generally embody restraint, particularly girls, for whom bodily discipline is intertwined with moral identity and closely associated with social acceptability, which results in heightened vigilance regarding their conformity to the principles of Hayâ, with their daily movements and postures scrutinized as markers of modesty and virtue. This gendered landscape of bodily regulation, wherein the concept of Hayâ, for instance, operates more restrictively for girls, is, of course, not unique to Iran. As Ringrose aptly states: "Women's bodies remain the prime site of sexual regulation, which is why whether it is clad in a bikini or a burqa it is a site of controversy and discipline from men and other women" (Ringrose, 2013, p. 6). At the same time, it is important to acknowledge that practices associated with modesty and Hayâ are not always experienced solely as externally imposed forms of restriction or subjugation. As Saba Mahmood aptly writes, "agentival capacity is entailed not only in those acts that resist norms but also in the multiple ways in which one inhabits norms" (2005, p. 15). In this sense, forms of bodily discipline and modest comportment may also be understood by some women as meaningful ethical practices connected to virtue, self-cultivation, and religious agency.

It is pertinent to the primary focus of this book that Hayâ exerts a significant influence on internal comfort with one's body and openness in discussing it. Many participants provided accounts of discomfort, silence, or even shame when addressing topics related to puberty, genital anatomy, and sexual health. Such challenges are equally evident within therapeutic settings, wherein clients may find it difficult to articulate embodied experiences, discuss sexual fantasies, or explore sexual concerns. The language of shame, in particular, is frequently associated with bodily functions and natural developmental changes, indicating that Hayâ has a psychological presence that can inhibit not only the acquisition of knowledge but also emotional and sexual expression.

Nevertheless, a potential countercurrent exists: perhaps a reframing of modesty that would permit enhanced bodily literacy and openness without forsaking the cultural value of Hayâ altogether. Modesty could coexist with education and bodily awareness, and the silence surrounding the body should not be misconstrued as a virtue. This more adaptable interpretation of Hayâ, though less prevalent, opens avenues for educational and therapeutic interventions that respect cultural sensitivities while facilitating informed and confident embodiment. Hayâ exerts a lasting impact on individuals' capacity to engage with topics central to psychosexual well-being, including body awareness, sexual health, and relational intimacy, and is not an attribute that can be swiftly altered or its presence in the therapeutic setting dismissed. Its influence must be acknowledged and carefully navigated.

In the therapeutic context, such a reframing can be supported through the therapeutic alliance itself. By building trust and rapport, therapists can create a space where clients feel safe enough to explore topics that may otherwise remain censored or laden with shame. They could gently challenge rigid manifestations of Hayâ while validating the values from which they stem, thus fostering a space where clients can renegotiate bodily awareness in culturally coherent yet psychologically liberating ways. Normalizing techniques, such as offering psychosexual education, validating embodied experiences, and using non-pathologizing language, can gradually help clients engage with areas of bodily awareness and sexual identity that may have been suppressed to conform to expectations of Hayâ. Thus, therapists can invite clients to consider alternative, personally meaningful interpretations of modesty, ones that support agency and self-respect rather than inhibition and guilt. Such explorations, however, must remain carefully paced and guided by the client's own readiness, particularly in contexts where reinterpreting values associated with Hayâ may evoke anxiety, moral conflict, or fears of social and relational repercussions. Through gentle and culturally attuned interventions, the therapeutic encounter can serve as a space where the rigid boundaries of Hayâ are neither dismissed nor imposed, but instead redefined in ways that foster psychosexual growth and emotional integration.

17.3.3 Docile Bodies and the Normalization of Privacy Violations

The final theme in this category concerns the disciplining of children's bodies and the normalization of privacy violations. This discussion conceptually draws upon Michel Foucault's notion of the "*docile bodies*," which are subjected, utilized, and transformed through disciplinary mechanisms to attain a state whereby individuals not only "may do what one wishes, but so that they may operate as one wishes, with the techniques, the speed and efficiency that one determines" (Foucault, 1979, p. 138). Foucault's notion of docile bodies illuminates the ways in which institutions, through mechanisms such as surveillance, routine, spatial organization, and normalizing practices, cultivate forms of self-regulation whereby individuals come to monitor and discipline their own bodies and behaviors. Foucault's framework helps illuminate how bodily control is not only enforced through external regulations but also becomes internalized as a moral and educational ideal. The study unveiled how the spatial arrangements and cultural practices within Iranian schools often encouraged compliance, surveillance, and monitoring of students' bodies. In numerous instances, this docility was treated not merely as a behavioral expectation but as a value in itself, something that signified good character. The prevalence of monitoring and regulation was so extensive that fostering docility among younger individuals was occasionally celebrated as a marker of educational and moral achievement.

Monitoring and regulation were particularly pronounced in terms of appearance, with students' bodies subjected to strict control, regardless of their awareness of this issue. Surveillance, both formal and informal, extended beyond disciplinary interventions and permeated routine aspects of students' lives. Adolescents were often required to keep their bedroom doors open, effectively removing any sense of private space and reinforcing a constant awareness of being observed, even within the supposed confines of their own home. In some private schools, for instance, mandatory swimming sessions created further avenues for invasive bodily monitoring. Girls were required to report if they were menstruating in order to be excused from participation, and similar disclosures were demanded for prayer room attendance. These procedures, presented as disciplinary, moral or hygienic measures, diminished young individuals' right to privacy and transformed private bodily processes into matters of public record, thereby reinforcing the notion of the body as a publicly regulated and monitored entity.

Male students were also monitored, although often unknowingly. For example, in one of the schools included in the study, during swimming sessions, teachers observed the physical development of students, particularly for signs of puberty and the emergence of secondary sexual characteristics. Based on the findings, this monitoring aimed to provide school authorities with a rough estimate of when a boy was entering puberty, thereby enabling increased control over his behavior. At times, this included interventions or conversations intended to inhibit sexual behaviors that, in reality, were developmentally appropriate for the age. Although not formally acknowledged and frequently conducted covertly, this practice effectively turned adolescent bodies into sites of surveillance.

For psychosexual therapists, the implications are profound. Clients who have grown up in such environments may arrive with limited awareness of their right to physical or emotional privacy. They may find it challenging to articulate their bodily boundaries or feel ashamed when asserting their personal space. In this context, therapy must become a reparative process, one in which privacy and agency are not only validated but actively restored. Therapists can support this work by gently affirming the client's right to bodily integrity and encouraging reflection on when and how they wish to be seen, touched, or heard. Techniques that center choice and agency, such as asking for consent before discussing certain topics or using grounding exercises that reestablish a sense of awareness and ownership over one's body, can be particularly beneficial. In therapeutic work with clients from contexts where privacy has been systematically denied, the act of creating and holding private space can itself be transformative, offering clients a pathway to envisage and embody more autonomous and self-determined relationships with their bodies.

17.4 Adab, Family, and the Interpersonal Landscape: Interpersonal Subjective Relationships Between Individuals and Groups

This section focuses on the second of the four interacting planes within Bhaskar's Four-Planar Social Being model, namely "social interactions between people" (Bhaskar, 2016, p. 83). It examines the values that shape interpersonal relationships, communication, and social expectations within the Iranian context, particularly as they pertain to sexualities and relationships. These values are not merely cultural backdrops; instead, they play an active role in shaping how individuals relate to one another and how authority, emotion, and intimacy are navigated.

Two themes that emerged notably from the fieldwork data are examined in this section: Adab and values surrounding family. For psychosexual and relationship therapists, understanding these values is essential. It facilitates a culturally sensitive approach that respects relational norms while recognizing how these may be expressed as silence, shame, confusion, or resistance within the therapeutic setting. This section provides insights into the interpersonal landscape in which such values operate.

17.4.1 Adab

At the heart of the exploration of interpersonal values and their relevance to psychosexual and relationship therapy lies the esteemed value of Adab, a concept often translated as etiquette or manners, but one that conveys much more profound implications, particularly the imperative of respecting adults and authority figures. In this context, Adab should be understood not only as etiquette, but as a moral-cultural framework governing respect, hierarchy, restraint, speech, bodily conduct, and social positioning. Adab is a nuanced and deeply ingrained cultural value in Iranian society that extends far beyond mere etiquette. It encompasses ideals of "proper form or conduct" (Kia, 2014, p. 282), respect, moral sensibility, and the internalization of culturally sanctioned values of respect. Among the interviewees, especially parents and teachers, Adab emerged as a central expectation for younger individuals, particularly in their interactions with adults. It was regarded not as an innate trait but as a culturally endorsed skill to be cultivated deliberately through education and practice.

Central to Adab is the principle of respecting adults, including parents, teachers, and other authority figures, which for many also encompasses doctors and therapists. This respect is demonstrated through various means, including dress, speech, and behavior. Sung and Kim (2003) identify five different forms of respecting adults as presentational, linguistic, salutatory, consulting, and acquiescent respect. For example, younger individuals are expected to dress modestly, employ formal language, adopt deferential body language, and demonstrate deference through obedience. Silence around topics such as sexualities and erotic relationships, particularly in the presence of adults, is also widely regarded as an expression of Adab. Several parents expressed concerns that engaging in sexual discussions, even in the framework of education, could erode this respect. Consequently, the misapprehension or misapplication of the value of Adab may result in the silencing and marginalization of younger individuals' voices.

Certain conceptualizations of Adab obscure the line between respect and obedience, leaving little room for individuals, particularly, though not exclusively, the young individuals, from critically questioning decisions, voicing dissent, or initiating open conversations concerning sexualities and relationships, which perpetuates hierarchical relationships and often equates deference with the true measure of the value of Adab. In therapeutic settings, such dynamics may hinder open dialogue, suppress curiosity, and prevent clients from expressing confusion, distress, or personal truths, particularly on matters concerning consent, identity, and intimacy.

Whether within schools, family settings, or broader community interactions, this dynamic often impedes the development of agency and trust, both of which are essential for psychosexual and relational well-being. It may also shape the dynamics within romantic and sexual relationships, where one partner might feel constrained in expressing desires, establishing boundaries, or voicing disagreement due to concerns about being regarded as disrespectful or lacking Adab. Recognizing

Adab as both a culturally esteemed ideal and a potential barrier to self-expression allows therapists to engage with Iranian clients in a more reflective manner. By acknowledging the intricacy and ingrained nature of this value, practitioners can more effectively navigate the delicate balance between respecting cultural norms and advocating for client autonomy.

17.4.2 Family

The second theme within this category, values surrounding family, explores a cluster of interconnected beliefs tied to family structure, the sanctity of marriage, perspectives on premarital relationships, and broader norms shaping family belonging in Iran. Although these values are neither fixed nor universally experienced, they play a significant role in shaping how clients navigate issues of intimacy, gender roles, autonomy, and moral expectations within relational contexts, often surfacing as sources of tension or internal conflict in therapeutic settings.

Families often serve as environments of support, love, and care; however, they may also function as sites of control, suppression, and silence. While during the interviews, many parents advocated for values such as trust, honesty, and emotional expression in principle, these were often hindered when it came to discussions around sexuality and sexual development. Additionally, affectionate gestures, such as parents kissing or hugging their children, were at times discouraged by school authorities, ostensibly to delay puberty or prevent the stimulation of sexual desire, which conveys problematic messages concerning the appropriateness of intimacy, familial affection, and emotional availability. Over time, such messaging can engender emotional confusion and inhibit both physical and emotional expressions of closeness. These constraints may impair a child's capacity to understand and engage in healthy intimacy, not only within their familial environment but also in later romantic and sexual relationships. When physical affection is censored and emotional openness restricted, individuals may develop a reduced capacity to recognize, trust, and communicate their emotional needs. Consequently, younger individuals may carry unresolved tensions into adulthood, as well as into therapeutic spaces, where intimacy may be perceived as unsafe, unfamiliar, or morally conflicted.

The dominant ideal of family structure in Iran aligns with the traditional model of a nuclear or extended family, typically defined as a heterosexual, legally married couple along with their children. This structure is not merely a matter of personal or religious preference but is institutionally reinforced, with diversity in family forms rarely being acknowledged, let alone celebrated. Marriage is perceived not only as the gateway to creating a family but as the only morally acceptable setting for sexual relationships. Long-term, monogamous heterosexual marriage, sanctioned both legally and religiously, maintains a privileged status, whereas alternative forms, such as cohabitation or short-term marriage, are often marginalized or stigmatized. Individuals who do not find themselves belonging to this framework often bear a deep cultural burden, even if they succeed in living according to their authentic preferences without facing any legal repercussions. Therapists must acknowledge this in clinical settings, as such individuals may exhibit internalized tensions, shame, or ambivalence that originate less from personal conflict and more from the dissonance between their lived experiences and prevailing cultural expectations.

Short-term marriage (Sigheh) presented a paradox for many interviewees because, although it is religiously permissible and legally recognized, it is culturally frowned upon and viewed as a last resort for those unable to suppress their sexual urges. Interview accounts demonstrated that it is occasionally employed in a selective and covert manner as a solution for young men experiencing sexual desire, considering that masturbation is both culturally and religiously forbidden. On the other hand, young women were strictly forbidden from short-term relationships, often encouraged and prepared for early, long-term marriage, with schools sometimes actively helping to facilitate matchmaking. This gendered split reflects broader societal discomfort with acknowledging sexual desire in younger individuals, and in particular, young girls. Instead of acknowledging or addressing such feelings in an age-appropriate fashion, the preferred response is often early marriage or, failing that, outright denial.

Tabatabaie writes:

> premarital sexuality in Iran is unacceptable to such a great extent that many parents and schools, even when aware of the risks associated with poor sexual health knowledge, may choose not to approach sex education, since to do so may be to acknowledge premarital sexuality and, supposedly, lead to premarital sex.
>
> (Tabatabaie, 2015, p. 204)

Considering the cultural and legal prohibitions against sexual relationships outside of marriage, premarital intimacy is rigorously monitored, particularly for girls. Virginity at the time of marriage remains highly esteemed, with practices such as virginity testing before marriage still prevalent (Naghizadeh et al., 2023). Although some younger individuals engage in romantic relationships, many abstain from premarital sexual activity due to personal, familial, or religious convictions. This finding aligns with national data indicating that premarital abstinence is customary (Khalajabadi Farahani, 2017; Khalili et al., 2020), despite the average age at marriage having increased substantially, resulting in an extended interval between sexual maturity and marital eligibility (Joodaki et al., 2020).

This prolonged period of abstinence is not just a personal or moral choice; it is actively reinforced through external mechanisms. The obligation to remain sexually inactive for a decade or more following puberty has prompted a range of preventative strategies, from self-restraint (referred to as Taghwâ in religious terminology) to occupying students in intensive physical, educational, or religious activities to suppress sexual desire or to eliminate free time or energy that could be used to act upon sexual thoughts. Schools and families actively discourage any discussion of sexual feelings, reinforcing a climate of silence and shame. Within my clinical experience, some clients raised in such environments appear to struggle with sexual fantasy or report limited familiarity with imaginative erotic life. For therapists, it is important to recognize that clients raised in such environments not only might have internalized sexual desire, thoughts and behaviors as inherently negative, but may also experience a significantly diminished capacity for sexual fantasy. This restricted imaginative range is a reflection of a value system that frames sexual desire as something nonexistent or as something to be suppressed. In therapeutic settings, it is therefore crucial to support clients in developing a more expansive and affirming understanding of their erotic inner worlds, helping them to access, articulate, and reimagine their desires without fear or self-censure.

Family structures are also shaped by deeply rooted gender roles and unequal power dynamics. Traditional Iranian families frequently operate within a patriarchal framework, wherein fathers hold overt authority, and mothers exert influence in a more subtle manner (Janan, 2013). Nonetheless, there are signs of change, particularly in urban regions such as Tehran, where an increasing number of families exhibit more balanced power distributions (Bakhshipour et al., 2019). As women gain greater access to education, employment, and resources, observable shifts in intra-family dynamics are becoming more prominent. Nonetheless, the legacy of gender-based hierarchies and societal expectations persists. This has direct implications for psychosexual and relationship therapy, as clients, especially women, may present with internalized conflicts regarding gender roles and societal expectations.

Among the most deeply held cultural values associated with family life in Iran is the expectation of having children, which occupies a central place in cultural constructions of family and is widely regarded not only as a personal aspiration but also as a moral and religious obligation. This pronounced pronatalist value exerts considerable pressure on individuals and couples, particularly those experiencing infertility, often giving rise to intense emotional distress, self-blame, and a sense of failure, compounded by societal expectations and familial scrutiny. Notably, some clients, while motivated by religious convictions to pursue parenthood, simultaneously express discomfort with assisted reproductive technologies, perceiving such interventions as religiously, ethically or spiritually contentious. This cultural pressure can also present significant therapeutic challenges, particularly in cases where psychosexual difficulties, such as genito-pelvic pain/penetration disorder or erectile dysfunction, are compounded by an urgent desire to conceive. Under such pressures, clients may seek rapid resolution of symptoms and a "quick fix" to achieve pregnancy, sometimes overlooking the psychological, relational, or embodied dimensions of their distress. For psychosexual and relationship therapists, it is essential to remain attuned to the cultural weight of reproductive expectations and to provide a therapeutic space that acknowledges both the urgency and the complexity of clients' experiences.

Cultural values and normative forces surrounding family, particularly those concerning marriage, sexuality, gender roles, and emotional restraint, could profoundly shape the inner worlds of Iranian clients. For psychosexual and relationship therapists, attunement to the weight of these cultural expectations is essential. A culturally sensitive approach not only validates the lived experiences of clients but also facilitates the gradual unpacking of shame, secrecy, and internalized conflict, supporting and enabling the co-construction of more autonomous, meaningful, and affirming narratives around intimacy and desire.

17.5 Structures of Power, Gendered Scripts of Silence and Shame: Broader Social Relations and Inherited Structures

> sexuality is so embedded in the social that it cannot be understood in isolation. It is through understanding societies that we can understand the meanings of sexualities, just as in understanding sexualities we begin to understand societies more effectively.
>
> (Holland et al., 2003, p. 242)

The third plane of Bhaskar's Four-Planar Social Being (2008) shifts the analytical lens toward social structures, encompassing broader social relations and inherited institutions that shape values related to sexualities and relationships. This section engages with systemic structures, with a particular focus on Iran's educational system. Social structures are powerful not only in shaping norms and institutional practices but also in regulating which cultural values may be expressed, encouraged, or institutionalized, and which must remain concealed, discouraged, or actively suppressed. They establish the parameters within which discourses on sexuality, gender, intimacy, and family are deemed either permissible or taboo. For instance, the structural endorsement of values such as modesty or obedience may elevate these themes within educational and social practices, while alternative values, such as autonomy, sexual self-determination, or pluralism, are sidelined or rendered invisible.

Nevertheless, social structures are inherently dynamic rather than static. They influence and are concurrently influenced by human agency, and policies, discourses, and institutional practices may evolve significantly over time. The insights presented here reflect the conditions that prevailed during the period of my doctoral research concerning the feasibility of sexualities and relationships education in Iran. Drawing on Margaret Archer's (1995) concept of "given structures," which refers to the institutional and normative frameworks inherited by individuals prior to their agency, this section concentrates on the educational and policy landscape as it stood during the period of fieldwork. These structures are not fixed; they may have already shifted or may be subject to significant transformation in the future.

For psychosexual and relationship therapists reading this chapter, it is crucial to recognize that sexualities are inherently multidimensional and context-dependent. Social structures, legal frameworks, and institutional regulations in one sociopolitical setting may legitimize therapeutic goals or methods that would be considered entirely inappropriate elsewhere. In particular, when certain behaviors are criminalized, it becomes even more important for therapists to be aware of the heightened difficulty clients may face in articulating their experiences, and to create therapeutic spaces that enable safe and meaningful exploration of those aspects of the self that social structures have rendered unspeakable.

17.5.1 Islamic Values?

To start with, Iran's legal and judicial framework is explicitly founded upon Islamic Sharia law, and this foundation permeates numerous facets of public policy, including the education sector. For instance, the Fundamental Reform Document of Education (FRDE, 2011) in Iran, which guides educational policy, is grounded in Islamic principles and considers the purpose of education as guiding students toward proximity to God and an ideal Islamic life. Nevertheless, Islam itself is not monolithic, as will be elaborated upon later in this chapter. While the government advocates a singular interpretation aligned with Shia jurisprudence, Iran's religiously diverse population, including intra-Shia variations, as well as non-Shia, non-Muslim, and secular perspectives, necessitates a more sophisticated understanding.

For culturally sensitive psychosexual and relationship therapists, it is essential to recognize that the imposition of a singular, authoritative reading of Islam in Iran can marginalize alternative interpretations and reduce the visibility of religious and cultural pluralism. Institutional frameworks prioritize values aligned with this dominant narrative, including chastity, modesty, heteronormativity, and religious observance, and integrate these principles into educational curricula, public discourse, and legal policies. However, even among those who actively practice Shi'a Islam, considerable variation exists in the comprehension and implementation of these values. People may differ in how they interpret proximity to God, prioritize certain virtues, or apply religious teachings to everyday life. Nonetheless, the state's promotion of what it refers to as "Islamic values" often relies on a reductive and essentialist interpretation of religion, one that may not accurately reflect the full spectrum of lived spiritual beliefs within the population.

17.5.2 Gender Inequality

Gender inequality was another prominent theme that emerged within the realm of social structures. Gender inequality in Iran is perhaps most conspicuously manifested within the legal structures surrounding marriage, divorce, and child custody. However, what emerged clearly from my research is that these inequalities are also profoundly ingrained within the educational system and institutionalized through both policy and practice. While legal codes make gender hierarchy explicit in areas such as inheritance, guardianship, and testimony, the educational environment serves as the cultural training arena where these hierarchies are perpetuated and normalized.

Gender equality is neither adequately represented in the FRDE nor in Iranian school textbooks. The FRDE reinforces traditional gender roles by idealizing distinct masculine and feminine traits and tends to accentuate differences rather than promoting parity (Mafi, 2023) and the existing research highlights persistent gender bias in curriculum content (Ansary & Babaii, 2003; Bahman & Rahimi, 2010; Foroutan, 2012), with textbooks frequently depicting men and boys in active, public roles and women and girls in domestic, supportive, or passive ones.

The tension arising from the lived experience of gender inequality, coupled with the structural messaging surrounding gender inequality, can contribute to confusion, frustration, and feelings of disempowerment, particularly among girls whose ambitions are constrained by the very institutions intended to promote their development. Furthermore, gender-based discrimination can lead to elevated rates of mood and anxiety disorders (McLaughlin et al., 2010) and be associated with increased depressive, anxious, and somatic symptoms (Klonoff et al., 2000). Additionally, for therapists, particularly couple therapists, working with relationship dynamics, it is imperative to recognize how these gendered educational experiences influence clients' self-image, aspirations, and relational expectations of themselves and their partners, in order to provide sensitive and effective care.

17.5.3 Gender Segregation

Another social structure of significance is gender segregation. The cultural value of Hayâ reappears in this context, this time manifesting structurally through gender segregation and the promotion of the Islamic dress code, namely the Hijab. For instance, according to the FRDE, fostering Hayâ is a central educational objective. However, Hayâ is frequently reduced to mere adherence to prescribed dress codes and gender separation, rather than being regarded as a personal, ethically grounded value. Even where physical segregation is absent, younger individuals are often encouraged to avoid interactions with the opposite gender as a demonstration of Hayâ. In such contexts, even basic social exchanges across gender lines were framed as inappropriate or shameful. This expectation reinforces a culture in which modesty is measured not only by attire but also by how individuals are seen, and not seen, within social spaces.

Many parents interviewed in my study believed that their children had internalized values such as modesty and viewed choices like premarital chastity as personal preferences; however, they still insisted on external measures such as gender segregation and mandatory Hijab. In particular, these expectations for girls exceed mere gentle requests: girls are subject to the compulsory Hijab, which is mandated by national legislation and monitored by relevant authorities. Whether this institutional framing aligns with Mernissi's argument that, in numerous Muslim societies, the perception of female sexuality as active and potentially disruptive leads to practices such as veiling and segregation to maintain social order and prevent "*Fitna*" (social chaos) (Mernissi, 1985), or whether it is rooted in the conceptualization of women and girls as more vulnerable, emotionally fragile, and at greater risk of harm in romantic or sexual relationships, thus justifying the necessity for enhanced control and protection, the underlying belief remains consistent: unsupervised interactions between genders pose a risk to be avoided. This external imposition has the potential to diminish the personal meaning of modesty and to transform it into a state-sanctioned obligation.

These gendered assumptions, reinforced through educational and legal policy, also marginalize individuals who do not conform to binary gender norms. Gender non-conforming and transgender individuals may find themselves excluded or punished under regulations that presume rigid roles and enforce gender-based segregation. Furthermore, when young people grow up with minimal cross-gender interaction, their understanding of others may become distorted or overly idealized, fueling further demands for segregation and entrenching gender-based mistrust, or cultivating romanticized yet unrealistic notions about the other gender that fail to reflect the complexities of real-life relationships.

For psychosexual and relationship therapists, these structural dynamics are not peripheral but central. Clients may arrive with deeply internalized myths and inaccurate assumptions about themselves and the other gender. Girls, for instance, may internalize the idea that they are inherently vulnerable and in need of protection, or conversely, that they are dangerously seductive and must exercise constant restraint. Boys, on the other hand, may develop misogynistic attitudes if they grow up perceiving girls as dangerously provocative, or may adopt paternalistic behaviors that limit girls' autonomy, viewing them as fragile individuals who need to be saved or managed, and have difficulty in navigating their relationships. Therapists must recognize how such policies may have severed the connection between values like modesty and personal autonomy, and work to reestablish those links in a way that honors the client's cultural background while also promoting psychological integration and choice.

17.5.4 Importance of Form

Finally, an observable and notable structural demand in Iranian educational environments pertains to the prioritization of outward presentation, including mere presence, visible conduct, attire, and speech, such as signing into the prayer room register regardless of personal belief, and adherence to obligatory hijab regulations, over inner belief or intent. This tendency to prioritize appearance over essence echoes Goffman's dramaturgical perspective (Goffman, 1959), which posits that social institutions such as schools serve as stages for meticulously choreographed performances. Students are expected to assume idealized roles aligned with institutional standards, irrespective of whether these performances reflect their internal beliefs. This performative focus may stem from the relative ease of overseeing external conformity, or perhaps from an aspiration that maintaining outward compliance will gradually realign inner beliefs and attitudes accordingly. Nonetheless, when values are reduced to observable manifestations, their ethical essence may be compromised.

The demand for consistency between outward expressions and institutional norms compels many individuals to conceal dissenting beliefs or practices, thereby cultivating a climate of psychological tension and duplicity. Such an approach can generate dissonance between internal values and public conduct, and this lack of congruity could give rise to psychological distress, known as "cognitive dissonance" (Festinger, 1962), wherein individuals struggle to reconcile their outward behaviors with internal beliefs. Over time, this phenomenon may also give rise to deeper experiences of "alienation" (Hartwig, 2007), a state in which individuals feel disconnected not only from their own values but also from the broader social institutions that impose such demands for conformity.

The impact is particularly pronounced when behaviors or identities, such as nonmarital intimacy, sexual orientation, or gender nonconformity, are not only socially discouraged but also subject to legal penalties. In such circumstances, the stakes for disclosure are significantly heightened. Clients may choose not merely to conceal aspects of themselves due to internalized shame but also because of the tangible threat of legal, social, or familial repercussions. The structural criminalization of certain identities compels many to perform compliance that does not reflect their actual internal realities, intensifying psychological distress and undermining self-trust. Therapists must recognize that when a particular behavior is criminalized, the fear of exposure permeates the therapeutic encounter itself. Even in settings designed for safety and reflection, clients may find it challenging to articulate their thoughts or experiences. It is therefore crucial for therapists to acknowledge these pressures and respond with heightened sensitivity. Cultural sensitivity, in this context, transcends mere empathy with cultural norms; it requires a critical awareness of the institutional structures that render certain truths unspeakable.

Sexualities and relationships are mediated not only through personal interactions or inner dispositions but also through deeply entrenched institutional and ideological structures. The intersection of religion, policy, and pedagogy can form a potent apparatus for shaping acceptable norms, often at the expense of autonomy, pluralism, and gender equity. Therapists must recognize that these structural forces shape not only what clients might have internalized but also what they feel permitted to articulate. When dominant social structures suppress or criminalize certain expressions of identity, the therapeutic space may become the only place where clients can begin to articulate unspoken aspects of their lives. Understanding this dynamic is essential to avoid reinforcing shame or silence and instead foster a sense of safety, validation, and complexity in therapeutic dialogue. Therapy must serve as a space where these enforced performances can be gently unpacked and where clients feel empowered to explore identities and desires that have been stifled by legal and social constraints. By facilitating clients' navigation of this dissonance, therapists support the gradual and cautious emergence of more integrated and autonomous selves.

17.6 Inner Worlds: Religion, Desire, and Meaning-Making: Inner Being, the Stratified Personality

The final dimension in Bhaskar's Four-Planar Social Being is the inner being, or the stratified personality, "the domain of an agent's own subjectivity" (M. Archer et al., 1998, p. 645). This plane concerns individuals' internal lives, including their beliefs, emotions, agency, and moral reflections. In the context of sexualities and relationships, it captures how people negotiate personal meaning in relation to broader cultural, relational, and structural influences. Drawing on data from my doctoral research, this section focuses on two key themes that emerged in relation to subjectivity: religious values and pleasure and sexual desire. These reflect the emotional and ethical complexities that shape how individuals make sense of their intimate and sexual selves.

17.6.1 Religious Values

Religion may be broadly defined as a system of beliefs, practices, and moral frameworks through which individuals interpret the world, form communal bonds, and derive existential meaning. Following Geertz (1973), religion can be understood as a cultural system comprising a set of symbols that act to establish powerful, pervasive, and long-lasting moods and motivations by formulating conceptions of a general order of existence and clothing these conceptions with an aura of factuality. This interpretive approach enables an exploration of how individuals make meaning of religious beliefs within the context of their lived realities.

This section does not seek to provide a doctrinal account of Islam, but rather to examine how participants in my study, as self-identifying Muslims, interpreted and attributed meaning to religious teachings in relation to sexualities and relationships. Their narratives reflected a nuanced engagement with religious values, shaped not by homogeneity but by discernment, negotiation, and selective adherence to them. As mentioned earlier, in developing this writing, I have also drawn upon my own experience as a psychosexual and relationship therapist, where similar dynamics frequently emerge in clinical encounters. Many of my clients grapple with reconciling religious obligations with sexual expression, and their therapeutic journeys often reflect the same patterns of individual interpretation, spiritual negotiation, and culturally mediated meaning-making observed in my study.

It is critical to recognize that, as Panjwani beautifully says, "no Muslim is just a Muslim" (Panjwani, 2017); each individual inhabits a complex social location shaped by intersecting factors such as age, gender, geographical background, education, and personal history. As such, their interpretations of Islam were often similar in structure but diverse in substance, reflecting personalized engagements with religious belief. Participants in my study, as well as my clients, exemplify the intra-religious diversity that challenges monolithic representations of Islam. While many identified as Muslim, their engagement with religious doctrine ranged from strict compliance with traditional jurisprudence to more context-sensitive, fluid, and emotionally informed interpretations. Some drew upon clerical authority or scriptural sources, while others relied on ethical reasoning, familial customs, or experiential insights. This diversity underscores the need for culturally sensitive psychosexual and relationship therapists to move beyond reductive or essentialist conceptions of religious identity and instead approach clients as meaning-makers whose relationship with religion is mediated through both cultural inheritance and individual agency.

Among the prominent themes that emerged during discussions of religious perspectives with the interviewees were the emphasis on hygiene and cleanliness, the centrality of marriage and sexual fulfilment, and the value placed on forbearance and self-control. These themes shed light on a moral framework informed by Islamic tradition, while also being profoundly influenced by lived experiences and personal reflections.

17.6.1.1 Hygiene and Cleanliness

Cleanliness, particularly through Islamic ritual practices such as Ghusl (full-body purification) and Wudu (ablution), was identified as a salient religious value with direct implications for psychosexual and relationship therapy. These practices are imbued with both religious and moral significance, functioning as ongoing reminders of bodily responsibility and ethical self-discipline. They carry considerable symbolic and spiritual weight, shaping individuals' perceptions of sexual conduct and bodily regulation. Ghusl is obligatory following each act of sexual intercourse, as well as after menstruation, in order to restore ritual purity and permit participation in daily prayers. For therapists, understanding these ritual dimensions is essential to appreciating how religious obligations may influence the practical and emotional dimensions of clients' sexual lives. For many, this requirement imposes practical constraints on the timing and spontaneity of sexual intimacy, particularly in light of the early morning prayer, with some individuals reporting disrupted sleep or the need for careful planning in order to uphold both religious obligations and sexual closeness.

The additional requirement of Ghusl following menstruation, alongside other religious expectations surrounding the menstrual cycle, further highlights the extent to which, for some people, sexual intimacy is governed by spiritual discipline. For instance, when recommending therapeutic assignments or between-session tasks, it is important to recognize that for many clients, penetrative sexual intercourse is religiously prohibited during menstruation and may therefore be entirely out of consideration during such times. These considerations can give rise to feelings of guilt associated with normal bodily functions, as well as hesitation or stress, which may in turn limit the frequency or spontaneity of sexual relations, even within the context of marriage.

These rituals, while spiritually meaningful, may also inadvertently contribute to the internalization of menstruation and sexual intercourse as inherently impure or contaminating, potentially giving rise to feelings of shame and discomfort regarding these issues, which could result in adverse psychological consequences over time. However, it is essential to recognize that these practices and the surrounding discourses hold significant potential for the development of culturally appropriate sexualities and relationships education programs in Iran. When reframed within a religious context, they can prompt more open discussions about sexual and reproductive health within families, legitimizing such conversations through the language of religious duty, cleanliness, and moral responsibility.

17.6.1.2 Marriage and Sexual Fulfilment

Some Muslims perceive Islam as a sex-positive religion that acknowledges and affirms the role of sexual intimacy within the framework of marriage. Rather than viewing sexuality as inherently shameful or problematic, many see it as a divinely sanctioned aspect of human life that, when expressed within marriage, contributes to emotional closeness and spiritual fulfilment. This perspective is supported by Yip and Page (2016), who found that a majority of Muslim respondents agreed with the statement "My religion is positive towards sexuality."

From this viewpoint, marriage is regarded as the only legitimate setting for sexual activity, where intimacy between spouses is not only permitted but valued as an ethical and religious responsibility. Classical Islamic texts such as *Imam Sajjad's Risalat al-Huquq* are sometimes cited in support of the idea that even one's sexual organs are owed certain rights and must be treated with dignity. In this framework, sexual fulfilment is not simply tolerated but encouraged, aligning personal pleasure with religious duty. However, as previously noted, sexual behavior is subject to well-defined moral boundaries. Premarital and extramarital relations are widely perceived as haram (prohibited), while early marriage or the cultivation of Taghwâ (God-conscious self-restraint) is recommended for managing desire.

Privacy and discretion are also central to Islamic sexual ethics as interpreted by many Muslims. Teachings that advise children to knock before entering their parents' room at specific times of the day reflect a religiously sanctioned effort to protect marital intimacy. This emphasis on modesty, respect, and sexual privacy serves to elevate marital sexuality as both spiritually valid and socially protected within Islamic culture.

17.6.1.3 Forbearance and Self-Control

The values of forbearance and self-control were often perceived by some Muslims as central to moral and spiritual development, particularly in the period preceding marriage. As Hodge observes, "the concept of lifelong singleness is foreign to Islam" (Hodge, 2002, p. 8), and while celibacy was not explicitly condemned, it was rarely idealized. At the same time, romantic and sexual relationships outside the bounds of long-term marriage were not endorsed and were, at best, reluctantly tolerated. As will be discussed later, for many, particularly parents, the existence of adolescent sexual desire was denied altogether, or when acknowledged, it was considered something to be strictly managed.

In such contexts, strategies of Sabr (patience) and Taghwâ (God-conscious self-restraint) were promoted as the religious means by which individuals, especially the young, could navigate their desires. The cultivation of self-control was not merely about avoiding sin, but about building character and preparing for the responsibilities of married life. As one headteacher of a boys-only school in my study noted, "More important than having or not having a sexual relationship before marriage, it is about having control over one's Nafs-E-Ammâreh." The Nafs-E-Ammâreh, often likened to the Freudian concept of the id (Kalbi & Basharat, 2020), refers to the part of the self, inclined toward impulsive desires. Resisting its temptations was viewed as a religious and moral exercise.

Importantly, this ethos of restraint was not only advanced through abstract principles but was operationalized through specific cultural and behavioral practices. The value of Hayâ, previously discussed, was commonly cited as a protective virtue that supports the development of modesty and self-regulation. Practical measures included maintaining gender segregation, discouraging interactions with members of the opposite sex, monitoring clothing choices, and restricting internet access.

Thus, forbearance was not presented as passive suppression but as an active, disciplined, and virtuous way of living that enabled young Muslims to resist temptation and cultivate ethical agency. These expectations, though deeply moral in intention, could also become psychologically burdensome, particularly when adolescents were navigating real and intense sexual feelings without a sanctioned outlet. For therapists working with clients from such cultural contexts, understanding these internalized expectations is vital to supporting clients with compassion and insight.

Taken together, the aforementioned themes illustrate how my interviewees and some of my Iranian clients perceive Islam as their religion concerning issues of sexuality and relationships. Their perspectives have been shaped through selective interpretation, negotiation, and engagement with lived experience, and should not be mistaken for uniform or prescriptive representations of Islamic doctrine. It is important to acknowledge that not all Iranians identify with Islam or any religion at all, and among those who do, intra-religious differences are both widespread and significant. That being said, these varied expressions of faith frequently intersect with common themes observed across religious traditions more broadly. For psychosexual and relationship therapists, this underscores the importance of cultural sensitivity that respects individual interpretations of religion while remaining attuned to the shared and diverse moral landscapes in which clients live.

17.6.2 On Pleasure and Sexual Desire

Among the most delicate and paradoxically revealing themes that emerged from my research was the discourse, or more aptly, the absence of discourse, surrounding sexual pleasure and desire, particularly in relation to younger individuals. When asked to describe their aspirations for their children in terms of sexual behavior and values, participants often referenced happiness and well-being. However, this notion of happiness was curiously circumscribed: it was primarily understood as the absence of desire rather than the cultivation of embodied pleasure. While parents occasionally expressed a wish for their children to become happy adults, this happiness was typically imagined as unburdened by sexual longing or activity prior to marriage, and preserved by robust self-control.

Indeed, sexual desire in younger individuals was framed mainly as a latent danger, something to be postponed, suppressed, or, if possible, entirely avoided. Desire was not perceived as an integral part of human development but rather as a disruptive force, a "dormant bear" or "latent dragon," to use the metaphors employed by several interviewees and clients. Participants consistently expressed the view that premature awareness of sexuality-related issues posed a threat to normative development and moral comportment. Consequently, younger individuals were routinely desexualized, subjected to discursive and behavioral strategies intended to prevent the awakening of sexual desire altogether.

Importantly, this desexualization was not gender-neutral. As previously noted, the management of sexual desire was markedly gendered, with girls more often directed toward early marriage and boys tasked with cultivating restraint. Educators and parents often characterized sexual desire in medicalized or pathologizing terms, as something that one might "contract" and from which one must recover. The onset of puberty itself was viewed with ambivalence, not as a developmental milestone, but as the opening of a dangerous window that must be swiftly and quietly managed. Participants frequently described elaborate tactics employed to subdue this emerging desire and to deny the very existence of sexual subjectivity in the young.

17.7 Sexual Desire as Agency and Autonomy

The stakes of this desexualization were not limited to bodily discipline or behavioral conformity. Rather, they reflected deeper cultural concerns about agency, autonomy, and noncompliance. Underpinning much of the adult anxiety was the fear that, if given the opportunity, younger individuals might make decisions about their sexual lives that diverge from those endorsed by their elders. The sexual desire of youth was not feared merely because it might lead to sexual activity, but because it represented a potential assertion of agency, an assertion that threatened to challenge, and possibly reconfigure, prevailing values around virginity, marriage, gender roles, and familial honor.

This preoccupation with control is perhaps best captured by the dual framing of young people as both sexually dormant and sexually dangerous. On the one hand, they were regarded as innocent and unaware, necessitating protection from corrupting influences such as "Western sexualities and relationships education programs," as some interviewees indicated. On the other hand, there was an implicit belief that, were these constraints to be removed, young people would become uncontrollably sexual, "skilled swimmers" the moment they were "shown the water," as one teacher graphically put it. This duality betrays a profound ambivalence: the child is imagined as both vulnerable and volatile, as simultaneously naïve and predisposed to transgression.

Consequently, the possibility of acknowledging pleasure, or of integrating it into a broader understanding of psychosexual development, was largely absent from participants' narratives. Pleasure, if it appeared at all, was reserved for the marital context and framed in service of relational or reproductive goals. Even here, references to pleasure were sparse and often couched in language of duty or reciprocity. The notion that young individuals might engage in sexual exploration as a site of personal meaning-making, bodily literacy, or relational growth was almost entirely foreclosed.

Nevertheless, as many scholars have argued, the absence of a discourse on desire does not prevent its emergence; instead, it leaves young individuals without the necessary tools to navigate it (Fine, 1988; Fine & McClelland, 2006). The suppression of desire may postpone its expression; however, it cannot eradicate its presence. In such a context, it is not unexpected that younger individuals actively seek out conversations about sexualities and relationships, often in secret or informal settings, despite considerable barriers. Their interest should not be interpreted as a moral failing, as some adults might presume, but rather as a testament to their profound need for meaning-making and relational comprehension.

For psychosexual and relationship therapists, this underscores the significance of assisting clients in acknowledging pleasure and desire not as problems to be resolved, but as legitimate and essential aspects of human experience, particularly for those whose developmental narratives have been shaped by cultural denial. Within my clinical work, some Iranian female clients, for instance, have appeared unfamiliar with the concept of seeking pleasure during sexual intercourse or appear detached from their own sense of sexual desire. For them, sexual relationships are often framed through the lens of duty: a responsibility to please their husbands, preserve the family unit, fulfil reproductive roles, or earn divine approval. Even those women who are more attuned to their desires sometimes express shyness or reluctance in articulating their needs.

On the other hand, many Iranian male clients describe experiencing a pervasive cultural pressure to constantly embody desire and to be ever ready for sexual engagement. However, within my clinical practice, I have observed a marked increase in the number of male Iranian clients reporting reduced sexual desire, often associated with anxieties related to economic insecurity and occupational stress, which has, in many cases, led to internal conflict and heightened anxiety, often manifested through concerns regarding masculinity and self-worth. This clinical observation is consistent with wider evidence suggesting that men's sexual difficulties are often shaped by the interaction of psychological distress, financial hardship, and pressures to conform to dominant masculine norms (Mengesha et al.,

2025). These gendered expectations further highlight the importance of a therapeutic space that promotes reflective and compassionate engagement with one's sexual subjectivity, beyond societal scripts rooted in obligation and performance.

17.8 Not Just Ticking Boxes: The Art of Feeling Culture

Cultural sensitivity extends far beyond merely ticking boxes or superficially reading about a culture and assuming a comprehensive understanding of it. It requires genuinely engaging with how diverse cultural backgrounds shape experiences, interactions, and therapeutic spaces. As explored throughout this chapter, true cultural sensitivity involves recognizing differing symbolic meanings, values, and expectations and actively responding to these complexities with genuine empathy, reflection, and awareness.

Reiss insightfully highlights that sensitivity does not require sharing the same perspective or worldview as another person and that it is possible to "be sensitive towards someone in respects of an issue without implying that one shares the same perspective (or world view) as the person to whom one is being respectful and considerate" (2019, p. 361). Practitioners can demonstrate sensitivity by respectfully and thoughtfully engaging with clients whose cultural values differ significantly from their own. Thus, effective cultural sensitivity explicitly acknowledges and respects individuals' rights to hold different values, beliefs, and sensitivities. Practitioners should consciously avoid assumptions about others' beliefs, desires, or motivations, consistently adopting an open stance and actively asking respectful questions to allow clients to articulate their unique perspectives clearly and authentically.

Henry and Heyes (2022) propose a valuable shift from structured dialogues, typically aiming for explicit resolutions, to more fluid and exploratory conversations, particularly when discussing sensitive topics such as sexuality and religion. Unlike dialogue, conversation invites participants into a shared, exploratory space where ideas can be passionately introduced, defended, and dynamically explored without necessarily seeking a definitive conclusion. This shift moves from "preserving what I am and what I say, think, or believe" to genuinely "being receptive to who the other is," fostering openness and authentic mutual understanding.

In therapeutic contexts, cultural sensitivity is paramount. It demands that therapists understand the sociocultural scripts shaping clients' sexual experiences and approach these scripts with curiosity, humility, and non-judgment. Cultural sensitivity does not imply acceptance or rejection of restrictive or harmful norms but rather a respectful engagement with the meanings clients assign to their sexualities. Therapists must remain attuned to the moral and emotional landscapes embedding these meanings, embracing ambivalence and reflection, and allowing space for tradition and transformation to coexist. This approach supports clients in articulating their desires, interrogating inherited norms, and cultivating empowered, fulfilling sexual subjectivities.

When reading *In the Footsteps of the Fathers: Psychosexual Therapy with the Orthodox Jewish Community* (Keshet-Orr & Collings, 2019), I was struck by the many resonances with my own research and clinical experience. The book explores therapeutic work with Orthodox and ultra-Orthodox Jewish individuals and couples, shedding light on the tensions between religious observance, cultural modesty, and embodied sexual experiences. The rituals, restrictions, and religious views described bore significant similarities to those encountered among my Iranian Muslim-identifying clients. These parallels suggest that while specific practices may differ, many underlying beliefs and values are remarkably consistent across cultural and religious traditions. At the same time, this observation comes with an essential caution: substantial variation could exist even among individuals who identify with the same religion or come from the same region. One must not assume cultural uniformity or religious homogeneity. The challenges of building trust, navigating faith-informed worldviews, and supporting clients toward sexual autonomy while respecting their values reveal universal therapeutic dilemmas. They also reaffirm the imperative of cultural humility in psychosexual practice.

Ultimately, cultural sensitivity demands active engagement in listening, conversing, reflecting, and clarifying. Therapists must recognize when cultural backgrounds influence dialogue, create silences, or present barriers to openness. This may sometimes necessitate referring clients to colleagues whose gender aligns more closely with their comfort level, ensuring a safer and more open therapeutic space. It also involves understanding that culturally embedded fears, internalized shame, and guilt often remain profoundly influential, even when individuals relocate to significantly different cultural environments. Thus, the art of feeling culture is an ongoing, reflective practice that profoundly enriches therapeutic interactions, transforming superficial awareness into deep cultural engagement and honoring the complexity and dignity of human experiences and relationships.

References

Alderson, P. (2013). *Childhoods real and imagined: Volume 1: An introduction to critical realism and childhood studies* (1st ed.) Routledge. https://doi.org/10.4324/9780203805350

Ansary, H., & Babaii, E. (2003). Subliminal sexism in current EFL/ESL textbooks. *Asian EFL Journal, 5*, 1–15.

Archer, M., Bhaskar, R., Collier, A., Lawson, T., & Norrie, A. (1998). *Critical realism: Essential readings* (A. Collier, R. Bhaskar, & M. Archer, Eds.; 1st ed.). Routledge. https://doi.org/10.4324/9781315008592

Archer, M. S. (1995). *Realist social theory: The morphogenetic approach.* Cambridge University Press.

Bahman, M., & Rahimi, A. (2010). Gender representation in EFL materials: An analysis of English textbooks of Iranian high schools. *Procedia—Social and Behavioral Sciences, 9*, 273–277. https://doi.org/10.1016/J.SBSPRO.2010.12.149

Bakhshipour, M., Aghajani Mersa, H., Kaldi, A., & Hosseini, S. A. (2019). The pattern of power distribution in family and social class of married women in Tehran. *Social Welfare Quarterly*, *19*(74), 9–46.

Bhaskar, R. (2008). *Dialectic: The pulse of freedom*. Routledge.

Bhaskar, R. (2016). *Enlightened common sense: The philosophy of critical realism* (M. Hartwig, Ed.). Routledge. https://doi.org/10.4324/9781315542942

Bleakley, A., Hennessy, M., Fishbein, M., & Jordan, A. (2009). How sources of sexual information relate to adolescents' beliefs about sex. *American Journal of Health Behavior*, *33*(1), 37–48. https://doi.org/10.5993/AJHB.33.1.4

Egan, R. D., & Hawkes, G. (2010). *Theorizing the sexual child in modernity* (G. Hawkes, Ed.). Palgrave Macmillan.

Engel, G. L. (1977). The need for a new medical model: A challenge for biomedicine. *Science*, *196*(4286), 129–136. https://doi.org/10.1126/science.847460

Festinger, L. (1962). *A theory of cognitive dissonance*. Stanford University Press.

Fine, M. (1988). Sexuality, schooling, and adolescent females: The missing discourse of desire. *Harvard Educational Review*, *58*(1), 29–54. https://doi.org/10.17763/haer.58.1.u0468k1v2n2n8242

Fine, M., & McClelland, S. (2006). Sexuality education and desire: Still missing after all these years. *Harvard Educational Review*, *76*(3), 297–338. https://doi.org/10.17763/haer.76.3.w5042g23122n6703

Fletcher, K. D., Ward, L. M., Thomas, K., Foust, M., Levin, D., & Trinh, S. (2015). Will it help? Identifying socialization discourses that promote sexual risk and sexual health among African American youth. *Journal of Sex Research*, *52*(2), 199–212. https://doi.org/10.1080/00224499.2013.853724

Foroutan, Y. (2012). Gender representation in school textbooks in Iran: The place of languages. *Current Sociology*, *60*(6), 771–787. https://doi.org/10.1177/0011392112459744

Foucault, M. (1979). *Discipline and punish: The birth of the prison*. Vintage Books.

Geertz, C. (1973). *The interpretation of cultures: Selected essays*. Basic Books, Inc.

Goffman, E. (1959). *The presentation of self in everyday life*. Anchor Books.

Hartwig, M. (2007). *Dictionary of critical realism* (M. Hartwig, Ed.). Routledge.

Henry, S., & Heyes, J. M. (2022). Sexuality education and religion: From dialogue to conversation. *Journal of Philosophy of Education*, *56*(5), 727–738. https://doi.org/10.1111/1467-9752.12704

Hodge, D. R. (2002). Working with Muslim youths: Understanding the values and beliefs of Islamic discourse. *Children & Schools*, *24*(1), 6–20. https://doi.org/10.1093/cs/24.1.6

Holland, J., Sharpe, S., Waites, M., & Weeks, J. (2003). *Sexualities and society: A reader* (J. Holland, S. Sharpe, M. Waites, & J. Weeks, Eds.). Polity P., in association with Blackwell.

Janan, T. (2013). *The difficulties of traditional Iranian parents have raising their first generation daughter in the United States* (Doctoral dissertation). The Chicago School of Professional Psychology, Illinois. ProQuest Dissertations & Theses. (UMI No. 3590404).

Joodaki, K., Nedjat, S., Vahid Dastjerdi, M., & Larijani, B. (2020). Ethical considerations and challenges of sex education for adolescents in Iran: A qualitative study. *Journal of Medical Ethics and History of Medicine*, *13*, 2–2. https://doi.org/10.18502/jmehm.v13i2.2664

Kalantar Motamedi, M. H., Ebrahimi, A., Shams, A., & Nejadsarvari, N. (2016). Health and social problems of rhinoplasty in Iran. *World Journal of Plastic Surgery*, *5*(1), 75–76.

Kalbi, H. E., & Basharat, T. (2020). A comparative study of the personality formulates of Ghazali and Freud. *Journal of Islamic Thought and Civilization, 10*(2), 223–242. https://doi.org/10.32350/jitc.102.13

Keshet-Orr, J., & Collings, S. (2019). *In the footsteps of the fathers: Psychosexual therapy with the Orthodox Jewish community—An overview from the therapist's chair.* Hadassa Word Press.

Khalajabadi Farahani, F. (2017). Meta analysis of premarital heterosexual relationships among young people in Iran over the past 15 years (2001–2015). *Journal of Family Research, 12*(3), 339–367.

Khalili, M., Mirzazadeh, A., Chegeni, M., Abedi, L., Rajaei, L., Ardalan, G., Haghdoost, A. A., Nasiri, N., & Sharifi, H. (2020). Prevalence of high-risk sexual behavior among Iranian young people: A systematic review and meta-analysis. *Children and Youth Services Review, 119*, 105526. https://doi.org/10.1016/J.CHILDYOUTH.2020.105526

Kia, M. (2014). Adab as literary form and social conduct: Reading the gulistan in late Mughal India. In A. Korangy & D. J. Sheffield (Eds.), *"No tapping around philology": A festschrift in celebration and honor of Wheeler McIntosh Thackston Jr.'s 70th birthday* (pp. 281–308). Harrassowitz Verlag. https://doi.org/10.7916/D85D8QH5

Klonoff, E. A., Landrine, H., & Campbell, R. (2000). Sexist discrimination may account for well-known gender differences in psychiatric symptoms. *Psychology of Women Quarterly, 24*(1), 93–99. https://doi.org/10.1111/J.1471-6402.2000.TB01025.X

Mafi, F. (2023). *Is sexualities and relationships education feasible in Iranian schools? An in-depth examination of selected stakeholders' perspectives and the vital role of values in sexualities and relationships education* (Doctoral thesis). University College London, IOE Faculty of Education and Society.

Mahmood, S. (2005). *Politics of piety: The Islamic revival and the feminist subject.* Princeton University Press.

McLaughlin, K. A., Hatzenbuehler, M. L., & Keyes, K. M. (2010). Responses to discrimination and psychiatric disorders among black, hispanic, female, and lesbian, gay, and bisexual individuals. *American Journal of Public Health, 100*(8), 1477–1484. https://doi.org/10.2105/AJPH.2009.181586

Mengesha, Z., Alem, A. Z., Gebremedhin, T. A., et al. (2025). Help-seeking for sexual difficulties among Australian men: Analysis of the ten to men longitudinal study. *Archives of Sexual Behavior, 54*, 2553–2565. https://doi.org/10.1007/s10508-025-03182-7

Mernissi, F. (1985). *Beyond the veil: Male-female dynamics in modern Muslim society* (Rev. ed.). Al Saqi.

Naghizadeh, S., Robatjazi, M., Abbasi, M., & Mohammadi, A. (2023). Midwives' views on virginity testing: A cross-sectional study. *Journal of Holistic Nursing and Midwifery, 33*(3), 203–213.

Panjwani, F. (2017). No Muslim is just a Muslim: Implications for education. *Oxford Review of Education, 43*(5), 596–611. https://doi.org/10.1080/03054985.2017.1352354

Raisi, F., Abbasiyan, S., Mafi, F., Firoozi Khojastefar, R., Abdi Masouleh, F., & Balizadeh Karami, A. R. (2022). Why Iranian women undergo aesthetic genital surgeries? A qualitative study. *Journal of Sexual Health Psychology, 1*(2), 65–76. https://doi.org/10.52547/JSHP.1.2.65

Reiss, M. J. (2019). Evolution education: Treating evolution as a sensitive rather than a controversial issue. *Ethics and Education, 14*(3), 351–366. https://doi.org/10.1080/17449642.2019.1617391

Ringrose, J. (2013). *Postfeminist education?: Girls and the sexual politics of schooling* (1st ed.). Routledge. https://doi.org/10.4324/9780203106822
Sung, K. T., & Kim, H. S. (2003). Elder respect among young adults: Exploration of behavioral forms in Korea. *Ageing International, 28*(3), 279–294. https://doi.org/10.1007/S12126-002-1008-Y
The Supreme Council of Cultural Revolution. (2011). *Fundamental reform document of education of the Islamic Republic of Iran.* Supreme Council of Cultural Revolution.
Tabatabaie, A. (2015). Constructing the ideal Muslim sexual subject: Problematics of school-based sex education in Iran. *Sex Education: Sexuality, Society and Learning, 15*(2), 204–216. https://doi.org/10.1080/14681811.2014.992066
Tervalon, M., & Murray-Garcia, J. (1998). Cultural humility versus cultural competence: A critical distinction in defining physician training outcomes in multicultural education. *Journal of Health Care for the Poor and Underserved, 9*(2), 117–125. https://doi.org/10.1353/hpu.2010.0233
Ward, L. M. (2016). Media and sexualization: State of empirical research, 1995–2015. *Journal of Sex Research, 53*(4–5), 560–577. https://doi.org/10.1080/00224499.2016.1142496
Warner, L. R., Leskinen, E. A., & Leyva, J. (2020). Sexuality and socialization. In N. A. Naples (Ed.), *Companion to sexuality studies* (pp. 160–178). Wiley. https://doi.org/10.1002/9781119315049.ch9
Yip, A. K. T., & Page, S. J. (2016). Religious and sexual identities: A multi-faith exploration of young adults. In N. A. Naples (Ed.), *Religious and sexual identities: A multi-faith exploration of young adults* (1st ed.). Routledge.

Chapter 18

Sexuality and Sexual Trauma Presentations in Those from Black and Minoritized/Global Majority Communities: Taking a Decolonized Approach

Divine Charura and Jodie Slee

Introduction

> Sara Baartman (AKA "Venus Hottentot") was a curvaceous South African teenager lured to Europe to perform for audiences in 1810. Her genitals and brain were posthumously dissected, pickled, and museumized. Sara Baartman's iconicity reveals the Western world's preoccupation with possessing the female body and controlling Black female sexuality.
>
> (Mackie-Stephenson, 2022)

> All I knew about sex was what my parents told me: "You hate boys, right?" "Yeah." "Keep your damn legs closed." And that's all.
>
> (Rouse-Arnett & Long Dilworth, 2006, p. 46)

This chapter will explore sexuality and the diversity of sexual trauma presentations in Black and minoritized/global majority communities. From our review of the research literature, we have identified increasing evidence that sexual minority status, ethnicity variables, and their intersections play roles in recovering from trauma. Consideration should therefore be given to how psychotherapeutic approaches can be made culturally appropriate and effective when working with those presenting for individual or couples psychosexual therapy. This chapter focuses on sexuality and sexual trauma presentations in individuals from Black and minoritized communities.

Firstly, we establish and broach our own positionality, philosophical, and theoretical underpinnings, as we believe that this is important for facilitating our discussions. It also serves to deconstruct stereotypes and challenge our preconditioned minds about sexuality and sexual trauma presentations in individuals from Black and minoritized/global majority communities. Given the abundant misrepresentation and negative portrayals of global majority communities, it is important for us to acknowledge the influence these portrayals have on our worldviews. Charura et al. (forthcoming) remind us that our lived experiences, both conscious and

DOI: 10.4324/9781003611387-18

unconscious, are informed by what has been introjected through the social conditioning process. Therefore, conceptualizations of others must be examined through an ongoing, dynamic process of confronting and challenging one's own internalized racism, relearning different ways of being, and applying this new learning.

In writing this chapter, we want to be upfront about elucidating and critically discussing sexual trauma from a uniquely decolonized lens. We will critically review the concepts, socio-historical-political contexts of sexual trauma, and explore the profound implications, effects, and impact this trauma has on Black and minoritized/global majority communities. Terms, language, and historical locations of salient constructs are examined and critiqued. Furthermore, we showcase the complexities of detangling often misunderstood concepts and the necessity of decolonizing psychosexual and relationship curricula and therapeutic practices.

A Note on Language

We hold a commitment to anti-oppressive practice and respecting *Gender Sexual Erotic and Relational Diversity* (*GSERD*), as well as transcultural sensitivities to sexual and relationship practices in different communities. In relation to the language used in this chapter, we have made a conscious effort to pay attention to our use of language. We are mindful that we do not speak for all people from minoritized or racialized communities. Therefore, we use the term "global majority communities." We do not speak for all people from these communities, but we write from the perspective of our extensive work with diverse communities in the United Kingdom (UK). We acknowledge that language evolves and changes quickly, and rather than using language that stigmatizes or perpetuates subjugation and oppression of others, we have aimed to use language that demonstrates our commitment to and awareness of respectful, culturally appropriate conceptualizations of psychosexual and relationship configurations. Our aim is to be neutral, without ignoring the existence of intersections of identity. Nevertheless, we are cognizant that the language we have used is inevitably subject to different interpretations depending on the positionality of the reader and the changing patterns of language and meaning over time. We, therefore, invite you, the reader, to hold in mind the diverse ways in which language and meaning can change depending on context. Our aim in writing this chapter is to uphold respect for all humanity, our diversity, and intersectionality.

Our Ontological and Epistemological Positioning

In describing ourselves, I (Divine, first author) describe myself as a Black British heterosexual man of African heritage. I am a psychologist and a psychotherapist with an interest in psychotraumatology, psychosexual, and relationship therapy. The second author, JS, is a White British woman, heterosexual, cisgendered, trauma-informed psychosexual and relationship therapist, and EMDR practitioner. We have been privileged to work jointly for over five years with individuals, couples, and families from diverse backgrounds, and we will in this chapter provide examples that are an amalgamation of our experiences. Having both trained at different institutions in the UK, we acknowledge our cultural biases and limitations, given that our education and epistemological influence in that domain was initially Euro-American-centric. However, we are also critical of the limitations this brings, as it asserts dominance over other theoretical perspectives, such as African, Judaic, Islamic, and Eastern psychology concepts.

We both have an interest in human diversity, psychosexual theories, and practice. Epistemologically, we acknowledge that human sexuality is complicated by the intersections of identity and behavior. The context of the global majority's diverse cultural practices, compounded by the minority stress these groups face, may lead to increased psychological distress and challenges in their sexual and relational domains. Racial stress or intergenerational trauma related to racial discrimination and oppression can increase PTSD symptoms in children who have experienced childhood sexual abuse. Specific practices or challenges in different communities include:

- The impact of religious expectations
- Female genital mutilation (FGM)
- Genitalia modification (e.g., labia elongation)
- Initiation practices to wo/manhood, cultural practices
- Expectations about relationships and sex

These factors impact individuals and relationships across the lifespan.

One of the quotes we started the chapter with mirrors what we have heard from many clients we have worked with, who spoke about the lack of dialogue and discussion with their primary caregivers or community about sex, sexuality, and pleasure. This paucity of psychoeducation, in our experience, results in challenges, including a lack of authentic understanding of one's body, anatomy, and unfamiliarity with one's own genitalia. For some, this lack of psychosexual education can be the etiology of disgust, shame, or difficulties in experiencing psychosexual pleasure. We also acknowledge that different communities, religions, and cultural practices may focus on the procreation aspects of sexuality and relationships and demonize or avoid delving into recreational pleasure discourses.

Our Theoretical Underpinnings

Our theoretical underpinnings for being trauma-informed and decolonizing psychosexual and relationship therapy draw from Intersectionality Theory (Crenshaw, 1991), Critical Race Theory (Delgado & Stefancic, 2001, 2012), and diverse cultural feminist-oriented theories (contextually relevant framing of feminism, challenging gender-based power structures, and advocating for girls and women's diverse sexual identities. See, for example, Africana Womanism (Hudson-Weems, 2000); dimensions of Chinese Feminism (Chen, 2011)). We also draw from trauma theories (e.g., Polyvagal theory, neuroscience, and somatic practices) (Porges, 2003, 2022); Systemic Theory (Harris & Crossley, 2021); and Transcultural Psychology, including literature on intercultural relationships (Yurtaeva & Charura, 2024). From Crenshaw (1991), we value the assertion that intersectionality recognizes that socially constructed identity categories (e.g., race, class, gender, and sexual orientation) simultaneously interact with one another and with wider societal and power structures to construct experiences of oppression and privilege unique to each individual. This chapter is informed by the importance of intersectionality, which aids understanding of diverse communities' experiences of sexual trauma and psychosexual dynamics (Cho et al., 2013; Crenshaw, 1991).

We value Critical Race Theory (CRT) because of its focus on engaging the voices of those with the lived experience of being marginalized by the dominant culture and the value of their counter-storytelling regarding how they experience racism. Their counternarratives include informing us within the therapeutic relationship context about their experiences of relationships within their own communities, from their perspective, as well as the embodied and culturally conceptualized nature of sexual trauma and its transgenerational and personal impact (Charura & Clyburn, 2023).

We have synthesized and composed a logical discussion on the contemporary issues and debates relating to sexual trauma. We align with those who have critiqued the history and origins of the concept of race, racism, colonialism, systemic oppression, injustices, and the historic sexual subjugation and abuse of Black and minoritized/global majority communities.

Context and Background Literature

The ideological underpinnings in Euro-American-centric psychology conceptualizations of the psyche have inadvertently positioned Western ideas of sexuality and relational dynamics as the norm, while those of other cultures have been labeled as primitive, odd, abnormal, uncontrollable, perverse, or hypersexualized. Furthermore, ideas of what constitutes a "normal" body or anatomy have been based on white European features. Charura et al. (forthcoming) assert that within some communities, this desire for an introjected ideal can manifest as colorism (preference for lighter skin), texturism (preference for straighter hair), and featurism (preference for features like a straight nose, thin lips, etc.). All of these preferences are rooted in the oppressive belief that physical attributes that are closer to white are more acceptable, presentable, and beautiful.

We argue that psychosexual therapy, as a Western and Eurocentric endeavor, is compromised by racism. This is due to the historical foundations of mainstream psychosexual theories, which are steeped in Eurocentric epistemologies that often fail to appreciate the diversity of perspectives on mental health from other cultures (Charura & Clyburn, 2023; Charura & Al-Murri, 2024). These limitations in psychosexual theory, which were historically rooted in Western thinking, still persist, marginalizing non-Eurocentric perspectives and overlooking the rich diversity of human sexual expression found in global majority communities. As a result, the frameworks for understanding sexual trauma and health are not universally applicable and fail to address the complexities of diverse cultural practices and beliefs regarding sexuality.

We begin this chapter with a reference to the case of Sara Baartman (also known as "Venus Hottentot"), a Khoekhoe woman who was exhibited as a freak show attraction in 19th-century Europe. Although Sara Baartman died on December 29, 1815, her exhibition continued, with her brain, skeleton, and sexual organs remaining on display in a Paris museum until 1974. Her remains were not repatriated to South Africa and buried until 2002. While this may seem like an exceptional case, the erotic projection and exhibition of Black women's steatopygic (fat-bottomed) body types continues today in various forms, such as in the sexualization and fetishization of Black women in mainstream media, advertising, and pornography. The sexualized objectification of women of African descent remains a deeply ingrained form of exploitation that underscores the continued legacy of colonial practices. The commodification of the Black female body as an object of desire and curiosity persists within the globalized economy of sexual consumption.

There is also a history of unethical medical experimentation, such as the Tuskegee Study of Untreated Syphilis in African American males, conducted between 1932 and 1972 by the United States Public Health Service (PHS) and the Centers for Disease Control and Prevention (CDC). This study, involving nearly 400 African American men with syphilis, highlights the intersection of ethics, race, ethnicity, sexuality, and trauma. The purpose of the study was to observe the effects of untreated syphilis, and the men were initially informed that the experiment would last six months, but it was extended to 40 years. The men were not informed of the true nature of the experiment, and more than 100 of them died as a result. Forty of the patients' wives were infected with syphilis, and 19 children were born with congenital syphilis. Furthermore, despite penicillin being widely available by 1947 and accepted as a standard treatment for syphilis, none of the men were offered the treatment. It wasn't until 1997 that President Bill Clinton formally apologized on behalf of the United States, calling the study "shameful and racist."

This incident highlights not only the medical and ethical violations committed but also the racialized nature of public health practices and the deep historical wounds left in the African American community by such acts. It emphasizes the intersection of race, health care, and sexuality, particularly how Black bodies have been subjected to exploitation and systemic neglect. The Tuskegee study is an example of how colonial mindsets regarding race and sexuality continue to shape contemporary health disparities and how the legacy of such studies continues to affect public health policies.

Our awareness of the stigma and shame associated with HIV and other STIs, along with their disproportionate impact on Black communities, is a crucial area that requires further exploration. The historical trauma, racism, and medical neglect surrounding health issues like HIV/AIDS have contributed to generational trauma within Black communities. Additionally, there has been a call for the decolonization of psychosexual research. Recently, there has been strong criticism of mass circumcision campaigns aimed at reducing HIV transmission in Eastern and Southern Africa, campaigns supported by the World Health Organization and implemented by the United States government and Western NGOs (Fish et al., 2021).

Fish et al. (2021) highlight the colonial undertones in these campaigns, referencing the *Maryland Medical Journal* (Maryland Medical Journal Editors, 1894), which argued for the enforcement of circumcision as a means to curb "the brutal and uncontrollable passion" of the "Black man" and to address "the perversion of his sexual instincts and ungoverned sexual passion." The proposal described by the editors as "worthy of consideration" had previously been put forward by Remondino (1894). This rhetoric perpetuates harmful stereotypes about Black sexuality and racializes sexual health concerns. Fish et al. (2021) also question whether the mass circumcision campaigns occurring in Africa today could be considered a "new Tuskegee." They argue that in the Tuskegee syphilis study, the researchers knowingly transmitted a lethal infection to unknowing partners while withholding life-saving information. A similar situation arose in Uganda's Rakai District, where a clinical trial resulted in 90 unknowing, seronegative partners contracting HIV. The researchers failed to inform participants about the possibility of infection, leading to what they term "criminal negligence" (Buddhakorale, 2013). This negligence, in turn, perpetuates historical trauma and colonial attitudes toward African communities and their health.

These current circumcision campaigns, while presented as a solution to the African HIV epidemic, reveal a deeper issue of cultural imperialism rather than sound health policy. The campaigns fail to sufficiently account for cultural differences and other contextual variables, and Fish et al. (2021) assert that African communities must have more robust representation in these health decisions. These medical practices cannot be separated from their racialized historical context and their potential to reinforce Western control over African bodies and health decisions. The ongoing influence of these colonial medical practices highlights the need for African communities to engage in and control their own health narratives, as they are more equipped to understand the intersection of their cultural, racial, and sexual identities.

Gregg (2020) reflects on the representation of history through visual iconography, emphasizing the intersection of race, masculinity, and sexuality. Charura et al. (forthcoming) similarly discuss how the long history of Black and Brown bodies as objects of projection and desire has been perpetuated. Although these bodies are often objectified, they have also been portrayed as grotesque. This polarization is rooted in the history of slavery and media representations of the sexualization of Black men, further cementing stereotypes. For example, the "Mandingo" image, which was popularized through depictions of sexual tension between plantation overseers and Black slaves, has contributed to the longstanding fetishization of Black male sexuality. Additionally, historic practices like castration, hanging, and scarring, as well as modern-day fetishization, have contributed to the continuing stereotyping of hypersexuality within Black communities.

Mainstream media frequently fails to present positive examples of Black sexuality, while exaggerating negative stereotypes, which are linked to increased psychological distress (Wooten et al., 2021). In relation to women, we draw on Fredrickson and Roberts' (1997) Objectification Theory, which helps to examine the psychological consequences of gendered oppression. The theory suggests that women's bodies are frequently subjected to a sexualized, objectifying gaze, which reduces them to body parts valued primarily for the pleasure and use of others. This positioning fosters the internalization of harmful stereotypes, contributing to issues like negative self-perception, mental health concerns, and the potential risk of sexual victimization (rape, incest, battering, sexual harassment) (Castillo et al., 2024).

In our facilitation of psychosexual therapist training and development, we have frequently been challenged and critiqued for "bringing up history." Some have argued, "That's all from the past, we must move on!" While we acknowledge these concerns, it is crucial to recognize that historical trauma, the legacies of colonial brutality, ongoing marginalization, subjugation, and experimentation on global majority communities persist. Acknowledging this history is essential in developing a therapeutic approach that is not only ethically sound but also holistic and trauma-informed. By consciously holding space for this legacy, practitioners can work to promote healing rather than risk reproducing harm.

Our Core Reflections and Lessons from Practice

As psychotherapists who have worked together in clinical practice and through clinical supervision, we have reflected on the individuals and couples we see in our clinical work. In this chapter, we present fictional case vignettes we have created based on our extensive clinical experience with individuals experiencing various sexual traumas and psychosexual challenges. These vignettes, though fictional, are informed by many years of hands-on work with individuals presenting with diverse issues. We have worked with people who have experienced childhood sexual trauma, trauma in adulthood, and complex sexual dysfunctions (Charura et al., 2024).

The spectrum of challenges we encounter includes individuals grappling with compulsive sexual behaviors, sexual phobias, orgasmic dysfunction, vaginismus (an involuntary tensing of the vagina during attempted insertion), dyspareunia (recurrent or persistent genital pain during, before, or after sex), erectile dysfunction, delayed ejaculation, premature ejaculation, and non-ejaculation. Additionally, we have worked with individuals struggling with body dysmorphia caused by genital mutilation, torture, or body modification practices such as labia elongation. Our therapeutic interventions also involve supporting individuals from diverse global majority communities, some of whom practice BDSM (Bondage, Discipline, Dominance, Submission, Sadomasochism) or explore kink and fetish behaviors (e.g., preferences for specific body parts, such as feet and toes, or objects like socks or shoes) as part of their sexual identity.

In our clinical practice, we have observed that many patients arrive at therapy with incomplete, stereotypical, and often false information about sexuality. Some lack adequate sexual education, which is evident in their unfamiliarity with common sexual terminology and a lack of understanding of their own anatomy. These gaps in knowledge can lead to confusion and distress. Furthermore, some patients share their feelings of incongruence with their cultural or religious practices in relation to their romantic or sexual relationships. Such incongruence can contribute to emotional conflict and sexual dysfunction.

The fictional case vignettes presented here serve as amalgamations of real-life experiences that incorporate aspects of identity, including names, gender, age, and relationship status. However, these vignettes are not representative of any specific individual or their personal experience. They are created solely for reflective purposes to enhance understanding and discussion. They do not correlate directly to any clients we have worked with.

Case Vignette 1: Psychosexual Therapy with an Intercultural Couple

Ru and Dan approached us for psychosexual therapy, and we both saw them as part of our joint practice. Ru describes herself as a mixed-race woman of Black and Asian heritage, and Dan as South-East Asian. Ru shared that she had a strict religious upbringing and had not been in any romantic or sexual relationships until the age of 28. Dan, on the other hand, disclosed that he had been in multiple relationships, which he said had "opened his eyes" to his own sexuality. These relationships included experiences with BDSM, kink, and Shibari. At one point in his sexual journey, he became involved with a "wrong crowd," and this experience nearly cost him his life. When we explored this further, Dan revealed that he had visited a self-styled "eunuch maker," who mutilated paying customers and streamed the procedure online.

By the time they arrived at our clinic, they had been married for five years. They had moved into Ru's parents' family home, living with seven other people, including Ru's parents and sisters, and had very little privacy. They also shared that, despite being married for five years, they were under pressure to conceive. During the initial four sessions of assessment, Ru disclosed that she had experienced "sexual trauma" in childhood and had not been able to successfully engage in sex since marriage. They were both preoccupied with whether Ru still had her hymen, and Dan found her genital modification practices disturbing. Ru described having a phobic response to her own genitalia, and she would vomit at the sight of her husband's genitals. Dan expressed feeling deeply depressed and mentioned that he was so desperate he had begun to consider separating from her.

Case Vignette 2: Working with Psychosexual Trauma and the Impact of Female Genital Mutilation

Pat attended an assessment following a referral from her GP. She described herself as a British woman of Middle Eastern heritage and indicated that she had been struggling with significant pain. Through the assessment, Pat shared that when she was a teenager, she was taken abroad and subjected to female genital mutilation (FGM). The details of her trauma emerged during the session: she had undergone the removal of the inner and outer labia, the removal of the clitoral glans, and her vulva was sewn closed (infibulation). In this process, a small hole was left for urine and menstrual fluid to pass, and the vagina was opened for intercourse and childbirth.

Pat also shared the additional trauma of witnessing two other girls undergoing the procedure, both of whom died. She spoke of flashbacks where she vividly remembered screaming, struggling, bleeding profusely, and being pinned down as she was cut. The pain and the violent, traumatic experience have left deep scars, and these memories continue to affect her emotional and psychological well-being.

Reflective Question 1.1

Having read the case vignettes on Ru and Dan, and on Pat, how would you approach working with them?

In both case vignettes, the individuals and couples bring complex, multifaceted issues into therapy that demand sensitivity, cultural competence, and an understanding of the deep psychological effects of sexual trauma. In Ru and Dan's case, their struggle with cultural identity, sexual trauma, and bodily autonomy requires a nuanced, trauma-informed approach that acknowledges the challenges faced by individuals from diverse cultural backgrounds. It's essential to work through the dynamics of sexual trauma in a way that respects Ru's experiences, her fear of her own body, and the emotional distress Dan is experiencing due to their inability to connect sexually.

For Pat, her experience of FGM necessitates a specialized approach that addresses both the physical trauma and the profound psychological impact of such an invasive and painful procedure. It would be crucial to explore her cultural background, her emotional responses to the trauma, and any spiritual or community-related implications of the FGM procedure in order to help her regain control over her body and heal from the shame and suffering she has endured.

Both cases underscore the importance of creating a safe, culturally responsive therapeutic space where trauma can be explored without judgment. It is essential to acknowledge the intersectionality of culture, race, gender, and sexual trauma and work collaboratively with clients to develop tailored therapeutic interventions that address both the individual's immediate distress and the broader sociocultural factors influencing their experiences of sexuality and trauma.

What Has Race Got to Do with It?

> As a younger woman, sexual expectations of being submissive or being a bottom... in terms of sexuality, was definitely a thing. I am kind of a dominant

> personality anyway, and so I was not going to allow somebody to put me in like a little Japanese sex toy box. I was never going to allow that to happen. – Sophia (Castillo et al., 2024)

Reflecting on our work with clients from global majority communities, the issue of the intersection between race, culture, trauma, and sexuality continually arises. Increasingly, literature is stimulating new ways of thinking about race, racial trauma, and antiracist practice, particularly in psychosexual therapeutic work (Ade-Serrano & Nkansa-Dwamena, 2025; Charura & Al-Murri, 2024; Charura & Lago, 2021a). Castillo et al. (2024) highlight how the intersectionality of race and gender-based oppression presents a nuanced understanding of how dehumanization and hypersexualization shape identity. They point to race-based stereotypes, such as the sexually provocative "Black Jezebel" and the submissive, loyal "China Doll," as examples of historical identity-based oppression of Black and Asian women. The quote from Sophia in this section illustrates the tensions that women from global majority communities often face in their resistance to hypersexualization. It highlights their struggle with sexual harassment, feelings of powerlessness in those moments, and the related trauma these experiences can induce.

Objectification Theory

Fredrickson and Roberts (1997) introduced objectification theory to explore the psychological consequences of gendered oppression. This theoretical framework has been instrumental in understanding how women's bodies are perceived within sociocultural contexts and in identifying the mechanisms through which sexual objectification occurs. Within a system dominated by white, heteronormative standards, women are routinely subjected to a sexualized, objectifying gaze. This gaze fragments the body, reducing it to parts that are valued primarily for the pleasure and use of others (Fredrickson & Roberts, 1997, p. 175).

Women from global majority communities often experience additional layers of sexualization, being objectified and fetishized in ways that overshadow other aspects of their identity. For instance, these women frequently report being labeled as "exotic" or receive sexualized comments about specific physical features, such as their lips, hips, genitalia, or "booty." They are often pressured to conform to racialized and sexualized stereotypes. For example, Asian women are sometimes expected to enhance features in line with hypersexualized portrayals rooted in colonial and orientalist narratives.

The problem of objectification extends beyond external pressures—it also operates within marginalized communities themselves. Cultural representations of Black women's sexuality, frequently reinforced in media forms (including popular rap music), often depict them using derogatory labels such as "freaks," "sluts," or "whores" (Rouse-Arnett & Long Dilworth, 2006). These portrayals not only contribute to the internalization of harmful stereotypes but also restrict authentic sexual expression. In many cases, they normalize harassment and abuse, particularly among young men who adopt these distorted views of gender and sexuality.

Challenging these harmful narratives is essential, as they reinforce cycles of shame, secrecy, and confusion. These narratives are often exacerbated by conflicting messages from parents, peers, media, religious teachings, and broader social institutions, all of which influence how individuals perceive their own sexual identities and how others perceive them.

The harmful consequences for women are evident in the formation of their self-perception. Self-conscious body monitoring, mental health concerns (such as shame, anxiety, and awareness of internal bodily states), and limited opportunities to experience peak motivational states are prevalent. These issues can increase the risk of direct sexual victimization, including rape, incest, battering, and sexual harassment. Colorism and texturism are also important dimensions of this broader conversation. Shadism, the prejudice against individuals with darker skin, remains an issue within the Black community, with darker-skinned women often perceived as less desirable, while lighter skin is equated with attractiveness, wealth, and social status. This beauty standard, based in Western society, has influenced non-Western countries and continues to perpetuate harmful racial hierarchies.

The dynamics of race, culture, and sexuality are intricately intertwined and require a culturally responsive and informed therapeutic approach. For therapists working with clients from marginalized communities, it is essential to understand the socio-cultural pressures that shape their sexual identities and experiences. Addressing these complex layers through a decolonized and culturally aware therapeutic lens can significantly impact clients' healing journeys, promoting a deeper understanding of their sexual and relational lives.

Perspectives on Kink and Play Brought in the Therapy Room Dialogue

Kink, play, and BDSM have been a feature in much of our clinical work, as illustrated by Dan in the first case vignette. We draw on the work of Labrecque et al. (2021), who explored *What is so appealing about being spanked, flogged, dominated, or restrained?* Their analysis of perspectives from those who engage with or practice sexual masochism and submission highlighted that prolonged, intense, contextual, anticipated, and consensual sexualized painful stimulation seems to induce both analgesia and ecstasy (Labrecque et al., 2021). A comparison has been made between this analgesic and ecstasy experience with the "runner's rush," "cross-fit's high," orgasmic birth, and other pain-related euphoric phenomena (Buckley, 2003; Labrecque et al., 2021; Mayberry & Daniel, 2016). These phenomena suggest that engaging in BDSM can serve as a mechanism for managing pain, trauma, and emotional release, potentially leading to a state of euphoria akin to the "flow state" experienced during intense physical or emotional exertion.

A definition from Wiseman (1998) provides a useful framework for understanding BDSM: "the knowing use of psychological dominance and submission, and/or physical bondage, and/or pain, and/or related practices in a safe, legal, consensual manner in order for the participants to experience erotic arousal and/or personal growth" (p. 10). This definition recognizes BDSM as an umbrella term encompassing various erotic activities often defined as non-normative or kinky, such as power exchange, role-play, fetishes, and other practices. The emphasis on consensuality and safety is central to the therapeutic understanding of BDSM, where it is not merely a manifestation of trauma but can also serve as an empowering practice for individuals seeking to explore and express their sexual identity.

While psychotraumatology and other approaches in psychosexual and relationship therapy traditionally focus on early life psychological adjustments to achieve an altered state of mind associated with managing traumatic experiences or dissociation, it is important from a decolonial perspective to recognize that BDSM practices should not be pathologized or automatically associated with previous trauma (sexual or otherwise) (Ansara, 2019). Martinez (2021) has highlighted the dominance of whiteness in BDSM literature, dating back to the 1970s, where most of the authors discussing BDSM appear not only as white but also as Westerners. This points to a larger issue of the colonial legacy of sexuality—where non-Western sexual practices, even those within marginalized racial communities, are often relegated to being "primitive" or "abnormal." A growing body of literature, along with voices encountered in clinical practice, points out that whiteness confers a certain privilege in sexual expression, providing flexibility and acceptance not always extended to people of color (Martinez, 2021).

For example, you can be a skater, a punk, a prep, a gamer, or someone into kink or BDSM in Western contexts without it being scrutinized or pathologized. However, when someone from a racialized community engages in diverse sexual practices, whether culturally informed, religiously motivated, or based on rituals of initiation or relationships, these practices are often viewed as "primitive" or "odd." This reflects a lack of acknowledgment that people from racialized communities are not just seen through the lens of race but are often reduced to this singular category without recognition of the intersections of other facets of identity (see Martinez, 2021). This view aligns with Crenshaw's (1989) concept of intersectionality, which facilitates a more nuanced understanding of how race and sex discrimination do not occur on a "single categorical axis." In the case of people from global majority communities, race and sexuality intersect with complex layers of oppression, making their experiences of kink and sexuality significantly more complicated.

Although our clinical experience with clients who practice BDSM has led us to conclude that BDSM can facilitate a person's reaching an altered state of mind associated with sexual arousal, there still remains a paucity of research in this area. It is important to note that BDSM is a multifaceted practice with numerous motivations behind it. For example, some individuals may engage in kink as a behavior, role-playing experience, or a form of identity expression, while others may view it as a form of orientation or a way of engaging in relationships. BDSM can encompass behavior, fantasy, exploration of sexuality, community engagement, role identification, or even personal growth. Kalafatis-Russell (2021) argued that some people are drawn to BDSM or kink for pleasure, intimacy-building, or as a leisure activity, while others may incorporate it as an essential part of their sexual identity, akin to their sexual orientation or gender identity. This understanding challenges the view that kink and BDSM are inherently tied to trauma or mental health disorders.

It is crucial that therapists avoid making assumptions about individuals who practice BDSM or sex work, presuming that these practices are indicative of unresolved childhood trauma (Anderson-Foster, 2023). Many individuals engage in these practices for a variety of reasons, some of which include exploring power dynamics, fulfilling sexual desires, or enhancing their intimate relationships. Therefore, assuming that these practices are pathological can be harmful and misleading.

From a decolonized approach to trauma-informed psychosexual therapy, we appreciate frameworks and modalities that emphasize the mind-body connection, such as mindfulness, meditation, physical activity, and embodied trauma work. Religion and spirituality may also play significant roles in understanding sexual and relational dynamics within different cultural contexts (Charura & Lago, 2021a, 2021b; Lago & Charura, 2015; Lago & Hirai, 2013; O'Brien & Charura, 2022, 2024). In the following section, we present an example of using body maps with clients, a culturally responsive and innovative method for facilitating sexual trauma processing that aligns with the principles of decolonization and cultural humility in psychosexual therapy.

Using Body Maps as an Innovative and Culturally Appropriate Method for Facilitating Sexual Trauma Processing

Use of Body Maps and Transculturally Appropriate Interventions

Our trauma work with Ru, Dan, and Pat exemplifies the necessity of decolonizing psychosexual and relationship therapy and focusing on embodied ways of working by moving beyond the pathologization of trauma. We assert that for psychosexual therapeutic approaches to be effective and inclusive in contemporary society, we must engage with a holistic framework that integrates bio-psycho-social-sexual-spiritual-existential assessment, formulation, and interventions, as noted by O'Brien and Charura (2024). This framework emphasizes the need to consider not just psychological symptoms but also the full range of human experience, including spiritual and cultural factors, and the complex ways in which trauma is embodied. It calls for a nuanced, person-centered approach that attends to the mind, body, and spirit, enabling a more profound and individualized form of healing.

Furthermore, our approaches and interventions should be anti-oppressive, culturally appropriate, trauma-informed, and socially just. This is critical in ensuring that therapy does not reproduce power imbalances or reinforce marginalization. Multidisciplinary collaboration is essential in such an approach, as trauma and sexual health can be complex and multifactorial, often requiring input from social workers, medical professionals, and community healers to create a holistic support system. The decolonial framework also necessitates a continual re-examination of Western-centric therapeutic modalities, ensuring they do not inadvertently uphold oppressive structures.

The body mapping intervention draws from neuroscientific and arts-based research (Nummenmaa et al., 2014; O'Brien & Charura, 2024; Volynets et al., 2020) and is an innovative decolonized approach in psychosexual trauma work. It offers an embodied, creative method for individuals to express trauma as they experience it in their bodies. This intervention recognizes that trauma often lives in the body, manifesting as physical sensations, muscle tension, and visceral responses. By providing a safe, non-verbal, and non-linear medium for expression, body mapping enables individuals to connect with their bodily experiences of trauma in a more accessible and integrative way.

In practice, the body mapping exercise invites patients to mark, draw, or write on body maps using any coloring tools of their choice, identifying where in the body they have experienced embodied trauma. This process provides a tangible representation of their inner world, where they can externalize and visualize their feelings, pain, or distress. For example, individuals may mark areas of their body where they have experienced genital modification, cutting, FGM, or other painful or traumatic experiences. The body map serves as a visual tool for dialogue about what the client has experienced and is a means for them to communicate feelings that may be difficult to articulate with words.

This exercise is not just an artistic endeavor, but a powerful therapeutic tool that helps clients process trauma and reconnect with their bodily sensations in a way that fosters healing. It can aid in trauma processing by enabling clients to re-engage with their sexually traumatized selves and integrate these fragmented experiences into their current sense of identity. Furthermore, it supports the re-embodiment process, where clients can re-establish a relationship with their body, often after it has been dissociated or alienated due to trauma.

From a decolonized perspective, body mapping helps to challenge and resist the pathologization of non-Western experiences of trauma. In many cultures, the body is not viewed merely as a biological entity but as a site of social, cultural, and spiritual meaning. This therapeutic intervention is adaptable to a wide range of cultural contexts, and it respects the lived experiences of individuals from diverse global majority communities. For example, in working with clients from African, Middle Eastern, or Indigenous backgrounds, body mapping can be an effective method to address the cultural significance of bodily experiences and to integrate healing practices that are informed by local beliefs and traditions.

This technique also fosters empowerment by giving individuals the tools to express their trauma in ways that are not only safe but creative and transformative. In therapy, this creative engagement with the body encourages patients

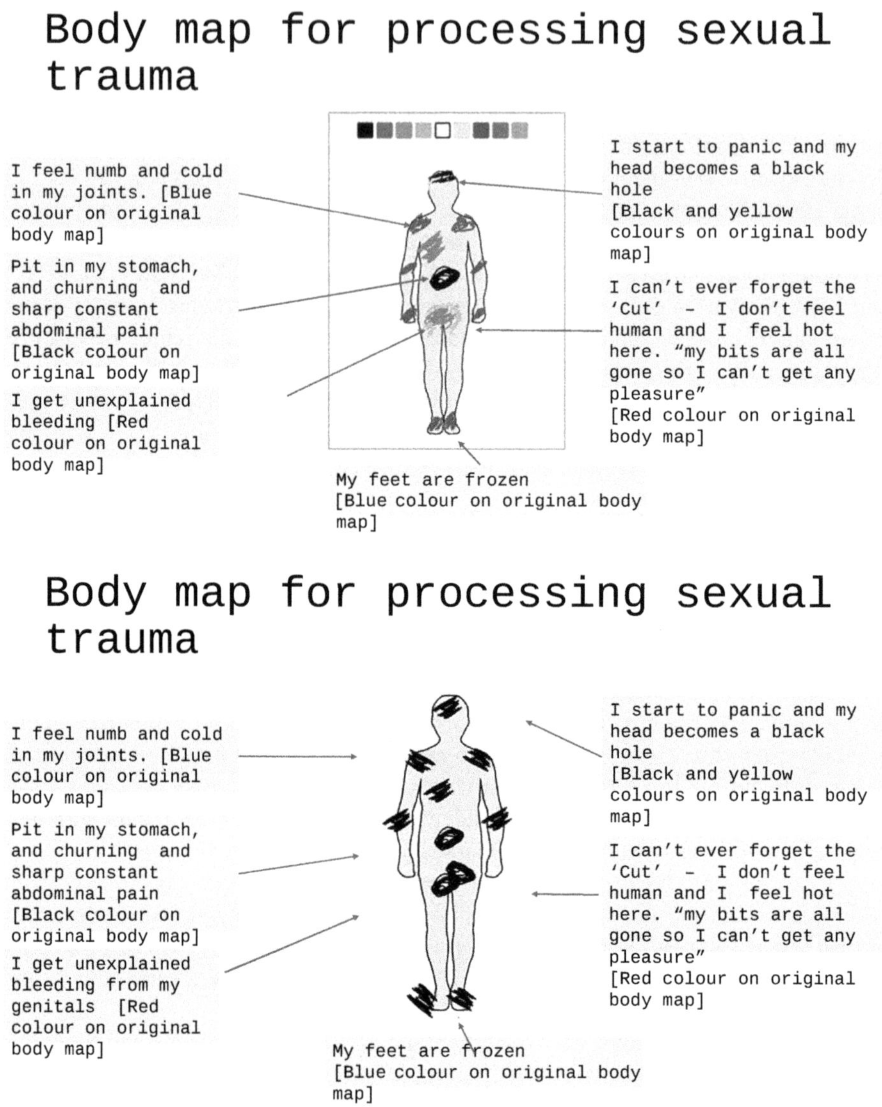

Figure 18.1 Example of a body map completed during sexual trauma processing

to take ownership of their healing process. By externalizing trauma through body mapping, individuals can experience a sense of agency in confronting and processing the hurt they carry. This therapeutic approach also aligns with the broader goals of trauma-informed care, which seek to empower individuals, acknowledge their resilience, and promote autonomy in the healing journey (see Figure 18.1).

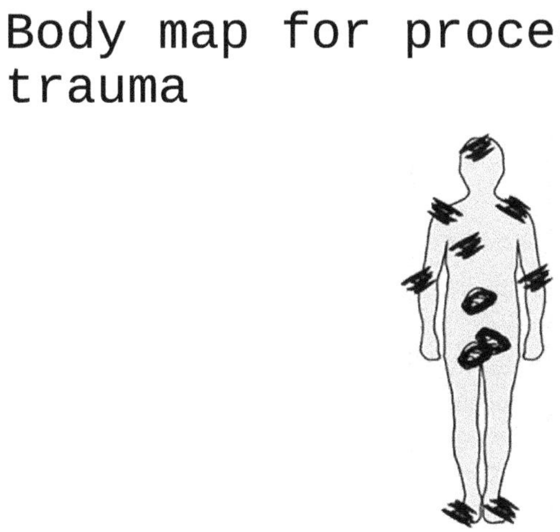

Figure 18.1 (Continued)

In reflecting on Pat's case, we observe the significant prevalence of FGM. As of 2024, UNICEF estimated that worldwide, approximately 230 million girls and women have been subjected to one or more types of FGM. The distribution of this practice is as follows: 144 million in Africa, 80 million in Asia, 6 million in the Middle East, and 1–2 million in other parts of the world (UNICEF, 2024). This vast number highlights the urgent need for culturally responsive and effective therapeutic interventions to support survivors of FGM.

Given the deep-rooted cultural, social, and physical consequences of FGM, it is crucial to provide methods that facilitate open dialogue and promote healing. In this context, using tools like body maps can be incredibly valuable. Body maps offer a culturally appropriate approach to working with embodied trauma, especially when dealing with gender-based trauma and human-rights-related experiences like FGM. The process of body mapping helps survivors express the trauma they've endured in a way that is not only therapeutic but also deeply respectful of their cultural context. It allows individuals to engage with their trauma nonverbally, which is particularly important when words may not fully capture the depth of their experience. This approach enables a safe and accessible space for survivors to begin processing and healing.

Furthermore, the use of body maps across diverse languages and cultural backgrounds offers a powerful, non-verbal means of communication, making it adaptable to different settings and communities. The universal nature of the body mapping technique ensures that survivors of FGM, regardless of language or cultural background, can express their pain and begin to reclaim control over their bodies and their narratives. By integrating body maps into psychosexual therapy, practitioners can offer a more inclusive, culturally competent, and holistic approach to trauma recovery, especially for marginalized communities who may face barriers to traditional forms of verbal therapy.

Implications for Psychosexual and Relationship Therapeutic Practice

Importance of Having an Awareness of the Histo-Socio-Cultural Determinants and Ethics

When working with individuals, couples, and communities from the global majority, it is crucial to maintain an awareness of historical, social, and cultural determinants. These factors include upbringing, sexual relationships, gender norms, broader social contexts, and the law (Popovic, 2006). Understanding these determinants provides an essential foundation for comprehending the lived experiences of those from global majority communities. For example, cultural beliefs about sexuality and relationships are deeply influenced by history and colonial legacies, which often contribute to gender-based oppression and racial trauma. This knowledge is vital for psychosexual therapists to work effectively with diverse populations, ensuring that therapy is grounded in cultural humility and sensitivity.

Furthermore, as ethical practitioners committed to the principle of nonmaleficence (alongside beneficence, autonomy, justice, and fidelity), "doing no harm" is paramount. This ethical obligation means that practitioners cannot afford to ignore or sidestep the dynamics that perpetuate sexual trauma and the "power-over" relationships that often define such trauma. As noted by Charura and Al-Murri (2024), sexual trauma and power imbalances often have deep historical and socio-cultural roots. Therefore, it is essential for therapists to engage critically with the oppressive forces that shape sexual violence, relational dynamics, and psychosexual distress. Without addressing these forces directly, therapy risks reinforcing harmful patterns that maintain inequality and trauma.

The importance of Practitioners Engaging with Antiracist Practice and Having an Awareness of the Intersection of Race, Power Dynamics, and Social Injustice

In our clinical practice, we have frequently encountered the challenge of clients questioning why race needs to be considered in therapeutic work, especially when discussing sexuality. While it is true that all humans share common experiences, it is essential to recognize that race, power dynamics, and social injustice have a significant impact on individuals' sexual experiences and identities. This is particularly true when working with individuals from global majority communities, where racial and gender-based oppression intersects and shapes sexual lives.

Liang (2022) highlights the importance of acknowledging power dynamics within sexual encounters, particularly in BDSM practices. Rather than eliminating power dynamics entirely, an anti-racist approach to BDSM focuses on the ways in which power is scripted and negotiated within relationships. This insight is crucial because sexuality—whether within or outside of BDSM—is not only a private sphere of intimacy but also deeply embedded in societal power structures (Bauer, 2014). To deny the influence of race-based fantasies or to avoid discussing racial power dynamics in intercultural sexual relationships is to ignore the realities of how race and sexuality intersect in complex ways. A refusal to engage with these dynamics perpetuates racial innocence, a false notion that race does not shape sexual experiences or relationships (Liang, 2022).

Furthermore, practitioners must be aware of the microaggressions and intergenerational trauma that clients from marginalized communities experience. These factors not only shape how clients experience their sexuality but also influence how they relate to their bodies, partners, and cultural practices. Engaging with the power dynamics at play allows therapists to develop a more nuanced understanding of the client's experience, leading to better therapeutic outcomes.

We emphasize that psychosexual therapists must challenge colonial discourses that categorize sexual practices from global majority communities as "primitive" or "irrational." These discourses, which originate from a Eurocentric worldview, have historically pathologized non-Western sexual practices. By confronting these harmful ideologies, therapists can create space for more inclusive and affirming therapeutic practices, respecting the sexual diversity and agency of global majority communities.

Taking a Non-Pathologizing Approach and Understanding the Diagnostic Debates and Shifts

The International Classification of Diseases and Related Health Problems, 11th Revision (ICD-11; WHO, 2019), remains the most widely accepted global diagnostic system. However, it is essential to recognize that the conceptualization of sexual behaviors in diagnostic frameworks is constantly evolving. For instance, the Diagnostic and Statistical Manual of Mental Disorders, Fifth Edition (DSM-5; APA, 2013), rejected the concept of "sex addiction" due to insufficient empirical evidence. This decision marked a significant shift in understanding sexual behaviors, with the field moving away from pathologizing sexual desire or expression. The ICD-11 introduced the concept of Compulsive Sexual Behavior Disorder (CSBD) but redefined it not as an addiction but as an impulse control disorder, reflecting the evolving understanding of sexual behaviors and the need for more precise and respectful terminology.

While these shifts are important, it is also crucial to acknowledge the limitations of Western diagnostic systems. These frameworks often fail to consider alternative models, such as the Chinese Classification of Mental Disorders (CCMD-3) or the Azibo Nosology, which provides a culturally specific model of mental health rooted in African-centered psychology (Atwell & Azibo, 1991). These models offer valuable insights into understanding mental health and sexual behavior from perspectives that challenge Western norms. When diagnosis is necessary, it should be accompanied by a thorough assessment that takes into account the cultural, historical, and social contexts of the client's experience.

As Charura et al. (forthcoming) advocate, therapists should adopt a "power-with" stance rather than a "power-over" one. This perspective encourages therapists to engage with clients as partners in the therapeutic process, acknowledging the expertise of both parties. By employing transculturally affirming therapeutic practices, therapists can provide more meaningful and effective support to individuals from diverse cultural backgrounds. Hall (2020) underscores the importance of critically examining how psychosexual therapy developed in Western contexts may need adaptation when working with culturally diverse populations. This includes recognizing the differences in cultural values and belief systems surrounding sexuality, relationships, and identity.

The Invitation to Move Beyond Conventional Systems

Therapists must not be bound by conventional systems that perpetuate a "power-over" approach, which leads to the pathologization of individuals and the denial of their humanity. Instead, psychosexual therapy should be grounded in an understanding of gender, sexual, erotic, and relational diversity (GSERD), acknowledging the intersecting identities and struggles that clients experience. It is vital that therapy moves beyond individualizing sexual issues and addresses the broader societal and historical forces that shape those issues. This approach supports a more comprehensive and compassionate model of therapy that prioritizes cultural humility, social justice, and the dismantling of oppressive systems.

Importance of Demonstrating Critical Social Awareness and Cultural Humility

As highlighted by Hernández and McDowell (2010), fostering an openness to discussing social identity, power, privilege, and cultural humility is essential for building trust and safety in therapeutic relationships. By demonstrating critical social awareness, therapists can create an environment that encourages clients to explore their identities, sexualities, and relational dynamics with greater ease. It is important to remember that cultural expertise is not required in every instance. Instead, therapists should remain curious and open to learning about their clients' unique experiences and cultural contexts.

Part of this openness involves questioning the dominant societal narratives about sexuality, particularly those that frame certain sexual behaviors or practices as deviant or shameful. For example, challenging the phallocentric notion that male sexuality is defined solely by penile erections and vaginal intercourse can help clients explore alternative ways of experiencing sexual pleasure. This process is crucial for clients who, like Ru and Dan, may struggle with shame, guilt, and trauma related to their sexual experiences.

Reducing Gendered Inequality in Sexual Pleasure

Since gender differences in sexual pleasure are not biologically predetermined, it is important to promote a more critical discourse surrounding sexual pleasure. By exploring and challenging existing inequalities, therapists can help to reduce the stigma that women, particularly those from marginalized communities, face when expressing their desires. Research suggests that women, especially those from global majority communities, often encounter significant barriers to sexual pleasure due to cultural, religious, and societal pressures (Laan et al., 2021). By fostering a more inclusive and equitable understanding of sexual pleasure, therapists can contribute to sexual justice movements and empower individuals to embrace their full sexual potential.

Being Culturally Responsive While Challenging Sexual Abuse

Cultural responsiveness does not mean avoiding difficult conversations about sexual abuse or harmful practices. It is crucial for therapists to be aware of harmful cultural practices that may be embedded in certain religious or social systems. For example, clients may present with long-term consequences resulting from harmful cultural or religious practices such as genital mutilation, forced marriages, or restrictive gender roles. By being curious and open to exploring these practices with respect and care, therapists can better understand the root causes of trauma and offer more effective therapeutic interventions.

Moreover, as therapists, it is essential to continuously develop our understanding of evolving sexual practices, rituals, and experiences. By keeping abreast of emerging research and maintaining a commitment to lifelong learning, therapists can ensure that their practices remain relevant, effective, and culturally competent. This commitment to cultural awareness, combined with a deep understanding of trauma, enables therapists to provide holistic and responsive care to clients from diverse backgrounds.

Importance of Supervision and Reflective Practice: Working with Transference and Countertransference Dynamics

In our work, we have come to recognize the significance of supervision and reflective practice in addressing transference and countertransference dynamics. These dynamics are particularly relevant when working with clients from diverse cultural and racial backgrounds, as the therapist's own identity and biases can influence the therapeutic relationship. For example, one of us, as a Black man, often encounters transference where clients project their experiences of cultural oppression onto him. Similarly, the White female therapist may be idealized or devalued based on perceptions of her authority or her ability to understand cultural sexual dynamics.

Supervision provides a space to process these complex dynamics and ensure that they do not interfere with the therapeutic process. Reflective practice allows therapists to examine their own reactions, biases, and assumptions, and to develop a deeper understanding of how their identity impacts their clinical work. This self-awareness is crucial for creating a therapeutic environment that is both respectful and effective.

Conclusion

In conclusion, human sexuality is complex and multifaceted. By adopting a decolonial lens, therapists can better understand the lived experiences of individuals from global majority communities and challenge pathologizing discourses. Through culturally affirming, trauma-informed practices, psychosexual therapists can help clients reclaim their narratives, heal from trauma, and develop healthier, more fulfilling relationships. As the field continues to evolve, it is essential for therapists to remain open to new ideas, approaches, and frameworks that respect the diversity of human experiences and promote social justice and healing.

References

Ade-Serrano, Y., & Nkansa-Dwamena, O. (2025). *Reimagining Race in Psychology* (1st ed.). Routledge. 10.4324/9781003415244

American Psychiatric Association. (2013). *Diagnostic and Statistical Manual of Mental Disorders* (5th ed.; DSM-5). American Psychiatric Publishing.

Anderson-Foster, N. (2023). Black Women and Compulsive Sexual Behavior. *Sexual Health & Compulsivity*, 30(1), 38–56. 10.1080/26929953.2022.2150918

Ansara, Y. G. (2019). Trauma Psychotherapy with People Involved in BDSM/Kink: Five Common Misconceptions and Five Essential Clinical Skills. *Psychotherapy and Counselling Journal of Australia*, 7(2), 1–24. 10.59158/001c.71102

Atwell, I., & Azibo, D. A. y. (1991). Diagnosing Personality Disorder in Africans (Blacks) Using the Azibo Nosology: Two Case Studies. *Journal of Black Psychology*, 17(2), 1–22. 10.1177/00957984910172002

Bauer, R. (2014). *Queer BDSM Intimacies: Critical Consent and Pushing Boundaries* (1st ed.). Palgrave Macmillan. 10.1057/9781137435026

Buckley, S. J. (2003). Undisturbed Birth: Nature's Blueprint for Ease and Ecstasy. *Journal of Prenatal & Perinatal Psychology & Health*, 17(4), 261. www.proquest.com/docview/198724973

Buddhakorale, K. (2013). Clinical Research in Third World Countries. *The Sri Lanka Journal of Venereology*, 1(1), 17. 10.4038/sljv.v1i1.5579

Castillo, K., Reynolds (Taewon Choi), J. D., & Elliot, J. (2024). A Qualitative Study on Biracial Black East Asian American Women and Their Experiences of Hypersexualization. *Qualitative Psychology*, 13(1), 121–141. https://doi.org/10.1037/qup0000312

Charura, D., & Al-Murri, B. (2024). Racial Trauma. In O. Nkansa-Dwamena, & Y. Ade Serrano (Eds.), *Race and Counselling Psychology* (pp. 73–89). Routledge.

Charura, D., & Clyburn, S. (2023). Critical Race Theory: A Methodology for Research in Psychotherapy. In K. Tudor, & J. Wyatt (Eds.), *Reflexive Research for Reflective Practice: Qualitative Research Methodologies for Psychotherapy* (pp. 72–86). Routledge.

Charura, D., & Lago, C. (2021a). *Black Identities + White Therapies* (1st ed.). PCCS Books.

Charura, D., & Lago, C. (2021b). Towards a Decolonised, Psychotherapy Research and Practice. In D. Charura, & C. Lago (Eds.), *Black Identities and White Therapies: Critical Positions and Radical Propositions* (pp. 185–198). PCCS Books.

Charura, D., & Smith, P. (2024). A Duoethnographic Exploration of Relational Psychotraumatology: Research, Training and Practice Considerations. *Counselling & Psychotherapy Research, 24*(3), 972–981. https://doi.org/10.1002/capr.12749

Chen, Y. (2011). *The Many Dimensions of Chinese Feminism* (1st ed.). Palgrave Macmillan US. 10.1057/9780230119185

Cho, S., Crenshaw, K. W., & McCall, L. (2013). Toward a Field of Intersectionality Studies: Theory, Applications, and Praxis. *Signs: Journal of Women in Culture and Society*, 38(4), 785–810. 10.1086/669608

Crenshaw, K. (1991). Mapping the Margins: Intersectionality, Identity Politics, and Violence against Women of Color. *Stanford Law Review*, 43(6), 1241–1299. 10.2307/1229039

Crenshaw, K. W. (1989). Demarginalizing the intersection of race and sex: A Black feminist critique of antidiscrimination doctrine, feminist theory and antiracist politics. *University of Chicago Legal Forum*, 1989(1), 139–167.

Delgado, R., & Stefancic, J. (2001). *Critical Race Theory*. New York University Press.

Delgado, R., & Stefancic, J. (2012). *Critical Race Theory* (2nd ed.). New York University Press.

Fish, M., Shahvisi, A., Gwaambuka, T., Tangwa, G. B., Ncayiyana, D., & Earp, B. D. (2021). A New Tuskegee? Unethical Human Experimentation and Western Neocolonialism in the Mass Circumcision of African Men. *Developing World Bioethics*, 21(4), 211–226. 10.1111/dewb.12285

Fredrickson, B. L., & Roberts, T. (1997). Objectification Theory: Toward Understanding Women's Lived Experiences and Mental Health Risks. *Psychology of Women Quarterly*, 21(2), 173–206. 10.1111/j.1471-6402.1997.tb00108.x

Gregg, R. (2020). On the Video Work of M. Lamar: A White Book for Decolonizing Queer White Fantasia on Black Bodies and Sexuality. *Framework*, 61(1), 85–87. 10.13110/framework.61.1.0085

Hall, K. S. K. (2020). Cultural Issues Impacting the Acceptance of Psychosexual Therapy. In D. L. Rowland & E. A. Jannini (Eds.), *Cultural Differences and the Practice of Sexual Medicine* (pp. 207–219). Springer. https://doi.org/10.1007/978-3-030-36222-5_12

Harris, R., & Crossley, J. (2021). A Systematic Review and Meta-Synthesis Exploring Client Experience of Reflecting Teams in Clinical Practice. *Journal of Family Therapy*, 43(4), 687–710. 10.1111/1467-6427.12346

Hernández, P., & McDowell, T. (2010). Intersectionality, Power, and Relational Safety in Context. *Training and Education in Professional Psychology*, 4(1), 29–35. 10.1037/a0017064

Hudson-Weems, C. (2000). Africana Womanism: An Overview. Out of the Revolution. In J. L. Conyers Jr. (Ed.), *The Development of Africana Studies* (pp. 205–217). New Brunswick, NJ: Transaction Publishers..

Kalafatis-Russell, A. (2021). Doing Kink vs. Being Kinky: A Systematic Scoping Review of the Literature on BDSM Behavior, Orientation, and Identity. (Master's thesis, University of North Florida). UNF Digital Commons. www.proquest.com/docview/2665127153

Laan, E. T. M., Klein, V., Werner, M. A., van Lunsen, R. H. W., & Janssen, E. (2021). In Pursuit of Pleasure: A Biopsychosocial Perspective on Sexual Pleasure and Gender. *International Journal of Sexual Health*, 33(4), 516–536. 10.1080/19317611.2021.1965689

Labrecque, F., Potz, A., Larouche, É, & Joyal, C. C. (2021). What Is So Appealing About Being Spanked, Flogged, Dominated, or Restrained? Answers from Practitioners of Sexual Masochism/Submission. *The Journal of Sex Research*, 58(4), 409–423. 10.1080/00224499.2020.1767025

Lago, C., & Charura, D. (2015). Working with Transgenerational/Intergenerational Trauma: The Implication of Epigenetic Considerations and Transcultural Perspectives in Psychotherapy. *The Psychotherapist Issue*, 59- Spring 2015, 23–25.

Lago, C., & Hirai, T. (2013). Counselling across Difference and Diversity. In M. Cooper, M. O'Hara, P. Schmid & A. C. Bohart (Eds.), *The Handbook of Person-Centred Therapy and Counselling* (2nd ed., pp. 436–452). Palgrave MacMillan.

Liang, M. (2022). Playing with Power: Kink, Race, and Desire. *Sexualities*, 25(4), 381–405. 10.1177/1363460720964063

Mackie-Stephenson, A. (2022). 'Venus Hottentot': Performance Ethnography, the Audience and Resisting Racism. *Research in Drama Education*, 27(1), 67–72. 10.1080/13569783.2021.1962269

Martinez, K. (2021). Overwhelming Whiteness of BDSM: A Critical Discourse Analysis of Racialization in BDSM. *Sexualities*, 24(5–6), 733–748. 10.1177/1363460720932389

Maryland Medical Journal Editors. (1894). Circumcision for the Correction of Sexual Crimes among the Negro Race. *Maryland Medical Journal*, 30(16), 345–346.

Mayberry, L., & Daniel, J. (2016). Birthgasm. *Journal of Holistic Nursing*, 34(4), 331–342. 10.1177/0898010115614205

Nummenmaa, L., Glerean, E., Hari, R., & Hietanen, J. K. (2014). Bodily Maps of Emotions. *Proceedings of the National Academy of Sciences*, 111(2), 646–651. 10.1073/pnas.1321664111

O'Brien, C. V., & Charura, D. (2022). Refugees, Asylum Seekers, and Practitioners' Perspectives of Embodied Trauma: A Comprehensive Scoping Review. *Psychological Trauma*, 15(7), 1115–1127. 10.1037/tra0001342

O'Brien, C. V., & Charura, D. (2024). Body Mapping Refugees and Asylum Seekers' Perspectives of Embodied Trauma: An Innovative Method for Psychotraumatology Research & Practice. *Qualitative Research in Psychology*, 21(1), 71–106. https://doi.org/10.1080/14780887.2023.2289964

Popovic, M. (2006). Psychosexual Diversity as the Best Representation of Human Normality across Cultures. *Sexual and Relationship Therapy*, 21(2), 171–186. 10.1080/14681990500358469

Porges, S. W. (2003). Social Engagement and Attachment: A Phylogenetic Perspective. *Annals of the New York Academy of Sciences*, 1008(1), 31–47. 10.1196/annals.1301.004

Porges, S. W. (2022). Polyvagal Theory: A Science of Safety. *Frontiers in Integrative Neuroscience*, 16, 871227. 10.3389/fnint.2022.871227

Remondino, P. C. (1894). Negro rapes and their social problems. *National Popular Review*, 4(1), 3–6.

Rouse-Arnett, M., & Long Dilworth, J. E. (2006). Early Influences on African American Women's Sexuality. *Journal of Feminist Family Therapy*, 18(3), 39–61. 10.1300/J086v18n03_02

UNICEF. (2024). *Female Genital Mutilation (FGM)*. https://data.unicef.org/topic/child-protection/female-genital-mutilation/. Retrieved 30 March 2024, from https://data.unicef.org/topic/child-protection/female-genital-mutilation/

Volynets, S., Glerean, E., Hietanen, J. K., Hari, R., & Nummenmaa, L. (2020). Bodily Maps of Emotions Are Culturally Universal. *Emotion*, 20(7), 1127–1136. 10.1037/emo0000624

Wiseman, J. (1998). *SM 101: A Realistic Introduction*. Greenery Press.

Wooten, L., Jordan, A., Simon, K. M., & Gold, J. A. (2021). This Is Us: A Case Examination on Black Men in Therapy. *Academic Psychiatry*, 45(6), 763–767. 10.1007/s40596-021-01528-6

World Health Organization. (2019). *International Classification of Diseases and Related Health Problems* (11th ed.; ICD-11). World Health Organization. https://icd.who.int/

Yurtaeva, E., & Charura, D. (2024). Comprehensive Scoping Review of Research on Intercultural Love and Romantic Relationships. *Journal of Social and Personal Relationships*, 41(6), 1654–1676. 10.1177/02654075241228791

Chapter 19

Sexuality in a Moving World: Psychosexual Therapy in the Context of Multicultural Relationships and Migration

Vinicius Jobim Fischer and Alice Einloft Brunnet

Introduction: Sexual Health and Multiculturalism

Sexual health, as defined by the World Health Organization, is not simply the absence of disease or dysfunction but a central aspect of overall health. It encompasses physical, emotional, mental, and social well-being in relation to sexuality, and it requires the possibility of pleasurable and safe sexual experiences that are free of coercion, discrimination, and violence (WHO, 2006). To understand sexual health, it is necessary to consider the broader definition of sexuality itself. According to the WHO, sexuality includes thoughts, fantasies, desires, beliefs, attitudes, values, behaviors, practices, roles, and relationships that are shaped by biology, culture, society, and personal history (WHO, 2017).

This means that sexuality extends far beyond reproduction or sexual functioning. It includes orientation and identity, intimacy and attachment, sexual pleasure, body image, masturbation, communication skills such as the ability to express consent, and even spiritual or moral dimensions (Mollen et al., 2018). Each of these aspects is influenced by the biopsychosocial and cultural environment in which a person grows, lives, and builds relationships.

When two people from different cultural backgrounds come together in an intimate partnership, they bring with them not only individual experiences but also entire sexual systems of beliefs and values. Negotiating these differences often requires adaptation, mutual curiosity, and openness. The task becomes even more complex when couples form in the context of migration, where they must also adjust to a new geographical and cultural environment with its own sexual norms and expectations.

To illustrate this, consider the case of Layla, a 29-year-old woman who fled Syria during the war and resettled in Germany. She met Markus, a German man, through community networks, and after several months they entered a relationship. While the couple shared affection and a desire for intimacy, they struggled with unspoken expectations around sexual initiation. Layla, raised in a conservative context where female modesty was highly valued, felt hesitant to express sexual desire openly. Markus, on the other hand, interpreted her hesitation as lack of attraction or rejection, which left him confused and hurt. In therapy, it became

DOI: 10.4324/9781003611387-19

clear that neither partner lacked interest in intimacy. Instead, they were navigating deeply ingrained cultural scripts about gender roles, sexuality, and communication. For Layla, expressing desire felt shameful. For Markus, not receiving clear signals of interest felt like dismissal. Therapy provided a space where these scripts could be named, respected, and renegotiated.

Stories like Layla and Markus remind us that sexual health cannot be isolated from cultural upbringing, migration history, and relational negotiation. What might seem like a sexual dysfunction in one context may, in fact, be a misalignment of cultural expectations in another. A lack of desire, difficulty with communication, or even conflict over contraception may reflect broader patterns of socialization, stigma, or religious teachings rather than pathology.

For therapists, this highlights the need to view sexuality through a multicultural lens. Multiculturalism is more than simply recognizing difference; it involves cultivating sensitivity to bias, discrimination, and power imbalances, while also respecting the values and experiences that clients bring to therapy (Vera & Speight, 2003; Pieterse, 2009). Within psychosexual therapy, this means building awareness of how cross-cultural dynamics shape intimacy and developing the skills to engage effectively with couples who may be navigating multiple, and sometimes conflicting, cultural frameworks.

This chapter therefore begins with the premise that sexuality is both profoundly personal and deeply social. It argues that psychosexual therapy for multicultural and migrant couples must integrate a biopsychosocial-cultural perspective, one that honors individual stories while also recognizing the broader forces that shape them.

Migration and Sexual Health: Global Context

Migration has become one of the defining features of the modern world. According to the International Organization for Migration, there were approximately 281 million international migrants in 2022, representing 3.6% of the global population (McAuliffe & Oucho, 2024). Within that figure, forced displacement has grown at alarming rates. The United Nations High Commissioner for Refugees reported that by the end of 2022, 117 million people were forcibly displaced, including refugees, asylum seekers, and internally displaced persons. These movements are driven by armed conflict, political instability, persecution, economic inequality, and increasingly by climate change.

Migration is not only a logistical transition but also a deeply personal and relational one. Migrants often carry the burden of pre-migration trauma, such as war, persecution, or family separation, while also facing post-migration challenges that include language barriers, insecure legal status, economic hardship, and discrimination (Aragona & Pucci, 2012; Jurado et al., 2017). These stressors can impact not only mental health but also sexual health and intimate relationships.

Sexuality is particularly sensitive to these pressures because it is tied to cultural scripts, values, and social norms. When individuals move to a new country, they encounter different ideas about intimacy, gender roles, consent, and family structures. For some, this is liberating, offering opportunities to express aspects of their sexuality that were previously suppressed. For others, it creates conflict, confusion, or even guilt, especially when navigating competing expectations from their culture of origin and the host society (Cook & Waite, 2016; Dean et al., 2017).

Consider the story of Ahmed and Noor, a married couple who fled Afghanistan and resettled in the United Kingdom. In Afghanistan, Ahmed had been the primary decision-maker in the household, while Noor's social role was largely limited to the private sphere. After resettlement, Noor began attending English classes and gradually gained confidence, independence, and exposure to new cultural norms about gender equality. She expressed interest in negotiating aspects of intimacy and contraception, topics that had previously been taboo in their marriage. Ahmed, struggling with unemployment and loss of his social status, experienced her growing independence as a threat. Their sexual relationship became strained, not because of a lack of affection but because of a clash between traditional scripts and new roles shaped by migration. In therapy, the focus shifted from identifying dysfunction to supporting both partners in renegotiating their expectations and identities in the context of their new environment.

This example reflects what scholars describe as acculturation stress. Acculturation theory suggests that migrants adapt to new cultural contexts through two processes: adopting elements of the host culture and maintaining elements of the origin culture (Sam & Berry, 2010). The tension between these two movements can affect how couples negotiate intimacy, gender roles, and sexual practices.

For many migrants, particularly those from conservative or collectivist societies, intergenerational conflicts also emerge. Younger family members may embrace aspects of the host culture more readily, including attitudes toward dating, sexual orientation, or reproductive autonomy, while older generations may see these shifts as a threat to tradition. Within couples, this can translate into disagreements about sexual education for children, expectations of fidelity, or the acceptability of premarital intimacy.

These challenges are compounded for LGBTQI+ migrants and refugees. Many flee their countries of origin precisely because of criminalization, stigma, or violence related to their sexual orientation or gender identity. Yet arrival in a new country does not always bring safety. LGBTQI+ migrants often face systemic discrimination in asylum procedures, lack of culturally competent healthcare, and exposure to new forms of marginalization in host societies (Nematy, Namer, & Razum, 2023). Detention facilities may place transgender individuals in unsafe environments, and the absence of supportive networks can intensify isolation. For these individuals, psychosexual therapy must attend not only to personal well-being but also to the broader structural forces that constrain their lives.

Several theoretical frameworks help illuminate these dynamics. Acculturation theory explains how individuals balance continuity with change in their cultural identities. Minority stress theory, originally developed in LGBTQ research, highlights the psychological burden that comes from living under conditions of stigma, prejudice, and discrimination (Meyer, 2003). For migrants, particularly those who are also racial or sexual minorities, the cumulative impact of minority stress can lead to elevated risks of depression, anxiety, and relational conflict. Cultural scripts theory further deepens our understanding by showing how sexual meanings and practices are guided by socially constructed narratives about masculinity, femininity, desire, and family roles (Simon & Gagnon, 1986). When partners bring different scripts into a relationship, mismatches can arise that require explicit negotiation.

Taken together, these perspectives remind us that sexual health in migration is never just about individual behavior. It is about the interaction between personal history, relational context, and the wider socio-political environment. For therapists, this means that working with migrant and multicultural couples requires an integrated approach that acknowledges trauma, migration stress, identity renegotiation, and the powerful influence of cultural narratives on intimacy and desire.

Cultural Dimensions of Sexuality in Migration

Culture is often described as the set of values, beliefs, customs, and practices that are shared by a group of people and passed down from one generation to the next. While this definition provides a useful starting point, it can also suggest that culture is fixed or uniform. In reality, culture is dynamic. It is constantly being reshaped through social interactions, generational change, and exposure to new contexts. Individuals within the same cultural group can have very different interpretations of its norms, and people adapt cultural teachings according to personal experience and circumstances (Causadias, Vitriol, & Atkin, 2018).

This dynamic quality is particularly visible in the realm of sexuality. Sexual beliefs and practices are shaped by multiple layers of cultural influence. Legal systems regulate marriage, divorce, and the age of consent. Religious institutions provide moral frameworks about sexual activity, contraception, and reproductive roles. Media portrayals of attractiveness and desirability shape expectations about romance and intimacy. Families and local communities communicate values about modesty, fidelity, and gender roles, often through silence as much as through direct instruction (Agocha, Asencio, & Decena, 2014). In migration contexts, individuals may find themselves caught between different and sometimes contradictory sets of expectations.

Elena's story illustrates this tension. Elena, a 33-year-old Catholic woman from Mexico, had grown up with the belief that contraception should be avoided because it interfered with God's plan for marriage and family. When she moved to Sweden for graduate studies, she met Jonas, a secular Swedish man who was strongly committed to gender equality and sexual autonomy. When they entered a relationship, Jonas assumed that discussions about contraception and family planning would be straightforward. For him, using contraception was both practical and responsible, ensuring that children would arrive when both partners felt prepared. Elena, however, felt deep internal conflict. On one hand, she wanted to share a future with Jonas and valued his perspective. On the other, she carried guilt and anxiety about violating her religious teachings. The couple found themselves in repeated arguments, not because of lack of love but because of the collision of two cultural systems around sexuality and family life. In therapy, both partners worked on understanding that their difficulties were not personal failings but reflections of deeply embedded cultural narratives. This recognition allowed them to approach the conversation with greater compassion and creativity.

Situations like Elena and Jonas's are far from rare. Couples across cultures differ in how relationships are formed, how partners are chosen, and how sexuality is expressed before and after marriage. In some contexts, arranged marriages or family involvement in partner choice are the norm, while in others individual romantic choice is expected. Dating practices, acceptable levels of public affection, and the legitimacy of premarital sex vary widely. For migrants, these differences are often magnified because they may be living in societies where host culture practices clash with those of their upbringing. This can lead to confusion, secrecy, or conflict within couples, particularly if one partner adapts more quickly to the host culture than the other.

It is also important to recognize that the level of distress attached to sexual or relational problems varies across cultures. In some societies, lack of desire or sexual dissatisfaction may be a source of shame, guilt, or even social ostracism, while in others it may be minimized or considered a private matter that does not require professional intervention. For example, in many collectivist cultures, fertility and reproductive capacity are given priority over personal sexual pleasure, and difficulties with arousal or orgasm may not be viewed as significant unless they interfere with childbearing. In more individualistic cultures, personal satisfaction and open communication about sexual pleasure may be emphasized, and sexual difficulties can quickly become central to a couple's sense of well-being (Hall, 2019).

For therapists, these variations require cultural humility. There is no single universal model of sexual health or relationship satisfaction. As Dermer and colleagues (2021) remind us, no cultural belief system is inherently superior to another. What matters most is the ability of couples to create consensual, respectful, and realistic expectations that are meaningful to them. This requires practitioners to suspend judgment and avoid imposing their own cultural values, while still upholding ethical principles such as consent, equality, and safety.

In migration contexts, the dual process of acculturation adds complexity. Migrants must balance two movements: adopting aspects of the host culture and maintaining elements of their culture of origin (Sam & Berry, 2010). Some individuals lean toward full assimilation, embracing the norms and behaviors of their new society. Others prefer separation, holding tightly to their original cultural practices. Still others seek integration, blending aspects of both cultures, or marginalization, where they feel disconnected from both. Each of these strategies has implications for sexual identity, intimacy, and family life. For example, a couple that integrates both cultures may develop hybrid practices around dating, communication, and family planning that allow them to feel grounded in their heritage while also adapting to their new environment.

Ultimately, cultural dimensions of sexuality in migration remind us that intimate relationships are never just personal. They are situated within larger social narratives that carry powerful emotional weight. Therapy in this context is not about erasing difference but about helping partners understand and navigate their cultural scripts with curiosity, respect, and a willingness to adapt. When couples are able to name and negotiate these influences, they often find that what once felt like a source of conflict becomes a foundation for growth and deeper connection.

Psychosexual Therapy Strategies in Multicultural Contexts

Psychosexual therapy is most effective when it is grounded in the biopsychosocial model of health, which emphasizes the interplay between biological, psychological, and social factors (Pascoal & Raposo, 2023). In the context of migration and multicultural relationships, it is important to extend this framework to include sociocultural factors as well. Sexuality is never experienced in a vacuum. It is shaped by cultural scripts, religious traditions, gender norms, and societal expectations, all of which influence how clients perceive their difficulties and how they approach therapy.

One of the most important elements of therapy in these contexts is the therapeutic alliance. Couples often arrive with feelings of shame, confusion, or mistrust, particularly if they have been raised in environments where sexuality was stigmatized or considered taboo. A therapist who approaches clients with empathy, openness, and cultural humility creates a foundation for safety. This allows partners to share concerns that they may have never expressed before, even to each other. Research consistently shows that therapeutic alliance is one of the strongest predictors of positive outcomes in psychotherapy, and this is especially true when cultural differences are involved (Anderson, Bautista, & Hope, 2018).

The first step in psychosexual therapy is a careful assessment. The therapist must work with the couple to clarify whether the primary concern is a sexual disorder, a relational difficulty, or a cultural difference that has become a source of tension. For example, a lack of sexual desire may reflect an individual sexual health issue in one case, but in another it may reflect cultural or religious norms that do not place emphasis on sexual pleasure. Identifying the source of the problem is crucial to tailoring treatment effectively.

Psychoeducation is often a vital starting point. Many couples carry sexual myths or misconceptions that perpetuate distress. For instance, the belief that penetrative intercourse is the only valid form of sex, or the assumption that men are always ready for sex while women are naturally passive, can place unnecessary strain on relationships. By offering accurate, accessible information about sexual response, anatomy, and communication, therapists can reduce shame and open pathways for healthier intimacy. Resources such as multilingual sexual health platforms (e.g., Zanzu.be) can be valuable tools in this process.

Religion, patriarchy, and stigma frequently play a central role in the difficulties that multicultural or migrant couples face. In many contexts, sexual desire is tightly regulated through religious teachings or family expectations, and deviation from these norms can evoke guilt or conflict. Patriarchal systems may reinforce unequal power dynamics between partners, which can limit open communication about needs and boundaries. Stigma, particularly around topics such as masturbation, homosexuality, or contraception, can leave individuals struggling in silence.

A case example illustrates this well. Nadia, a 27-year-old Pakistani woman, sought therapy with her husband because of a persistent discrepancy in sexual desire. She had grown up with strict religious prohibitions against masturbation and had been taught that female sexual desire was shameful. Her husband, raised in a more permissive environment, was comfortable with self-exploration and expected open discussions about intimacy. Nadia often avoided sexual activity, not because she lacked affection for her partner, but because the idea of expressing desire felt transgressive. In therapy, both partners began to explore how religious teachings had shaped their expectations and how these differences were now playing out in their marriage. With psychoeducation, normalization, and structured communication exercises, Nadia was able to begin reframing her beliefs, while her husband learned to approach her experiences with greater patience and respect. The process allowed them to develop new ways of connecting that honored both partners' values.

Therapists working with multicultural couples can benefit from keeping in mind some key principles for culturally sensitive practice. These principles can be summarized in Figure 19.1.

1. Recognize culture as central to clients' sexual values and behaviors
2. Build therapeutic alliance through empathy and cultural humility
3. Explore both individual identity and cultural scripts shaping sexuality
4. Respect differences while upholding universal principles of consent and safety
5. Use accessible and multilingual resources when appropriate
6. Involve both partners actively in goal-setting and treatment planning
7. Remain reflexive about the therapist's own cultural assumptions

When working with couples, guided exploration can help uncover hidden cultural dynamics influencing their sexual lives. Table 19.1 outlines some questions that can support this process.

Therapists also benefit from practical reminders of what to do and what to avoid. Table 19.2 summarizes culturally sensitive therapy practices in a simple format.

In sum, psychosexual therapy in multicultural contexts requires therapists to go beyond a standard biomedical or psychological model. It asks them to step into the complex intersection of personal history, cultural background, and relational negotiation. By combining careful assessment, psychoeducation, cultural sensitivity, and structured therapeutic tools, therapists can support couples in transforming

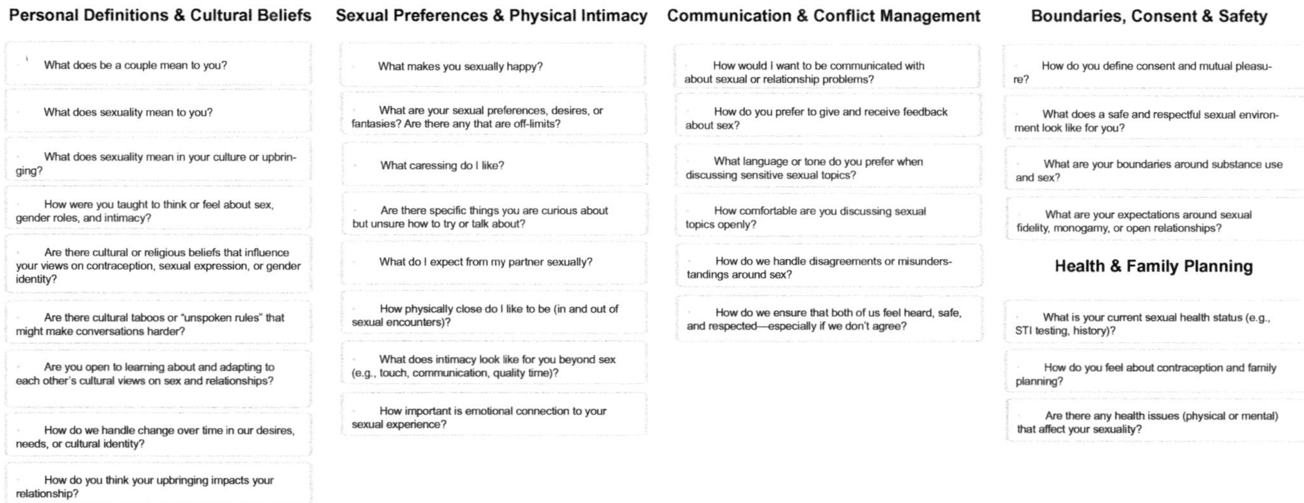

Figure 19.1 Key principles for culturally sensitive psychosexual therapy practice

Personal Definitions & Cultural Beliefs

- What does be a couple mean to you?
- What does sexuality mean to you?
- What does sexuality mean in your culture or upbringing?
- How were you taught to think or feel about sex, gender roles, and intimacy?
- Are there cultural or religious beliefs that influence your views on contraception, sexual expression, or gender identity?
- Are there cultural taboos or "unspoken rules" that might make conversations harder?
- Are you open to learning about and adapting to each other's cultural views on sex and relationships?
- How do we handle change over time in our desires, needs, or cultural identity?
- How do you think your upbringing impacts your relationship?

Figure 19.1 (Continued)

cultural differences from sources of conflict into opportunities for deeper understanding and connection.

Therapeutic Focal Points

While every therapeutic encounter is unique, there are recurring themes that often guide the work with multicultural or migrant couples. Organizing therapy strategies around these focal points helps therapists remain attentive to the multiple layers of influence on sexual health. Three of the most critical areas are open

Sexual Preferences & Physical Intimacy

- What makes you sexually happy?
- What are your sexual preferences, desires, or fantasies? Are there any that are off-limits?
- What caressing do I like?
- Are there specific things you are curious about but unsure how to try or talk about?
- What do I expect from my partner sexually?
- How physically close do I like to be (in and out of sexual encounters)?
- What does intimacy look like for you beyond sex (e.g., touch, communication, quality time)?
- How important is emotional connection to your sexual experience?

Figure 19.1 (Continued)

communication, intimacy, and treatment planning. Each of these requires cultural sensitivity as well as flexibility in approach.

Open Communication

One of the most common barriers couples face when addressing sexual concerns is a lack of open communication. Shame, guilt, and fear of rejection frequently silence conversations about intimacy. In many cultures, sexuality is surrounded by secrecy. Parents may avoid discussing it with children, religious communities may present it in purely moralistic terms, and families may reinforce the idea that sexual concerns should never be spoken of outside the home. These lessons carry forward into adulthood and often prevent partners from sharing their needs or anxieties with one another.

Therapy can serve as a corrective space where these silences are gently challenged. A central role of the therapist is to create an environment where it is safe to talk about topics that have long been hidden. This involves more than simply

Communication & Conflict Management

- How would I want to be communicated with about sexual or relationship problems?
- How do you prefer to give and receive feedback about sex?
- What language or tone do you prefer when discussing sensitive sexual topics?
- How comfortable are you discussing sexual topics openly?
- How do we handle disagreements or misunderstandings around sex?
- How do we ensure that both of us feel heard, safe, and respected—especially if we don't agree?

Boundaries, Consent & Safety

- How do you define consent and mutual pleasure?
- What does a safe and respectful sexual environment look like for you?
- What are your boundaries around substance use and sex?
- What are your expectations around sexual fidelity, monogamy, or open relationships?

Figure 19.1 (Continued)

asking questions. It requires building trust, normalizing discomfort, and explicitly validating that discussing sexuality is not shameful. In such a space, couples begin to experiment with naming their desires, disappointments, and worries.

A vignette illustrates this challenge. Farah, a young woman of Moroccan heritage, and David, her partner of mixed Irish and Jamaican background, came to

Health & Family Planning

- What is your current sexual health status (e.g., STI testing, history)?

- How do you feel about contraception and family planning?

- Are there any health issues (physical or mental) that affect your sexuality?

Figure 19.1 (Continued)

Table 19.1 Guiding Questions for Multicultural Couples' Exploration of Sexuality

Domain	*Guiding questions*
Personal definitions and beliefs	How do you each define sexuality? What messages did you receive about sex growing up?
Sexual preferences and intimacy	What kinds of intimacy feel natural or comfortable to you? Which practices feel unfamiliar or uncomfortable?
Communication and conflict management	How do you usually discuss disagreements? Are there cultural differences in how you express needs?
Boundaries, consent, and safety	What does consent mean to each of you? How do you signal yes or no in intimate settings?
Health and family planning	How do you view contraception, fertility, or family planning? How are these shaped by your cultural or religious background?

therapy to discuss recurring arguments about contraception. Farah had grown up in a family where conversations about sexual health were absent, and contraception was never mentioned. David, by contrast, had learned from an early age that discussing contraception was part of responsible adulthood. Whenever David brought up the topic, Farah felt overwhelmed by embarrassment, interpreting the conversation as evidence of distrust or accusation. David, in turn, felt frustrated that something he saw as essential to mutual care could not be spoken about. In therapy, the couple worked through structured communication exercises where Farah practiced expressing her discomfort in small steps, while David learned to approach the subject with sensitivity rather than frustration. Over time, what had been a silent and painful conflict became an opportunity for greater connection and shared responsibility.

Table 19.2 Culturally Sensitive Therapy Do's and Don'ts Summary

Do's	*Don'ts*
Acknowledge and respect cultural values	Assume all clients from a culture share the same beliefs
Foster open, non-judgmental communication	Dismiss cultural concerns as irrelevant
Tailor interventions to cultural context	Impose your own cultural norms
Engage in continual cultural competence training	Overgeneralize based on ethnicity or background
Use interpreters when needed for clarity	Ignore power dynamics within relationships

Therapists can help couples build adaptive strategies for communication, such as mindful listening, reappraisal, problem-solving, and gradual disclosure. These skills not only support sexual health but also strengthen overall relationship resilience.

Intimacy

Intimacy is more than physical closeness. It is a process of mutual disclosure and empathic response. According to the interpersonal process model of intimacy (Laurenceau, Barrett, & Rovine, 2005), intimacy is built when one partner shares personal experiences, emotions, or vulnerabilities, and the other responds in a way that communicates understanding, validation, and care.

In the context of sexual and relational difficulties, intimacy becomes especially important (Bergeron, Vaillancourt-Morel, Péloquin, & Rosen, 2024). When couples feel distant or misunderstood, sexual problems can quickly become magnified. For example, low desire may feel like rejection, or sexual pain may be misinterpreted as lack of interest. Working on intimacy allows couples to approach these difficulties with compassion rather than blame.

Therapy can focus on helping couples strengthen empathy and perspective-taking. This may involve guided exercises where partners practice responding to disclosures with validation rather than judgment, or mindfulness-based interventions that encourage partners to remain present during intimate interactions. When couples learn to recognize and appreciate the positive aspects of their sexual and relational lives, they often find it easier to navigate challenges without escalating conflict.

Treatment Planning

A clear treatment plan provides structure and direction for therapy. The evaluation phase is the foundation. Here, the therapist explores both the sexual and relational issues presented and the cultural context that surrounds them. The Cultural Formulation Interview (CFI) in the DSM-5 offers a valuable framework for this assessment. The CFI guides clinicians to ask about the client's definition of the problem, cultural perceptions of its cause, sources of support, and past help-seeking behaviors (American Psychiatric Association, 2022). Using this tool in psychosexual therapy helps uncover the cultural narratives and expectations that shape how couples understand their challenges.

Once the evaluation is complete, the therapist and couple move into the delimitation of goals. This stage requires careful attention. Goals must be meaningful to both partners, realistic within their cultural frameworks, and flexible enough to adapt as therapy progresses. Involving both partners actively in this process fosters ownership and commitment to change.

Interventions usually begin with psychoeducation. Providing accurate, accessible information about sexuality helps dismantle myths and creates a shared language for the couple. From there, cognitive restructuring can be introduced. This involves identifying and questioning unhelpful beliefs about sexuality, such as rigid gender roles or assumptions about what "normal" sex should look like.

Homework assignments often play a central role in treatment. Couples may be invited to engage in specific activities outside of therapy, such as practicing non-sexual intimacy, experimenting with new ways of expressing desire, or using structured communication exercises to discuss sensitive topics. These assignments provide opportunities to translate insights from therapy into lived experience.

The outcomes of this process typically include increased sexual knowledge, stronger communication skills, greater confidence in managing conflict, and an enhanced sense of self-efficacy. Couples often leave therapy with not only improved sexual functioning but also a more resilient partnership.

Taken together, open communication, intimacy, and structured treatment planning form the backbone of psychosexual therapy in multicultural contexts. Each requires sensitivity to cultural background while also supporting couples in building the tools they need for mutual understanding and fulfillment. When therapy succeeds in these areas, couples often find that cultural differences become less of a barrier and more of an opportunity for growth.

Ethical Considerations

Working with multicultural and migrant couples in the realm of psychosexual therapy involves a set of ethical challenges that are both complex and deeply personal. Sexuality is one of the most intimate aspects of human life, yet it is also profoundly shaped by cultural values, religious teachings, and social expectations. When cultural norms appear to conflict with principles of sexual health and human rights, therapists may find themselves in ethically delicate territory. The responsibility in such cases is to respect cultural diversity while also protecting the dignity, autonomy, and well-being of the individuals involved.

One of the key tensions arises from the balance between cultural relativism and universal human rights. Cultural relativism reminds us that beliefs and practices must be understood within their own cultural context, and it cautions against imposing outside standards. However, if applied uncritically, cultural relativism can lead to the toleration of practices that harm individuals, particularly women, LGBTQI+ people, and those in positions of reduced power. On the other hand, universal human rights, such as those outlined in the World Association for Sexual Health's Declaration of Sexual Rights (WAS, 2014), assert that every person has the right to sexual health, sexual pleasure, freedom from coercion and violence, and access to accurate information and services. For therapists, holding these two perspectives together requires discernment and humility.

Consider the ethical dilemmas that arise around gender roles. In some cultures, strict divisions of labor and authority between men and women are considered normal and even necessary. Within therapy, this may present as a husband expecting sexual availability from his wife regardless of her own desire, or a wife feeling unable to discuss contraception without fear of judgment. Similarly, issues surrounding LGBTQI+ identities can become ethically complex. Some clients may come from backgrounds where same-sex relationships or gender diversity are stigmatized or criminalized. A therapist who is too cautious may inadvertently reinforce silence, while one who is too forceful risks alienating clients or appearing to disrespect their cultural heritage.

Coercive practices, such as forced marriage, marital rape, or denial of reproductive autonomy, present even more urgent ethical challenges. In such cases, therapists must be clear that cultural differences do not excuse harm. Upholding clients' safety and autonomy is paramount, even if this involves gently but firmly challenging long-held beliefs or confronting harmful dynamics within the couple. These situations require careful navigation, since overt confrontation can sometimes lead to ruptures in the therapeutic alliance. A trauma-informed approach is particularly important here, as it ensures that clients feel safe, respected, and empowered rather than judged or pressured.

Strategies for addressing these dilemmas include psychoeducation, empowerment, and careful attention to context. Psychoeducation allows therapists to provide accurate information about sexual health in ways that respect cultural values while still challenging myths that perpetuate harm. For example, explaining the physiological realities of female sexual desire or reproductive health can open doors to conversations that clients had previously avoided. Empowerment involves helping clients recognize their right to make choices about their bodies and relationships, even when cultural scripts suggest otherwise. This does not mean pushing clients to abandon their beliefs, but rather supporting them in finding ways to navigate those beliefs while preserving their sense of agency.

Supervision and training in cultural humility are essential for therapists working in this space. No practitioner is immune to personal biases, and ethical dilemmas often evoke strong emotional responses. Supervision provides a forum for reflection, guidance, and accountability. Cultural humility, in turn, emphasizes that competence is not a fixed achievement but an ongoing process of learning, self-reflection, and openness to correction. By approaching therapy with humility, therapists are more likely to recognize the limits of their own knowledge and to remain curious about the cultural frameworks that shape their clients' experiences.

Ethical practice in multicultural psychosexual therapy therefore involves a balancing act. Therapists must hold respect for cultural diversity in one hand and commitment to universal principles of human rights in the other. They must be willing to sit with the discomfort of these tensions while remaining steadfast in protecting the well-being of their clients. When handled with sensitivity, transparency, and humility, these ethical challenges do not become obstacles but rather opportunities for growth, both for clients and for therapists themselves.

Conclusion

Migration and multiculturalism bring unique challenges to intimate relationships, but they also carry enormous potential for growth. When individuals from different cultural, religious, or linguistic backgrounds come together, they are invited to navigate not only their personal histories but also the legacies of entire social systems. Sexuality, which is deeply shaped by cultural scripts, becomes one of the most sensitive areas of negotiation. Couples may face conflicts around gender roles, family expectations, or sexual practices, and these conflicts are often intensified by the stresses of migration. Yet within these struggles also lies the opportunity to expand perspectives, to learn new ways of being intimate, and to co-create shared meanings around sexuality that reflect both continuity and change.

Culturally sensitive psychosexual therapy is not simply an added benefit in this process. It is essential for ethical and effective care. Without attention to cultural context, therapy risks misunderstanding clients' concerns, mislabeling cultural differences as dysfunctions, or imposing values that feel alienating. A therapist who approaches multicultural couples with empathy, curiosity, and humility can help transform difference from a source of distress into a foundation for resilience. By creating a space where couples can articulate their values and negotiate their sexual lives with honesty, therapy becomes not only a clinical intervention but also a site of healing and empowerment.

The strategies outlined in this chapter underscore the importance of focusing on open communication, intimacy, and structured treatment planning. Communication allows partners to break through silence and shame, intimacy creates the conditions for empathy and validation, and treatment planning ensures that therapy remains grounded, collaborative, and goal-oriented. Through these processes, couples gain tools to manage conflict, deepen their understanding of one another, and sustain fulfilling intimate lives.

At the heart of this work is the principle of empowerment. Psychosexual therapy in multicultural contexts is not about prescribing a single model of sexuality or intimacy. It is about supporting couples as they construct meanings that feel authentic to them while ensuring that these meanings uphold respect, safety, and mutual consent. Whether a couple chooses to maintain traditions, adapt to new cultural expectations, or create hybrid practices, the role of the therapist is to validate their choices and help them navigate the complexities with clarity and confidence.

The implications of this work reach beyond individual couples. In increasingly diverse societies, culturally sensitive psychosexual therapy contributes to broader goals of inclusion, justice, and collective well-being. It challenges systems of stigma and discrimination that marginalize migrants, racial and ethnic minorities, and LGBTQI+ communities. It affirms that sexual rights are human rights, and that every person deserves the opportunity to experience intimacy and pleasure without fear or shame. By addressing sexuality in the context of migration and multiculturalism, therapists also participate in building more equitable and compassionate societies.

In conclusion, migration and multiculturalism add complexity to sexual and relational lives, but they also open the possibility of richer, more expansive forms of intimacy. Culturally sensitive psychosexual therapy, grounded in humility, empathy, and ethical commitment, offers a pathway for couples to navigate these complexities with resilience and creativity. By empowering individuals to co-create shared meanings, build deeper intimacy, and sustain respect within their partnerships, this therapeutic approach honors both the diversity of human experience and the universal need for connection.

References

Agocha VB, Asencio M, Decena CU. Sexuality and culture. In: DL Tolman, LM Diamond, JA Bauermeister, WH George, JG Pfaus, LM Ward (eds), *APA Handbook of Sexuality and Psychology*. Washington: APA; 2014. Vol. 2:183–228.

American Psychiatric Association. *Diagnostic and Statistical Manual of Mental Disorders*, fifth edition, text revision. Washington: American Psychiatric Association; 2022.

Anderson KN, Bautista CL, Hope DA. Therapeutic alliance, cultural competence and minority status in premature termination of psychotherapy. *Am J Orthopsychiatry*. 2018; 89(1):104–14.

Aragona M, Pucci D. Post-migration living difficulties as a significant risk factor for PTSD in immigrants: a primary care study. *Ital J Public Health*. 2012; 9:1–8. https://doi.org/10.2427/7525

Bergeron S, Vaillancourt-Morel MP, Péloquin K, Rosen NO. Intimacy promotes couples' sexual well-being on a daily basis and over one year: the role of positive sexual cues. *Arch Sex Behav*. 2024; 53(7):2737–49. https://doi.org/10.1007/s10508-024-02912-7

Causadias JM, Vitriol JA, Atkin AL. Do we overemphasize the role of culture in the behavior of racial/ethnic minorities? Evidence of a cultural (mis)attribution bias in American psychology. *Am Psychol*. 2018; 73(3):243. https://doi.org/10.1037/amp0000099

Cook J, Waite L. "I think I'm more free with them"—conflict, negotiation and change in intergenerational relations in African families living in Britain. *J Ethn Migr Stud*. 2016; 42(8):1388–402. https://doi.org/10.1080/1369183X.2015.1073578

Dean J, Mitchell M, Stewart D, Debattista J. Intergenerational variation in sexual health attitudes and beliefs among Sudanese refugee communities in Australia. *Cult Health Sex*. 2017; 19(1):17–31. https://doi.org/10.1080/13691058.2016.1184316

Dermer SB, Dunham SM, Mercer ME. Utilizing a human rights perspective to train therapists in sexuality and sexual wellness. *Athens J Soc Sci*. 2021; 8(3):169–80. https://doi.org/10.30958/ajss.8-3-1

Hall KSK. Cultural differences in the treatment of sex problems. *Curr Sex Health Rep*. 2019; 11:29–34. https://doi.org/10.1007/s11930-019-00189-9

Jurado D, Alarcón RD, Martínez-Ortega JM, et al. Factors associated with psychological distress or common mental disorders in migrant populations across the world. *Rev Psiquiatr Salud Ment (Engl Ed)*. 2017; 10:45–56. https://doi.org/10.1016/j.rpsmen.2017.02.004

Laurenceau J-P, Barrett LF, Rovine MJ. The interpersonal process model of intimacy in marriage: a daily-diary and multilevel modeling approach. *J Fam Psychol*. 2005; 19(2):314–23. https://doi.org/10.1037/0893-3200.19.2.314

McAuliffe M, Oucho LA, editors. *World Migration Report 2024*. Geneva: International Organization for Migration (IOM); 2024.

Meyer IH. Prejudice, social stress, and mental health in lesbian, gay, and bisexual populations: Conceptual issues and research evidence. *Psychol Bull*. 2003; 129(5):674–97. https://doi.org/10.1037/0033-2909.129.5.674

Mollen D, Burnes T, Lee S, Abbott DM. Sexuality training in counseling psychology. *Couns Psychol Q*. 2020; 33(3):1–18. https://doi.org/10.1080/09515070.2018.1553146

Nematy A, Namer Y, Razum O. LGBTQI+ refugees' and asylum seekers' mental health: a qualitative systematic review. *Sex Res Soc Policy*. 2023; 20:636–63. https://doi.org/10.1007/s13178-022-00705-y

Pascoal PM, Raposo CF. How sexual problems are managed (by other professionals). In: S Geuens, AP Mivšek, WL Gianotten (eds), *Midwifery and Sexuality*. Cham: Springer; 2023. pp. 345–54. https://doi.org/10.1007/978-3-031-18432-1_29

Pieterse A, Evans S, Risner-Butner A, Collins N, Mason L. Multicultural competence and social justice training in counseling psychology and counselor education. *Couns Psychol*. 2009; 37(1):93–115. https://doi.org/10.1177/0011000008319986

Sam DL, Berry JW. Acculturation: when individuals and groups of different cultural backgrounds meet. *Perspect Psychol Sci*. 2010; 5:472–81. https://doi.org/10.1177/1745691610373075

Simon W, Gagnon JH. Sexual scripts: Permanence and change. *Arch Sex Behav*. 1986; 15:97–120. https://doi.org/10.1007/BF01542219

Song SJ, Kaplan C, Tol WA, Subica AM, de Jong JTVM. Psychological distress in torture survivors: pre- and post-migration risk factors in a US sample. *Soc Psychiatry Psychiatr Epidemiol*. 2015; 50:549–60. http://dx.doi.org/10.1007/s00127-014-0982-1

World Association for Sexual Health. Declaration of Sexual Rights [Internet]. 2014 [cited 2025 May 17]. Available from: www.worldsexualhealth.net/was-declaration-on-sexual-rights

World Health Organization. *Defining Sexual Health: Report of a Technical Consultation on Sexual Health*, 28–31 January 2002. Geneva: WHO; 2006.

World Health Organization, UNDP/UNFPA/UNICEF/WHO/World Bank Special Programme. *Sexual Health and Its Linkages to Reproductive Health: An Operational Approach*. Geneva: WHO; 2017.

Chapter 20

Sexual Culture of the Hans in Ancient China and Its Development

ML Ng

Introduction: The Early Chinese Sexual Culture

Similar to many ancient ethnic groups, the ancient sexual culture of the Chinese Hans, the major ethnic group native to Greater China, had a strong tendency to fertility worship, as demonstrated by the large number of existing rock paintings and unearthed painted potteries, symbolizing the male and female sexual organs and coitus. In terms of writing, the earliest sex education book in China can be traced back to the *Book of Changes* of the Zhou Dynasty (about 1,000 BCE), regarded as the foundational book of the Chinese concept of nature. The book assumes that nature comes from the interaction of the Yin (female) and the Yang (male) elements, and in human beings, the interaction is carried out by sexual intercourse. Hence, many specific descriptions of sexual intercourse and reproduction followed.

Slightly before the Han Dynasty (202 BCE), Su Nu (the name of a legendary goddess) wrote the *Su Nu Jing* (Su Nu Bible), most of which detailed the many methods of sexual intercourse, and the so-called "Seven Damages," "Eight Benefits," "Nine Methods," and a total of 24 sexual positions or moves. Another part talked about flirting skills, specifying the so-called "Five Signs," "Five Desires," and "Ten Moves." Another part of the book talks about the relationship between sexual intercourse and health maintenance, including the sexual postures and techniques that should be considered in relation to seasons, psychology, conception, contraception, and other sexual scientific theories and related social and artistic aspects. For example, there was the "Love music (harmony)" theory, which advocates that both the male and the female must be emotionally compatible before they can have sex, otherwise it will be harmful to the body, a very romantic and moralistic stance even in the eyes of modern people.

Scholarly and Scientific Context

These ancient texts were not purely poetic or spiritual in tone. They represented a systematic body of sexual knowledge deeply embedded in traditional Chinese medicine (TCM), especially in the domain of cultivating "jing" (essence), one of the three vital energies along with "qi" (energy) and "shen" (spirit). The regulation

DOI: 10.4324/9781003611387-20

of sexual behavior was seen as crucial for health and longevity. Excessive ejaculation, for instance, was thought to deplete one's vital essence, while harmonious intercourse could help preserve life energy (Fan, 2008; Furth, 1999; Sivin, 1987).

These texts also contained an early version of psychosexual understanding. Concepts such as mutual arousal, timing of intercourse with seasonal and emotional harmony, and spiritual connectivity demonstrate an integrated biopsychosocial model (Bullough, 1994) of sexuality, long before the term ever existed in Western medicine. The emotional compatibility emphasized in the "Love music" theory can be seen as an ancient Chinese precursor to what modern sex therapy describes as the necessity of emotional safety and attunement in sexual relationships.

Clinical-Historical Illustration

One prominent example of how these traditions may have influenced practice can be drawn from the imperial court physicians of the Tang Dynasty, who reportedly consulted texts such as *Su Nu Jing* when advising emperors suffering from sexual exhaustion or infertility. These cases, although filtered through mythological accounts, highlight how medical and sexual disciplines were deeply entwined in elite Chinese life. Today, modern practitioners of Traditional Chinese Medicine may still incorporate adapted versions of these principles when treating sexual dysfunction, especially in integrative clinics across China, Taiwan, and Hong Kong (Wile, 1992).

From Western Han to the Qing Dynasty

By the Western Han Dynasty (after 202 BCE), there were various books on Fang Zhong Shu (Bed Room Skills) recorded in silk books and bamboo slips, such as *Ten Questions*, *Integrating Yin and Yang*, *Tianxia Zhidao Tan* (The Heaven and Earth Top Methods), and several others. It is believed that the rise of these books at that time was related to the emperors, because it was assumed to be a "skill of the emperors that should be spread throughout the world." These writings reflected not only medical or erotic interest but also the ideological role of sexuality in consolidating imperial authority and maintaining physical vitality and dynastic longevity (Brook, 1999).

The Tang Dynasty that followed was described by historians as the era with "the most liberal sexual concepts in ancient China." (Schafer, 1963) In the royal family, incest and prostitution were commonplace. In society at that time, premarital sex and women's unchastity were also very common. It was not surprising that talented and beautiful women expressed their feelings through poetry and fell in love with males they simply met. The works of female poets such as Li Ye and Yu Xuanji express a rare female sexual agency in pre-modern literature, defying both moral norms and gender restrictions of their time (Chang & Saussy, 1999; Hinsch, 2010).

However, in the later Song Dynasty, due to the country's political instability and external threats, the government adopted increasingly conservative measures.

These efforts were executed through a centralized bureaucracy and an extremely rigid interpretation of Taoism and Neo-Confucianism. The state implemented strict control over society, including people's sexuality. These policies advocated the preservation of natural principles and the suppression of human desires, including erotic ones. As a result, the degree of sexual need and expression, especially women's humanity and autonomy, remained highly suppressed until the end of the Qing Dynasty in 1912. The late imperial era saw women increasingly confined to domesticity and chastity, while sexuality was linked with disorder or moral decay (Ebrey, 1993; Ko, 1994; Raphals, 1998; Rawski, 1998).

Confucian, Buddhist, and Taoist Sexual Concepts

Another force that brought conservatism to the Chinese sexual culture came from religious and philosophical teachings, namely Confucianism, Buddhism, and Taoism.

Confucianism has been, for most of Chinese history, the mainstream socio-philosophical foundation, with Confucius and Mencius considered sages and supreme teachers. It contains many taboos or prejudices on sexuality. For example: "Only women and villains are difficult to breed," or "Men and women must not have skin-to-skin contact on giving and receiving," and "When one is fed and warmed, one's sexual desires will come up." These proverbs conveyed a moralized control over bodily and sexual behavior. The Cheng-Zhu school of Neo-Confucianism in the Song and Ming Dynasties advocated "preserving natural principles and eradicating human desires," negating sexual needs even more thoroughly. The renowned 20th-century Chinese scholar Lu Xun furiously pointed out that the "feudal ethics are destroying people" (Cline, 2011; Lu Xun, 1930).

Buddhism, with its ultimate goal of liberation from worldly attachments, also had a significant impact. Although lay practitioners were allowed conjugal sex, celibacy was the ideal path for monks and nuns. The Buddhist emphasis on detachment, non-attachment to bodily pleasure, and viewing sex as a hindrance to spiritual development led to a moral tone in both doctrine and monastic life (Faure, 1998). However, Buddhism in China often took on syncretic forms, blending with Taoist and Confucian ideals, especially in family and reproductive ethics.

Taoism, especially in its early esoteric forms, had a very different view. If the *Book of Changes* can be considered Taoist in nature, it contains many well-known passages on sexual openness, such as "The heaven and the earth gather together, and all things will be transformed into 'Chi', with men and women breeding essence, and all things coming to life." Taoist classics like *The Classic of Sunü* and *The Art of the Bedchamber* advocated techniques for preserving sexual vitality, emphasizing emotional harmony, rhythmic breathing, and energetic balance between partners as health-promoting practices (Wile, 1992).

However, during the Wei, Jin, Southern, and Northern Dynasties (220–589 AD), as Buddhism gained popularity, the royal family reformed Taoism in an attempt to compete. This led to the suppression of its sexually liberal elements. Bedchamber arts were marginalized and, in many instances, condemned. In the Song Dynasty, with the rise of Neo-Confucianism, Fangzhongshu (Bed Room Skills) was even more thoroughly suppressed and banned as obscene, treated as superstitious or morally dangerous by the state (Despeux, 2008).

Sexual Culture of Ethnic Minorities Other Than Han

In China, aside from the Han people, there are officially recognized 55 ethnic minority groups, many of which maintain distinct cultural practices, including differing views on sexuality, gender roles, marriage customs, and sexual norms. These include traditions such as matrilineal inheritance, consensual trial marriages (e.g., the Mosuo's "walking marriages"), and greater sexual autonomy among women in certain southwestern groups like the Bai, Yi, and Dai (Harrell, 2001; Jamieson, 2000; Walsh, 2005).

However, when ethnic minority groups rose to power and became rulers of Han-majority populations—as seen during the Sui (Xianbei), Tang (Xianbei), Yuan (Mongol), and Qing (Manchu/Jurchen) dynasties—they generally respected, retained, and often absorbed Han customs, including sexual and marital traditions. These ruling dynasties did not attempt to radically alter or suppress Han sexual culture. Instead, they blended their own customs with prevailing Han practices in ways that reflected political pragmatism and a desire for legitimacy.

Because of this syncretism and the historical dominance of Han cultural norms, this chapter focuses specifically on the sexual traditions and transformations within Han society, which ultimately had a stronger and more enduring influence on the mainstream development of Chinese psychosexual perspectives.

The Conservative Influence of Western Culture

Based on the previous discussion of Confucian, Buddhist, and Taoist influences, it is clear that traditional Chinese philosophies promoted restraint and discipline in sexual conduct. However, the end of the Qing Dynasty (1911 CE) ushered in a new and powerful force of sexual conservatism: the introduction of Western cultural values through colonization, education, religious missions, and legal reform.

This "fourth wave" of conservatism was not rooted in indigenous Chinese ethics but emerged as a product of Western religious and moral philosophy—particularly Catholic and Protestant Christianity. Western missionaries brought with them Judeo-Christian ideals, including the belief that sex should occur only within monogamous marriage. These beliefs were encoded into both moral discourse and eventually legal frameworks.

For instance, in 1930, the Nanjing Nationalist Government initiated a modern family reform by promoting monogamy and abolishing traditional practices such as polygamy and concubinage. This move was aligned with Western moral systems, especially as found in Christian doctrine, which emphasizes marital fidelity. The Christian Bible, in the Book of Genesis, introduces the foundational couple—Adam and Eve—as the archetype for one-man, one-woman union. The Ten Commandments reinforce this notion, explicitly prohibiting adultery and coveting another's spouse (Exodus 20:14, 17).

This influence was further entrenched with the 1950 Marriage Law enacted by the People's Republic of China. This law formally outlawed polygamy and mandated monogamy as the only legitimate form of marriage, a radical legal reform that echoed the Western standard set during the Council of Trent in the mid-16th century, when the Catholic Church formalized monogamous marriage as the doctrinal norm (Ozment, 1983; Sommer, 2000). While presented as progressive, these legal shifts marked a sharp turn away from the plural marital structures traditionally accepted in Chinese society.

In Hong Kong, the trajectory was similar but uniquely shaped by British colonial law. Even after more than a century of colonial rule, polygamy remained legal under Qing family law until 1971. That year, the British colonial administration finally abolished the practice, aligning local family law with British Christian norms of monogamy (Smart, 1999).

Western conservatism also significantly influenced Chinese views on prostitution. In traditional Chinese society, prostitution was neither heavily regulated nor entirely condemned. Brothels were accepted in many urban areas, and courtesans often participated in cultural and artistic life. By the late 1920s, however, nationalist modernizers in cities like Nanjing and Shanghai attempted to abolish prostitution altogether, although they were largely unsuccessful. These efforts coincided with Christian anti-vice campaigns influenced by missionary work and Western public health movements.

In Taiwan, after the Nationalist retreat, prostitution remained technically legal and regulated until 2022, when the last official public brothel closed. In contrast, in mainland China, following the Communist Revolution of 1949, prostitution was criminalized outright as part of a broader campaign to "cleanse" society of feudal and capitalist remnants. This legal and moral approach was deeply shaped by Soviet Marxist ideology and also Western Puritanical values, both of which disapproved of commercial sex (Hershatter, 1997; Wang, 2017).

In Hong Kong, British authorities took a more pragmatic but still morally conservative approach. As early as 1932, the colonial government enacted formal laws to prohibit prostitution, although enforcement was inconsistent and certain forms of sex work continued in specific regulated districts.

The Sexually Conservative Influence of Western Literature

The spread of Western cultural influence in China was not limited to religion, legal structures, or family norms. It also penetrated deeply into Chinese intellectual life through literature, education, and reform movements. In the mid-19th century, following China's defeat in the Opium Wars, Chinese reformers began to look toward the West for models of modernization and national rejuvenation. This gave rise to the Westernization Movement, where young students were sent abroad to study, Western missionaries established schools, and translated Western works became increasingly popular among the Chinese intelligentsia (Schoppa, 2000).

By 1915, these efforts culminated in the New Culture Movement, a landmark intellectual shift that aimed to break with feudal traditions and embrace new values such as democracy, science, and gender equality. While the rhetoric of this movement advocated sexual openness and freedom, its deeper alignment with Western values—particularly Christian-influenced ideals of monogamy—reintroduced a form of sexual conservatism, albeit under a modern, progressive guise (Liu, 1995).

This duality is vividly illustrated in the lives and writings of the intellectual giants of the time. Kang Youwei, for example, a leading reformist during the 1898 Hundred Days' Reform, publicly proposed a modern marital law supporting "one husband, one wife" as part of China's civilizational advancement. Yet, in his personal life, Kang had six concubines from three different countries, all of whom were significantly younger than him. This stark contradiction between advocacy and personal practice reveals the complexity and perhaps hypocrisy embedded within early reformist narratives (Judge, 2008).

Similarly, Liang Qichao, another New Culture figure, co-founded the "World Association of Monogamy" with Tan Sitong. Together, they penned a manifesto pledging to uphold monogamy and reject both concubinage and prostitution. However, Liang himself maintained both a wife and a concubine, who bore him nine children. Despite promoting progressive values, his life remained rooted in older Chinese familial structures (Chang, 1985).

The case of Lu Xun adds another layer to this ideological contradiction. Known for his scathing critiques of feudal morality and his support for gender equality, Lu Xun espoused relatively open views on sexuality in theory. Yet his fiction often depicted sexuality through a lens of shame, corruption, or moral decay. In works like *Diary of a Madman* and *Medicine*, sexual desire is never celebrated, but portrayed as a symptom of larger social illness. This literary framing reinforced the idea that sex, especially outside rigid moral boundaries, was dangerous or dirty (Anderson, 1990; Lu Xun, 1925).

Lu Xun's personal life further complicates this narrative. In 1906, at the age of 25 and studying in Japan, he returned to China to marry a woman he had never met, as arranged by his mother. Although they remained legally married for decades, Lu later claimed that the marriage was entirely celibate. In 1925, he began a romantic and ultimately marital relationship with one of his female students, Xu Guangping, without formally divorcing his first wife. Despite being a vocal advocate of monogamy in his writings, his own experiences reflected the contradictions between idealized sexual morality and the complexities of lived human relationships.

This tension points to a broader truth about the imposition of Western marital norms in a transforming society. The promotion of monogamy was not always about sexual liberation or equality. Rather, it often came as a moral import tied to religious dogma, especially Christianity. While it was framed as progressive, the underlying message frequently reinforced sexual restriction, gendered control, and moral surveillance (Jeffreys, 2006).

In retrospect, these reformers may not have been hypocrites so much as victims of an unresolved cultural tension. On the one hand, they were trying to liberate China from the constraints of feudal patriarchy. On the other hand, they absorbed Western sexual ideals without questioning their religious and moralistic underpinnings. As a result, monogamy was treated not as one of many viable relational models, but as a singular ideal—often beyond the reach of real people's lives.

This legacy still shapes Chinese cultural attitudes today. Even as modern China undergoes rapid urbanization, globalization, and the emergence of diverse sexual identities and relationships, monogamy continues to be viewed as the normative, morally superior model. Yet, as history shows, its elevation was not purely indigenous but deeply entangled with imported values that were themselves contested and unevenly applied.

The Aborted Anticonservative Sexual Revolution

In the early years of the Republic of China, as Western conservative sexual values began to infiltrate the country, only a handful of voices dared to advocate for a more liberal and scientific approach to sexuality. One of the most notable among these was Zhang Jingsheng, a pioneering but often overlooked figure in the development of modern sexology in China.

Zhang, who earned a doctorate in philosophy from the University of Paris in 1916, returned to China with bold ideas about personal freedom, sexual liberation, and scientific progress. In 1926, he compiled and published sexual self-reports from seven university students, both male and female. This project was unprecedented in China at the time. These reports detailed the sexual experiences, desires, and challenges of real individuals, thereby introducing a form of sexological case study to Chinese readership (Pan, 2006; Zhang, 1926).

Zhang further advanced controversial ideas such as the physiological existence of "female ejaculation," which he referred to as the "Third Water," and he proposed new theories about marriage, sexual education, birth control, and romantic love. His work challenged traditional Confucian morality and rejected the sexual conservatism promoted by both indigenous and Western authorities. Unsurprisingly, his ideas met strong resistance. He lost his university position, his publishing ventures were shut down, and his name was widely maligned in conservative circles. Eventually, he turned to translation, notably of Rousseau's *Confessions*, in an attempt to continue spreading his views under the guise of foreign literature. During the Cultural Revolution, he was labeled a counterrevolutionary and died in 1970 in poverty and obscurity (Zhang, 1998).

Zhang's case represents a tragically aborted sexual revolution, one that could have positioned China at the forefront of scientific sexology had it not been thwarted by political conservatism and cultural repression.

Western Culture's Conservative Approach to Sexual Anomalies

The influence of Western culture on Chinese sexual norms extended beyond marriage laws and moral codes. It also reshaped how sexual and gender variance was understood, classified, and often criminalized. While premodern Chinese society had a history of relative tolerance toward various forms of sexual and gender diversity—including homosexuality, cross-dressing, and nonbinary gender expressions—these were rarely prosecuted unless they conflicted with public order or filial obligations (Hinrichs & Lin, 2012; Hinsch, 1990).

In contrast, British colonial rule introduced a more legalistic and punitive framework, especially in places like Hong Kong. As part of the British Empire, Hong Kong inherited Victorian laws such as the Offences Against the Person Act of 1861, which criminalized same-sex relations and cross-dressing. These laws were enforced well into the late 20th century, and they played a central role in shaping social attitudes and institutional policies around sexuality in Hong Kong and other colonial territories (Sibalis, 2004; Vitiello, 2012).

While modern China did not initially adopt such harsh legal sanctions against homosexuality or gender variance, the socio-political discourse around these topics began to reflect Western medical pathologization. Homosexuality was labeled as a psychiatric disorder in mainland China's diagnostic manuals until 2001, echoing similar classifications found in the DSM until its revision in 1973. Although attitudes are slowly shifting, significant stigma and structural inequality remain.

A turning point came in 2023 when Hong Kong's Court of Final Appeal ruled that the government had failed in its constitutional duty to provide a legal framework for recognizing same-sex partnerships. This ruling, which cited Article 14 of the Hong Kong Bill of Rights, represents a significant step forward. However, no new legislation has yet materialized, suggesting that institutional change remains sluggish despite legal advances.

The uneven progress seen in Hong Kong and mainland China reflects the enduring influence of Western-derived legal and psychiatric models, many of which still struggle to accommodate sexual and gender diversity within culturally appropriate frameworks (Jaspers, 1953; Wong, 2017).

The Subtle Influence of Western Religions

Among the most enduring and powerful vectors of Western sexual conservatism is religion—specifically Christianity. As a dominant cultural force in Europe and the Americas, Christianity brought with it a rigid framework of sexual morality centered on monogamy, chastity, and the suppression of bodily desires. These values have had a profound impact on the global perception of sex and continue to shape sexual attitudes in many societies, including parts of China.

Christianity first entered China in 635 CE during the Tang Dynasty through the Nestorian mission, but it remained a marginal influence for centuries. It was not until the 19th and early 20th centuries—during China's increased exposure to Western powers—that Christian institutions began to gain a foothold. This growth was particularly visible in urban centers like Shanghai and Qingdao, and most notably in British-ruled Hong Kong.

Hong Kong became a hub for Christian missionary activity, and its educational, legal, and cultural systems reflected this legacy. By 2022, Hong Kong reported approximately 480,000 Protestants and 379,000 Catholics, representing nearly 10% of the population (Hong Kong Census and Statistics Department, 2022). The influence of Christianity is also evident in the city's public life. About one-third of Hong Kong's annual public holidays are Christian in origin. Furthermore, around half of its secondary schools are Christian-run institutions, many of which are considered prestigious and influential.

The physical presence of Christianity in Hong Kong is striking as well. With nearly 100 churches, chapels, and Christian assembly halls serving a relatively small Christian population, the density of religious infrastructure far exceeds that of the United Kingdom. While in the UK there is roughly one church per 135,000 Christians, in Hong Kong the figure is closer to one for every 10,000 (UK Charity Commission, 2021).

This saturation has led to what some scholars call "institutional Christianization," wherein Christian moral codes subtly permeate secular institutions and influence cultural attitudes, particularly around sexuality. These codes often reinforce traditional gender roles, stigmatize non-heteronormative relationships, and limit public discourse on sexual health and rights (Liu, 2013; Yip, 2006).

Thus, even in a relatively modern and globalized city like Hong Kong, the combined effects of colonial history, religious institutions, and Western moral codes continue to uphold a conservative approach to sexuality.

Conclusion

Does Western Sexual Culture Lead to Sexual Openness in China?

Some readers may be surprised by the argument that Western culture has contributed to sexual conservatism in China and Hong Kong, especially given the widespread belief among modern Chinese that Western influence has introduced excessive sexual freedom. Popular discourse often claims that Western media, fashion, and entertainment have "corrupted" traditional values and morality. Yet, a closer look at historical and legal developments tells a different story.

If we examine the timeline of sexual regulation, it becomes evident that many restrictive practices currently seen in Chinese society actually mirror Western norms—particularly those rooted in Victorian and Christian traditions. These include the promotion of monogamy, the criminalization of sex work, and the suppression of open discussions around non-heterosexual identities. The assertion that Western culture brought sexual openness to China becomes difficult to sustain when we recognize that earlier Chinese societies, particularly during the Han and Tang dynasties, exhibited more tolerance for sexual expression than many parts of the West did during the same period.

Even Hong Kong, which is often considered a cosmopolitan bridge between East and West, has adopted Western-style sexual censorship and legal conservatism. The city's current pornography laws, for example, are on par with or even stricter than those found in many Western countries, with enforcement mechanisms that resemble those in the United States or United Kingdom. Only in particularly liberal regions of the West, such as the Netherlands or parts of Scandinavia, does one see markedly different legal attitudes toward adult sexual expression.

This contradiction reveals a deeper issue: rather than engaging critically with sexual norms, both Chinese and Hong Kong societies have absorbed imported ideals without always interrogating their historical relevance or adaptability. When sexual issues arise, many individuals instinctively blame outside influence instead of recognizing the need for internal dialogue and reform. This externalization of blame reflects a broader discomfort with sexuality itself, a discomfort that is often reinforced by educational gaps, cultural taboos, and rigid institutional frameworks.

This tendency to shift responsibility toward the "foreign other" might be an important subject for inclusion in contemporary sex education and psychosexual therapy programs. By addressing these cultural defense mechanisms, professionals can better guide individuals and communities toward healthier, more self-aware understandings of sexual identity and practice.

A Difficult Journey to Pursue

Sex education and therapy remain some of the most challenging and sensitive areas of public discourse in Chinese-speaking societies. They sit at the intersection of deep-seated cultural beliefs, religious influence, political ideologies, and globalized media. As highlighted throughout this chapter, the evolution of Chinese sexual culture—particularly among the Han majority—has not followed a simple trajectory from repression to openness or vice versa. Instead, it has been a complex journey marked by negotiation, contradiction, and external intervention.

Hong Kong, in particular, represents a unique case. As a society navigating its historical ties to both Chinese traditions and British colonial systems, it finds itself pulled in multiple directions. On one hand, there is a clear desire among segments of the population to modernize sexual discourse and advocate for inclusion, gender equality, and sexual rights. On the other hand, strong institutional, religious, and educational influences continue to promote conservative ideals, often under the guise of moral responsibility or cultural preservation.

The task for sex educators, therapists, and scholars is not to assign blame to one culture or another. Rather, it is to facilitate thoughtful, evidence-based conversations that allow individuals and communities to examine their own assumptions about sex, relationships, and identity. By understanding the historical and cultural forces at play—including the less acknowledged conservative influence of Western norms—professionals can better support those struggling with sexual anxieties, confusion, or conflict.

In conclusion, while the road ahead may be complex and challenging, it is also one of great potential. With cultural sensitivity, academic honesty, and therapeutic empathy, we can continue building a more open, informed, and compassionate approach to sexuality in China, Hong Kong, and beyond.

References

Anderson, M. (1990). *The Limits of Realism: Chinese Fiction in the Revolutionary Period*. University of California Press.
Brook, T. (1999). *The Confusions of Pleasure: Commerce and Culture in Ming China*. University of California Press.
Bullough, V. L. (1994). *Science in the Bedroom: A History of Sex Research*. Basic Books.
Chang, K. S. (1985). The late Qing reformers and the question of concubinage. *Republican China*, 11(1), 1–22.
Chang, K., & Saussy, H. (Eds.). (1999). *Women Writers of Traditional China: An Anthology of Poetry and Criticism*. Stanford University Press.
Cline, E. M. (2011). *Confucianism and Sexuality: The Cultural Construction of Moral Discourse*. University Press of America.
Despeux, C. (2008). "Taoist Alchemy and Sexual Practices." In Livia Kohn (Ed.), *Daoism Handbook*, pp. 464–497. Brill.
Ebrey, P. B. (1993). *The Inner Quarters: Marriage and the Lives of Chinese Women in the Sung Period*. University of California Press.
Fan, F. (2008). *Sexuality and Medicine in Ancient China: The Influence of Taoism on Reproductive Theory and Practice*. Routledge.
Faure, B. (1998). *The Red Thread: Buddhist Approaches to Sexuality*. Princeton University Press.
Furth, C. (1999). *A Flourishing Yin: Gender in China's Medical History, 960–1665*. University of California Press.
Harrell, S. (2001). *Ways of Being Ethnic in Southwest China*. University of Washington Press.
Hershatter, G. (1997). *Dangerous Pleasures: Prostitution and Modernity in Twentieth-Century Shanghai*. University of California Press.
Hinrichs, T. J., & Lin, L. L. (Eds.). (2012). *Chinese Medicine and Healing: An Illustrated History*. Harvard University Press.
Hinsch, B. (1990). *Passions of the Cut Sleeve: The Male Homosexual Tradition in China*. University of California Press.
Hinsch, B. (2010). *Mating Rituals and Courtship in Imperial China*. Rowman & Littlefield.
Hong Kong Census and Statistics Department. (2022). *2021 Population Census: Summary Results*. Hong Kong SAR Government.
Jamieson, N. (2000). *Understanding Vietnam*. University of California Press.
Jaspers, K. (1953). *The Origin and Goal of History*. Yale University Press.
Jeffreys, E. (2006). *Sex and sexuality in China*. Routledge.
Judge, J. (2008). *The Precious Raft of History: The Past, the West, and the Woman Question in China*. Stanford University Press.
Ko, D. (1994). *Teachers of the Inner Chambers: Women and Culture in Seventeenth-Century China*. Stanford University Press.

Liu, L. H. (1995). *Translingual Practice: Literature, National Culture, and Translated Modernity—China, 1900–1937*. Stanford University Press.
Liu, D. (2013). *Sexuality in China: Histories of Power and Pleasure*. Polity Press.
Lu, X. (1925). *How We Should Be Fathers Nowadays*. Reprinted in *Selected Essays of Lu Xun* (trans. Yang Xianyi & Gladys Yang), Foreign Languages Press.
Ozment, S. (1983). *When Fathers Ruled: Family Life in Reformation Europe*. Harvard University Press.
Pan, S. M. (2006). "Transformations in the Primary Life Cycle: The Origins and Nature of China's Sexual Revolution." In E. Jeffreys (Ed.), *Sex and Sexuality in China* (pp. 21–42). Routledge.
Raphals, L. (1998). *Sharing the Light: Representations of Women and Virtue in Early China*. SUNY Press.
Rawski, E. S. (1998). *The Last Emperors: A Social History of Qing Imperial Institutions*. University of California Press.
Schafer, E. H. (1963). *The Golden Peaches of Samarkand: A Study of T'ang Exotics*. University of California Press.
Schoppa, R. K. (2000). *The Columbia Guide to Modern Chinese History*. Columbia University Press.
Sibalis, M. (2004). Urban space and homosexuality: The example of the Marais, Paris's "Gay Ghetto." *Urban Studies*, 41(9), 1739–1758.
Sivin, N. (1987). *Traditional Medicine in Contemporary China*. University of Michigan Press.
Sommer, M. (2000). *Sex, Law, and Society in Late Imperial China*. Stanford University Press.
UK Charity Commission. (2021). *Statistics of Registered Charities in England and Wales*. UK Charity Commission.
Vitiello, G. (2012). *Sexuality in China: Histories of Power and Pleasure*. Polity.
Walsh, E. R. (2005). From nü guo to nü er guo: Negotiating desire in the land of the Mosuo. *Modern China*, 31(4), 448–486.
Wang, Z. (2017). *Finding Women in the State: A Socialist Feminist Revolution in the People's Republic of China, 1949–1964*. University of California Press.
Wile, D. (1992). *Art of the Bedchamber: The Chinese Sexual Yoga Classics Including Women's Solo Meditation Texts*. State University of New York Press.
Wong, W. C. W. (2017). *Sexual Health in Chinese Culture: Attitudes, Practices and Clinical Management*. Springer.
Yip, A. K. T. (2006). Sexuality and the church. *Theology and Sexuality*, 8(1), 1–9.
Zhang, J. (1926). *Sexual Life Self-Reports. Reprinted in Early 20th Century Sexual Thought in China*. Beijing Book Co.
Zhang, X. (1998). "Zhang Jingsheng and China's Sexual Revolution." In T. Barlow (Ed.), *Formations of Colonial Modernity in East Asia* (pp. 169–199). Duke University Press.

Chapter 21

Impact of In-Law Dynamics on the Heterosexual Couple's Relationship

Shobha Managoli

Introduction: The Cultural Framework of Marriage and In-Law Dynamics in India

India's rich cultural diversity holds one common thread across its many states and communities: the understanding that marriage is not merely a union between two individuals, but a merging of two families. This belief continues to deeply influence how relationships evolve, particularly within the framework of in-law dynamics.

Historically, Indian society has operated under a patriarchal and joint family system, where multiple generations coexisted under one roof. Prescriptive texts such as the Manusmriti codified gendered roles within the household, emphasizing a woman's duty toward her husband and his family, thereby reinforcing patriarchal authority and intergenerational hierarchy (Manusmriti, ca. 200 BCE/1886).

Within this structure, family harmony was largely maintained by elders, primarily the parents-in-law. The mother-in-law, in particular, was traditionally expected to mentor the incoming daughter-in-law, ensuring she upheld the family's legacy through adherence to household norms and the fulfillment of her reproductive role, often with a strong preference for birthing a son (Fischel, 2012; Habib, 1995).

Conversely, the groom maintained a primary allegiance to his natal family. He was often treated as a figure of status and authority within his wife's household, reinforcing gendered expectations that shaped power dynamics in marriages.

The gradual disintegration of the joint family system has been shaped by several pivotal societal changes:

- Urbanization and industrialization, which enabled geographic and economic mobility (Singh, 2010).
- The rise of individual aspirations, especially among the middle class.
- Increased access to education and financial independence among women, allowing for more equitable participation in household decision-making (Chandra, 2024).
- Legal reforms such as:
  - The Dowry Prohibition Act (1961, with subsequent amendments), aimed at curbing dowry-related violence and harassment.

DOI: 10.4324/9781003611387-21

- The Protection of Women from Domestic Violence Act (2005), which expanded legal definitions of abuse beyond physical harm (Kumar, 2017).
- Exposure to global cultural norms through modernization, media, and cross-cultural interaction.

Despite this progression, cultural beliefs still influence rituals, family values, and social expectations at every stage of marriage, from the choice of spouse in arranged setups to negotiations about dowry and ceremonial customs. Each interaction during the marital process holds potential for either fusion or friction, depending on how boundaries, respect, and emotional expression are managed.

A poignant linguistic insight lies in the Hindi word for mother-in-law, "*saas*," which also means "breath." This dual meaning metaphorically captures the tension in navigating this relationship, often breathless in its demands and expectations. The daughter-in-law enters a new family system laden with implicit instructions, fears, and cultural codes that influence her perception of and behavior toward the in-laws.

At their best, in-laws can serve as a stabilizing force, offering emotional guidance, fostering intergenerational bonding, and providing the couple space to nurture intimacy. However, in practice, this is often not the case.

Common Sources of Conflict Between Couples and In-Laws

Some recurring challenges include:

- **Hospitality Expectations During the Wedding**: Criticism or excessive scrutiny from the groom's family during wedding events often sets the tone for later in-law interactions. Even minor remarks can shape the groom's perception of the bride's family and vice versa (Banerjee, 2020).
- **Dowry Demands**: Despite legal bans, dowry-related pressure and dissatisfaction continue to be a source of long-term conflict.
- **Gift-Giving Rituals**: Expectations regarding gifts during festivals or childbirth are culturally loaded and can be a cause of friction if not aligned with familial norms.
- Deeply rooted social beliefs, such as:
  - A son-in-law should not frequent his in-laws' home, lest he lose respect in his own household.
  - A daughter's parents should avoid consuming food at her marital home and should focus only on giving, not receiving.
  - A wife is expected to sacrifice everything for her husband's family, while the husband's familial obligations are vague and culturally under-articulated.
  - Statements like, "If he's good, he's my son; if not, he's your husband," reflect a shifting of accountability onto the daughter-in-law for the husband's shortcomings.

- A pervasive belief that "a good husband is one who earns more than his wife can spend," perpetuates traditional gender roles and discourages male participation in domestic labor.

Research indicates that about 60% of couples experience conflict with their in-laws, contributing significantly to emotional distress, marital dissatisfaction, and, in some cases, divorce (Bryant et al., 2011). These dynamics are further complicated by factors such as family of origin values, sibling relationships, personality traits of parents, parenting styles, attachment histories, financial disagreements, and communication methods.

When in-law relationships are strained, the consequences are evident in the couple's private bond. These include a decline in emotional and sexual intimacy, frequent breakdowns in communication, and overall dissatisfaction with the marital relationship. In extreme cases, unresolved in-law tensions can escalate to the dissolution of the relationship.

This chapter will examine the complex interplay of these factors, cultural, emotional, systemic, and psychological, to better understand the mechanisms through which in-law dynamics influence the couple relationship in contemporary India.

Case Study 1: Between Two Homes—Navigating Loyalty and Autonomy in Marriage

Ranjan and Meera, a newly married heterosexual couple in their late twenties, presented for therapy citing frequent arguments, emotional distance, and a growing fear that their escalating conflicts could turn violent. Meera reported persistent irritability, while Ranjan described feeling caught between loyalty to his mother and commitment to his wife. The initial intake uncovered substantial emotional strain rooted in in-law involvement, particularly from Ranjan's mother.

Background and Context

The couple had been in a committed relationship for three years prior to marriage. Both hailed from traditionally rooted Indian families, though their upbringings differed in significant ways. Ranjan, an only child from South India, was raised solely by his mother after his father's early demise. As a result, a pattern of emotional reliance developed between them, with Ranjan's mother actively involved in most life decisions. In contrast, Meera, the youngest of three daughters from a North Indian family, was raised in a household that emphasized independence, gender equality, and assertiveness.

This culturally cross-regional pairing, North and South India, further compounded expectations around post-marital roles, familial obligations, and decision-making hierarchies, often referred to in family systems theory as "fusion versus differentiation" (Bowen, 1978; Goldenberg et al., 2020).

In-Law Dynamics and Marital Stressors

Key issues identified in therapy included:

- **Over-involvement from Ranjan's mother**: Decisions ranging from household décor (e.g., curtain colors, crockery types) to holiday planning were influenced or dictated by her. Ranjan often sought her input without involving Meera, which led to a sense of exclusion.
- **Pressure on Meera to conform**: She was expected to accommodate frequent visits to Ranjan's family home and to host extended family members with elaborate hospitality. These expectations triggered emotional fatigue and resentment.
- **Ranjan's conflict avoidance**: In moments of marital disagreement, Ranjan often turned to his mother for resolution, leaving Meera feeling isolated and undermined.

Meera verbalized her experience succinctly:

> I feel we are not two in this but three. Her shadow looms over everything. I don't feel I am married to him.

Ranjan, in contrast, expressed deep-rooted filial loyalty:

> I don't want to hurt my mom. She raised me alone.

During sessions, Meera appeared physically restless, often sighing or shifting in her seat. Ranjan either dominated the negotiation or became silent, returning later with pre-planned compromises that appeared to reflect his mother's input more than a collaborative marital decision. Meera frequently remarked, "So the mama's boy got his answer again."

This triangulation, a dynamic where one partner involves a third party to cope with relational tension, is a common issue in marital therapy and often stems from unresolved individuation issues with parental figures (Nichols, 2020).

Clinical Assessment

A genogram was constructed to visualize emotional interconnections and multigenerational transmission patterns (McGoldrick et al., 2008). Incident analysis was also employed to explore the cognitive-emotional responses of each partner to key events since meeting each other's parents.

Therapy goals were jointly set as follows:

- Improve communication and conflict resolution skills.
- Establish appropriate emotional and physical boundaries with extended family.

- Support Ranjan in processing loyalty conflicts and strengthening his autonomy.
- Facilitate assertive communication for Meera, particularly around needs and expectations.

Therapeutic Interventions

The intervention framework was integrative, drawing from family systems therapy, emotionally focused therapy (Johnson, 2008), and culturally informed couple therapy practices:

- Psychoeducation on enmeshment, family hierarchies, and boundary formation.
- Genogram analysis to explore and reflect on emotional over-dependence and triangulation patterns.
- Incident analysis, guiding each partner to unpack thoughts, emotions, and unmet needs around family interactions.
- Role-play exercises for assertive communication by Meera and non-defensive listening by Ranjan.
- Boundary mapping, a structured activity where decisions were visually categorized as either "couple-only" or "family-inclusive."
- Letter-writing exercise, where Ranjan wrote an unsent letter to his mother, exploring themes of autonomy, loyalty, and guilt.
- Weekly couple rituals, such as tech-free meals or shared recreational time, to promote reconnection and emotional safety.

Challenges in Therapy

Initial resistance was observed, particularly from Ranjan, whose loyalty conflicts were deeply ingrained. His perception of assertiveness as confrontation had to be restructured. Meera also struggled with articulating emotional needs without emotional escalation, a pattern addressed using emotional regulation strategies and reflective questioning.

Outcomes

- Ranjan began asserting the need for marital boundaries, expressing them respectfully to his mother.
- During a significant cultural festival, the couple mutually decided to spend time independently rather than with extended family, marking a turning point in their assertion of boundaries.
- Meera reported feeling emotionally seen and empowered in her marital role.
- Conflict episodes reduced in frequency and intensity, with greater collaboration and problem-solving evident.
- The couple collaboratively developed a structured plan to host Ranjan's mother with agreed-upon time limits and expectations.

Cultural Commentary

This case illustrates how intergenerational enmeshment and unresolved parental allegiance can complicate marital functioning, particularly in collectivist societies like India where parental involvement is normalized (Chandra, 2024; Uberoi, 2006). The case also highlights the gendered expectations faced by daughters-in-law, a theme echoed in numerous Indian ethnographic studies (Banerjee, 2020; Mukhopadhyay, 2021).

In clinical work with Indian couples, especially where family hierarchy plays a pivotal role, therapists must remain sensitive to deeply embedded values around duty (dharma), filial piety, and gendered responsibilities. Utilizing culturally attuned tools such as genograms, role plays, and structured rituals can facilitate transformative insight and healing.

Family Constellation and Its Impact on Marital Dynamics

Family constellation, referring to the structure and composition of the household, plays a critical role in shaping marital satisfaction, autonomy, intimacy, and conflict resolution styles. In the Indian context, three primary family setups are observed:

- **Nuclear Family**: Comprising only the husband, wife, and their children.
- **Joint Family**: Includes multiple generations living together, often involving in-laws and extended relatives.
- **Extended Family in Close Proximity**: The nuclear couple lives separately, but in-laws reside nearby and engage frequently in their daily lives.

Each of these configurations brings its own advantages and limitations that influence the couple's relational health (see Tables 21.1 and 21.2).

Studies have shown that nuclear family systems tend to support higher levels of marital satisfaction and autonomy, particularly for women, while joint family structures are more likely to impose traditional gender expectations and role rigidity (Kumar, 2011; Mukhopadhyay, 2021). However, joint families can provide financial security, childcare support, and continuity of traditions, which are valued in many Indian households.

The influence of family constellation is not merely structural but deeply psychological. For example, couples in joint families often internalize traditional expectations that can limit emotional expression, especially for women. Shared space also increases the likelihood of surveillance, especially regarding intimate matters, as seen in research on intergenerational boundary violations (Banerjee, 2020; Uberoi, 2006).

The following section presents three clinical case studies that illustrate how each family constellation uniquely shapes the relational landscape of Indian couples.

Table 21.1 Family Constellation and Its Influence on Marital Life

Aspect of marital life impacted	*Nuclear family*	*Joint family*	*Extended family*
Autonomy	High	Limited, especially for women	Variable depending on proximity
Family Involvement	Flexible and negotiated	Overinvolved in every decision	Often overinvolved, sometimes flexible
Gender Roles	Shared responsibilities	Traditional and discriminatory	Varies with degree of closeness
Conflict Resolution	Handled by the couple	Mediated by family, typically biased toward son	Family may intervene, not always neutrally
Satisfaction Levels	Higher	Often compromised	Varies across couples and settings

Table 21.2 Comparative Table of Advantages and Disadvantages

Family type	*Advantages*	*Disadvantages*
Nuclear family	Greater privacy and autonomy for the couple	Lack of immediate family support during crises Possible guilt or estrangement from elders
- Reduced exposure to intergenerational conflict	Lack of immediate family support during crises	Role conflict and generational misunderstandings Pressure to conform to gendered norms Reduced privacy and intimacy
- Possible guilt or estrangement from elders	Practical support during life transitions (e.g., childbirth, illness) Emotional proximity to elders	Frequent interference Guilt when asserting boundaries Ambiguous expectations

Case Study 1: Nuclear Family—Autonomy and Relationship Satisfaction

Riya and Arjun, both in their early thirties, are corporate professionals residing in Mumbai. Presenting to therapy with complaints of frequent arguments, emotional withdrawal, and a sharp decline in intimacy, they exemplified the nuanced challenges faced by nuclear families balancing modern work-life stressors with unmet relational needs. The couple reported that their relationship, once affectionate and connected, had over time devolved into repetitive conflict and growing emotional distance.

Initial assessments indicated a lack of effective conflict resolution and emotional attunement. Arjun expressed concern that Riya was "always on her phone," often busy with work and seemingly disinterested in sexual or romantic connection. He noted that her overreliance on social media and her tendency to devalue his family's advice exacerbated his feelings of being sidelined. Riya, on the other hand, described feeling emotionally neglected, stating that Arjun was largely unavailable during times of personal stress and crises. She perceived his repeated comparisons between her and his mother or sister as invalidating, particularly around expectations of domestic responsibilities and cooking standards.

The dynamics observed in this couple mirror findings in contemporary Indian research that point to an increasing strain in nuclear families where traditional gender norms often clash with modern egalitarian ideals (Kumar, 2011; Mukhopadhyay, 2021). Although nuclear setups typically offer autonomy and privacy, they may also reduce the buffer of extended social support during moments of relational strain (Uberoi, 2006). Furthermore, couples without established boundaries from their families of origin, especially concerning emotional and practical decision-making, may experience spillover effects in their communication and intimacy.

Therapeutic interventions focused on establishing differentiated roles, improving emotional responsiveness, and facilitating mutual understanding of how unresolved familial expectations were being projected into the marital space. Psychoeducation was provided on the importance of psychological safety for fostering intimacy. Additionally, behavioral exercises to increase shared time without digital distractions, and assertiveness training to articulate emotional needs, were integrated into the therapy process. Over time, the couple began re-establishing intimacy and restructuring their relational priorities.

Case Study 2: Joint Family—Conflict and Support in Traditional Roles

Anjali and Vikram, married for four years and living in a joint family setup in Jaipur, sought therapy due to chronic dissatisfaction in their marriage. Vikram's parents were co-residents, and the intergenerational setup amplified the couple's struggles. Anjali described the household as "hierarchical and rigid," citing frequent surveillance by her mother-in-law, who reportedly monitored their private space, including listening at the bedroom door.

From Anjali's perspective, the lack of financial independence was deeply problematic. She recounted not having direct access to money for personal needs, including basic hygiene products, as decisions were routed through her mother-in-law. Her autonomy in managing the household or expressing dissent was minimal, leading to growing resentment. Vikram, conversely, perceived Anjali as aloof and emotionally unavailable to his family. He noted that she would often isolate herself in the bedroom, resist conversations with his parents, and routinely vent to her mother about the family dynamics.

This case presents a clear instance of enmeshment within joint family systems where spousal boundaries are often blurred by extended family interference. Research has consistently shown that joint family arrangements, while offering collective economic benefits and child-rearing support, tend to perpetuate patriarchal structures, often at the cost of women's autonomy and emotional well-being (Chandra, 2024; Fischel, 2012). The lack of dyadic privacy in such setups often hinders sexual intimacy and conflict resolution, which typically requires emotional safety and confidentiality.

Therapeutic goals included empowering the couple to negotiate private time, enabling Anjali to assert her needs without fear of retaliation, and supporting Vikram in developing a more balanced allegiance between his natal and conjugal families. Techniques such as genogram mapping, conflict de-escalation training, and role-playing assertive communication were central to the intervention.

Case Study 3: Extended Family in Close Proximity—Balancing Support and Boundaries

Neha and Rohan, a couple from Pune, demonstrated the challenges of navigating boundaries within extended family proximity. Although they did not live with Rohan's parents, their daily involvement was substantial. Neha described incidents where her mother-in-law would visit unannounced, interrupting intimate moments, and pass remarks on her attire or household management. Moreover, Rohan's frequent comments about missing his mother's cooking and his expectation that Neha replicate his family traditions left her feeling invalidated.

Rohan, in turn, felt that Neha was irritable and dismissive toward his mother, further straining the relationship. He also noted a rise in hostility during minor disagreements, which occasionally escalated into verbal abuse. The couple's situation was marked by emotional dysregulation, rigid family loyalties, and unresolved hurt.

This dynamic reflects what scholars have termed the "transitional family constellation," where geographic separation does not equate to psychological individuation from the family of origin (Kakar, 2016). In such setups, the illusion of autonomy is often disrupted by daily involvement and commentary from nearby parents, leading to a breakdown in couple intimacy and shared decision-making.

Interventions in this case included boundary mapping, sensate focus therapy to rebuild emotional and sexual connection, and family-of-origin work to understand attachment scripts that influenced their responses. Education about emotional labor and equitable gender expectations also played a key role in helping the couple reshape their relational paradigm.

These three case studies underscore the significant influence that family constellation has on marital satisfaction, conflict patterns, gender roles, and emotional intimacy. Whether in nuclear, joint, or extended family settings, in-laws' involvement and societal gender norms continue to shape how couples experience and manage their relationships. As highlighted in cross-cultural marriage studies, therapeutic work in such contexts must attend not only to the couple as a dyadic unit but also to the intergenerational systems they are embedded within (D'Cruz & Bharat, 2001; Sharma, 2013).

Therapeutic Process: Intake and Intervention in the Context of In-Law Dynamics

Intake Process: Uncovering the Hidden Architecture of Conflict

In working with couples affected by in-law dynamics, the intake phase serves as more than a procedural beginning, it becomes a diagnostic window into the relational ecosystem shaped by cultural expectations, familial hierarchies, and generational roles. Particularly in Indian sociocultural settings, where marriages are often a union of families rather than individuals (Chandra, 2024), therapists must look beyond surface-level complaints to identify embedded patterns of enmeshment, triangulation, and covert loyalties.

The intake should begin with a joint session, establishing rapport and clarifying the therapeutic framework. The therapist should position themselves as a nonjudgmental facilitator focused on strengthening the relationship as the primary "client," rather than siding with individual partners. It is crucial to set the tone by normalizing conflict and acknowledging the bravery required to seek professional help in a culture that often stigmatizes therapy (Mukhopadhyay, 2021).

In cases involving parent-in-law stress, it is recommended that therapists adopt the principle of "in-laws can enter the therapy room symbolically, but not literally," particularly during the formative stages of therapy. Inviting in-laws too early can dilute therapeutic boundaries and reinforce power imbalances. Instead, therapists may use proxy techniques such as letter writing, role-play, or incident mapping to symbolically "bring" in-laws into the discussion, while maintaining the therapeutic alliance with the couple.

Individual sessions, conducted after the initial joint intake, often yield deeper insight. These sessions provide a safe space for each partner to discuss sensitive issues, such as loyalty binds, covert expectations, or trauma linked to parental figures, that may not surface in a joint format. Tools such as genograms (McGoldrick et al., 2008) can be especially helpful to visually map generational legacies, relationship triangles, and unresolved attachments.

By the third session, therapists can shift toward formulating a working hypothesis and treatment plan. Clarifying the couple's goals, whether they involve boundary setting, rebuilding intimacy, or renegotiating traditional roles, is crucial to aligning expectations and fostering motivation for change.

Intervention Approach: Rebuilding and Sustaining the Couple Bond

Rebuilding the Relationship: From Disconnection to Connection

The core of the therapeutic intervention lies in helping the couple transition from emotional reactivity to conscious relational engagement. This begins by restoring psychological safety and mutual empathy.

Key strategies include:

- **Boundary Negotiation**: Using tools such as boundary mapping, therapists help couples distinguish between decisions that belong to the conjugal unit versus those influenced by the extended family. This is critical in collectivist cultures where boundaries are often diffuse.
- **Assertiveness Training**: Many women in Indian marriages struggle with voicing needs due to internalized gender roles. Assertiveness skill-building, grounded in respect and nonviolence, can empower partners to express themselves clearly without escalating conflict (Kakar, 2016).
- **Psychoeducation**: Understanding systems theory, enmeshment, and the impact of triangulation can help partners depersonalize conflict and identify maladaptive patterns inherited from the family of origin.
- **Genogram Analysis and Incident Exploration**: Revisiting emotionally charged family interactions (e.g., wedding events, dowry discussions, or household rituals) helps couples identify how past events continue to inform present behavior. These reflections can reduce blame and foster shared meaning.
- Conflict resolution skills: Couples learn techniques such as time-outs, reflective listening, and structured problem-solving to move from blame to collaboration.

Therapeutic Techniques and Micro-Interventions

The following tools have shown promise in couples therapy addressing in-law conflict:

- **Role-Play Exercises:** Simulate high-conflict scenarios with therapist-mediated feedback to increase emotional awareness and practice respectful assertiveness.
- **Weekly Couple Rituals**: Encouraging regular, meaningful time together (e.g., shared meals, gratitude reflections, digital-free time) helps strengthen the dyadic bond amid external pressures.
- **Signaling Systems**: Introducing subtle gestures or "codes" can help partners indicate emotional overwhelm or the need for a pause during escalating moments, promoting de-escalation without public confrontation.
- **Emotional Regulation Tools**: Breathing techniques, grounding exercises, and body scans can be integrated to improve affect tolerance during stressful interactions.
- **Reflective Questioning**: Questions such as "What value are you honoring when you side with your parents over your partner?" invite deeper introspection and clarify competing allegiances.
- **Use of Humor and Positive Distraction**: Injecting playfulness and lightness into emotionally heavy therapy sessions can lower defensiveness and increase openness to change.

Maintaining the Relationship: Long-Term Success

The sustainability of therapeutic gains depends on the couple's ability to consistently apply the tools learned. Maintenance work includes:

- **Regular Check-Ins**: Scheduled follow-up sessions at decreasing intervals help track progress, reinforce new behaviors, and recalibrate strategies as needed.
- **Celebration of Milestones**: Acknowledging positive shifts, such as a festival successfully managed without conflict or a boundary upheld, reinforces hope and resilience.
- **Feedback Loops**: Ongoing therapist-client dialogue ensures that interventions remain culturally congruent, emotionally accessible, and practically useful.

Conclusion

Navigating In-Law Dynamics with Cultural Sensitivity and Clinical Insight

Addressing in-law dynamics in Indian marriages requires a unique therapeutic lens, one that honors cultural contexts while equipping couples to establish differentiated identities. As seen in the case studies, family constellation plays a pivotal role in shaping marital satisfaction, emotional resilience, and conflict patterns. Whether embedded in nuclear, joint, or extended families, couples must learn to negotiate traditions without erasing their individuality.

Therapists must act not as referees in intergenerational conflict but as facilitators of insight, autonomy, and empathy. By focusing on the relationship as the client, and using a structured, culturally informed, and emotionally intelligent framework, mental health professionals can empower couples to thrive, not just survive, within the complex tapestry of Indian familial life.

Ultimately, the therapeutic goal is not to eliminate in-law influence but to transform it from a source of tension into an opportunity for growth, maturity, and relational depth.

References

Banerjee, K. (2020). Mother-in-law and daughter-in-law conflict in Indian households: A psychosocial perspective. *Indian Journal of Social Work*, 81(3), 327–345.

Bowen, M. (1978). *Family therapy in clinical practice*. New York.

Bryant, C. M., Conger, R. D., & Meehan, J. M. (2011). The influence of in-laws on newlywed marriage: A longitudinal ana\lysis. *Journal of Family Psychology*, 25(2), 191–200. https://doi.org/10.1037/a0022413

Chandra, V. (2024). Changing landscape of Indian family. In V. Chandra & S. L. Blair (Eds.), *Indian families: Contemporary family structures and dynamics*. Springer Nature. https://doi.org/10.1108/S1530-353520240000026004

D'Cruz, P., & Bharat, S. (2001). *Beyond joint and nuclear families: Family systems and cultural context in India*. Tata Institute of Social Sciences.

Fischel, W. J. (2012). The role of the family in medieval Indian society. *Journal of the Economic and Social History of the Orient*, 55(2), 221–244. https://doi.org/10.1163/15685209-12341230

Goldenberg, H., Stanton, M., & Goldenberg, I. (2020). *Family therapy: An overview* (10th ed.). Cengage Learning.

Habib, I. (1995). *The agrarian system of Mughal India, 1556–1707*. Oxford University Press.

Johnson, S. M. (2008). *Hold me tight: Seven conversations for a lifetime of love*. Little, Brown and Company.

Kakar, S. (2005). Chapter 5. Hindu myth and psychoanalytic concepts: The Ganesha complex. In S. C. Chang, M. Nishizono, & W.-S. Tseng (Eds.), *Asian culture and psychotherapy: Implications for East and West* (pp. 65–78). University of Hawaii Press. www.degruyterbrill.com/document/doi/10.1515/9780824873868/html

Kakar, S. (2016). *Intimate relations: Exploring Indian sexuality*. Penguin Books India.

Kumar, N. (2011). *The Indian family in transition: Changing roles and relationships*. Sage Publications.

Kumar, S. (2017). *The gendered terrain of maintenance for women*. Notion Press.

Manusmriti. (1886). The laws of Manu(G. Bühler (Trans.)). In F. Max Muller (Ed.), *The sacred books of the East* (Vol. 25, pp. 1–600). Clarendon Press Oxford University Press) (original work published ca. 200 BCE).

McGoldrick, M., Gerson, R., & Petry, S. (2008). *Genograms: Assessment and intervention* (3rd ed.). W. W. Norton & Company.

Mukhopadhyay, C. C. (2021). *Women, education, and family structure in India*. Routledge.

Nichols, M. P. (2020). *Family therapy: Concepts and methods* (12th ed.). Pearson.

Sharma, A. (2013). The family in ancient India: A study of the Vedic and epic periods. *Indian Journal of Social Science Research*, 10(1), 1–12.

Singh, J. P. (2010). India's changing family and state intervention. *The Eastern Anthropologist*, 63(1), 17–40.

Uberoi, P. (2006). *Freedom and destiny: Gender, family, and popular culture in India*. Oxford University Press.

Chapter 22

Uniqueness of Sexual and Relationship Therapy Among Polygamy Patients

Wafaa Eltantawy

Monogamy vs. Polygamy

Many may wonder whether monogamy or polygamy is "better." Questions about these relationships often revolve around issues of morality or fidelity. However, the answer may not be universal and differs between people in most countries across the world. The differences in these types of partnerships can work for different people, and one may not sound right for you based on your values, opinions, or needs.

Anthropological and evolutionary psychology research suggests that monogamy and polygamy are both culturally constructed systems that have evolved in response to ecological, economic, and social factors (Henrich, Boyd, & Richerson, 2012; Zeitzen, 2008). Monogamy has historically gained prominence in Western societies due to legal regulation, Christian moral values, and shifting gender roles, whereas polygamy has often been practiced in agrarian or patrilineal societies where lineage, inheritance, and labor are critical (White & Burton, 1988).

Monogamous individuals may pair well with others seeking monogamy, just as polygamous individuals may be suited for others who participate in polygamy. However, relationships may exist between partners who have differing needs or preferences. A woman who has never wanted to be a wife may be more open to the potential of an open relationship without a permanent husband.

Clinical studies also show that relationship satisfaction varies based on the congruence between personal values and relationship structure. When individuals engage in relationship forms that align with their beliefs and emotional needs, they report greater satisfaction and psychological stability (Altman & Ginat, 1996, Sheff, 2014). In contrast, forced or involuntary participation in either structure can lead to distress, emotional fatigue, or dysfunction (Al-Krenawi & Slonim-Nevo, 2008).

While relationships can vary depending on wants and needs, there may be a societal debate on which type of relationship is "better." In many traditions, monogamy and being married may be viewed as indicative of a loving, faithful, or true union. In those contexts, marriage is perceived as a partnership that may only contain two spouses who commit to a life together until death.

DOI: 10.4324/9781003611387-22

Sociological critiques, however, emphasize that this binary view often ignores the diversity of human intimacy and kinship models across cultures. As such, it is increasingly important in therapeutic settings to approach all relationship types—including consensual non-monogamy, polygamy, and serial monogamy—with neutrality, cultural humility, and non-pathologizing attitudes (DeMaria et al., 2010).

Polygamy vs Polyamory

Polygamy and polyamory both involve multiple romantic partners, but they differ in keyways. Polygamy refers to the practice of having multiple spouses, while polyamory is a broader concept that encompasses having multiple romantic or intimate relationships, not necessarily marriage.

From an anthropological and legal standpoint, polygamy is typically embedded within religious, cultural, or traditional structures. It is most institutionalized in the form of polygamy, where a man marries multiple women.

In rarer contexts, polyandry (one woman married to multiple men) exists, such as in some Himalayan regions like Tibet and Nepal (Zeitzen, 2008). Polyamory, by contrast, is a more contemporary, Western-anchored relational model grounded in voluntary non-monogamy, with mutual consent and often without legal recognition (Conley et al., 2018; Sheff, 2014).

Polygamy

This term specifically refers to the act of being legally married to multiple people. It can take the form of polygyny (one man married to multiple women) or polyandry (one woman married to multiple men). It can be legal or illegal depending on the jurisdiction. It is often hierarchical, with a primary spouse and secondary ones (Popovic, 2006).

In many societies, polygamy is practiced as part of religious or customary law, often emphasizing lineage, inheritance, and patriarchal norms. Countries like Saudi Arabia, Nigeria, and South Africa recognize polygamous unions under specific legal frameworks (Al-Krenawi, 2014; Recognition of Customary Marriages Act, 1998). However, critics argue that polygamy can perpetuate gender inequalities, especially in contexts where consent is assumed rather than explicit (Bove & Valeggia, 2009).

Polyamory

This is a broader concept that focuses on having multiple romantic or intimate relationships, whether through marriage or not. It emphasizes consent, honesty, and open communication among all partners. Not illegal in most places if all parties are consenting. It is egalitarian, with all partners generally on equal footing. "Polyamory is about informed and enthusiastic consent," says Deepak Kashyap (Barlow, n.d.).

Polyamorous relationships emphasize ethical non-monogamy, where love, intimacy, and transparency form the foundation of multiple relationships. Unlike polygamy, polyamory is not inherently tied to legal structures or religious doctrine. Instead, it is rooted in contemporary philosophies of relational autonomy, fluid identity, and consensual negotiation (Sheff, 2014). Scholars like Barker and Langdridge (2010) argue that polyamory challenges dominant narratives of romantic exclusivity and opens space for more inclusive relationship models.

Clinical Note

From a therapeutic perspective, distinguishing between polygamy and polyamory is crucial, particularly in treatment planning. Polygamous clients may bring issues influenced by cultural or religious power dynamics, family hierarchies, and legal complexities (Al-Krenawi & Graham, 2006). In contrast, polyamorous clients often seek support in boundary negotiation, jealousy management, or societal stigma, especially when their relationships are marginalized or misunderstood (Conley et al., 2017).

Global Perspectives of Polygamy

Anthropological studies indicate that approximately 83% of human societies have permitted polygamous marriages. In many preindustrial societies, polygyny was accepted or even preferred, though it was seldom practiced by commoners or lower classes due to economic constraints (Joseph et al., 2012). This pattern is consistent with the findings of White and Burton (1988), who observed that the occurrence of polygyny often correlates with male status, wealth, or lineage preservation in stratified societies.

Polygamy is a culturally diverse marital practice that reflects a society's values, religious doctrines, gender norms, and socioeconomic structures (White & Burton, 1988). While monogamy is legally mandated in many countries today, polygamy—particularly polygyny—remains common and culturally accepted in others. According to Zeitzen (2008), the prevalence of polygamy is not simply a vestige of traditional life but remains an adaptive strategy in specific socio-ecological contexts.

Africa

In Africa, for example, polygyny is widely practiced in many countries and is often embedded in customary laws or traditional practices. Studies suggest polygyny is still practiced by approximately 11% of married women in sub-Saharan Africa (Demographic and Health Surveys, WHO, 1993). In countries like Mali, Burkina Faso, and Nigeria, polygyny can exceed 30% in rural areas (Bove & Valeggia, 2009). It is associated with wealth and status: in rural agrarian communities, more wives often mean more children to help with labor and enhance subsistence security.

It is also associated with lineage preservation: having multiple wives increases the likelihood of producing male heirs. Anthropologist Esther Goody (1973) explained how such reproductive strategies ensured labor continuity in lineage-based economic systems. In legal frameworks, countries like Nigeria and South Africa legally recognize polygamous marriages under customary law. In South Africa, polygamy is also protected under the Recognition of Customary Marriages Act (1998), affirming the cultural legitimacy of plural marriage.

Middle East

In Middle Eastern and Islamic societies, polygamy is religiously sanctioned in Islam, with polygyny permitted under the Quran (Surah An-Nisa 4:3), allowing a man to marry up to four wives if he can treat them equally. While this provision is embedded in religious jurisprudence (*fiqh*), cultural norms shape its application. Though permitted, it is not widely practiced, often due to economic constraints and rising support for monogamy. Legal structures in countries like Saudi Arabia, Iran, Pakistan, and Indonesia legally allow polygamy, though enforcement and conditions vary (Al-Krenawi, 2014).

Feminist critiques within Muslim societies challenge the patriarchal implications of polygamy and demand reform, especially around consent and equitable treatment (Joseph et al., 2012). In many cases, the religious ideal of justice among wives is difficult to uphold in practical terms, resulting in emotional inequities.

South Asia (India, Nepal)

Hinduism traditionally emphasized monogamy, though ancient texts mention polygynous kings and sages. In India, polygamy is banned for Hindus under the Hindu Marriage Act (1955) but permitted for Muslims under personal law. This legal pluralism has fueled ongoing political debate, especially around women's rights and the proposed Uniform Civil Code.

Nepal and Sri Lanka have seen historical polygamy among royals and elites, though it is now largely outlawed. Yet, in some tribal and mountain communities, such as those in Karnali and remote hill districts, vestiges of polygamy still exist within kinship systems.

Polygamy in Tibet and Polyandry

Tibet is one of the rare regions where polyandry, one woman married to multiple husbands, has historically existed. Fraternal polyandry, where brothers share one wife to prevent division of family land and preserve wealth, has been recorded in the Himalayan belt. Though less common today, it still occurs in remote villages in Nepal, Ladakh, and parts of Bhutan (Zeitzen, 2008).

This form of marital arrangement also reduces the population growth pressure in high-altitude, low-resource areas, underscoring the ecological rationale behind such systems (Goldstein, 1987).

East Asia (China, Japan)

Ancient China

Polygyny was practiced by emperors and wealthy men, though only one primary wife was officially recognized. Others were concubines with limited rights. These relationships were formally hierarchical and reflected Confucian norms of filial piety and male authority.

Japan

Polygamy was practiced until the Meiji era, particularly among samurai elites, but was officially outlawed in 1880 as part of modernization and Western legal reforms.

North America: Indigenous Cultures and Mormonism

Indigenous Cultures

Some Native American tribes practiced forms of polygyny before colonization. These arrangements were often functional, connected to labor-sharing, kinship expansion, or spiritual symbolism.

Mormonism

In the 19th century, The Church of Jesus Christ of Latter-day Saints (LDS) endorsed polygyny, citing religious revelations. The US government later outlawed it through the Morrill Anti-Bigamy Act (1862), and the church officially renounced it in 1890. However, fundamentalist Mormon sects in Utah and neighboring states still practice polygamy, though it is not legally recognized (Altman & Ginat, 1996).

Europe and the Western World

Polygamy is generally illegal across Europe, North America, and Oceania. However, immigration and multicultural populations have introduced complex legal and ethical debates. For instance, in the UK, Canada, and France, family courts occasionally face challenges in recognizing polygamous marriages performed abroad—especially regarding spousal benefits, custody rights, or inheritance.

While polygamy remains prohibited under civil law, family reunification policies and plural union recognition in welfare systems have added complexity to legal frameworks (Henrich et al., 2012).

Polygamy as Adaptation to Local Needs

In many societies, polygamy adapts to local needs. In subsistence economies, larger families improve survival; in patriarchal systems, it solidifies male dominance. Altman and Ginat (1996) describe how husbands and wives in plural families cope with their complex lifestyle in various facets of everyday life—including emotional boundaries, economic arrangements, and kinship obligations.

Modern Transitions

Urbanization, women's education, and legal reforms are steadily shifting norms toward monogamy, even in traditionally polygamous societies. Critics argue polygamy can lead to gender inequality, reduced women's autonomy, and child marriage. It also often becomes a source of conflict in the household, causing the aim of marriage—companionship, security, and love—to become obsolete (Ja'far, 2019).

Supporters counter that consensual polygamy is a valid cultural expression and can support kinship and care networks, especially in cases where economic collaboration and reproductive support are central to family structure.

Anthropological and Sociological Insights

Anthropology and sociology offer diverse perspectives on polygamy, exploring its social structures, cultural meanings, and potential consequences. Anthropologists study the prevalence and variations of polygamy across different societies, examining its relationship to factors like resource availability, kinship systems, and power dynamics (Zeitzen, 2008).

Sociologists focus on the impact of polygamy on family dynamics, gender roles, and social inequality, often considering its effects on the well-being of individuals, particularly women and children. Studies show that emotional strain, competition among spouses, and imbalances in sexual satisfaction can have lasting psychological effects (Al-Krenawi & Slonim-Nevo, 2008; Bove & Valeggia, 2009).

Intersections Between Polygamy and Sex Therapy

The practice of polygamy presents unique challenges, dynamics, and considerations for sex therapists. Despite sex and relationship therapy being concerned about individual and couple issues, polygamy introduces distinct therapeutic concerns. Issues such as jealousy, communication dynamics, and cultural or religious beliefs require sensitive and trauma-informed therapeutic approaches. Understanding the historical and cultural contexts of polygamy is essential for providing effective support to individuals in polygamous relationships (Al-Krenawi & Graham, 2006; Zeitzen, 2008).

Here's a more detailed breakdown of the uniqueness:

Understanding the System

Polygamous structures vary from monogamous systems. Different forms of polygamy exist (e.g., polygyny, polyandry), and each has its own set of rules, hierarchies, and dynamics. Therapists need to understand the specific structure and rules of the family they are working with.

- **Cultural and societal influences:** Polygamy is not universally accepted, and its prevalence varies across cultures and religions. Therapists need to be aware of the cultural context in which the relationship exists and the potential for societal stigma or bias. For example, Bove and Valeggia (2009) note that in sub-Saharan Africa, polygyny remains normalized within rural economies and kinship networks, yet in Western societies, it may carry significant social disapproval.
- **Power dynamics and hierarchies:** Polygamous relationships often involve a power dynamic between the primary partner and their other partners. Therapists need to be sensitive to these power imbalances and help ensure that all individuals feel heard and respected. This includes recognizing subtle forms of dominance that may not be overtly coercive but are embedded in tradition, economics, or religious doctrine (Altman & Ginat, 1996).

Addressing Individual Needs

Sexual Health and Satisfaction

Sexual dysfunction, low desire, and other sexual concerns can be more prevalent in polygamous relationships, particularly among women. In a cross-sectional study, it was found that women in polygamous marriages experience considerably higher psychosexual and psychosocial adverse effects as compared with their monogamous counterparts (White & Burton, 1988). Other studies, such as Barut and Mohamud (2023), further support these findings by revealing lower levels of sexual satisfaction and arousal among women in polygamous unions.

Emotional Well-Being

Polygamous relationships can be complex and emotionally demanding, leading to feelings of jealousy, insecurity, and low self-esteem. A meta-analysis was conducted to assess the psychological symptoms associated with marriage types. It indicates that women in polygamous marriages had worsened mental health as compared with women in monogamous marriages (Rahmanian et al., 2021). Thus, therapists must provide a safe and supportive environment for individuals to express their emotions and work through these challenges with validation and culturally sensitive care.

Relationship Dynamic

Conflict and communication issues can be amplified in polygamous relationships due to the multiple partners involved and the potential for competition and jealousy. Therapists need to help individuals develop healthy communication skills and navigate the complex dynamics of the relationship. This can include addressing triangulation, alliances, and rivalry, especially when co-wives compete for resources, attention, or status (Slonim-Nevo & Al-Krenawi, 2006).

Specific Therapeutic Approaches

Emotionally Focused Therapy (EFT)

EFT, with its focus on attachment and emotional regulation, can be particularly well-suited for working with polyamorous or polygamous relationships, as it helps individuals connect with their emotions and improve their communication (Johnson, 2004).

Systems Therapy

A systems approach, which considers the interconnectedness of all members of the polygamous family, can clarify and address the challenges of the relationship structure. Therapists should use culturally adapted systemic models that reflect kinship and religious frameworks relevant to the clients (Lago & Charura, 2015).

Narrative Therapy and Trauma-Informed Therapy

Incorporate narrative therapy to explore identity and values. Use sex-positive frameworks to affirm pleasure and bodily autonomy. Explore trauma histories, especially in women who may have experienced coercion or pressure to accept polygamous arrangements. These approaches are particularly important in helping clients rewrite internalized narratives around submission and self-worth (Joseph Henrich et al. 2012).

Individual Therapy

Individual therapy can be beneficial for addressing individual concerns such as low self-esteem, jealousy, or sexual dysfunction, within the context of the polygamous relationship. This also allows for private discussion around cultural shame or religious dissonance.

Group Therapy

Group therapy can provide a safe and supportive environment for individuals to share their experiences and learn from one another. Facilitated group work for co-wives can create space for shared understanding and healing where rivalry exists (Slonim-Nevo & Al-Krenawi, 2006).

Ethical Considerations

- **Cultural sensitivity:** Therapists must be sensitive to the cultural and religious beliefs surrounding polygamy. A non-pathologizing stance that honors the role of polygamy in the client's worldview is essential for building trust and therapeutic alliance.
- **Informed consent:** All individuals involved in the therapy must be fully informed about the therapeutic process and have the opportunity to give their consent. This is especially critical in contexts where younger or secondary spouses may have entered the relationship under familial or societal pressure.
- **Confidentiality:** Confidentiality must be maintained, even within the polygamous family, to protect the privacy of individuals. Particular care must be taken when clients reveal trauma, mental health concerns, or sexual dissatisfaction that may not be safe to disclose in a group setting.
- **Advocacy:** Therapists may need to advocate for the rights and needs of individuals within the polygamous family, particularly if they are facing discrimination or negative attitudes. Advocacy may also extend to navigating access to legal protection, healthcare, or social services, especially where polygamy is not formally recognized by the state (Zeitzen, 2008).

Additional Considerations

Sexual and relationship therapy for individuals in polygamous relationships can be complex due to the unique dynamics involved. In polygamous relationships, where one individual has multiple spouses or partners, the therapeutic approach must account for various factors such as jealousy, power dynamics, cultural context, and differing expectations across relationships. These variables shape both the clinical formulation and the intervention.

Psychosexual Dynamics in Polygamous Relationships

Desire, Arousal, and Satisfaction

Sexual dysfunctions (e.g., low desire, anorgasmia) may stem from unclear boundaries, performance anxiety related to comparison, resentment, or lack of emotional connection. Barut and Mohamud (2023) found in their study that women in polygamous marriages had significantly lower levels of desire, arousal, and sexual satisfaction.

Variability in sexual satisfaction may emerge between co-wives or partners due to perceived favoritism, unequal attention, or unmet emotional needs. Barut and Mohamud's (2023) findings also supported the phenomenon of the "first wife syndrome" among polygamous women, characterized by the highest levels of anxiety and depression in the first wife compared with other co-wives in the polygamous marriage.

These findings are supported by broader studies in the Middle East and sub-Saharan Africa that document how emotional neglect and inequality in sexual attention can lead to sexual dissatisfaction, psychological distress, and strained marital dynamics (Al-Krenawi & Graham, 2006; Slonim-Nevo & Al-Krenawi, 2006). In therapy, these patterns must be carefully assessed as part of a holistic psychosexual history, considering each partner's narrative about intimacy and fulfilment.

Sexual Scripts and Roles

Partners may adopt rigid sexual roles due to religious or cultural norms or gender expectations, inhibiting sexual expression. Female partners may internalize narratives that prioritize male satisfaction or reproduction over their own pleasure. Many women internalize messages that pleasure is secondary to male experience or the "success" of the act (Nagoski, 2015).

In traditional societies where modesty, obedience, and chastity are highly valued, sexual scripts often reflect patriarchal frameworks that place women's bodies in service to male pleasure and lineage continuation (DeMaria et al., 2010). These scripts can become deeply embedded in women's psychosexual self-concept, leading to guilt, shame, or aversion. Exploring these internalized beliefs in therapy is critical to empowering clients and validating their sexual autonomy.

Communication and Consent

Many polygamous unions lack open communication about sexual needs, especially in societies where patriarchy is dominant. Sex therapists may find that discussions around consent, mutual satisfaction, or personal agency are new or even taboo.

Involuntary polygamy (e.g., coerced by family or religious leaders) can result in psychological trauma or long-term relational distress.

Effective therapeutic work involves initiating culturally safe conversations about sexual expectations and consent. Research by Al-Krenawi (2014) shows that many women in polygamous marriages report a lack of agency in initiating or negotiating sexual activity, further exacerbating feelings of powerlessness and dissatisfaction. Therapists must also distinguish between consensual polygamy and polygamy imposed through social or economic coercion.

Jealousy, Competition, and Relational Power Dynamics

Jealousy and rivalry between co-wives or partners can manifest sexually or emotionally. Jealousy in polygamous or polyamorous contexts often centers on unequal sexual access, perceived favoritism, and emotional exclusivity. It can lead to reduced libido due to stress, anxiety, or relational insecurity, sexual withdrawal or performance issues, and feelings of competition or inadequacy (Sheff, 2014). These dynamics may affect libido and self-esteem, trust in the partner(s), and feelings of sexual rejection or inadequacy.

Therapists may need to address hierarchies within the relationship—who gets time, affection, or privileges.

Clinical studies confirm that perceived unfairness in resource allocation or affection fuels psychological stress, especially in cohabiting polygamous households (Slonim-Nevo & Al-Krenawi, 2006). Therapy should help partners negotiate clearer roles and boundaries to reduce triangulation and prevent breakdowns in emotional intimacy.

Cultural and Religious Contexts

Many clients in polygamous marriages come from cultural or religious backgrounds that value modesty, submission, or gendered norms of sexuality. Women, for example, in Middle Eastern, South Asian, some African, and conservative Christian contexts are taught that sexual modesty is virtuous, and open discussion of desire or pleasure is often taboo. This can lead to sexual shame or guilt, difficulty expressing needs or negotiating boundaries, and internal conflict between cultural expectations and personal experience. DeMaria, Weeks, and Hof (2010) explore how modesty norms can inhibit sexual communication, especially in culturally traditional marriages. Al-Krenawi and Graham (2006) found that women in polygamous marriages frequently internalize roles of submission, which contributes to lower self-esteem and mental health distress.

A culturally affirming approach involves respecting the spiritual meaning of polygamy for the client and navigating tension between religious values and therapeutic goals. In addition, therapists must be cautious of imposing Western ideals of monogamous, sex-positive frameworks. Misalignment between the therapist's values and the client's cultural context can lead to therapeutic rupture if not handled with care.

Studies by Bove and Valeggia (2009) further emphasize that in some societies, polygyny is intertwined with survival, economic sustainability, and religious duty. Any therapeutic intervention must be aware of these dimensions and use language and methods that do not frame traditional practices as inherently pathological.

Legal, Ethical, and Safety Considerations

In many countries, polygamy exists outside of formal legal protection, affecting inheritance rights, domestic abuse protections, and marital counseling access. Undocumented or unofficial wives may be especially vulnerable and may not feel safe disclosing concerns around abuse or coercion.

Legal disenfranchisement often creates barriers to justice, housing, and healthcare. It may also limit the ability of women in polygamous relationships to leave abusive marriages or advocate for themselves in court (Zeitzen, 2008). In such cases, therapists must be well-versed in local legislation, community resources, and safeguarding protocols. Trauma-informed risk assessment and inter-agency collaboration may be required where clients disclose abuse, trafficking, or child marriage linked to polygamy.

Sexual and Relationship Therapy for with Polygamous Patients

Sexual and relationship therapy for polygamous patients requires a specialized approach that acknowledges the unique dynamics and challenges inherent in such relationships. Therapists need to be sensitive to cultural and societal norms surrounding polygamy, as well as the potential for power imbalances and jealousy within the group. Additionally, they must be prepared to address the specific needs of individuals within the polygamous structure, including issues related to sexual satisfaction, emotional well-being, and relationship dynamics. Below is an elaborated guide to support clinical understanding and practice.

Understanding the Relationship Structure

Cultural and Religious Context

Polygamy is often influenced by cultural, religious, or personal beliefs. Understanding the context in which the polygamous relationship exists is essential for tailoring therapeutic interventions. Clinicians should clarify whether the polygamy is consensual versus coerced, legal versus informal, and religious or cultural versus lifestyle-based (Al-Krenawi & Graham, 2006).

Communication

The complexity of communication between multiple partners in a polygamous relationship is crucial. Therapy should encourage open dialogue among partners if culturally appropriate and address decision-making power, emotional intimacy, and sexual negotiation and consent (Bove & Valeggia, 2009).

A recent body of work also emphasizes that in some households, communication is filtered through the "primary wife" or male partner, contributing to power disparities that therapists must navigate carefully (Altman & Ginat, 1996). Therapy may focus on improving communication skills, resolving misunderstandings, and addressing unmet needs in the relationship.

Role of the Primary vs. Secondary Spouses

Sometimes, dynamic primary relationships can affect how secondary relationships are perceived and how individuals within these relationships feel about their place and status. Addressing these perceptions and feelings of inequality is an important part of therapy. Clinical studies suggest these hierarchical dynamics contribute to psychological distress and a perceived lack of fairness among spouses (Barut & Mohamud, 2023).

Sexual Health and Satisfaction

Sexual Issues

Sexual satisfaction can be complicated in polygamous relationships due to differing sexual needs and preferences across partners. Therapy can explore issues such as frequency, sexual preferences, and intimacy needs. It is also important to explore each partner's sexual agency, consent, and pleasure, particularly women who may feel disempowered or silenced (Sheff, 2014).

Infectious Disease Risk

In relationships involving multiple sexual partners, discussions around safe sexual practices, contraception, and the risk of sexually transmitted infections (STIs) are essential. According to WHO and Demographic Health Surveys data (1993), polygamous women in sub-Saharan Africa face a significantly higher risk of STI exposure, often due to imbalances in sexual autonomy and education.

Sexual Comparisons and Insecurity

Patients may experience insecurity or jealousy related to sexual comparison with other partners. Therapy can help address body image concerns, comparisons, and self-esteem issues. These psychological patterns can also impact orgasmic functioning, desire discrepancy, and relational disconnection (Nagoski, 2015).

Jealousy and Emotional Strain

Jealousy Management

Jealousy is a common issue in polygamous relationships, where partners may feel neglected, excluded, or overlooked by the individual with multiple partners. Therapy can help individuals develop healthy coping mechanisms for jealousy and establish boundaries to minimize emotional strain. According to Slonim-Nevo and Al-Krenawi (2006), jealousy was a significant predictor of marital dissatisfaction among first wives in polygamous marriages.

Balancing Emotional Needs

Therapy should explore emotional intimacy, affection, and connection with each partner. It is important to address the challenges of emotional balancing to ensure that each person feels valued and loved. Emotional equity is a central theme in maintaining long-term relational health in polygamous families (Altman & Ginat, 1996).

Power Dynamics and Equality

Power Imbalances

There may be a power imbalance within polygamous relationships, where one partner holds more power over the others. This can create emotional distress, feelings of inequality, and even exploitation. A therapist can help address these imbalances by focusing on fairness and equal distribution of power within relationships. Researchers such as Al-Krenawi (2014) note that patriarchal authority, particularly when religiously sanctioned, may prevent wives from voicing grievances.

Conflict Resolution

Disputes between partners may arise over issues of time, attention, and resources. Developing conflict resolution skills is key to maintaining peace within the relationship. Emotionally Focused Therapy (EFT) and culturally adapted systemic therapy can be particularly useful tools in this context (Sheff, 2014).

Individual vs. Collective Needs

Individual Therapy for Self-Exploration

It is important for individuals in polygamous relationships to have the space to explore their personal desires, fears, and boundaries. Therapy might include individual sessions to help each partner gain insight into their needs and how they interact within the group dynamic. Women, especially, may benefit from exploring internalized messages around obedience, silence, and sexual self-worth (DeMaria et al., 2010).

Couple Therapy

Each pair in the polygamous relationship might benefit from specific therapy sessions to address their unique concerns. Therapy should be adaptable to the needs of the couple or group, helping to resolve conflicts and promote stronger emotional connections.

Ethical Non-Monogamy and Consent

Clarifying Boundaries

Polygamous relationships can fall under the umbrella of ethical non-monogamy, where all parties are aware of and agree to the structure of the relationship. Therapy can ensure that clear boundaries are communicated, respected, and revised as needed.

Mutual Consent

Ensuring that all parties agree with the relationship dynamics and that no one feels coerced is fundamental. Consent in polygamous relationships should be clear, enthusiastic, and ongoing. Involuntary polygamy can have long-lasting trauma-related implications and must be distinguished clearly in intake and case formulation (Rahmanian et al., 2021).

Mental Health Support

Mental Health Considerations

The complexity of polygamous relationships can sometimes exacerbate issues such as anxiety, depression, or low self-esteem. Women in polygamous marriages are also at higher risk of sexual dissatisfaction and relational insecurities (Slonim-Nevo & Al-Krenawi, 2006). A therapist can provide psychological support, helping individuals cope with stress and emotional challenges in the relationship.

Support for Children and Extended Family

If there are children or extended family members involved in a polygamous family structure, they may need separate therapy to help navigate family dynamics and any impact of polygamy on their well-being. Research in Bedouin communities, for example, found that children in polygamous households report higher rates of behavioral and academic difficulties compared to monogamous family structures (Al-Krenawi & Slonim-Nevo, 2008).

Therapist's Role

Nonjudgmental Approach

A therapist must adopt curiosity and a neutral and nonjudgmental approach, especially when working with polygamous clients who may come from diverse cultural, religious, or personal backgrounds. It is important to respect their choices and beliefs while facilitating a safe space for open dialogue.

Tailored Therapy

There is no one-size-fits-all solution for sexual and relationship therapy in polygamous patients. Each case is unique, and therapy should be customized based on the specific needs, issues, and concerns of the individuals involved. Cultural humility, clinical reflexivity, and ongoing supervision are essential in sustaining ethical engagement and therapeutic efficacy (Hernández & McDowell, 2010).

Therapeutic Implications and Best Practices

Culturally Competent Inquiry

Ask open-ended, nonjudgmental questions:

- "How is your sexual relationship negotiated within the context of your marriage(s)?"
- "How are sexual needs and boundaries discussed between co-wives?"
- "How does faith or tradition shape your expectations around sex?"
- "What does fairness or satisfaction look like for you in this marriage?"

Use curiosity over judgment:

- "How are roles and responsibilities divided in your family?"
- "What does intimacy look like in your relationship?"

Therapists must be trained to frame such questions with cultural humility, recognizing the client's cultural and religious frameworks as valid points of reference. As Hernández and McDowell (2010) assert, demonstrating critical social awareness and openness to exploring social identity, privilege, and intersectionality supports trust and therapeutic safety in transcultural work.

Systemic Awareness

- Include exploration of family structures, community expectations, and power dynamics in the assessment.

Therapists should assess how broader systemic factors—such as patriarchal community norms, spiritual beliefs, and societal stigma—inform relational and sexual dynamics within the polygamous household. According to Lago and Charura (2015), a systems-informed lens also requires attention to transgenerational narratives, especially in communities where polygamy has historical or spiritual significance.

In clinical supervision, such systemic explorations can help therapists reflect on how their own cultural assumptions and biases may unintentionally shape the therapeutic process.

Empowerment Without Imposition

- Support each partner's agency and sexual well-being, even within traditional frameworks.

- Avoid imposing monogamous assumptions unless clients seek alternative models.

Therapists should validate the relational style of polygamy as legitimate when consensual and lawful, while ensuring that each member is supported in identifying their boundaries, pleasures, and psychological needs. Imposing Western ideals of intimacy, individualism, or linear fidelity may hinder engagement and result in client drop-out (Charura & Lago, 2021a).

Instead, therapeutic empowerment involves affirming the lived experiences of clients within their unique cultural frameworks and enabling self-defined goals for relational and sexual health.

Group and Couple Interventions

- Therapy may involve one-on-one, couple, or even multi-partner sessions if all parties are willing.
- Address dynamics such as sexual favoritism, emotional neglect, or sexual satisfaction.

Studies by Al-Krenawi (2014) have shown that structured group therapy among polygamous family members can increase empathy and reduce relational tension when facilitated with neutrality and respect for spiritual traditions.

Key Therapeutic Goals

- **Enhance Communication:** Teach partners how to express their feelings, desires, and concerns in healthy and constructive ways. Communication frameworks such as nonviolent communication (NVC) or emotionally focused communication techniques may be integrated, especially when cultural norms discourage directness.
- **Build Emotional Intimacy:** Foster strong emotional bonds among partners while recognizing the unique needs of everyone. Emotional intimacy in polygamous systems often fluctuates depending on time allocation, shared parenting responsibilities, and unresolved jealousy. Emotional validation in session can bridge gaps between relational tensions.
- **Resolve Conflicts:** Help partners manage jealousy, competition, or disputes in a way that maintains respect and fairness. EFT, particularly when culturally adapted, can be powerful in helping co-wives or partners validate each other's emotional pain and enhance attachment security.
- **Sexual Health Education:** Address any concerns related to sexual health, including safe practices, consent, and emotional intimacy. This may involve psychoeducation on sexual rights, contraceptive options, and negotiating intimacy without shame, particularly in patriarchal or religiously conservative settings (DeMaria et al., 2010).

In Summary

Therapy for individuals in polygamous relationships requires sensitivity to complex emotional, psychological, and cultural issues. It is important to provide support that allows for greater understanding, respect, and balance in such relationships while ensuring the mental and sexual well-being of all parties involved. The role of the therapist is not only to guide but also to learn—by creating space for diverse relational models to be understood, honored, and ethically supported.

Sexual and Relationship Therapy in Polygamous Relationships within the Muslim Population

Polygamy, specifically in the context of Muslim populations, is a practice that, while rooted in Islamic tradition, presents unique challenges in the areas of sexual and relationship therapy. The Islamic concept of polygamy allows a man to marry up to four women under the condition of fairness and equity between them. While this practice is legal in many Muslim-majority countries and supported by religious interpretations, it can create complex emotional, sexual, and relational dynamics that may benefit from specialized therapeutic interventions.

Cultural and Religious Context

Polygamy in Islam is governed by strict guidelines, emphasizing fairness, equal treatment, and the well-being of all parties involved. The *Qur'an* (4:3) allows men to marry up to four wives but mandates that they must treat each wife equally in terms of time, resources, and emotional care. While this legal and religious framework provides a structured approach, the practical reality of achieving true equity is difficult and often emotionally charged. Al-Krenawi (2014) found that while polygamy is religiously accepted, many women experience psychological burden, including low self-esteem and depression. This is corroborated by studies showing elevated levels of anxiety and depressive symptoms in first wives due to perceived emotional neglect or favoritism (Barut & Mohamud, 2023).

In therapy, it is essential to acknowledge the cultural and religious significance of polygamy while addressing the psychological and relational challenges that arise within these marriages. Therapists working with Muslim polygamous clients should be aware of Sharia-based principles and how interpretations of these can influence marital expectations and perceived duties (Slonim-Nevo & Al-Krenawi, 2006).

Communication and Conflict Resolution

In Muslim polygamous relationships, communication often becomes strained due to the emotional complexities of sharing a partner. The expectation of fairness between multiple wives can be difficult to manage, and issues of jealousy, neglect, and unspoken grievances may arise. Therapy must focus on improving communication within the relationship, fostering an environment in which all spouses feel heard and valued. The therapist's role is to mediate discussions between partners, facilitating respectful dialogue around sensitive topics such as intimacy, fairness, and emotional fulfilment.

Effective communication skills are essential for managing jealousy, a common issue in polygamous relationships. Therapy should explore the root causes of jealousy, such as insecurity, fear of neglect, or perceived inequities in emotional or sexual attention. Addressing these emotions openly allows for better understanding between partners and helps reduce feelings of resentment or rivalry. Additionally, promoting conflict resolution strategies that emphasize empathy and mutual respect can aid in preventing disputes from escalating.

Therapists may consider structured methods such as EFT or culturally adapted forms of systemic therapy to create safety for each partner to express concerns in line with their values and communication norms (Laan et al., 2021).

Sexual Satisfaction and Intimacy

Sexual satisfaction in polygamous relationships can be particularly complicated, as the sexual needs of each spouse may differ, and the husband may be attempting to balance intimacy with multiple partners. Therapy can help partners express their sexual needs and desires openly, fostering an atmosphere where intimacy is prioritized and not overlooked.

However, the issue of sexual fairness is a significant concern. Islamic teachings demand that a husband must treat each wife equally, including in terms of sexual relations. This can lead to stress and frustration, as it may be difficult for the husband to provide equal attention and satisfaction to each spouse. In therapy, the role of the therapist is to help individuals and couples navigate this challenge, providing tools for balancing sexual expectations with emotional connections.

Therapy can also address the psychological aspects of sexual relationships. Many women in polygamous marriages may experience feelings of inadequacy or low self-esteem if they feel neglected in favor of other wives. This can affect their sexual self-image and intimacy with their husband. Individual counselling, along with couples therapy, can work to heal these emotional wounds and improve sexual satisfaction.

The research by DeMaria, Weeks, and Hof (2010) shows that cultural modesty norms often suppress communication around sexual needs, which can be a barrier to resolving dissatisfaction. Therapists must therefore gently introduce language around sexual rights, pleasure, and mutual satisfaction, especially when cultural taboos prevent open discussion.

Mental Health and Emotional Support

The mental and emotional health of individuals in polygamous relationships is a critical aspect of therapy. Feelings of isolation, loneliness, and low self-worth may arise if a partner feels neglected or if there is perceived unfairness in the distribution of resources and attention. For the wives, therapy can address the emotional impact of polygamy, helping them feel validated and supported. For the husband, managing multiple relationships and the associated responsibilities can lead to stress, guilt, and burnout.

Therapists can play a crucial role in helping individuals and families develop coping strategies for managing emotional challenges, such as stress management techniques and self-care practices. Additionally, a therapist can guide the family through issues of power dynamics, helping to ensure that the emotional and physical needs of each individual are met in a way that respects Islamic teachings and the principles of justice and equity.

Research supports the notion that culturally sensitive interventions, particularly those grounded in family systems therapy and narrative approaches, can reduce psychological strain and restore emotional equilibrium (Al-Krenawi & Slonim-Nevo, 2008; Charura & Lago, 2021b).

Clinical Case Evidence and Next Section Preview

The following case studies illustrate the complexities and therapeutic interventions that may be necessary in addressing the sexual and relationship difficulties within polygamous Muslim households. These examples are drawn from peer-reviewed literature and field-based research to reflect real-life scenarios with clinical relevance.

Case Study 1: Jealousy and Emotional Distress in a Polygamous Marriage

Background

Ahmed, a 45-year-old Muslim man, is married to two women: his first wife, Fatimah, and his second wife, Amina. They live in a country where polygamy is practiced legally, and Ahmed believes he is fulfilling his religious duty by providing for and marrying both women. However, Fatimah has begun expressing growing feelings of jealousy and insecurity regarding her husband's attention toward Amina. Despite Ahmed's claims of fairness, Fatimah feels emotionally neglected and fears losing her husband's affection.

This scenario reflects a common pattern found in polygynous marriages, where the emotional needs of wives are often differentially met despite equal provision. Al-Krenawi and Graham (2006) found that first wives in polygamous marriages often report significantly higher levels of emotional distress and jealousy compared to their co-wives.

Presenting Issue

Fatimah's jealousy has led to frequent arguments between the wives, and emotional distress is becoming evident. Fatimah has even developed anxiety, and Amina feels caught in the middle, unsure of how to support her husband without antagonizing Fatimah. Ahmed is frustrated, as he believes he has been equally dividing his time and resources between his wives but is unaware of the depth of Fatimah's emotional turmoil.

Such emotional experiences are consistent with research by Slonim-Nevo and Al-Krenawi (2006), who reported that wives in polygamous unions often suffer from depression, anxiety, and decreased self-worth, especially when they perceive emotional favoritism.

Therapeutic Approach

In therapy, the first step was to establish open communication among all three individuals. Each spouse was encouraged to express their concerns in a safe and non-judgmental space. Through the therapy sessions, it became clear that Fatimah felt emotionally and physically neglected, as she believed Ahmed prioritized Amina's needs over hers. Ahmed had failed to recognize the subtle emotional cues from Fatimah, focusing instead on the material aspects of fairness such as financial support and time distribution.

A key intervention was a series of communication exercises that helped both wives articulate their emotional needs. Fatimah was guided to express her feelings of inadequacy without accusations, while Ahmed was taught to actively listen without becoming defensive. Amina was included in the discussions, as her role in this dynamic needed to be acknowledged as well. The therapist also worked with Ahmed to help him understand that emotional equity is just as important as physical or financial fairness.

This therapeutic strategy aligns with principles of EFT, which emphasizes the development of secure emotional bonds through improved communication and empathy (Laan et al., 2021). By reframing fairness to include emotional responsiveness, the therapist promoted mutual validation and deeper connection.

Outcome

Through multiple therapy sessions, the family learned to identify and discuss their emotional needs and set clearer boundaries regarding time allocation and intimacy. While Fatimah's jealousy did not disappear completely, her anxiety decreased as she felt more assured of her husband's commitment. Amina and Fatimah also developed a deeper understanding of each other's roles, reducing the competitive feelings between them. Ahmed learned that being fair to his wives involved not only the practical aspects of marriage but also nurturing their emotional well-being.

This outcome reflects broader findings in the literature on therapeutic interventions in polygamous families, where increasing emotional literacy and relational equity can significantly improve household harmony and reduce individual psychological distress (Barut & Mohamud, 2023).

Case Study 2: Sexual Dissatisfaction and Unrealistic Expectations in a Polygamous Family

Background

Yusuf, a 50-year-old man, has four wives, and his marital arrangement is viewed as a model of religious and social stability within his community. However, despite the outward appearance of harmony, there are underlying tensions related to sexual dissatisfaction. His first wife, Zainab, has begun expressing frustration about the infrequency of their sexual intimacy. Zainab feels neglected because Yusuf prioritizes the sexual needs of his younger wives, believing they are more sexually desirable.

This reflects a dynamic often reported in empirical studies, where age-related sexual preferences and unequal intimacy create distress for senior wives. Barut and Mohamud (2023) found that first wives in polygamous marriages often experience heightened dissatisfaction due to perceived or real sexual neglect.

Presenting Issue

Zainab is struggling with feelings of sexual neglect and resentment, which have begun to affect her self-esteem and emotional well-being. She often compares herself to Yusuf's other wives, feeling unattractive and rejected. Her distress is compounded by a lack of open discussion about her sexual needs. In contrast, the younger wives feel that they are receiving enough sexual attention. Yusuf is unaware of the emotional and sexual dissatisfaction his first wife is experiencing.

These dynamics are echoed in the literature on sexual satisfaction and role conflict within polygamous unions, where silence around intimacy often fuels misunderstanding and psychological strain (Sheff, 2014).

Therapeutic Approach

Therapy in this case focused heavily on sexual communication, as well as the concept of emotional intimacy within a polygamous marriage. The therapist emphasized the importance of open and honest conversations about sexual satisfaction, addressing not only the physical aspects of intimacy but also the emotional connections that are crucial for sexual fulfilment. Zainab was encouraged to express her feelings of rejection in a non-confrontational way, explaining how the disparity in sexual attention made her feel undesirable.

The therapist also worked with Yusuf to help him understand that sexual fairness involves more than just the frequency of encounters but includes emotional investment and ensuring that all wives feel valued in the relationship. A significant part of the therapy was addressing the unrealistic expectations that Yusuf had of his sexual relationships, as he viewed them through a transactional lens rather than focusing on emotional connection.

This approach is consistent with sex-positive therapy frameworks that promote mutual satisfaction, emotional bonding, and dismantling of internalized gender scripts (DeMaria et al., 2010; Nagoski, 2015).

Outcome

With the therapist's guidance, Yusuf acknowledged the emotional toll his actions had taken on Zainab. He was able to modify his approach to sexual intimacy by making sure that he devoted equal emotional energy to his first wife, including regular acts of affection and open dialogue about their sexual relationship. Zainab began to feel more secure in the marriage, as her needs were being addressed. The younger wives, too, were encouraged to express their desires and concerns in the relationship, leading to more harmonious sexual dynamics within the family.

The success of this intervention mirrors evidence from Al-Krenawi (2014), who emphasized that increased emotional presence and responsiveness in therapy often mitigates distress among senior co-wives in polygamous families.

Conclusion to Case Studies

These case studies highlight the multifaceted nature of sexual and relationship therapy within polygamous Muslim households. Therapy must consider the religious, cultural, and psychological dynamics that shape relationships. Issues such as jealousy, sexual satisfaction, emotional neglect, and power imbalances require a tailored approach that fosters communication, empathy, and fairness. Through therapeutic interventions that focus on emotional and sexual equity, individuals in polygamous relationships can find ways to navigate the complexities of their marriages, creating healthier and more fulfilling relationships for all involved.

Conclusion

Polygamy in Muslim communities is practiced under strict guidelines provided in the *n*, Qur'an where men are allowed to marry up to four women, provided they treat them equally and fairly (Qur'an 4:3) "…Then marry those that please you of [other] women, two or three or four. But if you fear that you will not be just, then [marry only] one…" While the practice aims to ensure fairness, many challenges emerge in the realities of polygamous relationships. These include emotional complexities, sexual dissatisfaction, jealousy, and issues surrounding time and resource distribution. In the context of therapy, these challenges require careful navigation of cultural, religious, and psychological factors.

Sexual and relationship therapy within the context of polygamous relationships in Muslim populations requires a culturally sensitive and nuanced approach. Therapy must honor the religious and cultural practices that shape these relationships while addressing the unique challenges they present. By focusing on communication, sexual satisfaction, conflict resolution, and emotional well-being, therapists can help individuals in polygamous relationships navigate the complexities of their lives, fostering healthier and more fulfilling relationships. Understanding the significance of fairness and emotional balance is key to providing effective therapy that respects the individual and collective needs of all involved.

References

Al-Krenawi, A. and Graham, J.R. (2006). A comparative study of family functioning, mental health, and self-esteem of polygamous and monogamous women. *International Journal of Social Psychiatry*, 52(1), 5–17.

Al-Krenawi, A., and Slonim-Nevo, V. (2008). Psychosocial and familial functioning of children from polygynous and monogamous families. *The Journal of Social Psychology*, 148(6), 745–764.

Al-Krenawi, A. (2014). *Psychosocial impact of polygamy in the Middle East*. Dordrecht: Springer. https://doi.org/10.1007/978-1-4614-8988-3

Altman, I. and Ginat, J. (1996). *Polygamous families in contemporary society*. Cambridge: Cambridge University Press.

Barker, M. and Langdridge, D. (2010). Whatever happened to non-monogamies? Critical reflections on recent research and theory. *Sexualities*, 13(6), 748–772.

Barlow, E. (n.d.). *Kinder Mind: Couples therapy for polyamorous relationships—What you need to know*. Kinder Mind. https://kindermind.com/blog/polyamorous-couples-therapy/

Barut, A. and Mohamud, S.A. (2023). The psychosexual and psychosocial impacts of polygamous marriages: A cross-sectional study among Somali women. *BMC Women's Health*, 23(1), 669.

Bove, R. and Valeggia, C.R. (2009). Polygyny and women's health in sub-Saharan Africa. *Social Science & Medicine*, 68(1), 21–29.

Charura, D., & Lago, C. (Eds.). (2021a). *Black identities + white therapies: Race, respect + diversity*. Monmouth: PCCS Books.

Charura, D., & Lago, C. (Eds.). (2021b). *Black identities + white therapies: Race, respect + diversity*. Monmouth: PCCS Books.

Conley, T.D., Matsick, J., Moors, A.C., and Ziegler, A. (2017). Investigation of consensually nonmonogamous relationships: Theories, methods, and new directions. *Perspectives on Psychological Science*, 12(2), 205–232. https://doi.org/10.1177/1745691616667925

Conley, T.D., Piemonte, J.L., Gusakova, S., and Rubin, J.D. (2018). Sexual satisfaction among individuals in monogamous and consensually non-monogamous relationships. *Journal of Social and Personal Relationships*, 35(4), 509–531.

DeMaria, R.M., Weeks, G.R., and Hof, L. (2010). Focus on the family: A cultural perspective on sexuality and intimacy. *Journal of Sex & Marital Therapy*, 36(2), 101–112.

Demographic and Health Surveys. (1993). *World Health Organization Report on Sub-Saharan Africa*. WHO.

Demographic and Health Surveys. (1993). *Polygamy in sub-Saharan Africa: Findings from the Demographic and Health Surveys*. Macro International/USAID.

Goldstein, M.C. (1987). When brothers share a wife: Tibetan polyandry and its demographic consequences. *Natural History*, 96(3), 39–48.

Goody, E.N. (1973). *Contexts of kinship: An essay in the family sociology of the Gonja of Northern Ghana*. Cambridge: Cambridge University Press.

Henrich, J., Boyd, R., & Richerson, P.J. (2012). The puzzle of monogamous marriage. *Philosophical Transactions of the Royal Society B: Biological Sciences*, 367(1589), 657–669. https://doi.org/10.1098/rstb.2011.0290

Hernández, P. and McDowell, T. (2010). Intersectionality, power, and relational safety in context: Key concepts in family therapy. *Journal of Marital and Family Therapy*, 36(3), 291–303.

Hindu Marriage Act. (1955). *The Hindu Marriage Act, 1955*. India: Government of India.

Ja'far, K. (2019). Polygamy in Islamic law: A contemporary perspective. *Al-Jami'ah: Journal of Islamic Studies*, 57(2), 347–372.

Johnson, S.M. (2004) *The practice of emotionally focused couple therapy: Creating connection*. 2nd ed. New York: Brunner-Routledge.

Joseph, H., Babore, A., and Trumello, C. (2012). Polygamy and mental health of women in Cameroon: Exploring the roles of jealousy and marital satisfaction. *Journal of Divorce & Remarriage*, 53(3), 211–228.

Laan, E., Both, S., van Lunsen, R., and Vignozzi, L. (2021). Sexual desire, arousal, and response: A biopsychosocial perspective. *The Journal of Sexual Medicine*, 18(3), 465–475.

Lago, C., and Charura, D. (eds.) (2015). *The handbook of transcultural counselling and psychotherapy*. Maidenhead: Open University Press.

Nagoski, E. (2015). *Come as you are: The surprising new science that will transform your sex life*. New York: Simon & Schuster.

Popovic, M. (2006). Polygamy. In H. J. Birx (Ed.), *Encyclopedia of anthropology* (Vol. 5, pp. 1882–1883). Thousand Oaks, CA: Sage. https://doi.org/10.4135/9781412952453

Qur'an. (n.d.). *Surah An-Nisa*, 4:3.

Rahmanian, P., Munawar, K., Mukhtar, F., and Choudhry, F.R. (2021). Mental health of women in polygamous versus monogamous marriages: A systematic review and meta-analysis. *Journal of Affective Disorders*, 280, 189–200.

Recognition of Customary Marriages Act. (1998). *Recognition of Customary Marriages Act 120 of 1998*. South Africa: Government of South Africa.

Sheff, E. (2014). *The polyamorists next door: Inside multiple-partner relationships and families*. Lanham, MD: Rowman & Littlefield.

Slonim-Nevo, V. and Al-Krenawi, A. (2006). Success and failure among polygamous families: The experience of wives, husbands, and children. *Family Process*, 45(3), 311–330.

White, D.R., and Burton, M.L. (1988). Causes of polygyny: Ecology, economy, kinship, and warfare. *American Anthropologist*, 90(4), 871–887.

Zeitzen, M.K. (2008). *Polygamy: A cross-cultural analysis*. Oxford: Berg.

Chapter 23

Psychosexual Work Among NRI Clients in India

Bishurul Hafi NA and NA Uvais

Introduction: Letters Across the Sea

The story of Indian migration to the Gulf is not only an economic narrative but also one of longing, intimacy, and emotional endurance. Few cultural expressions capture this better than the "*kathu patt*" or letter songs popularized by poet S.A. Jameel. These verses, exchanged between absent husbands and waiting wives, give voice to the ache of separation and the resilience of bonds stretched across distance, reflecting the complex emotional landscapes of transnational migration (King & Christou, 2010). A wife's words of devotion, mingled with sorrow, remind us that absence is not just geographic but deeply bodily and relational. A husband's reply, trembling with love and helplessness, reflects the enduring tension between duty abroad and intimacy at home. These songs were not just entertainment; they were public acknowledgments of the private struggles of separation that defined many households across South India.

Historically, Indian migration for work has always carried this dual weight of hope and sacrifice. In the early twentieth century, economic routes led many to Burma (now Myanmar) and Ceylon (now Sri Lanka), where remittances supported families left behind. The oil-driven economies of the Gulf Cooperation Council (GCC) states shifted this flow dramatically in the 1970s, creating a massive wave of labor migration, particularly from Kerala and other southern states. Today, more than 8.5 million Indians live and work in the Gulf, often in environments that are socially conservative, culturally restrictive, and physically isolating. For many, migration begins at a very young age, long before relational or sexual identities are fully matured, leaving individuals vulnerable to the influence of digital sexual scripts and pornography during critical developmental periods (Pathmendra et al., 2023).

Expatriate life shapes sexuality in ways that are rarely spoken about publicly, often manifesting as unique clinical challenges within immigrant populations (Huang & Akhtar, 2005). For some, the absence of family leads to loneliness and compulsive behaviors. For others, cultural scripts about purity, duty, and secrecy intensify the guilt that surrounds masturbation, pornography use, or premarital encounters. Long separations between spouses alter marital rhythms, setting up

DOI: 10.4324/9781003611387-23

cycles of anticipation, anxiety, and sometimes disappointment. Digital technologies offer new ways of sustaining intimacy but bring with them fears of exposure and surveillance. Some clients find themselves in clandestine relationships or sexual networks, entangled in secrecy, shame, and health risks. Across all of these realities lies a common theme: sexuality is lived not in isolation but in the push and pull of migration, culture, and longing (Kar & Singh, 2015).

This chapter explores these psychosexual realities with a focus on Non-Resident Indian (NRI) clients and their partners in India. It draws on clinical observations, cultural research, and the lived voices of migrants themselves. The stance taken is deliberately client-centered, culturally responsive, rights-respecting, and trauma-informed, aligning with international standards that define sexual health as a state of physical, emotional, mental, and social well-being (World Health Organization [WHO], 2006). This means honoring the values and beliefs clients bring, while gently correcting misinformation and reducing shame with evidence-based care. It means recognizing that cultural norms are not fixed but dynamic, and that each individual story carries its own nuance beyond the generalizations.

By weaving together clinical vignettes, theoretical frameworks, and cultural context, this chapter aims to shed light on the complex psychosexual world of expatriates. In doing so, it seeks to expand the therapeutic lens so that practitioners can respond with sensitivity, creativity, and ethical clarity to the unique challenges faced by NRI clients and their families.

Migration, Loneliness, and Psychosexual Health

Migration from India to the Gulf often begins at a young age. Many men, and increasingly women, leave their hometowns before they have had the chance to form stable adult relationships. They enter environments where employment is structured around long hours, strict contracts, and shared living quarters with little privacy. While social clubs, community associations, and places of worship provide some opportunities for connection, they rarely replace the comfort of family life. Over time, the absence of partners and familiar social networks creates a persistent risk of loneliness.

Loneliness is not merely an emotional state. Research shows that prolonged loneliness increases the likelihood of depression, anxiety, sleep disturbance, substance misuse, and suicidal thoughts. It also exerts physiological effects, heightening stress responses and increasing the risk of cardiovascular disease, diabetes, and other chronic health conditions, as systemic reviews of migrant health consistently demonstrate a high burden of physical morbidity linked to environmental and social stressors (Mucci et al., 2019). For migrants in the Gulf, this burden is amplified by additional stressors: the uncertainty of contract renewals, financial obligations to family in India, and restrictive social norms that limit open discussion of emotional or sexual needs.

Mental health systems in many Gulf states are not equipped to meet this demand. Ratios of psychiatrists and psychologists remain far below international standards, and among the available professionals, only a minority are trained in multicultural or multilingual care. This leaves expatriate workers in a vulnerable position, with limited access to safe and culturally attuned support. Many resort to self-managing distress through alcohol, stimulants, compulsive pornography use, or risky sexual behavior, which often worsen rather than relieve the underlying problems.

Clinical Vignette: Rasheed

Rasheed, a 27-year-old from Kerala, migrated to Abu Dhabi at the age of 20. He works in construction and lives in a crowded labor camp. Although he has friends at work, most conversations revolve around daily tasks, money, or brief jokes. He describes his evenings as long stretches of silence broken by phone calls to his family, which often leave him more homesick. To cope, Rasheed began watching pornography on his phone, at first occasionally, but later several hours each night. He also started drinking with colleagues on weekends. Over time, he noticed that his sleep became restless, his concentration at work declined, and he began experiencing frequent chest tightness and a sense of dread. When asked what troubled him most, he admitted that he felt "empty and useless" and feared he was "losing himself."

Rasheed's case reflects how loneliness interacts with sexual behavior, substance use, and mental health, creating a cycle that can spiral without timely intervention.

Screening and Assessment

Clinicians working with NRI clients can benefit from structured tools that help identify the depth of these concerns. The UCLA Loneliness Scale can measure the intensity of isolation, while the PHQ-9 and GAD-7 are validated instruments for depression and anxiety, aligning with standardized diagnostic frameworks (American Psychiatric Association [APA], 2022). The AUDIT-C can help detect risky alcohol use. Sexual function inventories, such as the International Index of Erectile Function (IIEF) or the Female Sexual Function Index (FSFI), may also be appropriate, depending on the client's concerns. Together, these tools provide a more complete picture of how migration stress and loneliness shape both mental and psychosexual health.

By recognizing loneliness not simply as a social inconvenience but as a driver of health risk, therapists and clinicians can better understand the lived experiences of NRI migrants and intervene with empathy, evidence, and cultural sensitivity.

Masturbation, Moral Injury, and Dhat Syndrome

India has a long history of sex-positive traditions, from the sculptures of Khajuraho to Vatsyayana's *Kamasutra*. These ancient texts and artistic expressions reflect a culture that once embraced sexuality as an integral part of life and spirituality. Yet over time, layers of colonial morality, conservative religious teachings, and shifting social norms have produced an ambivalent, often hostile stance toward solo sexual behavior. Masturbation, though medically recognized as a safe and normal expression of sexuality, is frequently framed as sinful, shameful, or physically damaging. For expatriates raised in this context, being alone in a foreign land often intensifies the inner conflict between bodily urges and moral codes.

One of the most striking clinical outcomes of this ambivalence is *Dhat syndrome*, a culture-bound syndrome widely reported in India, Pakistan, Bangladesh, and other parts of South Asia (Chadda & Ahuja, 1990). Derived from the Sanskrit word *dhatu* (elixir or vital substance), Dhat syndrome revolves around the belief that semen is a precious essence, painstakingly distilled from food and blood, and that any loss of it threatens vitality. Men who experience nocturnal emissions, pre-ejaculate, or semen mixed with urine may interpret these natural processes as catastrophic. Typical complaints include fatigue, body weakness, low energy, anxiety, depressed mood, sexual dysfunction, and somatic concerns such as back pain or palpitations (Grover et al., 2016). Many attribute these symptoms to past masturbation, erotic dreams, or "excessive desire," and see themselves as morally or physically damaged.

Dhat syndrome often overlaps with obsessive-compulsive spectrum concerns and health-related anxieties. Clients may check their urine repeatedly for signs of semen, avoid intimacy to "conserve" vitality, or become preoccupied with ruminations about past sexual behavior. The distress is not merely physical but existential, as men may feel they have violated family expectations or divine commandments.

Clinical Vignette: Vikram

Vikram, a 23-year-old unmarried man from northern Kerala, sought therapy after months of sleepless nights and declining performance at work. He reported feeling drained and weak, convinced that his semen was leaking during urination. He described waking from erotic dreams with a sense of panic, interpreting nocturnal emissions as proof that his body was failing. Vikram stopped meeting friends and avoided women, fearing that even casual arousal might worsen his condition. His greatest fear was that by the time he married, he would be impotent and would "shame" his family.

Therapeutic Frame

Working with clients like Vikram requires both cultural sensitivity and scientific clarity. A cultural formulation interview can help map his personal beliefs, family messages, and religious context, ensuring that interventions are framed respectfully. Psychoeducation is central: explaining semen physiology, normalizing nocturnal emissions, and clarifying that masturbation does not cause long-term harm. Cognitive-behavioral therapy (CBT) can address catastrophic interpretations of bodily sensations, while mindfulness practices help reduce guilt and foster non-judgmental awareness of arousal, utilizing a structured approach to cognitive restructuring and behavioral change (Metz et al., 2017) Values-congruent behavioral activation—such as reengaging with friendships or physical exercise—can restore a sense of vitality and dignity. When safe and appropriate, involving family members may help correct intergenerational myths and reduce pressure.

The broader lesson of Dhat syndrome is that psychosexual symptoms are never only biological. They are shaped by cultural scripts, moral landscapes, and personal histories. For NRI clients, the tension between solitary sexual practices and moral expectations can magnify distress, but with culturally attuned therapy, it is possible to reduce shame, restore confidence, and build healthier understandings of the body and sexuality.

Pornography Use in Expat Life

For many expatriate men, living far from partners and family creates both opportunity and temptation for solitary sexual outlets. In conservative Gulf societies, where premarital and extramarital sex is strictly prohibited, pornography often becomes the primary source of arousal and release. Large-scale studies confirm that pornography use is widespread in Arab countries, particularly among young men and those with lower educational attainment (Eljawad et al., 2021). While prevalence data on expatriates specifically is sparse, anecdotal clinical evidence suggests that consumption is common among men from Kerala and other Indian states who spend years working abroad without their spouses.

Pornography use itself is not inherently harmful. However, the context in which it occurs often shapes its impact. For some expatriates, pornography fills a temporary void without major consequences. For others, frequent or secretive use begins to erode relationship intimacy (Willoughby et al., 2021). Partners left in India may suspect infidelity when they discover browsing histories or hidden files. Some wives report checking their husbands' phones or computers, searching for "evidence" of betrayal, which can spark escalating cycles of mistrust and negative shifts in the couple's relational satisfaction (Minarcik et al., 2016). The emotional fallout is particularly severe when religious or moral frameworks cast pornography as sinful, adding layers of guilt and shame to an already fraught dynamic.

It is important to distinguish between high-frequency use and problematic use. While many men may consume pornography daily without major distress, a subset develop compulsive patterns that interfere with sleep, concentration, sexual satisfaction, or relational harmony (Reid et al., 2011). Screening tools such as the Compulsive Sexual Behavior Disorder Scale (CSBD-19), the Problematic Pornography Consumption Scale (PPCS), and the Sexual Compulsivity Scale can help clinicians identify when pornography use has shifted from habit to compulsion.

Clinical Vignette: Anu and Sajan

Anu and Sajan, married for six years, came for therapy shortly after Sajan returned from Dubai. During his stay abroad, Anu often felt emotionally disconnected from him and grew suspicious of his late-night phone habits. When she eventually discovered pornography files on his device, she confronted him angrily. Sajan admitted that pornography had become his nightly routine, but insisted it was "just a way to cope with loneliness." Anu, however, felt betrayed, interpreting his use as proof of diminished attraction to her. Their arguments became increasingly volatile, with Anu checking his phone and Sajan growing defensive. Both reported feeling distant and unsatisfied, and both carried strong religious guilt about pornography, though expressed differently.

Therapeutic Approaches

Addressing pornography-related distress requires a multifaceted and culturally sensitive approach. Motivational interviewing can help clients clarify their personal values, exploring whether their use aligns with or contradicts their relational and spiritual commitments. Couples may benefit from setting mutually agreed-upon boundaries, such as limiting or abstaining from pornography during periods of cohabitation, while discussing openly how each partner interprets its meaning. Content filters and accountability apps may be useful tools but should be implemented collaboratively, not as surveillance.

For those with entrenched habits, mindful arousal retraining can help shift focus from visual stimuli back to embodied experiences. Sensate focus exercises allow couples to rediscover intimacy through gradual, non-demand touch that emphasizes presence rather than performance. Structured communication protocols can reduce cycles of accusation and defensiveness, creating space for vulnerability. Finally, relapse-prevention planning can prepare clients for predictable triggers such as loneliness, stress, or boredom, offering healthier coping strategies like exercise, relaxation, or scheduled partner communication.

Pornography use among expatriates illustrates the intersection of migration stress, secrecy, religious guilt, and marital strain. Therapists who approach this topic without judgment, but with cultural sensitivity and evidence-based tools, can help couples move from mistrust to understanding and from shame to constructive intimacy.

Sexual Adventures, STI Fear, and Venereophobia

Expatriate life is often framed publicly as disciplined, lonely, and work-centered. Yet hidden sexual markets exist in most Gulf cities, ranging from massage parlors and sex workers to covert networks of men who have sex with men. For many migrants, these encounters happen only once or twice, often under the influence of alcohol or intense peer pressure. Masculinity norms play a powerful role, as refusing to join colleagues in visiting sex workers can be interpreted as weakness, naivety, or even inadequacy.

For some men, especially those raised in conservative religious households, even limited or non-penetrative encounters produce overwhelming guilt and fear.

Alongside this shame, a different anxiety emerges: the fear of sexually transmitted infections (STIs). Known clinically as *venereophobia*, this syndrome involves catastrophic interpretations of minor bodily sensations such as tingling, discharge, or rashes, reflecting the cognitive specificity characteristic of health-related anxiety disorders (Starcevic & Berle, 2006). The fear often spirals into obsessive checking, repeated internet searches, and avoidance of routine medical tests for fear of being exposed.

Clinical Vignette: Mansoor

Mansoor, a 32-year-old NRI electrician working in Qatar, described a single encounter with a sex worker arranged by colleagues. He did not have penetrative sex, but there was kissing and brief genital contact. Soon after, he noticed mild itching on his skin and became convinced he had contracted HIV. Mansoor began examining himself several times a day, avoiding communal meals, and withdrawing from friends. When he was asked to attend mandatory medical testing for his work permit renewal, he panicked and considered quitting his job to return to India. He repeatedly told himself, "Everyone will know I am dirty." Over time, his anxiety became so consuming that he stopped sleeping properly and began losing weight.

Evidence-Based Approach

Mansoor's case highlights how cultural shame, sexual secrecy, and health anxiety converge in the expatriate context. The first therapeutic step is *risk assessment.* Clinicians can provide accurate information about modes of STI transmission, clarifying that superficial contact carries minimal or no risk for HIV. Laying out *window period timelines* for reliable testing can also reduce uncertainty and prevent unnecessary repeated testing.

Second, *targeted testing* should be offered as reassurance, but framed within a non-stigmatizing narrative. Providing written materials about confidentiality policies and the difference between routine health screening and disclosure to employers can ease fears about exposure.

Third, *cognitive-behavioral therapy* (CBT) for health anxiety is effective. This involves identifying catastrophic thoughts ("a small itch means HIV"), challenging them with evidence, and introducing balanced alternatives. Behavioral strategies such as limiting online symptom checking and using graded exposure to medical settings can reduce avoidance.

Finally, *shame reduction* is crucial. Therapists can normalize the fact that many migrants experience peer pressure, clarify that sexual mistakes do not define one's worth, and use stigma-safe language that avoids labels such as "dirty" or "immoral." Incorporating mindfulness exercises may help clients like Mansoor observe bodily sensations without attaching catastrophic meaning.

With culturally sensitive care, clients who fall into cycles of venereophobia can regain emotional stability, protect their employment, and move forward without carrying the weight of secrecy and guilt.

Extramarital Relationships and Relational Fallout

One of the defining features of expatriate life in the Gulf is prolonged separation from spouses. Many migrants, particularly from Kerala and other southern states of India, spend eleven months a year abroad and return home for only a few weeks. While financial stability is the primary motivation, the cost often comes in the form of relational strain. Over time, loneliness, lack of intimacy, and daily companionship needs create fertile ground for alternative attachments.

In this context, workplace romances and clandestine affairs are not uncommon. Some migrants even enter secret second marriages abroad, often rationalizing them as temporary arrangements for companionship. The secrecy surrounding these relationships, however, creates an environment ripe for conflict, blackmail, and exposure. When these affairs unravel—due to job transfers, financial disputes, or a partner's anger—the fallout is often devastating. Women involved in such affairs may directly contact the man's wife in India, disclosing intimate details or even threatening to circulate messages and photographs. In other cases, blackmail emerges, with demands for money or material support in exchange for silence.

The emotional grief that follows the end of an affair is rarely recognized but can be profound. Migrants may feel torn between genuine affection for an extramarital partner and loyalty to their spouse. Returning home becomes emotionally charged, as guilt and fear of discovery intensify. Meanwhile, the spouse left in India often experiences betrayal, humiliation, and anger, compounded by cultural stigma and community gossip.

Clinical Vignette: Leena and Thomas

Leena, a 38-year-old homemaker in Kerala, was blindsided when she received a phone call from a woman in Dubai claiming to be in a long-term relationship with her husband, Thomas, who had worked abroad for over a decade. The woman forwarded screenshots of intimate chats and photographs, confirming the affair. Leena confronted Thomas upon his next visit, and what followed was a storm of anger, tears, and confusion. Thomas admitted to the relationship but insisted it was "only to survive loneliness." Leena felt betrayed not only as a wife but as someone who had sacrificed much of her own life to raise their children alone while he worked abroad. Their teenage son overheard arguments and began distancing himself from Thomas. The entire family system was shaken, with extended relatives weighing in and adding pressure.

Couple Therapy Tasks

In situations like Leena and Thomas's, therapy must address multiple layers of trauma and systemic pressure:

- **Trauma of Betrayal**: The injured partner requires space to process feelings of shock, rage, and grief without being rushed into premature forgiveness, noting that the specific ability to communicate about sexual intimacy is a critical component of overall relationship recovery and satisfaction (Montesi et al., 2011)
- **Structured Disclosure**: Therapists can guide conversations so that the disclosure is complete but not unnecessarily graphic, preventing re-traumatization.
- **Boundaries Around Devices**: Couples often need to renegotiate expectations about privacy, transparency, and communication technology to rebuild trust.
- **Safety from Harassment**: If the extramarital partner continues to harass or blackmail, therapists may support clients in documenting threats, seeking legal advice, and protecting their digital privacy.
- **Family System Pressures**: In collectivist settings, family members, in-laws, and even community leaders may demand involvement. Therapists can help couples clarify whose voices matter in their decision-making.
- **Pragmatic Decisions**: Finally, couples must decide whether reconciliation or separation is feasible. For some, rebuilding the marriage through therapy is possible, while for others, the injury to trust is irreparable.

Extramarital relationships among expatriates highlight the complex interplay between migration, secrecy, loneliness, and community stigma. Therapeutic work in this area requires both cultural sensitivity and strong boundaries, ensuring that while couples are supported in their decisions, the dignity and emotional safety of both partners remain central.

Long-Distance Marriages and Uncertainty

Among NRI families, long-distance marriages are often normalized as part of the migration experience. For many couples, especially in the Gulf context, the economic necessity of working abroad outweighs the emotional strain of separation. Yet over time, the emotional costs accumulate in ways that are distinct from the challenges faced by singles or families who migrate together.

Uncertainty Management Theory provides a useful lens for understanding this phenomenon (Dainton & Aylor, 2001). Couples in long-distance relationships experience heightened uncertainty about the stability of their bond and the trajectory of their future. They invest heavily in communication and rituals of connection to reduce that uncertainty. Video calls, letters, and, increasingly, WhatsApp messages become lifelines. At the same time, maintaining intimacy at a distance requires emotional bandwidth, and the constant vigilance to keep the relationship "alive" can drain energy that might otherwise be spent on friendships or social integration abroad.

The rhythm of home visits creates its own psychological cycle. For many expatriates, the countdown to annual leave is a mix of anticipation and pressure, as "return mobilities" often require navigating complex expectations of the ancestral homeland (King & Christou, 2011). Days at home are filled with shopping, gift-giving, and family obligations. In joint family systems, gift politics can be particularly fraught: the choice of what is purchased for each relative carries symbolic meaning and can either maintain harmony or spark conflict. In-law dynamics often intrude on the couple's limited time together, leaving spouses with little privacy for intimacy. When the expatriate departs again, partners may feel not only sadness but emptiness, as if the weeks of waiting did not yield the closeness they had hoped for.

Studies suggest that couples in long-distance marriages may experience higher loneliness than singles or families who migrate together. Singles often have more freedom to form friendships or community bonds, while co-residing families sustain daily routines together. Long-distance couples, in contrast, live in limbo—neither fully together nor fully apart (Sahlstein, 2004).

Clinical Vignette: Hiba and Nithin

Hiba and Nithin had been married for nine years. Nithin worked in Saudi Arabia, returning to Kerala once a year. In the months leading up to his visit, they both engaged in elaborate countdowns—sending each other photographs, planning purchases, and mapping out family visits. Yet when Nithin finally arrived, their time together was consumed by shopping trips, visits to relatives, and in-law obligations. Hiba longed for private moments of intimacy, but Nithin often seemed distracted, preoccupied with financial matters or family expectations. After he left, Hiba reported feeling "emptier than before," and Nithin admitted to feeling guilty for "never being enough." Their arguments intensified during the months apart, and even their online communication became strained.

Therapeutic Interventions

Supporting couples like Hiba and Nithin requires practical strategies alongside emotional validation. Therapists can encourage:

- **Ritualized Connection Plans**: Establishing small, predictable routines for communication (such as shared prayers, weekly video calls without family present, or joint activities like cooking the same meal) to maintain intimacy.
- **Future-Orientation Mapping**: Helping couples outline medium- and long-term plans for cohabitation, even if years away, to reduce the sense of endless waiting.
- **Planned Intimacy Windows**: Encouraging couples to protect time during visits for private bonding, explicitly negotiating boundaries with extended family in advance.

- **Caregiver Support for In-Law Stress**: Providing tools for boundary-setting and conflict resolution when joint-family expectations intrude on the couple's space.

Long-distance marriages show how love and commitment endure across separation, but also how fragile intimacy becomes when constantly deferred. Therapists who integrate cultural awareness with relational tools can help couples reduce uncertainty, sustain closeness, and resist the erosion of trust that long separations often bring.

Digital Intimacy, Privacy, and Fear of Exposure

In the era of smartphones, many expatriates maintain their sexual connection with partners through WhatsApp, video calls, and other digital platforms. These practices can sustain intimacy across borders, but they are also deeply complicated by conservative cultural norms around sexuality and modesty. While some couples experiment with voice notes or video intimacy, many feel trapped between the desire for closeness and the fear of exposure.

Gender plays a strong role in these dynamics. Women often express greater hesitation about sending intimate images or participating in video sex because of fears of screenshots, leaks, or revenge porn. Men, in turn, may interpret their partner's reluctance as rejection, leading to frustration and conflict. These anxieties are not unfounded—cases of leaked videos or hacked accounts circulate widely in communities, heightening paranoia.

For clients with pre-existing vulnerabilities, particularly those on the psychotic spectrum, these fears may intensify to the level of persecutory beliefs. Some worry that their phones are tapped, that family members are monitoring their devices, or that strangers have access to their private conversations. This techno-paranoia can freeze intimacy, cutting couples off from the very tools that might otherwise sustain them through separation.

Clinical Vignette: Rukhsana

Rukhsana, a 29-year-old woman whose husband worked in Oman, reported feeling distressed whenever he requested video intimacy. While she longed to please him, she could not bring herself to undress on camera. She feared that screenshots might be taken or that the video could leak to social media. These fears grew so overwhelming that she began avoiding all sexual conversations, even in text, and redirected discussions to household matters. Her husband, feeling rejected, accused her of withholding affection, which deepened the emotional gap between them.

Therapeutic Approaches

Therapists can support couples like Rukhsana and her husband by integrating *digital safety coaching* into psychosexual care:

- **Device Hygiene**: Teaching clients how to secure phones with passwords, update security software, and clear metadata from images.
- **Encrypted Platforms**: Encouraging the use of applications that prioritize end-to-end encryption.
- **Negotiated Boundaries**: Helping couples discuss what kinds of digital intimacy feel acceptable and safe, whether voice-only, clothed video, or gradual progression.
- **Consent Scripts**: Offering language that normalizes consent in digital settings, such as "I am comfortable with this today, but not with sending images."
- **Emergency Plan**: Preparing a step-by-step strategy if intimate content is leaked, including reporting mechanisms and emotional stabilization techniques.
- **Trauma-Informed Care**: Validating the real fear of exposure while helping clients regulate anxiety and reestablish intimacy through safer channels.

Digital intimacy can enrich long-distance marriages, but without safety and trust, it can also become a source of fear. Therapists must acknowledge both sides, guiding couples to balance closeness with caution.

Performance Anxiety, Aging, and the Refractory Period

For many expatriates, the anticipation of returning home for annual leave is filled with both excitement and pressure. Months of longing culminate in the expectation of frequent sexual activity, often framed as a way to "make up" for lost time. This buildup creates fertile ground for performance anxiety, particularly among men (Jannini et al., 2012).

Many clients prepare in advance by purchasing *PDE5 inhibitors* such as Viagra, sometimes even before leaving the airport. Others turn to unregulated "natural" enhancers marketed as herbal aphrodisiacs—products like "turkey jam" or "Yemeni honey" that may in fact contain high doses of sildenafil or tadalafil. The absence of regulatory oversight increases the risk of side effects, dangerous interactions, and inconsistent dosing. Some also buy sex toys abroad to enhance performance, fearing disappointment upon reunion.

One of the most common misunderstandings concerns the *refractory period*—the interval after orgasm during which a man is physiologically unable to achieve another erection. This period lengthens with age, yet many couples are unaware of the change. For partners who have waited months for intimacy, a husband's reduced capacity may be interpreted not as biology but as a lack of desire or evidence of infidelity.

Clinical Vignette: Divya and Harish

Divya and Harish had been married for fifteen years. Harish worked in Kuwait and visited once every two years. On his most recent trip, the first week was full of intimacy, but by the second week, Harish found it harder to sustain erections. Divya, who had carefully planned her cycle around his visit and had abstained from any intimacy in his absence, was devastated. She accused him of either not desiring her or of having another partner abroad. Harish, feeling ashamed, grew defensive and avoided sex altogether. Divya broke down in tears during therapy, saying, "I waited for him all this time, and now I feel cheated."

Therapeutic Approaches

Helping couples like Divya and Harish involves a combination of psychoeducation and practical strategies:

- **Education on the Sexual Response Cycle**: Explaining the refractory period and how it naturally changes with age, reassuring both partners that this is not evidence of disinterest or betrayal.
- **Sensate Focus Progression**: Encouraging couples to explore touch, intimacy, and pleasure beyond penetrative sex, reducing pressure on erections.
- **Scheduling Intimacy**: Planning sexual activity around times of rest rather than exhaustion, and spreading encounters over the leave period rather than concentrating them in the first week.
- **Medication Safety**: Guiding clients on the safe use of PDE5 inhibitors, discouraging unregulated products, and involving medical providers when appropriate.
- **Sleep and Jet Lag Management**: Highlighting the role of fatigue, disrupted sleep, and travel stress in sexual performance, and promoting realistic pacing.

Performance anxiety in the expatriate context is not simply a personal issue but a relational one, amplified by cultural scripts of sacrifice, loyalty, and obligation. With sensitive intervention, couples can move from disappointment and blame to mutual understanding, reimagining intimacy as more than frequency or performance.

A Practice Framework for NRI Psychosexual Care

Psychosexual work with NRI clients requires more than addressing symptoms, it necessitates a deep understanding of how cultural factors shape the clinical presentation and management of sexual dysfunction (Bhavsar & Bhugra, 2013) It calls for an integrated framework that attends to migration histories, cultural values, family obligations, and the specific risks that come with living in restrictive environments. Below are key pillars for building such a framework.

Assessment Pillars

A thorough intake should include not only sexual history but also the client's:

- **Cultural and Religious Background**, including moral codes around sexuality and family honor.
- **Migration History**, with attention to age of departure, length of separation, and home visit cycles.
- **Risk Exposure**, such as unprotected encounters, pornography use, or substance reliance.
- **Partner Access**, distinguishing those in long-distance marriages from those who have relocated families.
- **Digital Habits**, including sexting, video intimacy, and privacy fears.
- **Financial Pressures**, which often shape choices around secrecy or disclosure.
- **Legal Context**, especially in countries where adultery, homosexuality, or pornography are criminalized.

Culturally Responsive Psychoeducation

Many NRI clients arrive carrying shame or misinformation. Psychoeducation can be framed in a way that honors belief systems while gently introducing accurate knowledge. For example, explaining nocturnal emissions or masturbation in biological terms can help reframe guilt without directly invalidating religious messages. Therapists can draw on metaphors, narratives, and culturally resonant analogies to reduce defensiveness.

Individual and Couple Pathways

Therapeutic strategies vary depending on the presenting issue and relationship structure.

- **Communication Training**: Teaching partners how to discuss intimacy, expectations, and disappointments without blame.
- **Intimacy Scaffolding**: Gradual exercises that rebuild closeness beyond penetration or performance metrics.
- **CBT and ACT**: Addressing shame, catastrophic thinking, and avoidance through cognitive restructuring, mindfulness, and values-driven action.
- **Graded Exposure**: For health fears such as venereophobia, stepwise reintroduction to medical settings and testing.
- **Values-Consistent Goal Setting**: Ensuring that interventions align with what clients identify as meaningful, whether religious faith, marital fidelity, or personal dignity.

Digital Privacy Counseling

Therapists must treat digital life as part of sexual health. Counseling should include education on encrypted platforms, consent scripts for video intimacy, and safe storage or deletion practices. In high-risk legal environments, therapists should be cautious about what is documented in clinical records, prioritizing confidentiality.

Interprofessional Links

Many NRI clients benefit from referral networks. A coordinated approach might include:

- **Primary Care Providers** for general health and screening.
- **Urologists and OB-GYNs** for sexual dysfunction or pain.
- **Pelvic Floor Physiotherapists** for vaginismus or chronic pelvic pain.
- **Psychiatrists** for comorbid anxiety, depression, or psychosis.
- **Legal Aid Services** for clients facing harassment or blackmail.
- **Faith Leaders** who are supportive of client safety, informed consent, and dignity.

Clinical Vignettes Consolidated

- **Rasheed**: A single migrant whose loneliness spiraled into alcohol and pornography use. Key adaptation: linking isolation screening with psychoeducation on healthier coping strategies. Transferable lesson: loneliness must be assessed as a clinical risk, not just a social issue.
- **Vikram**: A young man distressed by nocturnal emissions and semen-loss fears. Key adaptation: reframing semen physiology in culturally resonant language. Transferable lesson: psychoeducation must dismantle myths without shaming belief systems.
- **Anu and Sajan**: A couple strained by secrecy around pornography use. Key adaptation: structured couple communication protocols to reduce accusation and build trust. Transferable lesson: pornography concerns must be addressed relationally, not only individually.
- **Mansoor**: An expatriate consumed by venereophobia after superficial contact. Key adaptation: integrating CBT for health anxiety with clear medical risk education. Transferable lesson: shame-sensitive language is essential when addressing sexual risk fears.
- **Leena and Thomas**: A marriage fractured by disclosure of an affair. Key adaptation: structured betrayal recovery work, including boundaries around devices. Transferable lesson: family and community pressures must be considered alongside couple dynamics.

- **Hiba and Nithin**: A couple living apart, cycling between countdown excitement and post-visit emptiness. Key adaptation: future-orientation mapping and planned intimacy windows. Transferable lesson: uncertainty management is as important as intimacy work in long-distance marriages.
- **Rukhsana**: A woman paralyzed by fears of digital exposure. Key adaptation: trauma-informed digital safety coaching. Transferable lesson: therapists must address digital sexuality as seriously as physical intimacy.
- **Divya and Harish**: A couple strained by mismatched expectations and performance anxiety during rare visits. Key adaptation: psychoeducation on the refractory period and pacing intimacy. Transferable lesson: biological education can transform relational blame into mutual understanding.

Together, these vignettes illustrate how NRI psychosexual realities are shaped by migration stress, cultural beliefs, digital fears, and relational cycles. Each case highlights the importance of combining empathy with evidence, and cultural sensitivity with clinical clarity.

Ethics and Legal Sensitivities

Working with NRI clients in the Gulf involves unique ethical and legal challenges. The host-country environment is often highly restrictive, and therapists must balance best practice standards with client safety.

Confidentiality under Host-Country Laws

Confidentiality cannot always be assumed. In some jurisdictions, medical records are subject to government review, and routine employer-sponsored health checks include mandatory HIV and STI testing. Positive results may trigger job termination or deportation. For this reason, therapists should practice *documentation minimalism*, recording only essential clinical details and avoiding unnecessary references to sexual behavior that could be misinterpreted if disclosed.

Non-Collusion with Harmful Practices

Therapists may encounter requests for interventions such as "conversion therapy," forced hymenectomy, or advice on suppressing masturbation. Ethical practice requires a clear stance: no collusion with practices that harm dignity, autonomy, or rights, adhering to global declarations that recognize the right to sexual health and the protection from harm (World Association for Sexual Health [WAS], 2014) At the same time, clinicians must avoid alienating clients by shaming their beliefs. The task is to remain *nonjudgmental toward behavior* (such as masturbation or pornography use) while safeguarding against compulsive patterns that cause distress or impairment.

Safety Planning for Blackmail and Retaliation

The risk of blackmail, particularly after extramarital relationships or digital intimacy, is real. Clients may also fear workplace retaliation if private matters are revealed. Safety planning should include documenting evidence of harassment, discussing strategies for non-engagement, and, where possible, consulting legal aid organizations. Therapists should help clients prepare emotionally for the possibility of exposure while reinforcing that shame belongs to the perpetrator, not the victim.

Telehealth Protocols

As many clients now use telehealth services, protocols for privacy and location safety are crucial. Therapists should verify that the client is in a private space, remind them of the risks of recording, and use secure platforms with end-to-end encryption (Martinez-Martin & Kreitmair, 2018). In some cases, location safety checks—asking whether the client is in a jurisdiction where certain disclosures could put them at risk—are warranted. Clients may need guidance on clearing digital footprints, such as deleting chat histories or disabling automatic cloud backups.

Ethical work in this setting is therefore not abstract. It involves daily decisions about what to record, how to frame interventions, and how to support clients who live with both emotional distress and real-world dangers.

Training and Service Development

To meet the needs of NRI clients, training and service development must go beyond generic psychosexual education. Practitioners require targeted preparation for the specific syndromes, fears, and relational patterns that dominate this clinical landscape.

Specialized Clinical Skills

- **Dhat-aware CBT**: Therapists should be trained in how to dismantle semen-loss myths through culturally sensitive psychoeducation combined with cognitive restructuring and mindfulness techniques.
- **Venereophobia Protocols**: Structured risk assessments, accurate STI education, and CBT for health anxiety must be embedded into practice.
- **Porn-Related Couple Interventions**: Training in motivational interviewing, boundary negotiation, and communication skills can help couples navigate pornography-related conflicts without escalation into secrecy or control.
- **Digital Safety Education**: Therapists should be fluent in guiding clients on encrypted apps, consent scripts for digital intimacy, and emergency steps if leaks occur.

Supervision for Moral Distress and Countertransference

Therapists themselves may experience moral distress when confronted with practices they find troubling, such as secret marriages, affairs, or requests for culturally sanctioned but harmful treatments. Supervision should help clinicians process countertransference related to gender norms, class differences, or the precarious lives of migrant workers. Peer groups can also provide space for reflective practice and emotional support.

Programmatic Partnerships

Finally, building service capacity requires partnerships beyond the therapy room. Diaspora associations can be engaged to promote awareness and reduce stigma, while GCC-based clinics can serve as referral points for medical testing or specialist care. Establishing *referral bridges* between community organizations, medical providers, and therapists ensures that clients are not left navigating fragmented systems alone.

Training and service development in this area are not simply about acquiring clinical tools. They are about building a responsive ecosystem that recognizes the complex realities of NRI migration, balancing cultural humility with evidence-based care, and placing dignity and safety at the center of psychosexual health practice.

Conclusion

The chapter began with the words of a *kathu patt* letter-song, a poetic exchange that has carried the emotions of longing, sacrifice, and devotion across seas for generations of Indian families separated by migration. These verses remain a powerful reminder that the heart of the NRI experience is not only economic but profoundly relational.

Psychosexual practice with NRI clients requires attention to both the beauty and the burden of this distance. The cultural respect embedded in songs, rituals, and community expectations must be honored, even as therapists bring evidence-based knowledge to reduce unnecessary shame, correct myths, and offer safe strategies for intimacy. By blending cultural humility with scientific clarity, practitioners can help clients disentangle guilt from physiology, love from secrecy, and loneliness from despair.

The task of therapy is not simply to treat dysfunction but to restore dignity. For some clients, this may mean reframing semen-loss beliefs that sap confidence. For others, it may mean easing the fears of digital exposure that freeze intimacy. Still others may need help navigating pornography use, extramarital entanglements, or performance anxieties shaped by long separations. Across all of these concerns, the unifying aim is to protect the client's right to safe, respectful, and fulfilling sexual lives.

For NRI couples and families, the journey is one of resilience as much as hardship. Therapists who walk alongside them, with openness to cultural nuance and commitment to ethical care, can transform migration's distances into spaces for healing, connection, and renewed intimacy. Just as the letter-song ends with hope of reunion, psychosexual work offers the possibility of bringing partners closer—not only across oceans, but across the silences created by shame, fear, and separation.

References

American Psychiatric Association. (2022). *Diagnostic and statistical manual of mental disorders* (5th ed., text rev.; DSM-5-TR). Washington, DC: American Psychiatric Publishing.

Bhavsar, V., & Bhugra, D. (2013). Cultural factors and sexual dysfunction in clinical practice. *Advances in Psychiatric Treatment*, 19(2), 144–152. doi:10.1192/apt.bp.111.009852

Chadda, R. K., & Ahuja, N. (1990). Dhat syndrome: A sex neurosis of the Indian subcontinent. *British Journal of Psychiatry, 156*(4), 577–579. https://doi.org/10.1192/bjp.156.4.577

Dainton, M., & Aylor, B. (2001). A relational uncertainty analysis of jealousy, trust, and maintenance in long-distance versus geographically close relationships. *Communication Quarterly*, *49*(2), 172–188. https://doi.org/10.1080/01463370109385624

Eljawad, M. A., Se'eda, H., Ghozy, S., El-Qushayri, A. E., Elsherif, A., Elkassar, A. H., … Islam, S. M. S. (2021). Pornography use prevalence and associated factors in Arab countries: A multinational cross-sectional study of 15,027 individuals. *Journal of Sexual Medicine*, *18*(3), 539–548. https://doi.org/10.1016/j.jsxm.2020.12.011

Grover, S., Avasthi, A., Gupta, S., Dan, A., Neogi, R., Behere, P. B., … Rozatkar, A. (2016). Phenomenology and beliefs of patients with Dhat syndrome: A nationwide multicentric study. *The International Journal of Social Psychiatry*, *62*(1), 57–66. https://doi.org/10.1177/0020764015591857

Hedman, E., Lekander, M., Ljótsson, B., Lindefors, N., Rück, C., Andersson, G., & Andersson, E. (2015). Optimal cut-off points on the health anxiety inventory, illness attitude scales and whiteley index to identify severe health anxiety. *PLoS One, 10*(4), e0123412. https://doi.org/10.1371/journal.pone.0123412

Huang, F.Y., & Akhtar, S. (2005). Immigrant sex: The transport of affection and sensuality across cultures. *American Journal of Psychoanalysis*, 65, 179–188. https://doi.org/10.1007/s11231-005-3625-1

Jannini EA, McMahon CG, & Waldinger MD (ed.). (2012). *Premature ejaculation: From etiology to diagnosis and treatment.* Milan: Springer.

King, R., & Christou, A. (2011). Of counter-diaspora and reverse transnationalism: Return mobilities to and from the ancestral homeland. *Mobilities*, 6(4), 451–466. https://doi.org/10.1080/17450101.2011.603941

Martinez-Martin, N., & Kreitmair, K. (2018). Ethical issues for direct-toconsumer digital psychotherapy apps: Addressing accountability, data protection, and consent. *JMIR Mental Health*, 5(2), e32. https://doi.org/10.2196/mental.9423

Metz, M. E., Epstein, N. B., & McCarthy, B. (2017). *Cognitive-behavioral therapy for sexual dysfunction.* Routledge, Taylor & Francis Group: New York, NY.

Minarcik, J., Wetterneck, C. T., & Short, M. B. (2016). The effects of sexually explicit material use on romantic relationship dynamics. *Journal of Behavioral Addictions*, *5*(4), 700–707. https://doi.org/10.1556/2006.5.2016.078

Montesi, J. L., Fauber, R. L., Gordon, E. A., & Heimberg, R. G. (2011). The specific importance of communicating about sex to couples' sexual and overall relationship satisfaction. *Journal of Social and Personal Relationships*, 28(5), 591–609.

Mucci, N., Traversini, V., Giorgi, G., Garzaro, G., Fiz-Perez, J., Campagna, M., ... & Arcangeli, G. (2019). Migrant workers and physical health: An umbrella review. *Sustainability*, *11*(1), 232. https://doi.org/10.3390/su11010232

Pathmendra, P., Raggatt, M., Lim, M. S., Marino, J. L., & Skinner, S. R. (2023). Exposure to pornography and adolescent sexual behavior: Systematic review. *Journal of Medical Internet Research*, *25*, e43116. https://doi.org/10.2196/43116

Reid, R. C., Garos, S., & Carpenter, B. N. (2011). Reliability, validity, and psychometric development of the hypersexual behavior inventory in an outpatient sample of men. *Sexual Addiction & Compulsivity*, 18(1), 30–51. doi: 10.1080/10720162.2011.555709

Sahlstein, E. M. (2004). Relating at a distance: Negotiating being together and being apart in long-distance relationships. *Journal of Social and Personal Relationships*, *21*(5), 689–710. https://doi.org/10.1177/0265407504046115

Starcevic, V., & Berle, D. (2006). Cognitive specificity of anxiety disorders: A review of selected key constructs. *Depression and Anxiety*, 23(2), 51–61. https://doi.org/10.1002/da.20145

Willoughby, B. J., Leonhardt, N. D., & Augustus, R. A. (2021). Associations between pornography use and sexual dynamics among heterosexual couples. *Journal of Sexual Medicine*, *18*(1), 179–192. https://doi.org/10.1016/j.jsxm.2020.10.013

World Association for Sexual Health. (2014). *Declaration of sexual rights.* Retrieved from https://worldsexualhealth.net

World Health Organization. (2006). *Defining sexual health: Report of a technical consultation on sexual health, 28–31 January 2002.* Geneva: WHO.

Chapter 24

Navigating Identity Conflict within LGBTQ+ Muslims

Saquib Ahmad

Identity Conflicts

Identity conflicts occur when different aspects of an individual's identity clash due to opposing values or beliefs. For example, someone might have the value of eating healthily but also crave fast food when tired or holding strong beliefs in both science and God. These conflicts don't necessarily mean the two identities are incompatible, but without a "bridging" value or belief, tension can arise. For instance, a person might resolve the first conflict by embracing the idea of "cheat days," or the second by believing, "My faith in God inspires my pursuit of science, as God encourages us to seek answers, and science is the way to find them."

When such harmony is absent, individuals may experience internal conflict, leading to questioning of themselves, others, or the world around them. This questioning can give rise to emotions such as guilt, anger, shame, despair, or fear, which, over time, may develop into mental health difficulties.

The intersection of LGBTQ+ identity and religious belief is a particularly challenging space, where such internal conflicts often lead to significant mental health struggles (Boppana & Gross, 2019).

This chapter does not argue for a redefinition of the Muslim *ummah* to explicitly include LGBTQ+ people. Instead, it advocates for improving mental health for all Muslims, which, in turn, fosters better individuals and communities. Resolving identity conflicts plays a crucial role in this process. This chapter does not seek to determine whether being Queer and Muslim is "acceptable." Instead, it highlights that there are Muslims who happen to be Queer (MQs) living very fractured lives due to identity conflicts. By promoting mental health and fostering environments where these conflicts can be safely explored, this chapter advocates for psychological and spiritual well-being for all Muslims—an approach that inherently expands the ethical and communal boundaries of the *ummah* towards greater inclusivity.

DOI: 10.4324/9781003611387-24

Shame

Psychological shame is a significant part of the Queer Muslim (MQ) experience, as it is for many others. However, for MQs, this shame is often magnified by an array of external pressures, especially for those living in the West, including:

- **Systemic Islamophobic Racism in the West**, which marginalizes Muslims broadly and compounds the challenges faced by Queer individuals within this group.
- **Systemic Queerphobia** that persists in societies around the world, perpetuating stigma and discrimination.
- **Queerphobia within Muslim Communities**, where LGBTQ+ identities are often rejected as incompatible with religious and cultural values.
- **Islamophobic Racism within the Queer Community**, where MQs face exclusion or are viewed and treated as anomalies, leading to feelings of isolation even among their peers.

These external pressures, combined with the internalization of Islamophobia, racism, and Queerphobia, make the MQ experience exceptionally challenging. Internalized oppression of this kind exacerbates feelings of shame and can profoundly impact mental health. This intersectional layering of racial, religious, gendered, and sexual marginalization reflects how dominant social imaginaries can obscure people whose identities do not fit single-axis categories (May, 2015).

Navigating these intersecting challenges is no small feat. Many MQs may live their entire lives in hiding, burdened by the cumulative stress of these pressures. Some may compartmentalize their identities, creating a private and public self. Others may feel forced to abandon their Queer identity altogether to maintain community acceptance. Tragically, some MQs may find these pressures so overwhelming that they see no other way out, and lives are lost as a result.

Islamophobia, Homophobia, Biphobia, Transphobia, and Their Internalization

When thinking about Islam and the LGBTQ+ community in the West, certain disturbing images may suddenly come to mind—whether real or imagined. These are the products of systemic Islamophobia, defined by the Oxford English Dictionary as "intense dislike or fear of Islam, especially as a political force; hostility or prejudice towards Muslims."

Like homophobia, Islamophobia operates within systems that sustain it at various levels, including legislation, media, education, and law enforcement etc. Numerous studies have highlighted the prevalence of Islamophobia in the Western media (Suryandari & Arifin, 2021), exacerbated more so recently by geopolitical events such as the war in Ukraine and the war on Gaza, and earlier wars in Iraq, Afghanistan, and Syria. The stark contrast in how refugees from Ukraine (predominantly White Christians) and Syria (predominantly Brown Muslim) are perceived exemplifies this systemic bias.

Growing up as a Muslim in such environments, it is unsurprising that many internalize Islamophobic narratives, just as homosexual people raised in homophobic environments often internalize homophobia (IH).

For MQs, however, Islamophobia can manifest differently. It often involves the complete erasure of Queer history within the Islamic world, even as Queer histories from ancient Greece or Rome are widely acknowledged and celebrated. As Mazama (2001) argues, dislocation occurs when people are made to understand reality through another group's cultural center; Diop's (1991) critique of Eurocentric historical narratives similarly underscores how such dominance marginalizes non-European histories, identities, and contributions.

Moreover, MQs frequently encounter whitewashed ideals of Queer liberation that are devoid of cultural contexts and historical relevance. Without access to their own historical narratives, MQs may struggle to connect with advocacy movements shaped predominantly by Western perspectives and contexts, leaving their unique challenges unaddressed.

Queer love and gender diversity have deep roots in Islamic history. During the Islamic Golden Age, scholars embraced Greek ideas of male love, Sufi poets wrote of boys with "cheeks of rose and lips of sugar," and rulers like Al-Amin (809–811 CE) openly loved male companions. Women also embraced same-sex relations though they are less documented due to patriarchal norms that were prevalent across the world at the time.

Rumi's devotion to Shams Tabrizi inspired homosensual poetry, and their 40-day isolation hinted at a deeper bond. South Asia's Hijra community, once holding power under the Mughals, were later criminalized by British rule.

Queerness was never absent from Islamic societies. The erasure is modern, not historical and exists in a colonial context with modern-day governments benefiting from the hangovers of their colonial past. In Pakistan for example, when looking at the Hijras and broader trans communities, for a time, the state seemed to be moving towards restoring their precolonial respect. Yet in 2023, the Federal Shariat Court revoked key protections from the *Transgender Persons (Protection of Rights) Act*, including the right to self-identify—undoing years of progress. As trans activist and politician Mehrub Awaz Awan explained in an interview with *Fighting Fear*,

> There is no understanding of Pakistan that is going to be complete unless it simultaneously is a class analysis of the country. Pakistan is a country that is divided along class lines, like many other countries, and how gender and sexuality is experienced across class lines becomes markedly different.
>
> (Awan, 2025)

This contradiction between progressive and conservative forces leaves Queer people—especially trans people from low socioeconomic backgrounds exposed to discrimination that is rarely policed and protections that go unenforced. Many are pushed into sex work as a means of survival, which, as in many countries, too often becomes a death sentence due to violence, exploitation, and substance misuse and other mental health issues.

What makes Islamic "Queerness" different from Western Queerness historically is how it's devoid of labels for sexuality. This means that often in Islamic literature, acts are labeled rather than the individual so one would not be labeled Gay, Bisexual, or Pansexual, they would be described as engaging in same-sex relations. Also, there is a level of fluidity that is pervasive across Islamic history in that though one may have had same-sex relations this did not mean heterosexual relationships were off the menu. Many prominent Muslim emperors were known to have had same sex relations and be married at the same time. Furthermore recently, in Siwa, Egypt, same-sex unions coexisted with marriage until banned in 1928.

That said, there is evidence of labels when it comes to gender identity. As mentioned above, Hijra's (transwomen) exist in the Indian subcontinent but also across the Islamic world. In Arabic the word mukhannath refers to gender-variant individuals, often referring to effeminate men or those with ambiguous sexual characteristics who exhibit feminine behaviors. There is much reference to them by scholars however Rowson's analysis indicates that the *mukhannathun* occupied a complex position within early Islamic society, balancing roles that were both integral to cultural practices and subject to moral scrutiny (Rowson, 1991) leading to periodic persecution on the basis of their "sinful" behaviors and not their identities.

It is essential for MQs to reclaim and or learn from their Queer historical and cultural contexts, rather than relying on narratives imposed by oppressive systems. Rediscovering and embracing these histories enables MQs to better understand their present circumstances and develop a sense of identity that is both empowered and authentically rooted.

Zahid, Bisexual Muslim

Consider the experience of Zahid, who was born in Pakistan and raised in the UK by his single mother. The youngest of three siblings, he first noticed his attraction to both men and women at the age of nine. Zahid grew up in a middle-class Pakistani household, where his paternal side lived in a large, multigenerational home with his immediate family, grandparents, and other relatives. He described his family's religious outlook as *Deen aur Dunya,* a philosophy that balances faith (*deen*) with everyday life (*dunya*). While his family was progressive by Pakistani standards, religion remained central to their identity.

Moving to the UK at the age of seven was an emotionally turbulent experience for Zahid. His once-vast social and emotional support network shrank overnight from over twenty people to just his mother, brother, and sister following his parents' separation. His mother, now the sole provider, became emotionally unavailable as she worked two jobs, leaving Zahid feeling abandoned and internalizing the belief that he was a *bad boy*.

As he entered adolescence, Zahid became more aware of his sexual feelings but had no framework to understand bisexuality. He knew what it meant to be Gay or Straight but never considered bisexuality as a possibility for himself. At school, he experienced homophobia—his more feminine traits were associated with being Gay, leading to teasing and slurs like "fag" or "queer." Though generally well-liked, he learned to *play a role* to avoid conflict, a form of masculinity policing rooted in both homophobia and misogyny (Kimmel, 2003).

Seeking escape and independence, Zahid left his home city for university, as far away as possible. This newfound distance provided the freedom to explore his sexuality in a way that had never been possible before. He had his first relationship with a man, fell in love, and slowly began to come out—to himself and to a select few friends—as Bisexual. Within a couple of years, he also came out to his mother, though his reasoning was deeply strategic. He saw *Bisexual* as a label that would allow him to be *Gay enough* to be accepted by his Queer peers while remaining *Straight enough* to justify marriage to a woman and maintain his family's expectations.

However, Zahid struggled with internalized biphobia (IBP). At his core, he did not fully believe bisexuality existed, despite his own experiences of attraction and satisfaction with both men and women. He had absorbed biphobic narratives from both within and outside of the Queer community. Gay friends would joke, "Bi today, Gay tomorrow" (MacDonald, 1981), reinforcing the idea that bisexuality was merely a transitional phase. Zahid himself internalized and perpetuated these attitudes, mocking those he deemed "too Gay" to be Bisexual, aligning with Kinsey's binary scaling of sexuality (Kinsey et al., 1948). Seeking religious clarity, he turned to the Qur'an and Islamic texts, which categorized Gay men, Lesbian women, and Trans people but made no mention of bisexuality. This absence further validated his biphobia.

Religious and cultural pressures led Zahid to marry in his mid-twenties. However, the marriage was short-lived, overshadowed by his belief that bisexuals were merely in denial about their true Gay nature. He further reinforced this belief through extramarital affairs with men, distorting any information that might challenge his IBP. His immediate family never explicitly condemned or disapproved of homosexuality, yet their silence on the subject spoke volumes.

Following his divorce, Zahid sought therapy to process the trauma of his failed marriage. However, his first experience with a therapist caused further harm—he felt his therapist subtly reinforced the idea that he was actually Gay and had married only to maintain the illusion of heterosexuality. This experience further deepened his shame. It was years before he attempted therapy again. This time, he found a knowledgeable clinician who provided psychoeducation on sexual orientation. Through this, he began to challenge his internalized biphobia and confront the inconsistencies he had previously ignored—particularly his self-imposed belief that he was *bad* for having married a woman and caused her pain.

Zahid's IBP did not stem solely from religious or cultural expectations but also from Queer spaces that dismissed his identity. Research shows that biphobia exists in both heterosexual and homosexual communities, often leading to double discrimination—where bisexuals face exclusion from both (Bennett, 1992; Mulick, 1999). This lack of bi-visibility—within both Islam and Queer communities—further contributed to Zahid's struggle.

Through continued therapy, exposure to literature, and connecting with other Bisexual people, Zahid was able to work on his IBP and become more accepting of himself. He resumed dating women, something he had avoided after his divorce due to the shame of *cheating* on his wife *with his sexuality*. However, this time, he was open about his identity from the start. He also began educating his friends and family on biphobia and its impact. Zahid found further solace in historical Islamic narratives, where sexual fluidity was more visible.

Zahid's story underscores the complex interplay of religion, culture, and Queer identity, particularly for those who experience not only homophobia but also biphobia within Queer spaces. His journey highlights the importance of culturally competent therapy, representation, and nuanced discussions of sexuality that go beyond binary thinking.

Visibility

IH is a deeply entrenched issue among Queer individuals, including MQs, shaped by systemic factors that are well-documented. For MQs, a key contributor to IH is the limited visibility of individuals like themselves. This invisibility is perpetuated not only by anti-Queer rhetoric within their own Muslim communities but also by Islamophobia in wider society (Rayside, 2011), including the LGBTQ+ community. MQs face fears similar to other Queer individuals, such as potential negative impacts on income, housing, social relationships (family and friendships), and their access to community—whether faith-based or Queer. However, when MQs do achieve visibility, it is often dismissed within the larger Muslim community as unrepresentative or inauthentic, further reinforcing their marginalization (Rayside, 2011).

To explore this issue further, a social media poll was conducted asking MQs, "*Do you see sufficient Queer Muslim representation around you?*" The options were Yes, No, Limited, and Not Sure. An overwhelming percentage answered *No* or *Limited*, while very few answered *Yes*.

Those who selected *No* or *Limited* were then asked, "*How do you relate to the representation you've seen?*" Responses included:

- "I felt I couldn't relate to the representations; they were nothing like me."

Another poll followed, asking respondents who said *No*, "*How much has this negatively impacted you?*" The options were *Not at all, A little, Quite a bit,* and *A lot.*

A significant percentage chose *Quite a bit* or *A lot*. When asked "*How?*," responses included:

- "I need people with the same lived experience to come forward and tell us how it's done, otherwise I keep going back to my previous coping mechanisms."
- "As a cultural Muslim, I didn't have a role model on how to navigate society growing up."

These findings underscore the pressing need for greater and more diverse MQ visibility. Representation is not just about being seen; it's about fostering connection, empowerment, and practical guidance for others navigating similar struggles.

For many MQs, navigating identity comes with shame and isolation, shaped by cultural expectations, religious pressures, and societal rejection. Social media has become a powerful tool for change, offering representation, community, and affirmation where traditional spaces fall short. Unlike Western legacy media, which often fails the "Riz Test"—a set of criteria developed to evaluate the portrayal of Muslims in film and television, inspired by actor Riz Ahmed's 2017 speech at the UK House of Commons addressing the lack of diversity on screen (The Riz Test, n.d.)—and portrays MQs through harmful stereotypes or erasure altogether, social media provides a more accurate, proportionate, and diverse representation, allowing MQs to reclaim their narratives.

Queer Muslim figures such as Taha Arshad, an influencer with a large following on Instagram and TikTok, Alloul Jaouad, a non-binary artist and author, Lady Bushra, a drag performer and comedian, and Blair Imani, an activist and educator, use their platforms to challenge erasure and offer visibility. Their presence provides MQs with role models who show that Queerness and Islam are not mutually exclusive and that one need not choose one or the other. These representations counter harmful stereotypes and challenge legacy media to do better by MQs.

For those struggling with shame and self-doubt, this visibility is more than representation—it is a lifeline. Visibility offers hope, belonging, and a path towards embracing their identity with pride rather than conflict. Social media gives visibility to faces and names that represent a nuanced and authentic MQ in the void created by legacy media.

Queer Phobia and Social Exclusion

Social inclusion is an important need for any human being and crucial for mental wellbeing, why would MQ's be any different? MQs in Western societies often face significant challenges due to homophobia and transphobia within their communities, leading to feelings of entrapment, especially among those who lack the means (social and or financial) for independent living, e.g., young people, those with familial responsibilities such as looking after vulnerable members of family.

Religious institutions and preachers have been documented delivering sermons that frame same-sex sexuality as incompatible with Islamic teaching and treat global LGBTQ+ rights discourse as pressure from Western human rights standards. This rhetoric can alienate MQs and foster environments where seeking support becomes threatening, if not impossible (Zulkffli & Rashid, 2016). This is by no means unique to Islam; many religious institutions have historically and currently propagated the message that to be in the club one must be straight and "normal," otherwise one is out, despite all religions having Queer people and Queer history in them.

The rising rejection of Queerness within religious communities reached a tragic peak with the assassination of Imam Muhsin Hendricks, the openly Gay Imam in South Africa, on February 15, 2025.

A pioneer in LGBTQ+ Muslim advocacy, Hendricks founded The Inner Circle (https://theinnercircle.org.za/about/) in 1996, which evolved into a nonprofit providing counseling, education, and anti-homophobia advocacy. In 2011, he established Masjidul Ghurbaah in Cape Town, a safe space for marginalized Muslims, including LGBTQ+ individuals and women, promoting female leadership and religious inclusivity.

Though his assassination highlights the deep-rooted dangers Queer individuals of faith face within society it also highlights the urgent need for collective action towards building acceptance. His legacy represents an alternative, reconciliation, love, patience and acceptance.

> Imam Muhsin made time for me via video call and helped me talk through some of my turmoils, reminding me that faith at its core is a personal connection with God. Speaking to him gave me a greater level of reassurance and allowed me to create more space for my faith, especially because it formed such a significant part of my identity
>
> (Queer male South Asian Muslim living in Australia)

Though we cannot be sure for what reason he was assassinated we can be sure that he did receive many death threats by religious sects within South Africa because of his Queer identity and religious practices.

Imam Muhsin Hendricks is not alone in his advocacy for LGBTQ+ inclusion within Islam. Globally, various initiatives have emerged to create inclusive spaces for Queer and marginalized Muslims. In Germany, Seyran Ateş established the Ibn Rushd-Goethe Mosque (www.ibn-rushd-goethe-moschee.de/en/), welcoming LGBTQ+ worshippers and promoting gender equality. In the United States, Imam Daayiee Abdullah, another openly Gay imam, founded the MECCA Institute (https://meccainstitutecommunity.org/index), advocating for progressive Islamic thought. Similarly, the Inclusive Mosque Initiative has been instrumental in creating safe, affirming spaces for Queer Muslims. These movements demonstrate that inclusive interpretations of Islam are possible and can be established, particularly in Western contexts.

Despite the efforts of these prominent figures, the prevailing narrative often suggests that Queerness and Islam are incompatible. This perception can lead to internalized conflicts among MQs, hindering their ability to envision a harmonious existence without compartmentalizing or concealing aspects of their identities.

Malik, Gay Muslim

Malik is a 34-year-old Gay Pakistani Muslim who immigrated to the United States during his teenage years. In Pakistan, discussions about sex were virtually non-existent in his conservative environment—not at home, school, nor among peers. Expressions of affection were subtle, and any sexual discourse was promptly suppressed. Upon relocating to the US, Malik encountered a stark contrast, with peers openly discussing sexual matters. He had experienced same-sex attractions but perceived them as normal due to the lack of discourse on sexuality in Pakistan. It was only in the US that he became aware of the label "homosexuality" and its associated stigmas, including its classification as a sin in Islam.

Malik remains closeted to his parents. However, his relationship with his sexuality has evolved from one of shame to acceptance, viewing it as an integral part of his identity. He neither explicitly shares nor hides it. Like many MQs, Malik faced familial pressures to marry. Achieving financial and emotional independence enabled him to assert boundaries, firmly communicating his disinterest in marriage and threatening to sever ties if pressured further. This assertiveness alleviated familial pressure. Malik believes his parents are aware of his sexuality but choose not to acknowledge it. His father once remarked that regardless of whom Malik brings home, he would remain his son and retain his support—a subtle signal of acceptance.

Malik's approach to reconciling his faith and sexuality highlights a deeply internalized belief system—one where same-sex behaviors, rather than being Gay itself, are considered sinful. His cognitive strategy of deliberately avoiding thinking about the sin and subsequently mitigating it by seeking forgiveness generally was not an attempt to challenge the belief itself but rather a necessary strategy to preserve his mental well-being. However, this avoidance did not eliminate guilt; instead, it heightened it, as he remained consciously aware that he was making a deliberate decision to sidestep the moral conflict rather than resolve it.

This reflects a broader reality for many MQs who navigate the tension between deeply ingrained religious teachings and their lived experiences and realities. Unlike those who may seek to challenge or reinterpret religious doctrine, Malik's approach was to maintain his belief while developing strategies to live more freely within its constraints. This reinforces the principle that religious belief, like any other belief system, is ultimately a personal choice. As therapists, our role is not to dictate or dismantle belief systems but to support individuals in living and coping more adaptively with their chosen values. Whether that means helping an individual integrate their faith and sexuality, providing space for questioning, or supporting their journey in whichever direction they choose, the goal remains the same—facilitating psychological well-being and autonomy over their own lives.

It is important to acknowledge that not everyone can employ cognitive avoidance in such an adaptive way to safeguard their well-being. For some, the very act of this type of avoidance may amplify distress rather than alleviate it. Malik's ability to navigate his internal conflict reflects a degree of cognitive flexibility, allowing him to prioritize his well-being without rejecting his beliefs. However, for others, this level of psychological adjustment may not be possible, particularly for those who experience cognitive rigidity—a tendency to see the world in strict black-and-white terms and this may be pervasive in many other areas of their life and so helping them reflect on this broader issue may be helpful as a starting point.

Islamophobic Racism, the Queer Community, and Interracial Relationships

Islamophobic racism (IR) is a multifaceted form of discrimination that merges religious intolerance with racial bias, leading to the systemic marginalization of those perceived to be Muslim. The Palestinian liberation movement provides an extreme yet illuminating example of how Islamophobic racism operates, particularly in the context of Western media narratives. The war on Gaza has starkly highlighted this bias, with Israel continuously framed as having the "innate right to defend itself" while Palestinians are either dehumanized—branded "human animals"—or reduced to mere statistics. This erasure ignores the fact that under international law, as per Article 1(4) of Additional Protocol I (1977), occupied people have the legal right to armed resistance.

For Queer Palestinians, existing under occupation presents a double marginalization. Not only do they face homophobia within their own communities, but they are also subjected to state-sponsored oppression under Israeli occupation. Queer Palestinians are expected to choose—their Queerness or their Palestinian identity—as though these aspects of identity could be separated out.

Furthermore, the Muslimification of Palestinians as a homogenous group is based on IR because Palestinians are also Christian and even Jewish. The conflation of ethnicity with religious identity is a deliberate attempt to reduce the Palestinian issue as a "radical Islam" issue rather than a human rights issue thus further perpetuating IR narratives.

In a discussion for *Queer Talk*, a podcast series by *Fighting Fear Community*, Ahmed Shihab-Eldin, a Queer Palestinian journalist and actor, describes how colonial occupation fuels social oppression, including homophobia:

> As serious of a problem homophobia is Palestine, in Egypt in many Arab countries, it's a very convenient narrative to officiate and distract from what I think, I would call a much more egregious violation of humanity... There is this dangerous narrative, this idea that Palestinian society is uniquely homophobic or that homophobia or violence, hatred or intolerance is somehow baked

> into Palestinian culture and what this framing does is it completely ignores the broader reality of occupation of a brutal military system that crushes any kind of social progress. Whether its women, whether its gender, whether it's sexuality… when people are denied basic freedoms when you're under siege, or under surveillance, you don't have freedom of movement, you're under constant military control, guess what that kind of pressure fuels all kinds of societal problems and limitations, including homophobia.
>
> (Ahmad, 2025)

Although an extreme example, the case of Palestine demonstrates how colonialism suppresses social mobility and justice, particularly for LGBTQIA+ communities. Palestinian liberation and Queer liberation are inseparable.

Dismissing Queer solidarity with Palestine as self-destructive with slogans like "Queers for Palestine is like Chickens for KFC" is not only deeply racist it also ignores the lived realities of Queer Palestinians, who reject the false binary between their Queerness and their Palestinian identity, as well as the shared struggles of Queer BIPOC people globally who have suffered under colonialism and its remains. Hijras in South Asia, two spirited people of Native America, Sister Brothers and Brother Sisters of Aboriginal Australia, or the Takatāpui in Maori culture just to name a few, have all had their Queer history, culture, and practices suppressed, erased, and or made illegal under colonial rule. For example, Thailand only this year legalized same-sex marriage, despite Queer identities being deeply present in both its past and present.

Beyond global politics, IR manifests in the everyday lives of MQs. In the Queer community, MQs experience both overt hostility and covert exclusions, particularly in dating spaces. Apps like Grindr and Tinder often expose them to direct racialized abuse. Many MQs in the West report experiencing Islamophobic microaggressions ("Why do you wear a hijab when you're Queer"), fetishization ("I love Arabs"), or outright rejection simply for being perceived as Muslim ("Try being Queer in Palestine, you'll be thrown off a building").

I personally recall being subjected to slurs like "sand monkey," "terrorist," and having to justify my faith to strangers on Grindr. One particularly notable experience was engaging in an unsolicited "debate" over the youngest wife of the Prophet Muhammad, a clear attempt to equate Islam with pedophilia. These interactions stem from two deeply ingrained assumptions:

1. That there is a "Muslim look"—defined by skin color, facial features, or dress.
2. That being Muslim is inherently bad, dangerous, or undesirable.

Such experiences are far from isolated. In 2025, *Fighting Fear* collaborated with *Queer South Asian Melbourne* to facilitate a workshop on the experiences of Queer South Asians in the West. Many attendees reported having experienced IR, including those who weren't even Muslim.

> I knew things like this happened in the US where Sikhs post 9/11 were perceived to be Muslim because of their turban but I didn't think this would happen in present-day Melbourne.
>
> (Participant at QSAM workshop 2025)

Islamophobic racism doesn't just shape social interactions, it also impacts romantic relationships. Tahir (2019) explores how power imbalances are embedded in BIPOC-White Queer relationships, often replicating the same structures of systemic racism found in wider society. Some of the key challenges that arise include:

- White Privilege in Queer Relationships: White partners hold unacknowledged power and social validation in Queer spaces.
- Desires for Assimilation and Privilege: Some Queer BIPOC may unconsciously seek white partners due to the social capital attached to whiteness.
- Cis heteronormativity and Its Influence: Even in Queer spaces, relationships still reinforce racialized gender roles prioritizing white, cis bodies.
- Color-blindness in Queer Interracial Relationships: White partners often dismiss race as irrelevant, claiming "love is love" while ignoring racial power imbalances.
- Symbolic Oppression and Representation: Queer media largely centers whiteness, erasing BIPOC narratives or reducing them to stereotypes.
- Colonial Power Dynamics in Intimacy: The historical legacy of colonialism continues to shape desirability politics in Queer spaces.
- Interracial Relationships and Societal Scrutiny: Black/white Queer couples face fetishization, erasure, and racist assumptions.
- Visibility and Erasure of Queer People of Color: Whiteness dominates LGBTQ+ spaces, sidelining the struggles and experiences of BIPOC Queer individuals.
- Structural Racism in Relationships: White partners can opt out of conversations on race, leaving their BIPOC partners to navigate oppression alone.

One of the most striking power imbalances in BIPOC-white relationships is the knowledge gap—where the BIPOC partner almost always knows more about the white partner's culture than vice versa. This cultural dominance is a direct consequence of colonial history and white social capital.

For MQs in such relationships, this often plays out through the erasure of their faith and traditions. While Christmas and Easter are widely acknowledged, Eid and Ramadan are frequently forgotten. Spirituality is glorified, while religion is ridiculed or vilified—especially when it comes to Islam.

When working with interracial couples, particularly where one partner is an MQ, these power imbalances must be addressed. Regardless of individual religiosity, many MQs experience culture, religion, and tradition as deeply intertwined. A failure to acknowledge these aspects in a relationship undermines their already precarious sense of identity.

Repeated experiences of unvalidated struggles can lead MQs to internalize the belief that there is a "right" and "wrong" way to be Queer. This can contribute to internalized homophobia (IH), which research has linked to lower relationship satisfaction, reduced commitment, and difficulties with intimacy (Thies et al., 2016).

In Queer spaces, MQs already exist at the margins—often caught between cultural exclusion and religious alienation. For those navigating interracial relationships, these tensions are only magnified. Addressing Islamophobic racism within Queer spaces is not just a matter of social justice; it is fundamental to ensuring the psychological well-being of MQs in their everyday lives and relationships.

Conclusion: Advancing the Discourse on Queer Muslim Realities

The experiences of MQs expose critical gaps in mental health, advocacy, and academic discourse, particularly where Western-centric models fail to account for the diverse ways MQs integrate faith and Queerness. Existing psychological frameworks often frame faith and sexuality as inherently conflicting, overlooking alternative identity formations that do not fit binary "coming out" narratives. Future research must explore culturally nuanced approaches to identity development that acknowledge the unique pressures and adaptive strategies of MQs.

This chapter also highlights Islamophobic racism within Queer spaces, yet little research exists on how MQs build resistance, solidarity, and alternative support networks. Studies on peer-led mental health initiatives, digital activism, and intracommunity advocacy could provide practical interventions for addressing the marginalization of MQs in both religious and LGBTQ+ spaces. Furthermore, the politicization of MQ identities—through pinkwashing, racialized Queerphobia, and slogans like "Queers for Palestine is like Chickens for KFC"—demands critical engagement to understand how colonial narratives continue to shape mainstream perceptions of Islam and Queerness.

Historical recovery remains a pressing need. While this chapter has outlined Queerness in Islamic history, much of it remains erased or overlooked. Further work must amplify these histories, not just to counter the myth of Queerness as a "Western import," but to provide MQs with culturally resonant narratives that affirm their existence.

Moving forward, the focus must shift from survival to self-determination. Rather than asking if one can be Queer and Muslim, the question should be how best to support those who are. Whether through mental health services, Queer advocacy, or religious reform, the goal is not to force reconciliation where it is not needed but to create spaces where MQs can define their own realities—on their own terms, in their own words, and free from imposed contradictions.

References

Ahmad, S. [Queer Talk]. (2025, March 07). Queer Talk S2E4 Ahmed Shihab-Eldin, Queer Palestinian Journalist [Video podcast]. *YouTube*. https://youtu.be/2PtHxGL-H9w

Awan, M. M. [Fighting Fear]. (2025). Queer Talk S2E7 Mehrub Moiz Awan, Transwoman, Politician & Writer in Pakistan [Video podcast]. YouTube. www.youtube.com/watch?v=A9S7xqlzc7k

Bennett, K. (1992). Feminist bisexuality: A both/and option for an either/or world. In E. R. Weise (Ed.), *Closer to Home: Bisexuality and Feminism* (pp. 205–231). Seal Press.

Boppana, S., & Gross, A. M. (2019). The impact of religiosity on the psychological well-being of LGBT Christians. *Journal of Gay & Lesbian Mental Health, 23*(4), 412–426. http://doi.org/10.1080/19359705.2019.1645072

Diop, C. A. (1991). *Civilization or Barbarism: An Authentic Anthropology*. Chicago: Lawrence Hill Books.

Kimmel, M. (2003). Adolescent masculinity, homophobia, and violence: Random school shootings, 1982–2001. *American Behavioural Scientist, 46*, 1439–1458.

Kinsey, A. C., Pomeroy, W. B., & Martin, C. E. (1948). *Sexual Behaviour of the Human Male*. Philadelphia, PA: W.B. Saunders.

MacDonald, A. P. (1981). Bisexuality: Some comments on research and theory. *Journal of Homosexuality, 6*, 21–35.

Mazama, A. (2001). The Afrocentric paradigm: Contours and definitions. *Journal of Black Studies*, 31(4), 387–405. https://doi.org/10.1177/002193470103100401

May, V. M. (2015). *Pursuing Intersectionality, Unsettling Dominant Imaginaries*. Routledge.

Mulick, P. S. (1999). *The Biphobia Scale: Development and Validation*. Master's Theses, https://scholarworks.wmich.edu/masters_theses/4124

Rayside, D. (2011). Muslim American communities' response to queer visibility. *Contemporary Islam, 5*(2), 109–134. https://doi.org/10.1007/s11562-011-0157-8.

Rowson, E. K. (1991). The effeminates of early medina. *Journal of the American Oriental Society, 111*(4), 671. https://doi.org/10.2307/603399

Suryandari, N., & Arifin, S. (2021, June). Islamophobia and media framing in west media. *Karsa: Journal of Social and Islamic Culture, 29*(1), 27–45. http://doi.org/10.19105/karsa.v29i1.3793

Tahir, S. (2019). Love is historically, institutionally, and societally constructed: Using intersectionality to examine racial issues of power and privilege in queer relationships. *Perceptions, 5*(2). https://doi.org/10.15367/pj.v5i2.206

The Riz Test. (n.d.). What is the Riz Test? Retrieved June 11, 2026, from www.riztest.com/

Thies, K. E., Starks, T. J., Denmark, F. L., & Rosenthal, L. (2016). Internalized homonegativity and relationship quality in same-sex romantic couples: A test of mental health mechanisms and gender as a moderator. *Psychology of Sexual Orientation and Gender Diversity, 3*(3), 325–335. https://doi.org/10.1037/sgd0000183

Zulkffli, M. A., & Rashid, R. A. (2016). A discursive psychological analysis of Islamic sermons on homosexuality. *International Journal of Applied Linguistics and English Literature, 5*(6), 190–198. https://doi.org/10.7575/aiac.ijalel.v.5n.6p.190

Chapter 25

Psychosexual Therapy: Hopes and Challenges in Bangladeshi Population

Mohammad Shamsul Ahsan, Leuza Mubassara, and Fatema Tuj Johra Joti

Background

Community-based research on sexual dysfunction in Bangladesh is scarce, yet available evidence suggests these conditions are widespread and under-reported. Clinical observations confirm that erectile dysfunction (ED) and premature ejaculation (PE) are the most common difficulties among men, while sexual interest/arousal disorder predominates among women (Maruf et al., 2024).

The first dedicated sex therapy clinic was established in Dhaka by clinical psychologists from Dhaka University, originally working in NGO-based sexual health clinics (e.g., Marie Stopes) with patients suffering from STIs. Their early interventions adapted the Masters and Johnson (1966) conjoint model, which emphasized dual-therapist couple work.

A turning point came in 2011, when Bangladeshi clinicians began receiving training at the European School of Sexual Medicine (ESSM). This led to the improvement of care of the Psychiatric-Sex Clinic at Bangladesh Medical University (BMU; formerly known as Bangabandhu Sheikh Mujib Medical University, BSMMU) in 2012 (Mozumder, 2024). The ESSM model, emphasizing biopsychosocial integration and sex therapy alongside psychiatry, has since been incorporated into clinical practice. The second major turning point was the establishment SASSM School Bangladesh by the members of South Asian Society for Sexual Medicine (SASSM). The SASSM launched this state-of-the-art educational initiative in 2017 at Dhaka to advance professional training in sexual medicine. Since its inception, the school has trained over 200 physicians who are enthusiastic about the biopsychosocial aspects of sexuality and have incorporated their learning into both research and clinical practice. A recent study demonstrated that the SASSM School Bangladesh significantly improved participants' knowledge of sexual medicine (Ahsan et al., 2025). Following its introduction, several local clinicians and researchers validated standardized assessment tools—such as the Premature Ejaculation Diagnostic Tool (PEDT) and the International Index of Erectile Function (IIEF), which have made the diagnosis of premature ejaculation (PE) and erectile dysfunction (ED) more objective and evidence-based (Islam et al., 2021). These tools have

DOI: 10.4324/9781003611387-25

also facilitated the use of well-defined and measurable outcome indicators in clinical and research settings.

However, despite these advances, challenges persist:

- A limited workforce of trained sex therapists.
- Reluctance among patients to disclose sexual concerns due to stigma.
- The dominance of a biomedical model in healthcare that often sidelines psychological and relational dimensions.

The gap between *Western models* and *local realities* remains wide, requiring clinicians to adapt evidence-based techniques to a South Asian cultural milieu shaped by Islamic values, collectivist family structures, and myths around sexuality.

Sex Therapy: Definition and Evolution

Sex therapy is broadly defined as the application of counseling and psychotherapeutic methods to treat sexual dysfunctions and relational difficulties. It involves structured psychoeducation, communication skills training, behavioral interventions, and deeper psychotherapeutic work as needed. Counselors play a facilitative role—helping patients overcome myths, build confidence, and pursue fulfilling intimate lives (Tripody, 2021).

Historically, sex therapy's lineage is traced from *Freudian psychoanalysis*, which pathologized certain sexualities and emphasized unconscious drives, to the revolutionary work of Masters and Johnson (1966). Their human sexual response model challenged prevailing myths, normalized sexual difficulties, and pioneered behavioral interventions such as sensate focus. Importantly, they advocated a "dual therapist" model (one male, one female working with couples), which was later streamlined to allow single-therapist approaches.

Early models often assumed male and female sexual responses were broadly similar, but subsequent work (Basson, 2000, Kaplan, 1979) and modern sexology demonstrate distinct physiological and psychosocial trajectories. For example, women's sexual response is now understood as more *circular*, *context-dependent*, and *relationally mediated*, whereas men's arousal often follows a more *linear trajectory* (Bhugra, 2009).

The Evolution of Sex Therapy and Medical Treatment in Sexual Health

For much of the twentieth century, psychodynamic or behavioral therapies dominated treatment of sexual difficulties. This landscape changed dramatically with the introduction of sildenafil (Viagra) in 1998, which marked the medicalization of sexual health. Pharmacological interventions—including PDE5 inhibitors (sildenafil, tadalafil) for erectile dysfunction, and SSRIs (dapoxetine, sertraline, paroxetine) for premature ejaculation—became widely prescribed.

While these drugs offered remarkable physiological benefits, they also reframed sexual health as a primarily biomedical issue. Uptake in Bangladesh followed similar trends to global practice, though access is constrained by affordability and distribution. Importantly, adherence remains poor: studies suggest that up to 50% of men discontinue PDE5 inhibitors within one year, despite symptomatic improvements (Sansone et al., 2025). Common reasons include side effects, loss of spontaneity, cultural reluctance, and dissatisfaction with purely mechanical improvements.

This points to a deeper reality: sexual well-being cannot be reduced to erections or orgasm alone. Patients consistently report that medications may restore performance, but not intimacy, self-esteem, or relational harmony. Thus, sex therapy retains a central role in addressing the cognitive, emotional, and interpersonal layers of sexual dysfunction.

Modern-Day Approach to Sex Therapy

Contemporary sex therapy emphasizes *integration* and *flexibility*. Rather than rigid adherence to a single school of thought, modern practice blends:

- **Cognitive Behavioral Therapy (CBT):** Challenging dysfunctional beliefs (e.g., "I am inadequate because my penis is small"), addressing performance anxiety, and restructuring sexual scripts.
- **Behavioral Therapy:** Techniques such as systematic desensitization, start-stop methods, and sensate focus.
- **Systemic and Couple Therapy:** Addressing relational dynamics, communication breakdowns, and cultural scripts within marriage.
- **Mindfulness and Acceptance-Based Approaches:** Growing in popularity for sexual pain disorders and anxiety-driven dysfunctions.

Masters and Johnson's dual-therapist model has given way to single-therapist practice, shown to be effective with couples (Leiblum & Rosen, 2000). Increasingly, *integrated treatment models*—combining pharmacotherapy with psychotherapy—are recognized as the gold standard (Althof et al., 2013; Leiblum et al., 2007).

In Bangladesh, ESSM-trained psychiatrists and psychologists have begun embedding these models into practice at tertiary clinics. However, implementation is limited to a few urban centers, and access in rural areas remains negligible. Workforce development, public education, and integration of traditional and biomedical approaches are urgent next steps.

Challenges and the Ongoing Role of Sex Therapy

Despite the undeniable progress in biological treatments for sexual dysfunctions, significant challenges remain in Bangladesh. Chief among them is the high dropout rate. Research indicates that 40–80% of patients discontinue pharmacotherapy for erectile dysfunction (ED), even when medications are effective in restoring erections (Brock et al., 2002; McCabe et al., 2016). The reasons are multidimensional: drugs often fail to address psychological factors such as self-esteem, body image, performance anxiety, relationship discord, and broader cultural beliefs about sexuality. Patients may also discontinue due to side effects, financial costs, or the loss of spontaneity associated with scheduled medication use.

These patterns highlight a fundamental truth: sexual health is not merely biomedical but profoundly biopsychosocial. While pills may restore penile rigidity, they cannot heal shame, improve partner communication, or dismantle myths surrounding masculinity and femininity. In Bangladesh, where cultural scripts about sexuality are deeply entwined with marriage, fertility, and family honor, sex therapy remains indispensable. It addresses the cognitive, emotional, relational, and cultural layers of dysfunction that pharmacology alone cannot reach.

Another challenge is the variability in therapeutic practice. Different schools of sex therapy—psychoanalytic, behavioral, cognitive-behavioral, and systemic—coexist, but, in practice, Bangladeshi clinicians often adopt an integrated approach. In psychiatric sex clinics, sessions are typically conducted by psychiatrists and postgraduate trainees who weave together psychoeducation, cognitive restructuring, sensate focus, and couple interventions. However, lack of structured training, stigma attached to sexual topics, and limited supervision mean that clinical styles can vary widely.

The following case vignettes illustrate the therapeutic model most commonly employed in Bangladesh, demonstrating both its potential and its challenges.

Case Vignette 1: Gone in 30 Seconds!

Patient History

Mr. KR, a 32-year-old textile engineer, had been married for three years to a 23-year-old graduate housewife in an arranged marriage. Initially, the couple reported a positive emotional bond. However, Mr. KR presented with longstanding anxiety traits and a pronounced inferiority complex about his body—especially his penile size.

He reported measuring his erect penis at 4.5 inches, which, compared to the cultural myth of the "ideal macho size" of at least 6 inches (often perpetuated by peers and pornography), reinforced feelings of inadequacy. Exposure to pornographic magazines during adolescence only intensified his anxiety and self-criticism.

Since puberty, he had engaged in regular masturbation but stopped after peers warned that masturbation could permanently damage his penis. This misinformation instilled a deep-seated fear of sexual inadequacy, which carried into adulthood. Despite excelling academically and professionally, he avoided marriage for years due to his self-doubt.

Upon marrying, Mr. KR developed premature ejaculation (PE), with ejaculation occurring within seconds of penetration. The condition worsened over time, fueled by his wife's frustration and his mounting performance anxiety. He was initially prescribed sertraline and escitalopram, but with little improvement. Having consulted five different doctors, he was eventually referred for psychosexual therapy. On the Premature Ejaculation Diagnostic Tool (PEDT), he scored 18 (scores >11 indicate PE).

Factors	*Predisposing*	*Precipitating*	*Maintaining*
Biological	Nil	Nil	Nil
Intrapsychic & Relational	Low self-esteem; neurotic traits; inferiority complex re: penis size	First-night sexual failure	Wife's rejection; performance anxiety; lack of medication response; worsening symptoms
Social & Cultural	Cultural myths re: penis size and virility; masturbation stigma	Wife's disparaging comment	Family pressure for conception and childbirth; gendered expectations

Therapeutic Intervention

1. **Psychoeducation**
   - Provided scientific explanations about the sexual response cycle, debunking myths around penis size and masturbation.
   - Reassured Mr. KR that his size was within the normal range; his wife was included in the education process to foster empathy.
2. **Sensate Focus Therapy**
   - *Step 1 (non-genital intimacy)*: Couple instructed to abstain from intercourse and genital contact; encouraged to rediscover intimacy through non-demand touch (e.g., back, chest, thighs), showering together, and using perfumes. Private masturbation was permitted. Follow-up included reflection on emotions and comfort levels.
   - *Step 2 (genital contact without penetration)*: Gradual introduction of genital touch in a safe, non-pressured environment. Focus on comfort, feedback, and playfulness.
   - *Step 3 (integration and intercourse)*: Progressive reintroduction of orgasm and penetration, maintaining emphasis on intimacy, communication, and comfort rather than performance.

Barriers and Progress

Initially, Mr. KR discovered new intimacy through non-genital touch, which improved confidence. He also benefited from adjunct pharmacological support with paroxetine. Before completing the full sensate focus program, he attempted intercourse successfully. However, emboldened by early success, he prematurely discontinued therapy and relapsed into PE. Upon resuming therapy, gradual improvements were achieved, and the case concluded with successful management of his condition.

This case underscores two themes:

- Dropout and relapse are common due to premature discontinuation.
- Combining psychoeducation, couple work, and sensate focus with pharmacological support can restore both function and confidence.

Case Vignette 02: Am I a Male!

Patient History

Mr. MMR, a 37-year-old married man with two children, presented with erectile difficulties persisting for three years. The problem emerged after a prolonged pause in sexual activity following the birth of his second child. Initially, during the early years of marriage (since 2018), he had occasional erectile difficulties but showed improvement with his wife's support.

He reported a history of daily masturbation between 1999 and 2005, sometimes multiple times per day, with no difficulty in excitement or erections. However, in 2006, he experienced testicular torsion requiring surgical removal of his left testicle. Following surgery, his masturbation frequency declined due to fears of losing sexual power.

Psychosocially, he had grown up in a turbulent family environment, frequently witnessing domestic violence (his father abusing his mother). This contributed to chronic insecurity and fragile self-esteem.

After resuming sexual activity post-pregnancy, Mr. MMR struggled with erections and began associating each failure with shame. His wife's response compounded the problem: she frequently accused him of deceiving her by not disclosing his unilateral testis and criticized him as "imperfect" or "not a real man." She also threatened to disclose his difficulties to extended family, heightening his humiliation and performance anxiety.

Biochemical tests showed no organic abnormalities. Antidepressant therapy provided no benefit, and he was referred for psychiatric sex therapy.

Factors	*Predisposing*	*Precipitating*	*Maintaining*
Biological	History of testicular torsion and orchiectomy (L testis)	Failure to achieve erection after long gap post-pregnancy	Persistent performance anxiety; repeated failures; non-response to medication

(Continued)

Factors	*Predisposing*	*Precipitating*	*Maintaining*
Intrapsychic & Relational	Insecure attachment; low self-esteem; inferiority re: one testis	Wife's criticism ("imperfect man," "deceived me")	Ongoing spousal rejection, fear of exposure, escalating anxiety
Social & Cultural	Cultural stigma equating virility with masculinity	Threat of social humiliation if wife disclosed issues	Reinforced shame, community expectations, pressure to prove masculinity

Therapeutic Intervention

1. **Psychoeducation**
   - Patient educated on sexual response cycle and the significant role of psychological factors in erectile function.
   - Reassurance given that psychogenic erectile dysfunction is reversible, and single-testis status does not necessarily impair sexual performance or fertility.
2. **Cognitive Restructuring (CBT)**
   - Addressed automatic thoughts ("I am incomplete," "I will fail again") through cognitive reframing, pros/cons analysis, and realistic self-appraisal.
   - Event analysis used to decouple isolated failures from global self-identity.
3. **Sensate Focus Therapy**
   - Introduced graded intimacy exercises without expectation of penetration, reducing pressure and restoring positive associations with touch.
   - Emphasized rebuilding emotional intimacy alongside physical connection.
4. **Couple Therapy**
   - Involved wife in counseling to address relational discord and communication breakdown.
   - Encouraged empathetic support rather than criticism. Wife was educated on the psychological underpinnings of erectile dysfunction to reduce blame and hostility.

This case highlights the intersection of biology, psychology, and culture: the loss of one testicle, combined with marital discord and gendered expectations of masculinity, converged to sustain dysfunction. Intervention required not only individual therapy but also relationship repair and cultural reframing of virility.

Case Formulation for Mr. MMR

Mr. MMR's presentation illustrates how biological history, psychological vulnerabilities, and sociocultural pressures intersect in Bangladesh.

Factors	*Predisposing*	*Precipitating*	*Maintaining*
Biological	History of testicular torsion with surgical removal of one testis (orchiectomy). Fears about reduced virility.	Erectile failure after long abstinence following second pregnancy.	Nil organic cause; psychogenic factors perpetuate dysfunction.
Intrapsychic and Relational	Insecure attachment style, low self-esteem, body image concerns about absence of a testis.	Wife's critical remarks: "imperfect man," "deceived me."	Escalating marital tension, spousal rejection, performance anxiety, non-response to medication, worsening cycle of failures.
Social and Cultural	Cultural emphasis on sexual power as proof of masculinity; myths about masturbation causing sexual weakness.	Threat of social embarrassment if wife discloses his sexual difficulties.	Ongoing fear of humiliation; social stigma around virility reinforces anxiety.

Therapeutic Intervention

1. **Psychoeducation**
   - Patient was educated about the human sexual response cycle, emphasizing the reversibility of psychogenic erectile dysfunction (McCabe et al., 2016).
   - Myths surrounding virility and single-testis masculinity were addressed with evidence-based reassurance.
2. **Cognitive Restructuring (CBT)**
   - Negative automatic thoughts ("I am incomplete," "I will fail again") were identified.
   - Pros-and-cons analysis and event reattribution techniques helped reframe failures as situational rather than global.
3. **Sensate Focus Therapy**
   - Introduced as non-demand intimacy exercises to rebuild trust in touch and reduce pressure for penetration.
   - Gradual exposure to intimacy without expectation of erection allowed for confidence restoration and relational safety.
4. **Involvement of the Wife**
   - Couples counseling focused on reframing her criticism into collaborative support.
   - Psychoeducation for both partners highlighted the role of empathy, patience, and shared responsibility in recovery.

Case Vignette 03: Genito-Pelvic Pain/Penetration Disorder

Patient Background

Mr. AK (28, banker) and Miss JR (22, student) had been married for 1.5 years. Since their wedding night, JR experienced pain during intercourse attempts, leading to genito-pelvic pain/penetration disorder (PVD).

- **History:** JR reported recurrent urinary tract infections (UTIs), now treated. The pain began during first intercourse attempts, which AK admitted were forceful and without adequate foreplay.
- **Current status:** For eight months, no successful penetration occurred. Conflict developed: AK felt JR was unwilling, while JR felt AK was impatient. Their distress led to consultations with gynecologists, who prescribed lidocaine and antidepressants—without success. Eventually, they were referred to psychiatry.

Factors	*Predisposing*	*Precipitating*	*Maintaining*
Biological	History of recurrent UTIs.	Nil.	Nil.
Intrapsychic & Relational	JR's neurotic trait; possible history of childhood abuse.	Painful first coitus (husband's rushed approach).	Wife's avoidance, catastrophizing; husband's frustration and impatience.
Social & Cultural	Pre-existing apprehension from cultural scripts ("first-night sex is painful").	Confirmation of this fear during rushed first-night intercourse.	Ongoing marital discord; separation due to unresolved intimacy.

Therapeutic Intervention

1. **Psychoeducation**
   - Couple educated on PVD, anatomy, and role of psychological and relational factors.
   - Aim: reduce stigma, enhance understanding, and promote collaborative coping.
2. **Couple Therapy**
   - Initial focus on relational repair and conflict resolution, especially since the couple had begun living separately.
3. **Cognitive Behavioral Therapy (CBT)**
   - Targeted JR's avoidance and catastrophizing through graded exposure and cognitive reframing.
   - Helped AK develop patience, empathy, and cooperative strategies.

4. **Vaginal Dilatation**
   - JR guided in self-exploration with mirror and touch; later included partner-assisted finger insertion.
5. **Sensate Focus Therapy**
   - *Non-genital stage*:
     - Stage 1: Individual self-touch with the right to stop at discomfort.
     - Stage 2: Partnered touch with feedback; intercourse/genital contact discouraged.
     - Encouraged shared activities (bathing, perfume use) to rebuild intimacy.
   - *Genital stage*: Gentle genital contact in safe, relaxed atmosphere.
6. **Vaginal Containment**
   - Gradual integration into intercourse, with JR in superior position to control penetration depth and pace.

Barriers and Progress

- **Challenges:** Frustration at slow pace; occasional resistance to structured sensate focus.
- **Progress:** Over six months, gradual improvements led to full penetration. At follow-up, the couple reported **satisfying and harmonious conjugal life**.

This case illustrates how cultural myths, medicalization without psychosocial care, and relational impatience perpetuate PVD. Holistic, stepwise intervention produced sustainable results.

Case Vignette 04: Male Hypoactive Sexual Desire Disorder

Patient Background

Mr. SM (34) and Miss WR (31) had been married for three years. Their relationship began with strong mutual attraction and eight months of high sexual activity. However, they presented with *discrepant desire*: WR reported high desire and distress over SM's lack of initiation.

- **Current Status:** No sexual activity for eight months. WR felt rejected and emotionally abandoned. Both partners feared the situation would worsen if they transitioned to parenthood.
- **Medical evaluation:** Endocrinologist excluded hormonal abnormalities. Comprehensive psychiatric and sexual history revealed **negative body image** (penile size concerns) and **conservative sexual attitudes** as contributory factors.

Factors	*Predisposing*	*Precipitating*	*Maintaining*
Biological	Hypothyroidism (treated).	Nil.	Nil.
Intrapsychic & Relational	Negative body image, penile size concerns.	Negative sexual encounters reinforcing avoidance.	Anticipatory failure, ongoing marital discord.
Social & Cultural	Conservative sexual upbringing and shame-based scripts.	Nil.	Nil.

Therapeutic Intervention

1. **Psychoeducation**
   - Normalized variation in desire.
   - Corrected misconceptions about penile size and masculinity.
2. **Couple Therapy**
   - Focused on reframing sex as a shared experience, not an obligation.
   - Encouraged empathy and role flexibility between partners.
3. **Cognitive Behavioral Therapy (CBT)**
   - Cognitive restructuring targeted negative body image and failure anticipation.
   - Introduced mindfulness and relaxation to reduce anxiety.
4. **Sensate Focus Therapy**
   - Emphasized non-demand intimacy to rediscover pleasure beyond penetration.
   - Encouraged exploration of diverse pathways to arousal and connection.

Progress

Over four months, the couple reported significant improvements:

- Weekly sexual activity re-established.
- Increased mutual desire and empathy.
- Reduction in anticipatory anxiety and body-image concerns.

This case demonstrates the role of psychological barriers and cultural scripts in hypoactive sexual desire, and how structured therapy can restore intimacy and prevent relationship breakdown.

Case Formulation for Mr. SM

Mr. SM's case highlights the complexity of *hypoactive sexual desire disorder* (HSDD) in men, where psychological, relational, and sociocultural dynamics often outweigh biological factors.

Factors	Predisposing	Precipitating	Maintaining
Biological	Hypothyroidism (treated, stable).	Nil.	Nil.
Intrapsychic and Relational	Negative body image, persistent insecurity about penile size.	Negative sexual encounters that reinforced avoidance.	Anticipation of failure, marital discord, escalating cycle of avoidance.
Social and Cultural	Conservative sexual attitudes limiting comfort with open exploration.	Nil.	Cultural silence around sexual communication; stigma around male desire variations.

Therapeutic Intervention

1. **Psychoeducation**
   - Provided clear information on genital anatomy, emphasizing the wide normal range of penile size and debunking myths equating masculinity with measurements.
   - Addressed the stigma around male low desire, normalizing variability across the lifespan (Clayton et al., 2018).
2. **Couple Therapy**
   - Reframed sexual intimacy as a shared journey rather than a duty or performance.
   - Helped WR cultivate empathy and reduce the cycle of rejection.
3. **Cognitive Behavioral Therapy (CBT)**
   - Cognitive restructuring targeted body image distortions ("I am inadequate because of my size") and anticipatory failure thoughts.
   - Introduced mindfulness and relaxation-based techniques to reduce anxiety and improve present-moment awareness during intimacy.
4. **Sensate Focus Therapy**
   - Structured non-demand intimacy exercises emphasized touch, playfulness, and communication without pressure for intercourse.
   - Reframed sexual encounters as opportunities for connection, pleasure, and exploration beyond orgasm.

Progression

Over four months of structured intervention:

- The couple re-established weekly sexual activity after eight months of abstinence.
- Mr. SM reported improved desire and reduced anxiety.
- WR felt emotionally reconnected, perceiving sex less as rejection and more as shared experience.

- The therapy highlighted how body image issues and cultural silence around male desire can be shifted through evidence-based, couple-focused care.

Experience from Patients Seen by Our Team

At the Department of Psychiatry, Bangabandhu Sheikh Mujib Medical University (BSMMU), a follow-up study of 112 patients offered sex therapy after limited success with pharmacological interventions (PDE5 inhibitors, antidepressants, or both) provides valuable insight into therapeutic realities in Bangladesh.

- **Common Presentations:** Misconceptions (37 cases), premature ejaculation (28), erectile dysfunction (22), vaginismus (9), female sexual interest/arousal disorder (12), orgasmic disorder (3), male hypoactive sexual desire disorder (1).
- **Treatment Approach:** Most patients underwent psychoeducation and sensate focus therapy, often supplemented with CBT techniques.
- **Key outcomes:** Longer therapy engagement (more than six sessions) consistently predicted better results, particularly for premature ejaculation, erectile dysfunction, and vaginismus.

Key Observations

	Pt No.	*Session No.*	*No. of Pt*	*Task*	*Responded*	*Did not respond*	*Drop out (<3 session)*
Misconception	37	1-2 session	37	Psychoeducation	28	9	
Premature Ejaculation	28	<6 session	16	Sensate Focus	1	3	12
		>6 session	12	Sensate Focus	10	2	
Erectile Dysfunction	22	<6 session	15	Sensate Focus	1	3	11
		>6 session	7	Sensate Focus	6	1	
Vaginismus	9	<6 session	2	Sensate Focus			2
		>6 session	7	Sensate Focus	6	1	
Female Sexual Interest and Arousal Disorder	12	<6 session	8	Sensate Focus	1	2	5
		>6 session	4	Sensate Focus	3	1	
Orgasmic Disorder	3	<6 session	1	Sensate Focus			1
		>6 session	2	Sensate Focus	1	1	
Male Hypoactive Sexual Desire Disorder	1	>6 session	1	Sensate Focus	1		

1. **Session Length Matters:**
   Patients completing more than six sessions had significantly higher improvement rates than those dropping out earlier. This aligns with international findings that psychosexual therapy requires time for behavioral and relational shifts (Althof et al., 2013).

2. **Misconceptions as a Major Driver:**
   Of the 37 cases rooted in sexual myths (e.g., masturbation causing weakness, penis size myths), 28 improved after just 1–2 sessions of psychoeducation. This underscores the importance of culturally tailored myth-busting in Bangladesh.
3. **High Dropout Rates:**
   Many patients abandoned therapy after fewer than three sessions. Possible reasons:
   - Frustration from repeated past failures with multiple providers.
   - Limited financial resources (services are out-of-pocket).
   - Cultural stigma making repeated clinic visits difficult.
4. **Therapist Adaptability:**
   Outcomes were best where therapists integrated psychoeducation, sensate focus, and relational counseling rather than relying on rigid models.

Treatment Outcome Data (Narrative of Table)

- **Misconceptions (37 cases):** Nearly three-quarters improved after targeted psychoeducation, showing the power of direct, culturally sensitive education.
- **Premature Ejaculation (28 cases):** Patients attending more than six sessions responded far better (10 of 12 improved) compared to those dropping out earlier.
- **Erectile Dysfunction (22 cases):** Similarly, 6 of 7 long-term attendees improved, while short-term attendees had minimal benefit.
- **Vaginismus (9 cases):** Almost all long-term patients (6 of 7) improved with sensate focus and gradual dilator work, while short-term attendees showed little progress.
- **Female Sexual Interest/Arousal Disorder (12 cases):** Mixed results, but longer therapy correlated with improvement (3 of 4 improved).
- **Orgasmic Disorder (3 cases):** Only 1 of 3 improved, highlighting the complexity of female orgasmic dysfunction in conservative contexts.
- **Male HSDD (1 case):** Improved with long-term sensate focus and CBT—mirroring Mr. SM's case.

Conclusion

Sex therapy in Bangladesh demonstrates both promise and limitation. It is not a one-size-fits-all approach (Leiblum & Pervin, 2007). The evidence from BMU (formerly BSMMU) highlights several critical lessons:

- **Integration Works Best:** Combining pharmacological support with psychosexual therapy yields the most sustainable outcomes.
- **Cultural Myths Are Powerful:** Addressing misconceptions head-on through psychoeducation can rapidly improve patient confidence.
- **Persistence Matters:** Patients who stay engaged for more than six sessions consistently show better outcomes, reinforcing the need for therapist encouragement and system-level support to reduce dropouts.

- **Structural Barriers Remain:** Limited trained professionals, lack of affordable services, and stigma around seeking therapy are ongoing obstacles.

Despite these challenges, the growing demand for psychosexual therapy in Bangladesh reflects a shift towards *holistic*, *human-centered care* that values dignity, relational intimacy, and long-term well-being over short-term medical fixes. This dual model—medication where necessary, therapy for depth and resilience—may be the most viable pathway for countries navigating resource constraints and cultural sensitivities.

References

Ahsan, M.S., Mubassara, L., Islam, A.K.M.A., Hasan, M.M., Selim, S., Ali, R., Hasan, M. and Hossain, M.K., 2025. South Asian Society for Sexual Medicine School, Bangladesh: a multidisciplinary training initiative in an under-resourced country. *Sexual Medicine*, *13*(2), qfaf028. https://doi.org/10.1093/sexmed/qfaf028

Althof, S.E., 2013. Integrated and combined therapy. In: Kirana, P.S., Tripodi, F., Reisman, Y. and Porst, H., eds. *The EFS and ESSM syllabus of clinical sexology.* 1st ed. Amsterdam: Medix, pp. 518–525. ISBN: 978-94-91487-10-1.

Althof, S.E., McMahon, C.G., Waldinger, M.D., Serefoglu, E.C., Shindel, A.W., Adaikan, P.G., Becher, E., Dean, J., Giuliano, F., Hellstrom, W.J. and Giraldi, A., 2014. An update of the International Society of Sexual Medicine's guidelines for the diagnosis and treatment of premature ejaculation (PE). *The Journal of Sexual Medicine*, 11(6), pp. 1392–1422.

Basson, R. 2000. The female sexual response: a different model. *Journal of Sex & Marital Therapy*, 26(1), pp. 51–65.

Bhugra, D., 2009. Leiblum, Sandra R. (Ed.), 2007. *Principles and practice of sex therapy* (4th edition). *International Review of Psychiatry*, 21(5), p. 487. https://doi.org/10.1080/09540260701284612.

Brock, G., McMahon, C., Chen, K., Costigan, T., Shen, W. and Watkins, V., 2002. Efficacy and safety of tadalafil for the treatment of erectile dysfunction: results of integrated analyses. *Journal of Urology*, 168(4, pt. 2), pp. 1332–1336.

Clayton, A.H., Goldfischer, E.R., Goldstein, I., Derogatis, L., Lewis-D'Agostino, D.J., Pyke, R., and Garcia, M., 2018. Validation of the decreased sexual desire screener (DSDS): A brief diagnostic instrument for generalized acquired female hypoactive sexual desire disorder (HSDD). *The Journal of Sexual Medicine*, 5(4), pp. 730–738.

Islam, T., Qusar, M.S., Ahsan, M.S., Morshed, A.S.M. and Haque, S., 2021. Adaptation and validation of Bangla version of premature ejaculation diagnostic tool. *Bangabandhu Sheikh Mujib Medical University Journal, 14*(4), pp. 132–137.

Kaplan, H.S., 1979. *Disorders of sexual desire and other new concepts and techniques in sex therapy*. New York: Brunner/Mazel.

Leiblum, S.R. and Rosen, R.C. (eds.) 2000. *Principles and practice of sex therapy*. 3rd ed. New York: Guilford Press.

Leiblum, S., Seehuus, M., Goldmeier, D. and Brown, C., 2007. Psychological, medical, and pharmacological correlates of persistent genital arousal disorder. *The Journal of Sexual Medicine*, 4(5), pp. 1358–1366.

Leiblum, S.R. and Pervin, L., 2007. Introduction. In: Leiblum, S.R. and Pervin, L., eds. *Principles and practice of sex therapy.* 4th ed. New York: Guilford Press.

Maruf, M.M., Mubasshara, L. and Ahsan, M.S., 2024. Psychosexual disorders in Bangladesh: From bench to community. In: Arafat, S.M.Y., ed. *Mental health in Bangladesh: From bench to community.* Singapore: Springer Nature Singapore, pp. 139–165.

Masters, W. H., and Johnson, V. E., 1966. *Human sexual response*. Little, Brown.

McCabe, M.P., Sharlip, I.D., Lewis, R., Atalla, E., Balon, R., Fisher, A.D., Laumann, E., Lee, S.W., Segraves, R.T. and Wespes, E., 2016. Risk factors for sexual dysfunction among women and men: A consensus statement from the Fourth International Consultation on Sexual Medicine 2015. *The Journal of Sexual Medicine*, 13(2), pp.153–167.

Mozumder, M.K., 2024. Psychosocial management of mental disorders in Bangladesh. In: Arafat, S.M.Y., ed. *Mental health in Bangladesh: From bench to community.* Singapore: Springer Nature Singapore, pp. 65–85.

Sansone, A., Guida, E., Dolci, S., Frangione, V., Asso, A., Bellia, G., and Jannini, E.A., 2025. Future perspectives for PDE5 inhibitors bridging the gap between cardiovascular health and psychological status. *Basic and Clinical Andrology,* 35(1), p. 3.

Tripodi, F., Gruenwald, I., Silvaggi, C., et al., 2015. Sexual response in men and women: models and critical issues. In: Reisman, Y., Porst, H., Lowenstein, L., et al., eds. *The ESSM manual of sexual medicine.* Amsterdam: Medix.

Tripodi, F. and Silvaggi, C., 2013. Sexual response: motivation and models. In: Kirana, P.S., Tripodi, F., Reisman, Y. and Porst, H., eds. *The EFS and ESSM syllabus of clinical sexology.* Amsterdam: Medix.

Tripody, F., 2021. Counselling and psychotherapy in sexual medicine. In: Lew-Starowicz, M. and Kruger, T., eds. *Psychiatry and sexual medicine.* Springer Nature Switzerland AG, pp. 161–190. Available at: https://doi.org/10.1007/978-3-030-52298-8_12 [Accessed 16 Mar. 2025].

Chapter 26

Towards an Anti-Oppressive Psychosexual Psychotherapy Practice

Julie Sale

Introduction: Who Am I

At the heart of anti-oppressive psychotherapy lies a fundamental requirement: to know ourselves. This entails acknowledging our social positioning and critically reflecting on how the intricate dimensions of power, privilege, and marginalization inherent in our identities shape our clinical work. Rather than assuming a false neutrality or adopting an authoritative third-person voice, I choose to begin this chapter by openly sharing who I am—recognizing that transparency is an ethical starting point for anti-oppressive practice.

My name is Julie. I am a white, cis-gender woman in my fifties, residing and working in England, UK. I embody a slim-bodied, non-disabled identity and come from a working-class, low-income background. I am a mother and serve professionally as a psychotherapist, educator, and organizational leader. Each aspect of my identity confers both privilege and constraint within the socio-cultural landscape I navigate.

Undeniably, my whiteness grants me significant, unearned privilege in British society, facilitating easier access to education, employment, and social capital, free from the structural barriers faced by racialized minorities (Khan, 2023; Mullan, 2023). My non-disabled status allows for seamless engagement with most physical spaces, a freedom not extended to many clients and colleagues with disabilities (Halacre, 2021). My professional roles afford me authority and power within therapeutic and academic settings. These privileges have shaped my career trajectory and life opportunities, positioning me advantageously in a system still deeply marked by inequity (Garcia & Timothy, 2020).

Yet, my identity also carries shadowed complexities. Being cis-gender offers social safety, but being a woman subjects me to gendered inequities pervasive in the UK, where older women, in particular, encounter patronization or invisibility (Burnham, 2013). My slim body aligns with dominant cultural beauty ideals, yet maintaining this status in a society driven by abundance and diet culture is demanding and fraught with its own pressures (Davies & Neustifter, 2021). Motherhood, while socially valorized, involves sacrifices and challenges that often go unacknowledged (Barton, 2024).

DOI: 10.4324/9781003611387-26

I want to emphasize that what I offer here is not a claim to definitive knowledge but an honest account of my ongoing learning. My understanding of anti-oppressive practice has been shaped and deepened by the rigorous labor of scholars and activists with lived experiences of oppression—people who have graciously shared their wisdom with those of us who have not lived their realities (St Aime, 2024; Ellis, 2024). I encourage readers approaching this chapter from a learning stance to engage deeply with the referenced works to broaden and enrich their perspectives.

Where I do speak with authority is in the field of psychosexual psychotherapy—a specialty where I have devoted significant clinical, supervisory, and educational work. My reflections here are informed by this professional expertise, alongside a commitment to ongoing humility and reflexivity.

Lastly, in my writing, I have been deliberate with pronoun usage. Words like "we," "you," "they," "our," and "us" carry relational and political weight. I strive to use them thoughtfully—avoiding assumptions of shared experience or the inadvertent othering of any group—to foster inclusivity and respect.

Anti-Oppressive Psychotherapy: Evolving Awareness and Practice

The recognition of psychotherapy's potential to perpetuate oppression has gained momentum in recent years (Brown, 2019; Garcia & Timothy, 2020; St Aime, 2024). Literature increasingly addresses how therapists can engage ethically and effectively with specific minoritized groups, with significant strides in acknowledging gender, sexuality, and relationship diversities (Czyzselska, 2021; Tilsen, 2021; Scarrone Bonhomme et al., 2023; Neves & Davies, 2023a; Neves & Davies, 2023b). Similarly, work focusing on culture, religion, and race has expanded (Khan, 2023; Mullan, 2023; Ellis, 2024), particularly since global racial justice movements like those sparked by the murder of George Floyd (Mullan, 2023).

However, certain areas remain underdeveloped. Disability awareness within psychotherapy, while growing, remains marginal (Institute of Psychotherapy and Disability, 2000; Halacre, 2021), and the understanding of neurodivergence is only recently filtering into practice guidelines (Waller, 2021; Strunz, 2024). Ageism persists as a neglected dimension of diversity, and many aspects of identity—such as body size, appearance, socioeconomic status, education, and relationship status—are often overlooked despite their profound impact on clients' lived experiences (D'Andrea & Daniels, 2001; Hays, 2008; Burnham, 2013).

Clinical Reflection: The Importance of Social Positioning

For example, consider a client presenting with sexual concerns who is an older, disabled, neurodivergent person of color navigating multiple layers of marginalization. Without therapists' conscious awareness of these intersecting identities and systemic oppressions, therapy risks re-traumatization or invisibility of critical contextual factors (Crenshaw, 1989; Meyer, 1995). Recognizing and naming one's own positionality allows therapists to hold space more safely for such clients, fostering trust and therapeutic alliance (Garcia & Timothy, 2020).

Conversely, therapists may also experience privilege or marginalization themselves. For instance, a white, cisgender therapist may inadvertently replicate white yy or cis-normativity in clinical assumptions. In contrast, therapists with marginalized identities might encounter countertransference linked to shared experiences of oppression, requiring heightened reflexivity and supervision (Hook et al., 2013; St Aime, 2024).

This foundational self-awareness and acknowledgement of socio-political contexts are indispensable for building an anti-oppressive psychosexual practice. It situates therapeutic work within the broader realities of systemic injustice and empowers both therapists and clients to engage authentically with the complexities of identity, power, and healing.

Diversity and Inclusion vs. Anti-Oppressive Practice

The evolution from working *with* diversity towards working *within* diversity marks a critical advancement in psychotherapy discourse, eloquently articulated by Myira Khan (2023). While traditional diversity frameworks tend to position clients as the "other" relative to a presumed normative therapist, the concept of working *within* diversity disrupts this binary by recognizing the complex interplay of identities present in the therapy room. Both therapist and client bring intersecting social locations—privileged and marginalized—that continuously shape therapeutic dynamics (Khan, 2023, pp. 27–36, 130–133). There is no neutral baseline, no blank slate against which difference can be measured; instead, every identity combination contributes uniquely to the therapeutic encounter.

This philosophy aligns with a broader professional shift beyond mere diversity and inclusion towards *anti-oppressive practice*—an integrative framework emphasizing the dismantling of systemic oppression across all identities (Garcia & Timothy, 2020; Khan, 2023; St Aime, 2024). This framework is increasingly reflected across specialties: guidance developed for racial and cultural competence (Khan, 2023; Mullan, 2023) resonates with best practices for LGBTQ+ affirmative therapy (Constantinides et al., 2019; Neves & Davies, 2023a) and disability-affirming work (Halacre, 2021; Katz Kattari, 2024a). These efforts highlight the interconnected nature of social justice struggles, reminding us—as Gzesh et al. (2024, p. 14) paraphrase Fannie Lou Hamer—that "nobody is free until everybody's free." Oppressions such as ableism, racism, and sexism are intertwined systems, demanding holistic approaches.

Core Principles in Anti-Oppressive Psychotherapy Practice

Across contemporary dialogues, several shared principles emerge as foundational for anti-oppressive practice:

- **Acknowledgement of Oppression:** Recognizing that systemic oppression is real and pervasive is non-negotiable. It demands awareness of power differentials and privileges shaping clients' lived experiences and the therapeutic relationship.
- **Recognition of Social Location:** Therapist and client social positions—including race, class, gender, and more—inevitably influence therapy processes, formulations, and outcomes.
- **Historical Awareness:** Understanding how histories—especially those of colonization, slavery, eugenics, and marginalization—shape current societal and personal realities is crucial.
- **Trauma-Informed Approach:** Appreciating the impact of both historical and ongoing trauma linked to minoritized identities enriches clinical empathy and safeguards clients.
- **Practice Flexibility:** Adapting standard therapeutic norms to meet diverse needs ensures inclusivity and cultural safety.

Oppression: Naming What We Often Ignore

To engage in anti-oppressive practice, therapists must confront the undeniable presence of oppression. As Khan (2023, p. 14) insists:

> We need to acknowledge our client's lived experience of power, privilege and oppression. To be blind to structural and systemic inequality is to be blind to our client's truth. To acknowledge the oppression, power, privilege and structural inequalities experienced by clients "out there" in the world, is to also acknowledge how they are experienced "in here," in the therapy room, in our therapeutic relationships and in our therapeutic process and culture.

Ignoring or denying systemic oppression not only distorts our and our clients' realities but violates core ethical principles by perpetuating harm and invisibility (Khan, 2023, p. 32).

Social Location: The Unseen Architecture of Therapy

Returning to the theme of self-awareness, social location remains pivotal. The chapters throughout this volume attest to the diverse cultural, geographical, and social contexts that shape therapeutic work globally (Garcia & Timothy, 2020; Khan, 2023; Mullan, 2023; Ellis, 2024; St Aime, 2024). Where a therapist and client live, their cultural norms, societal hierarchies, and personal identities inevitably influence perceptions, communication styles, and therapeutic goals. Psychotherapy, therefore, is never "context-free" but is deeply embedded in the socio-political milieu.

The Importance of History in Decolonizing Therapy

Decolonizing psychotherapy has brought renewed focus to the centrality of history in understanding oppression and healing (Khan, 2023; Mullan, 2023; Ellis, 2024;

St Aime, 2024). History is not neutral; it is selectively recorded and taught, often privileging dominant Eurocentric narratives while erasing or marginalizing others.

In the UK, for example, critical histories such as the transatlantic slave trade, British colonialism, and the experiences of the Windrush generation remain underrepresented in school curricula. A 2023 YouGov survey found that 75% of respondents admitted to knowing little or nothing about Black British history (Bloomsbury, 2023). Similarly, South Asian histories—such as the partition of India—are often absent from compulsory education, despite this group being the UK's second largest ethnic minority.

Even in progressive areas such as sexuality and gender identity, the shadow of past laws like Section 28—banning discussions of LGBTQ+ identities in schools—lingers, and parental opt-outs from sex and relationships education persist.

Disability, the largest global marginalized group, suffers similar erasure; though one in five UK residents has a disability (Snowden, 2023), the origins of eugenics—which advocated for forced sterilizations and systemic violence against disabled people—are rarely taught (Gzesh et al., 2024, pp.16–17). This omission perpetuates stigma and misunderstanding.

While the UK observes dedicated history months for Black, South Asian, LGBTQ+, and disability histories, the lived experience of many families and individuals reveals limited visibility of these observances in education, where World War II history dominates instead.

History and Our Profession: Facing Uncomfortable Truths

This historical awareness extends to the psychotherapy profession itself, which is steeped in white, Eurocentric values (Brown, 2019; Garcia & Timothy, 2020; Mullan, 2023; St Aime, 2024). Unacknowledged white supremacy, the appropriation and dismissal of Indigenous knowledge, the erasure of marginalized histories, and the racial and gender biases embedded in diagnostic criteria persist within clinical theory and practice. Additionally, trauma blindness—the failure to recognize oppression as a source of psychological distress—remains a critical concern demanding urgent attention.

Clinical Vignette: Reflecting on History and Social Location in Practice

Consider a Black British client presenting with sexual identity conflicts and mistrust of mental health services due to historical medical abuses and systemic racism. Without integrating an understanding of these historical traumas and social contexts, therapy risks retraumatization or superficial engagement (Garcia & Timothy, 2020; Neves & Davies, 2023a). In contrast, an anti-oppressive approach might involve explicitly acknowledging these histories, creating space for dialogue around cultural mistrust, and validating the client's experience within a broader sociohistorical framework.

By centering oppression, social location, history, trauma, and flexibility, therapists can begin dismantling harmful power dynamics and foster therapeutic environments that honor the fullness of clients' identities and experiences.

Trauma: The Invisible Burden in Minoritized Identities

Our contemporary understanding of trauma has expanded far beyond discrete events to encompass the enduring legacy of intergenerational trauma, epigenetic inheritance, and the cumulative impact of systemic marginalization. Scholars like Resmaa Menakem (2021) and Mullan (2023) underscore how trauma is embodied and transmitted through generations, particularly within communities that have endured colonization, racism, and systemic violence. Intersectionality, a concept pioneered by Crenshaw (1989), highlights how overlapping identities compound experiences of oppression and trauma, demanding that clinicians consider these complex intersections in assessment and intervention. Minority stress theory (Meyer, 1995) similarly elucidates how chronic exposure to discrimination and stigma contributes to psychological distress among marginalized populations.

In psychosexual psychotherapy, trauma manifests not only as direct abuse or violence but often as the internalized residue of societal rejection, invisibility, and devaluation. Behaviors that might initially appear disproportionate or enigmatic—such as hypervigilance, emotional withdrawal, or intense fear—must be understood within the broader context of these lived realities. Clients may present with symptoms labeled under depression, anxiety, substance use, or "sexual dysfunctions," but these diagnoses frequently veil the profound grief and rage rooted in oppressive experiences.

A poignant clinical reminder comes from Dr. Erica McInnes (2025), who urges therapists to shift from asking, "What is wrong with you?" to "What happened to you?" This reframing promotes a trauma-informed, compassionate stance, recognizing clients' reactions as survival strategies rather than pathologies. For therapists who share minoritized identities with their clients, this question becomes deeply personal—transforming the therapeutic encounter into a shared journey of healing, where "you" becomes "we."

Clinical Vignette

Consider Maria, a 34-year-old queer woman of color, presenting with chronic sexual avoidance and intimacy difficulties. Her initial reticence in therapy masked layers of trauma from racial discrimination and family rejection. Understanding her struggles through the lens of minority stress and intergenerational trauma enabled her therapist to validate her responses as adaptive rather than dysfunctional, fostering a therapeutic alliance rooted in trust and cultural humility.

Flexibility: Reshaping Therapy to Dismantle Oppression

Anti-oppressive practice challenges many of psychotherapy's traditional boundaries, which can inadvertently reproduce exclusion and harm (Constantinides et al., 2019; Tilsen, 2021; Mullan, 2023). The rigid adherence to fixed session lengths, punctuality, and physical attendance may privilege Western norms that do not translate universally. For example, a 50-minute session may be overwhelming or inaccessible for disabled or neurodivergent clients who require shorter or more flexible engagements (Strunz, 2024). Financial constraints may prevent clients from committing to weekly therapy, necessitating alternative scheduling or sliding scale models to improve accessibility.

Moreover, insisting on in-person sessions in office settings may alienate marginalized clients who experience these environments as intimidating or unsafe. Community-based, virtual, or hybrid models can help bridge this gap, enhancing reach and cultural responsiveness. The traditional Western ideal of therapist neutrality, expressed through limited self-disclosure, is also questioned by anti-oppressive paradigms, which recognize the power of shared identities and authentic connection in fostering safety and healing, particularly in marginalized communities (Brown, 2019).

Despite growing awareness, systemic change is slow. Marginalized therapists report feeling excluded or even traumatized by training environments, while clients from minoritized groups remain underrepresented or labeled "hard to reach" (Turner, 2025). This designation begs critical reflection: *Who* is not reaching *whom*? Such questioning invites therapists to interrogate their own practices and the structures that limit inclusion.

Applying Anti-Oppressive Practice to Psychosexual Psychotherapy

The core question for this volume is: How do these anti-oppressive principles translate into the specialized field of psychosexual psychotherapy? Sexuality is deeply personal yet profoundly political—intersecting with identity, culture, history, and power. Minoritized clients face unique vulnerabilities, not only socially but also within therapeutic contexts shaped by normative assumptions about sex, gender, and relationships.

Therapists must cultivate heightened reflexivity to dismantle normative biases that pathologize sexual diversity or impose culturally narrow scripts. The trauma-informed flexibility discussed above becomes essential when addressing sexual issues often compounded by historical stigma, shame, and systemic exclusion. By embracing anti-oppressive frameworks, psychosexual therapists can create spaces that honor complexity, validate diverse expressions of sexuality, and empower clients towards authentic sexual well-being.

Pause for Reflection

Before proceeding, take a moment to reflect on your internal responses to anti-oppressive psychotherapy:

- What thoughts, emotions, or physical sensations arise as you engage with these concepts?
- If you imagine a continuum from curiosity and openness at one end to resistance and rejection at the other, where do you situate yourself?
- What might your placement reveal about your current practice, assumptions, or areas for growth?

Engaging with these questions invites therapists into the ongoing, sometimes uncomfortable work of self-examination that underpins truly transformative, anti-oppressive care.

Anti-Oppressive Psychosexual Psychotherapy

Who Is Vulnerable?

An essential foundation for anti-oppressive psychosexual psychotherapy is to identify which clients are most vulnerable to experiencing oppression within therapeutic contexts. The *Equality Act 2010* (UK Government, 2020) codifies protected characteristics that legally safeguard individuals from discrimination: age, disability, gender reassignment, marriage and civil partnership, race, religion or belief, sex, and sexual orientation. Expanding on this, recent case law has confirmed protections for gender fluid and non-binary individuals under gender reassignment (UK Government, 2018) and for those holding gender-critical views under belief (UK Government, 2021). Neurodivergent people may be covered under disability protections. However, several identities remain legally unprotected: kinky individuals are not explicitly included, though some protections might be inferred under sex or sexual orientation; asexuality is not recognized as a protected sexual orientation; young people are excluded from age protections; and relationship statuses such as single, multiple partnered, divorced, or widowed are not protected under the marriage and civil partnership category. Nevertheless, the *Memorandum of Understanding on Conversion Therapy* (MoU Conversion Therapy, 2024) extends protections against conversion practices to asexual people, along with all sexual orientations and gender identities.

Moving beyond legal frameworks, social models of identity and oppression reveal further vulnerable groups that are often overlooked (D'Andrea & Daniels, 2001; Hays, 2008; Burnham, 2013). Body size and appearance, for instance, profoundly impact psychosexual well-being yet lack explicit legal protections. The pervasive stigma and discrimination tied to these characteristics create unique barriers and emotional burdens in therapeutic contexts.

Who Are the "Oppressors"?

Oppression is structurally maintained by those who benefit from systemic advantages linked to dominant identities. In the UK, this translates predominantly to white, cis-gender, heterosexual, monogamous, and non-disabled individuals. Psychosexual psychotherapists who hold some or all of these identities bear a responsibility to critically reflect on the privileges they inherit and how these shape prevailing social and sexual norms. The unexamined influence of these dominant identities risks perpetuating biases and blind spots in clinical practice. As such, kindness and liberal values, while necessary, are insufficient to dismantle deeply embedded structures of oppression (Neves, 2025).

The Oppressive Potential of Psychosexual Psychotherapy in the UK

The normative frameworks underpinning UK psychosexual psychotherapy reflect and reinforce the social positioning of white, cis-gender, heterosexual, monogamous, and non-disabled identities as default "norms" (Neves, 2025). These dominant social scripts shape understandings of sexual behavior, relationship models, and acceptable desires, often marginalizing or pathologizing deviations.

White Supremacy

White supremacy—the belief in the inherent superiority of white people and corresponding social privileges (Wiktionary, 2025)—is embedded within the Eurocentric foundations of psychosexual therapy. The field's historical and theoretical influences largely emanate from white male figures (Coleman & Ford, 2024), reinforcing exclusionary norms. Medical racism compounds this legacy (Sowemimo, 2023), evidenced in infamous historical abuses such as the non-consensual surgeries by James Marion Sims on enslaved African-American women (Shende et al., 2024), the Tuskegee Syphilis Study (Brandt, 1978), and the Guatemala Syphilis Experiments (Rodriguez & García, 2013). These abuses highlight how racialized bodies have been systematically exploited in medical and sexual health contexts.

Culturally embedded racist sexual scripts persist today, including the hypersexualization of Black men (Young, 2018), fetishization of Black women (Banks et al., 2024), desexualization of East Asian individuals (Kazumi, 2020), and stereotypes associating South Asian men with sexual offending (Gill & Day, 2020). Failure to recognize and address these scripts within psychosexual therapy perpetuates harm through invisibility and misinterpretation.

Clinical Vignette

Tariq, a 29-year-old Black British man, presented with difficulties in intimate relationships characterized by anxiety and avoidance. Therapy revealed internalized racial stereotypes impacting his sexual self-esteem and relational trust. Addressing these racist sexual scripts within a culturally affirming framework was crucial to Tariq's progress.

Progressive Perspectives with Oppressive Potential

Ironically, well-intentioned progressive values—feminism, inclusivity, sex positivity, and pleasure ethics—may inadvertently marginalize clients whose cultural or religious frameworks differ from mainstream UK perspectives (Hall & Graham, 2013). The valorization of autonomy and transparency risks invalidating collectivist values and honor-based cultural norms, potentially exacerbating shame or alienation (das Nair & Butler, 2012). For example, the compulsory "coming out" narrative celebrated in Western LGBTQ+ discourse may be deeply unsafe or alienating for clients from non-Western or religious backgrounds (Hall & Graham, 2013). Such dynamics necessitate sensitive, client-centered negotiation of cultural values and therapeutic goals.

Mononormativity

Mononormativity—the privileging of monosexual and monogamous relationship models as "natural" or "ideal" (Wiktionary, 2025)—is pervasive and often invisible in therapy. This bias pathologizes single individuals, those in consensually non-monogamous relationships, or cultures with multiple partnered family structures, often misattributing attachment styles or moral judgments (Barker, 2018). Even therapists educated in non-monogamous modalities may unconsciously uphold hierarchical polyamory norms or question the safety of children in multi-partner families, perpetuating erasure of diverse relational configurations.

Heteronormativity

Heteronormativity refers to the social and institutional privileging of heterosexuality, heterosexual relationships, and traditional gender roles as the fundamental and "natural" standards within society (Wiktionary, 2025). This framework not only marginalizes LGBTQ+ identities but also shapes societal expectations about sexual behavior, intimacy, and relationship legitimacy.

The harm heteronormativity inflicts on LGBTQ+ people is well documented. Privileging heterosexuality delegitimizes all other sexual orientations and fosters systemic discrimination (Neves, 2025). It is worth recalling that homosexuality was only removed from the ICD as a mental health disorder as recently as 1990, illustrating the relatively recent dismantling of pathologizing attitudes. The heteronormative assumption that "sex" exclusively means penis-in-vagina (PIV) intercourse erases the sexual experiences of those who do not fit this template, including same-sex couples, asexual individuals, and those with diverse bodies or sexual practices. This narrow script also reinforces the misconception that sex is primarily natural and essential for intimacy because it leads to reproduction, underpinning stigmatization of non-reproductive sexualities (Sale, 2019).

A particularly insidious consequence of heteronormativity is the conflation of asexuality with hypoactive sexual desire, which can lead to coercive "conversion" attempts to "normalize" sexual desire (Sale, 2019). The diagnostic category of Hypoactive Sexual Desire Disorder (DSM-5-TR, 2022) pathologizes lack of sexual desire, yet it rests on heteronormative assumptions about normative sexual behavior. Asking "Says who?" challenges the unquestioned authority of these norms.

Kink and Paraphilias

Psychosexual therapy's traditional framing of kink and non-normative sexual interests as paraphilias or disorders reflects heteronormative and pathologizing biases. The DSM-5 defines paraphilias as "intense and persistent sexual interests other than genital stimulation or preparatory fondling with phenotypically normal, physiologically mature, consenting human partners" (DSM-5-TR, 2022). This definition inherently privileges heteronormative and cis-normative standards. The terminology—especially phrases like "phenotypically normal"—is loaded with assumptions that dismiss the validity of diverse sexual expressions.

Despite the APA's distinction between paraphilias and paraphilic disorders, psychotherapeutic professions often conflate kink with trauma and pathology (De Block, 2013; Bennett, 2024). This stigmatization results in many kinky clients avoiding therapy altogether due to fears of judgement, misdiagnosis, or forced normalization (Nevard, 2018).

Maya, a 35-year-old bisexual woman engaged in consensual BDSM, hesitated to seek therapy due to past experiences where her sexual preferences were pathologized as signs of trauma or disorder. A trauma-informed, kink-affirmative approach allowed Maya to explore her identity without shame, fostering improved self-acceptance and relationship satisfaction.

Heteronormativity's Impact on Heterosexual Clients

Heteronormativity does not only harm non-heterosexual clients; it also imposes rigid expectations on heterosexual clients. The pervasive assumption that heterosexual people desire and enjoy penetrative sex contributes to diagnostic criteria for disorders such as Erectile Disorder and Genito-Pelvic Pain/Penetration Disorder (DSM-5-TR, 2022). While these diagnoses require "significant distress" for clinical relevance, the existence of such categories presumes distress in deviation from heteronormative sexual scripts (Ward, 2022). This medicalization of normative variability can create unnecessary shame and self-doubt among heterosexual clients.

Cis-Normativity

Cis-normativity—the assumption that all people have a gender identity aligned with their biological sex—upholds a binary and restrictive model of gender (Wiktionary, 2025). These scripts contribute to marginalization and clinical misunderstandings of transgender and gender-expansive people. Importantly, distinctions between biological sex and gender identity are recognized by the World Health Organization and the American Psychiatric Association (DSM-5-TR, 2022; WHO, 2025). The reclassification of gender incongruence as a sexual health condition rather than a mental disorder (WHO, 2025) and the shift from "gender identity disorder" to "gender dysphoria" in the DSM-5 represent progress towards depathologization (DSM-5-TR, 2022).

The British Psychological Society emphasizes that diverse gender identities are normal and not pathological (BPS, 2024). However, transgender and gender expansive people continue to face harmful conversion efforts, restricted access to affirming care post-Cass Review (Cass, 2024), and professional divisions over treatment approaches (National LGBT Survey, 2017; Mollitt, 2022).

Guidance on working with gender dysphoria exists (Scarrone Bonhomme et al., 2023), but attention to the sexual dimensions of gender diversity remains limited (Jacobsen et al., 2019). Psychosexual therapists must consider both the psychological impact of gender dysphoria and its effects on sexual experience, adapting interventions sensitively. For instance, dysphoria often centers on breasts, chests, or genitalia, necessitating careful language use and flexible therapy strategies that might avoid nakedness or direct touch (Jacobsen et al., 2019).

The Influence of Cis-Normativity on Sexual Scripts

Cis-normativity reinforces stereotypes such as women being sexually reluctant and men being sexually proactive, shaping relationship expectations and pathologizing variations in sexual desire and behavior. This dynamic generates shame in clients whose gender expression or sexual preferences diverge from these norms, including heterosexual women with high desire, men with low desire, or men engaging in same-sex or anal sex activities (Sale, 2023).

Ableism

Ableism, defined as discrimination in favor of non-disabled people (Wiktionary, 2025), is deeply entrenched in UK society, where disabled individuals are often infantilized and desexualized (Esmail et al., 2010; Gzesh et al., 2024). Legal frameworks such as the Sexual Offences Act 2003 (Legislation, 2003) restrict disabled people's access to sexual pleasure support, and professional ethical codes, including COSRT's (2022), enforce these protections, sometimes inadvertently limiting sexual autonomy.

Awareness of neurodiversity in psychotherapy is growing (Strunz, 2024), but knowledge regarding its impact on sexuality and relationships remains nascent (Katz Kattari et al., 2024). Neurodivergent individuals have diverse sexual interests and experiences; common themes include preference for solo sex, overlapping sex and gender diversity in autistic people, heightened sexual interest in some individuals with ADHD, and variable sensory processing affecting sexual response (Katz Kattari et al., 2024).

Ableist therapy approaches, such as traditional sensate focus exercises, may be inaccessible or harmful for disabled or neurodivergent clients without thoughtful adaptations (Katz Kattari, 2024b).

Alex, an autistic client, found standard sensate focus exercises overwhelming due to sensory sensitivities. Together, therapist and client developed an adapted approach emphasizing solo sensory exploration and gradual social engagement, enhancing Alex's comfort with intimacy and sexual expression.

Body Size, Appearance, and Age

Two unprotected characteristics of human identity in our culture that significantly influence experiences of sexuality are body size and appearance. Society often values slim female bodies, tall and athletic male bodies, and overall facial attractiveness. Those who fall outside these culturally reinforced standards frequently experience both internal and external shame and stigma, which can negatively impact their sexual desire, expression, and perceived relationship value. Conversely, some may experience fetishization and objectification based on their appearance, which also affects their sexual agency and relational dynamics (Davies & Neustifter, 2021).

When we add age to this dynamic, the narrative of desexualization resurfaces, particularly for older adults who are more likely to face sexual function challenges (DeLamater & Karraker, 2009; Dundon & Rellini, 2010). The societal assumption that older people are asexual contributes to rising rates of sexually transmitted infections (STIs) in the over-50s population, as well as correlates with injustices faced by disabled older adults in care settings, where sexual expression is often restricted or denied (Elias & Ryan, 2011; Johnson, 2013; Syme, 2017).

Transferential Dynamics and Therapeutic Implications

In psychosexual psychotherapy, therapists must be aware of how body size, appearance, and age influence transferential and countertransferential processes, as well as projections that may arise within the therapy relationship. The way a therapist and client perceive each other's bodies and ages can affect emotional safety, communication, and exploration of sexual issues.

For example, a therapist's unconscious bias regarding a client's body size could influence the therapeutic alliance or subtle non-verbal responses, potentially impacting the client's comfort in discussing intimate concerns. Clients may project societal shame or internalized stigma about their appearance or age onto the therapist, influencing engagement and trust.

Principles of Anti-Oppressive Psychosexual Psychotherapy

Our exploration so far reveals that, despite increasing liberal understandings of sexuality in the UK, oppression within psychosexual psychotherapy remains a tangible risk. Intersectionality (Crenshaw, 1989) highlights that clients holding multiple marginalized identities are exponentially more vulnerable to experiencing oppression in therapy, especially when therapists hold unexamined dominant identities.

Drawing from anti-oppressive frameworks in general psychotherapy, four foundational principles for anti-oppressive psychosexual psychotherapy practice are proposed as an initial scaffold for ongoing reflection and growth.

Principle 1: Know Yourself—Differentiating Personal Values from Professional Ethics

Acknowledging our social positioning and that of our clients—and understanding how these impact the therapeutic space—is essential. While self-awareness, reflexivity, and supervised reflective practice are ethical cornerstones, these often fall short of intentionally interrogating power, privilege, and bias embedded within our identities, values, and social conditioning. This applies regardless of whether therapists or clients hold dominant or marginalized identities.

Dominant cultural scripts and normative identities can cause harm in therapy, yet the oppressive potential of socially progressive positions—such as assumed "correct" social justice stances or sex-positive views—may be less apparent. Imposing these stances relationally, especially without attunement, can replicate oppression. Meeting ourselves, colleagues, and clients where they are, and developing non-defensive responses to perceived differences, is a key aspect of anti-oppressive practice.

Camille Sapara Barton's phrase "unkind eyes" in *Tending Grief* (Barton, 2024, p. 15) poignantly describes the white judgmental gaze on Black British identity. Unfortunately, those committed to social justice can redirect such "unkind eyes" onto others, such as heterosexual men, perpetuating a cycle of swapped oppressions rather than dismantling systemic ones.

For psychosexual psychotherapists, it is crucial to bracket personal sexual and relational beliefs, separating personal morals from professional ethics. For instance, a sex therapist refusing to work with a client involved in an affair due to personal moral conflict exemplifies how personal values can interfere with ethical obligations. Conversely, uncritical affirmation of client sexualities without sensitivity to safety or shame can fail to provide nuanced, attuned therapy (Sale, 2019).

Principle 2: Acknowledge and Deconstruct Dominant Sex and Gender Narratives

Therapists must consciously identify, name, and critically examine dominant societal norms that shape sexual self-concepts. It is vital to integrate social factors alongside biological and psychological aspects within a biopsychosocial framework (Potki et al., 2017).

Psychosexual psychotherapy provides a powerful space for unpacking and deconstructing restrictive gender and sexuality scripts. This includes challenging toxic masculinity in clients presenting with erectile difficulties or premature ejaculation, exploring femininity narratives that constrain sexual desire expectations, addressing racialized sexual stereotypes like hypersexualization or exoticization, and confronting sexual stigma experienced by disabled clients. The list of dominant scripts influencing client distress is extensive and complex, underscoring the necessity of socially informed therapeutic work.

Principle 3: Minoritization Creates Trauma

Trauma within psychosexual therapy extends far beyond overt histories of childhood sexual abuse, domestic violence, or sexual offenses. Anti-oppressive psychotherapy broadens this lens by acknowledging that individuals holding marginalized identities frequently endure cumulative trauma arising from systemic and interpersonal oppression. These include repeated macroaggressions—such as institutional discrimination—and microaggressions—subtle, often unconscious slights that perpetuate exclusion and invalidation. This ongoing minority stress profoundly impacts emotional regulation, relational capacity, and sexual well-being (Meyer, 1995; Menakem, 2021).

A trauma-informed stance in psychosexual psychotherapy is thus not optional but fundamental when working with clients from minoritized backgrounds, irrespective of the presence or absence of explicit trauma disclosures. For example, a woman presenting with vaginismus may find vaginal dilator exercises triggering if her lineage includes histories of sexual violence or non-consensual medical experimentation. Similarly, somatic approaches like sensate focus may inadvertently retraumatize a client with gender dysphoria or one whose body has been subjected to cultural stigmatization regarding beauty and normalcy.

Consider also a client who has experienced female genital cutting (FGC). The common sex therapy focus on "pleasure" might unintentionally evoke shame or disconnection if not sensitively contextualized within their cultural and trauma narrative. Neurodivergent clients may find typical relational intimacy exercises—such as encouraged eye contact or specific touch practices—distressing due to sensory processing differences, thereby exacerbating their trauma symptoms (Katz Kattari et al., 2024; Strunz, 2024).

It is critical to recognize the intersectionality of minoritizations. Clients with socially dominant identities may simultaneously possess marginalized erotic preferences, which often remain invisible. For instance, heterosexual individuals practicing kink without access to affirming communities may experience internalized stigma and social isolation, highlighting the diversity of oppression within psychosexual spaces (Nevard, 2018; Bennett, 2024).

Therapists with marginalized identities themselves must engage in ongoing reflexivity and self-care, maintaining awareness of how systemic oppression impacts their own lived experience and how this dynamic unfolds within therapy. The therapeutic encounter becomes a shared space where the "you" and "me" of trauma intersect, demanding a collective, compassionate approach to healing.

Principle 4: Flexibility in Practice

Flexibility is paramount in translating anti-oppressive principles into effective psychosexual psychotherapy. Every stage—assessment, formulation, intervention—must be critically examined through the client's unique social and cultural context.

For example, classical sensate focus exercises may need adaptation or replacement with alternative somatic therapies like body mapping or sensory exploration, especially for clients who are disabled, neurodivergent, gender expansive, or experiencing body image distress (Katz Kattari, 2024b). Attachment-based formulations should be reconsidered for clients from communities where intergenerational trauma shapes relational patterns differently, such as Black and Brown populations (Crenshaw, 1989; Mullan, 2023).

Autistic clients, who may prefer solitary sexual expression, benefit from solo sex therapy practices tailored to their sensory and emotional needs, whereas clients from certain cultural or religious backgrounds might prioritize relational sex therapy approaches that respect prohibitions against solo sexual activity (Katz Kattari et al., 2024).

Even technical interventions can be creatively applied: vaginal dilator techniques, for instance, may be adapted for clients struggling with anal penetration by using dilators with flanges, ensuring safety and comfort (Neves, 2021). This adaptability underscores that any "standard" therapeutic model must be fluid and client-centered to dismantle barriers and foster inclusivity.

At its best, psychosexual psychotherapy is inherently anti-oppressive, actively dismantling normative assumptions and creating healing spaces for all identities. While the field continues to evolve, ignorance is no longer a defensible excuse.

Final Reflections

- Reflect on the four principles of anti-oppressive psychosexual psychotherapy. Which are currently integrated into your practice, and which warrant further development?
- Consider the client identities you rarely or never encounter. What systemic or personal factors might contribute to their absence?
- How might your own attitudes, therapeutic approaches, or outreach practices be inadvertently limiting inclusivity?
- What additional anti-oppressive principles or practices would you propose to enrich this framework?

References

Banks, J., Monier, M., Reynaga, M. & Williams, A., 2024. From the Auction Block to the Tinder Swipe: Black Women's Experiences with Fetishization on Dating Apps. *New Media & Society*, 27(7), pp. 4228–4245.

Barker, M., 2018. *Rewriting the Rules an Anti Self-Help Guide to Love, Sex and Relationships*. 1 ed. London: Routledge.

Barton, C. S., 2024. *Tending Grief. Embodied Rituals for Holding Our Sorrow and Growing Cultures of Care in Community*. Berkely, California: North Atlantic Books.

Bennett, T., 2024. The Marginalization of Kink: Kinkphobia, Vanilla-Normativity and Kink-Normativity. *Journal of Homosexuality*, 1, pp. 1–21.

Bloomsbury, 2023. Bloomsbury. [Online] Available at: www.bloomsbury.com/uk/connect/latest-news/new-data-reveals-uk-knows-shockingly-little-about-black-british-history/#:~:text=Sophie%20Scott%20%7C%2027%20Oct%202023&text=New%20YouGov%20polling%2C%20commissioned%20by,in%20the%20transatlantic%20slave%2 [Accessed 1 February 2025].

BPS, 2024. British Psychological Society. [Online] Available at: https://explore.bps.org.uk/binary/bpsworks/a1c55aff38002b4b/1cdabdfd9a72f137aff5ff80c3693842703dedbdbde506985855c7475b9231dd/9781854338600.pdf [Accessed 9 February 2025].

Brandt, A. M., 1978. Racism and Research: The Case of the Tuskegee Syphilis Study. *The Hastings Center Report*, 8(6), pp. 21–29.

Brown, J. D., 2019. *Anti-Oppressive Counselling and Psychotherapy. Action for Personal and Social Change*. 1 ed. New York and London: Routledge.

Burnham, J., 2013. Developments in Social GGRRAAACCEEESSS: Visible-Invisible, Voiced- Unvoiced. In: I. B. Krause, ed. *Cultural Reflexivity* (pp. 139–160). London: Karnac.

Cass, H., 2024. The Cass Review. [Online]. Available at: https://cass.independent-review.uk/home/publications/final-report/ [Accessed 9 February 2025].

Coleman, E. & Ford, J., 2024. A Brief History of Sexology and Lessons Learned. *The Journal of Sexual Medicine*, 21, pp. 835–838.

Constantinides, D. M., Sennott, S. & Chandler, D., 2019. *Sex Therapy with Erotically Marginalised Client. Nine Principles of Support*. London and New York: Routledge.

COSRT, 2022. COSRT Code of Ethics and Practice. [Online] Available at: www.cosrt.org.uk/wp-content/uploads/2022/02/COSRT-Code-of-Ethics-and-Practice-2022.pdf [Accessed 25 February 2025].

Crenshaw, K., 1989. Demarginalizing the Intersection of Race and Sex: A Black Feminist Critique of Antidiscrimination Doctrine, Feminist Theory and Antiracist Politics. *University of Chicago Legal Forum*, 1989(1), pp. 139–167.

Czyzselska, J. C., 2021. *Queering Psychotherapy*. 1 ed. London: Karnac.

D'Andrea, M. & Daniels, J., 2001. RESPECTFUL Counseling: An Integrative Multidimensional Model for Counselors. In: D. Pope-Davis & L. Coleman H, eds. *The Intersection of Race, Class, and Gender in Multicultural Counseling* (pp. 417–466). Thousand Oaks, CA: Sage Publications.

das Nair, R. & Butler, C., 2012. *Intersectionality, Sexuality and Psychological Therapies: Working with Lesbian, Gay and Bisexual Diversity*. London: BPS Blackwell.

Davies, A. & Neustifter, R., 2021. Fat Fuckers and Fat Fucking: A Feminine Ethic of Care in Sex Therapy. *Psychology and Sexuality*, 14(1), pp. 294–305.

De Block, A. & Adriaens, P., 2013. Pathologizing Sexual Deviance: A History. *The Journal of Sex Research*, 50(3-4), pp. 276–298.

DeLamater, J. & Karraker, A., 2009. Sexual Functioning in Older Adults. *Current Psychiatry Reports*, 11, pp. 6–11.

DSM-5-TR, 2022. American Psychiatric Association. [Online] Available at: www.psychiatry.org/psychiatrists/practice/dsm [Accessed 8 February 2025].

Dundon, C. M. & Rellini, A. H., 2010. More than Sexual Function: Predictors of Sexual Satisfaction in a Sample of Women Age 40–70. *The Journal of Sexual Medicine*, 7(2), pp. 896–904.

Elias, J. & Ryan, A., 2011. A Review and Commentary on the Factors that Influence Expressions of Sexuality by Older People in Care Homes. *Journal of Clinical Nursing*, 20, pp. 11–12.

Ellis, E., 2024. *Transforming Race Conversations. A Healing Guide for Us All*. 1 ed. London: W.W. Norton & Company Ltd.

Esmail, S., Darry, K., Walter, A. & Knupp, A., 2010. Attitudes and Perceptions Towards Disability and Sexuality. *Disability and Rehabilitation*, 32(14), pp. 1148–1155.

Garcia, M. U. & Timothy, R., 2020. Anti-oppression Psychotherapy: An Emancipatory Integration of Intersectionality Into Psychotherapy. *Psychotherapy and Counselling Journal of Australia*, 8(2), pp. 1–15.

Gill, A. K. & Day, A. S., 2020. Moral Panic in the Media: Scapegoating South Asian Men in Cases of Sexual Exploitation and Grooming. In Ramon, S., Lloyd, M., and Penhale, B., eds. *Gendered Domestic Violence and Abuse in Popular Culture (Emerald Studies in Popular Culture and Gender)*. Bingley: Emerald Publishing Limited, pp. 171–197.

Gzesh, A. S., Katz Kattari, S., Juarez, N. & Mayer, M. J., 2024. *A (Very Brief) History of Disability and Sexuality Policy in Exploring Sexuality and Disability. A Guide for Human Sexuality Professionals*. Katz, Kattari, S (ed.). London and New York: Routledge.

Halacre, M., 2021. *Working with Disability Across the Counselling Professions*. London: BACP.

Hall, K. & Graham, C. A., 2013. *The Cultural Context of Sexual Pleasure and Problems. Psychotherapy with Diverse Clients*. New York and London: Routledge.

Hays, P., 2008. *Addressing Cultural Complexities in Practice: Assessment, Diagnosis, and Therapy*. 2 ed. New York: American Psychological Association.

Hook, J.N., Davis, D.E., Owen, J., Worthington Jr., E.L., and Utsey, S.O., 2013. Cultural Humility: Measuring Openness to Culturally Diverse Clients. *Journal of Counseling Psychology* (advance online publication). doi:10.1037/a0032595.

Institute of Psychotherapy and Disability, 2000. IPD. [Online] Available at: https://instpd.org.uk/ [Accessed 9 February 2025].

Jacobsen, J. et al., 2019. *Sex, Sexuality, and Trans Identities: Clinical Guidance for Psychotherapists and Counselors*. London: Jessica Kingsley.

Johnson, B., 2013. Sexually Transmitted Infections and Older Adults. *Journal of Gerontological Nursing*, 39(11), pp. 53–60.

Katz Kattari, S., 2024a. *Exploring Sexuality and Disability. A Guide for Human Service Professionals*. New York and London: Routledge.

Katz Kattari, S., 2024b. *No Spoons for Spooning: Navigating Sexuality, Chronic Illness, and Chronic Pain in Exploring Sexuality and Disability. A Guide for Human Service Professionals*. ed Katz, Kattari, S. London and New York: Routledge.

Katz Kattari, S., Gross, E., Sherwood, K. & Hostetter, C. R., 2024. *Infinity and Rainbow. Supporting the Sexuality of Neurodivergent People in Exploring Sexuality and Disability. A Guide for Human Service Professionals*. ed Katz Kattari, S. London and New York: Routledge.

Kazumi, A., 2020. The Depiction of Asians in Hollywood Films. *Global Studies*, 4(8), pp. 113–126.

Khan, M., 2023. *Working Within Diversity. A Reflective Guide to Anti-Oppressive Practice in Counselling and Therapy*. London: Jessica Kingsley Publishers.

Legislation, U. G., 2003. Sexual Offences Act 2003. [Online] Available at: www.legislation.gov.uk/ukpga/2003/42/contents [Accessed 25 February 2025].

McInnes, E., 2025. Nubia Wellness and Healing. [Online] Available at: https://nubiawellnessandhealing.co.uk/about-us/ [Accessed 8 February 2025].

Menakem, R., 2021. *My Grandmother's Hands: Racialized Trauma and the Pathway to Mending Our Hearts and Bodies*. 1 ed. New York: Penguin.

Meyer, I. H., 1995. Minority Stress and Mental Health in Gay Men. *Journal of Health and Social Behavior*, 36(1), pp. 38–56.

Mollitt, P. C., 2022. BACP. [Online] Available at: www.bacp.co.uk/bacp-journals/therapy-today/2022/june-2022/the-big-issue/ [Accessed 9 February 2025].

MoU Conversion Therapy, 2024. BACP. [Online] Available at: www.bacp.co.uk/events-and-resources/ethics-and-standards/mou/ [Accessed 1 February 2025].

Mullan, J., 2023. *Decolonizing Therapy. Oppression, Historical Trauma, and Politicizing Your Practice*. 1 ed. New York: W.W. Norton & Company Inc.

National LGBT Survey, 2017. UK Government. [Online] Available at: https://assets.publishing.service.gov.uk/media/5b3cb6b6ed915d39fd5f14df/GEO-LGBT-Survey-Report.pdf [Accessed 9 February 2025 2025].

Nevard, I., 2018. Counselling and the Kink Community: A Thematic Analysis. *Counselling Sexually Diverse Clients*, 49(4), pp. 617–628.

Neves, S., 2021. *Compulsive Sexual Behaviour. A Psycho-Sexual Treatment Guide for Clinicians*. 1 ed. London: Routledge.

Neves, S., 2025. Working with LGBTQ+ People in Our Current Society: Developing an Anti-Oppressive Practice. *European Journal of Psychotherapy & Counselling*, 27, pp. 67–81. https://doi.org/10.1080/13642537.2024.2398999.

Neves, S. & Davies, D., 2023a. *Erotically Queer. A Pink Therapy Guide for Practitioners*. New York and London: Routledge.

Neves, S. & Davies, D., 2023b. *Relationally Queer. A Pink Therapy Guide for Practitioners*. 1 ed. New York and London: Routledge.

Potki, R. et al., 2017. Bio-Psycho-Social Factors Affecting Sexual Self-Concept: A Systematic Review. *Electronic Physician*, 9(9), pp. 5172–5178.

Rodriguez, M. A. & García, R., 2013. First, Do No Harm: The US Sexually Transmitted Disease Experiments in Guatemala. *American Journal of Public Health*, 103(12), pp. 2122–2126.

Sale, J., 2019. Contemporary Institute of Clinical Sexology. [Online] Available at: www.theinstituteofsexology.org/blog/are-you-an-accidental-conversion-therapist [Accessed 8 February 2025].

Sale, J., 2023. Exploring Erotic Diversity in Heterosexuality: Keeping a Queer Eye for the Straight Guys. In: S. Neves. & D. Davies, ed. *Erotically Queer. A Pink Therapy Guide for Practitioners*. London: Routledge.

Scarrone Bonhomme, L., Davies, S. & Beattie, M., 2023. *Gender Affirming Therapy. A Guide to What Transgender and Non-Binary Clients Can Teach us*. Maidenhead: Open University Press.

Shende, P., Jagtap, A., Goswami, B., Jagtap Sr, A. & Goswami Jr, B., 2024. The Legacy of James Marion Sims: History Revisited. *Cureus*, 16(9), pp. 1–6.

Snowden, T. L., 2023. Shout Out UK. [Online] Available at: www.shoutoutuk.org/2023/11/28/why-you-should-know-more-about-disability-rights-history-and-i-should-too/ [Accessed 24 February 2025].

Sowemimo, A., 2023. *Divided. Racism, Medicine and Why We Need to Decolonise Healthcare*. London: Welcome Collection.

St Aime, F., 2024. *Anti-Oppressive Psychotherapeutic Practice: Finding Liberation Through Unlearning*. 1 ed. London: Routledge.

Strunz, R. M., 2024. *Neurodiversity-Affirming Psychotherapy: Clinical Pathways to Autistic Mental Health*. 1 ed. London: Routledge.

Syme, M., 2017. Supporting Safe Sexual and Intimate Expression Among Older People in Care Homes. *Nursing Standard*, 31(52), pp. 52–63.

Tilsen, J., 2021. *Queering your Therapy Practice. Queer Theory, Narrative Therapy and Imagining New Identities*. New York and London: Routledge.

Turner, D., 2025. *Decolonising Counselling and Psychotherapy. Depoliticised Pathways Towards Intersectional Practice*. 1 ed. London: Routledge.

UK Government, 2018. Employment Tribunal Decisions. [Online] Available at: www.gov.uk/employment-tribunal-decisions/ms-r-taylor-v-jaguar-land-rover-ltd-1304471-2018 [Accessed 25th January 2025].

UK Government, 2020. Equality Act 2020. [Online] Available at: www.gov.uk/discrimination-your-rights [Accessed 25th January 2025].

UK Government, 2021. Employment Tribunal Decisions. [Online] Available at: www.gov.uk/employment-appeal-tribunal-decisions/maya-forstater-v-cgd-europe-and-others-ukeat-slash-0105-slash-20-slash-joj [Accessed 25th January 2025].

Waller, N., 2021. *Neuroqueer Heresies: Notes on the Neurodiversity Paradigm, Autistic Empowerment, and Postnormal Possibilities*. 1 ed. London: Autonomous Press.

Ward, J., 2022. *The Tragedy of Heterosexuality*. New York: NYU Press.

WHO, 2025. World Health Organisation. [Online] Available at: www.who.int/health-topics/gender#tab=tab_1 [Accessed 8 February 2025].

Wiktionary, 2025. Wiktionary. [Online] Available at: https://en.wiktionary.org/ [Accessed 25th January 2025].

Young, S., 2018. The Myth of Promiscuity: Examining Black Male Sexual Narratives and Sexual Identity. [Online] Available at: https://dsc.duq.edu/cgi/viewcontent.cgi?article=2469&context=etd [Accessed 9 February 2025].

Chapter 27

Epistemic Power Wheel: How Dominant Western Sexuality Frameworks Marginalize Alternative Worldviews

Bernd Leygraf

Radiating outward are four contrasting epistemic and cultural domains—*collectivist/kinship-based relational models*, *religious and spiritual epistemologies*, *indigenous/local knowledge systems*, and *non-Western languages and frameworks*. Each represents ways of understanding sexuality, identity, and relationality that fall outside the Western canon, and are therefore often translated, negotiated, punished, or excluded. The diagram shows these interactions through directional arrows labeled *resistance*, *shaming*, *imposition*, *negotiation*, *punishment*, and *translation*, demonstrating the unequal power dynamics between dominant and marginalized knowledge systems.

The outermost ring represents *marginalized or excluded frameworks*, reminding us that many cultural perspectives become visible only at the borders of Western discourse, if at all. Collectively, the diagram critiques the assumption that Western individualistic models are universal. It highlights how global sex therapy and psychosexual practice must acknowledge multiple epistemologies and move beyond dominance-based paradigms to become culturally inclusive, flexible, and contextually attuned (Figure 27.1).

DOI: 10.4324/9781003611387-27

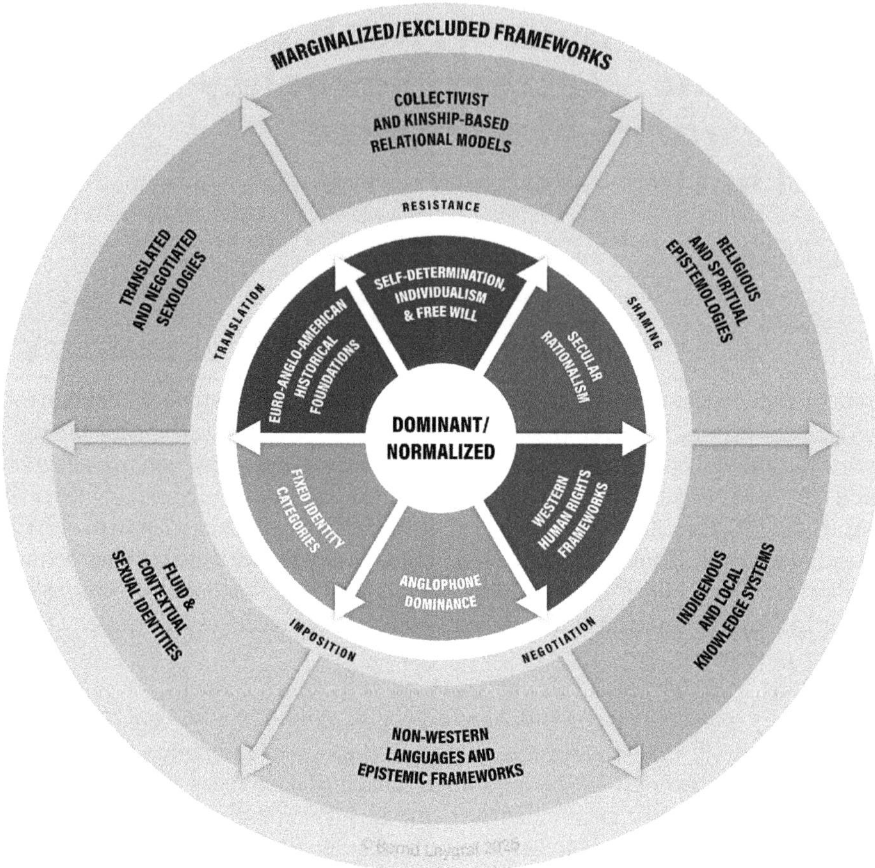

Figure 27.1 Epistemic power wheel: How dominant Western sexuality frameworks marginalize alternative worldviews

Index

Note: Page locators in **bold** and *italics* represents tables and figures, respectively. Endnotes are indicated by the page number followed by "n" and the note number e.g., 111n5 refers to note 5 on page 111.

For Product Safety Concerns and Information please contact our EU representative GPSR@taylorandfrancis.com
Taylor & Francis Verlag GmbH, Kaufingerstraße 24, 80331 München, Germany

www.ingramcontent.com/pod-product-compliance
Ingram Content Group UK Ltd.
Pitfield, Milton Keynes, MK11 3LW, UK
UKHW020156200926
475702UK00016B/2740
9781041007333